THE MIDDLE EAST

A HANDBOOK

D0875776

HANDBOOKS TO THE MODERN WORLD

AFRICA, edited by Colin Legum
ASIA, edited by Guy Wint
WESTERN EUROPE, edited by John Calmann
LATIN AMERICA AND THE CARIBBEAN, edited by Claudio Véliz
AUSTRALIA, NEW ZEALAND AND THE SOUTH PACIFIC, edited by Charles Osborne
THE SOVIET UNION AND EASTERN EUROPE, edited by George Schöpflin

In preparation:
THE UNITED STATES AND CANADA, edited by Richard Fisher

THE MIDDLE EAST

A Handbook

Edited by
MICHAEL ADAMS

ANTHONY BLOND

First published 1971 in Great Britain by Anthony Blond Ltd
56 Doughty Street London WC1

© 1971 Anthony Blond Ltd

This book was printed on F.1 Thinprint 70 gm²
Manufactured by Robert Fletcher & Son Ltd
Stoneclough, Lancs.

Printed in Great Britain by
Clarke, Doble & Brendon Ltd., Plymouth

218 51296 1

CONTRIBUTORS

Ibrahim Abu-Lughod
Edmond Y. Asfour
Nevill Barbour
Norman Bentwich
H. Bowen-Jones
Afif A. Bulos
John Carswell
Henry Cattan
Elizabeth Collard
David Cowan
Norman Daniel
Hubert Darke
Clement H. Dodd
Riggan Er-Rumi
Kevin G. Fenelon
Geoffrey Furlonge
David Holden
Doreen Ingrams
Jabra I. Jabra
Adel Kamal
Nabih Kamel

Abbas Kelidar
Helen Khal
Abdul Aziz El-Koussy
Jacob M. Landau
Tom Little
Barnet Litvinoff
Robert E. Mabro
Samir A. Makdisi
Ragaei El Mallakh
R. L. Morris
Hamid Mowlana
Seyyed Hossein Nasr
Peter J. Parr
Munif Razzaz
Maxime Rodinson
R. B. Serjeant
W. W. Stewart
Frank Stoakes
Arnold Toynbee
Geoffrey Wigoder
Marvin Zonis

CONTENTS

MAPS

EDITOR'S PREFACE

THERE is a wry joke among Middle East specialists to the effect that if you set out to write about the area and press on with all possible speed you will just be in time to see your work rendered out-of-date by the next crisis. The specialists whose work is gathered in this volume will have been as conscious as their editor of the danger confronting them. Never in modern times has there been a period when the future of this area has been more uncertain, when so many of its inhabitants—and its governments—have seen their fate hanging in the balance. For the whole world, indeed, the stability of the Middle East has been an anxious and enduring preoccupation.

Against such a cataclysmic backdrop it would show a lack of proportion to dwell for long on the purely technical problems which have confronted the editor and the publishers in the preparation of this volume. Yet it is fair to remind the reader that a task which has occupied, from the start to finish, some three years has been carried out in circumstances of peculiar difficulty. Even now, as the material goes to the printer, uncertainties persist—but decisions (editorial decisions, that is) can no longer be delayed, although they are bound to affect the accuracy, and so the usefulness, of the volume in its final form. Frontiers, which must be marked on maps, remain in some cases indeterminate. The future of the régime of government, and even of the whole political and social structure, of more than one country in the area is unpredictable. Statistics based on an existing set of data may need revision, if the data themselves become obsolete in the wake of political changes which can at this moment be apprehended but not foreseen. Throughout an area characterised in its recent past by instability, the few fixed points now rise like isolated rocks out of a sea of uncertainty.

In these conditions, one problem asserts itself above all others : the problem of objectivity. It is a problem to which there is no answer that will satisfy all comers, and it is perhaps well to explain here the editorial formula which I have adopted. After planning the structure of the volume and drawing up a list of contents as comprehensive as possible, I chose writers known to me, either personally or by reputation, as leading specialists in their own fields. Where I was in doubt I consulted a number of authorities, among whom I must single out Dr. Albert Hourani for grateful mention, and where possible followed their recommendations. Other things being equal, I preferred a Middle Eastern author to one from outside the area and I am especially grateful to those who found time, amid bitter preoccupations in their own homelands, to accept my invitation to contribute to the Handbook. My own choice of authors was then approved, with one or two suggested changes which I found sensible and acceptable, by the publishers of the volume, whose open-minded approach throughout I am happy to record.

For the most part, those whom I approached were willing to collaborate with me, although there were exceptions where one author or another declared himself unwilling to lend his name to a volume whose contents in their entirety he felt he would be unable to approve. Where this happened, I had no option but to accept his decision, although I was disappointed by the attitude which it expressed. If there is one thing that the problems and the realities of the Middle East need more than another, it is surely full and frank discussion and it gives me pleasure to know that, whatever other shortcomings this Handbook may have, it does make available between its covers an extraordinarily wide range of views. If the book has been compiled according to an editorial formula, as I have indicated, it is the expression of no editorial policy more precise than the policy of allowing experts to discuss, side by side, every aspect of life in the area extending from the Caspian Sea to the upper reaches of the Nile. Others may argue if they will about what constitutes objectivity; what matters to me is that the material assembled here should contribute to a more complete and a more constructive understanding than is normally shown of the nature and the problems of the Middle East.

Inherent in such an understanding is the knowledge that the period of instability which we are witnessing now is only one among many similar periods in the history of the Middle East; the knowledge, too, that this period in itself represents only a brief moment in relation to the more than 50 centuries through which civilised life has gone on in parts of this area. It is my hope that this Handbook will be read for the light it throws on the achievements of the past as well as for its detailed examination of the sorry state of affairs prevailing today. There is no area of the world of greater interest to the archaeologist and, by contrast with the triumphs of the human spirit revealed to us by archaeology in the Middle East, the lawlessness and strife of today, the loss of life and the waste of resources, constitute a sad denial of human progress.

With all our interest in the past history of an area which has contributed so much to our own spiritual and social development, it is the present that demands our attention. Where our own Western interests are concerned, here is an area on which we depend to a significant degree for the basic ingredient of our industrial development. For this and other reasons, this area has become the latest battlefield in the struggle for political influence between the super-powers of East and West. And because of this involvement, both economic and political, the outcome of the present conflict in the Middle East has become a matter of the most urgent concern, not only to the super powers, but to every country in the world, since all of us may find ourselves caught up, despite ourselves, in the results of East-West rivalry.

These are sufficient reasons for urging a greater awareness of the realities of contemporary life in the Middle East, but to me, even these are not the primary reasons for concern. They are but reminders of our collective failure to resolve the underlying problems of the area : reminders too of the dangers that may overwhelm us all if we do not correct that failure. The first reason for our concern, as I see it, should be that the present tension and instability throughout the Middle East condemns millions of human beings to endure a degree of misery and anxiety which are by any reasonable standard intolerable. The misery finds expression in refugee camps, in generally low standards of health, in the lack of opportunities for rapidly increasing populations. The anxiety reflects these handicaps but has still deeper roots in many parts of the area, where political uncertainty throws across the lives of the inhabitants the shadow of an insecurity which is total and unqualified. For them, the bitter reality is that they live daily under the threat of a disaster that may claim their homes or even their lives—and that there is no visible authority that can protect them.

That this should be true of an area which has provided the spiritual and ethical framework for the outlook of so large a proportion of humanity is no less than tragic. For us in the West, the sense of tragedy must be deepened by the knowledge that with such influence and such opportunities at our disposal in the Middle East we have, in the recent past, not merely failed to make proper use of our opportunities but have used our influence in the pursuit of policies whose result has been to complicate the problems facing the area itself. The political instability which is so prevalent in the Middle East today has among its causes the interference exercised yesterday, for their own purposes, by Britain, by France, by the United States of America and to a lesser extent by other Western nations. One of the results of that interference, and of its marked lack of success, has been the appearance of the Soviet Union as a major power in an area where, until a generation ago, its influence was severely restricted.

For all these reasons, the outside world, and especially the West, must accept a share of the responsibility for the present condition of the Middle East. By implication, we have also an obligation to do what we can to help in resolving the problems of the area, if only by trying to undo the ill-effects of what we have done in the past to create them. The obstacles to progress are not difficult to identify and it is towards removing them that our efforts should now be directed, towards combating under-development, ill-health, intolerance and the spread of a narrow and exclusive brand of nationalism. Against all of these, there is no weapon more potent than knowledge, no panacea more effective that the understanding that knowledge can bring. It is my earnest hope that this Handbook, by diffusing knowledge, will promote understanding. At the very worst, those reading it may learn to know better those whom they have come to think of as their enemies. At best, they may be encouraged to recognise in them old associates, whom fate and the turning wheel of fortune may yet reveal as potential friends.

M.A.

COMPARATIVE STATISTICS

COMPARATIVE STATISTICS

Symbols used : — a zero or insignificant value
n.a. suitable data not available

POPULATION OF MIDDLE EAST AREA

Country	Approximate Area (000 sq. km.)	Date of latest census	Population at date of census	Population estimate mid-1967[1]	% Estimated annual growth 1963-7[1]
Bahrain	0·6	Feb. 1965	182,203	193,000	3·2
Iran	1,648·0	Nov. 1966	25,785,210	26,284,000	3·1
Iraq	434·9	Oct. 1965	8,261,527	8,440,000	2·5
Israel	20·7	May. 1961	2,183,332	2,669,000[2]	2·9[2]
Jordan	97·7	Nov. 1961	1,706,226	2,039,000[3]	3·3
Kuwait	16·0	Apr. 1965	467,339[4]	520,000	7·6
Lebanon	10·6	—	—	2,520,000[5]	2·5
Oman	212·4	—	—	565,000	—
Qatar	22·0	—	—	75,000	8·1
Saudi Arabia	2,149·7	1962–3	(results repudiated)	6,990,000	1·7
Southern Yemen	287·7	—	—	1,170,000	2·2
Sudan	2,505·8	Jan. 1956	10,262,536	14,355,000	2·8
Syria	185·2	Sept. 1960	4,565,121	5,570,000	2·9
Trucial States	83·6	Apr. 1968	177,640	180,000	—
Dubai			57,469		
Abu Dhabi			46,500[6]		
Sharjah			31,480		
Ras al-Khaimah			24,482		
Fujairah			9,724		
Ajman			4,245		
Umm al-Quwain			3,740		
Turkey	780·6	Oct. 1965	31,391,421	32,710,000	2·5
UAR	1,001·4	May 1966	30,075,858	30,907,000	2·5
Yemen	195·0	—	—	5,000,000	1·5

140,187,000

Sources: *UN Statistical Yearbook 1968*, UN 1969
Census Report of Trucial States Development Council

[1] United Nations estimates.
[2] The population of E. Jerusalem is estimated at 60,000.
[3] Including the West Bank. An Israeli military census showed a population of 598,637 for the West Bank in 1968.
[4] Of which over 50% were foreign.
[5] Of which about 500,000 in Beirut.
[6] Official estimate.

4

ESTIMATED ACTIVE/EMPLOYED LABOUR FORCE BY MAIN SECTORS

Country	Year[1]	Agriculture 000	%	Industry 000	%	Services 000	%	Total 000
Bahrain	1965	4·7[2]	8·7	0·6[3]	1·1	32·8[4]	61·5	53·3
Iran	1966	3,540·2	47	1,284·8	17	1,732	23	7,493
Iraq	1963	1,750	67·4	129·6	5	468	18	2,595
Israel	1967	101·5	12	203·8	25	439·6	56	831
Jordan	1961	137·8	35	41·9	10·7	96·9	24·8	390
Kuwait	1965	2·0[5]	1·1	23·9[6]	13·3	115·6[7]	64·5	179·3
Lebanon	1961	220	38	60	10	143	25	580
Oman	—	n.a.	—	n.a.	—	n.a.	—	n.a.
Qatar	—	n.a.	—	n.a.	—	n.a.	—	n.a.
Saudi Arabia[8]	—	n.a.	—	n.a.	—	n.a.	—	n.a.
Southern Yemen	1965	345	78	13·3	3	53	12	440
Sudan	1961	4,155	85·8	241	4·9	354	8·3	5,572
Syria	1966	825·7	57	163	11	354·2	24	1,452
Trucial States	—	n.a.	—	n.a.	—	n.a.	—	n.a.
Turkey	1965	9,414	64	1,260·0	9	1,162	8	14,782
UAR	1965	4,660	59	800	10	2,175	28	7,860
Yemen	—	n.a.	—	n.a.	—	n.a.	—	n.a.

Source: National Government Statistics

[1] Latest year for which reliable figures are available.
[2] Of which 1,092 non-Bahraini.
[3] Of which 230 non-Bahraini.
[4] Of which 14,069 non-Bahraini.
[5] Of which 1,410 non-Kuwaiti.
[6] Of which 21,760 non-Kuwaiti.
[7] Of which 83,018 non-Kuwaiti.
[8] A limited survey was made recently, which only covers 25 cities, thus completely excluding the agricultural sector.

UNEMPLOYMENT

Of the Middle Eastern states only three produce statistics of employment which conform to any degree with ILO requirements:

Country	1966 Number (000)	Percentage of labour force
Iraq	(c. 38)	2·0 (1965)
Israel	(c. 6·5)	7·9
Syria	70	4·8

In all countries where rural employment predominates, disguised unemployment can be very high, 10—30%, and everywhere this element inflates the size of the service sector since petty trading absorbs much redundant urban labour.

DOMESTIC PRODUCT

Country	GDP per caput at factor cost $US		Estimated Gross Domestic Product at market prices (in national currencies)					Unit of currency millions
			1960	1963	1965	1966	1967	
Bahrain	n.a.	—	n.a.	n.a.	n.a.	n.a.	n.a.	▬
Iran[1]	265	(1966)	337	405	504	543	602	Rials 000
Iraq	292	(1966)	598	727	872	n.a.	n.a.	Dinars
Israel	1,320	(1966)	4,554	7,886	10,881	11,854	12,294	£1
Jordan	204	(1966)	98	129	168	170	194	JD
Kuwait	4,535	(1966)	n.a.	679	752	789	881	KD
Lebanon[2]	295	(1963)	n.a.	1,951	2,500	n.a.	n.a.	£L
Oman	60	(1958)	n.a.	n.a.	n.a.	n.a.	n.a.	—
Qatar	n.a.	—	n.a.	n.a.	n.a.	n.a.	n.a.	—
Saudi Arabia	227	(1963)	n.a.	8,898[3]	10,244[3]	11,514[3]	13,102[3]	SR
South Yemen	194	(1963)	n.a.	n.a.	69	n.a.	n.a.	£
Sudan	94	(1963)	388	458	485	n.a.	n.a.	£Sud
Syria[4]	192	(1966)	2,265	3,311	3,589	3,392	n.a.	£S
Trucial States	n.a.	—	n.a.	n.a.	n.a.	n.a.	n.a.	—
Turkey	292	(1966)	51	69	80	93	104	£T
UAR	167	(1966)	n.a.	1,888	2,403	2,494	n.a.	£E
Yemen	44	(1958)	n.a.	n.a.	n.a.	n.a.	n.a.	—

Sources: *UN Statistical Yearbook 1968*, UN 1969
National Government Statistics

[1] Twelve months beginning 21 March of year stated.
[2] Net Domestic Product at factor cost.
[3] These figures are for the Saudi financial year which does not correspond exactly to 12 calendar months.
[4] At factor cost.

FOREIGN TRADE
EXCHANGE RATES AND CURRENCIES AS AT JANUARY 1970

Country	Currency	£1	$1
Bahrain	Dinar (BD)	1·142	0·48
Iran	Riyal (IR)	183·2	75·75
Iraq	Dinar (ID)	0·857	0·36
Israel	Pound (£I)	8·39	3·50
Jordan	Dinar (JD)	0·862	0·359
Kuwait	Kuwait (KD)	0·857	0·36
Lebanon	Pound (£Leb)	7·75	3·29
Oman	Gulf Rupee (GR)	13·285	5·53
Qatar	Qatar/Dubai Riyal (QDR)	11·45	4·77
Saudi Arabia	Riyal (SR)	10·77	4·50
South Yemen	Dinar (SAD)	1·0	0·42
Sudan	Pound (£Sud)	0·835	0·35
Syria	Pound (£Syr)	10·0	3·82
Trucial States—			
Abu Dhabi	Bahrain Dinar (BD)	1·142	0·48
Others (Qatar & Dubai)	Riyal (QDR)	11·45	4·77
Turkey	Pound (Lira TL)	21·6	9·0
UAR	Pound (£Eg)	1·04	0·435
Yemen	Riyal (YR)	2·57	1·07

Sources: International Monetary Fund
Bank of England Financial Times

PRODUCTION AND CONSUMPTION OF ENERGY

Country	1967 Total production (million metric tons coal equivalent)	1967 Per caput consumption (kg)	1967 Electricity generated (million kwh)	1967 Coal & Lignite prod. (000 metric tons)	1969 Crude oil production (000 metric tons)
Bahrain	4·51	3,601	190	—	3,800
Iran	169·72	451	4,500	300[1]	167,600
Iraq	79·33	610	1,431	—	74,700
Israel	0·32	2,262	4,728	—	100
Jordan	n.a.	265	157	—	—
Kuwait	152·37[2]	6,648	1,335	—	129,000[3]
Lebanon	0·09	648	907	—	—
Oman	4·09	32	n.a.	—	16,300
Qatar	20·12	1,400	n.a.	—	17,100
Saudi Arabia	169·63[2]	440	377(1966)	—	148,300[3]
Southern Yemen	n.a.	2,023	237	—	—
Sudan	0·01	87	318	—	—
Syria	0·01	393	676	—	3,500
Trucial States	24·09[4]	338[4]	n.a.	—	28,800
Turkey	10·03	422	6,167	3,416 (coal) 5,031 (lignite)	3,600
UAR	7·69	267	5,895(1966)	n.a.	16,000[5]
Yemen	n.a.	10	n.a.	—	—

Source: *UN Statistical Yearbook 1968,* UN 1969

[1] Estimate of US Department of Mines.
[2] Neutral Zone production (28·8 million metric tons in 1967), shared 50/50 between Kuwait and Saudi Arabia, to be added to their total production.
[3] Neutral Zone production 23,700,000 metric tons shared 50/50 between Kuwait and Saudi Arabia, to be added to their total production.
[4] These figures are for Abu Dhabi only, although power stations exist in other Trucial States.
[5] Including production from Israeli-occupied Sinai.

CONSUMER PRICE INDEX
(All Items. 1963=100)

Country	1958	1959	1960	1961	1962	1963	1964	1965	1966	1967
Bahrain	n.a.	n.a.	n.a.	n.a.	n.a.	n.a.	n.a.	n.a.	n.a.	n.a.
Iran	79	87	96	99	100	100	104	106	106	107
Iraq	92	91	94	96	96	100	99	98	99	101
Israel	77	79	80	86	94	100	105	113	122	124
Jordan[1]	n.a.	n.a.	n.a.	n.a.	n.a.	n.a.	n.a.	n.a.	n.a.	n.a.
Kuwait	n.a.	n.a.	n.a.	n.a.	n.a.	n.a.	n.a.	n.a.	n.a.	n.a.
Lebanon[2]	91	94	98	97	98	100	n.a.	n.a.	n.a.	n.a.
Oman	n.a.	n.a.	n.a.	n.a.	n.a.	n.a.	n.a.	n.a.	n.a.	n.a.
Qatar	n.a.	n.a.	n.a.	n.a.	n.a.	n.a.	n.a.	n.a.	n.a.	n.a.
Saudi Arabia[3]	n.a.	n.a.	n.a.	n.a.	n.a.	100	101	101	103	107
South Yemen[4]	90	89	92	91	93	100	103	104	106	109
Sudan[5]	87	86	86	94	96	100	104	101	103	114
Syria	n.a.	n.a.	n.a.	n.a.	98	100	106	102	108	113
Trucial States	n.a.	n.a.	n.a.	n.a.	n.a.	n.a.	n.a.	n.a.	n.a.	n.a.
Turkey	65	82	87	90	93	100	103	107	116	133
UAR	101	101	102	102	99	100	104	119	130	131
Yemen	n.a.	n.a.	n.a.	n.a.	n.a.	n.a.	n.a.	n.a.	n.a.	n.a.

Sources: *UN Statistical Yearbook 1968*, UN 1969
National Statistics

[1] The Jordanian authorities produce cost of living statistics for selected areas which are not comparable with the rest of the data in this table.
[2] Beirut only.
[3] Wholesale price index.
[4] Aden only.
[5] Restricted samples of consumers.

MOTOR VEHICLES IN USE

Country	Passenger cars 000			Commercial vehicles 000		
	1965	1966	1967	1965	1966	1967
Bahrain	6·41[1]	6·81[1]	7·3	2·5	2·6	2·7
Iran	135·0	142·4	164·2	47·5	49·4	59·7
Iraq	54·5	58·2	60·7	34·4	37·0	39·2
Israel	75·5	88·0	99·3	40·0	47·5	50·9
Jordan	12·0	13·6	16·4	5·4	6·2	6·7
Kuwait	58·6	69·6	73·0	21·8	25·3	33·6
Lebanon	98·7	105·4	114·2	14·0	14·1	14·9
Oman	n.a.	n.a.	n.a.	n.a.	n.a.	n.a.
Qatar	n.a.	n.a.	n.a.	n.a.	n.a.	n.a.
Saudi Arabia	57·5	65·8	n.a.	47·0	53·0	n.a.
Southern Yemen[2]	12·9	13·1	13·6	2·8	3·1	3·2
Sudan	23·1	23·7	21·1	16·9	17·6	n.a.
Syria	27·2	28·3	30·0	14·3	13·3	14·4
Trucial States	n.a.	n.a.	n.a.	n.a.	n.a.	n.a.
Turkey	87·6	91·5	105·9	101·3	108·4	119·2
UAR	97·7	105·3	108·0	26·0	27·5	27·1
Yemen	n.a.	n.a.	n.a.	n.a.	n.a.	n.a.

Source: *UN Statistical Yearbook 1968*, UN 1969

[1] Including taxi cabs.　　　　[2] Aden area only.

8

HOUSING

Country	Year[1]	Urban–Rural	No. of private households	No. of occupied dwellings	Average no. of rooms per dwelling	Average no. of persons per room
Bahrain	1965	Total	31·061	26,300[2]	2·5	2·4
		Urban	n.a.	22,361[2]	n.a.	n.a.
		Rural	n.a.	3,939[2]	n.a.	n.a.
Iran	1966	Total	5,029,320	3,898,719	n.a.	n.a.
		Urban	1,960,701	1,300,828	n.a.	n.a.
		Rural	3,068,619	2,597,891	n.a.	n.a.
Iraq	1956	Total	n.a.	736,721	n.a.	n.a.
Israel	1966	Total	670,157	626,800	2·3	1·6
		Urban	563,857	556,200	2·4	1·5
		Rural	106,300	70,600	2·0	2·1
Jordan	1961	Total	313,613	n.a.	2·3	n.a.
		Urban	129,277	n.a.	n.a.	n.a.
		Rural	184,336	n.a.	n.a.	n.a.
Kuwait	1965	Total	72,464	72,464	n.a.	n.a.
Lebanon	1952–3	Beirut only	51,394	n.a.	4·3	n.a.
Oman	—	—	n.a.	n.a.	n.a.	n.a.
Qatar	—	—	n.a.	n.a.	n.a.	n.a.
Saudi Arabia	—	—	n.a.	n.a.	n.a.	n.a.
Southern Yemen	—	—	n.a.	n.a.	n.a.	n.a.
Sudan	1964–5	Khartoum only	31,610	n.a.	2·2	2·5
Syria	1961–2	Total	859,654	n.a.	2·5	2·3
		Urban	306,896	n.a.	2·9	2.1
		Rural	552,758	n.a.	2·4	2·5
Trucial States	—	—	n.a.	n.a.	n.a.	n.a.
Turkey	1965	Total	5,564,716	n.a.	2·3	2·2
UAR	1960	Urban	1,992,491	1,572,488	3·6	1·6
Yemen	—	—	n.a.	n.a.	n.a.	n.a.

Sources: *United Nations Yearbook 1968,* UN 1969
National Statistics

[1] Latest available year.
[2] Data refer to housing units.

HOUSING—FACILITIES IN DWELLINGS

Country	Urban–Rural	Year	electricity	% of dwellings with inside or outside running water	bath
Bahrain	U. & R.	1965	80	72·6	—
Iran	U. & R.	1966	25·5	14·5	—
Iraq	U. & R.	1956	17·1	20·8	10·3
Israel	U. & R.	1966	94·4	98·6 (89·5 inside)	87·5
Jordan	U. & R.	1961	17·0	36·2 (21·3 inside)	8·7
Kuwait	—	—	—	—	—
Lebanon	U.	1952–3	91·2	93·4	—
Oman	—	—	—	—	—
Qatar	—	—	—	—	—
Saudi Arabia	—	—	—	—	—
South Yemen	—	—	—	—	—
Sudan[1]	U.	1964–5	55·2	95·8	49·4
Syria	U. & R.	1961–2	38·0	41·9	—
Trucial States	—	—	—	—	—
Turkey	U.	1960	85·3	56·0	42·3
	R.	1963	2·4	2·2	53·5
UAR	U.	1960	37·8	39·5	—
Yemen	—	—	—	—	—

Source: *UN Statistical Yearbook 1967*, UN 1968

[1] Incomplete data. Khartoum City only.

RADIO, TV SETS AND TELEPHONES IN USE

Country	Radio receivers Year[1] R/L[2]	Radio receivers Number 000	TV receivers Year[1] R/L	TV receivers Number 000	Telephones 1967
Bahrain	R1967	210	R1967	18	9·1
Iran	L1967	1,790	R1967	131	220·1
Iraq	R1965	2,500	R1966	180	77·5
Israel	L1967	774	L1967	26	344·5
Jordan	L1965	269	R1967	15	33·0
Kuwait	R1964	175	R1966	80	43·0
Lebanon	L1967	451	R1967	150	130·0
Oman	—	n.a.	—	—	—
Qatar	—	n.a.	—	n.a.	7·5
Saudi Arabia	R1960	74	R1964	30	29
Southern Yemen	R1965	300	R1967	30	9·4
Sudan	L1964	225	R1966	11	42·5
Syria	R1965	1,745	R1966	100	91·4
Trucial States	—	n.a.	—	n.a.	n.a.
Turkey	L1967	2,789	L1966	2·5	427·8
UAR	L1965	1,613	R1967	399	352·3
Yemen	—	n.a.	—	—	n.a.

Sources: *UNESCO Statistical Yearbook 1967*
UN Statistical Yearbook 1968, UN 1969

[1] Latest year for which figures are available.
[2] R=estimated number of receivers in use.
L=number of licences issued.
In many cases a licence may cover more than one receiver in the same household.

PERCENTAGE ORIGIN OF GDP AT FACTOR COST
FOR LATEST YEAR AVAILABLE

Country	Year	Agriculture	Industry[1]	Services[2]
Bahrain	—	n.a.	n.a.	n.a.
Iran	1967	22	37	41
Iraq	1965	21	47	32
Israel	1966	8	32	60
Jordan	1967	22	16	62
Kuwait	1966–7	0·5	69·4	30·1
Lebanon	1964	13	21	66
Oman	—	n.a.	n.a.	n.a.
Qatar	—	n.a.	n.a.	n.a.
Saudi Arabia	1967	8	59	33
Southern Yemen	—	n.a.	n.a.	n.a.
Sudan	1964	54	12	34
Syria	1966	28	19	53
Trucial States	—	n.a.	n.a.	n.a.
Turkey	1966	37	24	39
UAR	1966–7	28	27	45
Yemen	—	n.a.	n.a.	n.a.

Sources: *UN Statistical Yearbook 1968,* UN 1969
National Statistics

[1] Including petroleum and construction.
[2] Including transport and trade.

PERCENTAGE EXPENDITURE ON GNP (AT MARKET PRICES)

Country	Year	Private consumption	Public consumption	Fixed capital formation	Change in stocks	Net trade balance (exports less imports) Goods & services	Net factor income from Abroad
Bahrain	—	n.a.	n.a.	n.a.	n.a.	n.a.	n.a.
Iran	1967–8	71	13	18	n.a.	5	−8
Iraq	1965	58	25	13	2	18	−17
Israel	1966	67	22	20	1	−10	−1
Jordan	1967	77	23	13	−1	−18	6
Kuwait	1966–7	35	19	20	1	53	−31
Lebanon	1964	80	8	21	—	−13	4
Oman	—	n.a.	n.a.	n.a.	n.a.	n.a.	n.a.
Qatar	—	n.a.	n.a.	n.a.	n.a.	n.a.	n.a.
Saudi Arabia	1966–7	38	19	18	1	55	−32
South Yemen	—	n.a.	n.a.	n.a.	n.a.	n.a.	n.a.
Sudan	1965	78	13	10	1	−1	0
Syria	1963	63	17	19	1	1	−1
Trucial States	—	n.a.	n.a.	n.a.	n.a.	n.a.	n.a.
Turkey	1966	74	13	15	—	−2	0
UAR	1966–7	67	20	14	2	−1	−1
Yemen	—	n.a.	n.a.	n.a.	n.a.	n.a.	n.a.

Sources: *UN Statistical Yearbooks*
National Statistics

TOTAL IMPORTS
($ millions c.i.f.)

Country	1955	1960	1963	1966	1967	1968
Bahrain	n.a.	27	69	88	95	108
Iran	309·7	559[1]	523	930	1,126	1,386
Iraq	272·2	389	319	493	423	404
Israel	325·6	503	672	835	769	1,081
Jordan	75·8	120	152	191	154	161
Kuwait	n.a.	242	324	463	593	611
Lebanon	259	311	386	533	463	602
Oman	n.a.	n.a.	n.a.	n.a.	n.a.	n.a.
Qatar	n.a.	28	28	30	29	42[2]
Saudi Arabia	200·2	235	320	457[3]	502[3]	492[3]
Southern Yemen	207·1	214	272	285	200	203
Sudan	140·1	183	285	222	214	195
Syria	179·2	239	235	289	264	331
Trucial States[4]	n.a.	n.a.	n.a.	66	100	160
Turkey	497·6	468	688	725	691	770
UAR	525·2	668	1,070	916	754	700
Yemen	n.a.	n.a.	n.a.	53	n.a.	n.a.

Sources: International Financial Statistics—International Monetary Fund
National Statistics

[1] March 1960–1.
[2] Provisional.
[3] Figures for Hijri years 1965–6, 1966–7, 1967–8, which are slightly shorter than the Grigorian year.
[4] Dubai re-exports quantities of goods to the other Trucial States (which are then shown as imports in customs returns) so that it is difficult to obtain reliable figures relating to all the states.

TOTAL EXPORTS
($ millions f.o.b.)

Country	1955	1960	1963	1966	1967	1968
Bahrain[1]	n.a.	23	22	26	31	39
Iran	168·8	845	933	1,309	1,930	1,879
Iraq	506·6	654	781	939	828	1,043
Israel	88·2	217	352	503	555	640
Jordan	8·0	11	18	29	32	40
Kuwait	n.a.	960	1,110	1,304	1,313	1,397
Lebanon	33·3	42	61	103	119	165
Oman	n.a.	n.a.	n.a.	n.a.	n.a.	n.a.
Qatar	n.a.	n.a.	n.a.	n.a.	n.a.	n.a.
Saudi Arabia	558·5	820	1,120	1,650	1,786	1,945
Southern Yemen	176·5	168	195	190	137	110
Sudan	147·3	182	226	203	214	245
Syria	128·3	120	189	173	155	168
Trucial States	n.a.	n.a.	n.a.	n.a.	n.a.	n.a.
Turkey	313·3	321	368	490	523	496
UAR	397·4	568	522	605	566	622
Yemen	n.a.	n.a.	n.a.	6·8	n.a.	n.a.

Sources: International Financial Statistics—International Monetary Fund
National Statistics

[1] Exports and re-exports, excluding oil and oil producers.

INDUSTRY
INDICES OF INDUSTRIAL PRODUCTION
(1963=100)

Country	1960	1961	1962	1963	1964	1965	1966	1967
Bahrain	n.a.	n.a.	n.a.	n.a.	n.a.	n.a.	n.a.	n.a.
Iran	75	81	92	100	114	127	143	170
Iraq[1]	n.a.	n.a.	100	101	112	119	122	123
Israel	67	77	88	100	114	125	127	123
Jordan	n.a.	n.a.	n.a.	100	108	136	147	108
Kuwait	n.a.	n.a.	n.a.	n.a.	n.a.	n.a.	n.a.	n.a.
Lebanon	n.a.	n.a.	n.a.	n.a.	n.a.	n.a.	n.a.	n.a.
Oman	—	—	—	—	—	—	—	n.a.
Qatar	n.a.	n.a.	n.a.	n.a.	n.a.	n.a.	n.a.	n.a.
Saudi Arabia[2]	n.a.	n.a.	n.a.	100	110	121	152	146
South Yemen	n.a.	n.a.	n.a.	n.a.	n.a.	n.a.	n.a.	n.a.
Sudan	n.a.	n.a.	n.a.	n.a.	n.a.	n.a.	n.a.	n.a.
Syria	83	88	97	100	114	124	128	136
Trucial States	n.a.	n.a.	n.a.	n.a.	n.a.	n.a.	n.a.	n.a.
Turkey	85	87	91	100	120	144	170	n.a.
UAR	52	65	77	100	116	121	117	111
Yemen	n.a.	n.a.	n.a.	n.a.	n.a.	n.a.	n.a.	n.a.

Sources: *UN Statistical Yearbook 1968,* UN 1969
National Statistics
Studies on Selected Development Problems in Various Countries of the
Middle East, 1969, UN

[1] Basic year 1962.
[2] Manufacturing only.

PRODUCTION A
MAJOR INDUSTRIAL AND AGRICULTURAL PRODUCTS

Country	Cement 000 metric tons		Total crude oil refining capacity barrels per day	Sugar[1]—raw value 000 metric tons		Tobacco Products Cigarettes millions		Tobacco metric tons		Cotton (Lint) 000 metric tons		Citrus fruit 000 metric tons		Cereals[5] 000 metric tons	
	1966	1967	1969	1966	1967	1966	1967	1966	1967	1966	1967	1966	1967	1966	1967
Bahrain	n.a.	n.a.	205,000	—	—	—	—	—	—	—	—	106	113	—	—
Iran	1,394	1,538	535,200	355·6	265·0	10,122	10,630	5,200	5,298	115	118	—	—	5,108	6,017
Iraq	1,279	n.a.	102,560	3·1	4·1	5,210	n.a.	n.a.	n.a.	11	12	905	1,082	1,858	2,055
Israel	1,168	805	120,000	40·0	34·0	3,087	3,236	112	110	25	29	57	523[3]	137	306
Jordan	374	321	7,500	—	—	1,502	1,829	72	37	—	—	—	—	128	311
Kuwait	n.a.	n.a.	489,000	—	—	—	—	—	—	—	—	—	—	—	—
Lebanon	1,095	1,016	35,500	13·6	10·9	1,594	1,400	2,560	2,695	n.a.	n.a.	250	238[4]	95	92
Oman	—	—	—	—	—	—	—	—	—	—	—	—	—	—	n.a.
Qatar	—[2]	—[2]	600	—	—	—	—	—	—	—	—	—	—	n.a.	n.a.
Saudi Arabia	323	410	279,000	—	—	—	—	—	—	—	—	—	—	252	255
South Yemen	—	—	178,000	—	—	n.a.	n.a.	n.a.	n.a.	4	5	n.a.	n.a.	42	49
Sudan	105	133	20,000	26·4	77·1	n.a.	n.a.	n.a.	n.a.	159	179	1	1	1,208	2,295
Syria	682	688	59,000	22·3	25·0	2,626	2,527	1,432	1,587	141	127	8	8	789	1,692
Trucial States	—	—	—	—	—	—	—	—	—	—	—	—	—	—	—
Turkey	3,854	4,236	137,000	651·2	722·7	35,844	33,300	3,408	3,060	382	396	457	545	16,511	16,962
UAR	2,629	2,754	170,000	360·0	364·0	13,432	12,750	3,687	3,250	455	437	634	705	6,482	6,759
Yemen	—	—	—	—	—	—	—	—	—	—	1	—	—	686	742

Sources: *UN Statistical Yearbook 1968*, UN 1969
World Petroleum
National Statistics
Middle East Economic Digest
Food and Agriculture Organisation Production Yearbook 1968, FAO 1969

[1] Sugar production figures, apply only to processing of locally grown beet or cane. A great deal of sugar is also imported for refining.

[2] Qatar National Cement Manufacturing Company started operations in 1969. Its output is about 100,000 tons a year.

[3] These are FAO estimates. Later UN figures give 54,000 and 62,000 tons for 1966 and 1967 respectively.

[4] These are FAO figures. Later UN figures give 240,000 and 210,000 tons for 1966 and 1967 respectively.

[5] Includes wheat, rye, barley, oats, maize, millet and sorghum, rice and buckwheat.

PRODUCTION B
OUTPUT OF MAIN PETROLEUM PRODUCTS

Country	Motor spirit 1966	1967	Kerosene 1966	1967	Jet fuel 1966	1967	Distillate fuel oils 1966	1967	Residual fuel oil 1966	1967	Bitumen (asphalt) 1966	1967	Lubricating oils 1966	1967	Liquified petroleum Gas 1966	1967
Bahrain	1,708	1,979	356	297	1,218	1,729	1,848	1,931	4,453	5,716	3	3	—	—	—	—
Iran	2,398	2,319	1,793	1,833	1,477	1,425	3,126	n.a.	n.a.	n.a.	248	340	56	49	26	38
Iraq	301	343	491	496	45	45	680	710	1,306	1,294	59	72	26	25	n.a.	n.a.
Israel	476	n.a.	258	n.a.	—	—	925	n.a.	1,592	n.a.	41	—	16	15	71	75
Jordan	77	72	71	69	46	51	136	118	91	88	39	29	—	—	10	10
Kuwait	314	314	43	47	—	—	2,928	2,563	6,459	6,480	—	n.a.	—	—	684	n.a.
Lebanon	310	303	154	180	—	—	232	269	883	891	—	—	—	—	23	21
Oman	—	—	—	—	—	—	—	—	—	—	—	—	—	—	—	—
Qatar	7	—	5	5	—	—	7	7	11	2	—	—	—	—	—	—
Saudi Arabia	2,115	2,416	248	372	1,323	1,215	2,217	2,243	9,113	9,765	108	139	—	—	488	574
Southern Yemen	406	335	744[1]	583[1]	n.a.	n.a.	1,505	1,179	3,659	3,154	—	—	—	—	5	3
Sudan	87	82	36	19	38	57	209	428	376	n.a.	—	—	—	—	2	1
Syria	167	168	144	172	—	—	281	254	419	456	31	n.a.	n.a.	n.a.	10	n.a.
Trucial States	—	—	—	—	—	—	—	—	—	—	—	—	—	—	—	—
Turkey	762	797	422	392	88	176	1,270	1,259	2,021	2,303	139	186	—	—	80	108
UAR	849	736	923	822[1]	24	n.a.	1,453	1,158	4,196	3,227	134	98	—	—	121	95
Yemen	—	—	—	—	—	—	—	—	—	—	—	—	—	—	—	—

Sources: *UN Statistical Yearbook 1968*, UN 1969
World Petroleum

[1] Includes Jet Fuel.

EARNINGS IN MANUFACTURE 1961–6
(D–day, W–week, M–month, m–male, f–female, mf–both)

Country	Code	Currency	Sex	1961	1962	1963	1964	1965	1966
Israel	D	£I	mf	11·1	12·3	14·0	15·4	17·5	20·4
Syria	M	£Sy	mf	129·0	130·0	132·0	132·0	133·0	135·0
Turkey	D	TL	mf	14·9	15·7	17·2	17·7	20·7	22·7
UAR	W	£Eg	mf	2·2	2·2	2·5	2·6	—	—

HOURS WORKED IN MANUFACTURING 1961–6
(W–per week)

Country	Code	1961	1962	1963	1964	1965	1966
Israel	W	42·3	41·9	41·8	42·7	42·2	41·6
UAR	W	48·0	47·0	44·0	44·0	—	—

Source: ILO

Notes: Revised method of estimation.

LAND UTILISATION
(000 hectares)

Country	Total land area	Year	Agricultural Area Arable[1] land under permanent crops	Arable land % of total area	Permanent[1] meadows & pastures	Forested land	Potentially productive[1] area	Waste-land & built-up land
Bahrain	60	1967	n.a.	n.a.	n.a.	—	n.a.	n.a.
Iran	163,600	1960	11,593	7·1	6,741	12,000[2]	4,127	130,339
Iraq	43,492	1964	7,496	17·2	4,264	1,951	29,781	
Israel	2,026	1967	411	20·3	822	101[3]	736	
Jordan	9,018	1965	1,140	2·6	212	67	302	8,053
Kuwait	1,600	1967	0·3	0·2	—	—	n.a.	n.a.
Lebanon	1,000	1967	306	30·6	10	95	358	271
Oman	21,238	1967	n.a.	n.a.	n.a.	n.a.	n.a.	n.a.
Qatar	2,201	1967	n.a.	n.a.	n.a.	—	n.a.	n.a.
Saudi Arabia	214,969	1965	373	1·7	85,028	1,700	2,880[4]	124,988
Southern Yemen	28,768	1966	252	8·8	9,065	2,590	1,554	15,307
Sudan	237,600	1964	7,100	3·0	24,000[5]	91,500	38,016	89,965
Syria	18,509	1967	6,130	33·1	5,412	477	6,499	
Trucial States	8,360	1967	n.a.	n.a.	n.a.	—	n.a.	n.a.
Turkey	77,076	1967	26,250	34·1	26,135	12,578	13,095	
UAR	100,145[6]	1967	2,801	2·8	—	2	97,342	
Yemen	19,500	1967	2,100[7]	10·8	n.a.	150	2,900[7]	n.a.

Source: *Food and Agriculture Production Yearbook 1965*, FAO 1969

[1] In certain cases, notably Saudi Arabia and Iraq, these figures include rough grazing.
[2] Includes unstocked land.
[3] Including potential land for afforestation.
[4] Of which 2,780,000 hectares for forests.
[5] Acacia short grass scrub.
[6] Of which inhabited and cultivated area accounts for 3,558,000 hectares.
[7] Yemen Ministry of Agriculture estimates.

INDICES OF AGRICULTURAL PRODUCTION
(1952-6=100)
(Countries with globally significant volume of production only)

Country	1959	1960	1961	1962	1963	1964	1965	1966	1967
Iran	126	122	131	130	138	135	147	147	159
Iraq	169	175	186	204	211	245	255	255	298
Israel	174	180	193	213	221	255	265	267	310
Jordan[1]	n.a.	100	181	134	158	246	230	130	206
Lebanon[2]	n.a.	n.a.	n.a.	n.a.	n.a.	n.a.	n.a.	n.a.	n.a.
Saudi Arabia[2]	n.a.	n.a.	n.a.	n.a.	n.a.	n.a.	n.a.	n.a.	n.a.
Sudan	135	131	129	156	154	141	158	165	191
Syria	98	92	112	158	142	154	153	115	145
Turkey	125	126	127	133	140	146	141	158	161
UAR	120	127	112	135	136	141	144	144	140

Source: *Food and Agriculture Production Yearbook 1968*, FAO 1969

[1] The Jordan index is based on production of cereals, vegetables, fruit, tomatoes and olives only.
[2] Data available not sufficiently consistent to calculate indices.

RAILWAYS

Country	Length of line operated (km.)	Passenger/km. (million)	Ton/km. (million)
Bahrain	—	—	—
Iran	3,499	1,142	2,232
Iraq	1,631	431	1,009
Israel	746	368	318
Jordan	366	n.a.	n.a.
Kuwait	—	—	—
Lebanon	417	7	46
Oman	—	—	—
Qatar	—	—	—
Saudi Arabia	577	34	52
South Yemen	—	—	—
Sudan	5,400	n.a.	2,253
Syria	992	68	85
Trucial States	—	—	—
Turkey	8,008	4,189	5,485
UAR	34	6,170	3,387
Yemen	—	—	—

Sources: *UN Statistical Yearbook 1968*, UN 1969
National Statistics

CIVIL AVIATION 1966 and 1967

Country	Number of airlines	Total scheduled passenger kilometres (millions) 1966	1967	Total scheduled cargo ton-kilometres (millions) 1966	1967
Bahrain	1	n.a.	n.a.	n.a.	n.a.
Iran	1	306·9	387·8	2·6	3·4
Iraq	1	88·8	72·1	1·0	0·8
Israel	2	1,452·8	1,531·7	35·0	45·7
Jordan	1	116·8	97·9	0·5	0·6
Kuwait[1]	1	244·5	248·5	3·6	4·5
Lebanon	3	615·1	695·6	42·3	63·0
Oman	—	—	—	—	—
Qatar	—	—	—	—	—
Saudi Arabia	1	n.a.	n.a.	n.a.	n.a.
Sudan	1	108·3	97·0	1·8	1·9
Syria	1	134·5	93·3	3·5	1·0
Trucial States	—	—	—	—	—
Turkey	1	271·9	310·5	1·8	2·3
UAR	1	658·3	573·3	6·6	5·8
Yemen	1	n.a.	n.a.	n.a.	n.a.

Source: *UN Statistical Yearbook 1968*, UN 1969

[1] Scheduled international flights only.

MERCHANT SHIPPING 1967
(000 tons gross)

Country	Total merchant ships	Of which, tankers
Bahrain	—	—
Iran[1]	30	—
Iraq	—	—
Israel	688	—
Jordan	—	—
Kuwait	137	102
Lebanon	598	102
Oman	598	—
Qatar	598	—
Saudi Arabia	598	102
South Yemen	598	—
Sudan	—	—
Syria	—	—
Trucial States	598	—
Turkey	611	104
UAR	236	—
Yemen	236	—

Source: *UN Statistical Yearbook 1968*, UN 1969

[1] National Statistics.

CONSUMPTION A
ESTIMATED AVAILABLE FOOD SUPPLIES—MAIN FOODSTUFFS

Net food supplies per caput grams per day

Country	Year	Cereals	Sugar	Meat	Milk	Fats & oils	Fruit and vegetables
Bahrain	—	n.a.	n.a.	n.a.	n.a.	n.a.	n.a.
Iran	1966	323	71	41	142	16	263
Iraq	1960–2	355	81	55	207	10	352
Israel	1966–7	286	111	144	374	50	747
Jordan	1966	290	113	28	137	26	545
Kuwait	—	n.a.	n.a.	n.a.	n.a.	n.a.	n.a.
Lebanon	1966	365	111	84	353	26	691
Oman	—	n.a.	n.a.	n.a.	n.a.	n.a.	n.a.
Qatar	—	n.a.	n.a.	n.a.	n.a.	n.a.	n.a.
Saudi Arabia	1966	337	29	48	101	4	538
Southern Yemen	—	n.a.	n.a.	n.a.	n.a.	n.a.	n.a.
Sudan	1966	310	33	76	352	24	194
Syria	1966	575	39	32	121	26	403
Trucial States	—	n.a.	n.a.	n.a.	n.a.	n.a.	n.a.
Turkey	1960–1	611	28	37	193	22	628
UAR	1965–6	551	49	36	122	19	522
Yemen	—	n.a.	n.a.	n.a.	n.a.	n.a.	n.a.

Source: *Food and Agriculture Production Yearbook 1968*, FAO 1969

CONSUMPTION B
ESTIMATED INDUSTRIAL CONSUMPTION—MAJOR RAW MATERIALS

Country	Cotton 000 metric tons 1967–8	Steel[1] 000 metric tons 1967	Fertilisers phosphate 000 metric tons 1967–8	Fertilisers nitrogenous 000 metric tons 1967–8	Newsprint 000 metric tons 1966
Bahrain	—	n.a.	n.a.	n.a.	n.a.
Iran	54·2	1,330	17·0	46·0	8·0
Iraq	6·5	234	2·1	5·8	1·7
Israel	24·3	316	11·8	28·3	18·4
Jordan	—	n.a.	1·1	2·0	0·6
Kuwait	—	n.a.	n.a.	n.a.	n.a.
Lebanon	5·4	225	7·0	12·5	3·3
Oman	—	—	—	—	n.a.
Qatar	—	n.a.	—	—	n.a.
Saudi Arabia	—	151	4·0	6·5	0·4
Southern Yemen	—	—	n.a.	n.a.	n.a.
Sudan	14·1	n.a.	0·8	34·0	1·6
Syria	23·9	165	5·5	16·9	1·2
Trucial States	—	n.a.	n.a.	n.a.	n.a.
Turkey	160·4	777	132·2	138·1	44·1
UAR	188·6	745	48·0	220·0	52·0
Yemen	n.a.	n.a.	n.a.	n.a.	n.a.

Sources: *Food and Agriculture Production Yearbook 1968*, FAO 1969
UN Statistical Yearbook 1968, UN 1969

[1] Apparent consumption in terms of crude steel.

HEALTH SERVICES

Country	Year	No. of hospitals	No. of hospital beds	Year	No. of doctors	No. of nurses	No. of pharmacists	No. of dentists	No. of midwives
Bahrain	1968	10[1]	918	1968	89[2]	470	59[3]	2	n.a.
Iran	1966	397	28,130	1966	6,889	5,972	2,702	1,440	1,366
Iraq	1966	153	15,904	1965	1,606	1,135	664	369	786
Israel	1966	142	19,566	1966	6,339	10,422[4]	1,527	1,211	n.a.
Jordan[5]	1968	31	1,636	1968	571	328	254	78	191
Kuwait	1966	18	3,488	1966	587	1,060[4]	86	56	n.a.
Lebanon	n.a.	n.a.	9,791	1965	1,735[6]	861[6]	462[6]	510[6]	496[6]
Oman	1966	8	207	1966	23	n.a.	1	2	15
Qatar	1969	3	600	1966	60	143[7]	3[7]	57	n.a.
Saudi Arabia	1968	80	6,299[8]	1966	686	1,198[9]	385	n.a.	647[10]
Southern Yemen	1968	15	1,308	1968	117[11]	384	5	20	n.a.
Sudan	1965	601	13,439	1966	567	5,499[4]	72	43	n.a.
Syria	1966	83	6,281	1963	978	408	348	292	290
Trucial States	1969	4[12]	156[13]	—	n.a.	n.a.	n.a.	n.a.	n.a.
Turkey	1965	626	55,451	1966	11,335	5,039	1,933	2,140	4,964
UAR	1965-6	n.a.	65,864	1965	13,021[14]	5,865[14]	3,871[14]	1,283[14]	7,568[14]
Yemen	1967	24	3,695[15]	1967	84	185	n.a.	n.a.	n.a.

[1] Excluding sanatoria (2), health centres (15) and clinics (20).
[2] Government medical staff only. Excludes doctors in private practice and those attached to the Bahraini Petroleum Co. and the American Mission Hospital.
[3] Including trainees.
[4] Including midwives.
[5] Jordan data includes West Bank and military hospitals.
[6] Those registered in Lebanon only.
[7] Government personnel only.

[8] Excluding health centres (303).
[9] Male nurses only.
[10] Includes female nurses.
[11] Since 1966 many doctors have left the country but no later figures are available.
[12] Abu Dhabi and Dubai only.
[13] Dubai only.
[14] Those registered in UAR only.
[15] Excluding medical case centres set up by UAR forces.

Sources: *UN Statistical Yearbook 1968*, UN 1969
National Statistics

MIDDLE EAST DEFENCE EXPENDITURE

Country	Defence expenditure $ million 1968	Defence expenditure $ million 1969	Defence expenditure per caput $ 1968	Defence expenditure As % of Gross National Product 1965	Defence expenditure As % of Gross National Product 1966	Defence expenditure As % of Gross National Product 1967	Defence expenditure As % of Gross National Product 1968
Turkey	472	510	14	4·3	4·4	4·6	3·9
Iran	495	505	19	4·4	3·6	5·5	5·8
Iraq	252	280	30	10·2	10·5	10·3	11·2
Israel	628	829	224	11·7	12·2	13·8	16·1
Jordan	81	126	39	12·9	12·2	12·8	14·7
Saudi Arabia	321	343	64	8·6	12·1	11·9	11·9
Syria	137	195	25	8·4	11·1	11·9	12·6
UAR	690	805	22	8·6	11·1	12·7	12·5

Source: Institute for Strategic Studies

SUPPLEMENTARY SOURCES USED FOR COMPARATIVE STATISTICS :

Bahrain Finance Department. *Annual Statistical Abstract*, 1967 and 1968.

Bahrain Government. *Annual Reports and Statistical Abstracts*, 1959–63 and 1967–8.

Bank of Israel. *Annual Report*, 1968.

Bank Markazi Iran. *Annual Report*, 1968–9.

Bank of Sudan. *Annual Report*, 1968.

El Mallakh, Ragaei. *Economic Development and Regional Co-operation: Kuwait*, Univ. of Chicago Press, Chicago, 1968.

General Union of Chambers of Commerce, Industry and Agriculture for Arab Countries. *Arab Economic Report*, August 1968.

Iraq Ministry of Planning. *Annual Statistical Abstract*, 1967.

Jordan Department of Statistics. *Analysis of National Accounts*, 1959–67.

Jordan Department of Statistics. *Statistical Yearbook*, 1967 and 1968.

Jordan Department of Statistics. *The Jordan Economy—Some Economic Indicators*, 1968.

Kuwait Institute of Economic and Social Planning in the Middle East. *National Accounts of Kuwait*, 1965–6 and 1967–8.

Middle East Economic Digest.

National Bank of Egypt. *Economic Bulletin*, 1969.

Saudi Arabian Monetary Agency. *Annual Reports and Statistical Reports*, 1967, 1968 and 1969.

United Nations. *Industrial Development in the Arab Countries*, 1966.

US Department of Commerce. *Overseas Business Reports*, 1968 and 1969.

BASIC INFORMATION

IRAN

Features

IRAN is structurally and topographically extremely complex but some major elements can be picked out. The whole area was severely affected by Tertiary earth movements which produced three great swathes of mountains. On the west the Zagros ranges extend from Azerbaijan in the north along the Iraqi border and sweep arcuately south-east into the Makran and Baluchistan overlooking the Indian Ocean; summits rise to over 14,000 ft./4,400 m. Also from the north-west knot the narrower but equally high and rugged range from the Elburz stretches to the east, separated from the Caspian by a relatively narrow coastal plain and sweeping eastward into the Afghan-Hindu-Kush complex; volcanic Mt. Demavend rises to 18,700 ft./5,800 m. On the eastern borders lie the confused highlands of the Afghan-Baluchi systems. Between these main mountain range complexes lies the basin and range high plateau of central Iran, over the lower parts of which extend the alkaline basins of the Kavir and the gravel deserts of the Dasht-i-Lut, areas completely repellent to man. Most of Iran, except for the Zagros periphery, drains into a series of interior basins, the hydrology and sedimentation history of which largely determine the agricultural potential. Climate in almost all regions of Iran is harsh. Except for the Caspian littoral and Khuzistan, winters are cold and snowfalls can be heavy, these extremes accentuated in the highlands. Summers are everywhere hot except in the highest mountains. Precipitation is highest in the highlands of the north and west but there is a net annual moisture deficit in all regions and irrigation is necessary for successful cultivation. The relatively pluvious highlands form the traditional homeland of many groups of nomadic pastoralism although sedenterisation is now proceeding fast. The centres of settlement and political importance have for the most part been sited in those major oasis-basins in the central region which lay on the great piedmont land-routes between Central Asia and the Indus Valley on the one hand and Mesopotamia and the Gulf on the other, Tehran, Isfahan, Mashhad and Kerman. Mineral resources are varied although not extensive (with the exception of oil and ore mainly associated with the western highlands).

Area
628,000 sq. mi.–1,648,000 sq. km.

Mean max. and min. temperatures
Tehran (35°41′N, 51°19′E; 3,750 ft./1,191 m.) 99°F/37°C (July), 26°F/—3°C (January); Abadan (30°22′N, 48°15′E; 10 ft./3 m.) 113°F/45°C (August), 45°F/7°C (January).

Relative humidity
Tehran 45%–65%; Abadan 35%–90%.

Mean annual precipitation
Tehran 9 in./224 mm.; Abadan 3 in./146mm.

POPULATION

Total population
26,284,000 (1967 UN estimate).

Chief towns and populations
(1966) TEHRAN (2,719,700), Isfahan (424,000), Mashhad (409,000), Tabriz (405,000), Shiraz (269,000), Ahwaz (207,000), Kermanshah (188,000), Hamadan (124,000), Rezaiyeh (110,000).

Distribution
The urban population, 38% of the total in 1966, is increasing three times as fast as the rural population. Average densities are highest in the lowlands of Khuzistan, the Caspian and irrigated basins on the interior flanks of the Zagros and Elburz mountains. Measures are being taken to decelerate the growth of Tehran.

Language
Farsi, Persian, is the dominant language but as a result of ethnic diversity there exist minority languages such as Turkish in the north-west and north-east, Baluchi in the south-east, Kurdish and Luri in the Zagros tribal areas and Arabic in the south. English and French are extensively used by educated people.

CONSTITUTIONAL SYSTEM

Constitution
Iran is a constitutional monarchy under an Imperial Decree of 1906.

Head of State
His Imperial Majesty Muhammad Reza Shah Pahlevi.

Head of Government
Prime Minister Amir Abbas Hoveida.

Executive
Executive power is the prerogative of the Shahinshah, the hereditary monarch. The Shah is military C.-in-C., declares war and peace, may appoint or dismiss ministers, and dissolve Parliament and rule by decree. Normally the Prime Minister is chosen by Parliament and appointed by the Shah; he in turn chooses, dismisses or accepts the resignation of ministers by the approval of the Shah. Parliament may force the resignation of the Premier or other ministers by votes of no-confidence. The power of the Shah to rule directly has been of considerable importance to the progress of several policies, notably land reform; between 1961 and 1963 Iran was thus ruled by decree at a crucial period.

Legislature
The legislature is bicameral consisting of the National Consultative Assembly (*Majlis*) and the Senate. The size of the *Majlis* is proportional to that of the population (now with 219 members) and it sits for a four-year term.

26

Election is by secret ballot; the franchise includes all Iranian nationals over the age of 20, excluding members of the police and armed forces and the normally debarred categories. Women were enfranchised in 1963. Normal candidates must be Muslim since special arrangements are made for the representation of minorities. Two vacant seats are reserved for Bahrain. The Senate also sits for four years; it has 60 members, half nominated by the Shah, half elected on a provincial proportional representation basis. The assembly has the power to deal with all laws, the Senate acting as an advisory house with limited reserve powers.

The 22nd Majlis
The majority party is the Iran Novin with 180 seats; the Mardom party had 31 seats, the Pan Iranists 5, the Minorities 5. Of the elected senators 27 were members of Iran Novin, 2 of Mardom.

Political parties
Iran Novin is a development of the former Progressive Centre group. Formed in 1963, essentially a moderate progressive organisation very active in most parts of the country, it has formed governments ever since. The Mardom Party with the only sizeable opposition in Parliament tended to be somewhat left of the majority National Party of a decade ago. The Pan-Iranists stand for nationalism above all else. The Communist groups are proscribed from political activity; the Tudeh Party (still active underground) is conventionally associated with Russian thinking but a Maoist revolutionary wing is active outside Iran.

Leading figures
(September 1970) Amir Abbas Hoveida, Premier; Ardeshir Zahedi, Minister of Foreign Affairs; Ata'ollah Khosravani, Secretary-General of Iran Novin party; Mansur Rouhani, Minister of Water and Power; Yahya Adl, Secretary-General of Mardom.

Local Government
For purposes of local administration Iran is divided into 14 provinces (*Ostan*) administered by governor-generals (*Ostandar*) who are appointed by and responsible to the Ministry of the Interior. The *Ostan* are subdivided into counties or cities (*Shahrestan*) which in turn are formed of municipalities (*Bakhsh*) and districts (*Dihestan*). All municipal administrations are assisted by elected councils. Judicial system : A Ministry of Justice oversees the administrative and judicial structure. The Supreme Court and the Chief Justice in Tehran are the final legal authority and the final appellate court. In each provincial capital there sits a Court of Appeal with civil and criminal branches; in addition there is an independent Criminal Court which deals with serious criminal offences remitted to it from lower courts. Courts of First Instance, single-judge courts, sit in most districts and deal with the bulk of civil and all intermediate criminal cases. Magistrates and Municipal courts deal with minor offences. Special courts include religious courts with limited jurisdiction (mainly family and marriage problems), government employee courts and permanent and temporary military courts, the former established in each *Ostan* and dealing with matters of state security.

RECENT HISTORY

Modern Iran dates from 1925 when Reza Khan, who came to power in the chaos following World War I, became Reza Shah and set about restoring the authority of the central government and establishing externally the national status of the country. Internally, modernisation and the breaking of regional and feudal power interests, as in Turkey, were accompanied by authoritarianism. Externally, the extra-territorial rights enjoyed by foreign governments and nationals were abrogated, concessions (including oil concessions to Anglo-Persian interests) deemed to be unfavourable were re-negotiated. In both spheres interests seem to harmonise with those of the Axis powers in the late 1930s and, since German influence appeared to be dangerously strong, the Allies invaded Persia in 1941. Britain and the USSR in 1942 signed a treaty guaranteeing Persian independence and securing the vital communications between Russia and Allied forces in the Levant and the Gulf. Reza Shah abdicated in favour of his son Muhammad Reza who became the second Pahlevi dynastic ruler. During the closing years of World War II the USSR brought increasing political and military pressure to bear and the Caspian area and Azerbaijan became virtually occupied territories. In 1946 British and American forces left Persia as agreed but Russia attempted to set up an autonomous state in Azerbaijan and only after UN and other pressures were applied did Russian forces evacuate the northern regions. They left as a legacy the Tudeh Communist Party and disaffection in the Kurdish areas. Nationalist sympathies, strengthened by these events, led to the disputing of agreements with the Anglo-Iranian Oil Company and to some xenophobia led by the National Front Group and Dr Mossadeq, the Premier. At the same time the economic needs of Iran, particularly for development capital, were becoming acute. In 1951 the oil industry (essentially AIOC) was nationalised, diplomatic relations between Iran and the USA and Britain became increasingly strained. During 1952 Mossadeq became unpopular in the *Majlis*, but received the backing of the Tudeh party while the young Shah was advised to leave the country. Oil revenue virtually disappeared and financial aid was not forthcoming. In 1953 the Shah left Iran and issued a decree appointing (as Premier) General Zahedi, who promptly arrested Mossadeq and restored central authority. Following the return of the Shah an emergency financial grant was made by the USA and the AIOC dispute resolved by the creation of an international consortium. By 1955 the Shah had become sufficiently experienced to realise the need for pressing reforms on and through governments, having taken the first personal steps by distributing his own estate to peasant farmers. Between 1955 and 1963, however, the main internal problems were associated with making a parliamentary democracy (in a largely illiterate country with most power residing in the 'thousand families' of large landowners) an effective means of achieving progress. A series of political parties, National, People's, National Front, National Union, etc., emerged under a succession of notable premiers, Manoutcher Eqbal, Jafar Sharif Emami, Ali Amini and Assadollah Alam, each one in turn securing some progress, meeting opposition sometimes with over-authoritarian zeal, sometimes by internal fission. However, except for short periods of rule by decree the 1960s developed with the definite progress of land reform law and the maintenance of government by election. This development, in 1963, culminated in the introduction of female suffrage and the passing of the Land Reform Law— a victory for the National Union's policy of reform and planning. Externally, Iran joined the Baghdad Pact in 1955, but retained her place in what became the CENTO system, and in particular developed Regional Co-operation for Development (RCD) links with Turkey and Pakistan; relations with the USSR were also improved very rapidly. The assassination of Premier

28

Mansur by right-wing elements in 1965 was followed by an attempt on the Shah's life by extreme radicals in 1966. Since that time internal affairs have become generally stable as development plans accelerate and the benefits of reforms appear. In October 1967 the Shah was formally crowned and Iran has assumed a full and significant role in international affairs. A cloud on the horizon has been the less than cordial relations with some Arab countries following Iran's clear disengagement during the Israeli war in 1967 and her anxiety to retain her claimed rights in the Gulf and in the Shatt al-Arab.

Defence
Iranian armed forces are second only to Turkey in strength among the countries of the Middle East. The army numbers at least 160,000 men, including armoured and parachute divisions. Armour until recently, has been mainly American, as is the equipment of the air-force, which has at least five fighter squadrons and a transport section. Naval forces, mainly light, are stationed in the Gulf and the Caspian. Under CENTO arrangements an extensive radar and communications network has been installed. Russian arms have recently been supplied in significant quantities.

ECONOMY
Background
The Iranian economy in recent years has been the fastest growing of any in the Middle East. During the Third Five Year Plan period, 1962–8, the rate of economic growth averaged 8% *p.a.* rising to over 11% at the close. The Fourth Plan, 1968–73 is designed to give an average growth rate of over 9% *p.a.* At current prices the *per caput* income rose from $85 in 1965 to $240 in 1967 and is planned to rise to $320 by 1973; a remarkable increase, given the considerable price stability which has been maintained. Agriculture still makes the largest single contribution to the GDP but declining slightly from 27% in 1963–4 to 23% in 1967–8[1] and also with the slowest growth of all sectors. Approximately 70% of the occupied population is engaged in agriculture and one of the major tasks is to raise productivity through technology and through harnessing the forces liberated by land reform. One of the major difficulties is that about 80% of the cultivated area is under wheat and barley, over 70% of this area unirrigated and worked in small units of production. Only in the extreme south-west in Khuzistan and along the Caspian shore is there relatively easily exploited under-used potential for irrigation and for extending the crop-range. Annual growth rates have averaged 3% and are planned to rise to 5%, important not only for raising domestic consumption levels but also for exports and for import-substitution. Iran is now a major producer and exporter of cotton, is almost self-sufficient in sugar, and meets two-thirds of tea requirements; imports of wheat, wheat flour and rice are however still rising. Government monopolies handle tobacco, cereals, tea and sugar.

Industry and mining together contribute about 13% to the GDP, a little more than commerce, banking and insurance taken together, and approximately the same as oil (excluding income paid abroad), but the growth rate over the period 1962 to 1967 was 85%. Particularly encouraging was the fact that while public sector investment was inevitably preponderant

[1] These figures signify the Iranian years 1342 (1963–4) and 1346 (1967–8), which run from March to March.

(since most capital is derived from oil revenue received by the state), private sector investment has accelerated more rapidly than expected.

Oil is not only a source of revenue but also of fuel and raw material. Iran is the sixth largest producer in the world, 95% of production coming from Iranian Oil Participants.[2] Since 1957 the National Iranian Oil Company has extended the range of its activities. NIOC now has 12 agreements for joint oil exploitation with a variety of foreign companies and production is more than 141 million metric tons *p.a.* The Consortium refinery at Abadan is now outstripped by NIOC installations, completed at Tehran and under construction in Shiraz. Persian crude oil exports all travel via the Gulf terminal at Kharg Island; internally the Tehran refinery is supplied by pipeline from Ahwaz. A recent development has been the agreement to supply the USSR with natural gas at a rate rising to 20,000 million cubic metres annually from 1976 onward. A gas pipe-line system is planned and first construction contracts placed for about 1,100 kilometres of pipeline connecting Ahwaz and Shiraz in the south with the central Serajeh gas field, Tehran, Rasht and Astara in the USSR. A number of other towns will also be connected, making power available for various uses. Major petrochemical plants are being constructed at Abadan, Kharg Island and Bandar Mashur, in conjunction with American chemical interests. Fertilisers for domestic use will form one major product.

Industrialisation is rapidly changing from the position in 1960 when only 30 out of 4,440 factory units employed over 500 people. Between March 1967 and March 1968, 179 permits were used for new industrial plants, providing over 5,000 new jobs. Industrial activity as a whole grew by 13%. Major developments include the continued expansion of the Isfahan industrial complex with a Russian built steel mill (eventually of 1.2 million tons capacity), the construction of an aluminium smelter and a variety of engineering and processing plants at Ahwaz. Cement production of about 1.8 million tons *p.a.* gives an export surplus at the moment, but consumption and production is expected to treble during the Fourth Plan. The cotton textile industry is in a similar position. Much recent industrialisation is based on a rapid increase in electricity generating capacity increasingly based in multi-purpose hydro-plants. In 1966 plant to the capacity of 1.3 thousand MW was purchased or on order, in addition to the five-fold increase in capacity between 1953 and 1965. In the Fourth Plan the supply of electricity should increase by 166%.

As noted earlier, investment capital has in the main come from oil revenue and for the massive advance on all fronts projected in the Fourth Plan, which will require c. £4,500 million in fixed investment, £2,700 million is to come from oil. In order to achieve this target considerable pressure has been exerted on the Consortium to increase income from sales by 20% *p.a.*, almost the same as the increase achieved during the Arab oil embargo to the West in 1967. Much depends on the reactions of other OPEC members.

Foreign Trade

Exports (including oil) in 1967–8 increased by 41% over 1966–7; oil contributed 133 million riyals out of a total of 147,100 million. Cotton and fruit, the next most important, rose by 31% and 7.5% while foreign earnings

---

[2] Gulf Oil Corporation (7%), Mobil Corporation (7%), Standard Oil (New Jersey) (7%), Standard Oil Co. of California (7%), Texaco Inc. (7%), B.P. (40%), Shell (14%), C.F.P. (6%), Iricon Agency (5%).

from carpets also rose. The main purchasers of Iranian goods (excluding oil) were the USSR (16%), West Germany (14%) and the USA (11%); Britain took 5%. Imports rose by 22% to 90,000 million riyals in 1967–8 with iron and steel (crude and manufactured), machinery, electrical equipment and vehicles making up 15% of the total; tea imports constituted over 9% of import value. Iran's major suppliers were West Germany (23%), the USA (18%), Britain (11%) and Japan (7%). Iran has a balance of payments deficit on current account of about $100 million p.a., but this is both incurred and covered by aid-sponsored development. Very large credits have been made available through US agencies, the World Bank, USSR and Western and Eastern European countries. Special industrial and trade agreements have also been entered into with Iran's RCD partners, India and the Gulf States.

Employment
The active population was estimated at the 1966 census to be c. 7.5 million, although data from the rural sector are imprecise; the industrially employed population was 22%, later estimates are unreliable. Unemployment was estimated at about 9% but in order effectively to eliminate unemployment, open and disguised, it is estimated that a million new jobs will have to be created by 1973.

Price and Wage Trends
Prices have remained very stable since 1961, rising at less than 1% p.a. Minimum wage levels under the labour law are negotiated in various industries and in the public sector. There is considerable variation in rates and the pressure for unskilled employment depresses the market rates. Wages of urban labourers average about 180 riyals a day.

Consumption
Private consumption expenditure in 1967–8 made up 71% of the GNP, public consumption expenditure taking 13%. The ratio of state expenditure to the National Income has however been rising rapidly to about 44% at present.

SOCIAL SERVICES

Social Insurance
The Social Insurance Organisation, affiliated to the Ministry of Labour and Social Services, covers all employed workers. In return for an 18% insurance premium on wages and salaries (5% from the insured, 13% from the employer) the organisation provides medical treatment, disability allowances, compensation, maternity, marriage and death allowances, and retirement pensions. In 1965 1,550,000 people, insured or dependants, were receiving benefits and over 1,500 million riyals were disbursed. The income of the fund exceeded 2,000 million riyals. The organisation then had 12 hospitals, 45 large and 22 small clinics of its own. In January 1968 there were 510,000 insured persons (more than two million including dependants). Insurance provision for agricultural workers, many of whom are now self-employed, is being introduced.

Health
A general department of health services has responsibility for medical facilities, health education and public health. By the end of 1964 there were 28,130 hospital beds in 397 general hospitals and 22 specialised institutions. Over 1,600 clinics and 32 medical centres had been established in

various parts of the country. Approximately half the facilities belong to the Ministry of Health, the remainder being run by organisations such as Social Insurance, NIOC and Banks, by charitable institutions such as the Red Lion and Sun Society, The Imperial Organisation for Social Services and the Pahlavi Foundation. Medical facilities can be obtained free by the poor in all except the most remote areas.

EDUCATION

During the last decade there has been an intensive campaign of education in Iran, particularly aimed at improving literacy. The 1966 census showed that of the population aged seven or over 70% were wholly or partially illiterate. During the Third Plan 19% of current annual budgetary allocations (c. 4·5% of GNP) went to education, 60% of this to primary schooling. In addition to normal provision a Literacy Corps was founded in 1962 to direct high school graduates from normal military service into teaching. In December 1968 there were 14,740 primary schools with 2,400,000 pupils and 19,000 teachers. By March 1968, 35,000 Literacy Corps teachers were sent to schools and were teaching 230,000 primary children and 106,000 adults. Also in 1968 female members of the Literacy Corps started work. Secondary education is not compulsory but is generally free. In 1968 there were 600,000 pupils. The structure and function of secondary schooling is being redesigned to provide a broader basis than hitherto. Technical education is carried out at various secondary schools. There are some 30 technical, 17 agricultural, 17 commercial and over 50 trade schools; in all they have over 16,000 pupils.

Higher education includes the Tehran Polytechnic Institute established partly with UNDP funds and designed for technical training; 67 Teacher Training Schools and Colleges with 7,000 students during 1967–8; eight universities. The state University of Tehran has a complete range of faculties and some 16,000 students. Also in Tehran are the National University (3,000) and the Arya Mehr Industrial University (Technological). Gondishapour University in Ahwaz (400) specialises in medicine and agriculture, the University of Isfahan has separate Colleges of Medicine, Arts, Science and Teacher Training (2,200), Mashhad University has all but technological faculties (2,000), Pahlavi University in Shiraz specialises in the applied sciences and medicine (1,400) and, lastly, Tabriz University has most faculties (2,000). There were some 37,000 students in Iranian Universities and another 25,000 studying abroad during the session 1966–7. Scholarships are available for both categories.

MASS MEDIA

There is no direct press censorship in Iran but a certain number of loosely applied regulations concerning irresponsible anti-national statements and covering the licensing of journalists; both newspaper proprietors and journalists know how far they can go in publishing and writing what the government will allow. Communist publications are banned. The main newspapers and periodicals are all produced in Tehran and are almost all privately owned by publishing groups. The principal publications are :

The Press
Dailies : *Echo of Iran* (also weekly and monthly), Tehran (6,000); *Erfan*, Isfahan (3,000); *Ettela'at and Ettela'at Hawaii*, Tehran (70,000 and 3,000);

Farman, Tehran (15,000); *Kayhan* (also in English edn.), Tehran (70,000); *Kayhan Havai,* Tehran (55,000); *Kayhan International* (English), Tehran (10,000); *Khorasan,* Meshed (15,000); *Le Journal de Tehran* (French), Tehran (5,000); *Mehre Iran* (Mardom Party), Tehran;
Periodicals: *Ettela'ate Banovan* (women's) (w), (40,000); *Ettela'ate Haftigwe* (w), (20,000); *Ettela'ate Kudekan* (children) (w), Tehran; *Javanan* (w), Tehran (10,000); *Kayhan Bacheha* (children) (w), *Tehran* (30,000); *Kayhan Varzeshi* (sport) (w), Tehran (55,000); *Khandaniha* (w), Tehran (25,000); *Sepid va Siyah* (m), Tehran (30,000); *Tehran Chamber of Commerce* (English) (m), Tehran (15,000); *Tehran Economist* (English) (w), Tehran (10,000); *Tehran Mossavar* (w), Tehran (35,000); *Towfigh* (w), Tehran (35,000).

Broadcasting
Radio Iran, part of the Ministry of Information, transmits domestic radio programmes through 12 regional services. Home service programmes are in Farsi. Foreign service programmes use Arabic, Armenian, Assyrian, English, French, Russian, Turkish and Arabic. At Ahwaz, Kermanshah and Zahedan high-power transmitters send out programmes in Arabic, Kurdish and Baluchi.

Television programmes are transmitted by Television of Iran, a private commercial company, from stations in Tehran, Abadan and Ahwaz.

The United States Armed Forces broadcast their own radio and television programmes in Tehran.

IRAQ

GEOGRAPHY
Features

THE Republic of Iraq has its heartland in the central lowlands of the Euphrates-Tigris system (Mesopotamia), to the north of which lie the Assyrian hill-lands and the mountain highlands of Kurdistan, and to the south and west of which extends the Iraqi-Syrian desert. Sand and gravel deserts superficially cover the sedimentary overlay of the ancient and relatively stable Arabian platform. The northern highlands on the other hand lie in an area of structural disturbance, most vigorous in Tertiary times, resulting in extensive faulting, folding and mountain building. It is in this region that most of Iraq's mineral wealth lies. Mesopotamia is essentially a median zone, depressed between the flanking regions and infilled with recent river sediments, a northern extension of the Gulf zone.

The south-western deserts are virtually uninhabitable because of aridity but the Assyrian hills and Kurdistan receive sufficient precipitation to support sedentary cultivation and a relatively concentrated pastoralism, which extends into the neighbouring countries. In Mesopotamia, the Euphrates north of lake Habbaniyah, as in Syria, is virtually without tributaries and flows in a relatively narrow valley marked by escarpments on its western edge. Southward it enters the extensive silt lowlands and becomes increasingly used for irrigation. The régime of the Euphrates is relatively simple, maximum flow following the Anatolian snow melt occurring in May. (See also 'Agriculture' p. 415.) The Tigris on the other hand receives water from a large number of east bank tributaries draining from the Zagros system and since these can be affected by storm rains at all times in the year the fluctuations in Tigris levels can be extreme and varied.

Baghdad lies at the head of great plains with indeterminate levels, low gradients and riverbeds higher than the surrounding land. The human utilisation of these lowlands has never been easy and the control of floods and of irrigation water is still not complete, but without the water of the great rivers Mesopotamia would be an arid wilderness. Settlement based on sedentary irrigated agriculture is concentrated in the zone between Baghdad and Basra. Mosul and Kirkuk have grown in recent years as oil and industrial centres, Mosul also being the chief town of an expanding cereal-growing region.

Area
167,300 sq. mi./434,900 sq. km. (UN estimate).

Mean max. and min. temperatures
Basra (33°20′N, 44°25′E; 7 ft./2 m.) 111°F/44°C (July), 42°F/5°C

(January); Mosul (36°20'N., 43°08'E; 730 ft./230 m.) 110°F/43°C (July), 32°F/0°C (January).

Relative humidity
Basra 20%–100%.

Mean annual precipitation
Basra 7 in./180 mm., Mosul 15 in./380 mm.

POPULATION

Total population
(1967) 8,440,000.

Chief towns and populations
(1965) BAGHDAD (1,108,497), Basra (423,000), Mosul (389,680), Kirkuk (224,000), Kerbela (246,800).

Distribution
In 1965 just over 40% of the population was officially classed as urban but a large proportion of this represents agriculturalists living in pseudo-urban settlements. More than one quarter of the population lives in Baghdad *liwa* (province) with 12% and 9% in Mosul and Basra *liwas* respectively.

Language
The official language is Arabic, used by 75% of the population. In the northern and eastern provinces there are large minority groups of Kurdish, Turkish and Farsi speakers.

Religion
Islam is the religion of the state and of over 90% of the population. Both Sunni and Shi'a sects are strongly represented. There are many relatively small Christian communities, Uniates associated with the Roman Catholic Church, Nestorian, Gregorian and Orthodox. The once-numerous Jewish population of Baghdad has rapidly declined to some 10–15,000. In addition there are the religious groups of Yazidis and Sabaeans, mainly in the highland zones.

CONSTITUTIONAL SYSTEM

Constitution
At present (April 1970) Iraq is governed under a provisional constitution promulgated in 1968 after the 17th of July *coup*, although a new provisional constitution is in preparation. The republic is declared to be a democratic socialist state in which all discrimination, whether based on race, religion or language, is forbidden. The rights of the Kurdish people are guaranteed within the framework of Iraqi unity. The highest authority is the Council of Command of the Revolution which will promulgate laws until a National Council is elected.

Head of State & Prime Minister
President Ahmed Hassan al-Bakr.

Executive
The President is the chief executive. He appoints the Prime Minister and other ministers (as well as all Civil Servants), and heads the Cabinet. The President declares war and peace and decrees internal emergency powers; he is the final court of appeal in all judicial matters.

Political Parties

The Ba'ath party, in its various sections, includes most active Iraqi politicians. At various times moderate groupings within the Ba'ath become united under more specific titles. The Arab Socialist Union, partly Ba'athist, is closely associated with the Arab Socialist Union of the UAR. The Iraq Communist Party is banned but sometimes operates closely with left-wing Ba'athists.

Leading political figures

President Ahmed Hassan al-Bakr; Lieutenant-General Salih Mahdi Ammash, Vice President; Dr. Abdel Karim Shaikhli, Foreign Minister; Air Marshal Hardan Takriti, Vice President.

Local Government

Iraq is divided for administrative purposes into 15 *liwas*, these are subdivided into *nahiyas* (districts) and these, in turn, into *gadas*. Central planning takes precedence over all other requirements.

Judicial System

Under a Ministry of Justice, Iraqi law is administered by a series of courts. The Court of Cassation in Baghdad is the highest judicial level and court of final appeal; a subsidiary technical bureau is in charge of all legal formulation. There are five judicial districts of appeal, Baghdad, Basra, Hilla, Kirkuk and Mosul, each with its own appeal court which considers the decisions of the lower court of first instance. These sit in various of the centres of local government, deal with civil and commercial cases and are separated into limited and unlimited courts according to their powers. Courts of first instance also include penal courts which, together with the courts of sessions in the appeal districts, consider cases under the penal proceedings law. Parallel with the courts of first instance are also the *Shariah* courts presided over by *qadis* who deal with matters of religion and personal status, these derived from traditional Muslim procedures. Revolutionary courts deal with all matters which are deemed to affect the security of the state, whether political, economic or financial. A special three-man committee was set up in December 1969 to try espionage cases.

RECENT HISTORY

Iraq was born in the collapse of the Ottoman Empire, first under British military administration, then as a mandated state under British protection in 1920. Arab nationalists with 'Greater Syria' ideas, together with separatist-minded Iraqis, rebelled against British domination and conspired against each other. In 1921 Iraq became a monarchy under Emir Faisal, but the associated Anglo-Iraqi treaty guaranteeing special British interests and rights was not ratified until 1924 and then only in the face of much opposition. Sunni-Shi'a disagreements together with inter-regional disputes accompanied other conflicts. In 1932 the Mandate was terminated and Iraq became an independent state but faction remained. In Assyria during 1933 and in the Euphrates desert region in 1936 tribal rebellion led to severe military repression. The small literate and articulate urban groups were clique-ridden, xenophobic as well as nationalist, and completely cut off from the general peasant population. Baqr Sidqi became the first army general to establish a practice of military coups in 1936, only to be assassinated in 1937. Economic development of hydrological and agricultural potential accelerated as oil revenue flowed from the Kirkuk field after 1934, but the

36

physical difficulties of harnessing the Tigris and Euphrates and the lack of effective political continuity of policy retarded progress. During World War II anti-British sentiment, exacerbated by events in Palestine and encouraged by German diplomatic efforts, resulted in policy changes, an army coup and the British occupation of Basra and Baghdad, this last particularly associated with the need for supporting Russia. Iraq joined the Allies in 1943 and the United Nations in 1945. Following World War II Iraq was torn between a pro-Western fear of Russian penetration, the safeguarding of her growing oil wealth as the Mosul and Basra fields were developed and, on the other hand, anti-Zionist, anti-British and anti-American sentiments. Troops were sent into Palestine in 1948 and considerable Jewish emigration commenced. Baghdad was the scene of many disturbances in 1951 and 1952. In the years 1955 and 1956 the official pro-Western line, associated with the formation of the anti-Communist defensive alliance of the Baghdad Pact and the rather tentative reactions to the Suez affair, led to further rioting and the imposition of martial law in 1956 and 1957. On the other hand disputes with Syria, over the IPC pipelines to the Mediterranean and deeper political rivalries, resulted in Iraq and Jordan declaring themselves an Arab Federation in the face of the Egyptian and Syrian creation of the United Arab Republic. In 1958 the explosive situation blew up in the Revolution in which King Faisal II and Nuri as-Said, Chief Minister, were assassinated, a republic proclaimed and power seized by a military junta led by another soldier-politician, General Qasim. Since that time the power-struggle between nationalist left-wing socialists, pro-UAR Arab nationalists, and communists has been acute. Qasim, as a nationalist, put forward claims to complete sovereignty over the Shatt al-Arab region, thus disturbing Iran, Kuwait and Britain. Shatt al-Arab navigation rights are still the subject of dispute with the Iranians; in 1961 British and other Arab forces supported Kuwaiti independence against Iraqi claims. In 1959 Iraq left the Baghdad Pact but at the same time took active measures to curb the growth of communist elements; again there were riots, assassination attempts and martial law. Most serious was the outbreak of Kurdish disaffection in 1961, when Mustapha Barazani declared an independent Kurdish state, and the beginning of a period in which civil war alternated with amnesties. In 1963 came another military coup, the assassination of Qasim and the appearance of a strong Ba'athist movement, Arab socialist in general ideology but divided into savagely differing groups, pro-UAR, left-wing crypto-communist, independent nationalist and socialist-idealist. In general the extremist Ba'ath members have striven for close links with Egypt and Syria while the moderate group has stood for an independent line. At first successful, the extremists lost power in late 1963 and President Abd-el Salam Aref came to power. He announced the merger of all political parties into an 'Iraqi Arab Socialist Union', and managed to foil an attempted *coup* in 1965. In April 1966 he was killed in an air crash, and his brother, Abd el-Rahman Aref, succeeded him as president. He, too, put down an attempted *coup*.

Kurdish and Iranian problems appeared to be nearing solution towards the end of 1966 but relations with Syria deteriorated severely in the winter of 1966–7 with the dispute between Syria and the Iraq Petroleum Company over the revenue from the IPC pipeline through Syria, and agreement was not reached until March 1967. Meanwhile, internally, industrial and commercial nationalisation policies were implemented, the IPC concession area was severely curtailed, and land reform plans were being executed.

In 1967, the June War induced a rapprochement between Iraq, Syria and Egypt and since the 1968 *coup* a more militant line has been adopted by General Hassan al-Bakr who became President and Prime Minister. The most recent internal development has been the ending of the Kurdish war in March 1970 and the drawing up of a programme of agreement which accords recognition to the Kurds as an ethnic entity within the state of Iraq, and allows them a certain amount of autonomy.

Diplomatic relations with Britain were broken off in 1967 but resumed in 1968. In general Iraq remains independent-minded but with the moderate Ba'athist socialists able only to keep power rather than to impose unity. Iraq is almost the only non-Communist country to accord full diplomatic recognition to East Germany, although the Iraqi Communist party remains proscribed.

ECONOMY

Background

Iraq has considerable resource potential for agricultural and industrial development but its exploitation has been slow. The effective labour force is relatively small, some 2·6 million, and the largest part of this is still untrained and illiterate. The proper exploitation of the only large under-utilised land and water resources in the Middle East requires expensive and advanced engineering works to harness and tame the Tigris-Euphrates system, and skilled farming based on sound irrigation practice. Until recently oil production, transport and refining also depended on foreign expertise. Even more important, Iraq has not had sufficient political stability and continuity to allow indigenous expertise and capital to be properly employed.

Oil production of 74 million tons in 1968 showed a 23% increase over the war- and boycott-affected 1967 figures although production only increased by 0·9% between 1968 and 1969. Revenue from oil is now probably estimated at £141 million *p.a.* The Iraq Petroleum Company (IPC) operates the Kirkuk, Mosul and Basra fields but since 1964 a state-owned company, the Iraq National Oil Company (INOC) has taken over virtually all other concession areas including the newly-discovered Rumailah field west of Basra. Further oil finds by the French company ERAP are reported from the south. Iraq has five refineries with a total annual capacity of some five million tons and a large sulphur-extraction plant at Kirkuk. Approximately two-thirds of the crude oil is moved by pipeline from the northern fields through Syria to Baniyas and Tripoli. Most of the southern production, about one-third, is shipped from Basra through the Gulf. Discussions are proceeding concerning the long-term supply of natural gas to Turkey.

In the current Development Plan, 1965–70, almost one-third of public investment is allocated to industry, equal to that allotted to agriculture. Factory industry is not well developed and present estimates of industrial employment include a large number of bazaar-scale workshops. Recent developments include cement and textile production. Sugar refining is being expanded at Kerbela, Mosul and Sulaimaniyah, in association with the introduction of sugar-beet into improved rotations in the cereal growing areas. The policy of nationalisation has led to the dominance of the state in virtually the whole of manufacturing and mining and with this has developed the practice of governmental control of foreign participation and the growth of special arrangements with communist bloc countries. Planned developments include the exploitation of sulphur deposits at Mishraq, the completion of a nuclear reactor plant and an artificial silk factory (both with

Soviet assistance), an ammonia and urea fertiliser plant at Basra, together with many smaller and diverse projects. The very considerable expansion in electricity generation is in part based on hydro-electric installations on the Zab at Samarra, and at Dokan and Derbendi.

In the agricultural sector agrarian reform and the expansion of the irrigated area are most important. Sequestration and redistribution of lands of large estates has affected over half-a-million acres of land and about 50,000 cultivators. River-control schemes, on the headwaters of the Diyala and Lesser Zab rivers and the further development of the Habbaniyah and Samarra installations are already in hand. Completion of present plans will increase the irrigated area by about 100%. Cereals occupy the greatest acreage but dates, of which two-thirds are exported, are the only important export crop.

Development and welfare expenditures have risen to a point where budgetary deficits have become normal. External assistance has been obtained from the Kuwait Fund for Arab Economic Development and the UN, as well as in credits from Russia.

Foreign trade

Over 90% of the value of Iraqi exports is contributed by oil, for which Italy is the chief customer, followed by Holland and France. Exports of manufactured goods continue to rise, although cement accounts for over 80% by value. A special export subsidy fund has now been created. Imports are regulated by currency allocation, the total for 1969 being ID156,800 million. The proportions available for current consumption and for con-summer durables are planned as 34% and 9%, and 56% was allocated to the purchase of capital goods. During the last decade the communist countries have become increasingly important suppliers, part of this, as in the case of Syria, resulting from aid agreements but also partly a result of a certain degree of ideological affinity. Japan, Britain, the USSR and West Germany were, in 1968, the main sources for imports and imports from China exceeded those from the USA. As can be seen from the import quotas, Iraq gives priority to the purchase of capital equipment but imports of these items in 1968 did not show the expected increase over 1967. Iraq continues to maintain a large trade surplus, ID227 million in 1968. However, since Iraq does not receive the full value of oil exports as shown in the trade figures, the true surplus is about ID53 million, still very considerable.

Employment

In spite of rapid and accelerating industrialisation it is estimated that some 85% of the population is dependent on agricultural employment.

SOCIAL SERVICES

The strong subsistence element in the large farming community and the traditional character of many parts of society, particularly in Kurdish areas, results in the restriction of most effects of welfare provisions to the towns. The Ministry of Health and the Ministry of Labour and Social Affairs are jointly responsible for most social services. Medical services range from a rapidly increasing number of clinics and dispensaries to special and general hospitals at Baghdad, Basra and Mosul. The ratio of physicians to population is still low but the university medical faculties are among the most effective training establishments in the Middle East. Medical care at clinics and hospitals is free to the poor and disabled but as in many other states is not adequate for total needs. Trade Union organisations have their own aid funds for disability and unemployment and various projects for adult vocational training are being linked to labour placement policies.

EDUCATION

While Baghdad shares with Cairo the literary leadership of the Arab world, illiteracy is a major national problem with one 1968 estimate suggesting that only 2–3% of the population were literate. This proportion is much higher, over 20%, in the younger age groups as a result of rising expenditure on education. Twenty-five per cent of the 1968–9 ordinary budget was allocated to education and culture. In 1965–6 there were 4,500 primary schools with one million pupils, and 630 secondary schools (of which 45 were vocational). Iraq is self-sufficient in teachers, trained at 30 training colleges. Higher education is organised in technical and other colleges, almost 80 in all, and the three universities of Baghdad, Basra and Mosul.

MASS MEDIA

All private newspaper publication was prohibited in 1967 and replaced by five official dailies. New publications may now be established under licence from the Ministry of Guidance. Many other periodicals and journals are produced by political and professional organisations and by ministries.

The Press
Dailies: *Al Jumhuriya*, Baghdad (20,000); *Al Masa*, Baghdad; *Al Mouata*, Baghdad; *Al Thawra al Arabiya*, Baghdad (Arab Socialist Union). In addition there is one Kurdish language paper, *Al Taakhia*, and one in English, the *Baghdad Observer*.
Periodicals: *Al Adib* (f), Mosul; *Al Amal wal Ummal* (w) (Trade Union), Baghdad; *Al Anba al-Jadida* (w), Baghdad; *Al Aqlam* (m), Baghdad; *Al Aswaq al-Tijariya* (w), Baghdad; *Al Fikr al-Arabi* (f), Mosul; *Al Hadaf* (f), Mosul; *Al Khalij al-Arabi* (w), Baghdad; *Majallat-al-Majma al-'Ilmi al-Iraqi* (m), Baghdad; *Saut al-Ummal* (w) (Trade Union), Baghdad; *Al Watan* (w), Baghdad.

Broadcasting
Domestic and foreign radio programmes are transmitted by the Broadcasting Station of the Republic of Iraq. Home service radio uses the Arabic, Kurdish and Turcoman languages; foreign broadcasts are in English, French, German, Persian, Turkish and Urdu.

Television programmes are the responsibility of the Ministry of Culture and National Guidance. Transmissions are made from Baghdad, Kirkuk and Mosul and a Basra station was opened in 1969.

ISRAEL

GEOGRAPHY

Features
WITHIN the state of Israel as defined by the *de facto* frontiers of the period
1948–67 lie a number of clearly definable regions. The Levantine coastal
plain extends southwards from Lebanon to Haifa and Mount Carmel. Behind
this plain rise the hills of Galilee, an extension of the Lebanon range, these
hills falling precipitously to the rift depression of the upper Jordan, Lake
Huleh and Lake Tiberias (the Sea of Galilee). South of the Galilee hills the
structural depression of the Vale of Esdraelon extends from Haifa to the
Jordan rift. Southward still, from the Carmel massif to the Gaza strip and
the Egyptian border extends a wide coastal plain backed by the hills of
Samaria and Judea, which formed part of the kingdom of Jordan after the
1948 Armistice and were occupied by Israel in 1967. Eastwards and southwards Israeli frontiers extend to the shores of the Dead Sea and through the
Negev to the head of the Gulf of Aqaba. The northern coastal plains and
the Galilee hills are relatively well-watered and have a Mediterranean
climate. Esdraelon and the northern Jordan valley have high temperatures
and high humidity but good potential for irrigation agriculture. The southern
coastal plain becomes progressively more arid to the south and the Judean
hills merge with the Negev in desert steppe and desert.

Area
8,000 sq. mi./20,700 sq. km.

Mean max. and min. temperatures
Jerusalem (31°45′N, 35°17′E; 2,485 ft./750 m.) 76°F/24°C (August),
48°F/9°C (January); Eilat (29°33′N 34°57′E; 10ft./3 m.) 92°F/33°C
(August), 60°F/16°C (January).

Relative humidity
Jerusalem 59%, Eilat 85%–50%.

Mean annual rainfall
Jerusalem 20 in./510 mm., Eilat 1 in./25 mm.

POPULATION

Total population
(1968) 2,773,900.

Chief towns and population
(1968) Tel Aviv (388,000), Haifa (209,900), JERUSALEM (East and West)
(266,300), Ramat Gan (106,800), Petach-Tikva (73,500), Holon (75,900).

41

Distribution
The urban population made up 82% of the 1967 total. The greatest concentration of population still lies on the coastal plain between Haifa and Ashdod.

Language
Hebrew is the dominant and official language, Arabic remains important mainly in the non-Jewish population, and among the great varieties of other languages brought in by immigrants English is the most important second language of Israelis.

Religion
Of the 1967 population 2,384,000 were Jews, these following two distinct rituals, the Ashkenazim and the Sephardim. The former, mainly coming from Central, Northern and Western Europe, are culturally dominant although the Israeli Hebrew language formally follows the Eastern, Sephardim usage. Of the non-Jewish population the great majority is Muslim.

CONSTITUTIONAL SYSTEM

Israel is governed under a series of laws and edicts which *in toto* make up a working constitution and under which Israel is a parliamentary state with an elected unicameral legislature.

Head of State
President Zalman Shazar.

Prime Minister
Mrs. Golda Meir.

The Executive
The President is elected by the *Knesset* (see below) for a period of five years; he invites one of the members of the *Knesset* to form a government. The Prime Minister forms a cabinet from members of the *Knesset* or from outside, the ministers being responsible to the Premier for the specialist ministries. The cabinet usually includes members other than of the majority party. The Premier proffers the resignation of his government after each presidential election but remains in office until a new government is formed. The government, through the Premier, may be forced to resign in the event of the *Knesset* declaring a loss of confidence.

The Legislature
A single-chamber assembly (*Knesset*) is elected by universal adult suffrage every four years. Enfranchisement law excludes senior state employees, senior military officers, judges, rabbis and priests. Election of the 120 members is by proportional representation. The *Knesset* elects the President and must approve all legislative actions of the government.

Political Parties
The largest party is the Israel Labour Party, an alliance of *Mapai* (Party of the Workers of Israel, the strong party of the centre), *Achdut Ha'avoda-Poalei Zion* (Union of Labour), the Zionist Socialist Party and the *Rafi* (List of the Workers of Israel), a splinter group of former *Mapai* members. In the elections of October 1969 the Labour Party remained the largest but not the majority party, with 56 seats and Mrs. Meir's administration remains dependent on some form of coalition, with the other two large parties, the right wing *Gahal* party, which holds 26 seats and the National Religious Party, with 12 seats.

Leading political figures
Mrs. Golda Meir, Premier and Labour Party Leader; Abba Eban, Foreign Minister (Lab.); Gen. Moshe Dayan, Minister of Defence (Lab.); Pinhas Sapir, Minister of Finance (Lab.); Yigal Allon, Deputy Premier and Minister of Education (Lab.); Teddy Kollek, Mayor of Jerusalem.

Judicial System
This incorporates inherited elements of British law as introduced into Palestine, Ottoman law, religious laws of various religious communities, all these as modified by the actions of the Israeli legislature. Civil courts are based on municipal courts in the five largest cities empowered with criminal jurisdiction in so far as municipal by-laws are affected, and the 25 magistrates courts which deal with civil actions involving claims or goods of value less than £I.3,000 and with criminal matters as courts of first instance and with misdemeanours. District courts at Jerusalem, Tel-Aviv, Haifa and Beer-sheba are courts of first instance in matters beyond the jurisdiction of magistrates courts and as appellate courts to those below. The supreme court is the final court of appeal in matters civil and criminal and the court of first instance in matters concerning civil rights and the actions of administrations. Religious courts include Jewish Rabbinical, Muslim, Christian and Druze courts. Their judgements cover matters of personal status, marriage and divorce in their particular communities but officers of the civil courts are responsible for the execution of those judgements. The defence laws (state of emergency) introduced by the British Mandate Government in 1945 have been retained and are used as a means of controlling the Arab minority.

RECENT HISTORY
The state of Israel was born out of bitter conflict between Arabs, Jews and Britain, the mandatory power, between July 1920 and May 1948. The concept enunciated in the Balfour Declaration of 1917 of a national home for the Jews in Palestine led to steady immigration which together with natural increase raised the Jewish population in Palestine from c. 70,000 to 700,000 between World War I and World War II. The acceleration of immigration, the large scale of land purchase by the Jews and the activities of the World Zionist Organisation provoked Arab hostility which flared into Arab rebellion against British power. In 1939 Britain issued a White Paper prohibiting further land purchase and curtailing further immigration. Jewish and Zionist attacks on this policy ceased during World War II but after 1945, and against the background of the Nazis' savage anti-Semitism in Europe, grew into open warfare both between Jews and British and between Arabs and Jews. The United Nations was unable to resolve the conflict and recommended partition, a solution unacceptable to the British Government. Anarchy finally forced Britain to declare unilaterally a surrender of the Mandate and in 1948 an Arab-Israeli war broke out. A UN negotiated armistice left Jordan in control of most of the Samarian and Judean hills (the Nablus-Hebron upland) together with half of Jerusalem, Egypt in control of the Gaza strip, and the new State of Israel in control of the remainder of Palestine. Some 800,000 Arabs fled from the areas of conflict and from the Israeli state to form the first wave of Palestinian refugees, moving in the first place into Jordan, Lebanon, Syria and the Gaza strip. UN resolutions calling for the return of the refugees were disregarded by Israel.

43

After 1948 a great wave of immigration and colonisation resulted in a 24% increase each year in the population of Israel in the period 1948–51. Between 1948 and 1967 Jewish immigrants numbered over one-and-three-quarter million, of which some 450,000 were from Arab countries. While the majority of immigrants settled in the towns, planned colonisation of the maximum territorial area took the form of co-operative agricultural settlements, the Kibbutzim and Moshavim; military pioneer rural settlements of the Nahal type were established in dangerous frontier areas.

The first elections were held in 1949 and under the proportional representation system employed Israel has been governed by a series of coalitions in which *Mapai* has consistently figured as the largest single party. The sole advantage of this situation is that in the state of siege in which Israel has always existed the central, relatively moderate group has always prevailed. In the early 1950s as the Arab states, in particular Egypt, built up their armed strength, frontier raids became frequent. Tension exploded in 1956 when Israel attacked Egyptian forces in what it regarded as a major preventive action, this in association with an Anglo-French military invasion of the Suez Canal area. Israeli armies occupied the whole of Sinai and points on the Gulf of Aqaba, the latter to break the blockade imposed by Egypt which had also closed the Suez canal to Israeli shipping. UN action resulted in the withdrawal of Anglo-French forces and the establishment of a UN emergency force on the Sinai border and at Sharm el Shaikh, which commanded the Straits of Tiran at the entrance to the Gulf of Aqaba. Egypt continued to deny Israel the use of the Suez canal.

The underlying hostility between Israel and her Arab neighbours remained, along with continuing tension on the borders, especially along the armistice line between Israel and Syria. On a global scale Israeli connections with the Western countries (in which most of the c. 85% non-Israeli Jews reside) ensured a steady flow of capital without which the state could not have survived. German reparation payments which ended in 1966 were of critical importance. This alignment however was also an element in the 'cold war' situation, encouraging Arab reliance on the USSR and other communist countries. Diplomatic and economic relations, in part based on trade and on the technological development expertise available in Israel, extended rapidly with African and Asian countries, mainly non-Muslim.

Between 1959 and 1963 David Ben Gurion, leader of the *Mapai* party, headed a series of coalition governments in which Moshe Dayan and Abba Eban, senior members of the present administration, held ministerial appointment. Internally a new economic policy appeared, based on a more liberal attitude to trade and foreign capital and on the needs of a new surge of immigrants. Externally, Ben Gurion sought UN and Western backing for Iraeli security in the face of a build-up of the UAR's armed forces and her closure of the Suez Canal to Israeli shipping. The administration of Levi Eshkol, which after 1965 became centred around *Mapam* (United Labour Party), on the one hand eased internal restrictions for the Arab minority but on the other pushed ahead with the National Water Project involving the large scale extraction of water from the Sea of Galilee for an irrigation grid-system, a policy deeply resented by Israel's Arab neighbours. During 1966, in spite of public efforts by President Bourguiba of Tunisia and private efforts by other Arab leaders, Israeli-Arab relationships, particularly with Syria, grew worse. An escalating confrontation between Israel and Syria, the growing strength and activity of Arab guerilla organisations and a crescendo of suspicion, ended in President Nasser's demand that UN forces be withdrawn from Egyptian territory in Sinai; the imposition of a blockade in the Straits of Tiran and the build-up of Egyptian forces in Sinai. King Husain of Jordan joined President Nasser in a defence agreement.

Israeli reaction was to form a national coalition government including all parties and on June 5th 1967, Israel attacked on the Egyptian, Jordanian and Syrian fronts. The Egyptian air force was virtually destroyed in three hours and within four days the Israeli army was established along the Suez Canal line. The Jordanian counter-offensive was equally rapidly defeated and within three days all the territory west of the Jordan and the Dead Sea, including Old Jerusalem, was occupied by Israel. During the sixth day Israeli forces, advancing over the Golan heights towards Damascus, accepted a UN cease-fire arrangement with Syria. The repercussions of the June Six Days War have been immense. The early Arab accusation of active Anglo-American support to Israel has since been withdrawn but anti-American sentiment has remained strong. Although France had equipped the Israeli air force, Arab goodwill was regained by President de Gaulle when he stopped all arms deliveries to Israel, branding her as the aggressor. The Security Council eventually adopted a resolution linking Israeli withdrawal from the occupied territories with an end to the state of belligerency, the solution of the refugee problem and the establishment of secure boundaries, and appointed Dr. Gunnar Jarring as UN special representative to explore the ground for a peace settlement. The Arab countries however refused to negotiate until Israel agreed to withdraw, while Israel refused to move until she could negotiate terms which would ensure her security. The impasse remains, but al Fatah (the Arab guerilla organisation founded 1965-6), the Palestinian Liberation Front and other Palestinian Arab military groups have increased the scale of hostile action ranging from armed raids to hi-jacking of Israeli planes and bomb attacks on Israeli property in the West. (In September 1970 the Popular Front for the Liberation of Palestine, a Marxist-Leninist guerrilla group, organised the hi-jacking of planes of those West European countries—Switzerland and West Germany—that held Arab guerrillas as prisoners; by holding the air passengers as hostages they succeeded in putting pressure on the governments of these countries to release the prisoners.) Regular forces are in constant contact on the Egyptian, Jordanian and Syrian fronts in spite of the presence of a UN observer force along the Suez Canal, and Israel has recently made air raids on areas far inside Arab territory, notably on Damascus and the Nile Delta region. Internally, in spite of the flight of more than 400,000 Arabs from the occupied areas, Israel is now faced with a very large Arab minority within the territory it controls, a minority which could become a majority within a decade. None of the various proposals for creating some form of buffer areas between Israel and the Arab countries, still less for constituting a bi-national Jewish-Arab state in Palestine, have seemed to be acceptable to both parties. The consultations of the great powers, begun in 1969, did not succeed in establishing a peace settlement. But in the summer of 1970 Egypt, Jordan and Israel accepted an American peace initiative, known as the Rogers Plan, which envisaged a temporary cease-fire and the holding of peace negotiations under the auspices of Dr. Gunnar Jarring on the basis of the Security Council's Resolution of 1967. The Palestinians, however, rejected this plan, and Israel refused to participate after the Egyptians violated the cease-fire. Negotiations continue for the resumption of talks; but the final outcome of this latest attempt at a settlement is uncertain.

ECONOMY

Background

The Israeli economy is now essentially a war economy. During 1968–9 almost 20% of the GNP was devoted to defence and about half of 1969–70 budgetary expenditure was allocated to security. It is in these siege terms that the Israeli economy must be viewed. In 1966, the last year of relative peace, agriculture, forestry and fishing contributed 8% of the GNP, manufacturing and mining 23%, government and central institutions 22%, and trade services 25%. Between 1966 and 1967 the GNP rose by 3·2%, the lowest rate of increase in Israel's history, but the growth between 1967 and 1968 was 13%. Manufacturing employed, in 1967, 25% of the occupied population. The food, beverages and tobacco, and textile industries are by far the greatest employers of labour. In 1966–7 40% of industrial workers and 54% of industrial establishments were located in Tel-Aviv.

Agriculture is characterised above all by heavy investment and advanced technology. Of the 1968–9 development budget 4% was allocated directly to agriculture, 3% to national water projects and 10% to industry (28% went to debt repayment); indirect investment in agriculture should include part of the costs of extending the coverage of strategic farming colonies. Wheat, barley, sorghums, and hay are the most important field crops by area, cotton and sugarbeet (both mainly irrigated) the most extensive cash crops. Citrus fruit provides the most valuable products.

Foreign trade

Between 1949 and 1967 Israel had a trade deficit averaging $250 million *p.a.* In *per caput* and absolute terms the position showed signs of improvement as industrial development increasingly diversified commodity exports but the effect of hostilities in 1967 and since has been to increase the annual trade deficit to $450 million in 1968 of which about one-half was incurred by defence imports. In 1968 18% of Israeli exports was made up of agricultural produce and live animals (14% by citrus alone). A further 36% was of precious and semi-precious stones. Of the imports 53% was of industrial raw materials and precious stones, 5% agricultural input raw materials, 3% transport equipment, and 6% and 10% respectively of petroleum products and industrial equipment. Of Israeli exports in 1968 25% went to the European Common Market, 12% to Britain and 19% to the USA; W. Germany and UK received large shares of the total citrus exports; the USA was the largest single market for polished diamonds. Imports (70% raw materials, 19% capital goods) come mainly from EFTA, the USA and the Common Market (24%); the USA, Britain and West Germany were the largest single suppliers. The considerable trade deficit has been covered by capital inflow estimated at $5,000 million between 1950 and 1968 (including c. $2,000 million in reparations from W. Germany); the annual rate is now c. $500 million. Israel plans through expanding diversified exports to reduce her dependence on this inflow.

Employment

The 1967 civilian labour force numbered 926,900. Of the employed persons (830,700) 25% were engaged in industry, 16% in education, health, religion and the judiciary, 14% in commerce, banking and insurance, 13% in agriculture, forestry and fishing and 8% in government and public administration. Compulsory military service takes up 12–15% of adult working life.

Prices and wage trends
The consumer price index rose from 100 in December 1959 to 138·5 in December 1964. The subsequent index (December 1964=100) showed a slower rate of increase, December 1967=118. Price inflation was c. 3% during 1968 and wage increases have stabilised at c.3% *p.a.*[1]

Consumption
Private consumption expenditure accounted for 60% of available resources in 1967, with 21% and 19% respectively accounted for by government consumption and gross fixed capital formation.

SOCIAL SECURITY

Social security arrangements in Israel are unique in that the part played by labour unions, the General Federation of Labour (usually known as the *Histadrut*), in particular, is preponderant. Founded in 1920 *Histadrut* has a membership of some 700,000 workers—three-quarters of all wage-earners—who together with their families form over half the population. Wives also have membership status, bringing numbers up to about one million. Voluntary membership is drawn from all occupational classes and includes c. 41,000 Arabs. Affiliated to *Histadrut* are the Organisation of Working and Student Youth, the Agricultural Workers Union and two religious labour organisations. 90% of all Israeli workers come under the trade union and welfare services of *Histradut*.

Dues of between 3% and 4·5% of wages cover all health and social services as well as trade union activity, and together with employers' contributions meet pension and sickness benefits, form provident funds and until recently redundancy and dismissal payments. The trade union section is responsible not only for negotiating pay and working conditions but also the employers' social security contributions. Benefit scales are linked to contributions and the retail price index. Accumulated funds total £I.1,750 million. Expenditure covering the whole field of social, educational, employment, housing and welfare for both Jews and Arabs totalled over £I.53 million in 1969. Governmental services are, in this context, relatively limited and mainly concerned with the provision of technical services, hospitals and medical centres.

In addition there are the National Labour Federation, the Mizrahi Workers' Organisation and the Agudat Israel Workers' Organisation.

EDUCATION
Primary
Since 1953 universal, compulsory, free primary education for all between the ages of 5 and 14 years has been established and in 1968 the *Knesset* approved the reorganisation of the system into 6 years' primary, 3 years' junior secondary and 3 years' senior secondary with free compulsory schooling up to the age of 16. Parents may choose between state and non-state education systems. Hebrew is the language of instruction in Jewish schools, of which there were 4,982 in 1967–8, and Arabic is the language of instruction in the 192 schools provided for Arab children. These are attended by 95% of Arab boys and 75% of girls. There are some state religious schools for Jews. All teachers' salaries are paid by the central government but the

[1] These are national figures.

schools are provided, maintained and equipped by local authorities. Private schools, mainly religious, are supervised and subsidised by the education authorities.

Secondary
The Ministry of Education administers, at a selective post-primary level, secondary, vocational and agricultural schools. The 188 Hebrew and 10 Arab secondary schools receive state and local government financial assistance only through the payment of grants to scholars on a sliding-scale according to family income. Pupils number 58,000 Jewish and 2,360 Arab children (1967–8).

Vocational training
Including apprentice training, schemes cover most areas of skill and are available to adults as well as to the post-14 age groups. As in the case of agricultural training, vocational education is given at many levels and organised by many voluntary and governmental organisations. Teacher-training colleges, 48 Hebrew and one Arab, enrol each year c. 7,000 Hebrew and 300 Arab students.

Universities
There are three full universities, one in embryo together with two institutes of university status. The Hebrew University of Jerusalem (f. 1918) has a full range of faculties, some 1,800 academic staff and over 12,000 students. Bar-Ilan University at Ramat-Gan (f. 1953) is less well-developed in the applied studies; c. 550 academic staff, 3,800 students. Tel-Aviv University (f. 1953) is especially strong in medicine; c. 1,000 academic staff, 3,500 students. Haifa College is the nucleus of a new university and is strongest in the Humanities and social sciences; c. 250 staff, 2,900 students. Also at Haifa is the *Technion* (Institute of Technology), home of undergraduate and postgraduate work in technology, agriculture, architecture and planning. The Weizman Institute of Science at Rehovoth is a private centre for scientific research and has a considerable world reputation. In 1969 the People's University at Dimona was founded in association with the Hebrew University, with 60 students and 3 teachers. There are in addition eleven other learned higher institutions, mainly, but not all, theological.

MASS MEDIA
Possessing the highest level of literacy in the Middle East, a special place in the lives of the 85% of world Jewry living outside Israel, and literary traditions brought from many regions, Israel has a very vigorous tradition in publication. The Press is subject only to the normal restraints on defamations and on state security. The latter is regulated by an Editors' Committee and the military censorship authority.

The Press
There are 29 daily newspapers, 17 in Hebrew, 2 in Arabic, one in Yiddish and one each in 8 other languages. The only important independent papers are : *Ha'aretz*, Tel-Aviv (45,000); and *Hayom*, Tel-Aviv. All other dailies have union, political or religious affiliations and almost all are published at Tel-Aviv: *Al Hamishmar*, Mapam (c. 18,000); *Davar*, Histadrut (c. 40,000); *Hatzofeh*, National Religious Front (c. 11,000); *Lamerhav*, Archdot Ha'avoda (c. 18,000). The largest circulation papers are popular evening productions : *Ma'riv*

(c. 118,000) and *Yediot Aharanot* (c. 90,000). The Arabic daily, *Al Yaum*, is also published at Tel-Aviv and has a circulation of c. 5,500.

There are more than 400 periodical papers and magazines, 260 in Hebrew and most with specialist interests; the weekly *Hapoel Hatzair* is the organ of *Mapai*.

Broadcasting

The Israeli Broadcasting Authority transmits medium and short wave radio programmes in eleven languages. Kol-Israel's main station is in Jerusalem with studios in Tel-Aviv and Haifa. Television transmissions to the public and to schools commenced in 1967.

JORDAN

GEOGRAPHY

Features

THE land of the Hashemite Kingdom of Jordan is made up of three clearly differentiated physical units. The largest of these is the eastern plateau which grades imperceptibly into the arid uplands of Jordan's Arab neighbours, Syria, Iraq and Saudi Arabia. Dominantly calcareous rocks overlie an almost completely concealed basement of older rock and are in turn covered in places by extensive lava-flows. To the east and south, sand, gravel and rock pavement desert predominates and rainfall is extremely low and sporadic (annual totals less than 5 in/200 mm.). Altitude and rainfall are highest along the heights overlooking the Jordan valley which supports degraded oak and pine forests. The Yarmuk and Zerqa are the only rivers with a permanent flow, both entering the Jordan, the former with a normal flow almost as great as that of the Jordan.

From the Gulf of Aqaba north to the Syrian border extends a great down-faulted rift much of which lies below sea-level, including the whole of the Jordan valley between Lake Tiberias (686 ft./210 m. below sea-level) and the Dead Sea (1,300 ft/400 m. below sea-level). Summer is characterised by extreme heat while winters are warm. Irrigation, utilising water from side tributaries of the Jordan, is restricted by the dissected and saline nature of the soils of the plain, while south of the Dead Sea it is only possible in the vicinity of springs aligned along the complex fault lines.

The Dead Sea, which has a maximum depth of 1,310 ft./400 m. has a high concentration of sodium and magnesium chlorides and other salts which gives it an average salinity some seven times that of sea-water and which forms the basis for some commercial activity.

The Palestinian hills to the west were heavily disturbed during the Jordanian rift faulting and form a rugged area of hills in which a mediterranean climatic régime predominates. Here are normally concentrated three-quarters of the population and cultivable land of Jordan, and, with the exception of Amman, its most populous and prosperous cities, Nablus, Hebron and Jerusalem.

Area
38,000 sq. mi./97,000 sq. km.

Mean max. and min. temperatures
Amman (31°57′N. 35°57′E; 2,515 ft./m. a.s.l.) 96°F/36°C (July), 28°F/−2°C (January).

Relative humidity
Amman 30%–90%

Mean annual rainfall
Amman 13 in./321 mm., Jerusalem 20 in./503 mm., Ma'an 1·5 in./39 mm.

POPULATION

Total population
(1968 estimate) 2,100,000.

Chief towns and populations
AMMAN (1968 estimate) (400,000).

Distribution
It has been estimated that 350,000 refugees entered free Jordan from the occupied West Bank in the six months following the war of June 1967. This movement has considerably distorted the previous pattern in that the urban population of the East Bank has grown faster than has economic activity while the establishment of several large refugee camps and the spread of 'squatting' by separate families has affected the rural position very considerably. In addition there are upwards of 15,000 regular and irregular troops from other Arab countries stationed in Jordan. In 1967 53% of the population was classified as urban-dwelling.

Language
Arabic is the official language. Circassian is also spoken by small groups of *Cherkez* who migrated from the Russian Caucasian territories at the turn of the 19th and 20th centuries.

Religion
Islam is the religion of the state, 80% of the population being Sunni Muslims and the rest Christian or belonging to other Muslim sects.

CONSTITUTIONAL SYSTEM

Constitution
The form of government in Jordan is parliamentary with a hereditary monarch, the present constitution dating from 1952.

Head of State
King Husain Ibn Talal.

Head of Government
Prime Minister, Ahmad Touqan. Executive power is vested in the King who exercises his power through his ministers. The King appoints, dismisses or accepts the resignation of the Prime Minister and, on the recommendation of the Prime Minister, appoints, dismisses or accepts the resignation of other members of the Council of Ministers. The King also appoints the President and members of the Senate (see *Legislature*) and accepts their resignation from office. The Council of Ministers is responsible for the conduct of all affairs of the State and if the House of Representatives should withhold a vote of confidence in the Council or in any minister then the council is bound to tender its resignation while an individual minister is bound to resign. The King is Head of State but takes an oath to respect and observe the provisions of the constitution. He is supreme commander of the armed forces and declares war, concludes peace and signs treaties.

Legislature

This consists of a bicameral national assembly with a senate of 30 members (see *Executive*) and a house of representatives of 60 members. Senators are appointed and representatives elected for four years. If either house rejects a law acceptable to the other or if the King withholds his approval of a law then power to promulgate lies with a joint session of both houses.

Political Parties

Political parties have, officially, been banned since 1963. Various groupings survive, ranging from the extreme nationalism of the Ba'ath National Front through the nationalist blocs of the National Socialist Party, the Arab Palestine group, the Liberation group and the Muslim Brotherhood to the moderates of the Arab Constitutional Group and a Coalition Party which seeks the right to full political activity. Differing reactions to non-official forces organised in fighting units for guerila action against Israel has produced additional complexity into the present situation and the position of leading political figures is liable to change rapidly.

Local Administration

The kingdom is divided into ten districts or *Liwa*, these in turn divided into sub-districts (*Qada*), governed respectively by district governors (*Muhafez* or *Mutassaref*) and sub-district governors (*Qaem Maqam*). In some sub-districts there are in addition *Nahiyas*, smaller administrative units, governed by *Mudirs*. All these administrative divisions are under the jurisdiction of the Minister of the Interior. Of the districts, Amman, Zarqa, Salt, Irbid, Karak, Ma'an, Jerusalem, Nablus, Jenin and Hebron, the last four are now in Israeli-occupied territory.

Judiciary

There are three distinct types of court in Jordan, the civil courts, the religious courts and special courts. The high court of justice sits in Amman and is the final appellate court above the courts of appeal, one in Amman and one in Jerusalem. As interpreter of the law it also acts as supreme court of judiciary. Below the courts of appeal are the courts of first instance which have powers in criminal and civil matters which exceed those of the magistrates' courts. These latter are normally limited to dealing with criminal cases where maximum punishment is for one year and with civil cases where the actionable matter has a value not exceeding £J250. Religious courts include the *Shariah* courts for Muslims and ecclesiastical courts for Christians. The *Shariah* courts deal with personal status cases and with matters concerning Muslim religious and charitable endowments (*Waqf*). Tribal courts are of the traditional kind evolved in pastoral societies. Their standing is rapidly diminishing and they tend to be confined to domestic settlements among the small number of tribal groups, particularly in the south-east of Jordan. The land settlement court is the only effective special court established and its purpose is the implementation of the 1933 land settlement law.

RECENT HISTORY

Jordan was created in the post-World War I settlement, in which Britain first received the Mandate for a general Palestinian area and then recognised Transjordan as a separate mandated state. Emir Abdullah, son of King Husain of Hedjaz and brother to the king of the new state of **Iraq**, became the first ruler in 1921. Transjordan was excluded from the Balfour commitment in 1917 to create a national home for the Jews in Palestine, but for the whole of its history has suffered the consequences of that action. Through treaties signed in 1924, 1934, 1939 and 1946 Transjordan ultimately attained virtual independence but Britain retained various military privileges while guaranteeing financial aid.

By 1948 growing tensions had resulted from King Abdullah's overtures to Iraq and Syria concerning the formation of a greater Syria and the hostility thus produced in Baghdad, Cairo and Damascus. In May British forces left Palestine and the existing anarchic state of war between Zionists and Arabs flared up as the armies of Transjordan with those of Egypt, Iraq and Syria entered Palestine. The 1949 armistice left Transjordan in occupation of the central Palestinian hills from Jenin through Jerusalem to Hebron. For almost two decades the incorporation in 1950 of Arab Palestine into the new Hashemite Kingdom of Jordan has been symptomatic of Jordan's independent line in this matter, an attitude which provoked the hostility of her Arab neighbours as also did her pro-Western tendencies. In 1951 Abdullah was assassinated and his son, Talal, reigned only for a year before abdicating in favour of his son Husain.

King Husain, in an endeavour to ensure the survival of the state by steering a middle course between the various international forces, became more and more the controller of policy. Between 1950 and 1955 Jordan remained outside both the Baghdad Pact and the Egyptian-Saudi-Syrian bloc. In 1957 the 1948 Treaty with Britain was abrogated but Syrian and Egyptian involvements with the USSR produced a revulsion from Eastern bloc policies, internal party politics were banned and relations with other Arab states became strained. Between 1958, when a merger between Iraq and Jordan lasted two weeks before the Iraqi monarchy was destroyed by revolution, and 1966, relations between Jordan and her neighbours (except Saudi Arabia) varied between cool and non-existent. Syrian and Iraqi Ba'athist groups also associated with Russian policies were ever-present external dangers, while on the Israeli border incidents became more frequent and extensive. In 1967 Husain signed a defence pact with the UAR as tension mounted but after the June War Jordan had effectively lost her richest territory on the West Bank and virtually all her armaments, gaining in exchange only some 350,000 refugees.

Since that time Jordan has become even more dependent on continuing British and American aid and on that of Kuwait, Libya and Saudi Arabia who, under the terms of the 1967 Khartoum Conference Agreement, jointly contribute a total of £135 million until hostilities end. Internally the presence of Iraqi troops and of thousands of independent commando troops organised by the several Palestine liberation organisations creates a challenge to the authority of the Government—a challenge that became a very real threat in the civil war between Government troops and guerrillas in September 1970—and through attacks on Israel puts the survival of Jordan itself at hazard. King Husain himself appears to be the indispensable nucleus.

Defence

The Jordanian army and air-force were almost destroyed in the June War and the process of rebuilding and re-equipping them is slow and expensive. Of expenditure in the 1969 draft budget about 70% was devoted to national defence and security, and the 1970 budget has allocated 48% of total expenditure to defence.

53

ECONOMY

Background

It is no exaggeration to say that the June War shattered the economy of Jordan and the progress of development associated with the 1964–70 Seven Year Plan. Between 1964 and 1967 the contribution of agriculture to the GDP declined by 3% while the total GDP increased by almost 30%, a measure of growing economic diversification. The 35% of the working population engaged in agriculture, fishing and forestry in 1961 changed little, but productivity in this sector was increasing and development plans, particularly in the East Ghor (Jordan valley) were coming to fruition. Improvements in husbandry were greatest in Palestinian Jordan where potential and productivity were already high. All production in West Bank territories has now been lost to Israeli occupation while the East Ghor is almost a no-man's-land and the East Ghor canal has been extensively damaged. The other main element in the primary production sector has not been affected, that is the production and export of phosphates from the Rusaifa area, northeast of Amman, and more recently from Wadi Hasa at the southern end of the Dead Sea. Production in 1966 exceeded one million tons and extraction rates are increasing rapidly. Manufacturing industry in 1967 was still dominated by small-scale simple processing establishments, 55% of all establishments being engaged in the making of shoes and clothing, bakery work or oil seeds pressing. The tourist-based craft industries lay mainly on the West Bank. Larger-scale development was and is receiving especial encouragement although the effect on the balance of payments of increasing the great dependence on imported fuel, raw material and machinery has to be carefully regulated. In 1968 a new planned industrial policy was announced. Special studies to select new growth industries have been started and the feasibility is being considered of setting up an industrial 'free zone' in the Amman-Zarqa area. Heavy industrial production is not contemplated except in the expansion of cement production and the processing of raw phosphates and the key factor is to be export orientation. The earlier development plans assumed an external contribution of over 50% to investment funds and this proportion is certain to continue. GNP *per caput* at current prices was £J82 in 1964 and £J77 in 1968.

Foreign Trade

The external trade of Jordan has been that which might be expected from a developing country with a preponderant primary economic sector. Exports during the period 1965–7 fluctuated slightly around the £10 million mark while imports increased to over £68 million in 1966, but fell in 1967 to £55 million. The 1968 figures showed a slight rise to £57 million. The main commodity exports before the June War were fruit and vegetables (c. 40% by value), derived mainly from the West Bank and the Ghor, and crude phosphates (c. 30%). Half of the import bill was chargeable to consumer goods and 55% of these were foodstuffs and beverages, heavily weighted by the staple cereals. The very large adverse balance on visible trade was only partly covered by invisibles such as the £10 million derived from tourism (much of this now lost) and the £1,500 million royalties from Tapline, the oil pipeline from Saudi Arabia to Sidon. IMF estimates showed a deficit of over £35 million on current account in 1966, a deficit covered by budget support, grants and development assistance from the USA, Britain, West Germany and Kuwait. Since June 1967 Jordanian trade has not yet re-established any firm pattern and budgetary and external deficits have been met by the joint annual grant-in-aid of £40 million a year from Kuwait, Libya and Saudi Arabia. British aid has continued and American assistance resumed after a short break in 1967–8.

Employment
The last reliable statistics available were based on the 1961 census. At that time the working population numbered 390,000, 23% of the total population. Over one-third was engaged in agriculture, forestry and fishing. Since that time there has been a massive influx of rural refugees into urban and country districts and unemployment, open and disguised, is very high.

Price and Wage trends
Actual movements of prices and wages have shown considerable fluctuations since 1967 but the general trend has averaged + 10% to December 1968.

Consumption
Private consumption in 1967 was estimated to take about 75% of available resources, a proportion little changed since 1963. It is probable that, given the subsistence character of most agriculture in unoccupied Jordan and the costs of supporting the large refugee population, this level is now exceeded.

Social Services
Under normal conditions the Ministry of Social Welfare and Labour administers unemployment and other relief and controls labour relationships in private industrial employment. For the rural majority of the population, relief in cases of poverty or disablement and ex-service and official pensions are of the greatest importance. UNRWA assists Jordanian and other Arab organisations in caring for Palestinian refugees of which there are still over half-a-million living in special camps. Medical facilities which are free to the poor included 56 hospitals of different sizes and rural clinics; only one-quarter of these units remain in unoccupied territory.

Education
Education for a minimum of nine years became compulsory in 1965 and by 1967 there were over 2,000 schools with more than 13,000 teachers, organised on a two-part primary and secondary basis. Compulsory education comprises six years' primary education and three years' secondary whilst the higher- and post-secondary levels are entered by selection. Secondary and post-secondary education includes (on the East Bank only) seven vocational schools, five teacher training colleges and the University at Amman. Public schooling, vastly predominant, is free and there is no segregation of sexes. The success of the still growing educational sector before June 1967 can be measured by Kuwait and Saudi activities in recruiting young trained teachers from Jordan. 830 schools are now in occupied territory and efforts are being made to expand east bank facilities.

Mass Media
Since March 1967 various measures of Press control have been in force and the state has financial interests in some of the publishing houses.

The Press
Dailies: Al-Destour, Amman (14,000) (Govt. backed); *Al-Difaa,* Amman, (12,000) (independent).
Periodicals: Amman al Masa'a (w); *Huna Amman* (m), Dept. of Guidance and Information; *Sawt El Damir* (m).

Broadcasting:
The Hashemite Jordan Broadcasting Service; Arabic, English, and Spanish.
The Jordan Television Corporation; Arabic and English.

56

KUWAIT

GEOGRAPHY

Features

THE Emirate of Kuwait is set in desert country in the north-western corner of the Arab/Persian Gulf, around the Bay of Kuwait. On the bay's southern shore Kuwait City occupies one of the rare firm coastal features lying between extensive areas of shoal, mudflat and coral reef; the city is now rapidly expanding south-eastward towards Mina al-Ahmadi, the oil port on the Gulf proper. Inland a few small oases lie in the waterless undulating desert which rises in altitude to the west. Medium depth aquifers of slightly brackish as well as sweet water have allowed small-scale traditional oasis agriculture but the economy of Kuwait is almost entirely dependent on the exploitation of vast on- and off-shore oil deposits, export of which commenced in 1946 and which has overwhelmed the traditionally dominant marine trade. To the south lies the Neutral Zone, jointly administered with Saudi Arabia and completely unproductive except for oil. To the north and east lie scattered islands of the marshland complex of the Shatt al-Arab.

Area
6,200 sq. mi/16,000 sq. km. Neutral Zone, condominium with Saudi Arabia, 2,500 sq. mi./5,700 sq. km.

Mean max. and min. temperatures
Kuwait City (29°20′N, 48°00′E; 10 ft./3 m. a.s.l.) 112°F/44·4°C (July/August), 64°F/17·7°C (January).

Relative humidity
85%–45% January, 40%–12% June.

Annual rainfall
1–7 in./25–175 mm.

POPULATION

Total population
(1967 estimate) 516,000.

Chief towns and population
KUWAIT CITY (250,000), Ahmadi (20,000).

Distribution
Except for c. 3,000 inhabitants of the islands virtually the whole of the population in Kuwait is concentrated in the L-shaped urban complex fringing the south side of Kuwait Bay and the Gulf shore. Approximately half the population does not possess Kuwaiti citizenship.

Language
The official language is Arabic.

Religion
Islam.

Constitutional System

Constitution
The present constitution was promulgated in 1962 and under it Kuwait is a hereditary emirate in which an elected National Assembly must approve the Emir's choice of heir apparent, a unique situation.

Head of State
Shaikh Sabah as-Salim as-Sabah, Emir of Kuwait.

Prime Minister
Shaikh Jaber al-Ahmad al-Jaber as-Sabah.

Executive
Power is vested in the Emir who exercises his powers through a council of ministers. The Emir appoints the Prime Minister, dismisses him or accepts his resignation and after consultation appoints, dismisses or accepts the resignation of ministers on the recommendation of the Prime Minister. All Ministers are *ex officio* members of the national assembly (see *Legislature*). The Emir promulgates laws and sets up public institutions; as head of state he is supreme commander of the armed forces, can declare defensive war, conclude peace and sign treaties. The function of the council of ministers is to lay down the government's general policies. Individual ministers are responsible to the national assembly for the affairs of their ministries and can be forced to resign by a vote of no confidence by the deputies.

Legislature
A unicameral national assembly consisting of 50 deputies is elected by literate male Kuwaiti citizens over the age of 21; the police and armed services are disenfranchised and only native-born Kuwaitis have the right to vote. The assembly may be adjourned or dissolved by the Emir with the safeguard of new elections which must be held within two months. The council of ministers collectively and individually must answer to the assembly for policies, and laws must be approved by the deputies as well as by the Emir before they become valid. If the assembly expresses no-confidence in the Prime Minister the Emir must either dismiss him or dissolve the assembly.

Political Parties
There are no officially recognised political parties in Kuwait.

Local Government
There are three provincial governorates, Ahmadi, Hawalli and Kuwait. Kuwait City has its own municipal administration, the oldest government department in the state, dating from 1930. The municipality, the head of which is the Director-General, is one of the largest financial units in the state with near-ministerial status. A central committee chosen by the municipality staff controls four main departments, in one of which, the technical department, is located the city planning section, which is responsible for the planning of one of the most rapidly growing urban centres in the world; in many ways the most important element in the life of Kuwait,

its decisions have immense economic and social consequences in what is essentially a city-state.

Judiciary

Since 1960 a codified judicial system under the supervision of the ministry of justice has been in force. The Court of First Degree is made up of two criminal courts and other specialised courts. The lowest criminal court has a single judge and deals with cases in which maximum punishment does not exceed three years' imprisonment. The higher criminal court with a president and two other judges deals with more serious cases. Specialised courts include the Domestic Court which deals with problems of personal status, marriage, inheritance and Islamic religious endowments (*Waqf*)—this court is subdivided so as to deal separately with Sunni, Shi'a and non-Muslims— the Civil, Commercial, Rent and Labour Courts. The Court of Appeal has civil and criminal sides and only in the latter is there an unconditional right of appeal. Death sentences may be delivered but are commuted to life imprisonment.

RECENT HISTORY

Early in the 18th century members of the Anaiza tribe occupied the site of the present town and developed marine and trading interests which dominated the life of Kuwait until recently. By 1760 a fleet of more than 800 *dhows* was based on the port which grew even faster after the East India Company established its head of Gulf base at Kuwait following the Persian occupation of Basra in 1776. Even so the population was no more than 10,000 or 12,000 until the end of the 19th century.

In 1756 the head of one of the leading Anaiza families, the *Sabah*, was chosen as first Emir of Kuwait and his line has ruled continuously ever since. Shaikh Mubarak the Great, 1896–1915, was first to assert the independence of the Emirate, this at a time when German negotiations with the Turkish Government for the southern part of the Berlin-Baghdad rail line and its extension to the south and Russian attempts to secure a naval supply station at the head of the Gulf were giving some anxiety to Britain. In 1899 Shaikh Mubarak's request for British support and protection was acceded to and the treaty was further extended to include recognition as an independent state under British protection. Turco-British negotiations over the status of Kuwait, which started in 1909, and the establishment of a British Political Agency in 1904 were landmarks in the establishment of the new state. By 1910, as a result of the increased trade which was associated with growing world interest in the region, the population had increased to c. 35,000, the first stage in a rapid period of growth.

In the period of post-World War I negotiations the most crucial was the 1922–3 conference to settle the Kuwaiti-Saudi Arabian frontiers in which the interests of the newly established kingdom of Iraq, under British Mandate, were also involved. Two neutral zones were established, one to the west between Iraq and Saudi Arabia and one to the south, adjoining the coast, the latter being jointly administered by Kuwait and Saudi Arabia. During the 1920s and 1930s Shaikh Salim and Shaikh Ahmad ensured that economic growth in Mesopotamia and the oilfields of Iraq and Iran contributed to the mercantile wealth of Kuwait whose population increased to c. 75,000 by 1937. During the same period oil exploration commenced. Politically, relations with Saudi Arabia improved from the nadir of the Saudi blockade of Kuwait in 1919, although the land frontier remained closed for almost another 20 years. Fears of Iraqi expansionism have however never been completely eliminated and her dependence on the supply of fresh water from the Shatt al-Arab near Basra, a traffic which lasted from 1925 to 1951, made Kuwait conscious of vulnerability.

The first oil concession was granted in 1934 for a period of 74 years to the Kuwait Oil Company, representing the Gulf Oil Corporation and the D'Arcy Exploration Company (a subsidiary then of Anglo-Iranian, now of British Petroleum). The first well was drilled north of Kuwait at Bahra in 1936 but not until 1938 was oil found at Burgan, 25 mi./40 km. south of Kuwait Town. World War II prevented the full exploitation of what appeared a rich field and the wells were plugged until 1946 when production really started. Shaikh Ahmad, then Emir of Kuwait, officiated at a ceremony for the first tanker loading and gave his name to the KOC oil township of Ahmadi and the port of Mina al-Ahmadi. Between 1946 and 1961 KOC drilled an average of 26 wells a year and production rose by 1961 to over 81 million tons.

Much of the history of Kuwait in the last 25 years has been associated with the results of the great accession of wealth resulting from oil. During the rule of Shaikh Abdullah there developed a domestic policy of welfare provision and the inception of a period of planned urbanisation which is not yet complete; both of these are considered in subsequent sections.

New wealth, new regional and world circumstances also changed the character of Kuwait's external relationships. In 1961 the independent and newly viable state, with British agreement, terminated the old special relationship and Kuwait took full charge of her foreign policy. One of her first acts was to join the Arab League while at the same time she established diplomatic missions in friendly countries. Also in 1961 a constituent assembly was selected to draft a constitution under which the policy of the state, internal and external, could be formulated. The first threat to Kuwait's independence appeared almost immediately from the claims of General Qasim's régime in Iraq, claims which were countered in the first place by British military assistance, this being quickly replaced by an Arab League Force from Jordan, Saudi Arabia, Sudan and the UAR. No overt action was taken by Iraq and in 1963, the year in which Kuwait became a member of the United Nations, the Iraqi Government announced its recognition of Kuwait's complete independence and special agreements regarding the supply of water from Iraq to Kuwait and trade between the two countries were signed.

Arab policy regarding Israel has had more permanent consequences for Kuwait. On the one hand Kuwait joined nine other Arab countries in 1965 in breaking off diplomatic relationships with Federal Germany when that country recognised Israel; on the other hand, in the same year Kuwait asserted her economic independence by declining to join an Arab Common Market with Iraq, Jordan, Syria and the UAR. Similarly, in 1967, Kuwait joined in the Arab oil embargo on exports to Great Britain and the USA on the grounds of their supposed complicity in the Arab/Israeli war. But in 1968 she became a founder member, together with Libya and Saudi Arabia, of the Organisation of Arab Petroleum Exporting Countries, expressing the need of states whose economies are dominated by the export of oil, particularly to the West, for commercial freedom from political pressures.

Defence

Offensive war is prohibited by the Constitution. The Emir can, as in the case of the June War of 1967, decree that other Arab countries may be assisted in defending themselves. Kuwait maintains an Army which is responsible for air as well as ground defence and a well-equipped Air Force of pursuit planes. Kuwait Airways, with a fleet of international network jet airliners, can be called on to supply military transport needs. A naval flotilla for Gulf defence is being built up. No official figures of military strength are released.

ECONOMY

Background

Kuwait's GNP *per caput* of $4,535 (according to the UN, although the Kuwaiti estimate is somewhat lower) ranks with that of the USA and Abu Dhabi as one of the highest in the world in spite of the state's having virtually no commercially viable agriculture, of being dependent on desalination plant and on Iraq for fresh water and of having very limited manufacturing activity. Oil is the dominant factor in the country's economy, with revenue from its production and sale, estimated at $670 million in 1969, accounting for c. 92% of total budget revenue. Of the GNP approximately one-third is directly derived from exports, another one-third from private consumption, c. 20% from government expenditure and c. 20% from fixed investment. Approximately 93% of the oil (which totals c. 6% of world production) comes from the Kuwait Oil Company (50% each BP and Gulf Oil). Kuwaiti private foreign investment is estimated at over £350 million. The major channel to the private sector of oil revenue has been through major expenditure on urban renewal and development, in particular through land acquisition by the state. Oil revenue has risen relatively slowly since 1966 as a result of the embargo on oil exports to the west and the closure of the Suez Canal. Major industrial developments have been based on domestic oil and natural gas, the main features being the opening of a five million ton crude capacity oil refinery and a fertiliser plant producing ammonia and sulphuric acid (with their products) at Shaiba, the Kuwait industrial area. Other manufacturing activity is confined to the production of basic consumer goods such as bread, soft beverages, bricks and tiles, almost all other products being imported. Further developments in petro-chemical based manufactures have been considered but the small size of the domestic market, high labour costs and resource limitations tend to outweigh the plentiful supply of capital. Through the Kuwait Fund for Arab Economic Development with a capital of $560 million aid investment is made in other Arab countries who have also been assisted from the general reserve. Jordan and the UAR receive special emergency aid. In the 1969–70 budget it was still possible to allocate KD 67 million to development and property acquisition, and KD 3 million to general reserve after meeting all these commitments together with the most lavish domestic welfare expenditure in the world. Gold holdings are estimated at $86 million and foreign exchange holdings are about the same.

Foreign trade

Exports consist almost entirely of oil and have been increasing in value by c. 8% per annum since the 1967 interruption. Receipts from foreign investment are not known but are considerable. Kuwaiti imports running at a level of over 200 million dinars *p.a.* give the state the highest *per caput* import rate in the world. Kuwait's chief suppliers are the USA (1967 22%), Britain (12%), Japan (13%) and West Germany (9%), with the Japanese share growing faster than that of Western Europe. There is a permanent balance of payments surplus and only a relatively small range of commodities bear an *ad valorem* import duty of 4%. The import of alcoholic beverages is prohibited and protection is given to the local bottled gas industry by a 100% *ad valorem* import.

Employment

The 1965 census showed that the occupied population made up 180,000 of the total of 470,000. Of the industrially employed population over 64% were employed in commerce, finance and services. The effective service sector excluding true manufacture and the primary industries probably absorbed over 80% of the labour force. 53% of the total population was non-Kuwaiti of which three-quarters was Arab and one-third Jordanian/Palestinian by origin. 77% of the occupied population was non-Kuwaiti, most strongly represented in the group described as craftsmen (91% of 62,000) and in the professional and technical group (75% of 13,000). Since May 1968 non-Kuwaitis have been encouraged to resign and retire (with appropriate inducements) from official and administrative posts to make way for the increasing number of trained Kuwaitis. The university and judiciary alone are exempt from restrictions on the employment of expatriates in official posts.

Prices and wages

The steady increase in money supply noticeable in recent years was to some extent checked in 1968 by a relative slowing down in the rate of increase in government expenditure. Money supply in Kuwait largely reflects the volume of trading activity and the competition of many large and bazaar type financial institutions has tended to regulate general price levels. Commodity prices are a function of import prices and external trading competition also regulates this. The other main factors have been a general stability in official salaries, the semi-skilled labour pool of non-Kuwaitis, the high level of savings and the lavish provision of free education, health and welfare services. While the cost of living and the level of wages remains high there is no sign of any significant inflationary tendency.

Consumption

Since the supply of many utilities such as electricity, housing and water is either highly subsidised or free and since Kuwait is the most extensively developed welfare state in the world, any measurement of personal consumption is highly artificial. Much of the demand is for commodities which in many countries would be classified as luxuries and the rate appears to vary little from year to year.

SOCIAL SERVICES

The Ministry of Social Affairs and Labour established in 1962 is in general control of social welfare but separate ministries administer special services.

Health

The Ministry of Health is in charge of a first-class, totally comprehensive and totally free health service which includes hospital provision of all kinds, health education and regional clinics. Ordinary budgetary expenditure on public health totalled over £16 million in 1969–70.

Disability

Rehabilitation and retraining facilities are provided by the Ministry of Social Welfare as are also full free services for the old and permanently disabled.

Pensions
Non-contributory pension schemes are guaranteed for all Kuwaiti workers, rates being graded according to need and previous income, but with a very high minimum level.

Unemployment
Unemployment benefits, probably the highest in the world, are provided on a similar basis to pensions for all Kuwaiti workers.

Other benefits
Education and telephone services are also free. There is no income tax or other taxation. Water and electricity charges are nominal. For Kuwaitis of limited income (less than c. £150 a month) interest-free loans are available to cover subsidised house purchase in state housing projects. Unskilled Kuwaitis are eligible for interest-free loans to establish their own businesses. Kuwaiti workers are given absolute protection under the ministry-operated labour law. Sporting, athletic and cultural facilities, all of high standard, are provided free.

EDUCATION

Illiteracy, except among the very old and the non-Kuwaiti unskilled immigrants, is on the point of disappearing as a result of a vast Ministry of Education programme culminating in compulsory education introduced in 1966–7. There are at present c. 110,000 pupils attending some 180 schools, staffed by over 6,000 teachers. All normal teaching is in Arabic and all provision is free.

Primary education
Kindergartens, state and private primary schools are available to all children. The normal primary period lasts four years.

Intermediate and secondary education
A range of state and private schools offers full academic and technical opportunities in two four-year stages. The ratio of teachers to children in secondary schools is 1 : 12. A special centre for the education of handicapped children has been established.

University and higher education
Kuwait University, opened in 1966, will produce its first graduates in the faculties of Science, Arts and Education in 1969. Postgraduate training is planned to follow immediately although there are already several hundred Kuwaiti students continuing their studies at postgraduate level at foreign universities. A technical college has an enrolment of some 800 students. There are in addition five specialised institutes and three commercial colleges.

Adult education
There are 49 government-sponsored centres.

General
In addition to lavishly equipped and financed facilities in Kuwait which in 1969–70 received a budget allocation of over KD 30 million (in addition to more than £3 million for higher education), the Government of Kuwait has established and supported 35 schools with 10,500 pupils in the Arab/Persian Gulf States.

MASS MEDIA
The Press
Freedom of the Press is guaranteed under the constitution. Circulation figures are not available for all publications.

Dailies: *Akhbar Al-Kuwait* (*Kuwait News*); *Al-Rai Al-Aam* (*Public Opinion*); *Daily News*; *Kuwait Times*.

Periodicals: *Kuwait Al-Youm* (w), the official gazette; *Adhwa al-Kuwait* (w); *Al-Araby* (m), Ministry of Guidance and Information; *Al-Bayan* (m); *Al-Hadaf* (w); *Al-Nahda* (w); *Al-Raed al-Arabi; Al-Wai al-Islami* (m), Ministry of Islamic Affairs; *Al-Yaqdha* (w); *Al-Siasseh*. There are in addition the journals produced by KOC, by medical associations and various literary groups.

Radio and television
Administrative control of the Ministry of Guidance and Information is exerted through the Kuwait Broadcasting Service, and Television of Kuwait. Radio programmes in Arabic and English are transmitted on short and medium wave bands; there are an estimated 350,000 radio receivers. Two television programmes are transmitted to the c.75,000 television sets in use. Kuwait is establishing a television transmitter and station in Dubai, providing finance, staff and training.

LEBANON

GEOGRAPHY

Features

The character of the terrain of the Republic of Lebanon closely conforms to the relatively simple pattern of geological structure. From the Mediterranean littoral with its narrow and discontinuous coastal plain rise the Lebanon ranges, reaching just over 10,000 ft./3,000 m. in the Qornet es Sauda, formed of a faulted anticline of Jurassic and later rocks. The eastern limit of this north-south aligned massif is marked by a great fault-line and the associated linear depression of the Bekaa in which flows the Litani river. Further eastward still another great parallel anticlinal fold forms the Anti-Lebanon massif which falls away gradually into the Syrian plains. Calcareous rocks predominate but the presence of impermeable cretaceous beds gives rise to a great series of spring-lines at all altitudes which support agriculture and settlement. Climatically there is a west to east transition from lowland Mediterranean, through subtropical highland to elevated desert plains. The Lebanon ranges have relatively heavy precipitation, over 40 in./1,000 mm., much of which falls as snow and which in winter has encouraged the growth of winter sports in a region which in summer is a cool haven from the heat of the plains and has given rise to a regular seasonal migration from Beirut. There is no mineral or raw material wealth, other than that derived from agriculture.

Area
4,100 sq. mi./10,600 sq. km.

Mean max. and min. temperatures
Beirut (33°53'N, 35°27'E; 110 ft./30 m.) 89°F/32°C (August), 54°F/12°C (January).

Relative humidity
Beirut 40%–65%.

Annual rainfall
Beirut 35 in./880 mm.

POPULATION

Total population
(1967 estimate) 2,520,000.

Chief towns and population
BEIRUT (500,000), Tripoli (145,000).

Distribution
It is estimated that almost half the Lebanese population lives in the coastal

65

cities : Beirut, the political and commercial capital; Tripoli, terminal of the IPC oil pipeline from Iraq; and Sidon, terminal of the Trans-Arabian pipeline from Saudi Arabia. Rural concentrations lie mainly on the coastal periphery and in the Bekaa. The population includes a very large number of non-Lebanese temporary residents while over a million Lebanese who are still assumed to hold citizenship now live abroad.

Language
Arabic is the official language but English and French are widely used.

Religion
There is no official state religion. The population is divided more or less evenly between Christians and Muslims and Shi'a and Sunni Muslims while the Druzes, who combine Shi'a rites with some pre-Islamic elements of religion, are fewer but important in the south. Christian sects include Greek Orthodox and Greek Catholic groups and the Maronites, a Roman Uniate sect. This last is the largest and most important community of all. The numerical balance between the various communities is important since seats in the Chamber of Deputies are allocated on the basis of religious representation.

CONSTITUTIONAL SYSTEM

Constitution
The present constitution is based on that of 1926 with subsequent amendments which in toto define Lebanon as a democratic republic with an elected President as head of the executive and an elected legislature.

Executive
The President is elected by an electoral college (the Chamber of Deputies) for a period of six years and is not eligible for immediate re-election at the end of his term of office. As head of State he appoints the Prime Minister and other members of the Council of Ministers. The Maronite community has the chief voice in the selection of the President who must be a Maronite Christian; the constitution also requires that the Prime Minister shall be a Sunni Muslim and for other Ministers to be drawn from the other communities, this reflecting the apportionment of seats among the various Christian and Muslim sects[1] (see Legislature). The President may initiate legislation or impose various delays in the passing of laws in the Chamber; he may also adjourn or dissolve the House. The Council of Ministers headed by the President of Council (the Prime Minister) together with the President of the Republic form the Government of Lebanon. Ministers may be chosen from within the Chamber of Deputies or from outside it.

Legislature
A unicameral Chamber of Deputies is elected by Lebanese citizens over the age of 21. The seats, 99 in total, are allocated by religious community with a formal ratio of 54 : 45, Christian to Muslim. The Maronites are allotted 30, the Sunni Muslims 20, the Shi'a 19 and so on down to single representatives of the Protestants and Armenian Catholics. Political parties provide quite separate lines of cleavage and seats may be contested by politically different candidates within each community while loyalties will, with circumstances, vary between allegiance to the Republic or to a government,

[1] This is the 'unwritten' constitution, a custom so strong as to have become constitutional. The actual written constitution does not contain this provision.

to a particular sectarian community or region, or to a political party. Deputies are elected by secret ballot for a term of four years. The Chamber must pass all legislation by simple majority, elects or impeaches the President by a two-thirds majority and can force the resignation of Ministers by a majority vote of no confidence.

Political Parties

There are ten recognised political parties in the Lebanon including a Constitutional Party (*Destour*), National Liberal and National Blocs, the Phalangist and Progressive Socialist Parties and two which represent particular regional interests, the Armenian Tachnek and the southern Muslim El-Assad. The Arab National Socialist Party, the Ba'ath, has been banned. Power however tends to reside with two main alliances which represent linked political party and sectarian community interests, the Triple Alliance led by the Maronites and the Democratic Group which tends to be further to the left and to be more influenced by Arab affairs.

Leading political figures

Given the state of transition in which Lebanese political life finds itself it is impossible to ascribe simple political allegiances to leading figures. They include all the present Council of Ministers as well as Pierre Edde, former Minister of Finance and a leading banker. There are in addition Abdullah Yafi and Husain Oweini, past Prime Ministers, and Camille Chamoun, past President and leader of the National Liberal Party.

Head of State

Suleiman Franjiya.

Prime Minister

Saeb Salaam.

Minister of Foreign Affairs

Khalil Abu Hamad.

Judiciary

Legal codes dating from 1930 and covering all civil and criminal legislation are enforced by three tiers of court. At the lowest level there are single-judge courts dealing with civil and criminal cases of a petty kind. Fifty-seven of these courts sit at various centres throughout the country. Above these are eleven courts of appeal, each with three judges, who deal with more serious civil and criminal cases. Normally the final courts are the three civil and one criminal courts of cassation. The senior, the first court, is presided over by the First President of the Court of Cassation. The Council of State deals only with the Administrative Law while a Court of Justice is the ultimate authority in matters concerning state security. Each of the main sectarian communities has its customary courts which are recognised as possessing legal authority in affairs of domestic and personal status.

RECENT HISTORY

The state of Lebanon was created in 1920 by France, as mandatory power for the Syrian region, in a deliberate act of policy designed to utilise the religious differences, particularly between Christian and Muslim, to ease the task of French administration. However, by so doing, France also gave geo-political recognition to the individuality of the non-Palestinian Levant with its ancient tradition of commercialism, cosmopolitanism and ethno-religious variety. The Franco-Lebanese treaty of 1936 gave considerable autonomy to the state which finally achieved independence during and immediately after World War II.

Three main themes are of especial significance. The first has been concerned with maintaining a working unity within an area whose fractional tendencies are an integral characteristic of the state. Politically this has meant that successive administrations, elected on a community basis, have had to recognise the divergent interests of these communities, Maronite, Druze and Sunni and Shi'a Muslim, as well as the national interest. Since 1952 the present electoral system has, in practice, effectively served its purpose of balanced reconciliation of interests. The second theme, closely integrated with the first, has been that of maintaining an independence of outside pressures, Middle Eastern and international. Since 1955 Lebanon has maintained no more than conventional diplomatic relationships with the Communist bloc but also refused to join the Baghdad pact in 1958. Invitations to join the UAR of Egypt and Syria, the Arab Federation and all other alliances have similarly been declined. Lebanon is however a member of the Arab League, an active member of the Union of Arab Chambers of Commerce and of all UN organisations except GATT. Pan-Arab nationalism, particularly in 'Greater Syria' guise, is the great danger to national unity, as was shown in 1958 when President Chamoun requested US military and diplomatic assistance, and in the unsuccessful *coup* of 1961–2 which was suppressed by internal efforts. The problem of Israel has increased the difficulty of maintaining a position of 'neutrality but inclined to the West'. In 1965 relations with Federal Germany were the subject of considerable dissension while in 1967 and later considerable Arab pressure has been exerted to persuade Lebanon to lessen her reliance on America and Western Europe.

This reliance stems from the third element, the importance to Lebanon, which has pre-eminently a service-sector economy, of maintaining the optimum spread of amicable relationships. Seventy per cent of the GNP derives from the service sector and much of this activity is international. Banking, tourism, transportation and general commercial activity are of vital importance but are also very susceptible to changes in political circumstances. Receipts from tourism during 1967 were half the 1966 total; the Intra-Bank crisis of 1966 was essentially a manifestation of the fragility of domestic banks compared with the major international corporations; a dispute with Iran, the *Bakhtiar* affair, has endangered the use of Beirut airport by Iranian airlines. The prime rule for Lebanese political policy is circumspection and this has led to continuous efforts to lessen tension. The activities of the Palestinian Liberation Front and other guerilla groups are controlled as far as is possible but in 1969 tension became so strong that the government was compelled to take action against guerillas operating from Lebanese territory. The dispute with the Palestine commandos has caused Lebanon losses both in political stability and economic progress. The present Government, formed in November 1969, represents all political parties except the National Bloc, and sees as its main task the preservation of Lebanese sovereignty.

Defence

Lebanon normally maintains only small armed forces for internal purposes including a flotilla of coastal craft and a small air force. Compared with her Arab neighbours Lebanon has not greatly expanded these forces since 1967 and the present position is obscure.

ECONOMY

Background

The Lebanese economy is dominated by the service sector, sectoral contributions to the GNP in 1966 being : commerce 26%, public administration 9%, banking 8%, transport 8% and other services 7%; agriculture and industry contributed only 15% and 12% respectively. The ratio of merchandise imports to exports, 4 : 1, is another aspect of the same basic characteristic. At the end of 1969 there were 87 registered banks in the Lebanon of which one-third were wholly or partially controlled by foreign corporations. Lebanon, which maintains a virtually free market in capital, became the financial and commercial centre of the Middle East as regional oil revenue soared and as confidence in Alexandria and Baghdad became eroded by changing political circumstances. Both of these relative advantages have declined in importance, particularly as the oil states developed their own institutions, but as a regional headquarters for non-Arab companies Beirut is still supreme. More recent has been the growth of tourism which earned over £40 million in foreign exchange during 1968 while transit dues paid on the movement of Iraqi and Saudi oil through the Mediterranean pipe-line terminals of Sidon and Tripoli contributed a further £6 million. The rise of Beirut airport as a major international junction has been paralleled by the development of MEA and Trans-Mediterranean Airways, the latter a freighting service. Total invisibles including overseas remittances and receipts from investment were estimated to produce a balance of payments surplus of £46·1 million in 1966, falling to £12·7 million in 1967 through the repercussions of the June War.

Agriculture is generally intensive and commercialised. Citrus fruits are especially important; together with tobacco, suger-cane and olives they are chiefly grown on the coastal fringe. Vines, other treecrops (notably apples) and grain become more important in the interior. Extensive development is now planned in agriculture. Manufacturing industry is growing very rapidly both for the domestic market and soaring exports. Small-scale light manufacturing of a very varied nature predominates together with food-processing, textiles, and the new cement industry. New power-generating installations are planned including the multi-purpose HEP and irrigation Litani River project. GNP *per caput* in 1963 was c. £123.

Foreign Trade

The Arab-Israeli war reduced the volume and distorted the pattern of trade during 1967 but even so imports totalled $463 million with exports of $119 million, diminishing considerably the normal visible trade gap. Britain was the main supplier—c. 20% of all imports—and alone among Western countries actually increased her volume of sales. The USA, France, West Germany and Italy provided a further 30%. Within the Middle East most imports came from Syria, Iraq and Saudi Arabia. Arab countries took over half Lebanon's exports, with Saudi Arabia and Kuwait in the lead. Britain and USA provide the largest non-Arab markets. The largest group of imports consists of machinery, textiles and vehicles, followed closely by precious metals, stones, jewellery, etc. Lebanon is a net importer of vegetable and animal products and of beverages and tobacco. The main exports were of agricultural products (c. 40%) followed by precious metals, etc.

Employment

A 1961 survey registered a working force of 580,000 of which over one-third were employed in agriculture, and some 10% in industry (including construction). Since that date the proportion engaged in industry has increased.

Price and wage trends
This is one of the many sectors in which Lebanese data is not wholly satisfactory. Estimates suggest that after a long period of relative stability there was a sharp rise in prices during the winter of 1968–9. Wage-levels seem to be responding more slowly.

SOCIAL SERVICES

Responsibility in this field is shared by the ministries and departments of social and labour affairs, public health and education, expenditure by which, as a proportion of the 1968 Budget, 2%, 3% and 16% respectively. The social security system provides for four main fields of benefit, sickness and maternity insurance, labour accidents and professional diseases insurance, family allowances and indemnity for termination of service. All benefits and indemnities are based on previous earnings and funds are made up of subscriptions paid by employees, employers and the State. A new Social Security Law has been the subject of much debate and controversy, since management and unions have disagreed over its provisions. A new workers' insurance scheme is to be implemented in 1971. The National Social Security Fund's budget for 1970 totalled £Leb 73,700,000.

EDUCATION

By 1967 there were 1,900 state primary schools offering free education for five years. The mainly fee-paying state and private schools above this level include four-year upper-primary schools and seven-year secondary schools. There are vocational schools and colleges and teacher-training institutions of various types. There are four universities, all at Beirut, including the American University of Beirut; what is essentially a French eqivalent, the Université St. Joseph (both of these dating from the late 19th century); the state-run Lebanese University; and the Arab University of Beirut, established in 1960. In all there are approximately 20,000 students, many from other parts of the Middle East. In addition there are almost a score of private and foreign cultural institutions engaged in teaching and in research.

MASS MEDIA

Lebanon is literate, multi-lingual and articulate; as a result there is an amazing proliferation of newspapers and journals. The Press is entirely in private hands and serves the domestic needs of differing communities and a large cosmopolitan element as well as those of other countries. Of the almost 100 regular publications only the most important and large-circulation names are listed here.

The Press
Dailies: *Al-Hayat*, Beirut, Arabic (c. 25,000); *Al-Ahrar*, Beirut, Arabic (c. 17,000); *Al-Anwar*, Beirut, Arabic (c. 45,000); *Al-Kifah*, Beirut, Arabic (c. 21,000); *Lisan-ul-Hal*, Beirut, Arabic (c. 23,000); *An-Nahar*, Beirut, Arabic (c. 22,000); *An-Nidal*, Beirut, Arabic (c. 25,000); *As-Safa*, Beirut, Arabic (c. 15,000); Armenian : *Ararat, Aztag* and *Zartonk*, all of Beirut;

English : *Daily Star*, Beirut; French : *Le Jour, L'Orient* and *Le Soir*, all of Beirut.

Periodicals: Achabaka (w) Beirut, Arabic; *Al-Adib* (m) Beirut, Arabic; *Al-Ahad* (m) Beirut, Arabic; *Al-Anba'* (w) Beirut, Arabic; *Al-Hurriya* (w) Beirut, Arabic; *Al-Intilak* (m) Beirut, Arabic; *Al-Iza'a* (w) Beirut, Arabic; *Al-Jamhour* (w) Beirut, Arabic; *Al-Usbua al-Arabi* (w) Beirut, Arabic; *Assayad* (w) Beirut, Arabic; *Commerce du Levant* ((m) and twice weekly editions) Beirut, French.

Broadcasting
The Lebanese Broadcasting Station is run by the Ministry of Guidance and Information. Transmissions are in Arabic, English and French. Television transmission is from two independent commercial stations, Compagnie Libanaise de Télévision and Télé Orient; Arabic, English and French are used on a total of six channels.

PERSIAN GULF STATES

BAHRAIN

GEOGRAPHY

Features

THE Shaikhdom of Bahrain comprises a small group of low-lying limestone islands located in generally shallow waters some 20 miles offshore from Saudi Arabia and from the Qatar peninsula. From over 500 drilled wells and natural springs sweet water is obtained in quantities which have always seemed inexhaustible and which, utilised for irrigation, have provided the basis for sedentary settlement for five millennia and encouraged the growth of the port of Manama on the main island of Bahrain and of the second most important island of Muharraq.

Area
260 sq. mi./670 sq. km.

Mean max. and min. temperatures
Manama (26°12′N, 50°38′E; 70 ft./22 m.) 100°F/38°C (August), 58°F/14°C (January).

Relative humidity
12%–100%.

Annual rainfall
3 in./75 mm.

POPULATION

Total population
(1965 census) 182,200.

Chief towns and population
MANAMA (79,100), Muharraq (34,400), Isa Town (15,000).

Distribution
Manama, the capital and chief commercial centre, has now been provided with an overflow residential satellite, Isa Town, which is planned to accommodate 35,000 people by 1975. Approximately 17·7% of the total population can be regarded as non-urban.

Language
Arabic is the official language but Farsi and other South Asian languages are used in the non-Arab communities which make up c. 20% of the population.

72

Religion
Islam is the official religion and both Sunni and Shi'a sects are represented.

CONSTITUTIONAL SYSTEM

The Ruler of Bahrain has sovereign powers and up to January 1970 was assisted by a Council of Administration composed of other members of the ruling family and the appointed heads of certain government departments. On 19 January 1970 Bahrain's Council of State was announced.

President
Shaikh Khalifa Ben Sulman al-Khalifa.

Defence Minister
Shaikh Hamad Ben Isa al-Khalifa.
By various treaties, dating in the first instance from 1820, Great Britain has special responsibilities for defence and foreign affairs.

Judiciary
Bahrain courts administer justice to citizens of Qatar and the Gulf shaikhdoms, most other Arab states and some other Muslim countries, the remainder coming under the jurisdiction of British courts. The codes and regulations framed for the latter are utilised to some extent in Bahrain criminal courts which otherwise, as is the case with other courts helped by a judicial adviser, administer traditional customary law modified after Egyptian practice. There is a Chief Justice who advises on final appeal procedure and who is head of the judiciary. The full court and the chief court for the Persian Gulf, both British, are based on Bahrain but can sit anywhere in the Gulf; the Judges are nominated by the Privy Council, appeal lying to the British Privy Council.

RECENT HISTORY

Background
In 1783 the chief family of the Utub tribe, the al-Khalifa, were instrumental in expelling the Iranians from Bahrain and became hereditary rulers. Iranian claims to sovereignty are based on their control of this region of the Gulf prior to that date. Until 1935 the history of Bahrain was closely associated with entrepôt trade and pearling and it is as a mercantile centre victualled by spring-watered agriculture that Bahrain developed. During the 19th century this fundamental characteristic involved Bahrain in the changing geo-political scene in a new way. The British desire to maintain a free and fluid position in the Gulf ran counter to Ottoman and Iranian political claims and to German politico-economic ambitions; in 1861 Britain supported the independent sovereignty of Bahrain in return for anti-piracy and anti-slavery agreements. Further treaties in 1880 and 1892 resulted in the British government assuming all responsibility for external affairs. Bahrain became the seat of the British Resident in the Gulf and of the chief and full courts for the Gulf. Following the discovery of oil Bahrain became the first of the Gulf States to experience the difficulties of socio-economic change, particularly after 1948. In 1956 the first non-traditional administrative councils were established and in 1957 the powers of the Bahrain judiciary were extended to their present limits. Education and welfare services date from the 1920s, the earliest in the Gulf. These did not prevent Bahrain from being the scene of socio-political trouble, notably in 1956 when anti-British

sentiment, inflamed by the Suez affair, exacerbated internal (but externally-encouraged) unrest, the outward manifestations usually taking the form of strikes in the oil industry.

Bahrain is now developing a socio-political internal maturity during a difficult period in which the British military presence first reached its peak (1966-7) and is now being run down in the process of withdrawal by 1971. Linked very strongly by trade with Saudi Arabia and with the southern Gulf, vulnerable to Iranian claims, Bahrain has recently been involved in the discussions concerning the Federation of Arab Emirates (see Trucial States). A United Nations representative was appointed in March 1970 at the request of the Iranian Government and with the full approval of the British government, to ascertain the wishes of the Bahrainis as to the future of the island.

ECONOMY

Bahrain has been an oil-exporter for longer than any other Arabian state. Since shipments started in 1934 and the refinery began processing local crude in 1936 oil revenue has increased to over £7 million a year. Production, entirely by the Bahrain Petroleum Company (BAPCO)-Caltex Group, is in the main from onshore wells but since 1963 the offshore field of Abu Saafa, shared with Saudi Arabia, has been of increasing importance. The future for oil seems uncertain since reserves are now rapidly declining and no significant new discoveries have been made. Natural gas however exists in considerable quantity and is the resource base for the most important new industrial development—aluminium smelting. An Anglo-Swedish consortium (with a $27\frac{1}{2}\%$ Bahrain financial interest) is establishing a £30 million smelter with a capacity of 85,500 tons a year, the alumina being shipped from Australia. By 1972 this, together with ancillary industries, will provide full-time employment for 400. The oil refinery which has a throughput of 90 million barrels a year increasingly relies on Saudi oil and in 1968 three-quarters of the crude handled was from Saudi Arabia. Other aspects of recent efforts to diversify the economy include plastics and a modern fish-processing plant.

Fortunately Bahrain has always been a trading centre. During 1968 customs dues contributed over £2 million to state revenue. Bahrain is also an important regional airport and telecommunications centre. An earth station, the first of its kind in the Middle East, was installed at Ras Abu Jarjur in July 1969, and there is a tropospheric scatter installation at Jebel Dukhan and a transmitter centre at Hamala. Agriculture has steadily declined in importance as other employment possibilities have appeared but a revival based on the more efficient use of groundwater resources is planned. The Bahrain Development Bureau was set up in 1967 to encourage industrial investment.

Foreign Trade

1968 imports were valued at BD52,051,000 while exports and re-exports, excluding oil, were BD18,494,000. Britain remains Bahrain's chief supplier—25% of commodities, of which nearly half are household goods. Japan, as everywhere in the Middle East, has increased her share (chiefly textiles and clothing), which is now slightly ahead of the USA's 12%. Saudi Arabia is the chief trade recipient taking over 50% of Bahraini exports and re-exports (half of these are textiles). The other main destinations lie in the Gulf, including Iran.

Employment
Of the occupied population of 54,000 in 1965, 40% was non-Bahraini. The largest number of these were employed in the construction industry and in the service sector, 4,800 and 11,000 respectively. The employment pattern among Bahrainis is rather similar except for a higher proportion in administrative and clerical work and a far larger number in the agricultural sector. BAPCO employees are almost totally Bahraini.

Price and wage trends
Prices, as elsewhere in the Gulf, are largely a function of world trading competition and low import dues. Domestic agricultural production serves to stabilise the prices of vegetables, an important dietary element. Levels of wages and prices have long recovered from the first oil-based inflation and appear relatively stable.

Consumption
There are available only a few indicators in this sector. The 1965 population of 182,200 possessed 5,700 private cars and while the population increases by about 3·5% *p.a.*, the number of private cars rises by more than 6% *p.a.*

SOCIAL SERVICES

These are in part the direct responsibility of the Council of Administration which assists the ruler, in part the province of the urban and rural municipal councils and, lastly, are partly administered by the health and education councils. These last two councils, together with other committees contain at least half elected members. This pattern results from the long period over which social services themselves have evolved. Public health and education alone now absorb over half normal budgetary expenditure; some relevant items are also financed in the separate development budgets.

There are no insurance provisions but rather direct assistance in the form of finance and retraining for unemployed Bahrainis. All medical services including hospitalisation are free. The first hospitals were established by British and American contributions in 1900. In 1925 a state medical service was established and the first state hospital completed in 1942. In 1968 Bahrain became a member of the WHO and had a medical budget of £2,300,000. Not only are there village dispensaries, five maternity hospitals, four centres for specialised treatment (chest, psychological, contagious diseases and tuberculosis), a first class general hospital and public health services, but Bahrain now trains its own nurses and has Bahraini doctors and specialists.

Isa town, the new urban centre, makes special provision in the form of subsidised high-quality low-cost accommodation and full free urban facilities and services.

EDUCATION

Bahrain has also pioneered education in the Gulf.

1968–9—Schools and Pupils

Primary Schools	Boys	42	Pupils	20,106
Primary Schools	Girls	29	Pupils	14,636
Intermediate Schools	Boys	12	Pupils	3,032
Intermediate Schools	Girls	9	Pupils	2,322
Secondary Schools	Boys	3	Pupils	3,334
Secondary Schools	Girls	3	Pupils	1,904

| Technical and Higher Schools | Boys | 3 | Pupils | 773 |
| Technical and Higher Schools | Girls | 1 | Pupils | 96 |

All state education in Bahrain is free and government bursaries support students attending foreign institutions. Two teacher-training colleges have been established and 74% of the education department's teachers are Bahraini citizens.

MASS MEDIA

The Press

There is one private Arabic weekly, *Al Adhwaa*, with a circulation of 5,000. In addition: *Al Najmar al Asbuʿa*, Arabic (BAPCO) (7,000); *Huna al Bahrain*, Arabic (Information Dept.) (4,000); *Al Hiya al Tijariya*, Arabic and English (Chamber of Commerce); *The Islander*, English (BAPCO) (7,000).

Radio

Bahrain Broadcasting Station broadcasts in Arabic from 2 kw. transmitters. English language broadcasts by the US Air Force in Dhahran, and by ARAMCO can be received in Bahrain.

PERSIAN GULF STATES

QATAR

GEOGRAPHY

THE Shaikhdom of Qatar is a low-lying peninsula composed of calcareous rocks approximately 100 mi./160 km. from north to south and with a breadth of up to 50 mi./80 km. The stony desert surface merges imperceptibly into the Arabian deserts in the south and into the shallow waters which lie off-shore everywhere except off Umm Said, the oil port in the south east. Hundreds of low capacity shallow wells tap water of varying degrees of brackishness and support life in a number of small oasis settlements.

Area
12,500 sq mi./20,000 sq. km. (Qatar territorial claims).

Mean max. and min. temperatures
Doha (25°15′N, 51°36′E; 20 ft./13 m. a.s.l.) 118°F/47·8°C (July), 43°F/6·1°C (January).

Relative humidity
68%–94%.

Annual rainfall
1 in.–5 in./ 25 mm.–125 mm.

POPULATION

Total population
(1967 estimate) 75,000.

Chief town and population
DOHA (60,000).

Distribution
Approximately 80% of the population lives in Doha, the capital and traditional trading port. Umm Said, the oil terminal, is QPC headquarters with a population of c. 5,000 while Dukhan on the west coast is a new oilfield town (pop. c. 3,000).

Language
Arabic.

Religion
The majority of the population are Sunni Muslims, the second largest religious group (some 3%) being Christian.

77

CONSTITUTIONAL SYSTEM

All executive and legislative power rests with the ruler of Qatar who, through the deputy ruler and appointed ministers and with the help of an Advisory Council, carries out direct rule. By treaty, Great Britain has special responsibilities for external affairs.

Head of State
Shaikh Ahmad Bin Aly al-Thani, Ruler of Qatar.

Deputy Ruler and Heir Apparent
Shaikh Khalifa Bin Hamad al-Thani.

Judiciary
Qatar courts administer justice, through laws and regulations formulated by a department of legal affairs, to nationals of Qatar, other Arab states, Iran, Indonesia and Somalia, except for matters under the jurisdiction of the Labour Court in which case there is no separation. The series of laws enacted since 1961 mainly deal with non-criminal affairs while criminal justice is still based on traditional non-codified practice. For all other residents British jurisdiction is administered through magistrate and higher courts and HBM chief court for the Gulf. *Shariah* courts of the traditional kind deal with domestic and personal status matters.

RECENT HISTORY

The Al-Thani family for many years ruled an almost barren peninsula whose fringing seas held a wealth of pearls but hazards for shipping. Doha grew, unlike many Gulf towns, as a small fishing village with little trade. Not until 1916 did Britain make an agreement with Qatar for taking over external responsibilities and giving defence support. During the late 1930s the discovery of oil gave Qatar a new importance although commercial production did not start until 1949 and oil revenues only passed the £100,000 mark in 1951. Since that time the history of Qatar has been politically unexciting but economically rewarding particularly during the last few years of administration by Shaikh Khalifa, the Deputy Ruler. Links with Dubai on a family as well as on a commercial basis have been strong, one element in recent discussions concerning membership of a Federation of Arab Emirates; Shaikh Khalifa is chairman of the Provisional Federal Council.

ECONOMY

Background
The economy of Qatar is completely dominated by oil. Revenue from production exceeded £33 million in 1968, contributing over 90% of the state income (although no financial or budgetary details are published). Production has chiefly been from the central Dukhan oilfield but, as in the case of Bahrain, reserves are limited and more attention is being paid to offshore areas. Qatar Petroleum Company (QPC), an affiliate of IPC, has levelled off production to about nine million tons *p.a.*, while the Shell Company of Qatar is steadily increasing the yield of the marine fields to the east, Id al-Sharqi and Maidan Mahzam, now about seven millions tons *p.a.* An increasing proportion of revenue has gone into government investment (£30–£35 million), and into economic development and social welfare. Im-

portant elements in development have been the Qatar National Fishing Company (Ross Group), pumped irrigation schemes which have already achieved some success, the Qatar Fertiliser Company which will produce ammonia and urea from natural gas by 1972 and the newly completed cement plant. The new deep-water berths at Doha are now virtually complete, reducing dependence on lightering and on the deep seaport-cum-tanker terminal at Umm Said.

Foreign Trade

Imports during 1968 are estimated at £17,500,000 of which the British share was nearly 40%; British goods have been chiefly machinery and transport equipment and electrical appliances. Re-exports are estimated to be between 10% and 14% of all imports, these going to neighbouring states. Exports other than oil are small but vegetables are becoming significant.

SOCIAL SERVICES

As in most other Gulf states assistance to the needy is carried out on an *ad hominem* basis of financial relief. Subsidised housing is being provided, on a rent or more usually on a loan basis, for low income groups and the disabled. The Department of Labour and Social Affairs is responsible for these services and for the new social welfare services. The Department of Medical Services and Public Health is responsible for health service centres and clinics as well as for three hospitals including the large Rumailah General Hospital at Doha. All medical services, including treatment abroad if necessary, are free.

EDUCATION

The Ministry of Education has been the chief social interest of the Qatar government. In 1968 it was estimated that 11% of budgetary expenditure went on education, about £3 million. Primary, secondary and specialist schools in 1968–9 had 16,000 pupils and over 900 teachers. Teacher recruitment has been assisted by the establishment of a training college. Free educational facilities include boarding and clothing where necessary, and overseas training in further education. Adult vocational training is organised by a Department of Career Development and Vocational Training. Technical training is now receiving special attention as part of the economic development programme.

MASS MEDIA

Radio

The Qatar Broadcasting Service, state-owned, has now commenced transmission in Arabic from 100 kW. and 50 kW. installations.

Information Department

Publication plans are well advanced.

PERSIAN GULF STATES

TRUCIAL STATES

GENERAL

THE Trucial States consist of seven sovereign states: Abu Dhabi, Ajman, Dubai, Fujairah, Ras al-Khaimah, Sharjah and Umm al-Quwain. Their territories lie on the southern shores of the Gulf, extending eastwards to the Gulf of Oman. Following a series of treaties between individual rulers and Great Britain, dating from 1820, the UK Government assumed responsibility for their defence, for settling inter-state disputes, and for external affairs. In addition to the notes which follow, further information is given, individually, for the two largest states.

GEOGRAPHY

Features

The Trucial Gulf coast, extending between Qatar and the rocky headlands of the Ras Musandam headland (in Oman) is characterised by shallow seas, a fringe of sand bars, coral reefs and islands and by stretches of saline/alkaline mudflats (*sabkha*). Wherever groundwater seepage has allowed human settlement of relatively firm sandspits, bars and islands, small marine-based communities have become established. At Dubai, Ras al-Khaimah and Sharjah, the presence of creeks encouraged greater than average growth based on Gulf and long-distance trade. Inland lies a zone of inhospitable sand desert which grades into an arid gravel and silt outwash belt at the foot of the Omani mountains. Where this belt opens on to the coast at Ras al-Khaimah, settlement extends inland from the sea. Where water from the highlands percolates at shallow depths into this belt, oasis agriculture, on a large scale in the Buraimi complex, has been established. The spinal mountains themselves are inhospitably rugged except for small upland valleys and basins, where surface water derived from higher rainfall supports grazing and crops. On the east coast rugged headlands alternate with small emboyments in which communities subsist on fishing and garden-oases. Khawr Fakkan, the only true port, has grown around one of the few safe harbourages. Aridity is general, and on the coasts high summer temperatures and humidity make the climate very oppressive. Drier air and greater temperature ranges characterise the interior.

Area

32,000 sq. mi./83,000 sq. km.

Mean max. and min. temperatures

Sharjah (25°12′N, 55°12′E; 30 ft./10 m.) 110°F/43°C (July and August), 53·5°F/12°C (December and January).

Relative humidity
42%–85%.

Annual rainfall
0 in./0·3 mm.–10·3 in./258·2 mm.

POPULATION

Total population
(1968 census) 180,200.

Shaikhdom of Abu Dhabi	46,500 (estimate)
Shaikhdom of Ajman	4,240
Shaikhdom of Dubai	59,092
Shaikhdom of Fujairah	9,724
Shaikhdom of Ras al-Khaimah	24,482
Shaikhdom of Sharjah	31,480
Shaikhdom of Umm al-Quwain	3,740

Chief towns and population
ABU DHABI TOWN (22,000), Dubai Town (57,400), Sharjah Town (20,600), Ras al-Khaimah Town (5,244).

Distribution
Approximately half the population may be described as urban and is concentrated on the Gulf coast. In the interior, apart from Al'Ain in the Buraimi complex, and on the east coast, the population lives in oasis villages of up to about 1,000 inhabitants. Non-Arab immigrants are numerous and associated with the towns.

Language
Arabic is dominant but Farsi and other languages of South Asia are used in the immigrant communities.

Religion
The majority of the indigenous inhabitants are Sunni Muslims.

CONSTITUTIONAL SYSTEM

Each ruler has absolute power over his own subjects, this power being exercised through traditional institutions. Each state has full sovereignty save for the limitations of British treaty responsibilities for external affairs. Since 1960 a Trucial States Council on which all rulers are represented meets regularly to discuss problems of mutual interest and to coordinate various activities. Its executive arm is the Development Office financed principally by the Ruler of Abu Dhabi and the UK Government.

Following the announcement by Britain in 1968 that its forces would be withdrawn from the area by late 1971, various discussions concerning federation have taken place between the seven Trucial States, Bahrain and Qatar. No final agreement has been reached but attempts to draw up a federal constitution and to replace a temporary federal council by one more permanent are continuing. Difficulties arise principally because of the disparities in size, wealth, sophistication and oil expectations between the nine states which exacerbate the differences which stem from local tribal loyalties, as well as the uncertainties caused by Iran's claim to Bahrain.

Rulers
Ajman : Shaikh Rashid Bin Humaid; Abu Dhabi : Shaikh Zaid Bin Sultan al-Nahayyan; Dubai : Shaikh Rashid Bin Said al-Maktum; Fujairah : Shaikh Muhammad Bin Hamed al-Sharqi; Ras al-Khaimah : Shaikh Saqr Bin Muhammad al-Qasimi; Sharjah : Shaikh Khalid Bin Muhammad al Qasimi; Umm al-Quwain : Shaikh Ahmed Bin Rashid al-Mu'alla.

Judicial System : Citizens of the Trucial States and of all Muslim countries are subject to the jurisdiction of the legal courts within each state. All other residents are under British jurisdiction which is administered according to British orders in council by the Judges of the British courts of the Gulf and the British chief court. With the exceptions of Abu Dhabi, where there is an appointed professional judge, and Dubai, where there is a full-time traditional Islamic judge (*qadi*), the rulers or nominated members of the ruling families deal with judicial cases.

RECENT HISTORY

The British presence in the Trucial Region derives from the quasi-official status of East India Company agents in the Gulf during the early 18th century. From 1770 onwards the Royal Navy became increasingly active in the protection of maritime trade and expeditionary forces were landed in Ras al-Khaimah, where Qasimi power was strong, several times in the early 19th century. Treaties signed in the 1820s binding the rulers to refrain from piracy, developed into annual truces negotiated through the Gulf political residency and the resident's agency established at Sharjah in 1823. Suppression of the slave trade was the purpose of other British diplomatic interventions and local and dynastic disputes, while not eliminated, became less frequent. From 1892 onwards the rulers conducted all their external affairs through the British Government and local political officers were finally superseded by a political agent in 1953. Since the main purpose until recently was to maintain a *Pax Britannica*, a central military force able to intervene in inter-state disputes was established in 1953, the Trucial Oman Scouts. Active in 1953 and 1955 in the Buraimi area, in Oman at various periods since 1957 and on Fujairah/Ras al-Khaimah frontiers in 1959 as well as on many smaller prophylactic missions, the Scouts, who have Arab as well as British officers, have maintained stability most effectively. The base for the British military forces is Sharjah. The expansion of Imperial Airways led to an airstrip being established in 1932 and in 1940 it became an RAF base. After 1945 Sharjah became the main air-staging base for the Gulf and following the British withdrawal from Aden there was in addition an Army build-up. This considerable base is scheduled to be abandoned as part of the British withdrawal from the Gulf in 1971. The future of the smaller shaikhdoms as independent states has always seemed doubtful and the prosperity of Sharjah will be drastically reduced unless it also can benefit from the proposed federation, or can succeed in striking oil. Ras al-Khaimah is the only state which possesses significant agricultural resources and its oil prospects (offshore) seem superior to those of the other oil-deficient states; the ruler has tended therefore to take a somewhat independent line over the Federation although an active member of the Trucial States Council.

Present negotiations concerning a Federation of Arab Emirates are crucial but complex, especially complicated by the involvement of Bahrain and Qatar. Qatar, Dubai and Ras al-Khaimah, one oil state, one trading city state now with oil and one with a little trade and no oil, are bound together to some extent by family alliances, cemented in the case of Dubai and Qatar by mutual investment interests. Qatar and Saudi Arabia have close religious links while Bahrain is closely commercially tied to Saudi Arabia. Iran, the greatest power on the Gulf, has never given up claims to Bahrain, and this attitude has made the Saudi and Kuwaiti Governments take a more fervent interest in a federal solution. To the Western world the finding of oil in ever greater quantities, onshore from Oman almost continuously north to Kuwait, and offshore in the south and central Gulf as well as in the north, makes it imperative that political stability should be established as rapidly as possible.

ECONOMY

The most important factors in the region as a whole have been the work of the Trucial States Council's Development Office and, in part through this office, financial and technical assistance from Britain, Kuwait and Saudi Arabia. Since 1965 there has been a rapid build up of development expenditure through the council, this now mainly concentrated on inter-state projects such as road-building, technical education, health and agricultural advisory services and on the five states without oil revenue. 1968 expenditure totalled about £2 million and 1969 estimates show a 50% increase. Abu Dhabi now contributes £1·7 million annually, Britain £1·2 million. Kuwaiti assistance has chiefly taken the form of setting up schools and medical centres while Saudi Arabia has financed major roadworks, housing and agricultural projects. Excluding Dubai and Abu Dhabi the states' revenues are obtained from low *ad valorem* import taxes, traditional tribal contributions and the sale of postage stamps.

PERSIAN GULF STATES

TRUCIAL STATES—ABU DHABI

GEOGRAPHY

Features

THE Emirate of Abu Dhabi extends along the shoal southern coast of the Gulf between the states of Qatar and Dubai and into the mainly sand desert interior of the Empty Quarter. Until recently the only areas at all attractive to human settlement were some of the 200 islands, including that of Abu Dhabi itself, on which small fishing and trading communities existed, and the oasis complexes of Liwa, near the Saudi Arabian frontier, and Buraimi, on the edge of the Oman mountain ranges and the border of the Sultanate of Muscat and Oman. Abu Dhabi is now connected by a causeway with the mainland, Das Island is the headquarters of the offshore oil extracting companies, Sir Beni Yas Island possessing deep waters is an oilport facing the Dhanna oil terminal of the inland Murban oilfield, and Al'Ain is the centre of a developing agricultural area in the Buraimi region. There are no material resources other than limited groundwater, marine pearl banks and oil, export of which started in 1963 and which is revolutionising the Emirate.

Area

31,000 sq. mi./80,000 sq. km. (Abu Dhabi territorial claim).

Climate

See Trucial States.

POPULATION

Total population
(1968) 46,500.

Chief towns and population

ABU DHABI TOWN (22,000), Al'Ain and associated villages (13,000).

Distribution

Almost half the population is located in the seaport capital and this proportion is growing as from the interior, the Liwa oases in particular, inhabitants move to the centre of economic growth and also as immigration increases. The population of the oil centres, Das Island, Dhanna and Tarif is 2,500 and growing. Al'Ain, the official residence of the ruler is being developed as a full urban centre whilst to the east the new town of Zaid is under construction. The indigenous population still sets store by tribal groupings which consist of the Bani Yas, the al-Manasir, al-Dhawahir and al-Awamer tribes. The rulers of the Emirate are members of the al-Nahayyan branch of the Bani Yas.

Constitutional System

The ruler possesses all executive and legislative power. Through decrees dating from 1966 a number of government departments have been established with specialised administrative responsibilities; the ruler appoints chairman and directors of these departments and through his *Diwan* exercises central authority. In 1968 a Planning Council was established with the ruler as president, appointed members consisting of departmental chairmen and directors and seven others.

Ruler
Zaid Bin Sultan al-Nahayyan, Ruler of the Emirate of Abu Dhabi.

Deputy Ruler
Shaikh Khalid Bin Sultan al-Nahayyan. A British Political Agency is located at Abu Dhabi.

Judicial System
The traditional Islamic courts at Abu Dhabi and Al'Ain are now being complemented by civil courts which, under the supervision of the Department of Justice, administer the new codified laws and procedures, civil and criminal, published since May 1968 in the official gazette.

Recent History
See also Trucial States

By the end of the 18th century the land-based tribal group of the Bani Yas under Shaikh Dhiyab Bin Isa al-Nahayyan had made the island of Abu Dhabi, with its wells of potable water, their main centre, while the Al-Dhawahir tribe remained in the Buraimi region. The Emirate since that time has remained in the Al-Nahayyan line while Shaikh Zaid Bin Khalifa (Zaid al-Kabir) during the latter half of the 19th century established sovereignty over what is approximately the present territory of the state, in particular establishing a *modus vivendi* with Oman which left Al-Buraimi proper in the Sultanate and brought Al'Ain, Qattara and Hili into the Emirate.

Between 1909 and 1928 the Emirate was ruled by Zaid the Great's sons on a provincial basis and for the period between 1928 and 1960, under Shaikh Shakhbut Bin Sultan, the Emirate remained little changed. Abu Dhabi, a low-grade fishing port, was the residence of the Emir, while al' Ain with its *falaj*-based traditional agriculture was administered and developed by the ruler's brother Shaikh Zaid. Border disputes between Abu Dhabi, Dubai, Oman, and Saudi Arabia were not infrequent and British intervention was regularly necessary. In 1966 Shaikh Shakhbut, overwhelmed by the problems of oil affluence, was deposed by family agreement and succeeded by Shaikh Zaid, the present ruler. Since 1966 the history of Abu Dhabi has been marked by increasingly successful domestic policies of social and economic development, pacific and generous dealings with its Trucial neighbours and a growing international stature in the Arab world and beyond.

Defence
Shaikh Zaid has established a well equipped defence force, independent of the Trucial Oman Scouts. This includes armoured land units, naval patrol boats and an embryo air force. The total armed force numbers approximately 2,000 men.

ECONOMY

Background
Previous to the discovery of oil in 1960 the economy of Abu Dhabi was extremely poor. The difficult coast prevented all but the most limited marine activity, including pearl fishing, while inland subsistence agriculture at Al'Ain and Liwa was the only alternative to desert nomadism. Abu Dhabi is now the twelfth largest oil producer in the world and her proven oil reserves are approximately one-third of those of the North American continent.

Unlike Dubai, Abu Dhabi has neither the tradition of nor the physical suitability for large-scale marine trade but does possess agricultural potential in the Buraimi region. The main elements in present economic development are therefore expenditure on urban modernisation at Abu Dhabi town, Al'Ain and the new City of Zaid.

Oil revenue in 1968 totalled almost £70 million, approximately £1,400 per head of the population. Oil production is controlled by five main groups, Abu Dhabi Petroleum Co. (IPC associate) and the ENI/Phillips/AMINOIL Consortium onshore, Abu Dhabi Maritime Areas (BP and CFP), Mitsubishi and a Japanese consortium offshore. The main producing fields hitherto have been at Murban and near Das Island. In the last concession agreement (Mitsubishi 1968) a commitment to construct a refinery is included and the development of petro-chemical industries is planned for the future.

The Five Year Plan for the period 1968–72 assumes a total allocation of over £295 million with the following sectoral allocations :

Communications	24%	Agriculture	5%
Municipalities		Education	5%
(inc. utilities)	17%	Public Buildings	3%
Electricity and Desalin-		Health	2%
ation	14%	Tourism	2%
Industries	6%	Labour	1%
Housing	5%	Loans and Investment	17%

Foreign Trade
Abu Dhabi is in the process of constructing major harbour facilities but at the moment imports, covering the whole range of consumer and capital goods and valued at about £18 million in 1968, are landed by lighter. Exports, almost entirely of oil, are shipped from Jabal Dhanna and Das Island; re-exports are insignificant.

SOCIAL SERVICES, EDUCATION AND MASS MEDIA

Abu Dhabi is unique among the Trucial States in having a full range of conventional social, educational and health services. A Department of Labour supervises the working of the labour law of 1966 which deals with worker/employer relationships, runs an employment bureau, inspects employment conditions and issues work permits to aliens. Education is free and the department controls seven elementary, two secondary and four special schools with 5,000 pupils and 220 teachers (1968). 150 students study overseas. A free health service includes new hospital facilities at Abu Dhabi, Al'Ain and Muweij'i, and infirmaries and clinics. Low cost housing is being provided in the three main urban centres.

A full radio and television service is planned and a 10 kw. medium-wave radio station is already operational.

PERSIAN GULF STATES

TRUCIAL STATES—DUBAI

GEOGRAPHY

Features

THE Emirate of Dubai is a compact territory almost entirely composed of sand desert and with a *sabkha* coast broken by Dubai creek, which provides safe anchorage for vessels of up to ten feet draught. From the nucleus of old Dubai, situated on a spit head at the mouth of the creek, the town has now expanded along the sides of the creek and south along the coast.

Area

1,500 sq. mi./3,900 sq. km. (estimate).

Climate

See Trucial States.

POPULATION

Total population

(1968) 59,000.

Chief town and population

DUBAI TOWN (57,400).

Distribution

97% of the population lives in Dubai Town, the leading port and merchant community of the Trucial States. Immigration is leading to a rapid rise in population.

CONSTITUTIONAL SYSTEM

The Ruler of Dubai exercises direct rule in the State. Because of the importance of Dubai Town, the most important administrative body in the State is the Dubai Municipal Council originally founded in 1957 and given a charter and corporate existence in 1961. The council of 16 appointed members represents different sections of the community. Its decisions must be ratified by the ruler but with his consent the council makes local orders, has power to make contracts and own land, and administers this most important element in the state through specialised committees and paid officials. A Land Registration Committee has responsibility for land registration and transactions and is an entity independent of the municipality.

Head of State

Shaikh Rashid Bin Said al-Maktum.

Judicial System
The main *Qadi's* Court administers traditional Islamic justice to citizens of Dubai and all other Muslim countries; all appeals are to the ruler.

RECENT HISTORY

Dubai Shaikhdom was established by the early 19th century secession from the Abu Dhabi tribal complex of a section of the Bu Falasah branch of the Bani Yas, the rulers being of the al-Maktum line. This assertion of independence was essentially a statement of the trading orientation of the people inhabiting the shores of Dubai creek but remained disputed into the late '50s and conflicts with Abu Dhabi and Sharjah were not infrequent. Shaikh Rashid, regent between 1939 and 1958 and ruler since 1958, has directed his state continuously along the path of commercial and trade development and Dubai has had a politically unexciting but rewarding 30-year history of consistent, single-minded progress which has made it, even without oil, the leading city-state.

ECONOMY

Background
The economy of Dubai until very recently was almost entirely based on international trade and trade of such a type that normal economic mensuration at all levels becomes largely meaningless. During 1968, the last year before oil production commenced, officially listed imports of £66·2 million were eight times larger than exports and re-exports. Customs dues levied on most imported goods at $4\frac{5}{8}\%$ produced a revenue to the State of £2 million, the largest (single) item, and the value of imports has risen by an average of 100% every two years. Not included in the normal customs statistics is the trade in gold although trade in bullion is perfectly legal. Dubai merchants purchase between £50 million and £70 million worth of gold each year, most of which is smuggled into India (and Pakistan) at premiums of 10%–30%. The direct effect of this trade on Dubai income is significant but not quantifiable; indirectly it has contributed towards making Dubai the financial and trading centre of the southern Gulf.

Oil was first discovered in the Fatah offshore field in 1966 and production started in 1969 by the Dubai Petroleum Company. Oil revenue accruing to Dubai is expected to rise to an annual rate of £12 million and will rise rapidly following the completion of a revolutionary type of underwater storage and tanker-loading installation 60 miles offshore.

Trade and oil, in the absence of virtually all other resources, are likely to make Dubai the leading commercial centre in any Trucial Federation and even one of the great commercial cities of the southern Middle East.

Foreign trade
In 1968 almost 500,000 tons of cargo were landed by ship and aircraft in spite of the necessity of offshore lightering all ships of over 5,000 tons burden. A deepwater port, Port Rashid, is now being constructed west of Old Dubai, the Ruler's birthplace. The main imported commodities are household and consumer goods, food and clothing, machinery and vehicles. Japan is the main supplier with c. 17% of total imports (1968–£67 million), Britain a close second with 16%, Switzerland third with almost 8%. Over 60% of Japanese goods consist of clothing, approximately half of British and American goods are machinery, while Swiss commodities are almost entirely household

goods. Trade with other Gulf regions consist mainly of re-exports of manu-factures and imports of food and raw materials.

Price and wage trends

As a result of the recent commercial and oil boom, prices and wages are now among the highest in the world.

SOCIAL SERVICES AND EDUCATION

There are no national social security arrangements and considerable problems are created by illegal immigrants, who from time to time can flood even this booming labour market and who are not sheltered by indigenous communal responsibility. The municipality and several societies assist cases of distress and disability when they occur.

Reliance until recently upon the re-investment of trading revenue has made Dubai lean relatively heavily on external assistance in this field. In addition to British activity (see Trucial States) there is the 106-bed Al-Maktum hospital, the 50-bed Kuwaiti hospital and the hospital under construction for the Iranian Red Lion and Sun Society. Hospital and medical mission fees are not charged to the poor or to government employees. Kuwaiti and private schools supplement the Trucial States Council's Trade School. Plans for the development of fuller, more formal services are now being considered.

THE REPUBLIC OF SOUTH YEMEN

GEOGRAPHY

Features
THE People's Republic of Southern Yemen extends for some 800 miles along the western part of the south coast of the Arabian peninsula. Between the sea and the generally ill-defined interior frontiers with Yemen, Saudi Arabia and Oman, relatively narrow and discontinuous coastal plains rise to the highland edge of the Arabian massif, 10,000 ft. high in the west, c. 1,000 ft. in the east. Fault and fracture-lines and igneous activity combine to produce an extremely accidented topography, further dissected by arid erosion processes. The Wadi Hadramaut valley is one of the few major and distinctive topographic features. In the highlands bordering Yemen relatively high summer rainfall supports agriculture and gives good grazing. The coastlands, interior plateaux and the east are all extremely arid. There is no known significant mineral wealth other than that derived from coastal salt-pans. Aden harbour is formed by two volcanic peninsulas.

Area
109,200 sq. mi./287,700 sq. km. (according to national claims).

Mean max. and min. temperatures
Aden (12°46'N, 45°00'E, 50 ft./15 m.) 95°F/35°C (June), 73°F/23°C (January).

Relative humidity
Aden 75%.

Mean annual rainfall
Aden 5 in./127 mm.

POPULATION

Total population
(1967 estimate) 1,170,000.

Chief towns and population
Aden conurbation (1964) (225,000), Mukalla (25,000), MADINAT-ASH-SHA'AB (est.) (10,000). Aden is the only considerable concentration of population although in the Hadramaut there are a few settlements such as Saiwun with populations of over 10,000. Rural settlement is most dense in the Yemeni highlands and the upper Hadramaut.

Language and religion
In this predominantly Muslim community Arabic is the most important and the official language. Hindi is used by the resident Indian community.

CONSTITUTIONAL SYSTEM

No permanent constitution has been drawn up for the Republic and Presidential authority backed by the National Liberation Front leadership tends to implement those existing laws which are relevant to the present situation. A committee has been formed, however, to draft a constitution.

Head of State
Presidential Council consisting of Salem Rubai Aly, Chairman; Muhammad Aly Haithem, Prime Minister; and Abdul Fattah Ismail, NLF Secretary General.

Political Parties
National Liberation Front (NLF), Arab nationalist and socialist; Front for the Liberation of Occupied South Yemen (FLOSY), proscribed left-wing Yemeni; South Arabian League (SAL), proscribed Saudi Arabian unity group.

Leading political figures
Members of the Presidential Council; Abdel Qawi Makkawi (FLOSY).

Local Government
The Republic is divided into six governorates with appointed governors, mainly military representatives of the central NLF régime. From time to time control has been seized by 'popular councils', FLOSY and SAL organisations.

Judicial system
In the territory once known as Aden colony, a supreme court and magistrates courts operate, along with traditional Muslim religious courts. In the ex-protectorate, customary law (*Urfi*) and Muslim religious courts are normal. Military courts deal with matters affecting state security.

RECENT HISTORY

Until 1959 the area now known as Southern Yemen was composed of Aden colony (a crown colony of Britain), the Eastern Protectorate States (including Socotra), and the Western Protectorate States. The two Protectorates remained under the internal administration of the emirs of the 23 separate states, Britain being responsible for defence and external affairs and playing an advisory role. In 1959 many of the Emirates were persuaded to enter into a Federation and most of the states had accepted by 1965. Yemeni claims to parts of the Protectorate were increasingly pressed in the 1950s and as armed incursions became more frequent the Sultan of Lahej, one of the key figures in the emirates, joined forces with Yemen. The Yemeni Republican régime in power after the 1962 revolution, led by President Sallal, maintained the traditional claims and was particularly sensitive concerning support for royalists and other dissidents emanating from Aden. After 1962, discussions were held which culminated in the inclusion of Aden in the South Arabian Federation in 1963. The federation was to be governed by a legislative council and an elected administration, Britain retaining reserve powers in the areas of defence and external affairs through a high commissioner and undertaking financial responsibility for economic development and for British military and air bases. In 1963 anti-federation and anti-British activities by the local Trades Union Congress and the Socialist Party led to repression by the federal authorities, and the declaration of a state of emergency. Growing internal dissension between a variety of groups in Aden and the inability of any party to agree to proposals made in the 1964 constitutional conference, the inability of the Arab league to induce unity between the crystallising forces now recognisable in NLF, FLOSY, and SAL, and the effect on opinion of UN resolutions of 1963 urging Britain to withdraw, led to the suspension of the Aden Government in 1965, following riots and strikes, the undermining of emirate authority and increasing violence, partly between the Arab groups but mainly directed against British forces. In 1966 Britain set out a timetable for the achievement of independence of Aden and expressed the hope that other states would join in a viable independent federation. Nationalism as understood by NLF and FLOSY became triumphant and other authority crumbled. The NLF organisation which had established effective control in most settlements turned its military effort against FLOSY and Britain was forced to recognise it as the only effective power. British evacuation was accelerated and in November 1967 Qahtan al-Sha'abi, leader of NLF became first President of the new Republic. The closure of the Suez Canal after the June War in part forced Britain's hand but had more serious consequences for Southern Yemen. During 1968 and 1969 Yemeni hostility to the independent régime, the success of FLOSY and SAL in exacerbating local and tribal dislike of central control and dissension within NLF have all been serious threats to political and economic stability.

ECONOMY

Aden is essentially a port and entrepôt, with associated light industries and construction work, together with an oil refinery at Little Aden designed for the bunkering trade and with an annual throughput capacity of five million tons. Mainly as a result of the closure of the Suez Canal, port revenues, refinery activity and the tourist trade have all fallen to one-half or less of the pre-independence position. Industry is confined almost exclusively to Aden, where, in addition to the refinery there are factories producing cement blocks, soft drinks, soap and dairy products. Also 84,000 tons of salt were produced in 1968.

In the remaining areas of the republic, the Abyan irrigation scheme, initiated in the protectorate period and covering some 50,000 acres (mainly under cotton) is virtually the only commercially-orientated element in otherwise peasant-type agricultural communities.

Normal trade with Western countries is only slowly recovering and considerable dependence on barter deals, associated with aid and arms purchases from the USSR and China, has appeared. Total imports in 1968 amounted to £84·4 million, of which Kuwait and Iran accounted for 15% and 13% respectively; most of this was made up of oil. Japan (13%) was the second largest supplier after Kuwait, while Britain supplied 10%. Exports totalled £45 million. The largest non-oil export was raw cotton, worth £1·2 million.

SOCIAL SERVICES

Those services established in Aden colony have generally been maintained. There is one general hospital at Khormaksar and 14 rural hospitals in the governorates, as well as more than 100 health units attached to the hospitals. Shortage of doctors is, however, acute. Unemployment and sickness benefits are usually only available to government officials and to employees of foreign establishments.

EDUCATION

Educational facilities are concentrated in the main at Aden, but primary schools have been established in many other settlements. Primary education lasts for four years and in 1965-6 there were 14,600 pupils in 38 schools in Aden, and 18,400 pupils in 208 schools elsewhere. Intermediate schooling for a further three years was available at 40 centres.

Of the 16 secondary schools, with courses of four to six years, 14 were in Aden. A technical institute at Aden gives technical training mainly at a secondary level. There were three teacher-training centres. Small traditional Islamic *medrasseh* serve the remoter communities.

MASS MEDIA

All but one of the ten newspapers and periodicals are published in Aden. The main publications are :

The Press
Dailies : *Al-Akbar, Al-Ayyam* (c. 8,000), and *Fatut Al-Jezirah* (c. 10,000); *Weeklies* : *Al-Thawra*, NLF, and *Sout Al-Junoob*, South Arabian Broadcasting Service.

SAUDI ARABIA

GEOGRAPHY

Features

THE United Kingdom of Saudi Arabia occupies over 80% of the Arabian peninsula extending from the Red Sea to the Arab/Persian Gulf and Qatar, bordered on the north by Jordan, Iraq and Kuwait, on the south by Yemen, South Yemen, Oman and Abu Dhabi. This great platform of ancient rocks rises abruptly from the Red Sea rift to the mountains of Hejaz and Asir in which ranges rise to over 6,000 ft./2,000 m. with peaks of over 9,000 ft./3,000 m. above sea-level. In these highlands lie the most extensive oases, as at Medina and Mecca, based on orographic rainfall of c. 10 inches (250 mm.) a year. To the east the tilted land mass falls away to the shallow shores of the Gulf. The interior is dominantly desertic but slight winter rainfall allows some shifting cultivation and relatively stable nomadic pastoralism in the north, away from the saline basins in central Nefud. Najd, the central region is drier and life is essentially based on the walls of many oases. To the south extend the great sand deserts of Rub al-Khali, the Empty Quarter.

Summers are extremely hot and the coastal areas very humid. Water resources are extremely limited and irrigation development requires the exploitation of very deep aquifers. Known mineral wealth consists almost entirely of vast oil resources extending along the Gulf from Kuwait to Oman.

Area
840,000 sq. mi./2,150,000 sq. km. (estimate).

Mean max. and min. temperatures
Riyadh (24°39′N, 46°46′E; 1,940 ft./600 m.) 103°F/40°C (July), 58°/14°C (January).

Relative humidity
Riyadh 35%.

Mean annual rainfall
Riyadh 3 in./70 mm.

Total population
6,990,000 (UN figures for 1967).

Chief towns and population
(1964) : RIYADH (169,000), Mecca (159,000), Jeddah (148,000), Medina (72,000), Taïf (54,000). It is estimated that over half of the population consists of Bedouin nomads. The remainder of the population is concentrated in pseudo-urban oasis settlements and in the five cities. Urbanisation is proceeding relatively quickly.

95

Language

The official language is Arabic.

Religion

The official religion is Islam and the majority of the population is Sunni.

CONSTITUTIONAL SYSTEM

Constitution

The United Kingdom of Saudi Arabia is a monarchy, the kingdom established in its present form in 1932 by King Abdul Aziz al-Saud.

Head of State and Head of Government

King Faisal Ibn Abdul Aziz al-Saud.

Executive

The King, as Prime Minister, appoints and dismisses heads of Ministries who form the Council of Ministers responsible to the Head of State.

Local Government

The basic element in local government is the tribe; less traditional are the municipalities of Mecca, Medina and Jeddah. Each tribe and tribal centre has a council consisting of the Shaikh, as president, a legal adviser and two notables. Districts, also demarcated on a tribal basis, are administered by a regional chief, appointed officers and leading local figures. The Municipal Councils are nominated by the cities' inhabitants and approved by the King. They are supported by appointed executive officials who form Administrative Committees.

Judicial system

Islamic Law is administered through a *Shariah* Affairs Department and supervised by a Judicial Committee. This Committee of four members sits in Mecca where the Chief Justice resides. Minor offences and actions are dealt with in essentially traditional courts (*al Omur al-Mosta'jalah*) from which there is no appeal. The higher courts (*al-Shariah al-Koubra*) sit at Mecca, Medina and Jeddah and deal with all more serious cases. Appeal can be made to courts of cassation sitting in Nejd and Hejaz. In all cases the Koran is the ultimate authority.

RECENT HISTORY

In 1901 Abdul Aziz al-Saud, ruler of Nejd and a descendant of Nejdi tribal chieftains who followed the teachings of Muhammad Ibn Abdul Wahhab, marched on Riyadh which was then in the possession of the pro-Turkish Emir of Shammar. As a Wahhabi he found it difficult during World War I to make common cause with the Sharif Husain of Hejaz in whose lands lay the holy but corrupted religious centres of Mecca and Medina; as a Nejdi he concentrated his anti-Turkish efforts on conquering Shammar, a task finally achieved in 1921. Husain, having alienated almost all other Arab groups (see Jordan and Syria) and broken with Britain, fell to Abdul Aziz's growing power and in 1926 Ibn Saud was proclaimed King of Hejaz, recognising Husain's two sons as Kings of Transjordan and Iraq. The northern boundaries of the dual kingdom of Nejd and Hejaz were determined by agreements in 1925 but the final settlements of the Jordanian demarcation line are still being negotiated. Conflict with Yemen continued until 1934 and sovereignty in respect of frontier zones is still not absolutely settled with Yemen, South Yemen, Oman and Abu Dhabi.

The early tasks of consolidation were continued with vigour in spite of all the problems of exerting authority over many nomadic tribes in a poor arid country four times the size of France. In 1933 the first oil revenues were received from Standard Oil in return for exploratory concessions in the eastern region, revenues which in part made up for a decline in receipts from pilgrimages to the holy places. The first oil exports occurred in 1938 but World War II prevented further exploitation development and Saudi finances became seriously over-stretched as expectation-based expenditure soared. In 1948 company reconstructions resulted in the formation of the Arabian American Oil Company (ARAMCO) which is still the major producing unit in Saudi Arabia. By 1949 there had been established an oil refinery and tanker terminal at Ras Tanura and a tanker terminal at Dammam, and construction had commenced of a pipeline (TAPLINE) to Mediterranean terminals. Oil production, export and revenue rapidly increased and in 1949 a first Development Plan was announced, the main features of which were an ambitious railroad building scheme, the enlargement of the Prophet's Mosque at Medina, and the foundation of the present social infrastructure.

A founder member of the Arab League since 1945, Saudi Arabia tended to maintain from the beginning an individualist approach to affairs within the region, a position maintained during the disturbed years which followed the death of King Ibn Saud in 1953. Relations with Egypt varied from cordial to hostile and as the contacts between the UAR and Syria on the one hand and the communist world on the other flourished, so Saudi Arabia frequently assumed the role of conservative mediator in various conferences. In 1964 King Saud relinquished the throne to his brother Faisal, under whose rule the country has developed even more rapidly, while in foreign affairs the main strands of policy have been : support (mainly financial) for Arab defence against Israel, an anti-Communist and anti-Ba'ath-Socialist line, an insistence on major responsibility for affairs in the Arabian peninsula whether in the Yemen or in the Arab/Persian Gulf, and the assumption of a role as a (if not *the*) premier spokesman for the Arab peoples.

During the last two years King Faisal has undertaken several major foreign diplomatic tours and following the 1967 Arab-Israel war formed the aid consortium of Saudi Arabia, Kuwait and Libya to assist Jordan and the UAR, contributing £50 million of the total of £135 million. At the same time strenuous efforts have been made to remove oil from the political armoury of the Arab states, notably by the forming of the OAPEC together with Libya and Kuwait. Within the country more political and administrative power has been delegated to the evolving cabinet structure, to a less patriarchal form of government and to planned, more diversified economic development. In the Gulf, Saudi policy has been concerned to avoid the appearance of a power vacuum following British withdrawal and to this end has recently favoured the creation of a Union of the Trucial Emirates.

ECONOMY

Background

Oil provides approximately half of the GNP, and over 85% of state revenue; it is through the latter that it dominates the Saudi economy. Production in 1969 of 171 million metric tons followed the continuing annual increase of over 8% which has characterised recent years, with ARAMCO supplying 87%, the remainder coming from onshore and offshore fields in the Neutral Zone (shared with Kuwait). Petromin, the Saudi national oil corporation, has linked with other foreign companies in exploratory work along the Red Sea and in the Rub'al-Khali. New reserves are continually being proved and are now estimated to be capable of supporting present rates of exploitation for more than a century. The fields include Ghawar, the largest oilfield in the world and Safaniya, the largest offshore field; extraction costs are extremely low and the range of crude oil available very great. Income from oil is likely to rise still further from the present annual rate of c. £400 million.

In 1960 a supreme planning board was established and in 1964 a central planning organisation, under whose auspices a policy of economic diversification is being implemented and under whose control more than 50% of budgetary allocations are invested in development projects. During 1968–9 almost 19% of development funds were devoted to transport and communications, 12% to education and training and 9% to Ministry of Agriculture investment in agriculture and water resources. While the annual growth rate of the GNP is estimated at 8% (1968 GNP c. £1,000 million), the manufacturing, mining and quarrying and construction sectors are growing by c. 12% a year. Petromin is the largest single industrial concern. Through subsidiaries and affiliates it controls the new refineries (operational at Jeddah and planned at Riyadh), the Saudi Arabian Tanker Company and the Saudi Marine Construction Company. In the petrochemical field SAFCO (Saudi Arabian Fertilisers Company) is already producing urea and ammonia at Dammam while a sulphur plant is planned for Abqaiq. In addition Petromin operates a 45,000 tons a year steel rolling mill at Jeddah. Consumer goods industries are also rapidly growing.

Foreign trade
The Saudi Monetary Agency's estimates indicate a surplus on current account during 1967–8 of c. £25 million. While this showed a decrease over the two preceding years, it should be noted that there was an outflow of over £250 million of investment income, only part of which was due to foreign investors, while aid to Jordan and the UAR exceeded £40 million. Crude and refined petroleum made up 94% of total exports of £750 million in 1967–8. Imports totalled £210 million, £66 million of which covered transport equipment, machinery and electrical appliances. The growth in the rate of import of capital goods of all kinds is particularly rapid. The USA is the leading supplier (1968 25%) with Britain, West Germany and Lebanon with an estimated 8% each. The main direct importer of Saudi oil is Italy; British imports totalled £47 million in 1968. The import of foodstuffs is still an essential element in Saudi Arabian trade, valued at £62 million, items in order of importance being rice, fruit and vegetables, milk products and meat.

Price and wage trends
Saudi Arabia contains all levels of economic activity from traditional subsistence nomadism to advanced technological and commercial enterprises; wage trends are largely meaningless in this context. Prices are equally impossible to assess generally and for many products are purely a function of import competition. The official cost of living index for the period 1962–3 to 1966–7 showed an annual increase of 1·5%.

SOCIAL SECURITY

Since 1960 a Ministry of Labour and Social Affairs, in co-operation with the Ministries of Education, Health and Welfare, administers economic and social care for Saudi workers and families in a variety of different ways. Because of the diffuse pattern of settlement the establishment of 16 development and training centres in the various regions has been given high priority. Each centre has several departments : women's and children's welfare, covering medical and cultural needs; health, with the main emphasis on sanitation and hygiene improvements; cultural, with responsibility for girls' and adults' education, and agricultural extension and advisory services. Consumer and agricultural co-operatives have been established under similar auspices.

Social welfare for the unemployed, handicapped and elderly takes the form of direct financial, medical and accommodation assistance (including pensions) but in the traditional societies of Saudi Arabia family and tribal responsibilities still play a very large part in this sector. State disbursements in aid and pensions are of the order of £2 million a year.

Social Institutes provide special facilities for orphans and delinquents as well as for other special categories. Voluntary societies, national and international, are supported. Youth Activities, in particular Sports Clubs, are also under the aegis of the Ministry.

The Ministry of Health similarly provides directly for personal needs through a free provision of all facilities in hospitals, health centres, dispensaries and mobile clinics, these last being of particular importance in the more remote and nomadically-populated regions. Within some of the ten medical and health regions there are special problems posed by the annual pilgrimage of the Haj. During 1968–9 375,000 foreign pilgrims (in addition to 700,000 Saudis) converged on Mecca, many of them also proceeding to Medina. Near Jeddah a main quarantine centre capable of handling 2,500 persons simultaneously has been built under WHO supervision in order to provide adequate health control. At Mecca itself is a 3,000-bed hospital exclusively for pilgrims and all regions visited by pilgrims are strictly supervised in matters such as accommodation, supply of water and food and sanitation. The income from visas and port and airport charges now barely covers the costs incurred by the State.

The main medical laboratories and the institute for medical officer- and nurse-training are established at Riyadh. Budgetary expenditure on medical and health services has been increasing by some 12% a year and in 1968–9 totalled almost £14 million.

EDUCATION

Education is more conventionally organised but again is free at all levels, costing in 1968–9 c. £70 million. In 1969 there were 1,419 primary schools with 327,000 pupils aged between 6 and 12 and 30,000 teachers, these latter coming from the seven teacher-training institutes. Secondary education for 12- to 18-year-olds is separated into academic and technical streams with special provision made for commercial, agricultural and industrial training. In 1967–8 there were 30 schools in this sector, these, as with the primary schools noted above, all for boys.

Girls' education since 1960 has been carried on in parallel in 233 primary schools with 81,000 pupils and in three secondary schools from whom come most of the recruits for the teacher-training centres. There are in addition 30 national, non-government, girls' schools.

Higher education is centred at six institutions. The oldest (established in 1957) is King Saud University in Riyadh with a complete range of faculties. Jeddah is the home of the new (1967) King Abdul Aziz University, while specialist institutions include the Higher Institute of Technology (Riyadh), the College of Petroleum and Minerals (1963, Dhahran), as well as the Islamic University in Medina and the Shariah College of Islamic Law at Mecca. The number of university students is estimated at some 6,000 with another 1,500 studying overseas.

MASS MEDIA

The Press
Dailies: *Al-Bilad*, Jeddah (15,000); *Al-Nadwah*, Mecca (15,000); *Al-Medina Al-Munwara*, Jeddah (12,000); *Al-Riyadh*, Riyadh (10,000).
Weeklies: *Al-Jazirah*, Riyadh (5,000); *Al-Ra'id*, Jeddah (2,000); *Al-Riyadhah*, Mecca (1,000); *Akhbar el-Dhahran*, Damman (1,500).
Periodicals: *Al-Manhal* (m), Jeddah (2,000); *Al-Mujtama* (m), Riyadh (2,000); *Nadwat al-Muwasalat* (m), Riyadh (official, 2,000).

Radio and television
The Saudi Arabian Broadcasting Company is controlled by the Ministry of Information. Radio transmissions are made from Riyadh, Jeddah and Dammam in Arabic, English, Parsi, Indonesian, Swahili and Urdu. The Saudi Arabian Government Television Service transmits from Riyadh and Jeddah. In addition there are non-commercial radio and TV transmissions from ARAMCO stations at Dhahran.

SUDAN

Features

SUDAN is the largest Middle Eastern country and extends over 18° of latitude. The climatic and vegetational zonation associated with this extension is even more important than regional physiographic features. In broad terms Sudan is the basin of the Central and Upper Nile but both the Blue and White Niles rise outside its territory. Southern Sudan includes the Bahr el Ghazal basin in which lies the Sudd region of marshes, shallow lakes and the indeterminate drainage of the White Nile, the high savannah with some thick forest of western Equatoria province and the dry, treeless savannah of western Equatoria and southern Upper Nile province. Northward lies the main savannah belt, between El Obeid and the Bahr el Ghazal, in which livestock can be kept on rain-fed grassland and precipitation is high enough to allow seasonal dry-farming of millets. Northward still, lies the steppe belt of dry scrub forest with acacia and poor grassland, stretching west to east from the Chad border through central Darfur province, Kordofan and Kassala to the Red Sea. Khartoum lies almost in the centre of this traditional homeland of semi-nomads through which flow the Atbara River and the Blue Nile. From Atbara to the Egyptian border lies desert through which the single Nile flows in a narrow cliffed flood plain. The White Nile on the one hand and the Blue Nile and Atbara have rather different régimes, the flow of the first controlled to some extent by its headwater lakes and varying from a minimum of c. 500 cu. m. per second to c. 1,250 cu. m. in October–November, the latter two having great floods—6,300 cu. m. on the Blue Nile in August and a low minimum flow of 100 cu. m. on the Blue Nile in March–April. Irrigation use of the great rivers is thus only feasible with major control works. The most suitable soils for agriculture lie in the steppe interfluves of the Niles and the Atbara. Mineral wealth is varied but no great deposits of any particular mineral have yet been discovered. Iron ore, copper, manganese and asbestos are the most important exploited resources.

Area
967,500 sq. mi./2,506,800 sq. km.

Mean max. and min. temperatures
Khartoum (15°33′N, 32°35′E) 108°F/42°C (May), 59°F/15°C (January).
Juba (4°50′N, 31°35′E) 100°F/37·7°C (February), 68°F/19·8°C (July).

Relative humidity
Khartoum 10%–41%, Juba 26%–60%.

Mean annual rainfall
Khartoum 6·5 in./163 mm., Juba 37·5 in./960 mm.

POPULATION

Total population
(1967) 14,355,000.

Chief towns and population
(1965) KHARTOUM (173,500), Omdurman (185,400), Khartoum North (80,000), Port Sudan (79,000), Wadi Medani (63,700), El Obeid (62,000).

Distribution
Eight per cent of the population is classified as urban and c. 25% is nomadic. The sedentary rural population is particularly concentrated in the provinces of Blue Nile and Khartoum, along the rivers and in the Gezira.

Language
Arabic is the principal language and the language of government, but the southern Hamitic and Nilotic peoples use several East African and Ethiopic languages. It is estimated that c. 30% of the population normally speak non-Arabic languages and the association of Arabic with the dominant Muslim north is one of the factors in the present disunity.

CONSTITUTIONAL SYSTEM

Sudan formally achieved independence in January 1956 and inherited a system of parliamentary government from the earlier period of internal self-government. Until a permanent constitution is adopted the transitional constitution established in 1955 is utilised by civilian régimes. A Supreme Council of five members is responsible, under the 1955 terms, for the appointment of a governing council and prime minister from members of a constituent assembly. A revolutionary council headed by General Jaafar al-Nimairi established a semi-military régime in May 1969, this following a period of chaotic dissension between the two parties forming a coalition government, the Umma party and the Democratic Unionist Party. The present régime declares itself dedicated to Arab socialism on a Nasserite model and to a one-party system.

Head of State
General Jaafar al-Nimairi is head of a revolutionary council of ten members and Prime Minister.

Political Parties
Umma—recently the largest political party, now banned; Democratic Unionist Party; Sudan African National Union (SANU)—seeking independence for the southern provinces; Southern Front—seeking autonomy for the southern provinces; Sudan Communist Party.

Government and leading political figures
Deputy Premier and Minister of Justice, Babikir Awadallah; Minister of the Interior, Major Abu-al-Qasim Ibrahim; Minister of Transport and Communications, Ahmad Jak.

Local Government.
Sudan is divided into nine provinces (*mudiriya*) each with a civil governor (*mudir*) and with a military governor for each of the six central and

northern provinces and one for the three southern provinces. Provinces are divided into 52 districts (*merkez*) some of which are divided into sub-districts. Each district has a commissioner (*mufatish*). The system is still basically colonial in concept with appointed officers and advisory councils. Since independence and during periods of stability, local self-government by elected councils was encouraged, especially in the municipalities but retrograde measures have been taken on occasion. Only two councils had control of local government in the southern provinces.

The formal administrative framework is linked to traditional tribal organisation through the *omodiyyah*, a group of villages or tribes, headed by a paid elected *omda* whose duty in the main is to reconcile village and tribal interests. Each village or tribe is headed by a shaikh appointed by the government after a consensus of the people. Both positions of *omda* and shaikh tend to become matters of family succession.

Judicial system
The Judiciary, headed by a chief justice, administers and controls three different types of court: civil, criminal and local. Provinces and districts each have single judge civil courts of first instance. The High Court sits as Court of Appeal and as court of first instance for major cases. Criminal courts include single magistrate courts for misdemeanours, minor courts presided over by a bench of magistrates for intermediate offences and major courts which deal with serious crimes and can impose death sentences. Major courts usually have a high court or provincial judge as president; appeal is to the High Court. The *Shariah* religious courts deal with matters of personal status, marriage, divorce and inheritance under customary Islamic law. Their President is the Grand Kadi.

RECENT HISTORY

In 1899 the Mahdist Sudan was reconquered in the name of the Khedive of Egypt by Anglo-Egyptian forces and the Anglo-Egyptian condominium was created. The borders of the new state were dictated by the result of British, German and French pressures at the climax of the short imperial struggle for power in central Africa. British influence and interests were dominant and in 1924 Egypt withdrew from the Sudan. Between 1924 and 1930 Sudan became a classic example of British indirect rule through tribal chiefs and shaikhs. While on the one hand this slowed the pace of social and economic change this period also saw the real development of the Gezira irrigation scheme, which, through the large-scale production of cotton as a cash-crop, became the basis of internal revenue and of external trade. The special characteristics of the mainly non-Arab and non-Muslim southern provinces were recognised by a series of special ordinances which implied direct British rule and education through mission schools, and which discouraged north-south movement. The culturally more advanced and united Muslim northerners increasingly regarded this special treatment as an affront to the country and themselves and, following Egyptian reassertion of its condominium position, became increasingly anti-British, nationalist and associated with the anti-British groups in Egypt itself. During and after World War II, Britain first created an advisory council for north Sudan, with mainly appointed members and then, in 1948, a legislative assembly for the whole country. Dissatisfied with the limited nature of self-government in the hands of the assembly and with the slow progress of local government organisation, the numerically small but growing élite of trained Sudanese and the Islamic religious groups were at one in putting pressure on Britain, but in conflict over future aims. The Umma party came to represent an independence front, supported by the Mahdists, while a Unionist group, supported by the Mahdists' chief rival, the Khatmiyya, stood for a 'Nile Valley Unity' and close association with Egypt.

In 1952 the revolutionary régime in Egypt first disowned Egyptian monarchical ambitions in Sudan and then in 1953 declared that Egypt was prepared to grant self-determination to the Sudanese if Britain was prepared to stand by this, her declared aim. The Anglo-Egyptian agreement provided for phased military withdrawal and an internationally supervised Sudanese election of an interim government. The National Unionist Party, led by Ismail El-Azhari and supported by Egypt, was victorious; the new government, partly swayed by Mahdist anti-Egyptian demonstrations, promptly took a nationally independent line within its powers of self-government. The appearance however of a north-dominated national government sparked off major military and civil disorders in the south. Faced with this major challenge to unity, the southern provinces were promised that a federal constitution would be considered. In 1955, Azhari unilaterally declared Sudan an independent republic and this was recognised in 1956 by Egypt and Britain.

The new and young administration plunged into rapid economic and social development which strained an economy too dependent on cotton for revenue and export; internally the Unionist Party became divided between the will of Khatmiyya, the religious body, and the non-sectarian politically orientated membership. A realignment of forces resulted in the appearance of a new party, Umma, representing the Mahdists, which entered into a coalition with a second new party, the People's Democratic Party (PDP), representing the Khatmiyya. Dissension rapidly followed as PDP tended towards pro-Egyptian and anti-Western sentiment and as Umma tended to rely on Western assistance to help in overcoming economic troubles and to be suspicious of Egyptian intentions over the common border and the division of the Nile waters. 1958 elections left the balance of power undecided and the government indecisive; there followed a military coup by General Abboud, whose intention was to improve internal stability and relations with Egypt. Parliamentary government was suspended.

Between 1958 and 1964 the military régime successfully implemented several development schemes on the Blue Nile and Atbara, obtained financial aid from several foreign sources and introduced a new system of self-governing provincial administrations. Political insensitivity however led to charges of corruption in a non-accountable administration, to heavy-handed military supervision of local government and most other institutions and to large-scale military action against southern dissidents. In October 1964 a very effective general strike and disaffection in the army brought the military autocracy to an end.

By 1965 political realignments enabled elections to be held, in which the temporarily dominant Communists were overwhelmed by the re-emergent Umma and NUP. Once again a coalition was inevitable in which Muhammad Ahmed Mahgoub of Umma became Premier and Azhari (Unionist) Head of State. Once more an uneasy coalition ran into trouble. Externally, relationships with Ethiopia became strained over the passage of arms to Eritrean rebels, Sudan's southern neighbours became increasingly incensed over a continuation of military action against southern non-Muslim rebels and gave support to SANU, the southern nationalist party. Egypt and other states became disturbed at growing right-wing tendencies. Internally the economic situation remained difficult, the Communist party was banned and dissension between Umma and the NUP was paralleled by conflict between the two wings of Umma itself. In 1966 Sadik al-Mahdi, President of Umma and hostile to his uncle Imam al-Hadi, leader of the Ansar more traditionalist group, forced the resignation of Mahgoub and became Premier of a new, more liberal, coalition government. Economic improvement followed stricter financial controls and discussions with southern representatives appeared to augur well. Sadik's presidential ambitions together with conflict between wings of the Umma party led to the re-emergence of Mahgoub as Premier in May 1967. The June War was followed by the establishment of closer links with Sudan's Arab neighbours and with the Communist bloc. Sadik's Umma wing, Deng's SANU and the PDP, in opposition, and the inability of NUP and the Imam's Umma fully to co-operate, led to a series of short-lived administrations, uneasy coalitions and an increasing distrust in politicians.

In May 1969 a military coup led by General Jaafar al-Nimari, an earlier rebel against General Abboud, brought into power a revolutionary council with pro-Nasser and socialist sympathies and with the Premier as its only civilian member. The appointed cabinet is without previous governmental experience and would seem only to be the executive arm of the Council. Umma has been proscribed. The new régime has established closer ties with Libya and Egypt and in November 1970 it was announced that the three countries had decided to form a federation. And in March 1970 an attempted coup, led by Imam Hadi al-Mahdi (who was killed), was successfully crushed.

ECONOMY

Background
According to the 1955–6 census, 86% of the national labour force was employed in the primary sector, almost entirely in agriculture and pastoralism. In these circumstances the estimation of GNP and of economic trends is particularly hazardous. Official figures record a decline in the contribution to the GNP by agriculture to c. 51% in 1963–4, and an increase in that of distribution and transport to 17% and of industry (including construction) to 13%. During the decade ending in 1966 the GNP is estimated to have grown at an annual average rate of over 4%. Significant productivity in agriculture depends entirely on irrigation and on associated commercial agriculture since the Government owns not only almost two million acres in the Gezira scheme but also considerable areas on the White Nile, the Tokar and Gash deltas and in the Roseires scheme area; of the proceeds from cotton sales between 30% and 36% go to central government, 2% to local government councils and 2% to social welfare funds. Agricultural diversification is encouraged, partly, as with sugar, for import-substitution and partly, as with fruit and vegetables, for export. Durra millet is the staple grain and normally provides an export surplus. Manufacturing is best developed in the non-durable consumer goods section but a protected cotton textile industry has been established and the Shell oil refinery at Port Sudan can meet most national requirements at present. Private foreign capital has been discouraged by recent attitudes and while most Western capital aid entering the public sector has been utilised for basic development in agriculture, irrigation, hydro-electricity and transport, many of the Eastern bloc barter arrange-

ments are for manufacturing installations and consumer goods imports; such barter deals are tending to limit Sudan's freedom of economic manœuvre. Moves towards the nationalising of banks and trading organisations have in part neutralised the effect of the Industrial Investments Act of 1968. The government wants foreign banks to invest more in development projects. Foreign debt is over £100 million, internal debt approximately half that level, government and international borrowing rates remain high and currency reserves are low. Economic potential is great but infrastructural needs, particularly in communications, and capital development work requirements are enormous.

Foreign trade
Approximately 45% of the value of exports is accounted for by cotton and variations in the price as well as production of cotton are reflected in considerable trade fluctuations. The value of cotton exports fell slightly in 1969 (£Sud 51·5 million) after increasing over the previous two years from £Sud 39·6 million in 1967 to £Sud 52·7 million in 1968. Groundnuts and gum arabic each make up c. 10% of exports with another 7% from sesame. India was the chief market for cotton in 1969, taking 20% of total exports, followed by Italy (15%) and West Germany (11%). Imports of textiles made up 16% of the 1968 total, machinery and transport equipment 14%. Britain, in 1968, supplied 14% of Sudanese imports and took only 6% of exports, while West Germany was Sudan's leading customer with 14%. The effects of trade pacts very recently entered into with Syria, Iraq and the Communist bloc countries cannot yet be assessed.

Consumption
In 1965 it was estimated that 78% of GNP expenditure was on private consumption and 13% on public. The recorded rate of fixed capital formation, 10%, was one of the lowest in the Middle East. These figures reflect the dominance of non-commercial agriculture, a fact which obscures wage, price and employment measurements.

SOCIAL SECURITY
Government officials including employees in education and transport are covered by various pension schemes. Free medical services are available to low income groups through health centres, clinics and hospitals in the main settlements. In rural areas the greatest part of the population relies on traditional village and tribal systems of mutual help. In all there are 601 hospitals, 1,186 dispensaries and 56 health centres (altogether 13,439 beds).

EDUCATION
In Sudan there exists a problem of mass illiteracy which is being tackled through a policy of concentrating upon primary education and of supporting a special campaign for adult instruction. The southern provinces have their own Under-Secretary for Education although the Ministry of Education in practice is integrating the whole country on the basis of the Arabic language.

Primary Education
A shortage of teachers has led to a distinction between elementary schools with qualified staff and junior elementary schools which also give instruction for four years but which are manned in the main by unqualified teachers.

The two-year course village schools, mainly in the south, are being rapidly closed down as elementary schools can be staffed. In 1967–8 there were 481,000 pupils in state and private schools. Secondary education is organised at 'intermediate' and 'secondary' levels, each giving four courses from 11 to 15 and 15 to 19. Entry is by competitive examination. In 1967–8 there were 72,000 pupils in state secondary and 64,000 pupils in private secondary schools. Secondary technical and vocational schools are being established.

Higher Education
Khartoum University (f.1956) retains, from the colonial period of Gordon College (f.1903), English as the language of instruction except in *Shariah* Law and Arabic departments. It has a full range of faculties, 200 academic staff and over 2,000 students. A Khartoum branch of the University of Cairo was opened in 1955. Concentrating on Law, the Humanities and Commerce, this is staffed by Egyptians (mainly seconded from Cairo) and has over 1,000 students. The Islamic University of Omdurman (f.1965) uses Arabic, French and English in courses which emphasise Arabic and Islam but also extend into the social sciences. Academic staff number c. 70, students c. 800. The Khartoum Technical Institute gives technical training at Intermediate, post-Intermediate and post-Secondary levels to over 3,000 pupils and Further Education courses to almost 3,000 part-time students.

Teacher-training colleges are financed by the Government and supervised by the Institute of Education. There are nine elementary standard and two intermediate colleges. The demand for teachers is particularly high as the result of the policy of integrating the south.

Mass Media

The Press
Dailies (all are published in Khartoum) : Arabic—*Al-Alam*, National Unionist; *Anbal-Sudan Al-Ayam* (c. 15,000); *Al-Gamahir*, PDP; *Al-Maydan*, Communist; *Al-Mithag Al-Islami*, Islamic Charter Front; *Al-Rai Al-Amm*, independent (c. 14,000); *Al-Sahafa* (c. 30,000); *Saut Al-Sudan; Al-Sudan Al-Gedid* (c. 7,000); English—*Morning News* (c. 4,500); *The Vigilant*, Southern Front.
Periodicals : There are more than 30 bi-weekly and weekly periodicals, most of them of specialist interest, most published in Khartoum. *Kordofan*, bi-weekly, Arabic, is one of the higher circulation magazines—c. 15,000.

Broadcasting
Sudan Broadcasting Service transmits radio programmes (in Arabic and English) from Omdurman. The Sudan Television Service transmits for c. 30 hours a week. Both services are government-controlled.

SYRIAN ARAB REPUBLIC

GEOGRAPHY

Features

THE largest part of the Syrian Arab Republic consists of the central and eastern plains of the middle Euphrates system, elevated semi-arid steppes of subdued relief except in the extreme north-east and merging into desert in the south. This area is lightly populated and low rainfall inhibits settlement except in irrigable areas. On the west however a north-south aligned zone of approximately parallel mountain ranges of the Lebanon and anti-Lebanon systems contains the Orontes valley and many upland basins, the whole characterised by extreme altitudinal range and a humid climate. Rainfall rises to over 40 in./1,000 mm. above 3,000 ft./1,000 m. altitude in the Al-Alawiyean Mountains, much of the winter precipitation falling as snow. The coastlands have a Mediterranean régime which becomes progressively more extreme in all respects inland until, east of a line Aleppo-Hams-Damascus, aridity becomes the dominant factor. Deepwater lies off the discontinuous coastal plain in Latakia and also in Iskanderun, still claimed by Syria though ceded to Turkey; along the coast are several excellent natural harbourages utilised by Latakia, Banias, Tartous and Jableh ports. The most easily exploited agricultural potential lies in the western zone while the only significant mineral resource—oil—lies in the north-east of the country.

Area

71,000 sq. mi./185,200 sq. km.

Mean max. and min. temperatures

Damascus (33°30′N, 36°19′E; 2,250 ft./700 m.) 73°F./23°C. (July), 50°F/10°C (January).

Relative humidity

Damascus 20%–52%.

Mean annual rainfall

10 in./250 mm.

POPULATION

Total population

(1967) 5,570,000.

Main towns and populations

(1967) DAMASCUS (584,000), Aleppo (528,000), Homs (190,000), Hama (148,000).

Distribution

39% of the population lives in the 52 urban administrative centres of the *Mohafazat* (Districts) and the *Mantika* (sub-Districts) although over 60% of the population is officially classed as urban. All the four cities with populations larger than 100,000 lie on the eastern interior periphery of the western highlands. In 1967 163,000 Palestinian refugees were registered as resident in Syria.

Language

The many different ethnic elements in the Syrian population including Semitic Bedu, Mediterranean Levantines, Kurds, Armenian and Turkic groups, together with a variety of cultural contacts have resulted in linguistic diversity. Arabic is the official language.

Religion

The constitution decrees that the chief of state shall be a Muslim. The majority of Syrians are Sunni Muslims but there is also a large minority of Shi'ites. In addition there are communities of Druzes combining elements of Islam with pre-Islamic esoteric beliefs, Alawites who blend primitive Christian and Islamic beliefs, Ismailis whose head is the Aga Khan, and small groups of animists and devil-worshippers.

CONSTITUTIONAL SYSTEM

The 1964 Constitution forms the basis of the present system although, legally, it has been suspended since 1966.

Constitution

The Syrian Arab Republic is a socialist republic based on Islamic Law and forming part of the Arab Homeland.

Head of State

There is at present no permanent Head of State. Lieutenant-General Hafiz Assad heads a 26-man 'national front', one-half of which is Ba'athist.

Executive

The edicts which since 1966 have modified the constitutional system have confirmed the ultimate executive power of a National Revolutionary Council. Membership of the Council is to be representative of the nation and the method a matter of decree. Implementation of executive policy shall be in the hands of a President's Council and, through this Council, of appropriate ministries. The Revolutionary Council shall choose the President and the President's Council, and through them, lay down general policies, control budgets and taxation, declare war or peace, draft a final constitution and support or withdrawn support from any minister or council of ministers. The President's Council is responsible to the NRC for activities on its behalf, these activities to be carried out by the council of ministers appointed by the PC. The Prime Minister will form a Government and a Cabinet of ministers whose decisions may be cancelled or modified by the PC.

Political Parties

The Ba'ath Socialist Party has been in power since 1963. Within it are sectarian groups whose dominance has varied from time to time. The Syrian

Communist Party is banned and the Arab Nationalist Movement proscribed. On 13 November 1970 a bloodless coup was staged by the military
wing of the Ba'ath Party.

Local Government

The Syrian Arab Republic is administratively divided into 12 *Mohafazat*
(Districts) which are subdivided into *Manatik* (Sub-Districts), 44 in number.
These are composed of *Nawahi* (pl. of *Nahia*) which in turn comprise the
smallest administrative units, the villages. The Ministry of the Interior
appoints, for each of these respectively, head officials, a *Mohafez*, a *Mudir
al-Mantika*, a *Mudir al-Nahia* and one (or more) *Mukhtar*. These officials
are responsible for all civil government matters within their areas.

Judiciary

The law of the Republic is administered by courts and special courts. The
latter include a single military court and several courts for minors. The
former in ascending order and diminishing number are : 'single-judge'
summary courts which sit in various centres and deal with relatively minor
matters, civil, commercial and penal; 'single-judge' courts of first instance
for more serious cases not subject to appeal; courts of appeal for all cases
subject to appeal and other cases placed in their jurisdiction; the Damascus
Court of Cassation, the final court of appeal. The Chief Justice is the head
of the judiciary. There are in addition three groups of religious courts
dealing in the main with matters of personal status and religious endowments, Muslim, Druze and Non-Muslim.

Defence

Precise figures for Syrian military forces are not available but were estimated
at 60,500 in 1968. Over 42% of ordinary budget expenditure went to the
Ministry of Defence. Legally, command of the armed forces rests with the
Head of State who is responsible to the National Revolutionary Council.

ECONOMY

Background

The largest contribution to national income still comes from agriculture
with wholesale and retail trade remaining more important than industry.
Economic growth has been surprisingly consistent given the constant political
turbulence, a fact which points to the considerable economic potential which
is still to be fully exploited in agriculture, oil, hydro-electric power and
trade. National income increased by c. 45% between 1956 and 1967 but as a
result of rapid population growth the *per caput* income rose only by some
6%. In the 1962–6 development budget the main sectoral allocations were :
transport and communications 26%; agriculture, irrigation and land reclamation 22%; power and fuel 15%; industry and mining 8%. The largest
single industry is textiles while recent developments include nitrogenous
and fertiliser production, oil refining and sugar refining, all at Homs.
Industrial employees totalled 26,000 in 1968. The principal cash export is
medium staple cotton and the major foodcrop wheat, although agricultural
production is highly diversified including tobacco, a large range of fruit and
vegetables and sheep and goats. Agriculture is still entirely in the private
sector, but as the result of nationalisation 43% of the domestic income
originating in industry stems from the public sector, with 64% in construction, 53% in transport and 99% in banking and insurance.

Foreign Trade
Trade figures show a large and growing balance of payments deficit which in 1967 totalled over £S400 million. In Syrian accounts the main offset items shown are expenditures and royalties of petroleum companies (£S215 million) and remittances from Syrians abroad (£S85 million). The trade figures are not however quite what they seem since in transactions between Syria and the Russian-East European bloc barter elements in development aid are in part concealed in import/export data and there is also a discrepancy between Russian and Syrian measurements of the same flows. For 1966 Russian estimates of the value of Syrian imports from the USSR were almost three times the Syrian estimate. Syrian data for 1967 suggests that in spite of the close links between Syria and the communist world, 45% of Syrian imports and almost 20% of Syrian exports are Western Europe orientated (4% and 1% respectively with USA/Canada), compared with 25% of imports from and 23% of exports to USSR/E. Europe. Italy is Syria's main supplier and Lebanon easily her most important market.

Employment
Unemployment in 1966 was estimated at 4·8% out of a labour force of 1·4 million. Numbers employed in industry are not known but are estimated at 11% of the total.

Price and wage trends
The index of wholesale prices after a period of stability between 1962 and 1965 showed a rapid rise to 119 points (1962 = 100) in 1967. This recent increase was heavily weighted by increased food prices from 100 in 1962–5 to 132 in 1967, this in turn largely a consequence of the poor harvests in 1966. Fuel prices however fell from 100 to 92 in the period 1967, building materials steadily rose to 116 points and the prices of industrial products first fell and then rose to 114. There is no information concerning wage-levels but it should be noted that the subsistence element in the agricultural sector is still strong.

Consumption
Total consumption represented 70% of expenditure on GNP in 1967, lower than in 1965 but higher than in 1963. Of total consumption the private sector share has declined from 81% in 1963 to 77% in 1967.

SOCIAL SERVICES

Responsibility for the social services lies chiefly with the Ministries of Social Affairs and Labour and of Health, although municipalities administer and finance some services. In the 1968 allocations to health, social services and juvenile reform were 2·5% of the total but 22% of budgetary expenditure was classified under culture and social welfare. Assistance for unemployed and disabled workers is in a large measure undertaken by the 126 Trade Union aid funds. Trade Unions had in 1967 a registered membership of almost 100,000. In recent years there has been a growth in the number of dispensaries, some 230 government and private. Private hospitals outnumber by 2 : 1 the 27 state institutions, being particularly numerous in the four largest cities. Government-run health centres have been established in most sizeable settlements. State medical services are free for the poor.

EDUCATION

Education at all levels absorbed 16% of 1968 general budget expenditure; Aleppo and Damascus Universities received further large grants in the Supplementary Budget; the total cost was over £20 million. In addition to the two universities, which had 31,600 students in 1967, there are 22 teacher-training colleges, 24 public and 2 private professional training institutes. The University of Damascus has a full faculty range while that at Aleppo has a greater concentration in applied subjects; law is very strongly represented at both. There is a strong private sector at the school level; of the 639 intermediate and secondary schools, 29 are run by UNRWA and 281 are private. Of the 4,875 primary schools, 71 are run by UNRWA, 306 are private, the great majority here being state schools.

MASS MEDIA

Under the socialist régime Syrian press publications have almost entirely become the official organs of trade unions, political, professional and religious organisations and of various branches of government. All papers and periodicals are licensed.

The Press

Al-Ba'ath, Damascus (Ba'ath Arab Socialist Party) (16,000); *Al-Jamahir Al-Arabia*, Aleppo (5,000); *Al-Fida*, Hama (3,000); *Al-Ouruba*, Homs (2,000); these together with the second Damascus daily *Al-Thawrah* with a circulation of c.20,000 are the most important newspapers. A very large number of specialised papers and periodicals are also produced, including: *Al-Dad* (m), *Hadarat Al-Islam* (f), *Al-Iktisad Al-Arabi* (w), *Al-Izzaa* (f), *Kifah Al-Oumal Al-Ishtiraki* (w), *Al-Majalla Al-Batriarquia* (m), *Al-Riada* (w), *Al-Sakafe Al-Isboui* (w), *Al-Talia* (f), *Al Yanbu Al-Jadid* (w), all at Damascus. Most monthly periodicals emanate from Damascus-based ministries.

Broadcasting

The General Directorate of Broadcasting and Television transmits domestic radio programmes in Arabic, English and French. Foreign programmes are broadcast also in Hebrew, Portuguese, Spanish and Turkish. Television transmissions cover the Damascus region.

TURKEY

GEOGRAPHY

Features

ONLY a small part of Turkey, north of the Dardanelles, lies in Europe. The greater part belongs to Asia Minor and consists of a plateau area (Anatolian Plateau), generally with elevations in excess of 2,500 ft./760 m., divided from the Black Sea in the north by the Pontine Mountains which rise to over 12,000 ft./3,650 m., and from the Mediterranean Sea in the south by the Taurus Mountains which rise to a similar height. The major areas of lowland border the Dardanelles and the lower part of the major river valleys.

Central Anatolia has arid summers and cold harsh winters (conditions becoming most extreme in the mountainous eastern region), a climatic régime which encourages cereal-growing and livestock-grazing. The coastal regions with their sub-tropical climates allow greater diversification and intensification of agriculture. Mineral wealth is varied and products of mining include, in order of value, coal, copper, lignite, chromite, boron minerals, iron, mercury, sulphur, magnesite. Petroleum production, mainly in the south-east, now equals the import volume. Turkey is the only Middle Eastern country with considerable forest resources.

Area

301,400 sq. mi./780,600 sq. km. (of which 9,150 sq. mi./23,700 sq. km. lies in Europe).

Mean max. and min. temperatures

Ankara (40°N, 33°E; 2,820 ft./860m.) 87°F/31°C (August), 24°F/–4°C (January); Istanbul (41°N, 29°E; 60 ft./18 m.) 81°F/27°C (July and August), 36°F/2°C (January).

Relative humidity

Ankara 72%, Istanbul 81%.

Mean annual rainfall

Ankara 14 in./355 mm., Istanbul 32 in./815 mm.

POPULATION

Total population

(1968) 33,539,000.

Main towns and populations

(1965) Istanbul (1,743,000), ANKARA (906,000), Izmir (412,000), Adana (290,000), Bursa (212,000).

113

Distribution
In 1965 15% of the population lived in centres of more than 100,000 inhabitants, 30% in centres of more than 10,000.

Language
The official language is Turkish. Arabic and Kurdish are spoken along the
frontiers with Syria and Iraq.

Religion
Over 98% of the population adhere to Islam.

CONSTITUTIONAL SYSTEM

Constitution
Republic. The 1961 constitution was adopted by referendum after the overthrow of the Menderes Government in 1960.

Head of State
President Cevdet Sunay.

Head of Government
Prime Minister Süleyman Demirel (Justice Party).

Executive
The President is elected for seven years by a two-thirds majority of the Grand
National Assembly (*Büyük Millet Meclisi*) from among the members of the
Assembly and is not eligible for re-election. On election the President
dissociates himself from his party and his membership of Parliament is terminated. He selects the Prime Minister, and then the other ministers on the
recommendation of the Prime Minister. No act of the President is valid
unless countersigned by a minister. He may return legislation—except budget
and constitutional laws—to the Assembly for reconsideration but if it is
passed again he must promulgate it. The Council of Ministers is responsible
to Parliament. Ministers are jointly and individually responsible for policy.
If the Council of Ministers is defeated on a vote of confidence three times
within 18 months, the Prime Minister may request the President to order
new elections.

Legislature
The Grand National Assembly is composed of two houses. The National
Assembly (*Millet Meclisi*) of 450 members is elected by proportional representation for four years. The Senate (*Senato*) has 185 members: 150 are
elected for six years by proportional representation, 15 are appointed by
the President of whom 10 must have no party affiliation, and 20 are life
senators. Legislation originates in the National Assembly and although the
Senate has the right of amendment and proposal the final vote is always
with the National Assembly. To become law a bill must pass both
houses.

Political Parties
The two main parties, the Justice Party which has emerged as the successor
to the proscribed Democrat Party of Menderes, and the Republican People's
Party founded by Atatürk, are not easily distinguished in conventional
western political terminology. The Justice Party tends to be associated with
free enterprise and to be conservatively traditionalist; when in power how-

ever its freedom of manœuvre is limited by the strength of modern economic *étatism*. The Republican Party is more strongly associated with development planning and therefore to some extent with change; it is however conservative in its support for state intervention on the Atatürk model and is by no means radical. The Turkish Workers' Party can be regarded as conventionally left-wing in character as opposed to the right-wing nationalistic Nationalist Action Party. The small Unity Party and the National Party are both conservative and based on religious and peasant support. The New Turkey Party is left-wing liberal. The Communist Party is banned. The Justice Party was returned to power in the 1969 elections.

Leading political figures
Süleyman Demirel, Prime Minister and Leader of Justice Party; Ahmet Topaloglu, Minister of Defence; Ismet Inönü, Leader of Republican People's Party; Osman Bölükbaşi, Leader of National Party; Yusuf Azizoğlu, Leader of New Turkey Party; Mehmet Aly Aybar, Leader of Turkish Workers' Party; Alparslan Türkeş, Leader of Nationalist Action Party.

Local Government
Turkey is divided into 67 provinces (*iller*) which are subdivided into 571 districts (*ilçe*) and then into 35,638 sub-districts and villages (*Buçaklar* and *Köyler*). Each provincial governor (*vali*) is appointed by the President upon the recommendation of the Minister of the Interior. He appoints the officials of the province and as a chief administrative officer of the province he is assisted by a staff of advisers and a provincial standing committee chosen from the provincial council which is elected for four years and over which the governor presides. The chief officer of the district is the *kaymakam*, of the sub-district *buçak müdürü*, and of the villages the *muhtar*. Every provincial and county capital and town of over 2,000 inhabitants is a municipality (*belediye*) and is headed by a mayor (*belediye reisi*) assisted by an elected municipal council.

Judicial system
The lowest civil courts, the magistrates' courts (*sulh hukuk*) have one judge and deal with cases concerning two parties but not the public. The civil courts of first instance (*asliye hukuk mahkemeleri*) are also single-judge courts dealing with cases that involve the public besides the two parties. The commercial courts (*ticaret mahkemeleri*) are sited in the major cities. They have a president and two assistant judges and deal with commercial cases involving sums above T£1,000 ($111); cases involving sums below this amount are dealt with by the courts of first instance. The lowest criminal courts are the single-judge criminal peace courts (*sulh ceza mahkemeleri*). Misdemeanours are dealt with by the criminal courts of first instance (*asliye ceza mahkemeleri*), also single-judge courts. The assize courts (*ağir ceza mahkemeleri*) composed of a president and four assistant judges have jurisdiction in all cases involving penalties of five years or more. The labour courts (*iş mahkemeleri*) deal with management-labour disputes and are composed of one judge and one representative of each of the two disputing parties. The courts of appeal (*temyiz mahkemeleri*) examine all court decisions when requested by the parties; they have several chambers each composed of a presiding judge and several members. Members of the courts of appeal are elected by the high council of judges. Jurisdiction in military cases is exercised by the *askeri mahkemeleri* which consist of a president and two military officers; there is a special military appeal court.

The highest administrative court is the Council of State (*Devlet Şurasi*) empowered to give its opinion upon projected legislation to the Council of Ministers. The Court of Jurisdictional Disputes (*Ulyuşmazlik Mahkemesi*) gives final judgement upon jurisdictional matters between the civil, administrative and military courts. The High Council of Judges (*Yüksek Hakimler Kurulu*) of 18 regular and five alternate members is concerned with all cases relating to the character and functions of judges. The Constitutional Court (*Anayasa Mahkemesi*) has 15 members and five alternate members. It rules on the constitutionality of legislation passed by the Grand National Assembly and its judgement is final. It is also empowered to try the senior officers of the state.

The judiciary is independent of the other organs of the state. Judges serve until they are 65 unless they are incapacitated by ill-health, convicted of a crime or pronounced unsuitable to remain in office. Capital punishment is maintained.

RECENT HISTORY

In 1920 a group of Turkish nationalists effectively took charge of what remained of the wrecked empire and in that year deposed the Sultan and rejected the terms of the Treaty of Sèvres, under which the Allies of World War I sought to dismember Ottoman Turkey. As a result of hard-won military success against Greek armies and the withdrawal of other Allied forces, Mustafa Kemal, who had emerged as the leader of the new nationalist movement, established control over Anatolia and eastern Thrace. In July 1923 the new Turkey, virtually in its present territory, was recognised by the Allies.

The state was forged and much of its form determined in the succeeding 15 years of Kemal's life. In October 1923 the Republic was proclaimed, governed by a single political party—the Republican People's Party—but with Kemal Atatürk as first President exercising autocratic powers. The drive towards modernism was based on three main lines of policy. The first was secularisation, formally recognised in 1928, this having a more than religious emphasis and closely linked with the second main line, that of education and female emancipation. Arabic orthography, the fez, the Ottoman legal codes and the Muslim religious hierarchy were replaced by specifically Turkish Customs and institutions. Thirdly, in the economic field also, the state became the dominant power through the policy of *étatism* designed to create an economically viable state.

During World War II, Turkey remained aligned with the Western powers although technically neutral until February 1945. Economically isolated, Turkey nevertheless survived considerable political and economic strains albeit at the price of greater authoritarianism. In November 1945 Inönü, President, leader of the Republican Party and once Atatürk's lieutenant, ended the one-party system. In 1946, following the first elections, Inönü was returned to power but opposition parties including the Democrats and Nationalists were represented in the Assembly. In 1950 the Democratic Party, headed by Adnan Menderes, regarded as more liberal and less authoritarian, came to power, had its mandate further strengthened in 1954, and lost ground only slightly in 1957. In the young democracy, however, challenges to established political power were met by a variety of measures, relating to electoral law, the press and official appointments; and the main parties were affected by internal dissension. The equally young economy entered a period of rapid but uneven growth which eventually led to inflation, an adverse balance of trade and strict economic controls. Externally, Turkey became even more firmly aligned with the West and became a member of NATO and joined the Baghdad Pact. During the whole of the 1950s Turkey remained strongly anti-Soviet, devoted over one-quarter of her GDP to the armed forces and received a large amount of aid, developmental and military, from the USA and other Western countries. Relations with Greece improved until, in 1957, the Cyprus question emerged to produce a bitterness and distrust which in part remains. Internally the decade ended with a crescendo of political conflict finally resolved by the intervention of the army which set up a committee of National Union headed by General Gürsel. The President, the Premier and many officials were arrested, the Democratic Party was proscribed and commissioners were set up to investigate affairs under the Menderes régime while, on the other hand, extreme elements in the committee were themselves expelled. In 1961, preparations for a return to civil government were made and party politics legalised; at the same time some 633 members and supporters of the previous régime were tried for offences against the state. The former Premier, Foreign Minister and Minister of Finance were executed, other death sentences, including that passed on the former President, were commuted to life imprisonment. In October 1961 free elections gave a non-absolute majority to the People's Party, the successor to the Republican Party, headed by Ismet Inönü, but the new Justice Party, which claimed many adherents from the defunct Democrat Party, formed a sufficiently strong opposition group for there to be a trend towards coalition. Opposed by those who viewed this as a betrayal of the revolution, Inönü finally formed a coalition of the People's Party, the New Turkey Party and the Republican Peasants' National Party. General Gürsel remained President.

The new Government turned its attention to economic development on a planned basis (see below) and with growing technocratic skill. Externally, the Cyprus situation hampered but did not prevent an improvement of relations with Russia. Internally, political dissension grew acute and after being forced into a minority People's Party Government in 1964 Ismet Inönü was forced to resign in 1965. Subsequent elections gave an absolute majority to the Justice Party under Süleyman Demirel and also gave representation, partly through the proportional representation electoral system, not only to a fairly strong People's Party but also to a right-wing National Party, the New Turkish Party, the Republican National Peasants' Party and the new left-wing Turkish Workers' Party. The new alignments were symbolic of an increasing sense of national independence also manifested in anti-American demonstrations, a deterioration in relations with Greece almost to the point of hostilities and new approaches to Russia, Eastern Europe and the Arab countries. Associate membership of the European Economic Community was a further assertion of maturity. Turkish links with the West are still strong and membership of NATO is maintained, as trust in the USSR remains less than complete. Through CENTO Turkey has further developed regional contacts with the other 'northern tier' states, Iran and Pakistan.

The President is head of the armed forces; compulsory national service lasts for two years. In 1967 Ministry of Defence expenditure made up 19% of general budgetary expenditure and almost 4% of the GNP, a total of T£3,897 million. The army (strength 360,000), airforce (55,000) and navy (38,000) are equipped with modern, mainly American, arms. The bulk of

117

Turkish forces are assigned to NATO command but American military installations have been considerably run-down in recent years.

ECONOMY

Background

The Turkish economy is still dominated by agriculture which (1965) employed 72% of the adult population and (1967) contributed 35% of National Income. The proportional contribution by manufacturing has however almost doubled in the last 20 years from 9·4% to an estimated 17·7%. The period 1923–50 was one of massive state intervention which, through financial and producing institutions, concentrated and deployed domestic and foreign capital and expertise—the policy of *étatism*. Manufacturing industry, mineral exploitation, internal and coastal transport and public utilities, together with the main purchasing and distribution facilities, within agriculture have all become dominated by these state institutions. A decade, 1950–60, of rather chaotic relative economic liberalism was followed by the present period of central planning. The First Plan, 1962/3—1966/7, succeeded in obtaining an annual average increase in net national product (value added at factor cost) of 6·4%, a figure which conceals the high rate of industrial growth, some 9%, and the slow agricultural progress—3·3%. The heaviest investment was in iron and steel, producing a fourfold increase, and in energy production and mineral resource exploration. Half Turkish oil requirements are now met domestically and some two-thirds of an electricity output which in 1967 was 80% higher than in 1962 is obtained from mainly new hydro-electric plants. Chemicals, plastics, cement and paper were other growth industries. In spite of relative stagnation in agriculture, Turkey in 1967 was self-sufficient in most agricultural products except for wheat.

The second and current Five Year Plan is designed not only to accelerate the rate of growth between 1967 and 1972 but to achieve a production capacity after which self-sustaining growth will be possible. Between 1962 and 1967 foreign capital inflow totalled $1,640 million, a rate of $350 million *p.a.*; the intention is to reduce this rate by 20% and to increase the non-aid component. 22% of gross investment, T£25,000 million, is allocated to manufacturing, one-fifth of which is destined for the iron and steel industry. Agricultural investment, designed to meet increased demand resulting from rising incomes and a growing population, is heavily orientated to soil and water resource exploitation, over one-quarter of the total being concerned with water resources. The remaining important aspect is that of trade balance (see below).

Foreign trade

During the First Plan exports rose more slowly than either GNP or imports and their character changed little. The balance of trade has shown a deficit in all years since 1946, that in 1967 totalling T£1,516 million. Agricultural products in that year accounted for 80% of all commodity exports while machinery and equipment made up 43% of imports, another 48% consisting of raw materials.

The intention under the Second Plan is to increase exports (1972) by 48% and increase the industrial share to some 27%. Imports are expected to rise in 1972 by c. 42%, the main increase being in raw materials and investment goods.

1967 TRADE-ORIGIN AND DESTINATION—%

Common Market Countries	35	34
of which: W. Germany	19	16
Italy	7	7
France	4	5
EFTA Countries	20	17
of which UK	13	6
USA	18	18
E. European Countries	13	17
of which USSR	4	6

Employment
The labour force was estimated in 1967 to number 13,739,000 of which 72% were employed in agriculture and 14% in industry (including construction). The Government estimates that 300,000 Turkish workers were employed overseas, mainly in W. Germany and their remittances home reached $137 million. Agricultural underemployment is very high, seasonally up to 40% of the sectoral force.

Price and wage trends
The national wholesale price index has shown a considerable rise since 1964 (1958=100, 1964=132, 1967=159). Consumer price indices for Istanbul and Ankara have shown a different pattern but an even greater rise to 203 and 182 respectively. The daily wages of the insured population (c. 10% of the total) rose by over 90% during the same period.

Consumption
In 1967 private consumption accounted for 72% of the GNP and public consumption accounted for 12%.

SOCIAL SECURITY
Social security is administered by the Workers' Insurance Institute under the general supervision of the Ministry of Labour. Amounts stated below refer to 1964. Insurance covers all employees in industry and commerce in undertakings of over ten persons, and is being gradually extended to cover small undertakings. Domestic and agricultural employees are excluded. There are special schemes for railwaymen and public employees. Maximum earnings for contributions and benefits are T£100 ($11) per day in all cases.

Health insurance
Employers and employees each pay 4% of wages. Medical benefits are usually provided directly by the Institute for a maximum period of six months (18 months if such treatment will reduce disability) and include free general medical care, hospital treatment, medicines, transportation, appliances and maternity care. Sickness benefits are paid for up to 18 months, and amount to 50% of daily earnings, rising to 66⅔% if the insured has dependants. Maternity benefits are equal to two-thirds of daily earnings and are paid for six weeks before and after confinement. Nursing grants are T£150 ($16·66) decreasing to T£100 ($11) where the mother is hospitalised.

119

Accident insurance

This is paid entirely by the employer at the rate of 0·3 to 5·2% of the employee's earnings according to the degree of risk. Medical benefits of the same order as for sickness are provided for a maximum of 20 months. Daily benefits for temporary disability (the same as for daily sickness allowances) are paid for 18 months. For total disability, pensions are paid at the rate of 60% of earnings, with a minimum monthly pension of T£200 ($22). This is supplemented by a further 30% for constant attendance. For less than total and more than 10% disability, a percentage of the full pension related to the degree of disability is paid. If this sum amounts to less than T£20 ($2·20) per month, it is converted into a lump sum. Widow's pensions, also payable to disabled widowers, are 30% of the insured's earnings. Orphan's pensions are 15% of total earnings, and 25% for full orphans, payable to each child under 18, under 25 if a student, and indefinitely if the child is an invalid.

Pensions insurance

Pensions are financed by employee and employer at the rates of 5% and 6% of the employee's earnings respectively (rising to 6·75% and 8·1% respectively in heavy industries). Pensions are paid at 60 for men (55 in heavy industries) and 55 for women. Old-age and invalidity pensions are 35% of average earnings during the whole period of insurance rising to 50% for one or more dependants. Minimum monthly pensions are T£200 ($22) or T£250 ($27·70) with dependants. Old-age pensions are reduced by 0·75% for each year that insurance has been paid for less than 35 years and increased by 1% for each year of insurance beyond the age of 60. Invalidity pensions are reduced by 1% for each year that the insurance is less than 20 years. Pensions amounting to two-thirds of the insured's pension are paid to widows and invalid widowers at any age. Part and full orphan's pensions are respectively 25% and 40% of the insured's pension. Parents receive 25% if the sum of all pensions does not exceed 100% of the insured's pension, with a minimum of T£200 a month. Any person who does not qualify for a pension is entitled to a lump sum refund of his own and his employer's contributions.

Unemployment insurance

The Turkish Labour Code requires an employer to pay a dismissal indemnity equal to 15 days' wages for each year worked over three.

EDUCATION

Turkish investment in education is immense and the rate is accelerating. The number of primary schools, between 1940–1 and 1967–8 has increased threefold, the number of teachers and enrolment fivefold. Compulsory primary education for all children between the ages of 6 and 14 who are within reach of a school has been particularly responsible for the rise in proportionate literacy which in 1927 was 10% of the population over 6 years of age, in 1940 19% and in 1965 49%. Even so approximately 25% of children of school age are not able to attend.

Secondary and vocational education has been recently given even higher priority in the national interest. There is selective entry from primary schools to junior high schools or to one level within vocational technical schools. The course of study lasts three years in the first case, two to six years in the second. From the junior high schools entry is possible to high schools and, mainly but not entirely, it is from this stream that entrants progress to universities. Between 1940–1 and 1967–8 the number of junior high and high schools and the number of teachers increased fivefold and enrolment sixfold. Vocational and technical schools had growth rates over tenfold.

Adult education
Covers general and vocational fields as well as public literacy courses and a great variety of institutions directly under the Ministry of Education as well as under the auspices of the Ministry of Village Affairs are involved.

Universities and higher education
There are now eight universities in Turkey (1967–8 enrolment figures): Ankara, eleven faculties (18,000), Middle East Technical University at Ankara, four faculties (4,500), Hacettepe, four faculties (1,600), Istanbul, ten faculties (30,700), Istanbul Technical University, six faculties (3,800), Ege University at Izmir, three faculties (2,200), Atatürk University at Erzerum, three faculties (1,800), and Karadeniz Technical University at Trabzon, one faculty (700). There are a further 81 public and private institutions of higher education, mainly concerned with vocational fields, with 62,400 students. A significant feature of Turkish education which differentiates it markedly from that of other Middle Eastern countries is that the fields grouped under 'engineering' have one-fifth of all the students. Universities are constitutionally autonomous and university education is free. Maintenance grants are made to students studying in places distant from their homes. In 1967, 3,800 students were studying abroad, financed by the State and under contract to enter government employment for a period after their return.

MASS MEDIA

The Press
The Press is free under the 1961 Constitution 'within the limits of the law'. Specific laws and articles in the Penal Code deal with defamation of state institutions and the protection of the state (including anti-Communist propaganda measures) but the application of the law varies in rigour with political sensitivities. A Board of Official Announcements supervises the right to publish official advertisements and announcements. Most of the large circulation newspapers are now group-controlled.
Dailies: *Hürriyet*, Istanbul, independent, (600,000); *Tercüman*, Istanbul, ind., (200,000); *Milliyet*, Istanbul, ind., (130,000); *Akşam,*, Istanbul, ind., (110,000); *Cumhuriyet*, Istanbul, ind., (90,000); *Son Havadis*, Istanbul, Justice Party, (50,000); *Ulus*, Ankara RPP, (40,000); *Dünya*, Istanbul, Ind., (40,000); *Ege Ekspres*, Izmir, JP (20,000); *Demokrat Izmir*, Izmir, RPP (15,000); *Adalet*, Ankara, JP, (100,000).
Periodicals: *Hayat* (w), Istanbul, family, (170,000); *Ses* (w), Istanbul, (80,000); *Akis* (w), Ankara, ind. political, (40,000); *Forum* (f), Ankara, political/economic; *Doğan Kardeş* (m), Istanbul, quality children's.

Broadcasting
The Turkish Radio and Television Institute (*Türkiye Radyo ve TV Kurumu*) is an autonomous public corporation that controls all radio and TV services. Its seven-man board of governors is composed of representatives of the Institute itself, prominent cultural institutions, the universities, the Minister

of Finance and the Minister of Tourism and Information. The director-general of the Institute is nominated by the board of governors and must be approved by the President of the Republic, the Prime Minister and Minister of Tourism and Information. The Institute has an independent budget financed by licence fees and is free to obtain foreign investment. TV is in a formative stage.

THE UNITED ARAB REPUBLIC

Features

BORDERED on the east by the structural rifts of the Red Sea/Gulf of Aqaba system lies a sedimentary covered ancient block through which runs the narrow valley of the Nile. Everywhere extremely arid except on the narrow Mediterranean coastal fringe, east of the Nile lie rugged highlands with some small mineral wealth, and west of the Nile stretches the Western desert. Extending from El-Kharga in the south through Farafra north to Siwa and Natrun are a series of depressions in which subterranean water is frequently sufficiently near the surface to support oasis agriculture. Elsewhere sand dunes alternate with *hamada* rock desert. Only in the Nile valley ribbon and on the broad delta do soil and water permit agricultural settlement and it is here that virtually all Egyptian life is concentrated apart from the Suez canal towns of Suez, Ismailia and Port Said, and the seaports of Alexandria and Damietta. During the last decade petroleum has been discovered first in Sinai and in the Gulf of Suez, more recently in the Western Desert near El-Alamein and Qattara. Natural gas is produced in the Delta.

Area
394,000 sq. mi./1,002,000 sq. km. (Inhabited 14,000 sq. mi./36,000 sq. km.)

Mean max. and min. temperatures
Cairo (30°1'N, 31°16'E; 65 ft./20 m.) 96°F/36°C (July), 45°F/70C (January).

Relative humidity
20%—85%.

Mean annual precipitation
1 in./30 mm.

POPULATION

Total population
(1970 estimate) 33 million.

Chief towns and populations
(1970 est.) CAIRO 5 million (1966 est.), Alexandria (1,801,000), Giza (571,000), Port Said (283,000),[1] Suez (264,000),[1] Tanta (230,000), El-Mahalla el-Kubra (225,000), Mansura (191,000), Subra el-Khema (173,000), Asyut (154,000), Zagazig (151,000).

[1] These figures are based on the 1966 estimate, but since the June War of 1967 all but about 10,000 civilians have been evacuated from the Suez Canal Zone.

Distribution
50% of the population is officially classed as urban; 35% of the population lives in the 17 cities with more than 100,000 inhabitants. The effective population density in the inhabited area is 847 persons per sq. km. (1967), an extremely high concentration bearing in mind that ten million agriculturalists are included.

Language
Arabic is the official language although most educated Egyptians also speak English and French. Cairo and Alexandria are cosmopolitan in this respect.

Religion
Islam is the official religion and almost all of the 90% of the population which is Muslim adhere to the Sunni creed. The largest minority is that of the Coptic Christians but there are also all other Christian faiths represented. There still exists a small Jewish group and minor pre-Islamic religious survivals.

CONSTITUTIONAL SYSTEM

Constitution
The Interim Constitution of 1964 is still in effect, under which the UAR is described as a Democratic Socialist State, Arabic and Islamic. The economic basis is founded on socialist planning and public as well as private ownership in all sectors.

Head of State and Prime Minister
President Anwar Sadat.

Vice-Presidents
Aly Sabri, Husain Shafei.

Executive
The President is in law head of the executive and elected by the submission to a national referendum of a nomination by the National Assembly. The presidential term is for six years. The President appoints, dismisses or accepts the resignation of vice-presidents and of the prime minister and all other ministers; he has the right to preside at cabinet meetings and, in collaboration with the government, decides upon state policy and its execution in all fields. The President convenes and terminates sessions of the assembly, under whose mandate he can issue personal decrees with full legal force. He is also in command of the Committee of National Defence which is responsible for safeguarding the country. The President appoints commanders of the armed forces and is himself Supreme Commander; he declares war and peace. The Prime Minister is head of Government under the President and the Committee of National Defence.

Legislature
A National Assembly of 350 members is elected for a term of five years under various legal provisions; its membership includes some Presidential appointees. All laws, all draft taxation levies, budgeting estimates and governmental programmes are submitted to the Assembly which has the right of rejection. The Assembly can be dismissed by the presidency with the safeguard of new elections within 60 days. If any minister loses the confidence of the Assembly he shall resign.

Political Parties

There is only one official political organisation, the Arab Socialist Union, of which President Nasser was Secretary-General.

The Arab Socialist Union has been restructured under a reform programme instituted by President Nasser on 30 March 1968. In October 1968, an eight-member Supreme Executive Committee was elected. This committee has an authority which surpasses that of the cabinet on many issues.

Local Government

The UAR is subdivided into 25 governorates (including Israeli-occupied Sinai). Governors are appointed by the President and Prime Minister and are responsible to the Minister of Local Administration. Governors are assisted by appointed officers, members of relevant ministries and by a council in which are elected members and party members of the Arab Socialist Union. A similar pattern exists at a lower city or rural area level.

Judicial System

There are no religious or traditional courts recognised in the UAR, only a conventional structure consisting of : a Court of Cassation, the final appellate court presided over in Cairo by the Chief Justice; six courts of appeal (in the most important governorates) which deal with felonies and also civil appeals; primary tribunals, one in each governorate, comprising several civil and criminal chambers; summary tribunals, single judge courts with limited power, in the various districts. The judicial system as a whole is the responsibility of an independent supreme judicial council. In February 1970, the UAR's first supreme court was established.

RECENT HISTORY

(See the United Arab Republic, p. 324)

ECONOMY

Background

Agriculture remains the most important sector in the Egyptian economy although its proportional contribution to the GNP is probably now little more than that of manufacturing industry, less than 25% compared with more than 20%. However almost 60% of the labour force is still engaged in farming and agricultural products made up about 70% of exports in 1966 (54% from cotton alone), the last full normal year for which data is available. Since the 1952 revolution economic growth and diversification has been considerable. The low *per caput* national income of £37 in 1952–3 increased to £43 in 1959–60 and to £67·5 in 1966, and has since been rising by c. $3\frac{1}{2}$% *p.a.* The 1960–5 plan laid considerable emphasis on lessening those income disparities which meant that large sections of the population were still abysmally poor.[2] Unfortunately the associated increased expenditure on welfare and on economic growth produced near-chronic foreign indebtedness (estimated in April 1970 at $1,900 million) which in turn has made external capital aid more necessary and also harder to obtain. Defence expenditure has risen astronomically to £Eg550 million in the 1970–1 budget compared with £Eg340 million for development. As a result taxation, particularly of consumption expenditure, has been heavily increased and industrialisation, especially for import substitution and exports, is being even

[2] A three-year 'accomplishment' plan was to have replaced a 1966–72 plan in July 1967. This was abandoned because of the 1967 war and has been replaced by annual development appropriations. A new development plan is scheduled to start in July 1970.

more strongly encouraged. In the 1969–70 budgetary development allocation 35% was devoted to industry, 14% to communications, compared with 18% to agriculture and irrigation (plus an additional 11% for the High Dam). In industry the most important elements in growth have been cotton spinning and weaving, food processing, chemicals and iron and steel. With cotton yarn production running at over 160,000 tons *p.a.*, Egypt is second only to Pakistan in this field. Food processing is extremely diverse and so also is the chemical industry which includes a strong pharmaceutical sector. The Helwan iron and steel centre is now being expanded to a capacity of 1·5 million *p.a.*, at a cost of almost 400 million. The basis of much of this industrial growth has been a phenomenal increase in electricity generation, fourfold since 1952 with a further 400% increase when the High Dam HEP installations are completed. Most of the growth has also been in the public sector which comprises three-quarters of industrial production by value. The private sector, characterised by a large number of very small units, is now being given emergency encouragement. All banking and insurance companies are nationalised. In agriculture the policy is to stabilise the annual cotton crop at about nine million cantars (c. 400,000 metric tons) and by raising yields to release land for foodcrops. The cereal crop, of which rice makes up one-third has been doubled since 1952. The high cost of intensive multi-cropping has increasingly turned attention to the possibility of major irrigation development of Western Desert depressions by tapping subterranean aquifers. Before the June War Egypt had attained self-sufficiency in oil from the Sinai fields. These are now occupied by Israel but production from the new Western Desert fields, near El-Alamein, is now running at a rate higher than the 1966 total. In 1966 oil production was 6·3 million tons : 16 million tons were produced in 1969. A pipeline from Suez to Alexandria, by-passing the Canal, has been projected, but would depend on large-scale foreign investment which has so far been discouraged by the attendant risks.

Foreign Trade

All import trade is officially nationalised under the Egyptian General Trade Organisation and most exports are from public sector sources. Foreign trade declined during 1967 but exports were worth £304 million in 1968–9, two-thirds of which is contributed by raw cotton, cotton yarn and textiles. Exports of industrial products (excluding petroleum) have been rising steadily : £66 million in 1966–7 to c. £92 million in 1968–9, and in 1968–9 the UAR recorded its first trade surplus—£Eg42·9 m.—for 30 years. This however does not take into account the complexities of barter deals with the USSR and other communist countries.

The regional trade pattern appears to be as follows :

	1966	1967	1966	1967
	% Exports to:		% Imports from:	
USSR	24	25	9	21
Czechoslovakia	10	7	3	3
India	7	5	5	6
China	5	4	3	4
W. Germany	5	4	7	8
E. Germany	4	5	4	4
UK	3	3	5	4
USA	2	3	20	9
France	2	2	5	5
(E. Europe & USSR	51	48	26	41)

Of the total of £Eg344 million of imports in 1967 the single largest item was unmilled wheat (60% from USSR), followed by machinery and motor vehicles (W. Germany and Czechoslovakia are most important suppliers), iron and steel products, and wheat flour (chiefly from W. Europe).

Employment

The total working force in 1965 numbered 7·9 million of which 59% was engaged in agriculture, 28% in services and 10% in industry. The industrial labour force has been growing at a faster rate than have the other sectors. Disguised unemployment is high in urban and rural areas; estimates range from 10–20%.

Price and wage trends

The cost of living index remained very stable between 1959–60 (100) and 1964–5 (109) but rose rapidly to December 1966 (120) and as a result of the June War still further by October 1967 (130). By late 1968 it had fallen to 126 and has remained approximately at this level. Minimum wages are fixed by law but the demand for work results in considerable evasion. Official figures for average annual wages in the public sector rose from £Eg227 in 1967–8 to £Eg274 in 1968–9. Profit sharing distribution rose from £Eg48 million to £Eg55 million to 400,000 workers.

Consumption

Private consumption during the last three years is estimated to have been growing at c. 5% *p.a.*, compared with a national income growth rate of c. 3%. Domestic credit is now being curtailed and there have been increases in taxes on consumer goods, particularly durables.

SOCIAL SERVICES

Health

Health insurance now covers c. 400,000 government and public sector employees in Cairo and Alexandria. Contributions are at the rate of 1% of salary from individuals and 3–4% from the State. The aim is to expand this service which covers medical care and hospitalisation. Every governorate and over 40 districts have general hospitals and there are some 14 special hospitals in addition to a full range of medical research institutions and teaching hospitals attached to the seven medical faculties which now train c. 1,500 physicians each year. School health and maternity and child welfare units (190 of the latter) have been established and there are plans to add another thousand rural health units to the 1,500 already in existence. Medical care is free or heavily subsidised to low income groups through regional and factory clinics. In the public health domain the main goal is the eradication of tuberculosis, trachoma and bilharzia, involving not only hygiene measures but housing and agriculture policies. Budgetary allocations to the Ministry of Health have risen from £7 million in 1952 to £34 million in 1968–9. Largely as a result of this expenditure, average life expectation has risen from c. 43 years to c. 53 years; as a corollary a ministerial executive committee for family planning has been established. The UAR now produces c. 85% of its pharmaceutical requirements.

EDUCATION

The Egyptian education service is in many ways one of the most advanced in the region and one of the oldest established; there remains a problem of

127

illiteracy in the rural areas and a shortage of the technologically trained. State institutions, vastly preponderant, are free or almost so. In 1967–8 primary schools for ages between 6 and 12 had 3·5 million pupils but another million children had no facilities. Preparatory schools lead on to secondary institutions with now about one million pupils; Girls make up one-third of this number as female emancipation becomes effective.

The general secondary system is open only to some 40% of primary school leavers, the remainder, those who continue in education, being guided into vocational and technical schools with c. 150,000 pupils. There are now 45 teacher training colleges and a variety of industrial training centres. The four state universities include Al-Azhar University and Ain Shams University at Cairo, and the universities of Alexandria and Asyut; in addition there is the private American University of Cairo. Cairo University (Al-Azhar) has 58,000 students and a complete range of faculties, many of them possessing high international prestige. In all there are about 150,000 university students, many from other Arab countries and also many becoming employed outside Egypt.

Present developments are aimed at providing complete primary coverage, at increasing the proportion of technical training and, lastly, at raising general standards through adult education.

MASS MEDIA

The Egyptian Press is the most advanced in the Middle East and radio has been developed as a major propaganda instrument. In both cases international as well as national impact is important. Only a few of the most important journals are listed below out of the very large number published in Alexandria and Cairo, (some of which are banned in other Middle Eastern states). The four chief publishing concerns are owned by the Government and editorial comment and news selection, particularly in foreign affairs, is subject to control.

The Press
Dailies: *Al-Ahram*, Cairo (250,000); *Al-Akhbar*, Cairo (250,000); *Al-Gomhouriya*, Cairo (Arab Socialist Union) (192,000); *Al-Ittihad Al-Misri*, Alexandria; *Al-Misaa*, Cairo (40,000). In addition, in the French language the *Journal d'Alexandrie*, *Journal d'Egypte*, Cairo; *Phare Egyptien*, Alexandria, and *Le Progres Egyptien*, Cairo; together with the *Egyptian Gazette*, Cairo, in English, and *Tachydromos-Egyptos*, Alexandria, and *Phos*, Cairo, in Greek.
Periodicals: *Akhbar Al-Yom* (w), Cairo (250,000); *Akher Saa* (w), Cairo (80,000); *Al-Ahd Al-Goumhouri* (w), Cairo; *Al-Guil Al Gedid* (w), (Women's journal); *Rose Al-Youssef* (w), Cairo; *Sabah Al-Kheir* (w), Cairo. Most periodicals published in Alexandria are commercial, financial and technical, e.g. *L'Économiste Egyptien* (w); *Egyptian Cotton Gazette* (q); *Revue des Questions Douanières* (m) and many more.

Broadcasting
The UAR Broadcasting and Television Corporation transmits 125 hours a day of home service radio programmes in six languages, Arabic, English, French, German, Greek and Italian. The foreign service, 'The Voice of the

Arabs', is the most powerful propaganda influence in the Middle East, transmitting for 23 hours each day in at least 20 languages; many of its programmes are relayed in other Arab countries. Television programmes are transmitted by the UAR Broadcasting Corporation of Cairo from stations in Alexandria, Aswan, Cairo and Mansura and from seven sub-stations.

YEMEN

Features
THE territory of Yemen extends inland into the Arabian peninsula from a 300-mile-long coastline at the southern extremity of the Red Sea. It includes within it a series of zones which, from west to east include a narrow arid coastal strip, equally barren adjacent hill-lands which rise to the El Jahal mountains, over 7,500 ft./2,400 m. in height. The highlands, relatively well-watered with 30–40 inches of rain *p.a.*, as with Saudi Nasir to the north, support rain-fed as well as irrigated agriculture. Further to the east the land grades downward into the southern deserts of Arabia across undefined frontiers with Saudi Arabia and South Yemen.

Area
75,000 sq. mi./195,000 sq. km. (estimate).

Mean max. and min. temperatures (estimates)
Hodeida (14°51′N, 42°55′E; 50 ft./16 m.) 95°F/35°C (July/August), 72°F/22°C (January); Sana (44°40′N, 16°45′E; 7,250 ft./2,200 m.) 80°F/27°C (June), 40°F/4°C (December).

Relative humidity
Hodeida c. 70%, Sana c. 30%–70%.

Annual rainfall
Sana 16 in./200 mm.

POPULATION

Total population
(1967 est.) 5 million.

Chief towns and population (estimated)
SANA (10,000), Taiz (80,000), Hodeida (45,000). With the exception of Hodeida, the Red Sea port, most of the population is concentrated in the mountain villages of the interior and in the twin capitals Sana and Taiz.

Language
Arabic is the official and only important language.

Religion
Islam is the official religion, with Sunnis mainly represented on the coast and Shi'a in the highlands.

CONSTITUTIONAL SYSTEM

The *de facto* government of the largest part of Yemen operates under the republican constitution published in 1965 and 1967. The President is head of state, is nominated by a consultative assembly and acts through a presidential council of ministers. The cabinet, headed by the Prime Minister, is composed of heads of specialised ministries through which administration is organised. In early 1969 the presidential council was chaired by its members in rotation. In 1970 Abdul Rahman al Iriani became head of the Presidential Council and thus President of Yemen. The consultative assembly is constitutionally the supreme legislature and is empowered to draw up a permanent constitution.

The judiciary in territory controlled by the Republican Government is independent and includes a supreme *Shariah* court.

The Republican Government has diplomatic relations with the communist states, India and Pakistan, and, in the Middle East, Iraq, Jordan, Kuwait, Libya, Morocco, Syria, Tunisia and the UAR; it is represented in the United Nations.

A small part of Yemen is in the hands of the Imam, spiritual head of the Zaidi sect of Shi'a Muslims. Under a royalist constitution published in 1965 provision was made for an appointed Consultative Assembly and an executive council of ministers, with the Imam as head of state.

A supreme Judicial council administers *Shariah* law. Throughout the whole of Yemen customary Islamic law remains dominant.

Recent History

In 1934 the peace treaty of Ta'if was signed between Imam Yahya of the Yemen, member of the thousand-year-old Rassid dynasty of Shi'a Zaidi rulers, and Ibn Saud. This, with the recognition of Yemeni independence by Britain, who for a century had held Aden, marked the establishment of the modern state of Yemen. Until 1948 the Imam maintained personal and despotic rule over a poor territory and a turbulent group of tribes. Following his murder during an abortive *coup*, Imam Ahmad, his eldest son, brought Yemen into the world of international relationships. Western technical and financial aid was sought, in particular for mineral exploitation, but anti-British sentiment arising from the existence of Britain's control of Aden and Aden Protectorate resulted in a series of imbroglios. These ranged from frontier incidents (which continued after the establishment of the independent South Yemen) through uneasy rapprochements with the USSR to negotiations with the UAR. Between 1958 and December 1961 a formal federation of Yemen and the UAR was in existence until it was unilaterally abrogated by the UAR. In the same year Imam Ahmad, who had opposed many of the internal changes made by the Crown Prince, died following an assassination attempt. Within a week a military *coup* supported by UAR forces overthrew the new Imam, Muhammad Badr, and a republican régime was established over the greater part of Yemen.

The Republic increased anti-British pressure on Aden, which was met by a refusal to recognise the régime as long as it was supported by the army of the UAR. Egyptian forces at their peak probably numbered some 50,000. The Imam appealed to Saudi Arabia as well as to the tribes of the interior and civil war became endemic. A series of attempts by President Nasser and King Faisal, notably in 1964, 1965 and 1967, to bring the war to an end were unsuccessful, partly because of mutual suspicion, partly because of external fomentation of the situation and partly because of dissensions within each of the rival groups. On the republican side General Al-Amri and President Sallal were frequently in conflict over policy which involved the

131

UAR and Yemeni groups who still possessed strong tribal allegiances. Sallal was deposed in 1968 and the South Yemeni NLF left-wing forces appeared as a further confusing factor. On the royalist side, tribal and personal dissension culminated in the deposition of Imam Muhammad al-Badr in favour of a relation. After the war of June 1967, Egyptian troops were withdrawn and both Saudi intervention decreased as the UAR concentrated on the more pressing problem of Israel and as Saudi Arabia viewed the danger on her southern border as being less immediate. At the beginning of 1970 there were still two *de facto* Governments but the Republicans were in effective control of most of the country.

ECONOMY

Background

There are no sound data on the present position of the Yemen's economy. Varied and diverse but mainly subsistence agriculture flourishes in the highlands. Wheat and barley are the staple crops, together with a very large range of temperate and sub-tropical fruits and vegetables, tobacco and some cotton. The traditional cash-crop, Moka coffee, has diminished in importance and irrigation developments in the Tihama coastal plain are mainly concerned with cotton. Communications are poor and highland livestock maintained on rich rangelands are extensively used for transport as well as for food. External aid comes from the USSR and China, in technical and budgetary form.

Trade

Reported figures show considerable fluctuations from year to year but exports to the UK average c. £20,000 *p.a.*, with imports generally higher. Japan and Italy, as well as the USSR and Eastern bloc countries, have significant normal trade relations with Yemen. In 1966 total imports were valued at 56·8 million riyals and total exports at 7·3 million riyals. In 1968 exports to the UK were valued at £8,000 with imports from the UK of £315,000.

SOCIAL SERVICES, EDUCATION AND MASS MEDIA

In the present disturbed situation the Yemeni population continues to rely on traditional communal responsibilities. Sana, Taiz and Hodeida have organised medical facilities and health centres and hospitals were established by the Egyptian forces in Yemen.

Taiz is the most important cultural centre with the Islamic University, and two of the three periodicals, *Al-Nasr* (10,000) and *Saba* (10,000). Literacy is low and technology primitive; a new secular educational system at primary, intermediate and secondary levels is being established on the Egyptian model in the main towns and there are seven vocational schools. The Islamic mosque-based *madrassah* remains most important.

The Republican Government maintains Radio Sana which broadcasts in Arabic. Al Jaug radio transmission is maintained by the royalist régime which is also supported by Saudi broadcasts.

PART ONE
GENERAL BACKGROUND

AN HISTORICAL OUTLINE
TO THE PRESENT

ARNOLD TOYNBEE

DELIMITATION

THE Middle East, within the geographical limits adopted in the present Handbook, is the central region of the Old World. In cultural terms it is also the geographical heart of the Islamic world, though this extends far beyond the Middle East's limits into Asia in one direction and into Africa in another. The population of the Middle East is predominantly Muslim in religion but the Muslims are divided between Sunnis (numerically predominant) and Shi'ites (in Iran, south-eastern Iraq and southern Lebanon). The local Christian and Druze minorities play important parts in the Middle East's cultural, economic, and political life, and these are not the only non-Muslim Middle Eastern communities—there are also, for instance, the Nusayris and the Yazidis. Within the Islamic world, the Arabs occupy a central position. (The African Arab countries to the west of the Nile valley fall outside the geographical scope of this Handbook.) What is true of the Islamic world as a whole is true of the Arab core of it. The Arab Muslims are divided between a Sunni majority and a Shi'ite minority. The non-Muslim Arabs are a small minority, but an important one. The Middle Eastern meeting-point of Asia, Africa and Europe is also the point at which the backwaters of the Atlantic and the Indian Ocean approach each other most closely, head to head. The Mediterranean is separated from the Red Sea only by the narrow isthmus of Suez; the portage from Gaza, at the south-east corner of the Mediterranean, to the head of the Gulf of Aqaba is not very much longer; and the dry land that lies between the Syro-Palestinian shore of the Mediterranean and the head of the Persian Gulf is an isthmus likewise. It is a much broader one, yet it is narrow enough to have made the portage across it a lively trade-route since the date of the earliest surviving records. As the Indian Ocean itself is a vast backwater of the still vaster Pacific, the Middle Eastern portages and ship-canals have played a key part in the world's maritime traffic.

The maritime aspect of the Middle East was of paramount importance in all ages down to the date of the invention of mechanical traction by rail; for, before this invention, transport and travel was far easier, quicker and cheaper by water than overland. Consequently it has paid to link the Mediterranean with the Red Sea by a continuous waterway. This was achieved at least as early as the reign of Pharaoh Necho II (609–593 BC). Necho cut, or recut, a canal from the head of the Gulf of Suez to the head

135

of the Delta of the Nile, and this canal was maintained, on and off, for the next eight centuries or so, until the latter days of the Roman régime in Egypt. The direct sea-to-sea canal between Suez and Port Said was not opened until 1869.

Maritime traffic between Europe and southern and eastern Asia has survived the invention not only of railways, but of aeroplanes and mechanical road vehicles too. In 1969 there is still no good road connection between Europe and the Indo-Pakistani sub-continent, and there is no through railway. Moreover, neither road nor rail can compete with maritime transport for the carriage of goods whose value is low for their weight and bulk. The Suez Canal has been put out of commission temporarily as a result of the Arab-Israeli War of 1967. A graver permanent threat to its future remunerativeness is the building of giant tankers, for an enlargement of the Canal to accommodate these would probably be prohibitively costly, and there is no knowing how much farther the dimensions and tonnage of super-tankers are going to increase.

However, the air-routes linking North America and Europe with southern Asia and Australia will always traverse the Middle East, unless of course, these air-routes, like the Suez Canal, were to be put out of action by war and politics. The regions connected by the air-routes through the Middle East—that is to say, the basin of the North Atlantic and the southern and eastern parts of Asia—are, and seem likely to remain, the two most populous regions in the world, and the Middle East's geographical location, in between them, therefore seems likely to preserve for this region its importance as a zone of communications, even in unpropitious circumstances.

When we take account of the Middle East's location, we may guess that this geographical asset was one of the features that made the Middle East the birth-place of civilisation about 5,000 years ago, and probably also the birth-place of agriculture several thousand years before that. The meeting and mixing of different peoples, each bringing special skills and manners and customs, has usually proved stimulating, and the configuration of the planet's land and water surface shepherds migrating peoples into a convergence on the Middle East from all quarters.

Beginnings of Civilisation

The evidence of archaeology down to 1970 indicates (though archaeology is constantly springing surprises) that Sumer (i.e. south-eastern Iraq) and Egypt were the two earliest seats of civilisation, and that the Sumerian civilisation was slightly older than the Egyptian. There is an economic, as well as a geographical, reason for the rise of civilisation at these two points. The creation, maintenance and advancement of civilisation become possible only when at least a minority of the population has been released, for at any rate part of its time, from having to work on the production of elementary material requirements : food, clothes, shelter—food above all. A surplus of food was won for the first time through the reclamation, for human use, of the jungle-swamps of the lower Tigris-Euphrates basin and the lower Nile valley and the Nile Delta. The alluvial soil reclaimed by large-scale drainage and irrigation works was converted into fertile fields. The irrigation-system of Egypt has never ceased to be a going concern, and the volume of its production will be notably increased as a result of the building of the High Dam. The irrigation-system of Iraq was allowed to fall out of repair, by stages, between the fourth century BC and the thirteenth century of the Christian era, but, since the end of World War I, it has been in process of being reconditioned, and the present 'population explosion' in the 'developing' majority of the human race makes it certain that the agricultural production of Iraq is going, once again, to be in demand up to the country's full capacity when its irrigation system has been completely restored.

The agricultural potentialities of Iraq and Egypt are much greater than those of the region in between them, and consequently civilisation started later there. However, the location of Syria, the Lebanon and Palestine is singularly favourable for the development of both trade and culture. These countries command the two portages between the two seas and the overland routes between the two main fields of irrigational agriculture, and their accessibility to cultural influences from both sides has proved stimulating. In the course of about one millennium ending in the middle of the sixth century BC, the peoples of this region performed three great feats. They invented the alphabet and monotheism and they discovered the Atlantic. The first two of these feats were intellectual; the third was a feat of enterprise and endurance. The Phoenicians' voyages of exploration were eventually surpassed by Portuguese and Spanish navigators more than two thousand years later. The Phoenician invention of the alphabet and the Israelite and Jewish invention of monotheism were feats of intellectual simplification—achieved by hard, deep and long-sustained thinking—that are at least on a par with the achievements of Copernicus, Newton and Einstein. An unwieldy jumble of ideograms and phonemes was replaced by a set of 20 letters representing basic consonantal sounds. A pantheon was replaced by a god who was conceived of as being unique, though he was also still conceived of as being a human-like personality: an autocratic monarch who was never completely transfigured into a loving and beneficent father. (The vision of ultimate spiritual reality as being something that is suprapersonal was attained, not in the Middle East, but in India.)

EARLIEST POLITICAL HISTORY

The Middle East's political history has been unstable by comparison with China's, though not more unstable than the political history of the Hellenic or the Indian or the Western worlds. The source of the Middle East's instability was Iraq, and Egypt was eventually involved in the turmoil that spread from the Iraqi centre of disturbance. Egypt, so long as it remained insulated, was as stable politically as China. In Egypt, as in China, bouts of political fragmentation and chaos were rare and relatively brief.

Egypt was unified politically at the dawn of the Egyptian civilisation; Iraq (known first as Sumer and Akkad and then as Babylonia) started out politically as a cluster of local sovereign 'city-states' that waged ruinous wars with each other for half a millennium before they were unified forcibly. (Egypt, too, had been unified by force, but this had happened early enough to spare her people the tribulations that the Sumerians brought on themselves.) The peoples of Syria and Palestine, like the Greeks in the last millennium BC, have preferred political disunity and have reverted to it repeatedly whenever they have been able to shake off the rule of imperial powers at whose mercy their political disunity has repeatedly placed them.

The political configuration of the Middle East has oscillated, in the course of the last 5,000 years, between three fundamental patterns. In 1970 the Middle East is a mosaic of local sovereign independent states, and this has been the most frequently recurring political dispensation in the Middle East taken as a whole. The present-day political map of the area resembles the map as it stood after the break-up of the 'Abbasid Caliphate and after the destruction of the first Persian Empire by Alexander the Great and after the destruction of the Assyrian Empire by the momentarily united forces of the Medes and the Babylonians. A rarer, but happier, political dispensation in the Middle East has been unification under the sovereignty of a single empire—a dispensation that was the rule in Egypt from about the beginning of the third millennium BC, but that has been an uncommon occurrence in the history of the Middle East as a whole.

The Empire of the Akkadian city-state Agadé, which imposed its rule on the Sumerian city-states in or about the 25th century BC, was perhaps the first empire to extend from the head of the Persian Gulf to the north-east corner of the Mediterranean, and, after its brief life, the same territorial extension was achieved, towards the close of the third millennium BC, by the still shorter-lived empire of the third dynasty of the Sumerian city-state Ur. At about the year 1700 BC, Sumer and Akkad were united politically for the third time by Hammurabi, a member of the first dynasty of the par-venu Amorite city-state Babylon, and this time the union of these two lands was more or less permanent, except for a persisting tendency towards separatism in the district at the receding head of the Persian Gulf. Hammurabi secured for Babylonia (as the united territories of Sumer and Akkad now came to be called) the unity that had been secured for Upper and Lower Egypt by Narmer 12 or 13 centuries earlier.

In the region between Babylonia and Egypt, spells of independence and disunity alternated with spells of subjection to imperial régimes, sometimes based on Babylonia and sometimes based on Egypt. The so-called 'New Empire' of Egypt (16th to 12th centuries BC) exercised a fitful and precarious suzerainty over Palestine and Syria which, at moments, extended as far north as the west bank of the Euphrates at the river's westward elbow. The first empire to embrace both Babylonia and Egypt was the Assyrian Empire (ninth to seventh centuries BC); but its hold on Egypt was weak and brief, and Babylonia was subjected by the Assyrians without being reconciled or being permanently subdued. The Assyrians waged their wars with such cruelty, and drew upon themselves such hatred, that towards the close of the seventh century BC the Assyrian Empire was overthrown and the Assyrian people itself was exterminated. However, the gruesome episode of Assyrian conquest and domination left a mark on the Middle East that was permanent. With a view to breaking the conquered people's spirit, disrupting their political and social structure, and so making effective insurrection difficult, the Assyrians deliberately mixed up the peoples of the Middle East by deporting the members of their political 'establishments' together with their skilled workers. As a result of this ruthless Assyrian policy, the population of the 'Fertile Crescent' (Babylonia, the Jazirah, Syria, Palestine) was knit together socially and culturally. Its unity was displayed in its common use of a series of *lingue franche* : first Aramaic, then Greek, then Syriac (a late form of Aramaic), finally Arabic. The Jews (i.e. the descendants of the people of the former tiny kingdom of Judah in the southern Palestine highlands) were singular in resolving to reassert their national and religious separateness, and in achieving this difficult objective in the course of the three or four centuries ending in the second century BC.

IMPERIAL PARTITION

The Assyrian peace had been purchased by the peoples of the Middle East at an intolerable price. Assyrian atrociousness had condemned the Assyrian Empire to suffer liquidation. Thereafter, the Middle East, together with Asian and African territories beyond its limits, was given political unity and peace by two milder and more tolerant imperial régimes : the first Persian Empire (mid-sixth century BC to 334–1 BC) and the Arab Caliphate (mid-seventh century AD to mid-ninth century AD). These two empires were more successful and more enduring than the Assyrian Empire had been, but they, too, found it difficult to keep an effective hold on Egypt from an Asian base.

The third of the three fundamental political patterns that have prevailed, in alternation, in the Middle East has been a pair of co-existing empires, one of them based economically on Iraq (alias Babylonia or Sumer and Akkad) and the other on Egypt. This pattern, in which the Middle East is partitioned between two great powers, has made its appearance three times so far.

During the century and a quarter between the sudden premature death of Alexander the Great in 323 BC and Rome's intrusion into the Middle East in the second century BC, there was a confrontation between the Ptolemaic Greek Empire based in Egypt and the Seleucid Greek Empire, whose economic base was Iraq, though its political base was Antioch in the north-west corner of Syria. After that, the Middle East was partitioned for seven centuries (the last century BC to the seventh century of the Christian era) between the Roman Empire and an empire ruled by an Iranian people, first the Parni and then the Persians—the authentic Persians from the province of Fars. This province was the homeland of the founders of the second Persian Empire (the Sasanian dynasty) in the third century of the Christian era, as it had likewise been the homeland of the founders of the first Persian Empire (the Achaemenidae) in the sixth century BC. The Parni, whom the Persians forcibly supplanted in the third century AD, were a pastoral nomad people from what is now the Soviet Republic of Türkmenistan. They had occupied Parthia (present-day Khurasan) in the third century BC under the leadership of the Arsacid dynasty, and consequently they came to be known as Parthians. Their economic base was Iraq, and their political capital was Ctesiphon, the east-bank suburb of the Seleucids' former regional capital Seleucia-on-Tigris. The Persian Sasanids simply stepped into the shoes of their Parthian Arsacid victims, and they carried on, with greater dynamism, the Arsacids' feud with the Roman Empire. The economic capital of the Roman Empire was Alexandria in Egypt, the former political capital of the Ptolemies.

The third pair of powers that have partitioned the Middle East between them are the Ottoman and Iranian Empires (16th century AD till the close of World War I). The Ottoman Empire was decisively stronger than Iran, and it succeeded in annexing Iraq permanently—an achievement that had been one of the Roman Empire's unfulfilled ambitions. The Ottoman Empire also occasionally occupied Azerbaijan, the home province of the Safavi dynasty who were the founders of the modern Empire of Iran. The Safavis had to remove their seat of government from Tabriz to Isfahan, where it was beyond the Osmanlis' reach. However, the Empire of Iran still survives in 1969, whereas the Ottoman Empire's Middle Eastern dominions were broken up after World War I. (The Ottoman Empire had previously lost all its European possessions to the west and north of Edirne, and its hold on Egypt had long since been reduced to a merely nominal suzerainty.)

The break-up of the Ottoman Empire was due to the same cause as the simultaneous break-up of the Habsburg monarchy. It, too, was a multi-national empire that had lived on into an age in which the standard type of state was one whose citizens were nationally homogeneous. The Iranian Empire has had the good fortune to be a state of this type. The non-Farsi-speaking minorities in its population are small and their geographical location is marginal. Hence the Iranian Empire's eventual escape from being partitioned between the Russian and British Empires—a fate that seemed to be Iran's destiny during the ten years 1907–17.

From about 3,000 BC till the 13th century of the Christian era, the Middle East was the cultural, economic, and frequently also the political centre of gravity of the western end of the Old World—a counterpart (senior by 15 centuries in the age of its civilisation) of China in east Asia and of India in south Asia. The western fringe of the Middle East includes Phoenicia, Israel and Ionia, three small countries that captured the lead in civilisation from Egypt and Babylonia in the last millennium BC. Ionia was the cradle of the Ancient Greek civilisation, and this Greek civilisation's political, economic, and cultural focus shifted from the Aegean basin to Alexandria and Antioch after the overthrow of the Persian Empire by Alexander the Great had brought the interior of the Middle East, except for Arabia, under Greek domination. From the last century BC onwards, the Roman Empire's portion of the Middle East was Rome's economic power-house. In the seventh century AD the Middle East, this time including Arabia, was united politically under the Arab Empire, except for Anatolia (the western half of present-day Turkey). For the next two centuries, the Arab Empire was one of the Old World's two super-powers (the other was China), and, for four centuries after the beginning of the 'Abbasid dynasty's slow decline, the Arabs were the leaders, at the western end of the Old World, in philosophy, science and medicine, and in poetry too. At this end of the Old World, the Arabs' only rivals were the contemporary Greeks, and the medieval Greeks were a Middle Eastern people. Their stronghold was not in Europe; it was in Anatolia. Constantinople (Istanbul) and Salonica were Greek beach-heads in a south-eastern Europe that by then had become predominantly Slav.

ECLIPSE

In the course of the 11th, 12th and 13th centuries, the history of the western end of the Old World took a surprising new turn. The Arabs and the Greeks fell on evil days; the Western Christian barbarians forged ahead, and this not only in military and economic power, but in culture as well. The Middle East now lost the leading role that it had played in this part of the world for more than 4,000 years; and after that it seemed for a time to have forfeited even the advantage of its geographical position when, in and after the 15th century, the Western peoples along the European section of the Old World's Atlantic seaboard mastered the art of oceanic navigation, discovered and appropriated the Americas, and found their way to India and eastern Asia by continuous voyage round the Cape of Good Hope. The rounding of the Cape by the Portuguese put out of business, for the time being, the age-old portages between the Mediterranean and the Indian Ocean across the Middle East. Even after the Ottoman Empire had gained command over these portages by conquering Syria, Palestine, Egypt and Iraq, it failed to wrest out of Portuguese hands the naval command of the Indian Ocean, though the Osmanlis held the interior lines and had an ally in western India, the Muslim kingdom of Gujerat.

The political unification of the western two-thirds of the Middle East under Ottoman rule did, however, save the Middle Eastern peoples from falling under Western rule so long as the Ottoman régime in the Middle East survived. Though the Middle East was weakened by the feud between the Ottoman and Iranian Empires, the partition of the Ottoman Empire between the Western powers and Russia was postponed by the rivalries between these harpies. India and Indonesia fell under Western rule before any Arab countries suffered the same fate, though north-west Africa and the Middle East lie on the West's threshold, whereas southern and eastern Asia could be reached from Western countries only by the long and circuitous sea-route round the Cape before the opening of the Suez Canal in 1869 and of air-routes over the Middle East since the end of World War II. As the Ottoman Empire lost its grip, its former Arab provinces were seized, one after another, by the Western powers : Algeria in 1830, Tunisia in 1881, Egypt in 1882, and the Asian Arab provinces in the Fertile Crescent in the course of, and at the end of, World War I.

RE-EMERGENCE

The decline and fall of the Ottoman Empire in the Middle East coincided in date with the emergence of the Middle East itself from its temporary eclipse. From the 15th century till the last years of the 18th century, the Middle East had not been one of the main targets of Western aggression, and this had been not only because the Ottoman Empire was tougher than the Mughal Empire in India and very much tougher than the empires of the Aztecs and the Incas. Another reason why the Middle East was spared was because India and the Americas had seemed to Westerners to be more lucrative fields for exploitation. Two changes have now brought the Middle East out of its temporary eclipse into the limelight again.

When the British had made themselves masters of India, the potential short cut between Indian and Europe via the Middle East came to the fore once again. British feelings on this subject were mixed. The opening up of routes across the Middle East might make communications between the British Indian Empire and Britain easier and quicker, but this would also make it easier and quicker for Russia or for Britain's West and Central European rivals to get at India if they felt so inclined. The British government promoted the installation of an overland telegraph-line between Britain and India, but it was opposed to the cutting of the Suez Canal by the French and to the building of the Bosphorus-to-Baghdad Railway by the Germans. The growing interest, whether favourable or hostile, that was being shown by Western powers in the development of Middle Eastern communications brought with it a growing risk to the survival of the Middle Eastern countries' independence. It is said that when Muhammad Aly, the Ottoman Viceroy of Egypt (1805–49) who had made himself virtually independent, was offered a plan for cutting a canal across the Isthmus of Suez, he replied : 'Why should I burden myself with an artificial Bosphorus and Dardanelles when Nature has not burdened me with one?'

The second change that brought the Middle East back into the limelight again was the discovery there of the world's largest proved resources of mineral oil. This discovery, and its commercial exploitation, have revolu-

141

tionised the economic relations between the Middle East and the West and also among the Middle Eastern countries themselves. The Middle East's oil reserves have made it once more an eldorado worth dominating, as it was in the days when the world's principal food surpluses were produced by Egypt and Iraq. As among the Middle Eastern countries themselves, Egypt's agricultural wealth has now suddenly become insignificant by comparison with the newly discovered mineral wealth of the previously poverty-stricken arid Arab countries: Saudi Arabia, Kuwait, the Gulf States, and, more recently, Libya and the Saharan hinterland of Algeria.

The Ottoman Empire, like the Habsburg Empire, was broken up by the impact of the post-Christian Western religion of nationalism, which had been brought to birth in the American and French Revolutions and had subsequently spread round the globe *pari passu* with the spread of the West's power and prestige. In retrospect it is obvious that these two multi-national empires actually shielded those subject peoples—the Czechs and the Arabs, for instance—who had worked for their overthrow in the expectation of national independence. So far from that, these peoples have discovered, too late, that they have merely exchanged King Log for King Stork.

When the Ottoman Empire's military intervention in World War I led to its break-up in the Middle East, as it had already broken up in south-eastern Europe, Britain and France rushed in to partition between them the ex-Ottoman Arab territories in the Fertile Crescent. (They did not try to lay hands on the Arabian Peninsula. Turkish experience had shown that, for imperialists, Arabia was a hornets' nest; for non-Muslim imperialists, the Hijaz was out of bounds, and the mineral wealth of Saudi Arabia was then still undiscovered.) At the Paris Peace Conference of 1919, the spokesmen for Asian Arab national aspirations assumed that the menace to these was the still-unsated appetite of French and British imperialism (especially French, since the French were less liberal than the British or more frank in disclosing their true intentions). In the event, the imposing colonial empires of the West European powers melted like snow during and after World War II. They were liquidated everywhere, and most easily in the Middle East, where they had established themselves only shortly before. One recently inaugurated Western colonising enterprise, however, did not disappear, but, so far from that, continued to grow, like the grain of mustard-seed in the parable, to the stature of a tree overshadowing the Middle East.

THE PROBLEM OF ISRAEL

This surviving Western colonising enterprise in the Middle East is the one that brought the state of Israel to birth in 1948. At the start, none of the parties concerned—except, no doubt, the Zionists themselves—had any inkling of the strength of the forces—emotional, financial, political, and eventually military too—that were latent in the Zionist movement. When the British government published the Balfour Declaration in 1917, their motive was the short-term war-aim of overtrumping the Central powers in a competition for winning Jewish support in Central Europe, and, still more, in the United States. A 'national home' for the Jews in Palestine was a card that the Central powers could not play, since Palestine was then part of the Ottoman Empire, which was the Central powers' ally. In playing this card, Britain and her allies and associates more than counteracted the odium that they had incurred, in Jewish minds, through their having been allies of Russia—a power which, at that time, was the Jews' principal persecutor.

The British government endorsed Zionism light-heartedly, under the illusion that this was a minor movement which they would be able to control and to direct to suit British interests. At the peace conference of 1919, the Emir Faisal came to terms with Dr Weizmann because he rightly held that the Arabs could not afford to fight a diplomatic battle on two fronts simultaneously, while he wrongly judged that the serious menace to Arab national aspirations was French colonialism, and that, by comparison, Zionism was a puny force.

In the course of the next half-century, the seed sown by the Balfour Declaration has raised the whirlwind. By December 1968 there had been three Arab-Israeli wars—in 1948, 1956 and 1967. There were, by then, about 1,500,000 Palestinian Arab refugees; all Arabs still remaining in Cisjordanian Palestine were either subjects of Israel or under Israeli military occupation; all Egyptian territory east of the Suez Canal was also under Israeli military occupation; the Canal itself was closed; hostilities were mounting along the 1967 armistice-lines; Israel and the adjoining Arab countries were still living in a state of war. Worst of all, this local calamity, which was bad enough in itself, threatened to engulf the rest of the world because the two superpowers, the United States and the Soviet Union, had allowed themselves to become locally involved by backing Israel and her Arab opponents respectively. Both powers were manifestly anxious not to be drawn into war with each other over the Middle East, but they were not fully masters of the situation, since they could not be sure of being able to control their respective protégés. Meanwhile, the Arab countries were at Israel's mercy, partly because of the Israelis' superiority in efficiency and, above all, in dedication and determination, and partly because the Arab states had failed signally to form a united front. Yet Israel's military ascendancy could not enable her to bring the war to a close, because the Arab world, like Russia and China, is virtually infinite in its geographical extent. In the hope of establishing a peace settlement, the great powers began consultations in 1969, but these proved sterile. In the summer of 1970, however, Israel, Egypt and Jordan accepted an American peace initiative, the Rogers Plan, which envisaged a temporary cease-fire and the holding of peace negotiations under the auspices of Dr. Gunnar Jarring on the basis of the Security Council's Resolution of 1967. The Palestinians denounced the settlement from the start, and Israel refused to participate after the Egyptian violation of the cease-fire. The outcome of the talks, when they resume, seems uncertain.

TURKEY

Turkey's history during the same half-century down to 1970 presented a striking contrast to the history of her former Arab provinces. At the end of World War I the Turkish people were in a desperate plight. The Ottoman Empire had been defeated militarily in the Balkan War of 1912 and then in World War I, but its most serious malady was depopulation. Since the creation of a Western-style Turkish army, recruited by conscription, in 1826, the Turkish population of Anatolia—the Empire's reservoir of loyal military man-power—had been reduced by constant casualties in rebellious outlying parts of the Empire (e.g., the Yemen and Albania). There had been three Russo-Turkish wars between 1826 and World War I—in 1827-8, 1853-6, and 1877-8. By 1922, when the Turks ejected the Greek invaders of Anatolia, Turkey had been at war almost continually for ten years. The Turkish population was estimated, whether correctly or not, to have dwindled, by this date, to about 8 million. In 1969 it stood at about four times that figure; for, by that time, Turkey had been at peace for 46 years, except for the participation of a Turkish expeditionary force in the Korean War. The standard of public health organisation had also greatly improved; and these two changes, between them, had produced a population explosion.

This dramatic turn in Turkey's fortunes had been brought about by the heroic efforts of the Turkish people itself under the inspiring leadership of Mustafa Kemal Atatürk, a great man who combined vision with the will-power to translate his aims into accomplished facts. Atatürk saw, and made his fellow-countrymen see, that the forcible detachment of the non-Turkish territories of the Ottoman Empire had been, for the Turkish people, a blessing in disguise. He diverted Turkish energies and aspirations to the task of renovating Turkish life in the Turkish people's homeland. The Ottoman imperial régime was jettisoned; and, in the new Republic of Turkey, Westernising reforms were carried out during the six years 1923–8 which it had taken the Western peoples themselves three or four centuries to accomplish. The emancipation of women, the concomitant abolition of polygamy, the replacement of the Arabic by the Latin alphabet, and the apprenticeship of the Turks in modern industry and commerce, previously left in the hands of non-Turkish minorities, are only four conspicuous radical reforms out of the many that were carried out under Atatürk's impulsion. The pace was unprecedentedly rapid; but the time was the last minute of the 12th hour; and the Turkish people's national survival was at stake. At the close of this half-century, Turkey still had many formidable unsolved problems on her hands. In this she was not peculiar; but there was an impressive contrast between her remarkable performance and the tragic course of events in the defunct Ottoman Empire's former Arab provinces.

PROSPECTS

In November 1970 the prospects of the Middle East as a whole were enigmatic. The most urgent task was to obtain the maximum practicable amount of justice and reparation for those Palestinian Arabs who had been evicted or subjugated as a result of the establishment, and subsequent expansion, of the state of Israel. These refugees were innocent victims of foreign political forces that they were powerless either to influence or to resist. Their misery was a moral scandal and a public danger to which world opinion had been callously insensitive. This shocking evil had been allowed to continue for 22 years. Redress, even though belated and incomplete, would be the most effective operation for de-fusing the time-bomb, ticking ominously in the Middle East, which was threatening to blow up the whole world.

On the political, as distinct from the moral, plane there would not be peace in the Middle East until the local belligerents took a decision from which, so far, they had shrunk. The Arabs had to accept the hard fact that the State of Israel had come to stay. This was hard, because Israel had been carved out of Arab territory whose lawful owners had been, at best, subjected, and, at worst, evicted and expropriated. The Israelis, on their side, had to accept the hard fact that the permanent survival of Israel could not be secured by any number of sensational military victories, but only by inducing the Arabs to reconcile themselves, in their hearts, to Israel's unwelcome presence in their midst. Even if the Arabs could have been compelled by Israel to sign a dictated peace-treaty under

144

military duress, this 'scrap of paper' would have been as worthless as the peace-treaty dictated to Germany after World War I.

If the United States and the Soviet Union could bring themselves to act in concert, they have it in their power to sponsor a peace settlement, and, if necessary, to impose one, between the Israelis and the Arabs. Practicable peace terms would necessarily be based on a compromise that would be uncongenial for both the local parties; yet, for them, it would be vastly better than an endless continuation of the present state of war, while, for their backers, the two super powers, the removal of the danger of an undesired collision in the Middle East would be far more valuable than any advantage that they might be able to extract, in competition with each other, from allowing the Middle Eastern war to continue.

Arnold Joseph Toynbee, CH. Director of Studies in the Royal Institute of International Affairs, and Research Professor of International History in the University of London until 1956. Member of British Delegation, Peace Conferences, Paris 1919 and 1946; Director, Research Department, Foreign Office, 1943–6; war work: Director, Foreign Research and Press Service, Royal Institute of International Affairs, 1939–43; Koraes Professor of Byzantine and Modern Greek Language, Literature and History at London University, 1919–24; member of Middle Eastern section, British Delegation, Peace Conference, Paris, 1919; Political Intelligence department, Foreign Office, 1918. Among his many publications are *A Survey of International Affairs, 1920–1946*, *A Study of History* (1934–1965), *Civilisation on Trial* (1948), *East to West: a Journey round the World* (1958), *Between Niger and Nile* (1965), *The World and the West* (1952 Reith Lectures, 1953).

THE PALESTINE PROBLEM:
THE PALESTINIAN POINT OF VIEW

HENRY CATTAN

THE Palestine problem is the problem which has arisen from the fulfilment of the Zionist ambition to create a Jewish State in Palestine at the cost of the forcible displacement of the original inhabitants and the usurpation of their ancestral homeland. It should be remarked at the outset that the Palestine problem does not involve a conflict between the Arabs, be they Muslims or Christians, and Judaism, for Arabs and Jews have lived throughout centuries in peace and harmony. The conflict is between the Arabs and Zionism, which, from a humanitarian concept seeking a place of refuge for persecuted Jewry, has evolved into what some consider to be a racist, nationalist and imperialist movement.

ORIGIN OF THE PROBLEM

The plan to create a Jewish State originated at the end of the 19th century with the idea of finding a home for the Jews of Europe, who for a long time had suffered from discrimination and persecution. In a pamplet named *Der Judenstaat* ('The Jewish State') published in 1896, Theodor Herzl, an Austrian journalist, developed this theme and suggested Palestine or Argentina as possible locations for the proposed State.

Herzl convened the First Zionist Congress at Basle in 1897. The Congress did not espouse Herzl's idea about the creation of a Jewish State but recommended the creation in Palestine of 'a home' for the Jewish people which would be secured by public law. The Congress also recommended the colonisation of Palestine by Jewish workers and the fostering of Jewish national sentiment and consciousness.

Herzl sought to interest the Sultan of Turkey in Jewish colonisation in Palestine but failed. Herzl died in 1904 and the Zionist plan then remained dormant for a while.

THE BALFOUR DECLARATION

During World War I the Zionists saw a chance of winning support for their programme and they succeeded in securing from the British government a declaration of sympathy with Jewish Zionist aspirations. This declaration

[1] Some of the material in this article is based upon the author's book *Palestine, The Arabs and Israel* published by Longmans, London, in 1969, and is here used with their permission.

was embodied in a letter dated 2 November 1917 addressed by Arthur James Balfour, then British Foreign Minister, to Lord Rothschild which stated :

'His Majesty's Government view with favour the establishment in Palestine of a national home for the Jewish people, and will use their best endeavours to facilitate the achievement of this object, it being clearly understood that nothing shall be done which may prejudice the civil and religious rights of existing non-Jewish communities in Palestine, or the rights and political status enjoyed by Jews in any other country.'

The number of Jews who then lived in Palestine did not exceed 56,000, representing 8% of the population, while the Arabs, both Muslim and Christian, numbered about 650,000, or 92% of the population.

It is important to note that the Zionist plan for a Jewish national home in Palestine was disapproved by the Jews of Palestine. Ronald Storrs, the first British military governor of Jerusalem, states : 'The religious Jews of Jerusalem and Hebron and the *Sephardim* were strongly opposed to political Zionism. . . .'[2] The opposition of the Palestine Jews to the creation of a Jewish national home in Palestine goes to show that this was a foreign concept, extrinsic to Palestine and alien to the Jewish community living there.

The Balfour Declaration was described as a document in which 'one nation solemnly promised to a second nation the country of a third. . . .'[3] The Declaration had no legal value for at no time, whether before or after it was made, did the British Government possess any sovereignty, dominion or other title in Palestine that would empower it to recognise any rights in favour of the Jews in or over that country. It was made in complete disregard of the rights and wishes of the inhabitants of the country. This is confirmed by Arthur James Balfour himself who on 11 August 1919, wrote :

'In Palestine we do not propose even to go through the form of consulting the wishes of the present inhabitants of the country. . . . The four great Powers are committed to Zionism. And Zionism, be it right or wrong, good or bad, is rooted in agelong traditions, in present needs, in future hopes, of far profounder import than the desires and prejudices of the 700,000 Arabs who now inhabit that ancient land.'[4]

The Balfour Declaration also conflicted with several assurances and pledges given by the British Government to the Arabs with respect to their independence from Turkey as soon as the war should come to an end.[5]

ZIONIST CLAIM OF A HISTORIC RIGHT

When Palestine was chosen as the location for the Jewish national home, Zionism invented the concept of a 'historic right' to Palestine. Such a concept has no foundation either in law or in fact because Palestine is the homeland of the Palestinians, who, as the descendants of the Philistines, Canaanites and other tribes, inhabited the country from the dawn of history until 1948, when the majority of them fled or were forcibly displaced by Jewish terrorist organisations. As to the Jewish occupation of Palestine in ancient times, this was a biblical episode and cannot give rise to a 'historic right' since many

[2] Storrs, Ronald. *Orientations*, Nicholson and Watson, London, 1945, p. 340. The *Sephardim* are the Oriental Jews who inhabited the Mediterranean basin in contradistinction to the *Ashkenazim* who are Jews of Slav and Central European origin.
[3] Koestler, Arthur. *Promise and Fulfilment*, Macmillan, New York, p. 4.
[4] *Documents on British Foreign Policy* 1919–1939, 1st series, Vol. IV.
[5] For the text of these assurances and pledges, see Cmd. 5974, 16 March 1939 and also Antonius, George. *The Arab Awakening*, Khayats, Beirut.

other peoples occupied and ruled the country during its long history. In point of fact, the Muslims and Christians possess a greater right based upon occupation than any other people for they have continuously held the country from AD 323 until the British occupation in 1917–18. The following table shows the various peoples who occupied Jerusalem from 1050 BC until AD 1950 :

		Years
Israelites	Davidic Kingdom to Fall of Jerusalem 1050–586 BC	464
Babylonians	Fall of Jerusalem to fall of Babylon 586–538	50
Persians	Cyrus to Macedonian conquest of Persia 538–332	206
Greeks	Alexander's conquest of Jerusalem to emancipation of city by Maccabees 332–166	166
Jews	Maccabean Kingdom 166–63	93
Pagan Romans	Roman conquest of Jerusalem to fall of paganism 63 BC–AD 323	386
Christian Romans	From Constantine to Persian conquest 323–614	291
Persians	Period of Persian rule 614–628	14
Romans	Reconquest by Byzantines 628–637	11
Arabs	Conquest by Muslim Arabs 637–1072	435
Turks	Rule by Moslem Turks 1072–1092	20
Arabs	Reconquest by Arabs 1092–1099	7
Christians	Crusading Kingdom 1099–1187	88
Arabs	Reconquest by Arabs 1187–1229	42
Christians	City ceded by treaty to Frederick II 1229–1239	10
Arabs	Revived Arab rule 1239–1514	278
Moslem Turks	Jerusalem under Ottoman Turks 1517–1917	400
Christians	British conquest and mandate 1917–1947	30
Arabs and Israelis	Jerusalem seized by Israelis and Arabs 1947–1950	3[6]

ARTICLE 22 OF THE COVENANT OF THE LEAGUE OF NATIONS

Palestine was occupied in 1917–18 by British forces under General Allenby. This occupation did not involve any annexation because the principles which President Wilson propounded towards the end of World War I—namely, the rejection of any territorial acquisition by conquest and the recognition of the right of self-determination of peoples—came to be generally accepted and were incorporated in 1919 in Article 22 of the Covenant of the League of Nations. The Covenant laid down that, to the peoples inhabiting territories which had ceased to be under the sovereignty of the State which formerly governed them, there should be applied 'the principle that their well-being and development form a sacred trust of civilisation'. Moreover, and specifically with regard to the communities detached from the Turkish Empire, namely, the peoples of Palestine, Syria, Lebanon and Iraq, Article 22 laid down that '... their existence as independent nations can be provisionally recognised subject to the rendering of administrative advice and assistance by a mandatory until such time as they are able to stand alone'.

[6] The above table is taken from the letter of Rev. Charles T. Bridgeman to the Trusteeship Council, 13 January 1950, General Assembly Official Records, 5th Session, Supplement No. 9, UN Document A/1286, p. 15.

THE MANDATE OVER PALESTINE

Accordingly, mandates were granted by the Council of the League of Nations to certain states for the administration of the territories severed from Turkey and Germany at the end of the First World War. The mandate over Palestine was entrusted to the British government in 1922. It embodied a provision for putting into effect the Balfour Declaration. This was done against the express wishes of the people most directly concerned, the Palestinians. Their wishes had been ascertained by the King-Crane Commission but its recommendations were concealed.[7] The inclusion of a provision in the mandate for the implementation of the Balfour Declaration resulted in the denial to the Palestine Arabs throughout the mandate of any right of self-government. In 1922, the mandatory power attempted to give the country a semblance of autonomy in the form of a legislative council, partly elected and partly appointed. But even this modest measure was defeated by Zionist opposition to the institution of any form of self-government while the Jews were still in a minority.

JEWISH IMMIGRATION DURING THE MANDATE

The mandate provided that while ensuring that 'the rights and position of others sections of the population are not prejudiced' the mandatory should facilitate Jewish immigration into Palestine. This provision opened the gates of Palestine to the influx of Jews. Between 1923 and 1932, only 84,454 Jews emigrated to Palestine[8] but after 1933, as a result of Nazi oppression, the Jews came to Palestine in large numbers. Within a quarter of a century the number of Jews in Palestine increased from 56,000 in 1918 to 608,000 in 1946; in other words, their ratio changed from one-twelfth to one-third of the total population.

Jewish immigration alarmed the Arab inhabitants. Zionist leaders sought to allay Arab fears by assurances that they entertained no idea of domination in Palestine or of the establishment of a Jewish state. Dr. Chaim Weizmann (who later became the first President of Israel) told Arab leaders in 1918 at Jerusalem : 'Let his hearers beware of treacherous insinuations that Zionists were seeking political power. . . .'[9] In 1919 Sokolow, Zionist leader and historian, wrote :

> 'It has been said, and is still being obstinately repeated by anti-Zionists again and again, that Zionism aims at the creation of an independent 'Jewish State'. But this is wholly fallacious. The 'Jewish State' was never part of the Zionist programme.'[10]

Norman Bentwich, a Zionist Jew and a former Attorney-General of Palestine, declared that 'State sovereignty is not essential to the Jewish national ideal'.[11] In 1930 he also wrote :

> 'The idea of a national home . . . signifies a territory in which a people, without receiving rights of political sovereignty, has, nevertheless, a recognised legal position and the opportunity of developing its moral, social and intellectual ideas.'[12]

[7] The King-Crane Commission's report was suppressed and kept secret for three years: Howard, Harry N. *The King-Crane Commission*, Khayats, Beirut, 1963, p. 221.
[8] For immigration figures to Palestine, see *Statistical Abstract of Palestine*, Office of Statistics of the Government of Palestine, 1941, p. 31.
[9] Storrs, Ronald, *op. cit.*, p. 341.
[10] Sokolow, N. *History of Zionism*, Ktav, New York, 1969, p. xxiv.
[11] Bentwich, Norman. *Palestine and the Jews*, Kegan Paul, London, 1919, p. 195.
[12] Bentwich, Norman. *The Mandates System*, Longmans, London, 1930, p. 24.

However, despite these assurances, it was becoming clear that Jewish immigration in Palestine was inspired, promoted and financed by Zionist organisations with one political objective : the creation of a demographic nucleus which would lead to the domination of Palestine and the establishment of a Jewish State. The original inhabitants of Palestine, Muslims and Christians, opposed the flow of Jewish immigration into their country. Their opposition took the form of protests, demonstrations, riots and civil disturbances and in 1936 an armed rebellion broke out against the mandatory government that lasted three years. Arab hostility to Jewish immigration to Palestine was not due to anti-semitism. The Jews have lived in peace and harmony with the Arabs throughout centuries and the persecutions which the Jews had suffered during their history were not committed by the Arabs. But the hostility shown by the Arabs of Palestine to Jewish immigration is understandable : they were in fear for their existence and for their homeland. As subsequent events have shown, their fears were justified.

THE WHITE PAPER OF 1939

Convinced that continued Jewish immigration into Palestine caused serious prejudice to 'the rights and position' of the Palestine Arabs, which Britain was bound by the terms of the mandate to safeguard, the British Government issued in 1939 a White Paper, in which it declared its intention to limit Jewish immigration to 75,000 persons over the next five years and to grant to Palestine its independence at the end of ten years. After the period of five years no further Jewish immigration would be allowed except with Arab consent.[13] But Zionist Jews fought this White Paper by a campaign of violence.[14]

Unable to permit any further Jewish immigration into Palestine against the wishes of the majority of its inhabitants, plagued by Zionist demands for more and more immigrants, subjected to pressure by the United States for increased Jewish immigration and harassed by the Zionist campaign of violence, the mandatory government in 1947 referred to the question of the future government of Palestine to the UN.

THE PARTITION RESOLUTION

The question of the future government of Palestine was the subject of discussion at two sessions of the General Assembly of the UN in 1947. A Special Commission appointed by the General Assembly (UNSCOP) suggested two plans for the future of Palestine : a majority plan and a minority plan. The majority plan proposed the termination of the mandate, the partition of Palestine and the creation of an Arab State, a Jewish State, and a *corpus separatum* for the City of Jerusalem which would come under a special international régime to be administered by the UN. The Arab and Jewish States would be linked by an economic union. The minority plan also envisaged the termination of the mandate but proposed the establishment of a

---

[13] *Cmd.* 6018, 17 May 1939.
[14] For details about this campaign of violence, see Government of Palestine, *A Survey of Palestine*, Vol. I, pp. 56–57; The British Statement on Acts of Violence, *Cmd.* 6873, 1946; also Fisher, S. N. *The Middle East*, Routledge and Kegan Paul, 1960, p. 579; Kirk, G. *The Middle East 1945–1950*, Oxford Univ. Press, London, 1954, pp. 209–213 and 218–223.

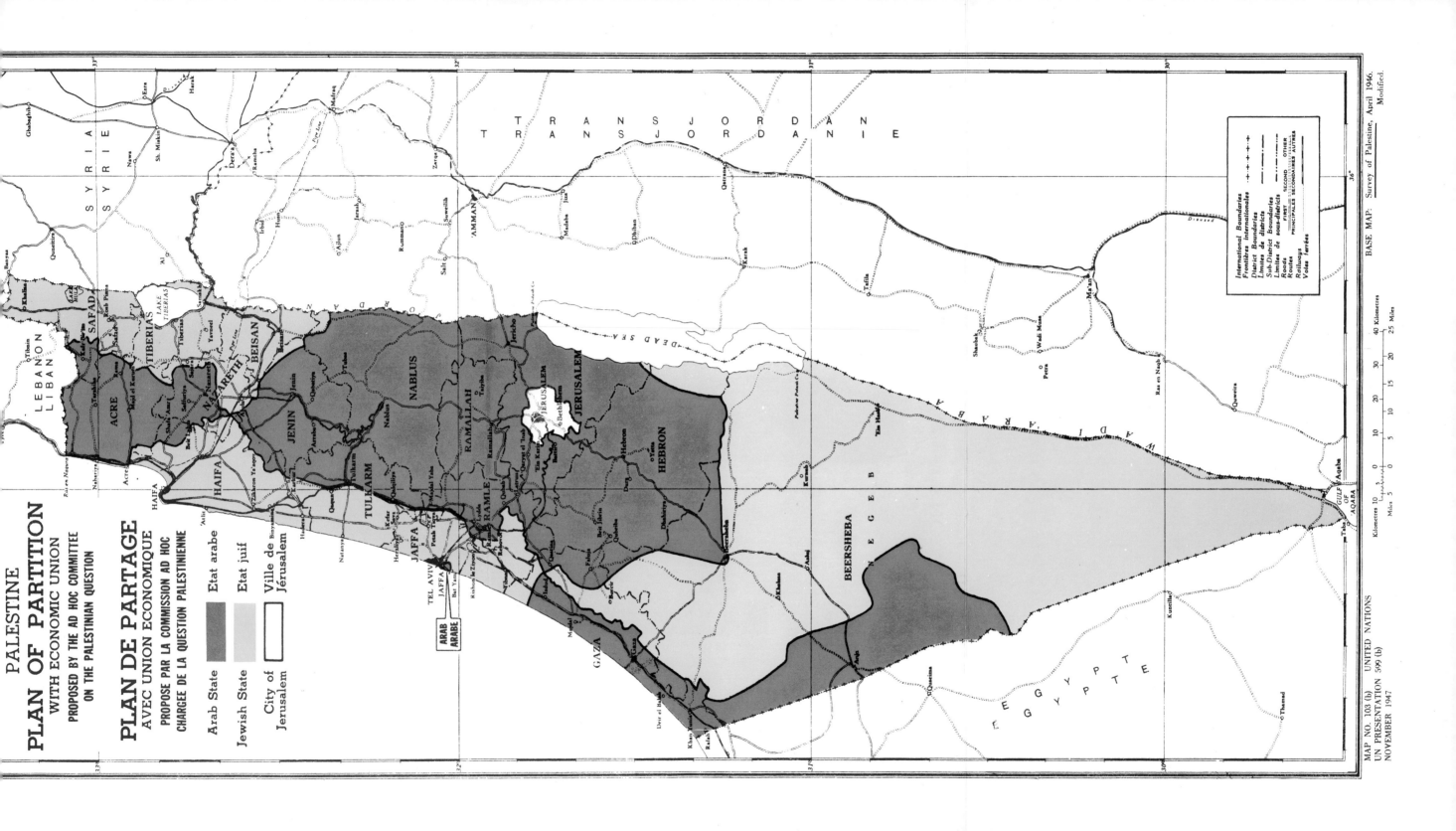

PALESTINE
PLAN OF PARTITION
WITH ECONOMIC UNION
PROPOSED BY THE AD HOC COMMITTEE
ON THE PALESTINIAN QUESTION

PLAN DE PARTAGE
AVEC UNION ECONOMIQUE
PROPOSE PAR LA COMMISSION AD HOC
CHARGEE DE LA QUESTION PALESTINIENNE

Arab State — Etat arabe

Jewish State — Etat juif

City of Jerusalem — Ville de Jérusalem

MAP NO. 103 (b)   UNITED NATIONS
UN PRESENTATION 599 (b)
NOVEMBER 1947

BASE MAP: Survey of Palestine, April 1946.
Modified.

International Boundaries — Frontières internationales
District Boundaries — Limites de districts
Sub-District Boundaries — Limites de sous-districts
Roads — Routes
Railways — Voies ferrées
FIRST — SECOND — OTHER
PRINCIPALES SECONDAIRES AUTRES

Federal State consisting of an Arab State and a Jewish State with Jerusalem as the capital.

The Arabs opposed the proposal to partition Palestine on the ground that it was incompatible with law and justice and the principles of democracy. They also questioned the competence of the UN to recommend the partition of Palestine. Their several requests to have these issues referred to the International Court of Justice were rejected.

The Zionists mobilised all their forces to secure a UN vote in favour of partition. They were able to enlist the support of President Truman, who put the weight of the US government in the balance in favour of partition. As a result, the General Assembly adopted on 29 November 1947, by a vote of 33 to 13 with 10 abstentions, a resolution for the partition of Palestine basically on the lines suggested by the majority report.[15]

In the view of the Arabs, the partition resolution was illegal and iniquitous.

The partition resolution was illegal because it constituted a trespass on the sovereignty of the original inhabitants. It gave away to alien immigrants a large part of the territory of the country and it denied to the Palestinians the exercise of their natural right of self-determination.

The partition resolution was also iniquitous, both in terms of population and in terms of land ownership.

In terms of population, the Jews constituted in 1947 less than one-third of the inhabitants of Palestine. Only one-tenth of them were part of the original inhabitants and these—consisting of Arabic-speaking and strictly Orthodox Jews—did not favour partition nor the establishment of a Jewish State. The rest of the Jews were foreign immigrants.[16] Thus, in effect, the partition resolution meant that foreign immigrants could break up the territorial integrity of the country in which they came to live and appropriate a part of its territory in order to set up a State of their own. The incongruity of the partition of Palestine becomes more striking when it is realised that even in the Jewish State as proposed by the UN the majority of the inhabitants were Arabs : 509,780 Arabs as compared with 499,020 Jews.[17]

In terms of ownership of land—exclusive of urban property—the Palestine Government's village statistics show that the Jews owned in 1945 only 1,491,699 *dunoms*[18] of land out of a total area of 26,323,023 *dunoms* for the whole of Palestine.[19]

Jewish land ownership thus represented a proportion of 5·66% of the total area of the country. In effect, the partition plan adopted by the UN meant that the Jews, who owned about 6% of the land, were given almost two-thirds of the country, i.e., a territory which was almost ten times the area owned by them. The distribution of land ownership between Arabs and Jews by sub-districts in Palestine is shown in UN map No. 94 (b) of August 1950.

The partition resolution was received by a wave of protests and demonstrations on the Arab side, jubilation on the part of Zionist Jews and consternation on the part of Orthodox Jews. The British Government decided

---

[15] Resolution 181 (II).

[16] See Government of Palestine, *Statistical Abstract*, 1944–1945, p. 42.

[17] Report of Sub-Committee 2 to the Ad Hoc Committee on the Palestinian Question, UN Document A/AC 14/32, 11 November 1947, Official Records of the 2nd session of the General Assembly, Ad Hoc Committee, 1947, p. 291.

[18] One *dunom* equals one thousand square metres. Four dunoms equal approximately one acre.

[19] Appendix VI to the Report of Sub-Committee 2 to the Ad Hoc Committee on the Palestinian Question, UN Document A/AC 14/32, 11 November 1947, p. 270.

EXTRACTS FROM VILLAGE STATISTICS
OF THE GOVERNMENT OF PALESTINE
(as at 1 April 1945, Summary for Palestine)

Areas in *dunoms*. 1 *dunom* = 1,000 sq. metres = 0·2471 acres

	Arabs	Jews	Total Public	Others	Roads, rail-ways, rivers & lakes	Total
SUB-DISTRICT						
GALILEE DISTRICT						
Acre	695,694	24,997	74,705	1,481	2,786	799,663
Beisan	159,812	124,755	73,070	184	9,266	367,087
Nazareth	258,616	137,382	88,354	4,429	8,752	497,533
Safad	474,973	121,488	91,500	7	8,163	696,131
Tiberias	226,441	167,406	33,122	5,085	8,915	440,969
Total	1,815,536	576,028	360,751	11,186	37,882	2,801,383
HAIFA DISTRICT						
Haifa	434,666	364,276	179,616	24,766	28,431	1,031,755
SAMARIA DISTRICT						
Jenin	701,965	4,251	126,179	73	2,746	835,214
Nablus	1,383,466	15	184,872	19,691	3,674	1,591,718
Tulkarm	650,646	141,361	27,257	15	16,081	835,360
Total	2,736,077	145,627	338,308	19,779	22,501	3,262,292
JERUSALEM DISTRICT						
Hebron	1,984,434	6,132	82,571	1,154	1,894	2,076,185
Jerusalem	1,326,571	33,401	146,361	55,765	8,687	1,570,785
Ramallah	681,996	146	2,569	489	1,364	686,564
Total	3,993,001	39,679	231,501	57,408	11,945	4,333,534
LYDDA DISTRICT						
Jaffa	158,413	129,439	11,981	16,917	18,616	335,366
Ramleh	670,392	122,159	47,380	11,640	18,621	870,192
Total	828,805	251,598	59,361	28,557	37,237	1,205,558
GAZA DISTRICT						
(Excl. Beersheba S/D)						
Gaza	830,314	49,260	206,196	349	25,382	1,111,501
Grand Total	10,638,399	1,426,468	1,375,733	142,045	163,378	13,746,023
Beersheba	1,936,375	65,231	10,574,925	5	464	12,577,000
Grand Total for Palestine	12,574,774	1,491,699	11,950,658	142,050	163,842	26,323,023

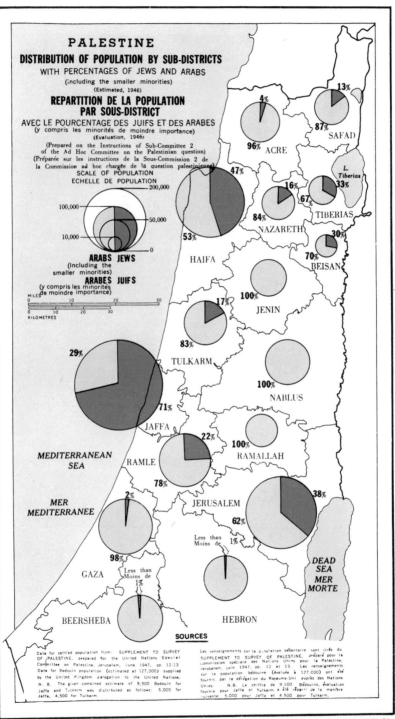

PALESTINE

DISTRIBUTION OF POPULATION BY SUB-DISTRICTS
WITH PERCENTAGES OF JEWS AND ARABS
(including the smaller minorities)
(Estimated, 1946)

REPARTITION DE LA POPULATION
PAR SOUS-DISTRICT
AVEC LE POURCENTAGE DES JUIFS ET DES ARABES
(y compris les minorités de moindre importance)
(Evaluation, 1946)

(Prepared on the Instructions of Sub-Committee 2
of the Ad Hoc Committee on the Palestinian question)
(Préparée sur les instructions de la Sous-Commission 2 de
la Commission ad hoc chargée de la question palestinienne)

SCALE OF POPULATION
ECHELLE DE POPULATION

200,000

100,000

50,000

10,000

0

ARABS JEWS
(Including the
smaller minorities)
ARABES JUIFS
(y compris les minorités
de moindre importance)

MILES
0   10   20   30

0   10   20   30
KILOMETRES

SAFAD 13% 87%

ACRE 4% 96%

HAIFA 47% 53%

L. Tiberias 33%

TIBERIAS 16% 84% 67%

NAZARETH

BEISAN 30% 70%

JENIN 17% 83% 100%

TULKARM 29% 71%

NABLUS 100%

JAFFA

RAMLE 22% 78% 2%

RAMALLAH 100%

JERUSALEM 38% 62% Less than / Moins de 1%

MEDITERRANEAN
SEA

MER
MEDITERRANEE

GAZA 98% Less than / Moins de 1%

BEERSHEBA

HEBRON

DEAD
SEA
MER
MORTE

SOURCES

Data for settled population from: SUPPLEMENT TO SURVEY
OF PALESTINE, prepared for the United Nations Special
Committee on Palestine, Jerusalem, June 1947, pp. 12-13
Data for Bedouin population (estimated at 127,000) supplied
by the United Kingdom delegation to the United Nations.
N. B. The given combined estimate of 9,500 Bedouin for
Jaffa and Tulkarm was distributed as follows: 5,000 for
Jaffa, 4,500 for Tulkarm.

Les renseignements sur la population sédentaire sont tirés du
SUPPLEMENT TO SURVEY OF PALESTINE, préparé pour la
Commission spéciale des Nations Unies pour la Palestine,
Jerusalem, juin 1947, pp. 12 et 13. Les renseignements
sur la population bédouine (évaluée à 127,000) ont été
fournis par la délégation du Royaume-Uni auprès des Nations
Unies. N.B. Le chiffre de 9,500 Bédouins, évaluation
fournie pour Jaffa et Tulkarm a été réparti de la manière
suivante: 5,000 pour Jaffa et 4,500 pour Tulkarm.

to terminate the mandate and to withdraw from Palestine by the middle of May 1948. With the decision of the mandatory power to withdraw without setting up in its own place some machinery of government for the maintenance of law and order, the explosion of an armed conflict between Arabs and Jews became unavoidable.

For this conflict, Arabs and Jews were differently and unevenly prepared. The Arab objective was to oppose partition by all means; but in their case these means were more in the nature of words and speeches than of acts. The Jews, on the other hand, acted more than they talked. They mobilised their secret paramilitary organisations, which counted more than 100,000 trained fighting men. They carefully planned the taking over of the country. Their objectives, as became clear from the unfolding of events, were twofold : one territorial and the other racist.

Seizure of Arab Territory

The territorial objective aimed at the seizure of as much of the land of Palestine as the Jews could lay hands upon, regardless of the geographical limits set upon the proposed Jewish State by the partition resolution. In furtherance of this aim and taking advantage of their superior military preparation and organisation, the Jews seized before and after the end of the mandate a considerable part of the territory of Palestine, including a number of wholly Arab cities, towns and villages.[20] The areas which the Jews seized in 1948 and 1949 amounted to 20,850 square kilometres[21] out of the 26,323 square kilometres constituting the total area of Palestine. The total area which thus fell under Israeli control amounted to almost 80% of the territory of Palestine. The Arabs, on their part, were left with one-fifth of their homeland.

Forcible Displacement of the Arabs

The second Jewish objective was to free the territory of the proposed Jewish state of its Arab inhabitants who, if allowed to remain, would have constituted the majority of its population. In other words, the Jews wanted what the UN partition resolution did not give them, namely, the land without its people. This, in the Zionist creed, was necessary in order to ensure the creation in Palestine of a state that would be racially, religiously and exclusively Jewish. Maxime Rodinson has observed that the Jewish character of the State is 'the prime aim and postulate of Zionist ideology'.[22] Dr. John H. Davis, former Commissioner-General of the UN Relief and Works Agency for Palestine Refugees in the Near East (UNRWA), has said that 'the extent to which the refugees were savagely driven out by the Israelis as part of a deliberate master-plan has been insufficiently recognized'.[23] The unique nature of the Palestine conflict was described by Sir John Glubb in the following words :

'It is quite essential vividly to grasp the unique conditions of the struggle in Palestine. We have witnessed many wars in this century in which one country seeks to impose its power on others. But in no war, I think, for many centuries

[20] See the chronology of events preceding the end of the mandate in *The Middle East Journal*, Washington, DC, 1948, Vol. 2, pp. 215–221 and 329–332.
[21] Israel Government, *Government Year-Book*, English edition, 5712 (1951/1952), p. 315.
[22] Rodinson, Maxime. *Israel and the Arabs*, Penguin Books, London, 1968, p. 228.
[23] Davis, John H. *The Evasive Peace*, John Murray, London, 1968, pp. 57–60.

past, has the objective been to remove a nation from its country and to introduce another and entirely different race to occupy its lands, houses and cities and live there. This peculiarity lends to the Palestine struggle a desperate quality which bears no resemblance to any other war in modern history.'[24]

In order to achieve their objective, the Jews turned against the Arab civilian population the terrorist machine which they had developed and perfected in their campaign of violence against the British in Palestine in connection with the White Paper of 1939. The chronology of events in Palestine during the six months preceding the end of the mandate reads like a horror story.[25]

Outstanding in savagery among the outrages of Jewish terrorism was the massacre on 9 April 1948 of almost all the villagers of Deir Yassin, a small peaceful village on the outskirts of Jerusalem. An account of this horrible deed was given by Jacques de Reynier, the chief delegate of the International Red Cross who visited the village and witnessed the aftermath of the tragedy.[26] 'Three hundred persons,' he said, 'were massacred . . . without any military reason nor provocation of any kind, old men, women, children, newly-born were savagely assassinated with grenades and knives by Jewish troops of the Irgun, perfectly under the control and direction of their chiefs'.[27] The objective behind the Deir Yassin massacre was achieved, with disastrous results : it led to the Palestine Arab exodus of 1948.

Where terrorism did not succeed in driving away the Arab inhabitants, the Jews resorted to actual expulsion, as in Haifa,[28] Lydda and Ramleh[29], Tiberias,[30] Safad,[31] Beersheba and several other towns and villages.[32]

The number of Palestinians displaced in 1948 has been variously estimated at between 750,000 and one million persons. At the time that UNWRA was constituted in 1950, their number was put at 960,000.[33]

Plunder of Arab Refugee Property

The Israelis consummated the tragedy of the refugees by seizing and taking over all their property. This was one of the greatest plunders in the history of Palestine. The contents of whole cities, towns and villages, hundreds of thousands of homes, thousands of shops, were seized and robbed in 1948. In a report dated 18 April 1949 the Israeli Custodian of Absentee Property stated that 'the Arabs abandoned great quantities of property in hundreds of thousands of dwellings, shops, store houses and workshops . . . placing the . . . victorious community before serious material temptation'.[34]

The looting and plunder were not confined to movables and personal

---

[24] Pasha, Glubb. *The Middle East Crisis,* Hodder and Stoughton, London, 1967, p. 41.
[25] See *The Middle East Journal, op. cit.,* pp. 215–221 and 329–332.
[26] Reynier, Jacques de. *A Jerusalem un Drapeau flottait sur la Ligne de feu,* Editions de la Baconnière, Neuchatel, Switzerland, 1950.
[27] Translation from Reynier, *op. cit.,* p. 213.
[28] *The Middle East Journal, op. cit.,* 1949, p. 325.
[29] In Lydda and Ramleh 60,000 persons were expelled by the Israelis; Kirk, G. *op. cit.,* p. 282.
[30] *The Middle East Journal, op. cit.,* 1948, p. 331.
[31] *Ibid.,* p. 332.
[32] Fisher, S. N., *op. cit.,* p. 589.
[33] Annual Report of the Director of UNWRA, 1953 (A/2470), p. 5.
[34] Peretz, Don. *Israel and the Palestine Arabs,* The Middle East Institute, Washington, D.C., 1958, p. 148.

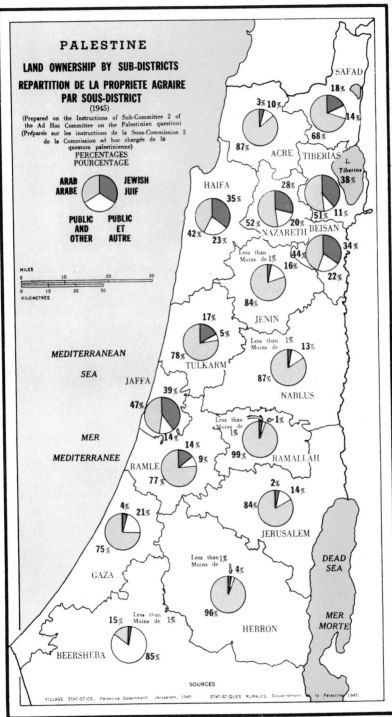

PALESTINE

LAND OWNERSHIP BY SUB-DISTRICTS

REPARTITION DE LA PROPRIETE AGRAIRE PAR SOUS-DISTRICT

(1945)

(Prepared on the Instructions of Sub-Committee 2 of the Ad Hoc Committee on the Palestinian question)
(Préparée sur les instructions de la Sous-Commission 2 de la Commission ad hoc chargée de la question palestinienne)

PERCENTAGES
POURCENTAGE

ARAB   JEWISH
ARABE   JUIF

PUBLIC   PUBLIC
AND   ET
OTHER   AUTRE

MILES
0   10   20   30
0   10   20   30
KILOMETRES

SAFAD
18%
14%
68%

3% 10%
87%
ACRE

TIBERIAS
L. Tiberias
38%

HAIFA
35%
42% 23%

28%
52% 20%
NAZARETH

51% 11%
BEISAN

Less than Moins de 1%
44%
16%
84%
34%
22%

17%
5%
78%
TULKARM
JENIN

Less than 1%
Moins de
13%
87%
NABLUS

MEDITERRANEAN
SEA

JAFFA
39%
47%
14%

MER
MEDITERRANEE

14%
9%
RAMLE
77%

Less than Moins de 1%
1%
99%
RAMALLAH

2% 14%
84%
JERUSALEM

4% 21%
75%
GAZA

Less than 1%
Moins de
4%
96%
HEBRON

DEAD
SEA

MER
MORTE

15%
Less than Moins de 1%
BEERSHEBA
85%

SOURCES

VILLAGE STATISTICS, Palestine Government, Jerusalem, 1945.   STATISTIQUES RURALES, Gouvernement de la Palestine 1945.

MAP NO 94 (b) UNITED NATIONS   UN PRESENTATION 574 (b)
AUGUST 1950

possessions. All immovable property of the refugees—whether lands or build-ings—was seized, confiscated or expropriated. The confiscation of Arab land extended even to the holdings of those Palestinians who remained under Israeli occupation. They were dispossessed of 80% of their land holdings.

END OF THE MANDATE

The Mandate for Palestine ended in chaos on 14 May 1948. Its principal result was that it had enabled the introduction and implantation in Pales-tine of an alien people who as a well-organised and militant group were determined to wrest the country from its indigenous inhabitants.

On the day on which the mandate ended the Jews proclaimed the State of Israel and formed a provisional government which was instantly recognised by the US government and three days later by Soviet Russia. There-upon military hostilities commenced between the new state and four neigh-bouring Arab states, namely, Egypt, Transjordan, Syria and Lebanon. The Arab states put into the field 'four armies with no central command, no concerted aim, and no serious and sustained will to win' to face the Israelis, who had proceeded with a total mobilisation of their manpower on modern lines.[35] The Arab armies which then moved into Palestine represented what in fact were token forces, a total of about 20,000 men.[36] As to the Palestinians, they had been systematically disarmed by the mandatory government during the mandate, on account of their opposition to Jewish immigration, and thousands of them had been sentenced by special military courts to long terms of imprisonment, and even to death, for the possession or the carrying of firearms.

On 22 May 1948 the Security Council issued an order of cease-fire and on 29 May called for a truce. Count Bernadotte, who had been appointed as UN Mediator for Palestine, arranged for a month's truce. On the expira-tion of this period, hostilities broke out again and continued until a second truce of indefinite duration came into force on 18 July 1948. The Palestine war of 1948 was concluded by four Armistice Agreements signed between Israel and Egypt, Lebanon, Transjordan and Syria. Armistice lines were delineated 'without prejudice to rights, claims and positions of either Party to the Armistice as regards ultimate settlement of the Palestine Question'.

UN PEACE-MAKING EFFORTS

As a result of the momentous events of 1948 the Palestine problem assumed new dimensions. The partition resolution, unjust and iniquitous as it was, had gone with the wind and a far more unjust and iniquitous situation had been created : a Zionist racist state (which had nothing in common with the Jewish State envisaged by the UN partition resolution) had emerged and was determined to maintain itself by force of arms. 80% of the area of Palestine was occupied by the Israelis and only an insignificant part of its territory was left to its original inhabitants. One million Palestinians were uprooted from their homes, their possessions plundered and their lands confiscated, and were turned overnight into refugees condemned to live in conditions of misery and destitution.

[35] Hourani, Albert. Arab Refugees and the Future of Israel, *The Listener*, 28 July 1949; Thicknesse, S. G. *Arab Refugees*, Royal Institute of International Affairs, London, 1949, p. 2.
[36] For an account of the Palestine war, see O'Ballance, Edgar. *The Arab-Israeli War*, 1948, Faber and Faber, London, 1956.

The UN, being largely responsible for this tragic situation, made efforts to restore peace, and a semblance of justice, in Palestine.

On 11 December 1948 the General Assembly adopted a resolution which provided that 'the refugees wishing to return to their homes and live at peace with their neighbours should be permitted to do so at the earliest practicable date, and that compensation should be paid for the property of those choosing not to return and for loss of, or damage to, property which, under principles of international law or in equity, should be made good by the Governments or authorities responsible'.[37] Although this resolution has been annually reaffirmed by the UN, Israel has completely ignored it and has refused to allow the repatriation of the refugees.

The UN also envisaged the settlement of the Palestine Question by means of conciliation. On 14 May 1948 Count Folke Bernadotte was entrusted with this function, but he was unable to secure any agreement between the parties and his peace mission was cut short by his assassination by Jewish terrorists in Jerusalem on 17 September 1948.

Following the Mediator's assassination, the General Assembly entrusted his functions to a Conciliation Commission which, on 12 May 1949, secured the signature of the parties to what has since been called the Lausanne Protocol. In accordance with the Lausanne Protocol, the UN partition plan was to be taken as the basis for discussion. However, the Commission's conciliation efforts failed because Israel refused to permit the repatriation of the refugees and refused also to give up any of the territories which it had seized, even though they fell outside the geographical limits of the Jewish state as defined by the partition resolution.

TWENTY YEARS OF TENSION

The situation created in Palestine in 1948 was provocative and explosive. Border incidents were frequent. Israel's policy from the outset was to impose itself by force and fear and to cow the neighbouring Arab states by massive raids, attacks and reprisals. While not a single Arab state was condemned for any aggression against Israel in violation of the Armistice agreements, the latter was condemned for more than 40 aggressions perpetrated against the Arab states in flagrant violation of these agreements. Thirty-four of these condemnations were pronounced by the Security Council. They include Israel's condemnations for its attacks on Huleh (1953), Qibya (1953), Nahalin (1954), Gaza (1955), the Syrian outpost on Lake Tiberias (1955), the Gaza Strip and the Sinai Peninsula (1956), the Syrian villages in the Lake Tiberias area (1960 and 1962), Samou' village (1966), Karameh (1968), Salt (1968), Airport of Beirut (1968) and certain villages in Southern Lebanon (1969). Outstanding among those aggressions was the Israeli invasion in 1956 of the Gaza Strip and the Sinai Peninsula in breach of the Armistice Agreement with Egypt. This invasion assumed the proportions of a war in which France and England were also involved. It was only as a result of combined pressures by the UN, the USA and Soviet Russia that Israel was forced in 1957 to withdraw from the territories which it had occupied.

AGGRAVATION OF THE PALESTINE PROBLEM IN 1967

Ten years later Israel went to war again and invaded the territories of three of its neighbours in breach of the Armistice agreements of 1949. After dis-

[37] UN Document A/810.

156

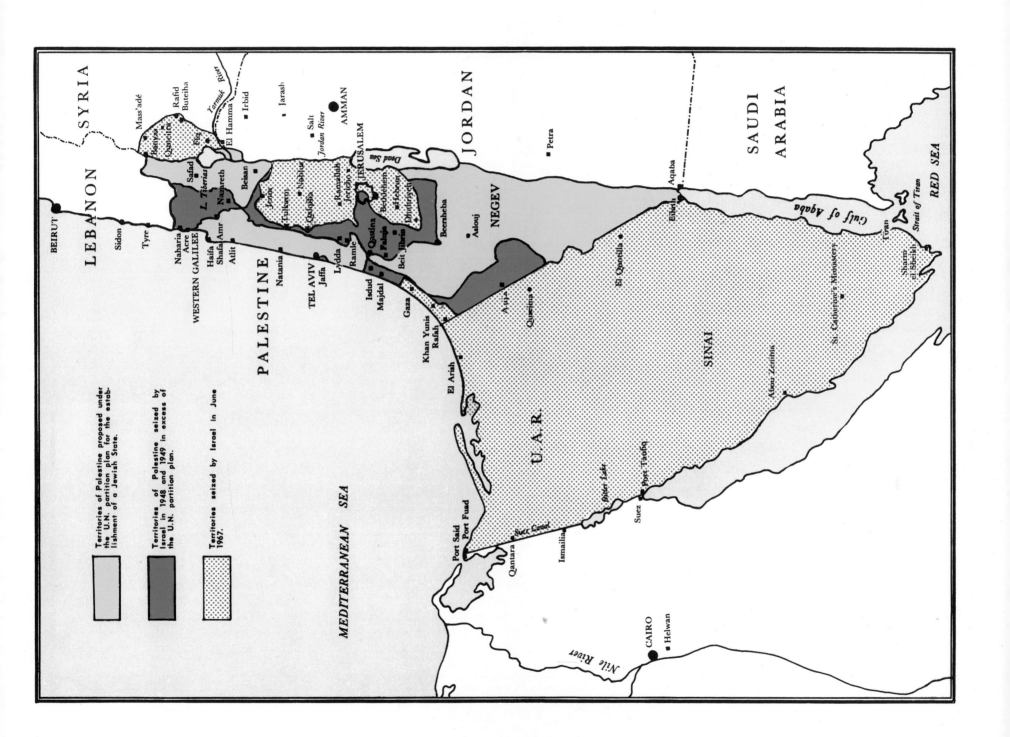

Territories of Palestine proposed under the U.N. partition plan for the establishment of a Jewish State.

Territories of Palestine seized by Israel in 1948 and 1949 in excess of the U.N. partition plan.

Territories seized by Israel in June 1967.

SYRIA

LEBANON

BEIRUT
Sidon
Tyre

Mass'adé
Rafid
Buteiha
Irbid
Jarash
Salt
Jordan River
AMMAN

JORDAN

Petra

SAUDI ARABIA

RED SEA

Yarmuk River
El Hamma

Banyas
Qoneitra
Fiq

Safad
L. Tiberias
Nazareth
Beisan

Naharia
Acre
Haifa
Shafa Amr
Atlit

WESTERN GALILEE

PALESTINE

Natania

TEL AVIV
Jaffa
Lydda
Ramle

Nablus
Qalqilya
Tulkarm
Jenin

Ramallah
Jericho
JERUSALEM
Bethlehem
Hebron
Dhahiriyeh

Qastina
Faluja
Beit Jibrin

Beersheba

Aslouj

NEGEV

Eilat
Aqaba

Gulf of Aqaba

Tiran
Strait of Tiran

Isdud
Majdal
Gaza

Khan Yunis
Rafah

El Arish

Arja
Quseima

El Qantila

Sharm el Sheikh

SINAI

St. Catherine's Monastery

Abou Zenina

U.A.R.

Port Said
Port Fuad
Qantara
Ismailia
Suez Canal
Bitter Lake
Suez
Port Taofiq

MEDITERRANEAN SEA

Nile River
CAIRO
Helwan

abling the Egyptian and Syrian air forces in a surprise attack launched on the morning of 5 June 1967, it invaded and occupied the Old City of Jerusalem, the Western Bank of Jordan, the Gaza Strip, the Sinai Desert and the Golan region of Syria. Four cease-fire orders were issued by the Security Council, but the fighting stopped only after Israel had achieved its territorial objectives.

The causes of this last conflict are the subject of dispute. According to the Israeli view, Israel started the war as a preventive measure, in self-defence against Arab threats. According to the Arab view, Israel engaged in a war of aggression and expansion. Charles W. Yost has advanced a third explanation, namely, that 'no government plotted or intended to start a war in the spring of 1967. . . .'[38]

If there exists a dispute about the causes of the war, none exists about the fact that it has seriously aggravated the Palestine problem. This aggravation can be viewed from three angles.

First, the basic Palestine problem has been aggravated in several respects, namely, by Israel's occupation of the remaining parts of Palestine (the West Bank and the Gaza Strip), by the displacement of several hundred thousand more refugees,[39] by the annexation of the Old City of Jerusalem and its Holy Places, by the subjection of one million Palestinians in the occupied territories to domination and oppression, and last, but not least, by the growth of Israel's expansionist and annexationist appetite as a result of its military success.

Secondly, by its occupation of the territories of three Arab states, Israel has now added to the original Palestine problem another conflict of a territorial nature, this time between itself and three of its neighbours. This territorial enlargement of the conflict carries unfathomable consequences by reason of Israel's declared intention to remain in occupation of the areas which it has seized until the Arab states agree to conclude a peace on Israel's terms and conditions, in direct negotiations.

Thirdly, by reason of the involvement of Soviet Russia and the USA in the Arab-Israeli conflict, the problem has assumed international significance. This widening in the dimensions of the conflict is the result of the conflicting attitudes adopted by these two great powers following the last war. In June 1967 Soviet Russia asked the UN for the condemnation of Israel's aggression and for the immediate withdrawal of its forces behind the armistice lines. The US government opposed Israel's condemnation and urged the conclusion of peace between Israel and the Arab states through 'negotiated arrangements' on the basis of the recognition of Israel's boundaries'. As a result of the division between the USA and Soviet Russia, the UN was paralysed and the practical result was a reward to aggression.

Contrary to Israel's expectations, the war which it launched on 5 June 1967 did not solve the Palestine problem nor enable the Israelis to impose on the Arabs a peace on their own terms. On the contrary, the last Israeli aggression released the Palestinian forces of resistance which for 20 years had been contained by illusions and by faith in UN resolutions. This has led to the emergence of a new military and political factor which is likely to shape the future evolution of the conflict in the Middle East.

[38] Yost, Charles W. The Arab-Israeli War : How it Began, *Foreign Affairs*, Vol. 46, No. 2, January 1968, p. 319.

[39] The Government of Jordan has estimated that the Palestinians displaced as a result of the 1967 conflict numbered 410,000 persons, some of whom were refugees of 1948. The total number of Palestinian refugees since 1948, taking into account those who are not registered with UNRWA, now exceeds 1,800,000.

Security Council's Resolution of 22 November 1967

Faced with a deteriorating situation, the Security Council adopted on 22 November 1967 a resolution which aimed at the establishment of ' a just and lasting peace' in the Middle East. This resolution emphasised the inadmissibility of the acquisition of territory by war and affirmed the necessity for the withdrawal of Israeli armed forces from territories occupied in the recent conflict, the termination of all claims or states of belligerency, the acknowledgement of the sovereignty, territorial integrity and political independence of every state in the area and their right to live in peace within secure and recognised boundaries, free from threats or acts of force. The resolution further affirmed the necessity for guaranteeing freedom of navigation through international waterways in the area and for achieving a just settlement of the refugee problem.

More than two years have elapsed and no progress towards peace has been achieved. Dr. Gunnar Jarring who was appointed by the Secretary-General of the UN to promote a settlement under the terms of the resolution met with no success in his mission. As a result, the four great powers—the USA, Soviet Russia, France and the UK—decided early in 1969 to consult together on how they could bring about a peaceful settlement on the basis of the resolution. However, these consultations have until now proved sterile. Although unanimous in 1967 in their adoption of the resolution, the great powers are now divided about its interpretation.

In the summer of 1970 Dr. Gunnar Jarring's mission was reactivated as a result of the acceptance by Egypt, Jordan and Israel of an American peace initiative which came to be described as the Rogers Plan and which envisaged a temporary cease-fire and the holding of peace negotiations under the auspices of Dr. Gunnar Jarring on the basis of the Security Council's resolution of 1967. The Palestinians, however, denounced the Rogers Plan and the Security Council's resolution on which it is based as an attempt to settle the conflict over their heads and in disregard of their rights. Thus the difficult process of peace-making has started again but, in the view of the Palestinians who are the people most concerned, this process has taken a wrong direction for it seeks to by-pass the root cause of the conflict.

Peace Without Justice?

Despite its positive aspects the Security Council's resolution suffers from one inherent deficiency : it seeks to put an end to the conflict without settling, or even attempting to settle, its root cause : the Palestine problem. What does the resolution offer by way of redress for the succession of wrongs done to the people of Palestine since 1947? It offers a return to the armistice lines that existed prior to 5 June 1967. However, a return to those armistice lines would only settle the aftermath of the last armed conflict but would not settle the Palestine problem. As has already been observed, the armistice lines of 1949 left only one-fifth of the area of their homeland to the Palestinians. The resolution also contains towards its end, and almost by way of an afterthought, a statement about 'achieving a just solution of the refugee problem'. Does such a vague statement offer a redress of the wrongs done in Palestine? The question is not simply or wholly a refugee problem. The issues involved are deeper and more fundamental and are not solved by being ignored. Basically the question concerns the uprooting of the people of Palestine and the usurpation of their homeland by an alien people. In

158

November 1967 it might have seemed to the Security Council that it could dismiss the Palestine question as 'a refugee problem'. Today this is not possible. Palestinian resistance has asserted the legitimate rights not only of the refugees, but of the Palestinian nation and the Security Council's resolution, inadequate as it is, can be considered to have been surpassed by events.

The great powers by their support of the Balfour Declaration, and the UN by its resolution for the partition of Palestine, have created the Palestine problem. This problem, seriously aggravated in 1967, is still entire and unresolved. Its peaceful solution is not in sight. No possibility exists of its settlement by agreement between the parties, for the obvious reason that the Israelis will not give up—except by coercion—what they have seized in 1948, 1949 and 1967. Likewise, no possibility of its settlement seems to exist at the hands of the UN and the great powers. Until now the UN, apart from the adoption of resolutions, has shown no readiness to resort to their enforcement. As to the great powers, they have shown more concern for the restoration of peace than for the restoration of justice. Peace without justice is illusory. And justice requires the undoing of many things which were done and the redress of many wrongs which were committed in Palestine. This is, in essence, the Palestine problem, which has convulsed the Middle East and will continue to convulse this area, and possibly the whole world, until it receives a solution consistent with right and justice.

FURTHER READING

Barbour, Nevill. *Nisi Dominus*, Harrap, London, 1946, reprinted by Institute for Palestine Studies, Beirut, 1969.

Burns, E. L. M. *Between Arab and Israeli*, Harrap, London, 1962; Astor-Honor, New York, 1963.

Cattan, Henry. *Palestine, The Arabs and Israel*, Longmans, London, 1969.

Davis, John H. *The Evasive Peace*, John Murray, London, 1968.

Esco Foundation for Palestine, Palestine: *A Study of Jewish, Arab and British Policies*, 2 Vols. New Haven, 1947.

Glubb, Lt.-General Sir J. B. *The Middle East Crisis*, Hodder and Stoughton, London, 1967.

Hadawi, Sami. *Bitter Harvest*, New World Press, New York, 1967.

Halderman, John W. *The Middle East Crisis: Test of International Law*, Oceana, Dobbs Ferry, New York, 1969.

Hodgkin, E. C. *The Arabs*, Oxford Univ. Press, London and New York, 1966.

Hurewitz, J. C. *The Struggle for Palestine*, Greenwood, New York, 1968.

Hutchison, E. H. *Violent Truce*, Devin-Adair, New York, 1956.

Jiryis, Sabri. *The Arabs in Israel*, Institute for Palestine Studies, Beirut, 1968.

Laqueur, Walter. *The Israeli-Arab Reader*, Weidenfeld and Nicolson, London, 1969.

Marlowe, John. *The Seat of Pilate, An Account of the Palestine Mandate*, Cresset, London, 1959; Dufour, Philadelphia, 1958.

Menuhin, Moshe. *The Decadence of Judaism in our Time*, Institute for Palestine Studies, Beirut, 1969.

Nutting, Anthony. *The Arabs*, Hollis and Carter, London, 1964.

Peretz, Don. *Israel and the Palestine Arabs*, The Middle East Institute, Washington, 1958.

Rizk, Edward. *The Palestine Question*, Seminar of Arab Jurists on Palestine, Algiers, 1967; Institute for Palestine Studies, Beirut, 1968.

Rodinson, Maxime. *Israel and the Arabs*, Penguin Books, Harmondsworth, 1968; Pantheon, New York, 1969.

Storrs, Ronald. *Orientations*, Nicholson and Watson, London, 1945.

Taylor, A. R. *Prelude to Israel*, Philosophical Library, New York, 1959.

Von Horn, Carl. *Soldiering For Peace*, Cassell, London, 1966.

Weizmann, Chaim. *Trial and Error*, Hamish Hamilton, London, 1949; Schocken, NewYork, 1966.

HENRY CATTAN. An international lawyer, he has practised in his native Palestine and in Syria. One-time lecturer at the Jerusalem Law School and until 1948 a member of the Palestine Law Council. Represented the Palestine Arab case at the second special session of the General Assembly of the UN and at the two ordinary sessions of the General Assembly 1947 and 1948. Arab League expert in connection with UN Mediation on Palestine 1948. Author of *The Law of Oil Concessions* (1967), *The Evolution of Oil Concessions in the Middle East and North Africa* (1967) and *Palestine, the Arabs and Israel* (1969).

THE JEWS AND THE MIDDLE EAST

BARNET LITVINOFF

THE region that is now generally designated as the Middle East encompasses many different peoples to make a tapestry of immense and frequently violent contrast. But one thing all these peoples have in common : their tendency throughout history to spread across the globe. The Greeks had a word for this condition of dispersal—Diaspora—and although it has been most usually associated with the Jewish situation, it can with equal truth be applied to the other peoples whose national identity originated in this area. Arabs, Armenians, Kurds, Christian and Muslim denominations of various kinds, all availed themselves of the waterways and land-routes conveniently accessible in the Middle East to escape annihilation, enslavement or assimilation as one conquest followed another, and empires rose and fell.

Thus all these peoples were sustained by a core that was able to elude the fate frequently suffered by other tribes throughout the world—in North and South America for example, and in Africa and Australia, where foreign occupation led to the extinction of the native races or to their subjection. As a consequence, the peoples of the Middle East fulfilled a strongly individualistic role in history. In the course of their migrations they exported their culture and religion to influence the thought and development of their host communities, which themselves became partly or wholly identified with the faiths emanating from the lands of the eastern Mediterranean; and because they retained from afar their own links with their places of origin they gave to the Middle East its unique location in the heart and mind of western man. Furthermore, these links were so powerful that they ensured the survival of the identity of the wanderers despite centuries of exile in remote parts.

The Middle East, therefore, has remained obstinately heterogeneous. Movements of national determination, while employing the instruments of modern politics for their fulfilment, bring in their train conflicts based upon ancient arguments concerned less with physical possession than with intellectual and emotional attitudes.

And just as, say, the Armenians have drawn the nourishment that ensured their survival from one small territory within this great area, so that throughout their dispersion they conserved their specific personality in terms of language and culture, the Jews too have remained largely what they were because of theirs. Judaism is exclusive to the Jews by reason of its being both a culture and a religion directly concerned with their national origin in the Holy Land (Canaan), their return there after exile, their identity with it during deportation, and because of God's promise that their ultimate permanent restoration there would accompany the Messianic transformation of the world into a place of universal justice and eternal peace—the way He intended it before the Fall. Judaism says all this in Hebrew, the language in which He is presumed to have spoken to Adam and Eve, and in which the Law and the Prophecies were written. The Hebrew equivalent of the term Diaspora is *Galuth*, which invests the idea of population dispersal with stultifying characteristics: a ghetto of the mind as well as of place, an inability to speculate in ideas, and a failure to live sincerely and fully as a Jew.

How real is this doctrine to the Jews of the present day? Can it have relevance within an immediate context, when nearly half the people live in the USA, and most of the rest have happily adapted to secular cultures wherever they are more or less permanently settled? The answer lies in the phenomenon of Jewish assimilation and revivalism. Throughout the ages there were many Jews for whom the doctrine commanded neither fascination nor obedience. They rejected it. The result has been the total assimilation of individuals and even complete communities. Had all the Jews subscribed to it all the time they would have been by now among the most numerous of nations, and the Return would no doubt have been achieved centuries ago.

It has never been possible to refute the philosophy of preparation for physical re-establishment in Palestine and still remain within the fold; a first generation might do so and resist extinction nevertheless, but its successors will succumb. For this philosophy was the very essence of the Jewish spirit. In this way all trace has been lost of vast numbers who were attracted to other cultures during the Roman Empire, in the rise of Islam, in the Empires of Turkey, Spain and France. The Jews recognisable as such today are the descendants of survivors from this constant process of assimilation (sometimes of course it was enforced).

Jewish identity is also fading in the world today. But always some are left to dream the ancient dream and carry its message of hope forward. It remains to be seen whether the re-establishment of the Jewish State after 2,000 years will bring about the complete disappearance of all who have denied themselves participation in it, or have been denied it by others.

The periods of Jewish revival have usually followed great catastrophes that the Jews would interpret as the apocalypse portending their redemption. These eruptions, which since the Middle Ages have been well documented, took place from earliest times, when periods of comparative tranquility and prosperity caused the Jews, they thought, to turn away from their God and forget their role as the 'chosen people'. The expulsion from Spain under Ferdinand and Isabella gave rise to the earliest of the modern messianic movements. During the next three centuries Jewry was in ferment, with pseudo-Messiahs who claimed supernatural capabilities gathering vast followings. On each occasion the restoration of Israel was looked upon as imminent. The most commanding personality of this kind was Sabbetai Zvi (1626–76), a Smyrna rabbi, who discovered his mission after the Thirty Years War and the massacre of East European Jews by the Ukrainian leader Bogdan Chmielnicki after 1648. The Sabbetaian movement gained the support of Jewish communities everywhere. It embraced the two branches of the people, Ashkenazim and Sephardim, swept through Europe and the Orient, and affected even as detached an intellectual as Spinoza. In its various guises it survived almost to our own times, in the Orient with secret rites and apocryphal scriptures, and in the West with the spread of Hassidism.

Although the Messianic hope involved divine intervention in the affairs of man, it was no part of the belief that the work should be left to God alone.

The process of redemption could and should be accelerated by the Jews themselves; recognition that the age of miracles had returned demanded their participation in it. This gives the religious sanction to modern secular Zionism, rendering law subservient to Law, and the lesser morality to the greater. Thus it was that the extermination of millions during the Hitler régime in Germany brought about determined Zionist defiance of the rules of the British Mandatory Government regarding immigration into Palestine and the accompanying restrictions on the purchase of land. The rabbis actively helped the Zionist underground to reinforce the Jewish presence where previously rabbis were not enthusiastic supporters of secular Jewish nationalism, and frequently numbered among its bitterest opponents.

The dream of the restoration of Zion was sustained throughout the dispersion not only because of the faith of the Jews alone. The gentile world also ensured that it would remain as the living expression of God's plan for universal redemption. This was possibly because the fulfilment would demonstrate that the Jews had completed their expiation for their refusal to accept Christ, or perhaps to excuse the Europeans' own treatment of the Jews. Lord Macaulay, in his famous essay of 1831 condemning the civil disabilities of the Jews in Britain, quotes one of the opposing arguments from *The Times* newspaper. This described the Jews as a people living in temporary sojourn in the various countries of the world, and consequently disqualified from the full enjoyment of political and civil rights in them. Many held, as Milton wrote in *Paradise Regained*, that the Jews' eventual return to Palestine would precede their conversion to Christianity : otherwise they were condemned, in Pascal's words, to exist in eternal misery, 'captives without hope'.

We are concerned here with an inextinguishable nostalgic yearning that, despite the vicissitudes of the Jews, was never remote from the realm of practical politics. The belief in their impending restoration not only re-echoes in the words of poets and philosophers, but also of calculating statesmen. In 1655 when Menasseh ben Israel of Amsterdam presented his petition to Oliver Cromwell for the rescinding of the expulsion of the Jews from England ordered in 1290, he based his plan on a widely accepted assumption that the formal reconstitution of the community in England was necessary to complete the dispersion (the Lost Ten Tribes having been 'discovered' among the native inhabitants of America), and this was the essential prerequisite to the Messianic New Age and the repossession of the homeland. The idea received strengthened encouragement with the defeat of the Turks before Vienna in 1683, an event that foretold the ultimate downfall of the Porte. In 1695 Holger Pauli, a Dane, submitted a plan for the rebuilding of the Jewish State in Palestine to the Kings of England and France, and of course Rousseau propounds a similar suggestion in some detail in his *Emile*. Bonaparte, with his army standing before the walls of Acre in 1799, issued a proclamation inviting the Jews to join him in dislodging the Turks, with a promise of the redemption of Israel's patrimony. Many Jews did in fact rally to his banner, though Haim Farhi, the leader of the Acre Jewish community and financial adviser to the governor of the city, restrained his people from going over to the invader and the French attempt to capture the port was abandoned.

Bonaparte's hasty enlistment of Jewish aid to facilitate his own ambitions in the Orient awakened British statesmen to the danger that their rivals across the Channel might exploit Jewish sentiment in such a way as to cheat them of their stake in the Middle East. Zionism (the term itself did not enter into daily usage until 1890) was now to gather supporters motivated at least as much by their own political ambitions as their desire to help the Jews; and with the Eastern Question pressing hard upon the preoccupations of the great powers, the British were not to be outdone. Under the stimulus of such idealistic figures as Lord Ashley (subsequently seventh Earl of Shaftsbury) and Colonel Charles Churchill, grandson of the fifth Duke of Marlborough, both Peel and Palmerston lent the authority of their office to Jewish aspirations.

In the meantime Jewish initiative had itself been gathering strength. They had just emerged from their own Middle Ages, which had endured much longer than for Europe as a whole. An 'enlightenment' movement, with the intention of bringing the Jews into the intellectual streams of the modern world, had been inspired by the German philosopher Moses Mendelssohn (1729–86) and been accelerated by the collapse of the ghetto walls brought about by the Napoleonic conquest of Europe. Soon these developments were to be given extra significance by the revival of the Hebrew language as a vehicle of daily intercourse. It was not surprising therefore that early in the second half of the 19th century the Jews began to visualise themselves as taking their place among the other subject peoples of Europe who were now seeking, and achieving, national independence. It was because the Jews had to await their cultural renaissance before leaders of their own could emerge that they found themselves the last European people to join the queue for political emancipation.

The climax of this evolving awareness that the Jews should intervene in their own destiny rather than wait for a happy alliance between God and one of the great powers was the creation in 1897 of the political Zionist organisation of Theodor Herzl (1860–1904). He proved immensely capable of bringing the movement to a stature whereby it could be noticed with respect by world leaders. At first Jewish men of influence gave him scant attention, but then he converted an English clergyman in Vienna, who brought him to the Grand Duke Friedrich of Baden. This opened a door to the German Emperor, Kaiser Wilhelm, but when he appeared hesitant Herzl directed his thoughts towards London. Here his project met with greater success. The Balfour Declaration was achieved in 1917, and by this act Britain not only gave the Jews their first modern opportunity to fulfil their historic religious role, but also succeeded in outwitting all the other wooers of the Jews for a place in this coveted corner of the Middle East.

The Historical Cycle

Because of the central position that the Holy Land occupies in Jewish existence—its fortunes constitute the barometer of their exaltation and demoralisation—it was natural for the people to place the Balfour Declaration beside the Cyrus Declaration 2,500 years earlier, and see many points of similarity between the two events. In each case the return to Jerusalem was facilitated by a power in triumph, motivated by a mixture of sentiment, generosity and self-interest. In each case it was greeted as a vindication of the Jews' fidelity to their covenant '. . . If I forget thee, O Jerusalem, let my right hand forget its cunning. . . .' In each case it was accompanied by the introduction of the benefits of a more advanced civilisation into a land less advanced—Ezekiel's vision of life breathed into the valley of the dry bones. For just as the long night of Turkish misrule in our times had never secured the complete departure of the Jews, only their destitution, so some had always remained in the Holy Land during the Babylonian conquest to feed the flames of faith in ancient days.

Also, in each case, the majority of Jews could not bring themselves to forfeit the material benefits of exile by returning to the land of Israel. We do not know exactly how many obeyed the injunction to go and rebuild the Temple, and how many continued to weep 'by the waters of Babylon'. But there can be little doubt that the resumed existence, on a substantial scale, of the people on their traditional soil made the difference between their survival or extinction as an identifiable nation.

During the next 600 years Judaea remained the focus of the Jewish spirit, simultaneously the symbol and the fact of the people's devotion to the law given them on Sinai. According to Josephus the national centre was 'very like to a ship in a storm which is tossed by the waves on both sides', but despite this it was sustained against all vicissitudes. Judaea was the scene of heroic struggles against overlords impolitic enough to stamp on the practice of the Jewish religion, it took the strains created by the attractions of Hellenistic ideas, it was wracked by social corruption and internecine conflict. But out of it was born Christianity, and a new body of Jewish moralistic writings that constituted the Jewish literary, legal and philosophical legacy to mankind : the codification under Yehuda the Patriarch between the first and second centuries AD of the Oral Law (all the rules handed down by tradition and custom since the conferment of the Mosaic Law) in the *Mishnah*. This in turn formed the basis of the Talmud, of which one version was created in Jerusalem and the other in Mesopotamia. The Talmud could be said to have set the domestic pattern of Jewish life and ensured the unity of the Jews as a people besides being their inspiration, consolation and guide, until the present day.

With the destruction of the Temple, the erasure of the word 'Jerusalem' from imperial Roman terminology and the abortive revolt of Bar Cochba in AD 135, the Jews compensated for the loss of their national centre by establishing 'temples of Jerusalem'—the synagogue—wherever they wandered. Their intention was to maintain their home in the spirit by remaining faithful, even in dispersion, to its customs, regulations and festivals. Rules such as those concerned with ritual purity, which have little validity outside Palestine, were sustained to the letter. Judaism preserved the Hebrew language, and it never ceased to be used for scholarship, prayer and social and commercial purposes between communities so widely separated that they could not comprehend each other's vernacular. The calendar regulating Jewish life was taken from the seasons where Jerusalem constituted the meridian, and the celebration of festivals was spread over two days, to ensure it would encompass absolutely the 'rising up' and 'going down' of the sun in the Holy City. The prayers spoken on the holy-days which are not, like the Day of Atonement, purely spiritual, reflect the agricultural cycle of ancient Palestine. Passover is the spring festival, and the Jew prays for the dew to nourish the soil. The Feast of Weeks marks the wheat harvest, and it comes seven weeks after Passover to preserve the meaning of the daily offering of barley in olden days. Seated in the tabernacle on *Succoth* the observant Jew may be enduring the rigours of a northern autumn, but his booth is decorated with the palm branch, myrtle, willow and citron, all seasonal in the Middle East at that time. The Fast of the Ninth of Ab, and the Feast of Lights, each commemorates tribulation or triumph in the Palestine of the dawn of the current era.

Additionally, the Holy Land evoked in the Jew the sensation of a per-

165

sonal relationship based upon an abiding mystical power. Its essence was expressed very early in the reproach David levelled against Saul in banishing him beyond the confines of Jewish territory, for it was as though the King was causing the shepherd to transgress a religious doctrine. To live in Palestine, said Nahmanides in the 13th century, was one of the 613 commandments of the Law of Moses, and thus the refusal of a wife to accompany her husband to Palestine is a legitimate reason for divorce in Jewish law. Conversely, voluntary emigration is condemned today as it was in previous epochs as *Yerida*, meaning descent or defection, and not exile. It produces a feeling of guilt impossible to exorcise, and is carried by many thousands today who have chosen the fleshpots of the Diaspora after having savoured national redemption in the homeland. Perhaps it is only another Jew who can recognise the psychological strain suffered by the Israeli living in Boston as compared with the sense of fulfilment experienced by an Irish emigrant there.

Past Efforts to Return

It is not therefore surprising that, ever since the beginning of the dispersion, the Jews have sought to return to their homeland *en masse*. Many such attempts are recorded, some of them quite practical expeditions with the help of powerful friends, others pathetic demonstrations of a futile if sublime faith. The more realistic efforts saw their opportunity when rival empires clashed for possession of Palestine, such as during the long period of conflict between the East Roman Empire and the Persians. As the Jews generally suffered restrictions of religious freedom under the yoke of the Caesars, they naturally allied themselves with the Persians. It became a tradition that a great Caesarea and a rebuilt Jerusalem could never exist side by side, and the revival of the latter entailed the destruction of the former. Thus it was that when Chosroes of Persia declared war upon the Christian conquerors, the Jews were roused to form their own liberating army. A force variously described as from 20–30,000 Jews was raised, mostly under a certain Benjamin in Egypt, and in the year 614 actually seized a major part of Palestine and administered it for 14 years. The attempt was repeated some 150 years later when a pseudo-Messiah named Abu-Issa raised a substantial force among the Jews of Syria and Mesopotamia, but the expedition came very quickly to grief.

The return of the Byzantines after Persia's short-lived rule in the seventh century brought Christian vengeance upon the Jews for their treachery against the country's masters. Their strongest concentration was in Tiberias, which was now the major religious centre of the people, its rabbis handing down rulings accepted as authoritative by Jews everywhere. The *Yishuv* (settlement), as those inhabiting Palestine were collectively described, was also spread over a large number of villages, with agriculture and cloth-weaving as their main pursuits. Their economy was of modest dimensions, but elsewhere in the Middle East Jews were attaining high standards of prosperity and social status. This was particularly the case in Egypt and Babylonia. In the latter an Exilarch of the Davidic line headed a largely autonomous community that won renown if not for its austere piety then at least as a fortress of Jewish literature and philosophy.

The Jews were destined to benefit by the rise of Islam, for they were not seen by the Arabs as representing a threat in any way comparable to that emanating from Byzantium. On the contrary, they were comparatively happily adjusted as just another Oriental sect in the Middle East. They rose to immense heights of achievement in the Arab service, not only in the Middle East but also in North Africa and Spain. They were numerous as governmental advisers, physicians, poets and scholars, and returned to Palestine in force (though exactly how many has never been established) with the Ummayads. Jerusalem revived once more, as did various other towns, and the period is noteworthy for having given impetus to a thorough revision of the Old Testament, with the standardisation of rules of punctuation and grammar that survives in present-day usage. Nevertheless this could hardly be termed a period of great harmony in Jewish life. Diversification was extensive, with communication between the various local communities in the Orient difficult to maintain. The result was to be seen in dynastic rivalries and schismatic heresy-hunting. At first the legality of the Exilarch in Babylonia was questioned, and this led to disputation over the authority of certain of the sacred writings, particularly the Talmud. One consequence of these developments was the birth of Karaism. The sect regarded themselves as 'mourners for Zion'. They recognised no holy writ except the *Torah* (Mosaic Law) and made living in the land of Israel an indispensable part of their belief. Of course, most of them were obliged to suffer their resentment of orthodox Judaism while remaining in the Diaspora, and it was only with the establishment of the modern State of Israel that their descendants, and the descendants of their converts in Europe besides the Middle East, have been able to fulfil their dream, even though some of the rabbis were to dispute their authenticity as Jews.

Unfortunately, the hopes that the ascendancy of Islam had raised about Palestine once again becoming a great centre of population were not destined to last. Although Jerusalem could not but be sacred to the Arabs, it possessed no glories that might rival Damascus and Baghdad. The country declined in military importance and economic stature. It became the prey of Bedouin tribes and the victim of civic incompetence. There were periodic outbursts of violence attended by massacre, causing the desertion of a large part of the settled population and the abandonment by the Christians of their monasteries.

Nevertheless, perhaps because of the influence of the Karaites and other ascetics who insisted upon an impoverished and perilous existence in the Holy Land rather than participation in the opulence and prestige obtainable through service in the Muslim cause in distant parts, the Jews weathered this crisis in Palestine's affairs. Indeed, despite the persecutions instigated during the Caliphate of Al-Hakim (996–1021) a more settled régime was about to dawn. Comprehensive evidence found in the Cairo *Geniza* (a repository of ancient manuscripts that came to light early in this century and is still only partially deciphered) tells of a vigorous Jewish existence in the Holy Land during the tenth and eleventh centuries. The records comprise legal transactions and communal correspondence between the Jews of Palestine and Egypt, identifying some 50 coastal communities from Tyre to El-Arish, besides Tiberias, Ramleh and Hebron. They were linked by an advanced autonomous administration under a Sanhedrin presided over by the Patriarch, with rabbinical seminaries dotted throughout the country.

Still, given the renaissance in Judaism that accompanied Jewish settlement in the greater Arab empire, the physical presence in Palestine was tenuous in the extreme. Certainly it had not the vitality to resist the fanaticism of the Crusaders, who had dealt savagely with the Jews in Europe and were no more generously disposed to their brothers in the Holy Land. Once again Hebrew poetry consisted of anguished appeals to God to restore Zion to its ancient greatness. Everywhere Jews looked to Saladin to be the agent to vent the Lord's wrath upon the Christians. They were not disappointed. Saladin issued a proclamation inviting the Jews' return to Jerusalem. It was heard in every corner of the known world. But in fact the move back had preceded the conquest of Jerusalem by the Egyptian sultan. The two greatest Jews of the Middle Ages, Yehuda Halevi of Cordoba (author of the *Kusari*, in which he expounds the differences between Judaism, Christianity and Islam), and Maimonides, author of the *Guide to the Perplexed*, both went to settle in Palestine, though Halevi died *en route*. Three hundred rabbis from England and France immigrated there in 1216, an act reflecting the eternal Jewish aspiration to safeguard their homeland as the people's spiritual home as well as their population centre.

To effect the reconciliation of the dispersed nation in its entirety with the soil of Israel seemed to the Jews of the Middle Ages to require disciplines transcending the pieties of ordinary daily life. There had always been a belief that men of great wisdom could, like Moses and the Prophets, communicate with God direct. Now mysticism became widespread, through the study of Cabbala. This doctrine took various forms, and on occasion gave rise to spurious practices. But it was also believed to provide the key to God's intentions regarding the place a rebuilt Jerusalem would occupy in the world to come. The Cabbalists regarded the Hebrew Bible as being composed not of mere words alone, but of hidden concepts, the meaning of which could be uncovered by the application of certain formulae in which the very shapes of the letters of the sacred alphabet were analysed.

The study of Cabbala was no transient phenomenon indulged in as a solace by a people temporarily dispossessed of their ancestral hearth and forced to live among strangers. Those who mastered its secrets claimed to be able to identify with all time, discern the unity of heaven and earth, and render the entire history and destiny of the Jews into one ordained plan. The tradition speaks of Cabbala as having been conveyed, through a work called the *Zohar*, by God to man at Meiron in the neighbourhood of Safad in the second century AD, though not put into written form until the 13th century in Spain. The work is charged with powerful emotional evocations of the physical uniqueness of Palestine, with each place-name analysed to show its special relationship with God; for, as the *Midrash* (homily) on the Book of Leviticus has it, 'the Holy One measured all countries, and he could not find any of them worthy to be given to Israel except the Land of Israel'. According to the same tradition, the air of Safad was the purest in the world; night fell later there, and dawn broke earlier, so that it was always destined to harbour poets and pietists with the loftiest thoughts and the clearest vision.

Safad assumed this role in fact following the Turkish conquest of Palestine in 1517. The first Hebrew printing press was established there, and its Jewish population expanded enormously. During the course of the next century Safad became the permanent or temporary home of almost every Jewish scholar of note, to make it also an economic centre of no small importance in Asia. This was in marked contradistinction to Jerusalem, where Turkish authority in the early days of the conquest was not well-established and Jewish life was consequently insecure.

Although Jewish fortunes in the Holy Land were to wax and wane, and the general demoralisation of the people wrought by the exposure of Sabbetai Zevi as merely another false Messiah became very marked towards the end of the 17th century, Safad's legacy was perceptible right until modern times. Indeed, its role was to be substituted by Jerusalem only about 1850, when the first rumblings of the modern return within the compass of a more secular movement began to be felt.

Because of what was being achieved in the Galilean hillside city, the Jews of the Diaspora, principally in Italy and Holland where they were wealthiest, began to systematise their financial support of the *Yishuv*. This was never contributed as charity, nor was it accepted as such. Frequently, as in Venice in 1601, it was instituted as a compulsory tax (and on occasion the aid of the Christian authorities was enlisted to collect it), a penalty as it were to be paid for not participating personally in the regeneration of the land of Israel. Here we have the historical basis of the massive fund-raising appeals of today. The upbuilding of Israel is regarded as a collective responsibility of all Jewry, a mark of identification where the symbol is as important as the action. Jews have invariably contributed greater sums to the cause of Israel than to other causes, properly called charitable, that confront them at home.

In the event, the Jews were disappointed in Turkey as a defender of their position in Palestine. The Porte proved no more sympathetic than had previous occupiers to their wish for large-scale immigration. The basic anomaly of the Jewish situation across the centuries remained unresolved. They were a people regarded as a nation—albeit a second or third-class one—in the lands of their dispersal, with civil disabilities and personal choice combining to keep them apart, but they were forbidden to translate this condition into self-determination in the land with which they were above all associated. We know of those who were eventually successful in reaching Palestine, but can only conjecture on the number who sought to go there but were prevented from doing so. As early as 1428 the Pope commanded the Italian cities controlling the sea-traffic to Palestine to stop transporting Jews to the Holy Land, and of course until the beginning of the 18th century the Mediterranean was the prey of Barbary privateers rendering unprotected travel hazardous in the extreme.

ALTERNATIVES TO ZION

Perhaps, then, the Jews could be lured to other 'Zions' that were available in the empty, unwanted spaces that scattered the globe? Schemes along these lines, sometimes on the initiative of Jews themselves, were produced throughout the 19th century, and even earlier. What gave them their urgency about a hundred years ago was the growth westward of the Russian Empire, placing the bulk of this people under Czarist oppression, and the Jewish population explosion in Eastern Europe. What these projects had in common was the need, made obvious by the city-bound, entrepreneurial role that aroused resentment against the Jews everywhere, to give them an opportunity to form a land-based society. It is necessary to recall the history of three such schemes to illustrate the hopelessness of associating Jewish independence with any region other than Palestine.

The first of them, conceived and financed by Baron Maurice de Hirsch (1831–96), the Parisian banker, entailed the migration of three million East European Jews to the Argentinian hinterland. This was begun in 1892. It had the willing co-operation of the Argentine Government and was more generously endowed than any colonisation project hitherto undertaken in Palestine. Although the transplantation across the Atlantic of hundreds of thousands of Jews was already in process, only 45,000 of the former ghetto dwellers were settled in the new colonies by 1914. Before long most of these had drifted to Buenos Aires and other towns, so that today only 2,000 families, of which half engage in agriculture, are to be found in the original settlement. Baron de Hirsch's experiment coincided with the inauguration of a rural economy in Palestine under the patronage of Baron Edmond de Rothschild (1845–1934). In many respects this endeavour was less auspicious than the one in Argentina, but it survived nevertheless to form the agricultural nucleus of modern Israel.

Even the founder of the contemporary Zionist movement, Theodor Herzl, feared that the winning of Palestine would take too long, and if the Jews of Eastern Europe were to be spared periodic pogrom, advantage should be taken of a British offer, tentatively made in 1903, to cede them an area of unspecified size in what is now Kenya, though it was then described as the 'Uganda project'. The reaction, from the East Europeans themselves, was so ferocious as to precipitate Herzl's death and goad a Polish student to attempt the assassination of his closest associate. The project was regarded as a betrayal of the cause, the act of assimilated Western Jews who could not comprehend the spiritual significance of Palestine and were therefore disqualified from leading the Zionist movement. Within 12 months of its birth this scheme was abandoned.

The most recent practical alternative to Zion had the official endorsement of the Soviet Government, and it came at a time when Jews were universally appreciative of Communism's role in liberating Russian Jewry from their abject condition during the previous régime. It envisaged an autonomous Jewish region in Birobidzhan, beside the Amur river adjacent to the Chinese frontier. Launched in 1928 with an accompaniment of blessings from distinguished Jews throughout the world and appeals to American Jewry for financial aid, the undertaking was promoted as the secular, non-imperialist alternative to Zionism in which the normal daily language would be Yiddish (Hebrew was deemed to have religious-superstitious counter-revolutionary associations). Autonomy was awarded in 1934, but already enthusiasm for the scheme was flagging, with more people leaving than coming in. The war increased the number of Jewish residents as Jews fleeing Nazi extermination found refuge in the deep recesses of the Soviet Union. The intention was to settle 300,000 in Birodbidzhan and eventually even grant it the status of a Soviet Republic. But the Jews failed to respond, and today the area contains fewer than 30,000 of them, a tiny minority of its total population.

JEWS AND ARABS IN PALESTINE

Manifestly, there was and can be no alternative to Palestine. The question remains, however, as to whether the Jews were justified in seeking to realise their ambitions there in modern times. For the area already had a settled population of Arabs, who were themselves awakening to their national rights after centuries under Turkish and other foreign rule.

The beginning of all wisdom in this tragic conflict is the recognition that Zionism is as much a legitimate movement of national liberation as is the Arab desire for independence. And it can only be fulfilled in this region, because this is where their constantly restrengthened roots have grown. Fortunately, it also happens to be a region of great diversity that cannot be said ever to have belonged to any one people. When the Jews began to return in substantial numbers after 1880 they were merely attempting to continue their historical role as described above (and not disputed in theory by any people). They welcomed the Balfour Declaration in 1917 not as a vindication of the legality of their claims, nor because of the possibility it gave them to fulfil themselves behind the shelter of foreign bayonets, but because it reflected a period when political change in the world apparently required the sanction of the great powers.

The Jews were prepared to accept governmental writ in Palestine provided this did not interefere with their intentions as to their ultimate destiny. They never made a secret of what that destiny was to be : a Jewish majority —there would have been no purpose in modern Zionism otherwise—and then not necessarily in the whole country. Under Turkish rule it became difficult for Jews not citizens of the Porte to immigrate there, so they came in illegally; likewise under the British mandatory régime. The point is sharply made by a comparison with the movement of Jews into other countries. The USA introduced restrictive immigrant quotas in the early '20s, and British Commonwealth countries followed with similar, though harsher, ordinances. The Jews were soon in desperate need of a haven. But they did not seek to circumvent these regulations, which they recognised as privileges, sometimes granted and sometimes withdrawn, by the Governments of the USA, Australia, etc. The same regulations translated to Palestine, however, and what the Jews saw was the transgression of natural justice.

The forces commonly called colonialism came into the picture not because the Jews were going to Palestine but because of the power vacuum threatened by Turkey's collapse. All the great powers (though in those days Britain and France especially) felt they were entitled to fill the vacuum, and consequently they used any instrument available, including the Jews, to attain their ends. Perhaps if Britain had worked harder in the early days of the Mandate to bring the Jews and Arabs into agreement (and this was by no means impossible, as witness their co-operation in the field of trade union organisation) the subsequent story would have been different. But it was no part of British policy to effect harmony between Jew and Arab, because this would frustrate her own function : superficially a trustee acting on behalf of the international community, fundamentally a protector of her own sphere of interest.

The Jewish national renaissance began about 1870 when Palestine was a loose geographical expression, having long been administered as the southern part of Syria. It had an Arab population, including Bedouin, of some 600,000. The hopes of the Arab world were turned to Damascus, Baghdad, Cairo and the holy cities of Arabia, while the hopes of the Jews were centred, as always, on Jerusalem. At that time the Jewish population of Jerusalem was 25,000 and outnumbered Muslims and Christians together. By 1905, without the assistance of any Western power, the number of Jews there had increased to 40,000, with 13,000 Christians and only 7,000 Muslims. The First World War caused the departure of many Jews of foreign (mostly enemy Russian) nationality, but by 1920 they had come back. In that year there were 60–70,000 Jews in the country, about one-ninth of the entire population.

The Jews largely overlooked the growth of a competitive national spirit among the Arabs. This was partly because few people in those days ascribed such a spirit to non-European peoples, and partly because the Arab leaders whom the Jews knew, and with whom they could treat, did not express disquiet at the prospect of a large-scale Jewish return. George Antonius, in his *Arab Awakening* (1938 edition, p. 269) quotes an article in a Mecca newspaper that he attributes to King Husain of the Hejaz as saying: ' . . . We saw the Jews from foreign countries streaming into Palestine. . . . The cause of causes could not escape those who had the gift of a deeper insight; they knew that the country was for its original sons (*Abnaihi l'asliyin*) a sacred and beloved homeland . . . The return of these exiles (*jaliya*) to their homeland will prove materially and spiritually an experimental school for their brethren.' Husain's son Faisal is described in the official record of the Peace Conference as demanding the independence of Arab areas with the exception of Palestine, which for its universal character he left on one side for the mutual consideration of all parties. (Quoted in Lloyd George's *Truth about the Peace Treaties*, 1938, Vol. II, p. 1042.) Similar sentiments were expressed on various occasions by other Arab spokesmen of the time.

These were of course aristocratic rulers who were not perhaps speaking for the common man. But ordinary Arabs gave evidence also that they recognised the benefits of the Zionist restoration, and the enterprise it was bringing to the area. They immigrated to Palestine from the moment of the Mandate's operation, and the Muslim population grew rapidly. The Royal Commission (in the Peel Report, 1937) pointed out that 'between 1922–31 the percentage increase of the Arabs in Haifa was 86, in Jaffa 62, in Jerusalem 37, while in purely Arab towns such as Nablus and Hebron it was only 7, and in Gaza there was a decrease of 2%.' Overall, the Arab population increased by 15% during the first 15 years of the Mandate alone, while in Transjordan it remained stationary.

Such statistics will be of small consolation to the Arabs today, when they find themselves dispossessed of most of the area they occupied at that time. But it should not be overlooked that every territorial issue in Palestine, whether arising from the Zionist presence or not, was solved in such a way as to involve painful compromise on the part of the Jews. The separation of Transjordan from the area originally envisaged as coming within the Jewish colonisation process entailed their permanent exclusion from two-thirds of biblical Palestine. The partition scheme of 1937 was accepted by Weizmann and Ben-Gurion on behalf of the Jews although it would have confined Jewish independence within one-fifth of what remained. Jerusalem was not even included as warranting independence, and the Jews were prepared to accept this too, knowing that it would produce grief throughout the world community. Remarkably enough, the British produced a reason for allocating Haifa neither to the Arabs nor to the Jews.

The Arabs had the misfortune of being so badly and autocratically led in Palestine that during periods of conflict they were never allowed to know that some of their most respected personalities were meeting with the Jews to discuss the future of the country on the basis of mutual co-operation. It was a misfortune also that their leader, Haj Amin al Husaini, began enlisting Hitler's aid in 1937, and in his appeals to his people from Berlin during the Second World War used words that savoured of the German dictator's paranoia. Thus they could hardly be aware, in the days before the Second World War, that many Jews in Palestine were in favour of a bi-national state and that practically all the others would have made important concessions to avoid a conflict.

The desire for an accommodation did not arise because the Zionists had encountered an unforseen obstacle in Arab intransigence, but rather through the nature of the Jewish revival itself. They had come to Palestine to realise a new society through association with the land, and in the view of many to bring about a fundamental change in the Jewish character that implied the absolute negation of exploitation. Modern secular Zionism was profoundly affected by the East European circumstances which gave it birth. It was based upon Tolstoyan ideas distilled through Marxian socialism : the soil tilled by the sweat of one's own brow, and the land shared by the community so as not to be the subject of speculation for private gain. Every Israeli Prime Minister since the establishment of the Jewish State has been a product of this philosophy.

Arab leaders today oppose Jewish immigration into Israel. It has not always been so. Prior to 1967 by far the largest source of Jewish immigration was from the Arab world, and Jews could not have left for Israel from such countries as Iraq, Syria, Egypt, Yemen, Tunis and Morocco without the concurrence of the respective Governments. In the case of the three largest sources of immigration, Iraq, Yemen and Morocco, it was as a result of arrangements formally agreed and for reciprocal advantage.

The impression is sometimes given to the outside world that the Palestine issue is the one thorn in the Arab flesh, and that were it not for Zionism the Middle East would be a place where the common man's life would be one of ever-increasing tranquillity and justice. The opposite is the truth. Civil unrest, rule by junta, denial of local self-determination and violent wars, have all occurred in Middle Eastern countries remote from the Holy Land. This region as a whole has not yet fully emerged from all the problems attending its transformation from a long period of servitude into an array of independent nations. The revival of the Jewish State, and its technological and social position in the Middle East, is a monument to the achievements of collective endeavour by the dispersed Jewish world, for the Israelis could not have done so much on their own. Surely this example of self-help crossing state boundaries is applicable to the Arab world also, which is not universally impoverished, to put an end to the great disparities in Arab living standards? Such a change may well bring about a new assessment of Arab-Jewish relationships, a rediscovery of fundamentals, and indeed lead to harmony among all the peoples from whose destiny this region cannot be divorced.

FURTHER READING

Antonius, George. *The Arab Awakening*, Hamish Hamilton, London, 1938; Putnam, New York, 1965.

Bein, Alex. *Theodor Herzl*, East & West Library, London, 1957.

Goldwater, Raymond, (ed.) *Jewish Philosophy and Philosophers*, McGraw, London, 1962.

Kobler, Franz. (ed.) *Letters of Jews throughout the Ages*, East and West Library, London, 1952.

Parkes, James. *A History of Palestine*, Gollancz, London, 1949.

Scholem, Gershom. *Major Trends in Jewish Mysticism*, London, 1941; Schocken, New York, 1961.

Shapiro, Harry L. *The Jewish People: a biological history*, UNESCO, 1960.

Sokolow, Nahum. *History of Zionism*, Longmans, London, 1919; Ktav, New York, 1969.

Tuchman, Barbara W. *Bible and Sword*, Redman, London, 1957; Minerva, New York, 1968.

Weizmann, Chaim. *Trial and Error*, Hamish Hamilton, London, 1949; Schocken, New York, 1966.

BARNET LITVINOFF. Born in London in 1917, a writer specialising in Jewish affairs. Served in Europe and the Middle East during the Second World War and was a prisoner-of-war for three years. Among his books are *Ben-Gurion of Israel* (1955), *Road to Jerusalem* (1966), *A Peculiar People* (1969).

ARAB LANGUAGE AND CULTURE

JABRA I. JABRA

It may sound like an oversimplification to say that one of the operative definitions of an Arab in the last hundred years has been : 'anyone who speaks Arabic as his own language and consequently feels as an Arab'. If the Middle East and North Africa have both been a melting pot of races, one factor has remained more or less constant for more than thirteen centuries : this factor is Arabic, which has been the language of the whole area. Whether as a medium of communication or of intellectual and literary expression, all through the area's long and turbulent history Arabic has remained forceful and dominant. Foreign rulers of all sorts, with their original languages, have come and gone : Arabic conquered them all. Indeed, such languages as Persian and Turkish, closely associated with Arab history, have themselves been permeated with Arabic and have utterly failed to displace it, leaving no more than a scratch on its surface.

There is something of a miracle about this language which made many ancient Arab scholars assume that it had burst fully-fledged upon the world through divine inspiration. Early in the seventh century it emerged from the Arabian peninsula with the Arab tribes, whose conquering horsemen swept over the domains of two long-established empires, Persia and Byzantium. In a matter of decades, the language of a semi-nomadic race established itself as the language of a far-flung empire : the medium of expression for a profound religion, a complex government, and a diversified pursuit of life.

During the first century of Arab expansion Arabic encountered at least three languages, all highly sophisticated and backed by a long intellectual tradition : Persian, Syriac and Greek, which were spoken in Iraq, Persia and Syria. It absorbed the full strength of each of those languages which were spoken by the new subjects of the conquering race, most of whom were soon converted to Islam. In Egypt, Coptic and Greek (the latter as a language of administration) soon gave way to Arabic; also in North Africa and later in Spain Arabic swept away, for all intents and purposes, a variety of local languages. Of course these languages did not always completely disappear : Persian remained spoken widely east of the Tigris, Syriac remained for a few more centuries a language of learning in many cities throughout Iraq and Syria, and Greek, which was pushed back beyond the Taurus mountains as a spoken language, remained for scholars a mine from which a great deal of philosophy and medical learning was extracted.

One Common Language

But Arabic had become the *lingua franca* of a vast, loosely-knit empire, where anyone, whatever his origin, who aspired to learning or to social or political distinction, had to perfect the language as his medium. The language had such a fascination for the new non-Arab converts to Islam that it was believed that those who had a greater mastery of Arabic were given places nearer to God in Paradise. Indeed, some of the greatest thinkers and poets of the Arab empire were not of Arab stock, nor did they have to be, and yet they were an integral part of Arab history and culture. Such was the unifying force of Arabic that, from the very start, it had become the essence of the Arab ethos.

A great deal of the credit for this goes to the Koran. Although it specified that 'an Arab is not better than a non-Arab unless he be more pious', the fact that the Koran was described as a direct revelation from God made its translation for the benefit of the new converts to Islam illogical : a Muslim, whatever his language, could only use for his devotions the Arabic words of the Koran, since they were God's very words. Its prose being so beautiful and evocative, its grammar so subtle and faultless, its teachings so terse and exact, God's Noble Book became the solid foundation of a whole new culture. Content and form seemed truly inseparable.

As Arabic spread among a diversity of peoples who were not originally Arabic-speaking, there was a real danger that the language in the long run would be corrupted by them. In fact its spoken forms were gradually vitiated by the indigenous languages of the population, and the Arabs soon noticed that grammatical errors of all kinds began to mark not only the people's language as they spoke, but even their more serious poetic and literary expression. This led to the appearance of the first grammarians and linguists who set about the task of codifying the language : in Basra and Kufa, both in Iraq, two famous schools of philology laid down the rules that governed the complexities of Arabic, including those of prosody which had hitherto been determined by ear. Whenever in doubt about a grammatical law, they referred either to the Koran as the touchstone of accuracy, or to the dialects of Bedouin tribes, who over the previous two centuries had penetrated the Iraqi and Syrian hinterland, preserving in the meantime the purity of their Arabic language. The first lexicographers (perhaps the first in any language anywhere) appeared at this time and compiled the extensive dictionaries that are still the bases of any modern attempt at Arabic lexicography. This drive for the purification of Arabic went on unabated for nearly 200 years, during which Arabic, as it enriched itself through translation from Greek, Persian and Syriac, acquiring in the process thousands of new words which were completely Arabised, became the language of a dynamic civilisation. By the 11th century the arts of peace, like the arts of war, had reached a peak of sophistication : magnificent poetry had been written, learned books, in spare, analytical, precise prose, such as that of Al Jahiz, had become the norm, and in scientific research the Arabs had assumed the leadership of the civilised world.

The Middle Ages

Arabic culture flourished at its best between the eighth and thirteenth centuries, when European civilisation was at its lowest ebb. Since points of contact with Europe, in conflict or in peace, were numerous all round the Mediterranean, Arab culture, having gained unquestioned supremacy, was bound to have a profound influence on Europe. Arabic, as a rich and resourceful language, played a decisive part in this. Although it did not supplant Greek or Latin, both of which were embedded in the matrix of Europe's developing vernaculars, it supplemented them in most spheres of thought and scientific endeavour. Medicine, astronomy, chemistry, mathematics, philosophy, though often reaching the majority of European scholars through Latin translations, were for ever marked with the stamp of the Arabic language and its modes of thinking.

In literature, foreign influences do not penetrate easily : the Arabs, for example, accepted Greek philosophy, but were impervious to Greek drama and epic poetry. Aristotle's *Poetics* was translated at least three times—in fact it reached Europe through its Arabic translation—but the book's real significance in connection with tragedy and comedy, as literary forms, was ignored by the Arabs. Arabic literary forms, however, did have an influence outside the Arabic-speaking world, especially in parts of Spain, Southern France, Sicily, Italy—and later in other countries. Andalusian Arabic poetry, with its rhyming schemes, lyrical structure and idealised amorous attitudes, was gradually between the tenth and thirteenth centuries to replace the earlier Latin and Greek unrhymed models; it helped in the emergence of poetry in the vulgar tongues. It thus contributed, both through direct contact and through the troubadours, to the creation of a new style in poetic composition in practically all European languages.

The Silver Age of Arabic Literature

After its golden age, Arabic literature went through a silver age of excessive refinement, when men of letters seemed to prize fancy rather than imagination, verbal ornament rather than original invention. Although massive historical, geographical and linguistic anthologies kept coming out in considerable numbers during and after the thirteenth century (in the middle of which the fall of Baghdad marked the end of that central power which had carried prestige and maintained the patronage of humanistic brilliance), a great deal of the old creative energy was wasted on verbal acrobatics and 'literary' tricks. All this, however, had one great virtue : the intoxicating love of language, which preserved it, however diminished in vitality, through the succeeding generations of decline. Little poetry or prose of note was created, but a great work of imagination was to come from an unexpected plebeian quarter : the *Thousand and One Nights*. It was written in a prose style which would have been utterly scorned by the writers of earlier times : semi-colloquial, heavy with the jargon of the markets and taverns of Cairo and Baghdad. Indeed it was completely ignored by the *literati* of later times, but this did not detract from its power or popularity. In fact, whoever assembled those great myths of a vast nation surviving foreign régimes and scheming non-Arab despots must have had the same passion for Arabic that had marked their more sophisticated predecessors. For they embellished the *Thousand and One Nights* with remarkable poetry—actual quotations of considerable length, some of which have been traced back to their authors. The book, which came orally to an increasingly illiterate audience over the centuries, became a kind of everyman's guide to poetry and fiction. It thus contributed to the maintenance of that fascination which the Arabs had always felt for the language, even at their lowest intellectual levels. It is ironical that the West, long after it had seemingly forgotten what the Arabs had done for its Renaissance, should again become alive to the magnificence of Arab culture through the popularised *Arabian Nights*, as the book was called through endless translations and editions throughout the civilised world in the 18th and 19th centuries.

DECLINE AND REVIVAL

Meanwhile the Arabic language had fallen on hard times. Its force, how-ever, remained merely dormant; centres of religious learning, such as at Al Azhar University in Cairo, preserved the language in its pristine purity. Colloquial forms had corrupted the language considerably : unless an Arab was quite literate, the grammatical subtleties and rhetorical intricacies of his language were a closed book to him. Different influences affected the vernaculars of the various parts of the Arab world in different ways, so much so that the vernacular of Iraq, for example, was almost incomprehensible in Egypt, and *vice versa*. But classical Arabic, *al-fus'ha,* remained the same. Religious education, if nothing else, kept it alive, and since there never was a tradition of writing down the vernacular in any serious way, any writing that had to be done, from the Arabian Gulf to the Atlantic ocean, was done in classical Arabic. When the Arab revival began towards the end of the 18th century, it simply began with the increasing use of the printing press and the ever-widening dissemination of the *written* forms of Arabic. Turkish, full of Arabic though it had become, was the prevailing medium of administration and the language of most of the ruling classes in the Arab world for nearly four centuries. But it failed to go much beyond that. The obstinate maintenance of Arabic among the people themselves preserved their Arab identity. (In Algeria and Morocco, French, imposed wilfully and forcibly on the nation, in later times, for more than a century, failed to defeat the Arabic language completely.) Not even the strong bonds of Islam between the Ottomans and the Arabs were to weaken the national bonds of the language itself, which kept the nation psychologically and culturally united and distinct. No wonder then that the Christians in Lebanon, who were among the first to revive classical Arabic studies, were also among the first to articulate the new concept of Arab nationalism, in spite of their numerical minority. Lebanon in the 19th century had a higher percentage of schools than anywhere else in the Arab world, and it seemed to produce more scholars, writers, journalists, *per caput*, than the rest of the Ottoman-dominated Arab lands. The intellectual and political influence of the Lebanese attested to the unifying force of the language, whose literature and thought had begun to be refurbished at their hands. In Khedival Egypt, in the meantime, a great translation movement had been started by a versatile and imaginative scholar, Rifa'a Tahtawi. From the mid-19th century onwards, the story of Arab cultural revival has been in many ways the story of Arabic revived along classical lines and enriched through translation from European languages. Creative writers in the last three generations have put this revival and enrichment to good use by producing much original prose and poetry of a modern significance. Whether a writer lives in Cairo or Casablanca, in Beirut or Baghdad, his work is likely to draw an immediate response in all Arab capitals. The forces of revival have been diverse and cumulative. Since the language regained its dynamism, its mystique has become even more magical, more operative than ever, lying as it does at the heart of the new political upsurge.

INTERNATIONAL COMMUNICATION

Arabic grammar, though complex, is basically as logical as mathematics. This has made the language capable of precision and subtlety. Rhetorically, since it has always had a tradition of oratory and poetic declamation (so much poetry is written to be *heard*, not *read*, in order to achieve a kind of lightning effect on an audience), it has an emotional resourcefulness deriving partly from an inherent grandiloquence the Arabs are fond of, and partly from an inherent verbal rhythm which to an Arab is as good as music, and gives him a comparable delight. Such a medium, profoundly conditioned by religious and historical associations, could hardly fail to be a bond to hold together a vast nation, whatever the races originally merged within it, spreading over much of Asia and Africa.

With the spread of education, classical Arabic has progressively surmounted all colloquial barriers. If vernaculars emphasise regional differences, it happens that Arabic vernaculars in order to cope with the uses of the modern world, resort to classical Arabic for expressiveness and exactitude. This has led to all vernaculars developing in the direction of *al-fus'ha*. Educated Arabs, who have always written the same language wherever they live, now tend in daily life to use a local vernacular modified by classical Arabic: thus dialects get closer to one another through its gravitating force, which makes colloquial differences between one Arab country and another of no serious consequence. In any oral discussion today, a Saudi Arabian and a Moroccan would be completely intelligible to each other, even if they did not have to write a single word.

Arabic then is in the essence of Arab culture today, exactly as it was a thousand years ago. A man who speaks Arabic as his own language could not help normally feeling as an Arab: for the verbal miracle is at work within him, unconsciously fusing him with 100 million others who speak the same language and who, therefore, share the same cultural experience.

FURTHER READING

Arnold, Sir Thomas, and Guillaume, Alfred (eds.). *The Legacy of Islam*, Oxford Univ. Press, London, 1947.

Hourani, Albert. *Arabic Thought in the Liberal Age*, Oxford Univ. Press, London, 1963.

Nuseibeh, Hazem Zeki. *The Ideas of Arab Nationalism*, Cornell Univ. Press, New York, 1956.

JABRA I. JABRA. Critic, novelist and poet, he occupies a senior post in the Iraq Petroleum Company in Baghdad. Taught English Literature at Baghdad University 1948–52 and 1955–64. Rockefeller Foundation Research Fellowship at Harvard University 1952–4. Writes in Arabic and English; among his works are *Cry through a Long Night* (1955), *Hunters in a Narrow Street* (1960), *Art in Iraq Today* (1961), *Tammuz in the City* (1959) and *The Closed Circuit* (1964).

ISLAM

SEYYED HOSSEIN NASR

ISLAM is both the religion of the vast majority of the people of the Middle East today and the most important factor that has moulded the civilisation of that region during the past 14 centuries. Moreover, because Arabia was the original homeland of Islam, the whole region of the Middle East has remained the centre of a religious community and a civilisation which has extended throughout a much larger region, from the Atlantic to the Pacific. Islam has unified the Middle East into a distinct cultural entity which, while being a unit within itself, forms a part of a larger cultural world which remains inextricably related to it.

Islam is not only a religion in the current Western understanding of the word, it is also a complete code and way of life encompassing all the phases of human existence. It is a pattern for all of human life and seeks to integrate all of human existence into the sacred. It is a way of unity and integration which does not recognise any legitimate boundary beyond the sacred. There is no room for the profane and the temporal. It is the matrix in which all phases of human activity from worship to art and from law to politics take place. The understanding of Islam can only be achieved in the light of its integrative character and total nature.

EARLY HISTORY—THE PROPHET MUHAMMAD

The historical career of Islam began during the early decades of the seventh century AD in Arabia. The Prophet Muhammad was born around AD 570 in Mecca in the aristocratic tribe of Quraysh. At the age of 40 he received his first prophetic message and began his mission among his own kinsmen and the other tribes of Mecca, but at first met with little success. In 622 he migrated to the city of Medina to begin a new phase in his career, and this meant a turning point in Islamic history, after which the new faith began to spread rapidly. This date was so important that it has become the beginning of the Muslim calendar. In a little over ten years in Medina, the Prophet succeeded in unifying Arabia for the first time in its history. Under the banner of the new faith a unified Arabia went on to make the most widespread and permanent conquest in history, one which brought a new religion and a new way of life to a region extending from the Pyrenees to the Himalayas. This region became henceforth the heart of the Islamic world (*dār al-islām*) to which Anatolia was later added by the Turks. A second wave of the spread of Islam by means of individual saints and scholars took place in

India and south-east Asia. The third phase of the spread of Islam began in the 19th century in negro Africa.

Islam addresses itself to man considered in his function as vicegerent of God on earth. It is a message of God in His Absoluteness to man. There is therefore no idea of incarnation in Islam. The message makes known to man, through revelation, something of the nature of the Divine. The unitary vision of Islam could not divinise anything but the Absolute Divinity or Allah Itself. All other orders of reality are reduced to nothingness before the Divine Majesty. The role of the Prophet Muhammad was to bring a message from Allah, the message being the Holy Koran which is the word of God itself. The messenger is not divinised but is represented as the most perfect of men, of all creation, who is emulated by all Muslims precisely because he is the perfect model of humanity.

Moreover, the Prophet is the 'Seal of Prophecy', bringing to a close the cycle of revealed religions. The Muslims have believed from the first that there will be no other revealed religion for humanity and later centuries of history have reinforced this view. This finality has given to Islam not only its integrative power of absorbing all that was positive of previous traditions, but has also bestowed upon it a universal character embracing the religions before it. No other sacred text speaks as much about other religions as the Holy Koran, in which it is explicitly stated that God has sent a prophet to every nation. More particularly Islam pays the greatest respect to the Semitic prophets, and Abraham, Moses and Christ play the most outstanding roles in Islam. Muhammad is considered by Muslims as the last in a long chain of prophets. He is considered to have come not so much to bring a new message as to reaffirm the primordial message of unity (*al-tawhīd*) which lies at the heart of every religion, which has always been and will always be.

The utterances of the Prophet of Islam, called *hadith*, and his practices, called *sunnah*, are the most important sources for Islam after the Holy Koran. The Word of God is too sublime to be understood by men unless it be with the aid of His Prophet. The Koran and *hadith* together form the pillar of the Islamic way of life. Therein is found the root of all Muslim beliefs and rites. The remarkable homogeneity of the Islamic world, which comprises ethnic groups as different as Malays, Persians and Sudanese, is due most of all to the common source of inspiration and the model which all have followed over the centuries.

THE CARDINAL RITES OF ISLAM

The basic Muslim rite is the daily canonical prayers, performed by the believer five times a day while facing Mecca. The prayers consist of certain verses from the Koran recited in Arabic combined with certain movements whch symbolise the various stages of man's approach and proximity to God, and are based on the practice of the Prophet of Islam. These prayers correspond to the sacraments in certain other religions such as Christianity. The sanctifying form which reveals the Divine content is provided by the Arabic language which is the sacred language of Islam. The form as well as the content is chosen by God. Man cannot reach the inner content of revelation without accepting fully the form. And Islam is itself the religion of submission to the Divine Will, from which comes peace. The word *islām* itself in Arabic is derived from a root which means both submission and peace.

There are other forms of prayers which complement the daily prayers. Some of these occur on special festive days of the year, and among the most important of these are the congregational prayers on Friday. Whereas the daily prayers may be recited anywhere and are in fact often recited at home, the Friday prayers are usually performed in a mosque and are accompanied by a sermon. They are an important element of the religious life of the community, although more emphasised in the Sunni branch of Islam than in Shi'ism. In some of the major mosques of the Islamic world tens of thousands of worshippers gather for the Friday prayers and often the most urgent social and political problems are discussed in the light of their religious implications, for in Islam there is no separation between the religious and the secular.

The second important Muslim rite is the fasting in the holy months of Ramadan, which lasts from dawn to sunset of each day and consists of complete abstention from both food and water. This trying period of the religious calendar is one during which Muslims seek to purify themselves and wear the armour of God against the world. The month of Ramadan always gives a particular colour to Muslim countries. During the day, life is somewhat slowed down and the atmosphere becomes austere while after sunset there is a great deal of gaiety and joy. It is a period of spiritual and religious rejuvenation for both the individual and the community.

The third cardinal rite of Islam is the pilgrimage or *hajj*. The pilgrimage *par excellence* is of course the one to Mecca, which every Muslim must perform at least once in his lifetime if he is financially and physically in a position to do so. In this great rite, in which hundreds of thousands of Muslims participate every year, the different parts of the Islamic community are brought together at the 'centre' and take with them something of the grace of the 'centre' to all the peripheral regions. Pilgrimage also includes visits to the tombs of saints and holy men, and in Shi'ism visits to the tombs of the Imams in Najaf, Kerbela, Meshed, etc. These other cities of pilgrimage, which are found throughout the Muslim world, are so many echoes of the 'centre' and therefore secondary centres of their own world. Pilgrimage is a major part of the religious life of Muslims everywhere. They interrupt their daily routines with visits to holy places which lie outside the time and space of everyday life.

THE CONDUCT OF LIFE IN ISLAM

The different aspects of the teachings of Islam meant to be followed by all members of the community are encompassed in the Divine Law or *Shariah*, which embraces all facets of human life. It defines man's duties towards God, his neighbour and himself. To live according to the *Shariah* is to live according to the will of God. The teachings of the *Shariah* include not only the rites described above and others which are circumscribed in Islamic teachings, but the social, economic and political aspects of life as well. To deal in the market place according to the *Shariah* is as much a part of a Muslim's religious life as to go to the mosque. The whole of life is integrated into the Divine order by means of the *Shariah*. Religion is not apart from life, nor is it even something that one can say enters into life. In the Islamic ideal it is life itself. And all the manifold activities of life that are legitimate and acceptable in the eyes of God are of a religious character.

The *Shariah* is actualised in Islamic society through both individuals and institutions. There is no priesthood in the commonly understood sense of the word in Islam. The priestly function is divided among all members of the community, especially among the male members, each of whom is the religious guide or *imam* of his own family. But the canonical prayers and other basic rites can be performed by all Muslims, male and female alike, directly before God without any intermediary. The 'church' of Islam corresponds to the whole Islamic community, called the *ummah*, and the clergy or priesthood to all members of this community. If, nevertheless, there is a class of men in the Islamic world, usually dressed in turban and long robes, who devote themselves completely to religious matters and are called *ulamā*, this does not mean that they form a priestly class. Rather, they are men learned in various Islamic sciences, especially the *Shariah*, and by virtue of this learning are more competent than other members of the Islamic community to interpret its teachings. But there is no rite which they can perform and which another Muslim would be denied the right to perform. Most individual rites can be performed by all, while certain collective rites, such as congregational prayers and prayers for the dead, can only be performed by males. The only conditions are knowledge of the rite and possession of religious and moral virtues as taught by the *Shariah*.

Beyond the individual, the most important unit within Islam is the family, which still forms the backbone of Islamic society. The religious instruction of the young is carried out mostly within the family, and the extended family is the most real and meaningful social unit for the Muslim. There is in fact the tendency in Islamic society to integrate all its members within the extended family system so as to provide social and economic protection for all. The Islamic practice of polygamy is closely related to this ideal. Polygamy has never been as widely practised in the Islamic world as is usually imagined. But to the extent that it has been practised, it has been with the twin aims firstly of integrating into the family system single women deprived of their husbands through wars or the like, or those who have simply not succeeded in finding a mate, and secondly of reducing promiscuous sexual relations to a minimum. On both accounts traditional Islamic society succeeded to a remarkable degree.

There are other Islamic institutions—social, economic and political—which have existed during different phases of Islamic history. Some of them, like the craft guilds, still survive, while others, like the caliphate—which was the most characteristic Islamic political institution—no longer exist in fact, although the latter as an ideal has not been completely abandoned. The different Islamic institutions have all been ways through which the teachings and ideals of the *Shariah* have been actualised. Of course all of these teachings have never been fully actualised in any society, men being imperfect by nature. But the *Shariah* and the principles of the Islamic institutions which are contained in it have stood before every Muslim generation as the ideal to be followed. The value both of the individual and of society has been always judged in the light of this transcendent ideal.

Islam has also another dimension which is meant for those who aspire to spiritual realisation and sanctity here on earth. This aspect of the Islamic tradition is called the *tariqah* or 'spiritual way' and has become known in Islamic history as Sufism. The teachings of Sufism have for the most part been organised within Sufi orders, which are spread throughout the Islamic world. In fact the spread of Islam in many regions of the world such as the Indian subcontinent, Indonesia and West Africa has been mostly due to the Sufi orders. Sufism contains the spiritual essence of the teachings of Islam and has expressed itself throughout the ages in exquisite poetry of which the Persian is generally the best known. It has also been closely associated with the other arts of Islamic civilisation such as architecture and music.

DOCTRINAL AND NATIONAL DIVISIONS

Within the all-embracing unity of Islam, of which the 'vertical' divisions consist of the *Shariah* and the *ṭarīqah*, there is also the 'horizontal' division of the community into Sunnism and Shiʻism. Both of these aspects of Islam derive directly from the Koranic revelation and are different interpretations of the same traditional truth. They differ concerning the function and identity of the successor to the Prophet and the question of who is the authority who is to interpret the religious message to men. On the question of rites as well as major theological points such as Divine Unity and eschatology there is little difference between them. The Sunnis comprise the great majority of Muslims, perhaps about four-fifths. The Shiʻites of the Imamite school, or the Twelve-Imam Shiʻites, comprise the overwhelming majority of the Persians, most of the Iraqis and many Pakistanis and Indians, as well as half of the Lebanese Muslims. The Ismāʻīlīs or Seven-Imam Shiʻites, whose spiritual leader is the Aga Khan, are scattered for the most part throughout India, Pakistan, Persia, Syria, Egypt and East Africa. A smaller group of Zaidis or Five-Imam Shiʻites comprise the majority of the Yemenis.

Besides its religious and spiritual teachings, Islam has also been the source of many metaphysical, theological and cosmological teachings of an intellectual order. Likewise it has given birth to an art which is spread throughout the Islamic world and contains some of the world's greatest artistic masterpieces. Islamic spirituality is in a sense an approach to the Divine through beauty, and traditional Islamic art reveals as much of the spirit and message of Islam as do the religious teachings of the *Shariah*. Both Islamic art and Islamic law are reflections of the form and grace of the Koran, each upon its own level of reality.

Today in nearly every Muslim land one can discern a struggle between Islam and Western ideas and institutions, both within the borders of each country and also within the souls of men. Nationalism has placed boundaries between Muslim peoples who, before, lived in a single world. A generation educated in the West or influenced by modern ideologies of different colours rules over most Muslim lands and upholds many ideas which are often in contradiction to the beliefs of the majority. In fact for the most part the vast majority of Muslims remain completely faithful to the teachings of Islam while the small but influential minority which holds power has ceased to belong completely and totally to the tradition because of the influence of the West. The pattern is not identical in every Muslim country but the general trend is similar. Faced with different kinds of economic and military pressures of the non-Muslim world, both Communist and Western, the leaders of the various Muslim countries concentrate all their energies on economic and material development, mostly along Western lines, and sometimes adopt measures that are not conformable with the Islamic view. This cleavage naturally creates a tension within society which characterises much of the Islamic world today.

Yet, even among the modernised classes many Islamic elements continue to survive, manifesting themselves at often unexpected moments. Islam continues as a living force which moulds the life of the vast majority of the Muslim peoples and still determines many of the values of the modernised classes. It is the most essential element in the life of that segment of the world which Westerners call the Middle East, and which for over a millenium has been the locus of a civilisation which had the closest contact and exchange with the West, particularly during the Middle Ages, before the West began to deviate from the common path followed by the two civilisations for so many centuries. To understand the Middle East, both past and present, one must gain an understanding of Islam, which has been and continues to be the most powerful moulding force of the life of individuals and societies in this region.

FURTHER READING

Asad, M. *The Road to Mecca*, Reinhardt, London, 1954.

Burckhardt, T. *An Introduction to Sufi Doctrine*, trans. D. M. Matheson, Muhammad Ashraf, Lahore, 1959.

Dermenghem, E. *Muhammad and the Islamic Tradition*, trans. J. M. Watt, Harper & Row, New York, 1958.

Fazlur, Rahman. *Islam*, Weidenfeld & Nicolson, London, 1966.

Jeffrey, A. (ed.) *A Reader on Islam*, Moulton & Co., Gravenhage, 1962.

Lings, M. *A Muslim Saint of the Twentieth Century*, George Allen & Unwin, London, 1961.

Nasr, S. H. *Ideals and Realities of Islam*, George Allen & Unwin, London, 1966; Praeger, New York, 1967.

Nasr, S. H. *Science and Civilisation in Islam*, Harvard Univ. Press, Cambridge, Mass., 1968.

Schuon, F. *Dimensions of Islam*, trans. P. Townsend, George Allen & Unwin, London, 1970.

Schuon, F. *Understanding Islam*, trans. D. M. Matheson, George Allen & Unwin, London, 1963; Roy, New York.

SEYYED HOSSEIN NASR. Dean of the Faculty of Letters and Professor of Philosophy at Tehran University. Member of the International Committee of the Temple of Understanding. First Aga Khan Professor of Islamic Studies, American University of Beirut 1964–5. Visiting Professor at the Centre of the Study of World Religions, Harvard 1962 and 1965. Associate Professor of Philosophy at Tehran 1958–64. Has lectured in universities throughout the world. Author of numerous books and articles, including *Three Muslim Sages* (1964) and *Ideals and Realities in Islam* (1966).

PART TWO

THE COUNTRIES OF THE MIDDLE EAST

IRAN

MARVIN ZONIS

IRAN has been called the oldest of the 'new nations', a distinction accurately reflecting not only its lengthy history and venerable culture, but also its impressive successes in avoiding the status of a European colony. Some 2,500 years have now passed since the formation of the first of the great Iranian national dynasties. Since then, Iran's fate has fluctuated. Her independence has been lost but regained, her unity shattered but reassembled, and her natural wealth ignored but then exploited for her own benefit. These fluctuations constitute the fascinating panorama of Iran's history.

IRAN AND THE FOREIGN POWERS

The periods of resurgence and prosperity are all marked by the coming to power of Iranian dynasties which overwhelm Iran's ethnic, linguistic and religious minorities, facilitate communication throughout the kingdom, and impose internal security and peace. The Achaemenids (550–330 BC), the Sassanians (AD 226–650), and the Safavids (AD 1500–1722) are counted the three great dynasties of Iranian history. All three made distinctive cultural and political contributions to world history; each was deposed by a foreign invader—Alexander the Great, the Arabs, and the Afghanis—succumbing from a pervasive inner decadence and lack of will. The interregnums were periods of fragmentation and cultural consolidation with the rise of provincial kingdoms or the loss of territory to other empires.[1]

More recent history has witnessed similar processes on a lesser scale. In the late 18th century the Qajars, a Turkic grouping from the north-west, extended their control and established another national dynasty. Under their rule, Iran was drawn into increased contact with Western powers—contact

[1] For references to early Iranian history see Girshmam, R. *Iran from the Earliest Times to the Islamic Conquest*, Penguin Books, Harmondsworth, 1954; Frye, R. N. *The Heritage of Persia*, Cleveland, 1963; Mallowan, M. E. L. *Early Mesopatamia and Iran*, New York, 1965; Olmstead, A. T. *A History of the Persian Empire: The Achaemenid Period*, Chicago, 1948; Rawlinson, G. *The Seventh Great Oriental Monarchy: Or the Geography, History, and Antiquities of the Sassanian or New Persian Empire*, London, 1876; Lockhart, L. *The Fall of the Safavi Dynasty and The Afghan Occupation of Persia*, London, 1958. For works of general history, see Sykes, P. M. *A History of Persia*, 2 vols., Macmillan, London, 1915; Browne, E. G. *A Literary History of Persia*, 4 vols. Cambridge, 1924; and Avery, P. *Modern Iran*, London, 1965.

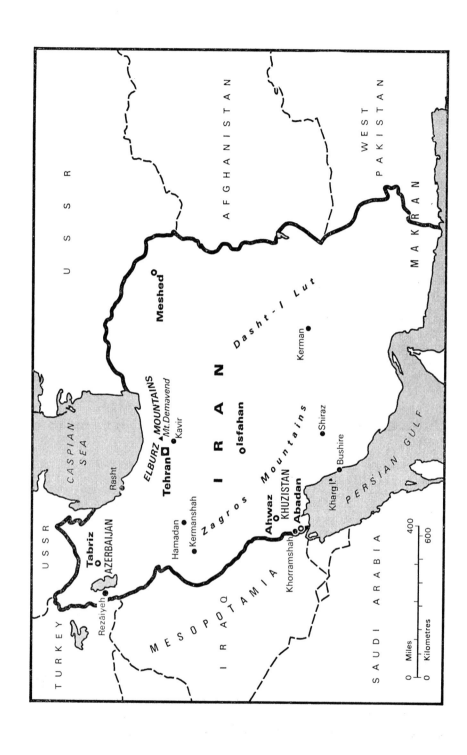

which proved almost totally disastrous for Iran.[2] This fateful half-century began with the assassination of Agha Muhammad Khan Qajar, the 'Eunuch-Shah', who secured the throne for the Qajar dynasty by pursuing his three passions—power, avarice and revenge.[3] There followed a series of missions from Napoleon seeking to draw Persia into alliance against the British in preparation for a French march on India. And equally rapidly, a series of British missions made their way to Tehran to prevent such an occurrence. Despite the fact that the recently crowned Fath Aly Shah was horrified at the regicide nation, in 1807 Persia signed the preliminary Treaty of Finkenstein with France, pledging mutual support for an invasion of India.[4] British pressure on the Shah increased. Finally, with the failure of the French to aid the Persians in their wars with the Tsar, Iran abrogated its earlier agreements and signed a new mutual assistance pact with Great Britain. Besides many provisos almost identical with the Treaty of Finkenstein, the new agreement had the added advantage of providing an *annual* subsidy to Iran of £150,000, to be spent under the supervision of the British ambassador.[5]

In addition to these intra-European political contests fought out on Iranian territory, Persia waged a series of debilitating and destructive wars with her more powerful neighbours to the north and west. From 1804 to 1812, Iran contested Russian pressures on Georgia and Armenia, but by 1813, in defeat, Iran recognised Russian demands on much of the Caucasus as well as ceding to her Baku and other Persian cities and agreeing to maintain no navy on the Caspian Sea. Only eight years later, Persia fought her last campaign with Ottoman Turkey. After a number of initial successes, the Iranian army was decimated by cholera and sued for peace. But Iran had yet to engage in her last major and degrading military encounters with Russia. These occurred from 1825 to 1827 and culminated in the Treaty of Turkomanchai. This document not only specified the cession to Russia of the Persian provinces of Nakhjavan and Yerevan and the payment of an indemnity of £3 million, but also marked the institution of extra-territoriality. Swiftly extended to the subjects of other European powers, these capitulations marked the end of an 'entirely independent' Persia, dramatised by the increasing intervention of the British and Russians in the internal affairs of Iran.[6]

Other events in the later years of the first half of the 19th century bore witness to the change in Iran's relations to the great powers. A Persian expedition of 1836–8 set out to wrest what it considered its rightful territory from Afghan control but was finally checked by pressure from the British. As the Persians laid siege to Herat, the British landed troops in Persian Gulf ports; when finally broached to the Shah, this 'invasion' had assumed

[2] For source material on Qajar history, see Balfour, J. W. *Recent Happenings in Persia*, Blackwood, London, 1922; Browne, E. G. *The Persian Revolution of 1905–1909*, Cambridge, 1910; Curzon, G. N. *Persia and The Persian Question*, 2 vols. London, 1892.
[3] Sir Percy Sykes, *op. cit.*, II, p. 295.
[4] Sykes reports that in his first audience with the French ambassador, Fath Aly Shah allowed himself to ask but three questions, 'How are you?' 'How is Bonaparte?' and 'What made you kill your king?' *Ibid.*, p. 304.
[5] *Ibid.*, p. 309. The subsidy was to continue indefinitely, to be halted only in the event that Iran engaged in a war of aggression.
[6] See Matine-Daftary, Ahmad. *La Suppression de Capitulations en Perse; L'ancien régime et le statut àctuêl des étrangers dans l'Empire du 'Lion et Soleil'*, Paris, 1930. These capitulations were in force until their unilateral revocation by Reza Shah on May 10, 1928.

gargantuan proportions. Later, British and Russian 'advice' resulted in the retirement of the Iranian Prime Minister.

ELITIST NATURE OF IRANIAN SOCIETY

By the accession to the throne of Nasr ed-din Shah in 1848, it was obvious to the young King and his Vizier, Mirza Taghi Khan, that the Western powers were clearly superior to Iran. In a response similar to that of France following the Franco-Prussian war, Iran's defeats were attributed to the backwardness and the non-Western, non-scientific orientation of its educational system. One result was the establishment of the Dar ul-Fonun. Admitting students aged 14 to 16, the school was an attempt to provide educated cadres for the government's civil and military bureaucracies. Entrance tended to be restricted to the children of the élite and no move towards mass education was made. The Dar ul-Fonun graduated some 1,000 members of élite families in its first 50 years of operation, graduates who did fill many of the key posts in government service.[7]

But the school is important, not so much for its output, as for its social implications. For the establishment of the nucleus of a state-supported education system widened and formalised the gap between the élite and the masses by the addition of yet another criterion for élite membership, a criterion which only the children of the élite could acquire. The élitist nature of Iranian society was institutionalised in its education system, a phenomenon which is only now being mitigated.[8]

PRESERVATION OF INDEPENDENT STATUS

But a second more positive outcome of the first half of the 19th century was the protracted success of Iran in avoiding a directly colonial status, a success which has continued to the present. Ever since the introduction of European power into the area following the invasion of Egypt by Napoleon, Iran has been considered a valuable prize. For the French, Iran represented a potential ally in her struggles with the British in India. When those struggles waned following the establishment of complete British hegemony, French interest diminished, leaving the field to the British and Russians.

It seems clear that from the late 17th century Britain's interests lay chiefly in protecting the north-western approaches to India—the only possible invasion route unimpeded by formidable mountains. With alterations of governments and circumstances, British policy fluctuated between the aggressive pursuit of active control over the Iranian government to a passive policy seeking only to prevent Russia from controlling Iran.[9] Russia seems to have been pursuing a variety of interests at different periods : control of territory

[7] For information on the Dar ul-Fonun, see Arasteh, R. *Education and Social Awakening in Iran*, Leiden, 1962, pp. 20–21 ; Sadiq, Issa. *Dowreye Mokhtasere Tarikhe Farhange Iran* ('The Contemporary Era of the History of Iranian Education'), Tehran, 1961, esp. pp. 163 ff.; and Farman Farmanyan, H. 'The Forces of Modernization in Nineteenth-Century Iran : A Historical Survey' in Polk, W. R. and Chambers, R. L. (eds.) *Beginnings of Modernization in The Middle East, The Nineteenth Century*, Chicago, 1968, pp. 126–128.

[8] See, for example, Zonis, Marvin. *Iran: The Politics of Insecurity*, Princeton, forthcoming, Chapter VI; and 'Higher Education and Social Change in Iran', in Yar-Shater, E. (ed.) *Iran in The 1960's*, New York, forthcoming.

[9] See Greaves, R. L. *Persia and the Defence of India, 1884–1892*, London, 1959.

for strategic interests, capturing warm water ports on the Persian Gulf, or simple economic imperialism.[10]

Iran's success in preserving her independence was based on the art of playing off one foreign power against the other. The last half of the 19th century illustrates a series of classic manœuvres of this type. Fearing for Iran's security, the Shah would turn to the Russians for support. When Russian influence was threatening to become too great, the Shah would turn to the British. When the British demanded a concession over Iran's railroads in return, a concession which the Shah was unwilling to give, he approached the Russians and urged them to demand a similar concession. Then he could return to the British and promise not to award the Russians rights for constructing railroads if they did not press their demands. Thus no concessions were granted and Iran retained her independence.

Two developments altered this balance. Firstly, foreign powers learned to make complementary rather than conflicting demands. No longer could the Shah refuse to grant demands for concessions on the grounds that the other foreign power would lose out. By the end of the 19th century, there were British and Russian banks, British and Russian trade companies, British and Russian capitulations (the right of citizens of those countries to be tried by their own rather than by Iranian courts), British and Russian control over Persian customs, etc.

Second, Britain and Russia, drawn together by the fear of a recently united and restless Germany, determined to settle their extra-European differences in order to concentrate on the new challenge. The Treaty of 1907 divided Iran and certain other countries, into 'spheres of influence'. The Russians were given a virtually free hand in northern Iran, including Tehran and Isfahan. The British received a small zone in the south-east flanking British India. In between was a large neutral zone including the city of Shiraz. Despite protestations to the contrary, Iranian nationalists viewed the treaty as a prelude to the dismemberment of their country. That fear was exacerbated by the failure of the signatories to consult or notify Iran about their agreement. Indeed, in the year preceding World War I, Russia adopted an imposing position of supremacy in her zone.

When the World War broke out, Iran immediately declared its neutrality, but this did not protect it from involvement. Russia and Britain on the one hand and the Ottoman Empire on the other invaded the country, established military bases, fought campaigns, and even went so far as to organise military units on Iranian territory. (These units were composed of Iranian recruits, equipped, officered, and paid by the British or Russians.)

As a result of the direct and indirect intervention of foreign governments and of her own internal weakness and decay, Iran's sovereignty seemed to be rapidly slipping away. Had it not been for the Bolshevik Revolution and the subsequent renunciation by Lenin of all Czarist, imperialist claims, it is likely that the 1907 agreement would have been formalised into the dismemberment of Iran and the end of its independence. But Iran was saved from that fate and, as one of the few countries of Asia and Africa to have preserved her independence in the age of imperialism, strengthened a deep-rooted sense of national pride and national identity. Moreover Iran became an astute participant in the game of international politics, a role which has been played up to the present day. When an outside power threatened, an appeal was made for protection to a second power, hostile to the first. (Hence

[10] See Kazedzadeh, F. *Britain and Russia in Persia, 1864–1914*, New Haven, 1968.

the vital role of the United States in post-World War II Iran when the Soviets supported the 'independent' Republics of Azerbaijan and Kurdestan in Iran's north-west and west. True to form, as the Shah saw that threat diminish and his own internal political position strengthen, the value of the USA to the Shah diminished and American influence accordingly fell. The Iran-USSR steel mill pact in 1965 and the provision of over $100 million worth of military supplies by the USSR thereafter were only the outward manifestations of a return to the 'normal' pattern of foreign relations for Iran.)

PERSIAN CONSTITUTIONAL MOVEMENT 1905–9

Besides these themes in Iran's foreign relations—the intervention of Russia and Great Britain (and more recently of the Soviet Union and the United States) in Iran's domestic affairs to advance their own interests, Iran's success in avoiding colonial status, the élite nature of Iranian society—additional major themes run through recent Iranian history. One is the Persian Constitutional Movement of 1905–9, which resulted in the first regulation by a formal constitution of the political affairs of any Middle Eastern state. The movement had its roots in the granting of concessions to foreign companies seeking to exploit Iran in the latter part of the 19th century. Then concession hunters from Great Britain and Russia competed for the right to control Iran's foreign trade, to develop its natural resources, to build railways and bridges, to monopolise any economic undertaking which promised sizeable economic benefit.

That such benefits could accrue to foreigners was due to the total corruption of the monarch and his court, the pervasive decay of public morality, internal administrative and political anarchy, and foreign pressures. These had contributed to the near bankruptcy of the government and a pressing need for funds. The monarch, Nasr ed-din Shah, who ruled from 1848 to his assassination in 1896, became infatuated with travel in Europe and his three trips in 1873, 1878, and 1889 created a need for vast sums of money.[11] The Shah's demand for funds, in combination with internal decay and external pressure, made Iran a fruitful arena for concession hunters ready to bribe Iranian officials.

The incredible backwardness of Iran at the end of the 19th century meant that a virtually limitless array of projects were available and worthwhile. One perceptive British traveller, Edward G. Browne, wrote :

'When I was in Persia [in 1888], the old régime held undisputed sway, and except for the existence of the Indo-European telegraph, the conditions of life were entirely medieval. There were no railways, no banks, no paper money, no cabs, no hotels outside the capital, and, of course, no telephones. The few newspapers which appeared at irregular intervals were lithographed, and, being produced by courtiers and officials, contained hardly any news and no criticism, had a very restricted circulation and no sale save such as was secured by supplying them to government employees and deducting the subscription from their salaries. . . . The only method of travel was on foot or horseback. . . . The Government was a pure despotism, mitigated by the lack of centralization and the quasi-independence of the provincial governors, which often made it possible to escape

[11] For a report by the Shah himself on one of these trips see Nasir ed-din Shah Qajar, *A Diary Kept by H. M. the Shah of Persia During His Journey to Europe in 1878 AD*, Hontum-Shindler, A. and Norman, Baron L. de (trans.) London, 1878.

oppression by the simple process of moving into another district under a more benign rule. . . ."[12]

Two concessions in the last half of the century served as rallying points to unite members of the élite in opposition to the Shah. The first was a concession to Baron Julius de Reuter to exploit all Iran's natural resources and for the construction of factories and communication facilities.[13] This breathtaking sacrifice of Iran's sovereignty led to an informal coalition of dissident elements who pressed the Shah into cancelling the concession. The second concession in 1882 was to a British firm for a monopoly over the production, distribution, and sale of tobacco. This concession struck directly at all sectors of society—as consumers or as producers—and generated an immediate and widespread reaction. In response to growing opposition this concession was also cancelled. For the first time in contemporary Iranian history, a popular outcry was able to change the course of the government.[14]

From these roots stemmed the Constitutional Movement. A revulsion against internal despotism and decay and external degradation grew. The mortgaging of the country's assets to finance foreign pleasure trips had brought Iran to the verge of colonial status. The tyranny and reaction of the Shah and his court contributed to the profound backwardness of the nation. Gradually over the last quarter of the 19th century the belief grew that Iran could be saved from these evils by the spread of the 'enlightened' culture of the more advanced societies and by the formulation of a code of laws. During 1905 and 1906 these beliefs resulted in demonstrations, economic strikes, and religious protests. Finally, in the summer of 1906, thousands of Tehranis, especially the merchants and religious leaders, encamped on the grounds of the British Legation and took sanctuary (bast) from their own government. The eventual result of these and other pressures was the granting by the Shah of a Constitution and Supplemental laws, which defined and limited his own powers. The Constitution also formally specified the creation of a Parliament with a lower house (Majlis) and an upper house.

From its first session, whenever the régime or reactionary landlords have been unable to control its elections, the Majlis has been the political seat of the most ardent nationalists. Moreover, given its constitutional function of limiting the power of the Shah, it has naturally been the subject of continual efforts by the throne to reduce its autonomy and thus its power to limit the freedom of action of the monarch. With the exception of one election during World War II and another during the Mossadeq period, no Majlis since this early period has been elected free of official control. The role of the Majlis, then, as a check on the royal prerogative has been severely limited.

One result is that opposition to governmental policies or to the Shah has frequently taken the form of demands for liberal democracy, parliamentarianism, or more basically, constitutionalism. The widespread appeal which such slogans generate has put 20th century Iranian monarchs on the defensive. Thus even while violating its provisions they have had to act in the

---

[12] Browne, E. G. *A Brief Narrative of Recent Events in Persia With an Appendix on the Persian Constitution*, London, 1909, p. 10.

[13] Frechtling, L. E. 'The Reuter Concession in Persia', *Asiatic Review*, XXXIV (July, 1938), pp. 518–533.

[14] Keddie, N. R. *Religion and Rebellion in Iran: The Iranian Tobacco Protest of 1891–2*, London, 1966 and Lambton, A. K. S. 'The Tobacco Regie: Prelude to Revolution', *Studia Islamica*, XXII (1965), pp. 119–157; XXIII (1965), pp. 71–90.

name of the constitution. But while the document alone cannot guarantee a constitutional régime, it does serve as a potent symbol around which Iranian political forces can find some degree of unity. It also serves as a hallmark against which to judge the performance of the régime. And it is a goal toward which the monarchs of this century have at least ostensibly directed the course of their rule.[15]

TOWARDS MODERNISATION

Another key theme of importance during the last two centuries of Iranian history is a drive towards modernisation initiated and supported by the state. After the granting of the constitution, Iran passed through two decades of internal dissension between nationalist politicians, seeking to implement the constitution, and the Shah and his supporters, who sought the abrogation of that instrument. The issue was decided by the parliament's refusal to approve a treaty proposed by Great Britain, which would have made Iran a virtual protectorate with British officials occupying key posts throughout the State. Shortly after the issue became a dead letter in February of 1921, a fiery Iranian journalist, Seyyed Zia ed-din Tabatabai, and the leader of the Iranian Cossak brigade, Reza Khan, staged a coup d'état. It appears that the coup was facilitated by the British who then withdrew their troops that still remained in Iran from World War I.[16] Reza Khan steadily consolidated his power, sending into exile first Seyyed Zia and then, in 1925, Ahmad Shah, the last of the Qajar monarchs. Installing himself as the first ruler of the Pahlavi dynasty, Reza Shah (as he was thereafter known) imposed rigorous taxes on sugar and tea and generated funds for the construction of the Grand Iranian Railway. He introduced a fledgling industrial system, built highways between cities and new roads within the major cities of Iran. The modern state-supported education system expanded at all levels, with new sections of the population finding an education within their grasp for the first time. He also established the first modern institution of higher learning in his country—the University of Tehran. In addition, his efforts at emancipating Iranian women, including the outlawing of the Iranian veil (*chador*), had a profound effect on the social structure. Modernising the civil and military bureaucracies and establishing a contemporary system of government finance were also important steps in the transition from a backward monarchy to a modern nation.

In short, Reza Shah gave impetus to and laid the basis for the more radical changes which have overtaken Iran since his rule. Often referred to as the 'Atatürk of Iran', Reza Shah operated within narrower limits than his Turkish counterpart. He himself was less worldly (his first trip outside the borders of Iran occurred toward the end of his rule with a visit to Atatürk), less well educated (it appears that at the time of his coronation he was but

---

[15] Some of the major sources of contemporary politics in Iran are Bayne, E. A. *Persian Kingship in Transition*, New York, 1968; Binder, L. *Iran: Political Development in a Changing Society*, California, 1963; Cottam, R. W. *Nationalism in Iran*, Pittsburgh, 1964; Marlowe, J. *Iran, a Short Political Guide*, New York, 1963; H.I.M. Mohammad Reza Shah Pahlavi. *Mission for My Country*, London, 1961 and *The White Revolution*, Tehran, 1966; Upton, J. M. *The History of Modern Iran: An Interpretation*, Cambridge, Mass., 1960; and Zonis, M. *op. cit.*

[16] Seyyed Zia ed-din has informed me in a personal interview that he is the author of a manuscript setting down his role in and interpretation of the coup d'état. The manuscript was in a vault in Switzerland with instructions that it be published on his death. This venerable figure has now passed away.

semi-literate), and less committed to democratic principles (with no pretence whatsoever he violated virtually every article of the constitution). Moreover, Iran at the time of his accession had much less than Turkey of the foundations of modernity—a smaller cadre of technically trained persons and a poorer economic and communications infrastructure.[17]

But working within these limitations Reza Shah began the state-directed development of Iran and established a strong central government with control over the farthest reaches of his domain. These two processes—state-sponsored development and the growing power of the central government—continue unabated to the present day.[18]

THE ROLE OF THE MONARCH

Another important aspect of contemporary Iranian history is the ruler's search for a political base of support. Suffice it here to trace the fate of Iran's present monarch, Shah Muhammad Reza Pahlavi, who acceded to the throne in 1941 following the deposition of his father by the British and Russians. Those two powers had launched a two-pronged attack from the north and south in August of 1941 to counter the threat which they perceived from Reza Shah's friendship with Nazi Germany. With Reza Shah exiled, his 21-year-old son's insecure throne depended on the graces of the British and Russians who had deposed his father. Supported by these foreign powers and by many of the élite who had served the ex-monarch, particularly his military generals, the Shah reconstructed his defeated army. Throughout the war years Iran was beset by economic disintegration, savage attacks on the 20-year rule of Reza Shah, and political chaos. But with his civil and military élites, the Shah was able to maintain a tenuous grip on the throne even after the withdrawal of the British and American troops, who had joined the occupiers in 1942, and after the ultimate withdrawal of the Soviets and the collapse of their ill-fated 'autonomous' People's Republics of Azerbaijan and Kurdistan.

An abortive assassination attempt on the life of the Shah in 1949 was followed by the outlawing and repression of the Iranian Communist Party.[19] Simultaneously, the National Front, a growing movement under the direction of Dr. Muhammad Mossadeq, became more vociferous about the need to nationalise the Anglo-Iranian Oil Company (a majority of whose shares were owned by the British government). Mounting pressures on the Shah led to the appointment of Dr. Mossadeq as Prime Minister and the Shah's acceptance of the Parliament's vote to nationalise Iranian oil. With the breakdown of diplomatic relations and of political and economic negotiations with the British over the fate of the disputed oil, Mossadeq vowed to go it alone with an 'oil-less' but truly independent and nationalistic government.

[17] See Banani, Amin. *The Modernization of Iran, 1921–1941*, Stanford, 1961.

[18] For information on the recent Iranian economy and economic development see Amuzegar, J. *Technical Assistance in Theory and Practice: The Case of Iran*, New York, 1966; Baldwin, G. B. *Planning and Development in Iran*, Baltimore, 1967; English, P. W. *City and Village in Iran: Settlement and Economy in the Kirman Basin*, Madison, 1966; Gittinger, J. P. *Planning for Agricultural Development: The Iranian Experience*, Washington, 1965; Issawi, C. 'Iran's Economic Upsurge', *Middle East Journal*, XXI, pt. 4 (1967), pp. 447–62; Lambton, A. K. S. *The Persian Land Reform 1962–6*, Oxford, 1969; and see Agah, M. (ed.) *Tahqiqat e Eqtesadi* ('Economic Research'), a quarterly journal published in Persian and English by the University of Tehran.

[19] See Zabih, Sepehr. *The Communist Movement—Iran*, Berkeley, 1966.

What followed was a struggle for power between the Monarch and his Minister. When the Shah dismissed Mossadeq, much of the population of Tehran took to the streets and the Shah relented. But over the course of the next year, this intense struggle for power, coupled with Mossadeq's increasingly autocratic rule and his inability to solve the oil crisis—thus preventing the inflow of large sums of money—disheartened his supporters. When the Shah again dismissed Mossadeq in August of 1953, crowds again took to the streets. But this time they were on the side of the Shah, who returned from a brief self-imposed exile to Rome in triumph. While the US Central Intelligence Agency played a key role on behalf of the Shah in those fateful days, it was primarily the Prime Minister's inability to maintain his coalition which was responsible for his collapse.

When the Shah returned he found himself in much the same position as he had been in 1946 and as his father had been in 1925, master of a throne with a centuries-long tradition of charisma but whose base of support was primarily the army. To strengthen that support, the Shah conducted an extensive purge of his Officer Corps, arresting or dismissing hundreds of officers accused of Communist inclinations or activities. With that base secured, he began to experiment with other forms of control.

From 1957 to 1960 a royally chartered and directed two-party system was created. One party was to serve as the government, with the other as the 'loyal opposition'. Both were under the direction of close personal friends of the Shah, but the 'tweedledum-tweedledee' character of the parties failed to provide any genuine outlet for political expression.

Simultaneously, the Shah convened the upper house of the parliament, provided for by the constitution but never previously organised. The constitution empowered the King to appoint half of the Senate's 60 members and with that power he was able to pack a second parliamentary body with established and conservative figures, who could at least serve as a check on what he considered the excesses of the first.

The 1960 elections to the parliament, however, revealed that the Shah's control over the political system was still tenuous and his support unreliable. As the elections proceeded, political disquiet and widely voiced complaints of electoral corruption led to the Shah's cancellation of the elections themselves. A second round of elections proved no more successful and the Shah prorogued the Parliament, installing a popular and liberal Prime Minister, Dr. Aly Amini, to rule unconstitutionally in the absence of a parliament. But Amini was distrusted by the Shah and with the return of at least a surface calm, he was dismissed and the Shah asked his closest boyhood friend, Assadollah Alam, to form a new government.

Alam was an ideal transition figure from the chaos of the early 1960s to the surface quiet of the late 1960s. He could be counted on to carry out His Majesty's wishes with little temporising. And this he did. He continued to rule without a parliament while submitting a series of reform measures. collectively known as the White Revolution, to a national referendum. These reforms constituted a series of initiatives from the throne designed to alter the base of political power in Iran. Aiming directly for support from traditionally excluded groups in society, the Shah sought to reduce his dependence on the military on the one hand and on the established political élites on the other while undercutting the National Front by leap-frogging directly to the farmers and workers and women, through land reform and profit-sharing in industrial enterprises and by extending the suffrage to women. The referendum resulted in an overwhelming vote of approval and served as a signal for going ahead with plans to hold a parliamentary election, an election whose outcome would be more favourable to the rule of the Shah.

These plans were disrupted, however, by the outbreak of three days of nation-wide rioting in June 1963, touched off by the arrest of Ayatollah Khomeini, the leading Shi'a *mullah* of Iran. Khomeini, a young and relatively unknown cleric, had achieved widespread popularity by his outspoken criticisms of the government for its allegedly 'anti-Islamic' policies. In previous years, such rioting would have toppled the government and shaken the roots of the régime. Coming as it did upon the heels of a month of tribal fighting in south-central Iran (fighting which resulted in the temporary capture by the tribes of the Shiraz international airport), these riots were especially threatening. But the ability and willingness of the government to employ military force and to act decisively in putting down both disturbances indicated that a new phase of Iranian politics had begun. The government could now boast a significant monopoly of physical force and a willingness to exercise it. The opposition was disorganised, their leaders having left the country, been jailed, or withdrawn from politics; their followers were demoralised or frightened, or worse. The Shah moved ahead with hardly an interruption.

New elections for the *Majlis* were organised and carried out far more efficiently than in the past, the members of the new parliament representing a considerable broadening of the social groups now participating in politics. On the other hand, the newly elected delegates, few of whom had been politically active in the past and thus had no political bases, were co-opted into the parliament to serve the interests of the régime. Thus the possibility of their challenging the régime in any way was negligible. (Moreover the senate, still composed almost entirely of the old élites, remained quiet.)

With the convening of the parliament in an atmosphere of tranquillity, the Shah's confidant and Prime Minister had successfully completed his mission. He stepped down and a new government was formed by Hassan Aly Mansur, head of a grouping then being billed as the New Iran Party, with a majority in the parliament. By the end of his first year in office, Mansur had managed to antagonise virtually all sectors of the politically aware. His arrogance and arbitrariness provoked widespread bitterness and ultimately a resort to a political weapon frequently used in Iran's past. Mansur was assassinated on the steps of the *Majlis* as he went to present a new government bill. It is significant however, that the Shah was able to appoint Mansur's Finance Minister as Prime Minister and to ensure the continuation of his policies with little alteration in the affairs of state.

The new Prime Minister and many of the younger men in their 30s and 40s with Western, technical education who were brought in by Mansur, have continued to serve until the present day. Their tenure of office is nearly the longest for any such officials in this century. Nor was the continuity of the régime shaken a few months after Mansur's death by yet another assassination attempt on the life of the Shah. A member of the Imperial Guards turned a machine-gun on the Shah in front of his office. While his two personal bodyguards were shot down, the King escaped injury. Once again he had been saved and once again his own sense of *baraka* or 'divine blessing' was heightened. Whatever the truth of the latter claim, it serves to bolster support among certain segments of the population, and to strengthen the confidence of the Shah in the correctness of the course he has established for Iran and for his régime. The failure of this assassination attempt to disturb the equilibrium of the régime seems to reinforce this view. With vir-

197

tually no exception, Iranian politics have continued to demonstrate 'stability' since that time.

And yet in the face of these widely admired triumphs, it is generally agreed that Muhammad Reza Shah has not succeeded in establishing the wide political base he has so ardently sought. The support of the masses does exist, but such support is an intangible base for Royal strength. The single party remains an artificially nourished collectivity of office seekers. Thus, the Shah maintains and continues to operate the Iranian political system only at the cost (and it is a debilitating one) of devoting a disproportionate amount of his resources to maintaining the processes of co-option which bind the political élites to his régime.

ECONOMIC AND SOCIAL AFFAIRS

Throughout the contemporary period, changes have occurred in the pattern of economic and social relations in the country. The state-initiated drive for industrialisation opened new avenues of investment for the existing upper classes. Correctly perceiving the opportunities for investment in light consumer-oriented industries, they began to switch capital from farming to the cities, especially following World War II. As Iran developed an extensive light industry sector, the landlords were able to preserve their economic positions following land reform. No longer relying on land as the sole or even the principal basis of their wealth, the loss of their rural estates did not affect their position in the structure of society.

The expansion of industry has also resulted in the creation of a substantial middle class located primarily in Tehran. Composed of the children of bazaar merchants and civil servants, these individuals obtained some modern education and then administrative positions in private or government industries. In addition, large numbers of them became part of the modern commercial sector by establishing shops or wholesale houses outside the traditional bazaars. The middle class has also expanded as a consequence of the phenomenal growth of the civil bureaucracy. Finally, an even larger growth of this middle class may be expected in the future as a vastly expanded system of higher education, including both universities and technical institutes, begins to turn out graduates in substantial numbers.

Perhaps the chief consequence of the growth of the middle class has been the expansion of the demand for physical amenities and material goods. The government has sought to win their support through urban development, luxury imports, the provision of private automobiles, etc., all of which requires that the government should devote substantial resources to insuring the satisfaction of consumer demands.

But despite these changes (the expansion in the size of the middle class, the growth in the economic role of the government, and the increase in industry) the bulk of Iran's population is involved in a pattern of economic relations which is traditional and persistent.[20] Some two-thirds of the population are rural dwellers engaged in food production and living at or near subsistence levels, with all the attendant problems of illiteracy, ill-health, and a lack of involvement in national political and social life. They are tied to local urban centres where they dispose of their limited agricultural surpluses in exchange for a few simple consumer goods.

And yet alterations in these patterns may be expected in the near future.

[20] For a definitive treatment of these relations see English, *op. cit.*

For the recent land reform in Iran has severed the ties between the landlords and the peasants, ties which are only now being replaced by organisations which will relate the peasants directly to the government through agricultural cooperatives and extension agents. The opportunities for government intervention in the society as a whole are thus unprecedented in Iranian history. But so are the risks which the government will assume, with the recognition of its responsibility for the welfare of the rural population.

In short, both the Iranian economy and social structure are at a significant crossroads. While it is still too early for major trends to have become evident, it is likely they will appear in the near future. Whether they bode well for the economy and polity remains to be seen.

The main themes of the last two centuries of Iranian history still characterise relevant issues of contemporary politics. Relations with the USA and USSR remain in flux, with the régime establishing closer relations with its northern neighbour and with Eastern Europe. The distribution of Iran's national wealth in overwhelming proportions to her social, political and economic élites continues. With the vast increase in available resources over the last decade, the actual disparities between the élite and the masses have become even more striking. The viability of the Persian Constitution remains an important issue for many politically active Iranians, and their efforts to give effect to its provisions have frequently resulted in their political downfall. The state-sponsored drive for modernisation proceeds vigorously. And as with the imbalances in the distribution of resources, so the state-sponsored modernisation drive serves to perpetuate and even create new impediments to social mobility. The régime is more powerful and less susceptible to challenge than at any time in recent history, while it continues to seek ways of mobilising political support without releasing powerful opposition forces.

Behind all these processes lie the person and the institution of kingship. The Shah remains the central actor and prime mover of political life in Iran. On his person and on the skills he can bring to bear on the politics of Iran depends the destiny of his country in the immediate future. His role in more distant times is less certain but there is every reason to expect the themes of recent history to remain key issues for the indefinite future.

MARVIN ZONIS. Assistant Professor of Political and Social Sciences and Acting Director of the Centre for Middle Eastern Studies at the University of Chicago since 1966; President of the American Institute of Iranian Studies and a member of the Joint Committee on the Near and Middle East. Instructor in Political Science at MIT 1965–6. Research Training Fellowship, Social Science Research Council 1963–5. The author of several articles, his *Iran: The Politics of Insecurity* is shortly to be published by Princeton University Press.

IRAQ

RIGGAN ER-RUMI

EARLY HISTORY

'NIMROD', Genesis tells us, 'was a mighty hunter before the Lord. And the beginning of his kingdom was Babel and Erech and Accad and Calneh in the land of Shinar. Out of the land went forth Asshur and builded Nineveh and the city Rehoboth and Calah.' This, for generations of Europeans, was the first mention of the land that is today Iraq. Archaeologists have been able to identify most of the places mentioned. Shinar (Sumer) is that part of Iraq that lies south of Baghdad, while Nineveh and Calah are in the north near Mosul. It is clear that the Bible recounts historical events, even if in garbled form and with a foreshortened time-scale. The violent overthrow of Babylon, the last kingdom in the land of Shinar, is also described in the Bible with some accuracy and great dramatic force. That occurred in 539 BC. For as long a period as separates us from the death of Belshazzar, Mesopotamia had been a centre of civilisation, from which even the Cretans and Ancient Greeks had learned skills and drawn ideas. But from now on, except for the brief splendour of the 'Abbasid caliphs—a splendour that owed much to Persia—Mesopotamia was to be a mere province in some alien empire until the 20th century. Her cuneiform writing dropped out of use and was forgotten; her art faltered and was lost. Although her agriculture and the intricate system of irrigation continued to function, if in declining fashion, for two millenia, only the Bible, a few mounds and some significant sounding place-names reminded the world of a great but lost civilisation. For Xenophon, at the beginning of the fourth century BC, Nineveh was a nameless 'large, undefended fortification near a city called Mescila'. For the next thousand years foreign armies—Greeks, Persians, Parthians, Romans, Sassanians—campaigned through the land and ruled it for longer or shorter periods. Then in AD 635 came the Muslim Arabs. The conquest was decisive. Mesopotamia has remained an Arab and a Muslim country ever since. But for yet another century the land was still ruled from a distant capital, in this case Damascus.

THE 'ABBASID CALIPHATE

Only in AD 749, when the 'Abbasids seized the caliphate, did the centre of power return to Mesopotamia. A few years later the caliph, al-Mansour, built his famous 'round city' on the right bank of the Tigris and for a century Baghdad became the wonder of the world. This was the Persian Baghdad of Harun al-Rashid, of the *Thousand and One Nights*, of *Sinbad*. The city

USSR

TURKEY

SYRIA

IRAN

KURDISTAN

Niniveh
Mosul
CALAH
Arbīl
Dokan
Sulaymānīyah
Shargat
Kirkŭk

Tigris
Diyala
Euphrates

Sāmarrā
Khanaquin
Adhamiyah
Ba'qûabāh
Baghdad

Rutba
Ramādi
L.Habbaniyah

I   R   A   Q

SYRIAN

Kerbelā
Al Hillah
Al Kŭt
Al Kŭfah
Al Amārah
Najaf
Ad Dīwānīyah

DESERT

As Samāwah

An Nāsirīyah
Shatt
al-Arab
Basra

SAUDI ARABIA

NEUTRAL
ZONE
KUWAIT

0 Miles	100	200
0 Kilometres		300

was at the centre of an efficient communications system. Merchants and messengers, commerce and political despatches moved freely to and fro along the seaways and roads to places as distant as China. Prosperity brought with it a period of brilliant achievement in literature, philosophy, science and the arts. There was a cultural give-and-take with both West and East. From the West came Greek works of medicine and science which were translated into Arabic. From the East came new ideas in mathematics and astronomy as well as decorative motifs. Many museums can show the high standards achieved in pottery, weaving, metal work and wall decoration. This was no one-way traffic. Influences were exported as well as imported. When a gold coin was struck for King Offa of Mercia in AD 774, the model chosen was an 'Abbasid dinar, presumably because 'Abbasid coins had a high reputation with the English. So slavishly was the original imitated that the Arabic inscription is still partly legible. But the writing had no meaning for the natives. The rubric *Offa Rex* appears between the lines of Arabic, but upside down.

Ominously, the style of government was no longer that of an accessible Arab tribal leader, as it had been under the Umayyads in Syria, but of an oriental despot. The brief century of 'Abbasid splendour was succeeded by four centuries of political fragmentation and decline. Turkish mercenaries were early brought in to guard the body of the caliph. Soon he became their captive. At the end of the 12th century there came the first of a series of swift and ruthless Mongol raids that destroyed all hope of revival. Iraq reverted to the position of a remote province in a distant empire, usually Turkish, but sometimes Persian. Journeys became dangerous, the government weak, the tribes uncontrolled, the land depopulated. Mongol destruction and Ottoman neglect have been variously blamed for Iraq's commercial and agricultural decline, but the neglect of the irrigation system and the flight from the land may have begun as early as the golden age of Harun al-Rashid and his rapacious tax farmers.

THE OTTOMAN *VILAYET*

Slowly, even the memories of the splendours of Baghdad faded. Mesopotamia became an unknown, desert land to be crossed at some risk by European travellers like Ralph Fitch (in the 1580s) on their way to India by caravan and raft down the Euphrates. Early in the 19th century world attention began to centre on Mesopotamia because of its position across the fastest route to India. Increasing numbers of Europeans began to come and look about them, to explore and to describe what they found. The accounts of people like Claudius Rich, Buckingham, Layard, the Blunts and Gertrude Bell make entertaining reading and give a vivid picture of the land in late Ottoman times. The *vilayets* of Iraq were still very much part of a universal Muslim empire, in which religion, laws, attitudes and institutions formed an accepted and integrated civilisation that included Persia, Turkey, Egypt, North Africa and much besides. Although ideas of Arab nationalism had begun to gain acceptance early in the 20th century, these ideas were based on language and culture and had nothing to do with a particular territory or a nation state. Yet when Turkey was defeated in 1918 the victorious allies could hardly do other than form such states out of the dismembered Ottoman empire. As Britain's forces had occupied Mesopotamia, she became its mandatory protector after the war. Britain gave the new state a king from the other side of the Arab peninsula, a constitution, a parliament and

202

an administration. It fell to Britain to rebut Turkey's claim to the *vilayet* of Mosul and by so doing to give Iraq, with minor exceptions, her present frontiers.

THE FRONTIERS

These frontiers are the result of administrative convenience, not of natural logic. Iraq has no natural defences. The mountains to the north and east have never been a serious obstacle to the movements of peoples or invaders. The Sumerians seem to have come from there, and they were followed by many others. To the west the steppe has been an easy highway for human beings ever since paleolithic times. It was used above all by peoples speaking Semitic languages : the Akkadians, for example, early in the third millenium BC and the Ammorites early in the second. This was the route by which Abraham travelled from Ur to the land of Canaan. Even Greeks and Romans were familiar with this way. Only to the south did the desert provide a safe frontier—until the camel was domesticated by Arab tribesmen. How easily it could then be crossed by well-mounted warriors was early shown by the Muslim conquerors, notably Khalid Bin Walid, the 'Sword of God', in 633.

INTERNAL DIVISIONS

Nor do the frontiers follow any obvious ethnic or religious boundaries. Many of Iraq's intractable political problems arise precisely from the inclusion within the country of religious and linguistic minorities. The Ottoman Turks were of the orthodox or Sunni branch of Islam, to which the majority of Arab Muslims outside Iraq belong, and the Ottomans naturally favoured the Sunnis among their subjects and relied on them to administer the country. It was impossible for a Shi'a Arab to rise to public office in Ottoman times. Yet half the population of Iraq was and is Shi'a, a sect adopted by Iraqis and Persians in the early decades of the Muslim era, almost it would seem as a protest against their Sunni Syrian rulers. This difference was adroitly exploited by the 'Abbasids to sieze power; the main shrines of the Shi'a world, Kerbela, Najaf, and Kadhimain, as well as the bulk of the Shi'a population are found from Baghdad southwards. In the north there are the Kurds, who though Sunni speak an Indo-European language akin to Persian. Their territory spreads across the area where Turkey, Persia and Iraq meet. They were there when Xenophon passed through, and their guerrilla tactics were the same then as they are today. There are other minority groups, each with its own religion, language and troubled history : Sabtis, white-robed baptists and silver-smiths; tragic 'Assyrian' Christians, who formed the bulk of Britain's Iraq levies; Armenians, bankers, musicians and craftsmen, who have stepped into the gap left by the Jews; and the Jews themselves. In 1914 Baghdad was largely a Jewish city, and the Baghdad Jews were a cultivated community, as was brilliantly shown by the Sassoon family. But now, after the creation of Israel, Jews are mistrusted by their Arab compatriots and most of them have left the country.

It is difficult for an outsider to understand the hold that a minority has had, and often still has, over its members in Iraq. Under the Ottomans a man lived and usually worked in a village or part of a town inhabited by others who believed as he did and spoke with the same accent. Here would be the mosque or church of his sect, presided over by a religious leader who would also dispense the group's laws and represent it with the central government. A man's whole allegiance would be given to, and his own identity depend on, the group. For him the concept of 'nation' would simply not exist. The Yazidis, who live north and west of Mosul, still form a group of this sort. A closed community, misunderstood by their immediate neighbours, they have often been wrongly described as devil worshippers. In fact they are virtuous, brave and self-respecting Muslims who believe in the primacy of the 'Peacock Angel'. Though he once fell, like Satan, he was reinstated by a forgiving God, and now outshines the other angels in splendour.

But the divisions within the population of Iraq do not end with the minorities. Other divisions arise from differing ways of life. The spread of primary education has proceeded at an unequal rate; in Baghdad attendance is 100%, in some country districts only 30%. It is hard to get teachers, doctors and nurses to serve in the smaller towns, let alone the villages, in spite of improved communications. The townsman soon forgets, if he ever knew, what it is like to live in the country. Nor do civilians always look without envy upon military privilege.

THE MONARCHY

So, although the creation of Iraq was entirely a British achievement, Britain gained no gratitude or credit; the new state corresponded to no national aspiration. The mass of the Shi'as could hardly be enthusiastic about a Sunni king, and as early as 1920 there was a rising against the mandatory power. But King Faisal I was an outstanding leader and kept the country together until independence was attained in 1932; Iraq was the first Arab country to reach that status. Unfortunately he died in the following year and the inherent weaknesses of the country quickly became apparent. The fashion of forming ministries by military *coups* began as early as 1936. The army soon realised that it was the sole source of real power in the country; since then it has intervened to change the government time and again. The astute Nuri es-Said, whose skill in manipulating ministries became a by-word, was himself put in power the first time by a military coup.

With the outbreak of World War II Iraq's friendship became vital to Britain, but Britain's past role as mandatory power had left it unpopular, and it was widely believed to be behind a hated régime. So when anti-monarchic forces gained power under Rashid Aly, it was natural that they should be pro-Axis. In May 1941 Britain drifted into hostility with the new régime, and after a brief campaign centred on the RAF base at Habbaniya the royal family and Nuri es-Said were restored. For the rest of the war Britain was able to count on the cooperation of Iraq, although Nuri es-Said's secret contacts with the Germans show that the support was one of cool appraisal, not sympathy.

When the war ended, Iraq was on the winning side and had fair hopes of prosperity. The greatest single reason for optimism was the increased pro-duction of oil after 1946. By 1954 the revenue had reached £67 million; 70% of this was originally allocated to national development projects. It seemed to be only a question of time before Iraq attained prosperity and with it stability.

REVOLUTIONS AND THEIR CAUSES

Such hopes were vain. The monarchy was bloodily overthrown in 1958, the ruling clique dispossessed and largely dispersed. From then until now, power has been held by various political groups of army officers, who have succeeded one another violently or with the threat of violence. Some of the reasons for this recurrent instability have already been given : Iraq was an artificial creation without historical roots; the sense of nationalism was not territorial and the territory contained several antagonistic minorities. But international issues played their part, the cold war and the Palestine problem above all.

Like other Arabs, Iraqis eagerly bought the amenities of the West and adopted many of its forms and appearances. They even borrowed its political ideas—fascism, communism and nationalism are all more European than Christianity is—and these ideas, together with the West's technology, seemed to offer progress, prosperity and power and were for that reason irresistible. But the new ideas made traditional customs, attitudes and beliefs seem old-fashioned and irrelevant. Very few Iraqis, even among those who had studied in the West, understood, much less accepted, the liberal values that underlie the Western way of life. So, while the West was sedulously imitated, it was also bitterly resented; young men eagerly training in England felt themselves to be at the same time the victims of England's political and economic interests.

Some Arab leaders in other countries had openly turned away from the West and commanded a great deal of support in Iraq. The result was that when British diplomacy and the government of Iraq tried to swing the country to the Western side by means of the Portsmouth Treaty (1948) or the Baghdad Pact (1955), they appeared to isolate her from her sister Arab countries and to betray the Arab cause. As there was no countervailing fear of Russia—indeed that country was felt to be a fellow-victim of Western aggression by virtue of the struggle against 'imperialism'—there were violent demonstrations on each occasion. The other international issue was the creation of Israel. This was widely regarded as an imperialist manœuvre to establish a base in the Arab heartland, and as such seemed to be merely an extension of the political exploitation of the Arabs by the West. The abortive Suez affair in 1956 only confirmed their worst suspicions. In spite of denials, the people of Iraq felt that their government had been compromised. They had long lost faith in a democracy that had never been understood and at best was a game of political intrigue played by a tiny monority. To despairing and frustrated outsiders the only way forward seemed to be offered by violence, and this was the way chosen by a group of left-wing army officers led by General Qasim in 1958.

The expected millenium did not arrive and dissension soon broke out among the revolutionaries. They had been drawn broadly from three groups; communists, supporters of the Syrian-based 'Ba'ath' (Arab national revival) Party, and officers of the armed forces, who had a belief in Arab, especially Sunni Arab, nationalism and a leaning towards their fellows in Egypt. Otherwise they adhered to no political party or programme. Each of the three groups was subdivided into moderates and extremists, opportunists and idealists, and all the groups were deeply susceptible to local and family factions. In fact it comes as a surprise to the onlooker to discover that the leaders of all three groups were drawn overwhelmingly from the small, Sunni Arab minority. (Although they formed only a fifth of the population, the Sunni Arabs had for long been preferred by their Sunni Ottoman rulers for positions of responsibility. It was then natural for the British, when they entered Iraq, to deal with the people already holding the reins of administration. Since these were almost always the people put there by the Turks, the British unwittingly reinforced the position of the Sunni Arabs 'establishment', who now had a monopoly of the senior administrative and army posts.)

To see the events of the ten years after the downfall of the monarchy as resulting from the struggles of these groups (the communists, the 'Ba'athists' and the nationalist officers) for power is an over-simplification, but it does give the onlooker a frame of reference by which to order those events in his mind.

At first Qasim had all these groups behind him, but as early as September one of his chief supporters, Colonel Abdul Salam Aref, was relieved of his post as C.-in-C. In October the Kurdish leader, Mulla Mustafa Barazani, returned from the Soviet Union with a large number of followers. In November Colonel Aref, who had been associated with the 'Ba'ath' movement and had played a key role in putting Qasim into power, was arrested and accused of treason. These events caused consternation in neighbouring Arab countries, because they seemed to show how deeply the new régime had come under communist influence. In December it was denounced by President Nasser. In March 1959 an abortive 'Ba'athist'-inspired military revolt in Mosul, provoked by a large government-sponsored pro-communist demonstration, apparently strengthened the position of the communists. Communist-dominated 'People's Courts' carried out reprisals against 'Ba'athists' suspected of complicity, and in April the communists demanded formal recognition and admission to the cabinet.

But Qasim was an ascetic Muslim, not the follower of any political creed, and he rejected their approach. In so doing he alienated the only remaining group capable of giving him organised support. For the next three years Qasim governed alone from his military headquarters, working incredibly long hours, often sleeping in his office, and aided by a dwindling, if devoted, staff. Weariness caused him at times to slip over the line that divides reason from unreason. In an attempt to divert attention from domestic difficulties—fighting against the Kurds led by Bavrazani had broken out in March 1961—Qasim plunged into foreign adventure. In June he laid claim to sovereignty over oil-rich Kuwait; the pretext was an Ottoman decree of 1871.

Kuwait enlisted the support, first of Britain, and then of the Arab League, and the affair eventually fizzled out, but it left Iraq internationally isolated. In February 1963 the inevitable end came with a successful *coup*. This was the result of a conspiracy between nationalist officers and the 'Ba'athists'. In spite of remaining popular with the poorer classes until the end—there was no popular demonstration in support of the rebels—the army did not rally to Qasim and he himself was captured and killed. The rebels appointed Colonel Abdul Salam Aref as President; he had been pardoned and reinstated by Qasim some 15 months earlier. The 'Ba'athists' lost no time in consolidating themselves. Through their 'National Guard' large numbers of communists and followers of Qasim were rounded up and subjected to mass trials and executions. Reaction followed. In November a group of nationalist officers, led by Colonel Aref, the President, overthrew the 'Ba'athists' by calling in the army. The 'National Guard' was disarmed and disbanded. A truce was declared with the Kurds and closer links established with Egypt.

The new government followed a policy of neutrality between East and West and held to the middle of the road in domestic matters. In September 1965 it even appointed a civilian, Dr Abdul Rahman Bazzaz, to the post of Prime Minister. Dr Bazzaz showed himself a competent politician and administrator. He managed to arrange a truce with the Kurds in January and, when in April the President was killed in a helicopter crash, it was

Bazzaz who ensured that the office of president was passed smoothly to the dead man's brother, Abdul Rahman Aref. But disagreements with the military members of the government led to the resignation of Bazzaz in September 1966.

The shock of the Six-Day War in June 1967 caused a precipitate rupture of diplomatic relations with Britain and the USA who were accused of sending planes to support Israel. It was the action of insecure men. Very soon the 'Ba'athists' were again in power and the usual public trials and executions followed. But Iraqi politics ran true to form. The new leaders, though ideologically 'Ba'athist', came not only from the Sunni establishment but largely from a single area, the district round Takrit.

Iraq will continue to be unstable and difficult to govern until the largest section of the population, the Shi'as, outgrows the minority mentality acquired through centuries of Ottoman domination and learns to govern.

THE PRESENT—GEOGRAPHY

The most important geographical feature of Iraq is formed by the twin rivers, the Tigris and the Euphrates, that run the length of the country from north-west to south-east where, for the last 70 miles before entering the Persian (Arab) Gulf, they join in a single channel called the Shatt al-Arab. For thousands of years these rivers have been the source of both life and misery for the riverain inhabitants. Even today all the large towns are on the rivers, for until the arrival of the railway and the lorry the only way to carry goods in bulk was by water. From Ramadi and Samarra southwards, in the flat alluvial plain that makes up approximately a quarter of the country's land surface, agriculture depends on irrigation from the rivers. The traveller who arrives at Baghdad by air at any season except spring sees little to relieve the flat monotony of the dusty landscape except the Tigris, meandering in extravagant loops to the horizon. Over most of its length the bare cracked desert comes right to the bank. There is no strip of bright green, as there is along the Nile for example. Only here and there a date garden, with orange trees planted between the palms, shows the potential fertility of the soil near some large village or small town built of mud bricks, of the same beige colour as the surrounding flatness. The beige gives way to varied green between the lower reaches of the twin rivers. Here are the marshes—lagoons divided by expanses of tall reeds—that offer a great, if dwindling, sanctuary to wild fowl, boar and fish. The canoes, reed huts and way of life of the tribesmen and their buffaloes are much as they were in Sumerian times, though now the transistor radio, the outboard motor and marine plywood are beginning to introduce irreversible changes.

North of Ramadi and Samarra the land begins to rise perceptibly. With the rising contours there is a slight increase of annual rainfall. This is the eastern end of the Jezira that starts in Syria, a treeless rolling steppe country, which for a brief three weeks in spring can become (in a good year—for the rain is always uncertain) a paradise of wild flowers. At this time, bemused flocks of sheep may be seen standing knee-deep in wild stock that carpets the ground for mile after mile. Here, from Shargat northwards, local merchants and shaikhs use tractors to plough up huge expanses for a sparse yield of corn, a cheap gamble that can bring a satisfactory return in a good year.

To the north-east of a line running from Mosul to Khanaqin is an area of some two thousand square miles. From low hills, the land rises quickly to wild mountainous country, with peaks over 3,000 metres high. This is the southern part of Kurdistan. The rainfall is relatively heavy, and the mountains are covered by forest, where they have not been denuded by soil erosion. In the narrow valleys, often terraced, the Kurds live in villages built of solid stone; they lead a hard but independent life as peasant farmers and herdsmen.

The rest of the country, about a half of the total, is desert. It provides scanty fodder for the herds of a decreasing number of bedouin whose political importance and way of life have been ended by the machine-gun and the aeroplane.

Even if the large area of desert is discounted, there is land in plenty and the twin rivers supply water in abundance. Above all there is oil to provide foreign exchange. The natural resources seem at first sight to be more than adequate for a population of just over eight million people, and the potential of the country appears immense. A closer look reveals serious impediments. The rainfall is scanty and unreliable; the rivers bring either too little water to the land or too much, and unlike the Nile, do so at the wrong seasons of the year. The spring floods, caused by the snow melting in the Turkish mountains, arrive when the grain crops are already standing; unless they are controlled, far from making the land more fertile, they can cause widespread destruction of buildings and produce. The secondary rise, caused by the winter rains, comes too late for general and easy use.

As early as 1903 the Ottoman Government realised that no agricultural development could take place unless barrages were built to hold back and store the flood waters for use during the dry reason. The lower reaches of the two main rivers were surveyed and a barrage for the Euphrates near Babylon was completed in 1912. After World War II, the rising oil revenues allowed grander schemes to be undertaken. By 1958, when the monarchy was overthrown, two further barrages had been completed, at Habbaniyah for the Euphrates and at Samarra for the Tigris (the Wadi Tharthar scheme), and others had been started. Today the risk of widespread flood damage is much less than it was 20 years ago. But safety still depends, as it has done for the past five thousand years, upon the steady maintenance of costly and intricate schemes of water control. If these fall into disrepair through war or civil upheaval, the danger returns.

AGRICULTURE

In spite of her oil Iraq is, and will be for the foreseeable future, a country dependent on agriculture. Agriculture employs the bulk of the labour force and must be at the centre of any development plan, for agricultural practice in Iraq remains primitive. Capital investment in flood control and water storage is the basic precondition of any attempted development. But simply to provide water and prevent flooding is not enough to turn Iraq from an underdeveloped country into a prosperous one. To see the problems in terms only of barrages, water supply and arterial roads is to ignore the intractable physical and social problems that must be solved before prosperity is brought back.

The single most serious physical problem is caused by excessive flatness. It is easy enough to bring water onto most parts of the alluvial plain but extremely hard to drain it off. Further, being one of the hottest and driest cultivated areas in the world, the rate of evaporation is extremely high during the summer, so that any trace of salt there may be in the water or in solution in the soil is brought to the surface and left there. This progressive salination of cultivated land has been the curse of Iraq since Sumerian times. Today anyone who travels from Baghdad in any direction will see long stretches of bare soil with dazzling white flowers of salt picking out the top of every ridge and hillock. The only cure is to leach the salt away with plenty of water, but this needs good drainage, and in an area as low and flat as the alluvial plain it is always difficult and sometimes impossible to arrange. (Baghdad, some 350 miles from the sea, is only 34 metres above it.) The normal practice has always been for the cultivator to move elsewhere when the land becomes too salty. Nature reinforces the traditional attitude of nomads to the land even in the 'settled' areas.

In Ottoman times most of the land was held by tribal custom. Each tribe had a larger or smaller territory over which it had customary rights of grazing and cultivation. These rights were collective; the territory was ill-defined. The tribe owed loyalty to a leader, who was usually elected from among the members of a single shaikhly family. Unfortunately, when land registration was introduced, the greater part of a tribe's territory was entered under the name of the ruling shaikh. At the stroke of a pen, the elected head of the tribal council became a landlord and the tribesmen his tenants. As the arrangement between the two was usually some form of share-cropping, the tenants soon got into debt and became little better than serfs, since they could not leave the land until they had paid off their debt. Feudalism was reintroduced into Iraq by bureaucracy in the 20th century. Some of the landowners in the south of the country possessed estates as large as an English county.

Many British and foreign advisers and experts believed that if only the large estates could be confiscated, Iraq's development would be assured. They were mistaken. Five-sixths of the land held in large estates was confiscated after the revolution of 1958; four years later the output of grain was less than half of what it had been during the last years of the monarchy, and the migration from country to town had swelled to frightening proportions. Squalid slums and suburbs of hovels built of mud, reeds and tin cans sprang up round the towns overnight. In an effort to stem the flow and to help the cultivators buy what they needed, loans were made to perhaps a quarter of their number. Many of them are said to have spent the loans on bus fares to the capital.

This was probably inevitable. Except in the north-east of the country among the Kurds, there were no cultivators with a long peasant tradition of attachment to the land. Rather, many of the Arabs had inherited from their warring nomad forbears a deep scorn for the settled peasant. Nature did not help. The flat, treeless land is parched by a pitiless sun for much of the year and swept by bitterly cold winds for the rest. Back-breaking toil for half the year and demoralising unemployment for the remainder yielded them only a bare subsistence that often ended in debt. No wonder they never developed pride in, or attachment to, the land they tilled.

With all their defects, the landlords had supplied services of sorts: they did not let their tenants actually starve, they gave credit at a price, as well as advice and marketing facilities. The problem was how to provide these services after the properties of the landlords had been confiscated. Foreign advisers suggested co-operatives, and for a time these were regarded by the city-based administrators as the nostrum for Iraq's agricultural troubles. But co-operatives need more than equipment in order to be of use. There must also be book-keepers, administrators and advisers with knowledge and experience. Such people simply did not exist in sufficient numbers to staff the cooperatives that were set up, and their resultant inadequacies did not commend them to the rural community, who were in any case suspicious of an idea that was strange to them. This failure is an example of the gap of understanding between the neon-lit townsman and the countryman living in a mud or reed hut whose appearance, size and comforts have changed astonishingly little through eight millenia.

HEALTH

To bring about an improvement in agriculture it is equally important to raise the standard of health in the country districts. In the south, malaria has been dramatically checked, though by no means eradicated; but even without malaria, many suffer from more than one major disease : bilharzia, tuberculosis, *bejel*—a non-venereal form of syphilis—and hydatid disease, to name only a few of the more common. The eradication of a disease like bilharzia, for example, is more than a medical problem; it demands social and engineering treatment, which is extremely difficult and costly. The bilharzia fluke spends part of its life-cycle in a water snail that abounds in the lower reaches of the main rivers of Iraq. When mature, the fluke leaves the snail and infests stagnant or slow-running water. If a human being comes into contact with infested water, the fluke will penetrate the skin and enter the blood-stream. It usually ends by forming a cyst in the bladder, from where in due time it is passed with the urine back into the water, to start the life-cycle over again. It is an unpleasant disease—a symptom is blood in the urine—and there is always a risk of reinfection even after a patient has been cured. It could be eliminated by introducing sanitation, but in a land as flat and low-lying as Iraq this is prohibitively expensive.

INDUSTRY

Social difficulties of a different type hamper the establishment of industry. There is no tradition of private investment in industry and the population of eight million is too small and too poor to form an adequate market for more than a few products. Most Iraqi Governments have been ambivalent in their attitude to successful industrialists. On the one hand, they have favoured industry for reasons of prestige; on the other, they have been suspicious of anyone who has made a profit. There is, too, an insufficient variety of raw materials and those that are available in economic quantities are usually also found in a neighbouring country. As a result Iraqi industry and trade tend to compete with, and not to supplement, the efforts of other states in the Middle East. (The export of cement to Kuwait is an exception.) Another difficulty is the lack of skilled man-power which is the cause of high costs and waste.

EDUCATION

Real progress in industry, as in agriculture and health, demands a steady and continuing process of education to change the practices and attitudes, not only of the men in the fields, but also of those who teach them, sell to them, or rule them, that is to say of the whole population. Iraq does not lack the means to build schools or to pay teachers to man them. Nor do Iraqis, parents and children alike, lack the desire for education. There is such intense pressure on secondary school places that many school buildings are used in shifts for more than one school. In the universities many faculties are grossly overcrowded, because no government dares to restrict entries too drastically. Only the faculties of science, engineering and medicine have been able to resist this tendency, because their numbers are restricted by the lack of laboratory space and equipment. Observers have sometimes asserted that Iraqis are athirst for education. This is only partly true. Like students everywhere, many are athirst only for the paper certificate gained by education. Even a secondary school certificate, let alone a degree, is believed to confer such status on the possessor that it puts him above practical work. The easiest way to pass exams is to learn whole passages from the textbooks off by heart. This fits in with the traditional view of education as the mere acquisition of knowledge. Little attempt is made to develop insight and independent thought. This state of affairs turns out a large number of arts graduates and secondary school leavers who cannot be employed in jobs of a practical nature or at the level to which they feel entitled. Large numbers of young men drift into semi-employment in the towns or swell the ranks of the ill-informed political malcontents.

Politics for these young men consists of reacting emotionally to 'trigger' words like 'imperialism', 'Arabness', 'progress', 'unity'. It has little to do with rational dialogue and nothing to do with individual liberty. The interest of the individual counts for nothing beside the fulfilment of the group's aspirations. Friends are shining white; enemies treacherous black. Hot opinions and violent policies result and it can be argued that only political instability has prevented Iraq from becoming a prosperous country. In this as in other fields there is need for a steady and continuous process of education, and the process must start with the teachers.

CONCLUSION—REASONS FOR OPTIMISM

It would be misleading to end on a despondent note. As every official guidebook says, Iraq is potentially rich : the oil revenues have not all been wasted; there has been effective large-scale investment in communications, electricity production, new industries—especially petro-chemicals—and irrigation. Less grandiose schemes for housing, agricultural machinery and storage have also attracted development funds. All this should in time create an expanding market and a stable middle class. And religion may be a steadying factor, for although there is much disbelief and agnosticism, Islam retains a remarkable hold upon the thoughts and habits of even the emancipated intellectual. Indeed, Arab nationalism seems to have strengthened at least the outward observances of Islam, for the two are subtly linked. All told, Iraq has the capacity, and the resources, to make real headway—but will only do so if an end can be put to the cycle of political disturbances which have frustrated development for more than ten years.

Over a quarter of the total government expenditure is devoted to educational and cultural projects and already the results can be seen. The competence of Iraqi professional men, especially of those in medicine, many of whom have close links with Britain, commands respect outside Iraq. There is a ferment and excitement among the writers, artists and architects that makes living in Baghdad a stimulating experience. Canvases by Iraqi artists are beginning to command fair prices in Europe and the United States. A lively school of local architects is at work in Baghdad, combining modern materials and traditional motifs. The most impressive proof of the cultural revival of Iraq is the rich and magnificently arranged archaeological museum. To visit it is a rewarding experience, and the British visitor will remember with pleasure the part played by British scholars and archaeologists in recovering the remarkable remains of Iraq's long history.

FURTHER READING

Bell, Gertrude. *Amurath to Amurath*, Heinemann, London, 1911.
Bell, Gertrude. *From her Personal Letters, 1889–1926* (2 vols), Ernest Benn, London, 1958 and 1961; Verry, Connecticut, 1961.
Caractacus. *Revolution in Iraq*, Gollancz, London, 1959.
Edmonds, D. J. 'The Kurdish War in Iraq', *The World Today*, Vol. 24, 12 December, 1968.
Lewis, Bernard. *The Middle East and the West*, Weidenfeld & Nicolson, London, 1963; Indiana Univ. Press, Indiana, 1964.
Lloyd, Seton. *Foundations in the Dust*, Penguin, Harmondsworth, 1955.
Longrigg, S. *Iraq*, Ernest Benn, London, 1958.
Longrigg, S. and Stokes, E. *Iraq 1900–1950*, Oxford Univ. Press, London, 1956.
Thesiger, Wilfred. *The Marsh Arabs*, Longmans, London, 1964; Dutton, New York, 1964.

RIGGAN ER-RUMI. Has a wide first-hand knowledge of the Arab world, where he spent 15 years, and of Iraq in particular, where he spent four years. A contributor to the bulletin of the School of Oriental and African Studies and the *Mariner's Mirror*.

ISRAEL

JACOB M. LANDAU

HISTORICAL NOTES

THE connection of Jews with Palestine started in Abraham's day; large-scale settlement occurred after the Exodus from Egypt, over 3,000 years ago. Despite two mass expulsions, by Babylon in 586 BC and by the Romans in AD 70, there were always some Jews living in Palestine, while others returned in fluctuating numbers. Palestine was ruled, successively, by Romans, Byzantines, Arabs (640–1517), Ottoman Turks (1517–1917), and the British (1917–1948) until the foundation of the State of Israel in 1948.

Migrations and the changes of ruler made up a heterogeneous population. Jews, returning in larger numbers from the 1880s onwards—out of religious or Zionist convictions—found a well-rooted Arab population, some of whose leaders welcomed the Jewish immigrants, while others mistrusted them. From early in the 20th century, the Jewish and Arab nationalist movements developed concurrently, which inevitably caused a conflict of interests and, later, tragic clashes in Palestine.

There were about 11,000 Jews in Palestine in 1839; 34,000 in 1878; and 85,000 in 1914,[1] despite Ottoman restrictions on immigration and land-purchasing. In 1914 there existed 43 Jewish agricultural settlements with 13,000 inhabitants. These produced some 30% of the orange crop, 90% of the wines and most of the almond crop, altogether approximately half of the total exports passing through Jaffa harbour. In the towns Jewish residents increased from about 18,000 in 1882 to 45,000 (in Jaffa, approximately from 2,000 to 9,000). These figures were somewhat reduced during World War I, due to the forced emigration of Jews who were citizens of those states fighting the Ottoman empire. Also, during the earlier part of the 20th century, the Arab population increased too (no exact figures are available, but it appears that the Arabs made up, in 1918, about 90% of Palestine's population).

There was a significant change in the ethnical composition and the ideological make-up of these Jews. Ashkenazi Jews, of East and West European origins, while still in a minority in Palestine, vied with Sephardi Jews, of South European and Middle Eastern origins, for status and leadership. New ideologies penetrated : the *Hovevey Zion* (Lovers of Zion), settling in Palestine from 1882, brought with them a passionate attachment to the land, soon reinforced by a revaluation of the importance of physical labour, by an ardent desire for revolutionary social change and a striving for an

[1] This figure was reduced by wartime emigration to 56,000 in 1918, when Jewish inhabitants constituted approximately 9% of the population of Palestine.

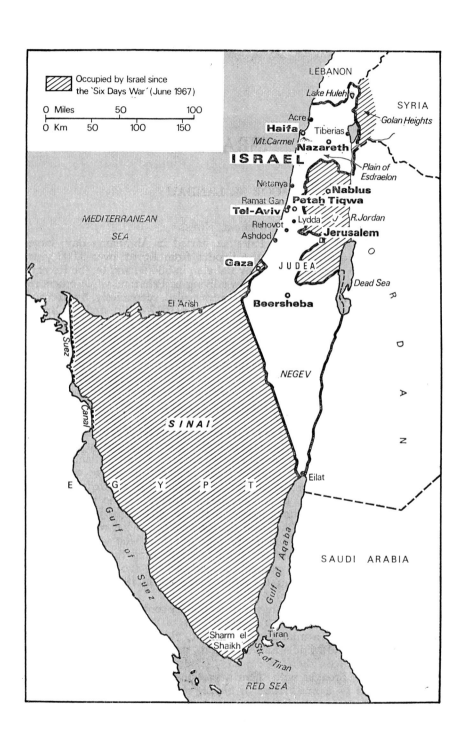

Occupied by Israel since
the 'Six Days War' (June 1967)

0 Miles 50 100

0 Km 50 100 150

LEBANON

Lake Huleh

SYRIA

Acre
Haifa Tiberias
Mt.Carmel Nazareth

Golan Heights

ISRAEL

Plain of
Esdraelon

Netanya

Nablus

Ramat Gan
Tel-Aviv

Petah Tiqwa

Lydda R.Jordan

Rehovot
Ashdod

Jerusalem

MEDITERRANEAN

SEA

Gaza

JUDEA

Dead Sea

El 'Arish

Beersheba

Suez

NEGEV

Canal

SINAI

Eilat

E G Y P T

Gulf of Suez

Gulf of Aqaba

SAUDI ARABIA

Sharm el
Shaikh

Tiran

Str. of Tiran

RED SEA

egalitarian society, by the struggle of a renascent Hebrew against Yiddish, ending in the victory of the former as a generally employed language of daily communication and instruction.

While the *Hovevey Zion* emphasised work in Palestine, and others advocated a spiritual regeneration of Judaism as a prerequisite to nationhood, a new Zionist movement strove for political solutions. Theodor Herzl, founder of the Zionist Organisation (1897), and his associates considered the very existence of a Jewish people as axiomatic, hence the necessity for a nation-state. Another innovation was the method of reaching an agreement on Jewish entry into Palestine, honourably negotiated through international political activity, as a matter of right, not as a favour. Naturally, the increase in Jewish numbers in Palestine and agricultural work there served as a lever for the diplomatic activity of the Zionist Organisation, whose leaders, Chaim Weizmann and Nahum Sokolow, obtained a commitment from the British Cabinet (the Balfour Declaration, 2 November 1917) for the creation of a Jewish national home in Palestine (provided nothing was done to prejudice the civil and religious rights of the 'existing non-Jewish communities' there). The Balfour Declaration was officially approved by Britain's allies—France, Italy and Japan; Weizmann also got the general approval of Prince Faisal of Arabia. Britain's victory in the war, her conquest and 30-year rule of Palestine made the Declaration feasible. The League of Nations approved the text of the British Mandate for Palestine (1922), explicitly mentioning the Balfour Declaration and assigning Britain to administer Palestine and prepare conditions for the foundation of a Jewish national home.

British Rule

British rule, military at first, was slow to make innovations and continued Ottoman practices, both legal and administrative. The Palestine Order in Council (1922), with six amendments, served as an organic law. It set norms for executive rule and legislation, both vested in a high commissioner, and for the judiciary—all subject to Whitehall. No borders were mentioned; indeed, on 1 September 1922, Eastern Transjordan became a separate unit under the Mandate. Britain's legacy to the State of Israel may be summed up under three main headings :

The Legal System. This perpetuated the co-existence of civil and religious courts. The first followed Ottoman decrees, along with orders published by the Mandatory in Palestine and the British common law and equity law, insofar as these filled gaps in Ottoman legal practice and did not conflict with local conditions. The second recognised the judicial privileges awarded to religious denominations in Ottoman times, in matters of personal status; but the Mandatory granted parallel authority, in several cases, to the civil courts.

Development. This was chiefly directed to forming an efficient, honest police force; economic progress; organised taxation; building harbours and airports, a good road network and a limited but useful railway system; and good postal services. Many local officials, Arab or Jewish, thus had an opportunity to acquire experience and training.

Fostering autonomous organisation. The phrase 'National Home' was interpreted differently by the British, Jews and Arabs, who disagreed on how to foster administrative advance and popular representation. The British had the final say. They organised a British administration, within whose framework they attempted to further Arab-Jewish co-operation. Most Arabs refused, and their refusal reflected their growing suspicion of Jewish immigration and economic development. The British were reluctant to form a British-Jewish administration, both out of an innate feeling for fair play and because of their apprehensions about rising Arab nationalism in Palestine and its growing ties with neighbouring Arab lands where British interests were involved. Hence a separate, semi-autonomous, Jewish administration arose, sometimes overlapping with that of the British. About 95% of Palestinian Jews voluntarily organised themselves into *Knesset Israel* (community of Israel), only a few ultra-orthodox Jews forming their own community. Both were officially recognised by the British. The supreme elected body of *Knesset Israel* was *Ha-Va'ad and ha-Le'umi* (National Committee). It supervised the education, health services, social welfare and security of Palestinian Jewry. These same matters were attended to, on a local level, by each Jewish settlement, while in religious affairs, every settlement was connected to the Chief Rabbinate. The Jewish Agency was the recognised representative of the World Zionist Organisation *vis-à-vis* the Mandate authorities, Whitehall and the League of Nations. Actually, *Ha-Va'ad ha-Le'umi* provided for services in addition to those of the British administration (e.g. in education). It also organised, contrary to British policy, its own military organisation, the underground *Hagana* (defence organisation), a meeting-ground of socio-economically and religiously heterogeneous groups, a foreshadowing of the Jewish political fragmentation in the State of Israel. Palestinian Arab society, on the other hand, although unequal economically, was less disparate politically.

FOUNDATION OF THE STATE

Throughout, the British in Palestine faced a difficult task. As the nationalist movements of Jews and Arabs grew in intensity, the voice of those who wanted an amicable settlement gradually became less influential. Extremism bred rival extremism. Whenever the British assisted one side, they were decried by the other; if they tried neutrality, both sides accused them of partiality. During World War II and immediately afterwards they inclined towards the Arabs, enforcing the policies of the 1939 White Paper which considerably restricted Jewish immigration and the sale of Arab land to Jews. After 1945, Britain was blamed for this attitude by Russia, France and the USA, where public opinion was incensed by the fact that Jewish refugees from Europe's DP camps were being driven away from Palestine's shores. Anti-British terrorism, successfully employed by Arab extremists in Palestine during the 1920s and late 1930s, was now used by those Jewish extremists who considered the *Hagana* as too moderate and hoped to harass the British forces into an evacuation of Palestine.

One of the results was to focus world attention on Palestine. Early in 1947, Ernest Bevin, the British Foreign Secretary, asked the UN General Assembly to consider the Palestine issue. The UN Special Commission on Palestine, representing several nations, recommended the creation of two states, Jewish and Arab. The UN adopted this recommendation (29 November 1947) and Britain announced that its Mandate would terminate on 15 May 1948. Sporadic fighting broke out in Palestine, mutual mistrust prompting both Jews and Arabs to prepare for a show of strength. This came about when the British left, as scheduled, with the armed intervention of all the neighbouring Arab states (who had voted against the UN's resolution and now set about to nullify it). The military victory of the newly-founded State of Israel ensured its existence, but not peace with its neighbours. Another war was fought with Egypt in October–November 1956, and with Egypt, Syria and Jordan (assisted by Iraq) in June 1967.

The same determination evident in the 1948 war characterised the preparations of Palestinian Jews during the last months of the Mandate for structuring the administration of their future state. With a rare unity of purpose, submerging socio-economic and political factionalism, bodies representing all shades of popular opinion prepared a detailed carry-over of the police and postal services, issued new currency, organised tax collection and the functioning of courts and banks, etc.

The 14 May 1948 Declaration of Independence was the birth-certificate of Israel. It was essentially a revolutionary document, in which a Jewish leadership had proclaimed the state's foundation several hours before the British left. Its preamble asserts the Jewish historical and international right to a state. A democratic régime, emphasising personal liberties for all, is guaranteed; but the state is envisaged chiefly as a Jewish body-politic. Separately, but concurrently, a proclamation was issued, maintaining all past legislation (except the 1939 White Paper and laws limiting Jewish immigration and land-buying in Palestine)—thus assuring legal and judicial continuity. This was elaborated in a longer document, issued in the Official Gazette on 3 June 1948; this first constitutional document of the state not only stressed direct transfer of power from the British, but set basic procedural rules for the new administration, some still relevant (though subsequently modified in part).

DEMOGRAPHIC CHANGE

In May 1948 Israel had a Jewish population of 649,000. In November 1948, Israel's first population count noted about 717,000 Jews and 156,000 Arabs; the other Palestinian Arabs, about one million, either remained in those parts of Palestine ruled by Jordan and Egypt, or moved there and elsewhere as war refugees. In the following years, substantial demographic changes occurred :

Growth. By December 1951, some 687,000 Jews had immigrated. The rate declined later, but a constant stream kept coming. At the end of 1967, there were about 2,400,000 Jews in Israel. The ratio of European and American Jews declined, compared to that of the Afro-Asian Jews, in the State's population. Those born in Palestine and Israel consistently numbered about one-third (1951 excepted, after the large immigration, when the proportion fell to a quarter). Since the average birthrate is higher in Sephardi and Oriental than in Ashkenazi families, Israel's Jewish population is almost evenly divided (1967) between these two groups.

Distribution. Israel's towns and cities grew visibly and some new ones were founded. However, while during 1947 only about 15% of the Jews lived in agricultural settlements of all types, the ratio had increased ten years later to approximately 22·5%. Partly this was the result of a deliberate official policy. Agriculture had an elevated place in Zionist ideology, which strove to channel Jewish energy into less urban and more productive work. The conquest of the desert, taken literally, caught the imagination of Israeli youth, and parts of the Negev were impressively reclaimed. Many unskilled immigrants were offered financial inducements, such as low-cost housing, to settle in agricultural villages, so as not to remain unemployed and become a burden in the towns. Sociologically, the added advantage was that such immigrants were not exposed to the economic and psychological pressures of town-life; in agriculture, representatives of the government, the Jewish Agency and *Histadrut* (the General Federation of Labour), were natural intermediaries. Of course, this had a reverse side, also, in that it tended to isolate immigrants from the mainstream of Israeli life.

Of those immigrants who chose agriculture, many preferred the co-operative *moshav*, where each family had its own private home and lands, though some of the heavy machinery was often owned jointly. Because of their socio-economic background, fewer went to the *kibbutz* or *kevutza*, the collective settlement where almost all property was owned jointly and physical labour was considered a satisfying achievement. While, from November 1948 to May 1961, Israel's Jewish population rose by 170%, the number of inhabitants in the collective settlements increased by less than 40%—from 54,000 to 70,000. Nonetheless, the very continuity of their growth, despite the attractions of city-life, is evidence of the vitality in this communal way of life, original to Palestine and Israel, and still appealing to the more dedicated youth.

Age. Due to the immigration of large families, an early marrying age and relatively numerous births under hygenic conditions which reduce infant mortality, Israel's population includes many children : on 31 December 1964, 33·1% Jews and 49·8% non-Jews were aged fourteen or under. Among the implications of this phenomenon : (i) *Housing problems.* Where many families have a large number of children, a constant search goes on for more spacious dwellings, resulting in a building boom and the mobility of large families; (ii) *Education.* Obviously, since education is compulsory and free during one year of kindergarten and eight years of elementary school (with many scholarships for the deserving poor during the four years of secondary school), it had to be provided for children of both sexes and all communities. During 1964–5, without counting kindergartens and university education, there were 516,238 pupils in Hebrew schools and 48,069 in Arabic schools, or a total of more than one-fifth of the State's population at the time.

The Arabs. Three main factors distinguish the Israeli Arabs demographically : (i) Little immigration, chiefly the limited number of refugees allowed to return and rejoin their families; (ii) A higher birthrate than the Jewish population—a net increase of over 4%, possibly the highest in the world; (iii) A tendency to live in monolithic groups, which happen to be near Israel's frontiers, thus posing certain security problems : across the border, there live more populous nations, officially at war with Israel, whose traditions, language and religions are identical with those of the Arabs in Israel (a military administration, imposed by Israel in these areas during 1948, was later eased and in December 1966 was totally done away with—thanks to the proven loyalty of the Arab minority to Israel).

At the end of 1966, there were in Israel over 300,000 Arabs (insufficient data prevents us from discussing the additional million Arabs in Israeli-ruled territories since June 1967). Of these, some 70% were Muslims (practically all Sunnites), 20% Christians and 10% Druzes. Most Druzes are farmers and live in villages. So are 67% of the Muslims (with 17% townspeople and 16% Bedouins in various stages of sedentarisation). The Christians, however, mostly reside in towns and cities (61%) and even the others choose to live in the *larger* villages; they are relatively more educated than other minority groups.

Some Socio-Economic Patterns

Limited in its natural resources, burdened by heavy expenditure on immigrant absorption, defence requirements, development and education, Israel has had to contend with serious economic problems. Although production increases annually by about 10–11% and Israel increasingly approaches self-sufficiency in several areas, its trade deficit is still considerable. Its imports mostly come from Common Market countries, the USA and Britain. Israel's major exports are diamonds, textiles, citrus products, mining and quarrying, chemicals and pharmaceuticals, steel products, fuel, paper and printing, and tyres. Since it can hardly hope for competitive agricultural exports, emphasis has been laid on industrial development. Industrial investment, both by the government and by local and foreign investors, grows yearly, world Jewry has invested generously in Israel. Particularly favourable conditions for investment, along with government loans, are granted to industrial plants in development areas. All this has created a serious shortage of skilled manpower and kept unemployment down to about 1%—mostly unskilled workers—a remarkable achievement in an immigrant economy. Both Jews and Arabs have benefited considerably from this economic boom, as is reflected in the widespread home use of most electrical appliances.

In addition to the private capital sector, the government and the *Histadrut* play an important part in Israel's economy. While the former has produced annually about 60% of the net national product, the other two have been responsible for about 20% each. The government has contributed impressively to housing (mainly for new immigrants) and the *Histadrut* has had an important share, besides housing, in agriculture and in transportation (which in Israel means chiefly road-transportation, carried out by *Histadrut*-affiliated bus co-operatives, and only a small part by the state-owned railways). The *Histadrut* has a substantial share of the public services, too, particularly through its countrywide clinics and other health-services.

Economic well-being was no panacea for social tensions, especially when confronted by rising prices. The melting-pot of Israeli society worked wonderfully well in creating a new nation, particularly cohesive when threatened militarily. However, basic differences between capital and labour, the middle class and the poor (few are truly wealthy), town and *kibbutz*, old and young, and especially groups of varying ethnic background, have persisted. While their overall solution may well take some time, these problems have caused no immediate social unrest—thanks not only to the relative prosperity of workers, many of whom have typical middle class salaries and live accordingly, but also to the far-reaching welfare policies of central and local authorities, as well as to the role of the *Histadrut*.

The *Histadrut* membership was close to a million persons in 1967 (members and their families, including many Arabs), or more than one third of Israel's population. It provides all these with health care and many educational services; it also watches over their professional interests. Since all coalition cabinets in Israel have been led by workers' parties, moderate in politics but deeply concerned with the material conditions of labour, there has been little social discontent among workers.

Credit is also due to Israel's womenfolk. Having brought an egalitarian mentality from Europe, Palestinian Jews encouraged their women to work and fight at their side, so that they maintained their status of equality quite naturally. However, since the waves of immigration to Israel in the early

1950s included some people who had other views concerning the status of women, as had some of Israel's Arab peasants (mainly Muslims and Druzes), a law for the equality of rights to women was passed in 1951. In 1955, 25·2% of Israel's women were employed; in 1964, 30·4%, and the proportion is growing. Legally, politically and economically the equal of men, Israeli women are accepted increasingly though perhaps grudgingly as social equals too, even by old-timers among Afro-Asian Jews and Israeli Arabs.

The Constitution Issue
and the
Secular-Religious Controversy

Israel has no written constitution. During 1948 a specially-appointed committee examined four drafts for a constitution and made its recommendations. The first *Knesset*, or Parliament, elected in January 1949, was to consider the adoption of a constitution. Its debates centred on the issue of having a written constitution. Those in favour argued that, Britain excepted, every state had a written constitution; that a new state particularly needed one; that it would limit autocratic tendencies and guarantee civil liberties; that a wish to avoid a clash of ideologies will cause only a postponement and successive future conflicts. The opponents of the idea held that, should a secular constitution be adopted, the religious parties might leave the cabinet coalition in a time of national crisis; that, in any case, preparing a constitution necessitated inspiration and patience; that a rigid constitution might impair Israel's dynamic progress; that a state's democratic character was not guaranteed by its constitution, but rather by the views of its citizens, as expressed by its legislators and safeguarded by its courts. As often happens in Israeli politics, a compromise was reached in the form of a resolution (1950) to prepare the constitution gradually, by adopting several basic laws which might later be joined in a constitution. This is being carried out, but the controversy over the issue is raised again during most election campaigns.

The controversy reflects one side of the multi-faceted public argument about the standing of religion in the State of Israel. For orthodox Jews, religious law is a complete code for everyday life, with compromise patently unacceptable; they would like to see all laws and customs in Israel regulated by Jewish sacred practice. Secular-minded Jews take a diametrically opposed view and argue that while orthodox Jews ought to believe and practise as they see fit, they should not impose their views on others. Actually, the issue is more complex. An orthodox Jew is deeply offended by motor-traffic on the Sabbath, or the breeding of pigs and public marketing of non-kosher meat—which he considers sinful temptation.

So the drafting of a constitution was postponed. A compromise was reached in some other matters : buses may not run on most roads on the Sabbath, but taxis may; pigs may be bred, but by non-Jews (Christians) only (1962); sellers of non-kosher meats must display signs accordingly. Compromises naturally satisfied nobody and the controversy was perpetuated by the official division of all state schools into secular and religious (by the parents' choice). The fact that the religious political parties have been an important component in practically all cabinets to date has added force to their point of view. It has meant also the continuation of the special prerogatives of religious officials and courts (Jewish, Muslim, Christian, more recently Druze) in sanctioning marriages, divorces and burials.

Parliamentary Régime and Party System

The Israeli State President is elected in the *Knesset* by secret ballot every five years. He is a symbol of leadership rather than a ruler. Effective power is vested in the *Knesset* and Cabinet, reflecting the multi-party system of the Israeli republic.

The *Knesset*, Israel's 120-member unicameral parliament, is elected every four years (unless it decides on earlier elections). The whole country is regarded as one constituency, and the elections are general, secret, direct and proportional. All Israeli citizens over 18 years of age, of both sexes, who on election day are within Israel's land-territories, may vote. Candidates have to possess essentially the same qualifications as ordinary voters, but have to be over 21; most state officials and military personnel are barred from running, unless they have resigned their posts. Elaborate regulations provide for the secrecy of the polling and the overall supervision of the elections through a commission chaired by a Supreme Court judge. Electoral propaganda is restricted, in conformity with democratic practice and good taste (no use of state property; disbursement of state funds to all parties as provided by law only). This has not prevented acrimonious charges by several parties, but all agree as to the punctilious honesty in voting and counting of results.

All legislation passed in the *Knesset* is binding. The President's signature on laws is a mere formality; cabinet ministers devise only the means of executing the law. The *Knesset* has exclusive rights in imposing taxes and tariffs and determining their rates (in practice, it fixes the maximum, and the ministers act within these limitations). It elects the President and is represented on the bodies appointing the Supreme Court. Its sub-committees not only discuss legislation, but also mould cabinet policy, generally at top-level decision-making. Equitable representation is assured on all these sub-committees to both government and opposition parties. Since their meetings are closed and their minutes classified, their work is reasonably speedy. Plenary sessions in the *Knesset* are open (with rare exceptions) and these debates serve to provide public control of the legislature. Yet another control is provided by the points of order and interpellations to the ministers about any matter concerning their offices to which the minister must reply within 14 days.

Since no party has obtained an absolute majority in the *Knesset*, all Israeli cabinets to date (1968) have been coalition cabinets. This has resulted in no less than 14 cabinets in the State's first 20 years. Many of these represented merely a reshuffle of parties and personalities, rather than a basic change of policy. While the prime minister must be an MK (Member of the *Knesset*), his ministers may be non-members. Each deputy-minister must be an MK. Since 1962, the law details the procedure for forming the cabinet : the State President designates an MK to choose a cabinet. Within a limited period, he must present his cabinet for *Knesset* approval. Other laws set forth the main tasks of ministers : directing all work in their ministries; participating in the collective decisions of the cabinet, and representing the ministry (and the cabinet) in the *Knesset*, where all ministers may speak up, but vote solely if they are MKs. Parallel to the *Knesset*, the Cabinet works on two levels—in subcommittees of ministers, chiefly to prepare law-bills, and in plenary sessions of the cabinet, presided over by the prime minister, who also draws up their agenda.

The participating parties in a new cabinet bind themselves in a written

221

'coalition agreement'. Subject to this, to *Knesset* control, and to public opinion as expressed in Israel's lively press, the State's political régime is cabinet-rule, whose effectiveness is not merely a matter of personalities, but a constant reflection of the multi-party system. Political parties in Israel are mostly a continuation of the parties which existed during pre-statehood days, with subsequent splits and fusions; indeed the origins of several go back to Europe. They get an immense share of popular interest. Numerous Israelis, both Jews and Arabs, are passionately concerned with politics and argue at length the ideologies and merits of the political parties; the parties' dailies, weeklies and other publications are extensively read and commented upon; most political parties provide inexpensive housing, job opportunities, or social clubs for their members and sympathisers. This explains, though only in part, the extraordinary fact that proportionate electoral support for groups of parties has remained almost unchanged. Although in Israel's seven parliamentary elections (1949, 1951, 1955, 1959, 1961, 1965, 1969), there was naturally some shift in the electoral results, the combined vote obtained by the left-of-centre, the centre, and the religious parties, respectively, follows a consistent pattern, despite a threefold rise in the number of valid votes, from 1949 to 1969.

Hence, until the formation of the 1967 National Cabinet on the eve of the June 1967 war, when Israelis felt the State to be in serious danger, all Cabinets had certain similar features. The extreme left, the tiny communist group, was constantly excluded (as was the case in 1967, too, when they were the only ones to oppose Israel's foreign and military policies). So, until 1967, was the right-wing *Herut* (Freedom) Party, whose militant slogans had meanwhile become more a matter of lip-service, but whose past antagonism to labour was still remembered. The mainstay of all cabinets was *Mapai* (Party of the Workers of Israel), very close to the centre, which consistently obtained about 32 to 38% of the popular vote in parliamentary contests. Thus *Mapai* has had the choice of forming coalition cabinets with either (a) the left-of-centre parties : *Achdut ha'avoda* (Union of Labour), with which it actually fused early in 1968 in the Israeli Labour Party, or *Mapam* (United Labour Party), a Marxist-Zionist party; (b) the centre party of the Liberals (later split into two parties, one of which united with *Herut* in 1965, under the appellation of *Gahal*, the *Herut*-Liberals' Bloc); or (c) the religious parties, which, in various degrees of militancy, wanted orthodox Judaism to shape the laws and life of Jews in the State. Generally, *Mapai* succeeded in playing each of these against the other, often striving to form as wide a cabinet as possible, while retaining key ministries for its own members. This meant easier manœuvring, since *Mapai* was thus less dependent on any one of its allies. A splinter from *Mapai*, *Rafi* (List of the Workers of Israel), which ran separately for the 1965 *Knesset* elections, led by ex-Prime Minister David Ben-Gurion, reunited with *Mapai* (but without Ben-Gurion) within the Israeli Labour Party during 1968.

THE LEGAL SYSTEM

Court procedures and precedents in Israel are greatly influenced by British (and less by Ottoman) law, supplemented by Israeli legislation and rulings. This coexists with religious law : Rabbinical *Shariah* (Muslim), church laws, etc. The Israeli Ministry of Justice works at rephrasing old laws (such as the Ottoman *Mejelle*, already abolished in Turkey itself), but this is a long and slow process. Indeed, when the interpretation of a law issued by the

British Mandate is in doubt, it is still the English version, rather than the Hebrew or Arabic, that is binding. The conservatism of the Israeli jurists finds expression also in their frequent search for precedents in British equity or common law. Most matters of personal status are generally decided in the courts of the religious communities, as inherited from the Ottoman empire, continued during the Mandate, and formalised by legislation in Israel. Another legacy of the Mandate authorities is the defence laws (state of emergency), enacted by those authorities in 1945, and denounced then, in strong terms, by Jewish lawyers. They are nonetheless renewed by the *Knesset*, annually, as a temporary measure in a state which is still at war. This has been done despite some opposition by lawyers and others, who feel that the defence laws may be used by the government for arbitrary measures. This danger, however, is offset to a large extent by the Israeli courts, which often serve as the guardians of civil rights and individual liberties.

All judges in Israel are appointed by ranking legal scholars and public functionaries, on the sole merit of their legal distinction, without any political considerations. Hence the prestige enjoyed by judges, who are often invited to head public bodies, including the central commission supervising parliamentary elections. Especially high standing is attached to the Supreme Court. One of its tasks is to sit as the High Court of Justice, safeguarding individual rights and liberties. The High Court of Justice may consider all requests not pertinent to other courts, particularly claims by any individual (or his legal representative) who feels he has been unjustly imprisoned or illegally dealt with by any of the state, municipal or other public authorities. Since it is bound solely by consideration of law, which it also sets out to interpret, and not of political conflicts, the Supreme Court, sitting as the High Court of Justice, has rendered judgments for the individual against the authorities, and its very prestigious functioning has served to deter any would-be authoritarianism.

Israel's Armed Forces

According to the 1949 Compulsory Service Law, later amplified, all Israeli men and unmarried women have to serve in the military forces. Since 1969 this law has stipulated that men have to serve up to three years and women two years. Reserve-duty of a few weeks per year applies to men until the age of 55 and women until 36; mothers are automatically exempt. The Minister of Defence is empowered by law to use his discretion for excusing from military service any group of people. He has used his discretion, in Israel's first 20 years, to excuse orthodox Jewish girls, students in the *yeshivas* (orthodox Jewish institutions of higher studies), and both Muslim and Christian Arabs. Orthodox girls and *yeshiva* students were excused chiefly due to the pressure of the religious parties, a component of most Israeli coalition cabinets. The prevailing consideration for excusing Muslim and Christian Arabs seems to have been avoiding the possibility of their having to fight their brethren across the borders. Such considerations hardly applied to the Druze community in Israel, whose men (but not women) are liable to the same military service laws as the Israeli Jews.

Israel's military forces were conceived as a small, modernised army, with relatively large reserves. It is thus a popular army, service in which is regarded as prestigious. By general consensus, politics have been kept out of the armed forces, which have consequently remained a major unifying factor in Israel's pluralist, highly politicised society. Indeed, the military have considered it one of their main tasks to assist integration : courses in elementary Hebrew and rudiments of civics were taught to new immigrants in the armed forces; teachers in military service were regularly provided for small settlements in which other instructors were not immediately available; and *NAHAL* (Pioneer Fighting Youth) units, made up of volunteers, spent their compulsory military service in outlying posts, combining military training with agricultural work in their host-*kibbutzim*.

EDUCATION AND CULTURE

The free and compulsory education law (1949, elaborated 1953) has ensured the education of practically all children in the kindergarten and eight elementary grades. While there is still some illiteracy among adult Jews and Arabs —despite an adult-education campaign—the generation of schoolchildren is nearly 100% literate. Over half of Israel's schoolchildren continue into secondary, vocational, agricultural or evening schools. The State and municipalities have been investing considerable efforts and funds in promoting the education of the poor and underprivileged. The Hebrew University in Jerusalem had (in 1968) over 12,500 students, Tel-Aviv University over 9,000, Bar-Ilan University in Ramat-Gan close to 5,000. A college flourishes in Haifa, as well as a very successful polytechnical institute. The Weizmann Institute of Science in Rehovot is mainly concerned with doctoral and post-doctoral research. Academies for the Hebrew language, art, and music are highly regarded.

Learning in all elementary and high schools in Jewish neighbourhoods is in Hebrew; in all Arab neighbourhoods it is in Arabic. Both Hebrew and Arabic are official languages, spoken in government offices, courts and the *Knesset*, which generally seats seven or eight Arabs. Both are used on currency, stamps and so forth. Despite frequent contacts, however, both Hebrew and Arab cultures seem to have had little mutual impact. This is true of literature, the press, theatre, art and music.

ISRAELI-ARAB RELATIONS

While the Israeli consensus is that the very existence of the State is an incontrovertible and non-negotiable fact, there are many currents of opinion regarding the significance of the State's geo-political situation and the means of guaranteeing its future. Most Israelis disagree with those Arabs who consider Israel responsible for all the troubles in the Middle East; they point out that the Kurdish revolt in Iraq, the war in the Yemen, and tensions in the Maghreb have nothing to do with Israel. On the contrary, they maintain that their own State and the Arab States obviously need peace, and that Israel's technical skills might assist Arab industry, agriculture and health services in the same way that they have successfully helped some other countries in Africa and Asia, with no political strings attached. (The Rogers Plan is the latest bid for peace (see p. 45).) Of course, much would depend on lessening mutual distrust and on the attitude of the major world powers, who now appear to consider events in this area as affecting their own interests. A sincere hope for a better future may undo the bitter legacy of the recent past.

FURTHER READING

Akzin, Benjamin and Dror, Yehezkel. *Israel: High-Pressure Planning*, Syracuse Univ. Press, New York, 1966.
Baker, H. E. *Legal System of Israel*, Israel Univ. Press, Jerusalem, 1968.
Bentwich, J. S. *Education in Israel*, Routledge & Kegan Paul, London, 1965.
Czudnowski, M. M. and Landau, J. M. *The Israeli Communist Party and the Elections to the Fifth Knesset, 1961*, The Hoover Institution, Stanford, 1965.
Eisenstadt, S. N. *Israeli Society*, Weidenfeld & Nicolson, London, 1967.
Fein, L. J. *Politics in Israel*, Little & Brown, Boston, Mass., 1967.
Hurewitz, J. C. *The Struggle for Palestine*, Norton, New York, 1950.
Khouri, F. J. *The Arab-Israeli Dilemma*, Syracuse Univ. Press, New York, 1968.
Landau, J. M. *The Arabs in Israel: a Political Study*, Oxford Univ. Press, London, and New York, 1969.
Matras, Judah. *Social Change in Israel*, Aldine, Chicago, 1965.
Patinkin, Don. *The Israel Economy: the First Decade*, Falk Project for Economic Research, Jerusalem, 1960.
Perlmutter, Amos. *Military and Politics in Israel: Nation-Building and Role Expansion*, Frank Cass, London, 1969.

JACOB M. LANDAU. Associate Professor of Political Science at the Hebrew University of Jerusalem. Among his publications are *Parliaments and Parties in Egypt* (1953), *The Jews in Nineteenth-Century Egypt* (1969) and *The Arabs in Israel—a Political Study* (1969).

JORDAN

GEOFFREY FURLONGE

GEOGRAPHY AND CLIMATE

THE Hashemite Kingdom of Jordan is bounded on the north by Syria, on the east by Iraq, on the south by Saudi Arabia, and on the west by the temporary armistice line dividing it from Israel. Its total area is about 37,000 square miles,[1] the eastern seven-eighths of which forms part of the Great Syrian Desert, while the remainder ('The Sown') consists of two plateaux to the west which average 900 metres in altitude and are separated by the deep trench of the Jordan Valley.

The desert is subject to great extremes of temperature, and its rainfall, concentrated in the three winter months and averaging less than five inches annually, suffices for no more than pasture for nomads. The plateaux are temperate in summer and cold in winter, and receive enough rain—up to 30 inches annually on the western side of the Jordan Valley, rather less on the eastern—to support cultivation where adequate fertility exists. The Jordan Valley, burning hot in summer and warm through most winters, receives between 10 and 15 inches of rain annually and has now been proved to be cultivable along almost its entire length.

ECONOMY

No oil has been found, and the only bulk mineral production is natural phosphates. Agriculture and grazing are therefore the main occupations, though of late light industry has been increasing. Wheat, barley, olives, fruit, and sheep, goats and camels form the principal items of production. Exports, consisting mainly of phosphates and agricultural produce, plus the profitable 'invisibles' of the tourist industry,[1] have never sufficed to pay for essential imports and the deficit has been filled by foreign subsidies and loans.

POPULATION

This was estimated in 1966 as 2·1 million, divided almost equally between the parts east and west of the River Jordan and including about 650,000 refugees from what has now become Israel. The vast majority are Arabic-speaking Semites, 95% of them Muslims and the remainder Christians.

The principal towns east of the Jordan are Amman, the capital, with a

---

[1] Since June 1967 the whole area west of the River Jordan has been under Israeli occupation. This situation, if perpetuated, would alter these facts.

226

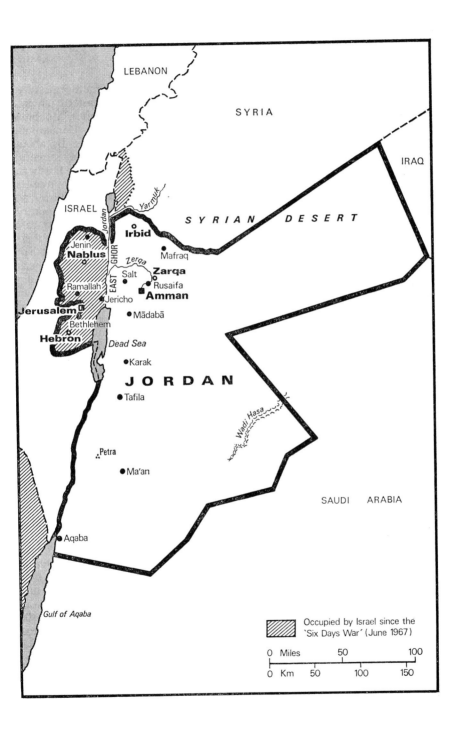

LEBANON

SYRIA

IRAQ

ISRAEL

Yarmuk

S Y R I A N   D E S E R T

Irbid

Jenin

Mafraq

Nablus

Zerqa

Salt

Zarqa

Ramallah

Rusaifa

Jericho

Amman

Jerusalem

Bethlehem

●Mādabā

Hebron

Dead Sea

●Karak

J O R D A N

●Tafila

Wadi Hasa

˙.Petra

●Ma'an

SAUDI   ARABIA

●Aqaba

Gulf of Aqaba

Occupied by Israel since the
'Six Days War' (June 1967)

| 0 | Miles | | 50 | | 100 |

| 0 | Km | 50 | | 100 | 150 |

population now estimated at 500,000, Irbid, Salt, and Ma'an. On the west are the Old City of Jerusalem, Bethlehem, Nablus, Jenin and Hebron.

ANCIENT HISTORY

The desert has been roamed by nomadic Bedouin since remote antiquity. The Sown emerges into history in Biblical times with its eastern plateau already occupied by (from north to south) Amorites, Ammonites, Moabites and Edomites, and the Jordan Valley and western plateau by Canaanites, all Semitic tribes whom modern Arabs claim as their forbears. By about 1000 BC the Israelites had established themselves in Judaea and Samaria, on the western plateau, in the Jordan Valley, and in Gilead, on the northern end of the eastern plateau, and for the next 1,000 years held greater or smaller areas as their fortunes varied. Between the eighth and fifth centuries BC the Assyrians, Babylonians and Persians in succession established temporary domination over the northern part of the Sown, while in the south-east another Arab tribe, the Nabataeans, founded a state which, centred on their impregnable stronghold of Petra, was to last for 600 years. In the fourth century BC the Seleucids, successors of Alexander the Great, held the northern regions and gave them a Greek veneer, while the south-west was fitfully occupied by the Ptolemies from Egypt. In 64 BC Pompey's invasion from the north ushered in a Roman occupation which eventually extended over the whole country; in AD 70 the Romans destroyed Jerusalem and caused the Jewish Diaspora, and in 106 they conquered and destroyed the Nabataean state. As elsewhere, they brought security and prosperity, and, in the fourth century, Christianity.

In 636, however, the region was wrested from their successors, the Byzantines, by the newly Islamised Arabs. Flooding in from Arabia, the Arabs fused with the original inhabitants and gave them the language and religion which predominate in the region today. From then until 1918 the population remained almost entirely Arab, but the region knew different masters: a series of Caliphates, based in turn on Damascus, Baghdad and Cairo; Seljuk Turks from Central Asia; Crusaders, whose Frankish Kingdom lasted 84 years; Egyptians; and, from 1517 to 1918, Ottoman Turks.

THE BRITISH MANDATE

In November 1918, towards the end of World War I, British forces under General Allenby, advancing from Egypt against the Turks, occupied the region and set up a military administration. Operating on their flank was an Arab army under the Emir Faisal, the third son of the Sherif Husain of Mecca who, in 1916, had led an Arab revolt against the Turks. The two armies, continuing northwards, reached Damascus and there Faisal, with British assent, set up an Arab administration over Syria. In 1920, however, at a Great Power Conference at San Remo, the French, obtaining a mandate over Syria, found the presence of Faisal and his administration incompatible with their ambition to control it permanently, and so expelled both. This enraged his father (then King Husain of the Hejaz), who in February 1921 sent his second son Abdullah and a Bedouin force into the area east of the River Jordan with the intention of invading Syria from the south and recovering it for his family. This area, however, formed part of the 'Palestine' for which the British, at the same San Remo Conference, had obtained a mandate, so that to let Abdullah proceed would have caused a clash with the French, whereas to stop him by force would have caused a clash with Husain. The British decided, therefore, to do a deal with him, and in March Winston Churchill, the newly appointed Colonial Secretary, summoned him to Jerusalem and there offered him the Emirate, under British authority, of the eastern portion of Palestine, henceforth to be designated 'Transjordan', on condition that he gave up any idea of invading Syria. The Emir accepted, and the new State was accordingly established, under a separate mandate but with the same High Commissioner as Palestine. It was agreed that a pledge to promote the establishment of a 'Jewish National Home' in Palestine, which the British Government had given in the Balfour Declaration of 1917, and which had been written into their terms of the mandate, should not apply to Transjordan.

The area thus allocated to the Emir was extremely poor. Most of it was desert, over which the Ruwalla, Beni Sakhr, Huwaitat and lesser tribes grazed their livestock. The lesser cultivable areas, mostly dependent on varying rainfall, were owned either by smallholders, communally by villages, or occasionally by town landowners. Amman and the other towns were small and served merely as markets for produce or the basic essentials of life. The country lacked most amenities and social services were rudimentary.

For the next 18 years the Emir, supported by the British Resident and a small group of devoted British and Arab officials, ruled this backward territory modestly and well. Trouble with surrounding states was avoided, internal order maintained, and essential services gradually built up. The Arab Legion, a Bedouin gendarmerie force, was developed to a high pitch of efficiency by two outstanding British commanders, Peake and Glubb Pashas; and the latter, by skilful use of armoured cars and aircraft, ended the wasteful inter-tribal raiding which for centuries had formed part of the desert way of life.

In 1928 the Emir, at British instance, promulgated an Organic Law setting up an elected Legislative Council, as a first step towards constitutional government, and the same year the British government negotiated with him a treaty recognising his country's independence but reserving to Great Britain certain military and financial powers. In practice the country continued as before to be ruled paternally by the Emir in close collaboration with the British Resident, and no one doubted where the real authority lay. But opposition remained minimal : the Emir's rectitude, common sense, humanity, and sense of humour brought him first the respect and then the devotion of the vast majority of his subjects, and despite the general poverty, amounting sometimes to starvation for the tribes when the winter rains failed, most Jordanians who remember that epoch speak of it nostalgically as 'the time when we were all happy'.

On the outbreak of World War II the Emir immediately offered the British Government his full co-operation and placed the Arab Legion at their disposal. Its 3,500 men proved of great value in 1941 in assisting British forces to put down a revolt in Iraq, and in 1946 the Emir's loyalty was rewarded by a new Treaty under which Transjordan attained full independence and the Emir became King; at the same time he changed the name of his realm to 'Jordan'. Two years later this instrument was replaced by a formal Treaty of Alliance, under which each country pledged itself to come to the aid of the other if attacked, and a separate agreement providing for an annual British subsidy to pay for Jordan's armed forces. The King now promulgated a constitution, which is still in force. This substituted for the Legislative Council a Parliament composed of a nominated Senate and a House of Representatives elected by universal male suffrage, to which the Cabinet was responsible. 'The People' were designated as the supreme power, but wide powers were reserved for the King, who could dismiss parliament and individual ministers, had the right to choose the prime minister, the senators, and the judges, and was commander-in-chief of the armed forces. In practice, during King Abdullah's lifetime, all major decisions continued to be made by him and the powers of parliament remained limited.

Independent Jordan, 1948–67

In May 1948 Jordan was drawn into the troubles besetting its neighbour Palestine. There the British Government, no longer prepared to hold the ring between the violently opposed Arab and Jewish communities, had the previous year remitted the problem to the United Nations, which had voted for partition of the country into Arab and Jewish states. The Arab League, of which Jordan was now a member, had rejected the decision and agreed that its members should send troops into the country when the British left, as announced, on 15 May 1948, in order to preserve all of it for the Arabs. King Abdullah, though with misgivings, felt obliged to comply, and in the event the Arab Legion bore the brunt of the fighting which ensued and was mainly responsible for the retention by the Arabs of most of Judaea and Samaria, and the Old City of Jerusalem. In late 1948 the Jordan Parliament approved the union of this area—which became known as the West Bank—with Jordan, and its annexation was formally voted by the Parliament, and recognised by the British government, in 1950.

Meanwhile Jordan had given refuge to over 600,000 Arab refugees from what was now the State of Israel. Their influx entirely changed its character. This had already been affected by modern inventions and the spread of education : already the Bedouin, far easier to control by car and poorer because trucks had reduced demand for the camels they bred, had lessened in importance, and an educated urban intelligentsia had begun to challenge the monopoly of power hitherto held by the tribal chiefs and landowners. The Palestinians, usually better educated and more sophisticated than the people of the East Bank, and often possessed of substantial capital or professional qualifications, accelerated this trend. Settled in Amman (which quadrupled in size) or in the other towns, they swelled the ranks of the new middle class and their abilities ensured for them a leading part in both the commercial and the political life of the country. On the other hand, they had no loyalty to the throne and no experience of self-government; but they were experienced in the techniques of opposition and obstruction, learned in the long struggle against Jewish pretensions and mandatory policies. They thus had an unsettling effect, so that the formerly peaceful kingdom for the first time knew urban unrest and political extremism.

It was in fact a group of Palestinian extremists who, in September 1951, contrived the assassination of King Abdullah in a Jerusalem mosque because he had allegedly engaged in secret peace-talks with Israel. His elder son and successor, Talal, was mentally unstable and was deposed in 1952. Thus, at the age of 18, Abdullah's grandson Husain came to the throne.

Between 1952 and 1967 Jordan evolved rapidly. Education, the demand for which was stimulated by the Palestinians, expanded considerably, though not fast enough to meet the demand. Primary and secondary schools were provided by the Government, by private bodies and religious communities, and by UNRWA (the United Nations Agency set up to look after the refugees). The latter also established three technical colleges for boys and one for girls, as well as a teacher-training college. As a result, illiteracy, especially amongst women, declined markedly from its formerly high figure. In the economic field, progress was striking. A development board, founded in 1952 and financed by British, and later American, grants and loans, was able to accomplish much despite the lack of natural resources. Jordan's only port, Aqaba, was modernised and linked to Amman by an asphalted road, thus reducing the country's dependence on Beirut and facilitating external trade. Irrigation schemes, notably one which diverted the waters of the Yarmuk down the Jordan Valley, substantially increased agricultural production. Reafforestation was pushed ahead, and an electrical grid scheme was begun. A flourishing tourist trade was built up with the aid of new roads and hotels. The rehabilitation of the railway which formerly linked Damascus with Medina, but which had been destroyed south of Ma'an in World War I, was put in hand and a spur to connect it with Aqaba was projected. The Royal Jordan Airline established services with all Middle Eastern capitals and with London and Paris.

Despite the improved standard of living resulting from these and many private enterprises, political evolution during those years was less healthy. The West Bank never fused with the East. From 1954 onwards Husain and his régime were faced with the growth of an extreme nationalist, left-wing, middle class movement, which professed admiration for President Nasser of Egypt and became subversive under the stimulus of funds and venomous radio attacks from Cairo. Its main targets became the King's dependence on the West and his retention of a foreigner, Glubb Pasha, in command of the Arab Legion. In late 1955 a British attempt to induce Jordan to join the Western-sponsored 'Baghdad Pact' was frustrated by Cairo-inspired intrigues, which brought down the government on the issue. In 1956 the King found it necessary to dismiss Glubb, who was blamed for the Legion's inability to prevent Israeli destruction of Jordan villages accused of raiding into Israel, whereupon the Legion was renamed 'the Arab Army'; and in March 1957, as a result of the Suez affair, the Jordan Parliament overwhelmingly voted to abrogate the Anglo-Jordan Treaty of Alliance, even though this meant the end of the British pledge to protect Jordan and to subsidise her armed forces. Three Arab states which had previously undertaken to make good the amount of the British subsidy failed to do so, but the United States Government decided to shoulder the burden and under their care the Arab Army, which had already been expanded with British money, was still further developed and re-equipped and the nucleus of an air force established.

In April 1957 the same movement attempted to overthrow the monarchy and to set up a republican régime under Egyptian domination, but the plan was foiled by King Husain's courage and by his astute use of loyalist Bedouin army units. In 1958 the King caused Jordan to join Iraq in a union intended as a counter to the United Arab Republic of Egypt and Syria, which Nasser had just formed, but this was dissolved a few months later when his cousin King Faisal II of Iraq was assassinated and his monarchy destroyed in a *coup d'état*, and for the next six years Jordan was largely isolated in the Arab world. Husain nevertheless consolidated his authority during this period, and in 1964 felt strong enough to respond to a popular demand for the end of Jordan's isolation by attending an Arab 'summit meeting' in Cairo, where he undertook to place the Jordan Army under the nominal authority of an Egyptian-led 'Arab Military Command' which the Arab League had instituted. He also felt obliged to consent to the formation of a 'Palestinian Liberation Organisation', intended to operate against Israel from Jordan territory, and his problem thereafter was how to maintain his own position despite the fact that the PLO openly flouted his authority. That he succeeded was due partly to his own firmness and tact, but also to the generally improving standard of living caused by economic betterment, which had now reached the point where 'viability by 1970' was seriously envisaged.

THE 1967 WAR AND ITS AFTERMATH

By June 1967 Arab commando raids into Israel, Israeli reprisals against both Jordan and Syria, and manœuvres by Nasser intended to score propaganda successes against Israel, had so much raised tension in the region as to convince the Israelis, probably erroneously, that the Arabs were bent on war. They accordingly decided on the preventive strike which, within six days, had destroyed the bulk of the Arab armed forces. Once fighting had begun, King Husain (who had just signed a defence agreement with President Nasser) could not avoid involvement without the certainty that his Palestinian subjects, all of whom saw the chance to take revenge on Israel, would dethrone him. As a result, his army and air force were smashed and the Israelis captured the Old City of Jerusalem and the whole of the West Bank, some 400,000 of whose inhabitants, including most of the refugees in camps there, fled to East Jordan and had to be accommodated anew.

The armistice which ended the fighting found Jordan in a greatly enfeebled condition. Her armed forces needed a complete re-equipment, which she could not afford, and her normal suppliers, the United States and Great Britain, showed no enthusiasm about providing it. The loss of the Old City of Jerusalem, which was keenly felt by all Arabs in view of its religious significance to Muslims and Christians alike, had also involved the disappearance of 95% of Jordan's tourist trade. The need to absorb the new influx of refugees imposed a heavy burden. Worst of all was the lowering of morale, and the mutual recriminations, which resulted from the realisation that Jordan had suffered another humiliating defeat. It is a tribute to King Husain's leadership and prestige that the country did not disintegrate during those first weeks.

PRESENT SITUATION

No progress has been made towards a settlement with Israel. A General Assembly resolution of July 1967, instructing Israel not to annex the Old City of Jerusalem, was successfully defied by the victors. A Security Council resolution, voted in November 1967, which provided for Israeli evacuation of 'occupied territories' and for a 'just settlement' of the refugee problem, in return for an Arab recognition of Israel, renunciation of belligerency, and an undertaking to allow freedom of navigation in the Suez Canal and the Gulf of Aqaba, remained unimplemented. Great Power talks on the Middle East situation had little practical effect. As time passed the attitude of the conflicting parties hardened, and the main development was the growth of the resistance organisations composed of ex-Palestinians, which, well supplied with money from the richer Arab countries and operating from Jordan and Syrian soil, kept the Israeli security forces on constant alert and maintained tension, while constantly threatening to undermine Husain's authority.

232

On the other hand, by Arab League decision, the oil-producing Arab States agreed to compensate the countries which had suffered losses as a result of the 1967 war. Jordan's share of this compensation amounts to £40 million annually, a sum which allows her economy to be sustained and economic development to be continued in such fields as the completion of the electric grid, telecommunications, and the further improvement of the road system and of Aqaba Port. At the end of 1968, Jordan's reserves stood higher than before the 1967 war. Some re-equipment of the armed forces was carried out; thanks to the efforts of UNRWA the situation of the 1967 refugees was approaching that of the former (1948) ones; public morale was higher; and Husain's personal position appeared stronger. The whole position was precarious and could have been changed overnight by either an Israeli decision to evacuate the West Bank, thus enabling the refugees from it to return to their homes or permanent camps; or, alternatively, by a resumption of hostilities with Israel. The lack of any real internal stability was demonstrated, in September 1970, by the civil war between government troops and guerrillas of the several Palestine liberation organisations who felt that Husain ought not to have accepted the American peace initiative, the Rogers Plan, with its temporary cease-fire and plans for peace negotiations with Israel. After much bloodshed and loss of life, the government eventually succeeded in suppressing the revolt. But the overall situation of Jordan remains precarious, with spasmodic fighting continuing between the guerrillas and government forces.

FURTHER READING

Dearden, Anne. *Jordan*, Robert Hale, London, 1958.
Glubb, Lt.-General Sir J. B. *A Soldier with the Arabs*, Hodder & Stoughton, London, 1957; Verry, Connecticut, 1957.
Husain, H. M. King. *Uneasy Lies the Head*, Heinemann, London, 1962.
Harris, George L. *Jordan*, Grove Press, New York, 1958.

SIR GEOFFREY FURLONGE, KBE, CMG. Ambassador to Ethiopia until 1959. Minister to Bulgaria 1954–6; Minister (later Ambassador) to Jordan 1952–4. One-time Head of the Middle Eastern Department of the Foreign Office. Political Officer with British Forces in Syria and Lebanon 1941–6. Entered Levant Consular service 1926 and served in Morocco, Saudi Arabia, Libya and Lebanon. Though retired since 1960 he continues to write and lecture. Author of *The Lands of Barbary* (1966) and *Palestine Is My Country: the Story of Musa Alami* (1969).

KUWAIT

RAGAEI EL MALLAKH

Backdrop to Development

Lying near the head of the Persian Gulf, bordered by Iraq and Saudi Arabia, comprising some 6,000 square miles (excluding the Neutral Zone),[1] and with a population of half a million, is the State of Kuwait. The terrain is flat and riverless, the climate inhospitable, particularly during the summer months when temperatures exceed 100 degrees Farenheit with high humidity. Kuwait is known widely today for its extraordinary wealth from oil and its swift rise from poverty. At the close of World War II, its *per caput* income was estimated at $21; at present it enjoys the world's second highest level at $4,535 (1966).

The history of Kuwait begins in the first part of the 18th century, with the movement of two families of the Anazah tribe from the Arabian peninsula. The Khalifah and Sabah settled on the coast where a fort or *kut* stood. 'Kuwait' is derived from the diminutive of that word. The Khalifah house moved on in the second half of the 1700s, finally settling in Bahrain. Since that time, the Sabah family has provided the rulers for Kuwait. Succession to the Emirship is based upon election by the family, not primogeniture. In 1963, the creation of an elected National Assembly marked the move from an absolute to a constitutional monarchy. The National Assembly has proved unexpectedly energetic in exercising and protecting its prerogatives and authority.

Although Kuwait was historically poor in natural resources, its geographical location gave it certain advantages. As early as 1775 Kuwait served as the starting point of a desert mail route to Aleppo and the Mediterranean. In the late 18th century, the British East India Company transferred its trade headquarters for the northern Gulf from Basra to Kuwait. Kuwait was once considered as the possible terminus of the Berlin-Baghdad railway as well as the beginning of a Russian line from the Gulf to the Mediterranean. The potential threat of these railroad schemes to the interests of British shipping spurred an Anglo-Kuwaiti treaty of protection in 1899. The major stipulation in this agreement was that Kuwait could not cede territory to, nor have relations with, any nation unless British consent had been received. Until full independence was achieved on 19 June 1961, Kuwait's foreign affairs were handled through the British Foreign Office. This relationship between the two nations, spanning more than half a century, may be seen in such

---

[1] The Neutral Zone, lying between Kuwait and Saudi Arabia, has been jointly administered by these two states since 1922.

234

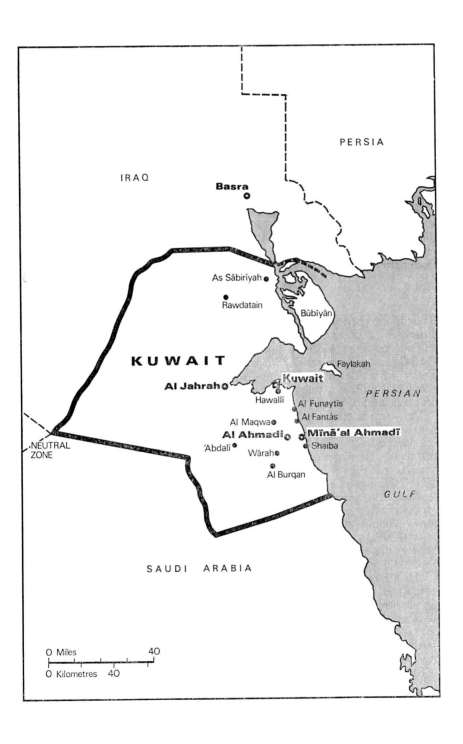

fields as trade, oil concessions, and the early direction of Kuwaiti investment.

Prior to independence, Kuwait participated as a non-member in the Arab League, co-operating in economic and social projects. In 1961, it became at once a full member of the League. Internationally, Kuwait became the 111th member of the United Nations in May 1963.

There are certain social and economic conditions, many deriving from the early days of Kuwait, which still mark the pattern of Kuwaiti development and growth. Kuwaitis are among the Gulf's most ambitious and mobile traders, with a long tradition of commercial entrepreneurship and geographically scattered contacts. Before the discovery of oil, the sea, which offered the means of transport for trade, also provided Kuwaitis with their second form of national economic vocation : fishing and pearling.[2] Moreover, Kuwait was fortunate in having an excellent natural harbour in Kuwait City. Thus, if a national characteristic can be identified, it is the predominantly mercantile mentality of Kuwaitis, with a relatively high degree of tolerance based upon contact with other countries and cultures. Into this milieu came the discovery of crude oil and with it Kuwait's meteoric rise from extreme poverty to affluence.

THE OIL INDUSTRY

Kuwaiti prosperity to date directly mirrors the development of the oil industry. In 1950, government revenues from oil were estimated at $11·5 million, reaching $281·4 million five years later, $648·5 million in fiscal 1966–7, and an estimated $667 million for 1968–9. In addition, the oil industry has made substantial purchases in the local market, of the order of about $60 million a year. Oil is responsible for approximately 95% of total governmental revenue.

The largest company holding concessions on mainland Kuwait is the Kuwait Oil Company (KOC), jointly owned by British Petroleum and Gulf Oil Corporation. The offshore concession was granted to Kuwait Shell Petroleum Development Company Limited. Onshore Neutral Zone concessions of the Kuwaiti portion are held by American Independent Oil Company (Aminoil) and those offshore were granted to the Arabian Oil Company, a Japanese enterprise which also holds Saudi Arabia's offshore concession share of the Zone. The single local company holding a concession is the Kuwait National Petroleum Company (KNPC), established in 1960 with a 60% subscription by the government to the original shares. The national company is becoming increasingly involved in varied activities, including refining and marketing.

The advantages for Kuwaiti crude are considerable with its production cost placed at about six cents a barrel. Kuwait Oil Company, by far the largest producer, lifts its crude from such fields as the Greater Burgan and (because the country is very small) has to move it only a short distance to Ahmadi ridge, from which it flows by gravity to waiting tankers. Until 1967, Kuwait was the leading producer in the Middle East and the second largest exporter in the world, led only by Venezuela.

The oil industry is of an enclave nature, highly detached (with perhaps

[2] With the growth of the oil industry, these second forms of economic activity suffered a drastic decline, although fishing is now undergoing a revival. The development of cultured pearls had undermined the pearling industry even before oil exploitation caused a further decline by offering more attractive employment opportunities.

the exception of petrochemicals) from the socio-economic mainstream of life in the country. Oil is a capital, not a labour-intensive enterprise; it employs about 7,000 persons, yet it accounts for more than 61% of the gross domestic product. By comparison, the government employs over 80,000, or one out of every six persons. The sudden wealth, and the limited extent to which the population is occupied in the actual productive processes of the source of this wealth, have endangered the relationship between economic effort and reward.

Moreover, the method of income-distribution for governmental revenues, while it has succeeded in spreading the wealth, has simultaneously weakened incentives and entrepreneurial ability in many instances. The pattern followed has been one in which the government purchased land owned by Kuwaitis at excessively high prices, and then resold it to citizens at prices far lower. Over $1,000 million has been paid out through this programme.

The beneficial aspects of the oil industry's development in Kuwait still outweigh the drawbacks which tend to accompany rapid and extremely one-sided economic growth. The most compelling factor in basing prosperity on such a single product is that crude oil is a wasting, non-renewable asset unlike, for example, primary products based on agriculture. There is a vulnerability connected with a one-product economy which is reinforced and deepened by the lack of any agricultural base in Kuwait. The country is dependent upon imports of foodstuffs and, more recently, of growing amounts of capital and consumption goods, the reflection of economic growth and affluence. The level of imports per person is the highest in the world, reaching approximately $1,000 in 1968. In short, without diversification, the Kuwaiti economy can suffer extreme fluctuations which depend entirely upon the conditions prevailing in the world oil industry.

Sociologically, the sudden expansion of economic activity has directly accounted for the influx of non-Kuwaitis. The population rose from 206,473 in 1957, to 321,621 four years later, reaching 467,339 in 1965. In the latter census, non-Kuwaitis accounted for 247,280, or slightly under 53% of the population. Thus, while Kuwaitis form the largest single grouping by far, they are not a majority within the entire population.[3] This imbalance will undoubtedly change in the future through education, as more Kuwaitis are trained to hold specialised positions. Nonetheless, the indications are that certain categories, especially of manual labour, will continue to be supplied by non-Kuwaitis.

SOCIAL GROWTH AND CHANGE

The astounding strides taken in education can be attributed to the sufficiency of capital and the small size of the population. In the past two decades, the number of students has increased 60 times. There were two schools in 1936; by 1966 there were some 160. Compulsory education is now required from four to 16 years of age. School is free to everyone residing in the country, from kindergarten through to higher education. This includes, at no cost

[3] In 1965, non-Kuwaiti Arabs accounted for 40·2% of the total population and 76% of all non-Kuwaitis. When they seek employment in Kuwait, non-Kuwaitis must obtain a work permit which is granted for specific periods; with the termination of their work non-Kuwaitis must leave the country. The national origins of the foreign population in the 1965 census were: Jordan, 77,712; Iraq, 25,897; Lebanon, 20,877; Syria, 16,849; UAR, 11,021; Oman, 19,520; other non-Kuwaiti Arabs, 16,047. The number of Iranians is around 26,000, largely unskilled labourers; the figure is uncertain as the majority of those entering Kuwait do so illegally.

to the student, books, supplies, lunches, and even clothing. In a society where participation of women in economic and social activities outside the home has been severely limited (in 1957, only 2% of the labour force was contributed by women), the stress on girls' education is an encouraging factor. Today over 40% of the total student enrolment is of girls. This should have a cumulative economic and social effect in the years ahead.

Two Kuwaiti institutions of higher instruction were opened in 1966. The University of Kuwait was established with the idea of providing Kuwaiti high-school graduates and others from the Gulf area with college-level instruction at home. The initial enrolment of 500 in the 1966–7 academic year is projected to reach a level of approximately 15,000 by 1977–8. The second education centre is the Kuwait Institute of Economic and Social Planning in the Middle East, of which the executing agency is the United Nations Special Fund. The objective of the Institute is to offer a special programme to train financial, economic and social planning specialists, as well as serve as a planning advisory service. The trainees at the Institute consist of Middle Eastern government employees and members of the staffs of economic organisations, who undergo a course in theoretical and practical planning procedures.

The extent to which Kuwait depends for human resources on its Arab neighbours is evident in the total number of teachers (5,036), of whom only 68 are Kuwaitis. This proportion should be modified as the number of educated Kuwaitis increases.

In health services the advances similarly have been impressive. Within a twenty-year span, the facilities have been expanded from one hospital to 15 and from four physicians to about 500, or a ratio of one doctor for every 750 persons. All medical services are free to persons residing in the country, regardless of nationality. As with education, most doctors and nurses are non-Kuwaiti, largely drawn from other Arab countries. Allocations for social services consistently have been around 25% of total budgetary expenditures for the fiscal years 1963–4 through 1966–7. Health and education account for about 20% alone.

Every citizen is guaranteed a minimum standard of living.[4] Additionally, any Kuwaiti whose monthly income is less than $420 is eligible to participate in low-income housing programmes. (To judge just how liberal this stand is, it should be recalled that there is no personal income tax in Kuwait.) Dwellings are purchased over a 25-year period, interest free. The home may not be transferred to an individual who is not a member of the owner's family, which ensures that such housing remains in the hands of low-income Kuwaitis. There are, as well, pension programmes and state care for the aged when needed.

DEVELOPMENT AND PLANNING

The most pressing problem in Kuwait's continued growth and modernisation is economic diversification to reduce its excessive dependence on a single product. This aspect underlies the framing of a five-year development plan,

[4] Monthly payments range from $42 for a single person to $140 for a family of eleven, plus a maximum of $56 per month for a family living in rented premises. This guarantee of a certain standard of living, as well as participation in low-income housing, is restricted to Kuwaiti citizens. Citizenship is difficult to achieve through naturalisation as relatively long periods of residence are required. Only Kuwaitis can own land and vote, and a Kuwaiti partner must be included in all business ventures.

drafted in 1966 and revised in the following year. Among the objectives are (1) support for the development of industries other than the oil industry, (2) a continued high rate of economic growth, (3) an attempt to restore a Kuwaiti majority in the total population, by natural increase and by reducing the number of non-Kuwaitis, (4) raising the proportion of Kuwaitis in the labour force, (5) an improvement in education and training standards, and (6) a drive toward economic activity which will complement that of other Arab states.

Because of the dearth of natural resources other than oil, industrial diversification has been launched first within the oil sector itself, through the establishment of the Shaiba industrial complex which includes the Kuwait National Petroleum Company's all-hydrogen refinery and the Kuwait Chemical Fertilisers Company. The output of both plants has reached the export stage. So far, Kuwaiti fertilisers have been exported to the Indian sub-continent, east Africa, and countries of the Middle East.

Free enterprise, trade and capitalism are traditionally the basic characteristics of the Kuwaiti economy. The term 'welfare state' often applied to Kuwait actually refers to the field of social services. Recently, however, the government has undertaken participation in mixed public and private business ventures. The *raison d'être* of this move has been the need to stimulate a shift in private investment away from the more accepted and comfortable areas of trade, retail and real estate into industry and large-scale enterprises which are new, and for this reason somewhat suspect, to the average Kuwaiti investor.

A peculiarity of the Kuwaiti economy, which is shared by few other countries, is the almost consistent condition of capital surplus. This surplus, traceable to the swift and massive development of oil production, is manifested in three areas: (1) a favourable balance of payments, (2) a budgetary surplus, and (3) a high savings rate compared to investment.[5] The savings rate of 44% of the gross national product is one of the world's highest, yet only 45% of these savings has been absorbed locally. So the question remains of what to do with the relatively abundant capital.

A major factor limiting internal investment is the narrowness of the domestic market; a population base of only half a million simply rules out the efficient manufacture of many products. And, as has been mentioned earlier, since this capital emanates from the depletion of a wasting asset, gradual though the depletion may be, it should be utilised in a manner which ensures the perpetuation and renewal of that capital. With this in mind, the government has followed a policy of accumulating reserves with widespread external investment, particularly in the United Kingdom and the United States. By 1968, the state reserves and various participations were placed at about $1,400 million. The return from government investment of these reserves is now somewhere in the region of $100 million annually. Having built up reserves and met the requirements of the social and economic infrastructure, alternative outlets for private as well as public Kuwaiti capital have been sought, particularly in the Middle East region.

KUWAITI FOREIGN ASSISTANCE PROGRAMMES

Foreign economic aid in general includes two elements: the investment content and political interests. Kuwaiti assistance offers no exception to this

[5] For example, the budgetary surplus from 1960 through 1964 averaged over $100 million annually and it is estimated that it will reach $190 million by 1969–70.

overall rule. As a small but exceedingly rich state in a region which predominantly lacks capital, it is a politically astute policy for Kuwait to share some of this increasing wealth with its larger, poorer and more populous neighbours. Moreover, political stability in the area is particularly desirable to an affluent state like Kuwait. To assert, however, that Kuwait's foreign aid programme is only politically motivated would be a serious oversimplification. In the light of the capital surplus and the limited absorptive capacity of the Kuwaiti economy, investment represents a very real factor in this programme.

There are three major methods or agencies through which Kuwaiti assistance is dispensed : the General Authority for South Arabian and Gulf States (known until 1966 as the Gulf Permanent Assistance Committee), the Kuwait Fund for Arab Economic Development, and loans from the state reserves. Outright grants have been given to the formerly isolated and poor shaikhdoms of the Trucial coast (Dubai, Sharjah, Himriyah, Umm al-Quwain, Ajman, Ras al-Khaimah and Fujairah) and certain support extended to Yemen. About 0·5% of Kuwait's national income has been set aside for this type of aid.

After Kuwait had achieved independence, the Gulf Permanent Assistance Committee (GUPAC) was formalised to support the development of the area. The agency assists in financing resource surveys, soil analysis, and water requirements and potential. Such basic knowledge is a prerequisite for the formation of any development plans or programmes. Social infrastructure, specifically health and education, received GUPAC attention and support. By 1965, Kuwait had participated in the construction of and was fully operating some 32 schools, two hospitals, and seven clinics in the Trucial area, at no cost to the local population. Yemen has similarly received Committee financing for 20 schools, a teachers' college, seven clinics, and a hospital. Whereas the GUPAC retained responsibility for, and met the cost of operating, all its supported installations in the Trucial states, the Yemeni government assumed responsibility for such facilities in the Yemen. Kuwaiti involvement in aid projects in this area is likely to diminish as substantial finds of oil are being made along the Trucial coast, particularly in Abu Dhabi, which is expanding its own assistance to its immediate neighbours.

The most formalised and autonomous aid agency is the Kuwait Fund for Arab Economic Development (KFAED). Designed to follow the businesslike procedures of the World Bank, the Fund has participated in lending for creditworthy projects throughout much of the Arab world. The terms of KFAED loans have compared favourably, in the rate of interest charged, with most other sources available to the developing countries. The capital of the Fund is $560 million, with a potential of $1,680 million when utilising its right to issue bonds and to borrow. The capital is to be revolving, so that any project supported must be economically sound and financially remunerative. The investment element is dominant in Fund credits.

By the spring of 1968, a total of 16 loans had been extended to seven Arab nations. Algeria received two loans for an oil pipeline, while agricultural, sugar manufacturing, and railroad development in the Sudan benefited from three Fund credits. Tunisia gained support through three agreements for electrical power expansion and agriculture; Lebanon also received a loan for power generation. Two agricultural projects in Morocco were selected for KFAED support and Jordan contracted loans for the Yarmouk River development, phosphate production, the upgrading of Jerusalem Electric Power facilities, and tourism expansion through the construction of Intercontinental Hotels in Jerusalem and Amman. Finally, the United Arab Republic received two loans for the improvement of the Suez Canal and marine transport. The KFAED, by mid-1968, had committed a total of almost $190 million.

In contrast with the Fund are those loans extended through the state reserves. These credits, given on a general support and programme basis, often for meeting balance-of-payments requirements, carry liberal terms and are occasionally interest-free. Political considerations have operated here, since ratification by Kuwait's National Assembly has been required for all loan agreements financed from state funds. In 1965 the Assembly voted to halt the negotiating of any further agreements of this type. A total of $348·74 million has been committed in 15 loans to Algeria, Dubai, Iraq, Jordan, Lebanon, Morocco, Sudan, Tunisia and the UAR.

In addition, Kuwait has participated, with the UAR, in establishing the Arab-African Bank, to carry out banking and development lending activities throughout Africa and the Arab Middle East. Total Kuwaiti aid has been running at about 10% of the country's national income annually, a proportion much higher than aid given by the advanced nations, such as 0·5% by the United States and 6% by the United Kingdom of their respective incomes. Following the June hostilities in 1967, Kuwait joined with Saudi Arabia and Libya in undertaking substantial crisis assistance to Jordan and the UAR. Kuwait has been paying $109·2 million of the total of $266 million promised to the UAR annually and $44·8 million of the three-nation contribution of $112 million to Jordan. The crisis aid has been on such a scale that it has apparently curtailed the amount of funds available for bilateral developmental lending, as these activities have decreased somewhat since 1967.

The most important aspect of Kuwaiti aid has been the encouragement it has given to intra-aid among the developing Arab countries. With a surplus in capital, Kuwait has been and still remains dependent upon the import of human resources and consumption goods from its Arab neighbours, among whom surpluses in these factors exist. Moreover, regionalism increases the investment opportunities open to Kuwaiti capital, both public and private.

FROM AFFLUENCE TO DEVELOPMENT

The rapidity of the economic growth taking place in Kuwait is indisputable and the resulting affluence is almost unprecedented elsewhere. However, sustaining this level of growth in the future will depend increasingly upon the extent to which Kuwait is successful in extricating herself from dependence upon a single product, and on the manner in which this is accomplished. One of the most critical approaches may be the fuller utilisation of regionalism whereby Kuwait could develop specialised products for such a larger market. The present inter-dependence points to the feasibility of this approach; Kuwait has a surplus of capital, but is deficient in labour, agriculture, and a domestic market of adequate size. The fact that Kuwait is investing in the region does not imply its withdrawal from wider international investment opportunities which offer sound returns.

Domestically, Kuwait could develop those industries which require high initial capital investment, and could promote research into the use of arid lands, weather modification, desalination, hydroponics and petrochemistry. Kuwait has started certain of these enterprises which ultimately can be of benefit to the entire Middle East and North Africa.

The commitment of the Kuwaiti population to development in general and to greater participation in the continued economic and social growth of the country is crucial. The relative abundance of capital eases the strains of planning for the future but does not remove the necessity for it. The challenge for Kuwait is to channel its wealth into a pattern of sustained development so that coming generations also will have prosperity.

FURTHER READING

Abu Hakima, Ahmad Mustafa. *History of Eastern Arabia 1750–1800*, Khayats, Beirut, 1965.

Abu Hakima, Ahmad Mustafa. *The Rise and Development of Bahrain and Kuwait*, Khayats, Beirut, 1965.

El Mallakh, R. *Economic Development and Regional Cooperation: Kuwait*, Univ. of Chicago Press, Chicago, 1968.

Frank, Helmut J. *Crude Oil Prices in the Middle East*, Praeger, New York, 1966.

Longrigg, Stephen H. *Oil in the Middle East*, Oxford Univ. Press, London and New York, 1961.

RAGAEI EL MALLAKH. Professor of Economics and Chairman of Middle Eastern and African Studies at the University of Colorado, Boulder. Has received fellowships from the Rockefeller Foundation, the Social Science Research Council and Harvard University, and served as economic consultant to the World Bank. Author of *Economic Development and Regional Cooperation: Kuwait* (1968), co-author of *The Arab Nation: Paths and Obstacles to Fulfilment* (1961). Contributor to *The World Today*, *American Economic Review*, *International Development Review* and *Middle East Journal*.

LEBANON

DAVID COWAN

HISTORICAL SUMMARY

THE Lebanese Republic has only existed within its present boundaries since the establishment of Greater Lebanon by the French mandatory authorities on 1 September 1920. Prior to that, Lebanon was confined to Mount Lebanon, north of the Beirut-Damascus gap, the coastal areas, the fertile Biqaa plain and the Anti-Lebanon forming part of Syria. Of all the Middle Eastern states, Lebanon is most noted for the diversity of its inhabitants—not racially speaking, for the vast majority are of basically Semitic Aramaic stock, although the innumerable conquerors who have come and gone over many centuries have all left traces of their occupation. The diversity lies in the multiplicity of faiths and sects, the delicate balance between which is the constant preoccupation of Lebanese politicians : a balance on which the future, indeed, the very existence of the country depends. The largest community is held to be that of the Maronite Christians, which comprises about four-fifths of the inhabitants of Mount Lebanon. The Maronites, descendants of the early Monothelites, were finally reconciled and affiliated to the Church of Rome in 1736. Then there are Greek Catholics and Greek Orthodox, Syrian Catholics and Syrian Orthodox, Armenian Catholics and Armenian Orthodox and some Protestants. The Muslims are divided almost equally into Sunnis and Shi'is, the former having their strongholds in Tripoli and the Basta quarter of Beirut, the latter predominating in the Biqaa and the South. In addition to the main Christian and Muslim communities, there are the warlike Druzes of the Metn and Chouf mountain districts, north and south of the Beirut-Damascus gap, and of the Mount Hermon region. The cause of the existence of so many sects in Lebanon lies in the complex religious and political history of the Middle East and in the fact that Lebanon is at the cross-roads of three continents.

Historically, Lebanon, that is Mount Lebanon, played no great role in the ancient world. Its only importance lay in the fact that its well wooded slopes supplied vast quantities of timber for the Phoenician fleets which set sail from Tyre and Sidon and for the carpenters of Ancient Egypt. In the Middle Ages, incredible though it may seem, its snow was shipped to Egypt to fill the ice-boxes of the Mameluks of Cairo ! During the Roman and Byzantine eras, which began with Pompey's occupation of Syria in 64 BC and ended with the Islamic invasion in AD 636, Lebanon was ruled as an integral part of the Syrian province and the inhabitants enjoyed the *Pax Romana*, being left to live their own lives provided they paid their taxes like good subjects. This peaceful existence was only shattered towards the end of the Byzantine period by the tremendous struggle waged between Byzantium and Sassanid

MEDITERRANEAN
SEA

● Halb

Al-Mina
Tripoli ● Zagharta
El-Hermel ●

▲ Qornet es Sauda

● Batroun

LEBANON

Baalbek ●

Beirut

Zahlé

SYRIA

○ **Sidon**

Djezzine ●
Marjayoun ●

Tyre ●

L.Tiberias

ISRAEL

JORDAN

▨ Occupied by Israel since
the 'Six Days War' (June 1967)

0 Miles   20   40

0 Kilometres   40

Persia from 502 to 628 during which Lebanon suffered a devastating incursion of the Persian army in 613–4. This terrible war left both Byzantium and Persia exhausted and an easy prey for the Arab armies united in Islam. For the next two centuries Lebanon enjoyed peace and oblivion as part of the Arab empires, firstly under the Umayyads of Damascus until 750 and then under the 'Abbasids of Baghdad. With the weakening of 'Abbasid power at the end of the ninth century, Syria (and with it Lebanon) became an appendage of the independent Egyptian rulers, first the Tulunids (868–905), then the Ikshidites (935–69) and lastly the Shi'i Fatimids (969–1171). Byzantium, never reconciled to the loss of Syria and anxious to protect the Christian communities living there under Muslim rule, attempted to recover the holy lands in the latter part of the tenth century, but the rise of the Seljuk Turks in the eleventh century tipped the balance in favour of Islam and at the battle of Manzikert in 1071, in which the Seljuks were triumphant, Byzantine hopes were finally dashed.

With the collapse of Byzantine power it fell to Western Christianity to conceive the hope of wresting the Holy Land, of which Lebanon was a mere appendage, from Islam and that in spite of the fact that the local Christian communities led a comparatively free and untroubled existence under Muslim rule, untouched by the dynastic and religious quarrels which were ravaging Islam. Hence we have the Crusades, which were facilitated in their early stages by the quarrels between the Seljuks and the Fatimids. Jerusalem fell to the first Crusaders in 1099, Tripoli in 1109 and Beirut and Sidon in 1110. Apart from a period of six years after 1187, when Beirut fell to Saladin, Sultan of Egypt and Syria, most of the Lebanese coastlands were part of the Crusader domains until 1291 when they finally came under the rule of the Mameluk Sultans. From the time of the Crusades the personality of Lebanon began to take shape, for the Maronites who had settled in Mount Lebanon in the sixth and seventh centuries acted as allies and willing subjects of the crusading Franks. Since then the Maronites have looked to the west, especially France, for protection and moral support in a sea of Islam and other Christian sects. Throughout the 14th and 15th centuries the Mameluk Sultans of Egypt remained masters of Syria and Lebanon and the mountain lands of the latter were left to their own devices under local chiefs or Emirs, Tanukh Emirs in the north and Druze Emirs in the south. All of these of course owed allegiance and paid tribute to the Mameluk Sultan, but were practically autonomous in their own districts. The most powerful were the Tanukh Emirs of Mount Lebanon, descendants of a Christian Arab tribe of Iraq which had emigrated to the Aleppo region after the Islamic conquests and had not been converted to Islam until the reign of the 'Abbasid al-Mahdi (775–85). It is almost certain that they were secretly converted to the Druze heresy before they settled in Lebanon. Thus the principal feudal lords of Mount Lebanon during the Mameluk period were Druzes.

When the Mameluks were confronted with the increasing power of the Ottoman Turks, the Tanukh Emirs sided with the Mameluks, whereas Emir Fakhr al-Din Al-Ma'ni, the principal Druze Emir of the south, took the part of the Ottomans. When the Ottoman Sultan Selim I was victorious at the battle of Marj Dabiq in 1516, the fortunes of the Tanukh Emirs fell with those of the Mameluks and the supremacy of Ma'ni Emirs was ensured under Ottoman overlordship. These Ma'ni Emirs and their offshoot the Shihabs were to play an increasingly important role in Lebanese history during the Ottoman period which lasted from 1516 to 1918.

The capitulation treaty between the French King François I and Sultan Suleiman the Magnificent (1520–66) authorised the French to open up trading posts in some Syrian towns, among them Tripoli and Sidon, and thus the long-standing link between France and Lebanon was maintained. The local Emirs were allowed a great deal of autonomy in their mountain fiefs by the Ottoman Sultans and at times, when the Ottomans were weak or at war with their neighbours, they even rebelled and tried to set themselves up as independent rulers. The most successful of these was Emir Fakhr al-Din II (1572–1635), who spread his authority over much of Mount Lebanon and waged war against the Ottoman governors. He did much for agriculture, visited Europe and encouraged trade between Lebanon and Western Europe. To gain European support for his attempt to achieve independence from the Ottoman Sultanate, Fakhr al-Din spread the legend that the Druzes were descendants of the Crusaders and that their name was derived from that of the Comte de Dreux! Faced with this attempt at secession, the Ottomans made a supreme effort against Fakhr al-Din's valiant little army of mountaineers. The Emir had finally to submit, was exiled to Stamboul and finally executed in April 1635. In order to calm Mount Lebanon, where hopes had risen so high, the Ottomans appointed a Ma'ni-Emir, Melhem, nephew of Fakhr al-Din, who had continued the resistance after his uncle's submission, but from then on for the next hundred and fifty years Turkish control of Lebanon remained very tight under governors specially chosen for their strictness and heavy hands.

When the Ma'ni Emir Ahmed died in 1697 the role of vassals of the Ottomans in Mount Lebanon passed to the Shihab family of Rashaya and finally to Haydar Shihab of Hasbaya. The Shihab family, one of the most ancient and noble families of the Middle East, trace their ancestry back to the Quraysh, the tribe of the Prophet Muhammad. They were renowned for their warlike qualities and were allied by marriage to the Ma'ni Emirs. Sometime in the latter half of the 18th century, the Shihab Emir Yusuf was converted secretly to Christianity, becoming the first Christian Emir of the country. Towards the Ottomans he remained a Muslim and his Druze subjects considered him one of themselves. From this time the Shihab family has been split into two parts, one Christian and Maronite and the other Sunni Muslim. Both branches have served Lebanon in high positions. The first Shihabi Emir to announce publicly that he was a Christian was Bashir the Second who, as we shall see, came out in open revolt against his Ottoman suzerain.

In 1789 insurrections broke out against Yusuf owing to the heavy taxes he imposed on the country and he was forced by the redoubtable Ahmed Jezzar Pasha, governor of Sidon, to retire in favour of Bashir, son of one of his cousins, who was then aged 21 years. Bashir ruled in Lebanon for just over 50 years, a period so full of events and so momentous for Lebanon that the Lebanese have called him Bashir the Great. The beginnings of Bashir's reign were not easy, for the means by which he had won the favour of Jezzar Pasha were by no means laudable and he had made many enemies. Supported by the Jumblat party he was able to put down several revolts and impose his rule on the country. Bashir proved a useless tool of Jezzar and soon fell out with him; but before Jezzar could turn his attention to the removal of the Lebanese Emir by his usual ferocious means, he was distracted by the arrival of Bonaparte in Palestine. Summoned to support the Ottoman cause, Bashir neither refused nor helped much and when the French danger receded he had to face the wrath of Jezzar, who was not appeased by the fact that Bashir enjoyed the favour of the Ottoman Sultan. Jezzar did not hesitate to engage his forces even against regular Ottoman troops and Bashir was forced to withdraw. He was taken on a British warship to Al-Arish in Sinai where the Ottoman troops were concentrated but his exile did not last long, for the death of Jezzar in 1804 freed Bashir from such a ferocious enemy and paved the way for his trimphant return to Lebanon as sole master under the Ottoman Sultan.

Bashir's main concern in his heyday was to maintain a strong army in order to curb the turbulent spirit of the mountain factions. In this he was supported by the powerful Druze chieftain, Bashir Jumblat, and together they rendered valuable assistance to the Sultan by repelling attacks of the Wahhabis on Syria and forcing the local Ottoman governors to carry out the dictates of Stamboul. Those who suffered mostly under his rule were the Shi'i factions of the Biqaa. However, the Porte could not tolerate a vassal who was becoming too powerful and turned Jumblat against his master, Bashir. Lebanon fell into such a turmoil that Bashir was forced to go into exile once more, this time to Egypt where he was well received by Muhammad Aly Pasha. In return for Bashir's promise to assist Muhammad Aly in the war in Greece, the latter obtained Bashir's pardon from the Sultan. Back in Lebanon once more he gathered his troops to punish Jumblat, and although the majority of the Druzes rallied to Jumblat, the latter's army was routed at Mukhtara, the heart of his own fief. Jumblat was strangled and many Druze notables put to death, a massacre which was not forgotten, the Druzes taking their revenge on the Maronites in 1860. After this victory, Bashir was at the height of his power and feared far and wide in Lebanon and further afield, but it transpired that he had tied his fate more than he realised to the fortunes of Muhammad Aly, Pasha of Egypt.

Lebanon, as part of Syria, could not remain isolated when in 1831 Ibrahim Pasha, son of Muhammad Aly, marched into Syria to further his father's dream of a strong militarist Egyptian empire. Bashir embraced his benefactor's cause from the beginning, not, it is certain, from any sense of gratitude for the Pasha's previous help, but as a means of throwing off the last vestiges of Ottoman control. In this he made a profound miscalculation for the Egyptians, or rather the Albanian officers, dealt with Lebanon as everywhere else with a heavy hand. Egyptian pro-consuls were installed in the coastal cities and Albanian troops camped at Dair al-Qamar and Bait al-Din, Bashir's magnificent mountain residence. Finally the Lebanese, especially the warlike Druzes, were conscripted into the Egyptian army and sent to fight in Arabia, Anatolia and the Sudan. Bloody revolts broke out all over the country and were put down with the utmost severity. The Christians were totally disarmed. As the Egyptian successes against the Sultan went on, despair spread through Lebanon. However, these successes were viewed with mounting apprehension by the European powers, Russia, Austria, Prussia and, above all, Britain, the corner-stone of whose oriental policy was the maintenance of the tottering Ottoman Empire. In concert these powers forced France to withdraw her support for Muhammad Aly; threatened with European military intervention, he was forced to evacuate Syria in 1841 and renounce his dreams. While the 'oriental crisis' was boiling, a general insurrection broke out in Lebanon and members of the several communities, even the Maronites who were dreading the day when they might be conscripted by the Egyptians, assembled at Antelias where they pledged themselves to work together to obtain fair play from Emir Bashir and some say in the government of the country. The 'National Pact' signed on 10

November 1943 is considered the charter regulating relations between the various Lebanese communities; but its forerunner and perhaps its model was the agreement of Maronites, Greek Orthodox, Muslims and Druzes at Antelias on 8 June 1840 to band together and link their destinies for what they saw as the common good. The 'Day of Antelias' paved the way for British intervention and on 11 November 1840 a British fleet bombarded Beirut. Bashir abdicated, realising that by supporting the lost Egyptian cause he had lost the confidence of his subjects, but not without first attempting to gain British support for his remaining in Lebanon. He went into his last exile from his native land on board a British warship which took him to Malta. A year later he was allowed to settle in Stamboul, where he died a rich and honoured guest in 1850, at the age of 87 years. In 1948 his mortal remains were brought back to Lebanon and buried with all ceremony in the Palace of Bait al-Din which he had built for himself early in the 19th century. Thus ended a period in which, not for the first time, Lebanon had bid fair to achieve its independence from the Ottomans and Egyptians.

Bashir II's successor, Bashir III, was a weakling who could not control the prevailing anarchy and rancour of the Druzes against the Maronites; when fighting broke out in the autumn of 1841 between the two factions he remained inactive. The Ottoman authorities intervened and Bashir III, the last Shihabi Emir, surrendered his power to the Sultan and went to live in Stamboul. In 1860 occurred the terrible massacre of the Maronites by the Druzes, who had never forgotten their harsh treatment by the Christian Bashir II. They were probably encouraged by the Turks, who had reason to doubt the loyalty of the Maronites who, with the abandonment of the Egyptian cause by France, tended once more to look to her as their traditional protector. In a few days 6,000 Christians were killed in Lebanon and 5,000 in Damascus and some estimate that in all 22,000 Christians were victims of Druze vengefulness. A French army was rushed to Lebanon and occupied the scene of carnage for a year, working with the Ottoman Army to restore order. A commission representing France, Britain, Prussia, Austria, Italy and Russia was set up in Beirut to work out a statute for Lebanon with the Ottoman government. As a result of their deliberations Lebanon (but only Mount Lebanon) was made an autonomous *mutasarrifate*, under a Catholic governor appointed for five years by the Porte and accepted by the powers. In his functions he was assisted by an elected council of the various communities and a local militia; Beirut, the coastal strip and the Biqaa remained under direct Ottoman rule. Under a series of able and benevolent governors, Mount Lebanon entered into a golden age when peace and security reigned. Agriculture was developed and flourished, roads built and many villages expanded into delightful summer resorts, to which Syrians and Egyptians flocked. French and American schools increased in number and the inevitable pressure of population on the small area led to large scale emigration to Egypt and to the United States and later to South America and Africa. Emigrant Lebanese remained devoted to their homeland and every year remitted large sums to their relatives, thus adding to the general prosperity and well-being. This happy state of affairs lasted from 1864 up to 1915 when, as a result of the Ottoman Empire's becoming a belligerent in World War I, direct Ottoman rule was once more imposed on Lebanon.

During World War I Lebanon suffered greatly. Early in 1915 the autonomy of Mount Lebanon came to an abrupt end with occupation by Ottoman troops. Remittances from abroad, on which the economy depended so much, ceased, as did the tourist traffic. Crops were earmarked for the army and a reign of terror began. Anyone suspected of sympathising with the western allies, i.e. the majority of the Christians on the Mountain, or with the incipient Arab nationalist movement, as did many Sunnis, was arrested and many ended their days on a Turkish gallows in the main square of Beirut. The allied blockade, a plague of locusts and an epidemic of typhus completed the Lebanese misery. However the allied entry into Syria and Lebanon was assured by Allenby's victory at Sarona in Palestine on 19 September 1918 and on 1 October Allenby entered Damascus. That same day the Turks evacuated the Lebanese coast and their 400-years-long preponderance in Lebanese affairs came to an end. At the conference of San Remo in 1920 France was given a Mandate for Syria and Lebanon. On 1 September 1920 General Gouraud proclaimed 'Greater Lebanon', roughly within the boundaries of Fakhr al-Din II's emirate, and its detachment from Syria. The Lebanese Republic was proclaimed on 23 May 1926 as an independent state, although the French still held all the reins of power. On 26 May 1926 the Constitution was promulgated which has remained substantially in force up to the present day, although modified by an amendment of 17 October 1937 which abolished the Senate. The first President of the Republic was a Greek Orthodox, Charles Debbas, but since his period of office the President has always been a Maronite, with a Sunni Prime Minister, although this arrangement is not laid down in the constitution. Given the Lebanese independent spirit and love of freedom the French, while being considered sincere friends and well-wishers of Lebanon by the majority, did not find it an easy task to rule Lebanon. Much dissatisfaction was caused by the French parliament's refusal to ratify the treaty of 1936 between Lebanon and France, which provided for the complete transfer of power to the Lebanese Government. France remained firmly entrenched until the arrival of British and Free French troops in July 1941.

At the end of 1943 General Catroux, General de Gaulle's representative in the Levant, proclaimed the complete independence of Syria and Lebanon, but the war having still to be brought to a successful conclusion the French authorities were hesitant in handing over power. The French thought to stifle the ferment and demand for independence by arresting the Lebanese President Bishara al-Khoury, with his Prime Minister Riad al-Solh and several ministers on 8 November 1943. The result was a closing of ranks among all sections of the Lebanese people, the formation of a 'resistance government' and the proclamation of the 'National Pact' on 10 November. General Catroux was sent back from Algiers and had the arrested politicians released. In 1945 most of the powers were transferred at British insistence to the Lebanese government and on 31 December 1946 the last French soldier left Lebanon and the country became completely independent, a member of the Arab League and of the United Nations Organisation.

Since achieving full independence the course of Lebanese affairs has not run altogether smoothly. Although a democratic republic with universal suffrage, Lebanon has not succeeded in establishing true democracy, for the allegiance of the Lebanese voter is not to a party or to a political theory, but rather to a particular politician. These politicians, descendants of the feudal lords who kept the country in turmoil for many centuries, have their own feuds and confederacies and it might appear to an outside observer that they put their personal interests before the welfare of the country. They, of course, would be the last to admit this and it must be said that on the whole the country has prospered and been a haven of tolerance and liberty under their erratic guidance. The last years of the presidency of Bishara al-Khoury (1943–52) were marked by a mounting wave of popular indignation at the corruption and nepotism which he seemed unable to control. There was also resentment in some quarters at the President's alleged francophobia and rapprochement to the neighbouring Arab States in collaboration with his able Prime Minister Riad al-Solh. Al-Solh was assassinated in July 1951 in Amman by members of the proscribed fascist pan-Syrian party, the PPS, whose leader and founder, Antoun Sa'adeh had been convicted of actively plotting to overthrow the Lebanese Republic and executed in July 1949.

On 17 August 1952 an enormous political meeting was held at Dair al-Qamar which paved the way for the resignation of the President on 19 September. Ten days later Camille Chamoun was elected President of the Republic. His presidency was marked by the rising tide of Arab Nationalism which could not fail to appeal to the Sunni Muslims, the second largest community. Chamoun's acceptance of the 'Eisenhower Doctrine' of March 1957 met with increasing hostility and finally led to the 1958 insurrection of the Muslims of Tripoli and Beirut, who were encouraged by the formation of the United Arab Republic and infuriated by the proposals of Shamoun's faction to renew his presidency for a further period of six years. The landing of American troops at Beirut on 15 July 1958 (they did not have to fire a shot) and above all the neutrality of the Lebanese Army under General Fuad Shihab cooled tempers and in spite of a short and bloody counter-revolution in September the unity of the country was preserved. Shaken by these events which had rocked Lebanon to its foundations, the communities accepted and rallied round Fuad Shihab who was elected President on 31 July and took up his office on 23 September. He was succeeded in the summer of 1964 by Charles Helou, the present President.

In June 1967 Lebanon, as part of the Arab World, was profoundly shocked and affected by the defeat of the Arab armies at the hands of Israel, whose foundation in the heart of the Arab World has been the cause of the instability endemic in the Middle East for the past 20 years and more. But now a new factor of instability has appeared on the scene. This is the Palestine guerilla movement, which has given a new personality to the Palestinian Arabs who have waited inactive and in vain for the neighbouring Arab states to restore them to their homelands and who now seem to have taken their destiny into their own hands. Drawing their strength from the destitute exiles in the refugee camps (Lebanon has more than 150,000 Palestinian refugees) and having the sympathy of the masses, they have become a power with which the governments of Lebanon and Jordan, and to a lesser extent Syria, have to reckon. The Government's effort to restrict their use of Lebanese territory in April 1969 led to clashes between the Lebanese Army and the guerillas; the government, torn between Christian condemnation of its leniency and Muslim disapproval of the Army's action, resigned and for most of the rest of that year a caretaker government ran the country. An accommodation was worked out, restricting to some extent the activities of the guerilas in South Lebanon, but it was an uneasy one and the Lebanese live in fear of Israeli reprisals. But the greatest problem facing present day Lebanon is the demographic one and the question of maintaining a working partnership of the seven principal communities. At the time of the 'National Pact' of 1943 the total population was in the neighbourhood of 1,000,000 whereas it is estimated at over 2,600,000 today. No census has been held for over 30 years for fear of revealing the unreality of the present communal distribution; it is probable that both the Sunni and Shi'i Muslim communities are now (owing to higher birth rates and lesser emigration) greater than the Maronite Christian one. Not until a realistic balance between the communities can be worked out will the country achieve a true and viable democracy. Even then, stability will be out of reach, for the Lebanon as for its Arab neighbours, until the fundamental problem of Arab-Israeli relations is solved.

SOCIAL AND ECONOMIC

In spite of, perhaps because of, the many political and confessional problems endemic since its foundation, Lebanon is by far the most advanced and outward-looking of all the Arab states. The Lebanese are by nature industrious, ambitious and enterprising and this is most evident in the fervent desire of all classes and sections of the population for education. The rate of literacy is much higher than in other Arabic speaking countries and compares favourably with that of most of the countries around the Mediterranean. There is an abundance of primary and secondary schools (whether government-run, privately-owned and directed, or financed and run by foreign countries) and Beirut is the home of four universities : the American University of Beirut (the AUB), the Jesuit St. Joseph University, both 19th-century foundations; the Lebanese National University, established after the Second World War; and the recently established Arab University, a branch of Alexandria University. All of these attract not only the best Lebanese minds but also many professors and students from other Arab countries and even further afield. The result is that Beirut (and, to a lesser extent, Tripoli) is a centre of intense cultural activity. There are hundreds of bookshops which display an ever-increasing flood of literature of all topics. It has even been said, with some exaggeration, that the centre of Arab culture has moved from Cairo to Beirut. A sign of the awareness of Lebanese intellectuals is that hardly a month passes after a book has made its mark in the United States, Britain, France or elsewhere before its Arabic translation appears in the Beirut bookshops, perhaps after being discussed at length in one or more of the many literary periodicals.

In Lebanon the Press is free and uncensored and reflects the kaleidoscope of Lebanese society and the stresses and strains of the outside world. In this country, half the size of Wales, there are some 40 daily newspapers, three in French, two in English, four in Armenian and the rest in Arabic. Many newspapers are mere mouthpieces for local factions or external Arab movements but a few, including the influencial L'Orient, Al-Nahar and Al-Hayat, are truly independent, reflecting the most rational and constructive Lebanese and Arab thinking. In addition there are over 30 literary, satirical, political or scientific periodicals. In marked contrast to the versatility and liveliness of the Press are the Lebanese radio and television, which are government-run and reflect in their mediocrity and lack of intellectual challenge the careful course the government has to plot through the quicksands of local and Arab politics.

Another factor which gives Lebanon an importance out of all proportion to its size is that Beirut has become, since World War II and especially since the Suez Affair of 1956, the banking and commercial centre for the whole eastern Arab world. As an area of comparative stability and freedom from government interference, it has attracted the activities of international agencies such as the regional office of Unesco and the Middle

Eastern headquarters of many international companies. In addition to the large sums remitted by expatriate Lebanese, Lebanon has also attracted vast amounts of capital from other Arab countries, whether sums salted away by politicians of less stable countries or the surplus capital of oil-rich shaikhs or successful merchants. Most of this capital has been invested in real estate, resulting in the breathtaking expansion of Ras Beirut in the past 20 years, with innumerable blocks of luxury flats and hotels to suit the most exacting tastes.

A valuable asset—at present endangered by political uncertainties—is the country's potential for the tourist trade. With one of the best climates in the world and an abundance of attractions, whether natural scenery, excellent beaches, Crusader castles or the magnificent ruins at Byblos or Baalbeck, Lebanon has everything to offer those in search of pleasure and relaxation. The Lebanese flair for the hotel business and tourist trade has put everything within easy reach, from skiing at the Cedars to swimming and water-skiing on the Mediterranean, from Lebanese folksinging and dancing and European orchestral and theatrical performances at the annual Baalbek Festival to extravagant floorshows at the Casino du Liban, equalling in sophistication and cosmopolitanism anything that can be enjoyed in Paris or Las Vegas.

FURTHER READING

Evans, L. M. *Portrait of a People, Lebanon*, Dar el-Machreq, Beirut.
Hachette World Guides, *Lebanon*, Hachette, Paris, 1965.
Hitti, P. K. *Syria: A Short History*, Macmillan, London, 1951; Crowell, Collier & Macmillan, New York, 1961.
Hourani, A. H. *Syria and Lebanon*, Oxford Univ. Press, London, 1946.
Penrose, S. B. L. *That They Have Life: the Story of the American University of Beirut 1866–1941*, Princeton Univ. Press, New Jersey, 1941.
Thubron, Colin. *The Hills of Adonis*, Heinemann, London, 1968; Little, Brown, Boston, 1969.

DAVID COWAN. Senior lecturer in Arabic at the School of Oriental and African Studies, London University. One-time principal instructor in the Middle East Centre for Arabic Studies in Lebanon. Author of *An Introduction to Modern Literary Arabic* (1958).

PERSIAN GULF STATES

DAVID HOLDEN

THE area around the Gulf is pre-eminently one of division and flux. Historically, this has often been true owing to the natural instability of the area's many small and scattered communities and the antagonism between its Persian and Arab cultures. Today the instability may be accentuated because two new factors of uncertainty have been added : (i) the forces of rapid social and political change promoted by the sudden acquisition of enormous oil wealth in many Gulf territories, and (ii) the decision of the British Government, announced in January 1968, to withdraw from all Britain's military commitments east of Suez, including the Persian Gulf, by 1971. With all these factors operating simultaneously, the territories of the Gulf are involved in a process of political, diplomatic, economic and social transformation whose outcome is unpredictable and whose speed and thoroughness may be unsurpassed anywhere in the world.

GEOGRAPHY

A shallow and almost land-locked arm of the Indian Ocean, measuring some 600 miles from the Straits of Hormuz to the mouth of the Tigris and Euphrates rivers at the Shatt al-Arab, the Arab Persian Gulf is an area of extreme summer heat whose coasts are largely barren and thinly populated. The north-eastern or Persian shore has generally been the richer of the two sides of the Gulf. It is now occupied by the single state of Iran, the greatest of the contemporary local powers. The south-western or Arab shore, on the other hand, has always seemed especially inhospitable, being merely the termination of the Arabian desert. Except for part of the coast of Muscat and the mountainous interior of Oman, south of the Gulf proper, where there is some natural fertility, most of the Arab communities were until this century tiny, scattered, impoverished and isolated.

Their natural fragmentation is expressed today in the division of the Arab shore of the Gulf among no fewer than 13 separate states, including some of the richest and some of the poorest and smallest in the world. Running from north to south they are as follows : Iraq, Kuwait, Saudi Arabia, Bahrain, Qatar, the seven shaikhdoms of the Trucial Coast of Oman—Abu Dhabi, Dubai, Sharjah, Ajman, Umm al-Qawain, Ras al-Khaimah and Fujairah—and finally the Sultanate of Oman which, although it lies beyond the mouth of the Gulf, has many connexions with the area. As Iraq, Kuwait and Saudi Arabia, as well as Iran, will be dealt with separately elsewhere, we are chiefly concerned here with the remaining ten Arab

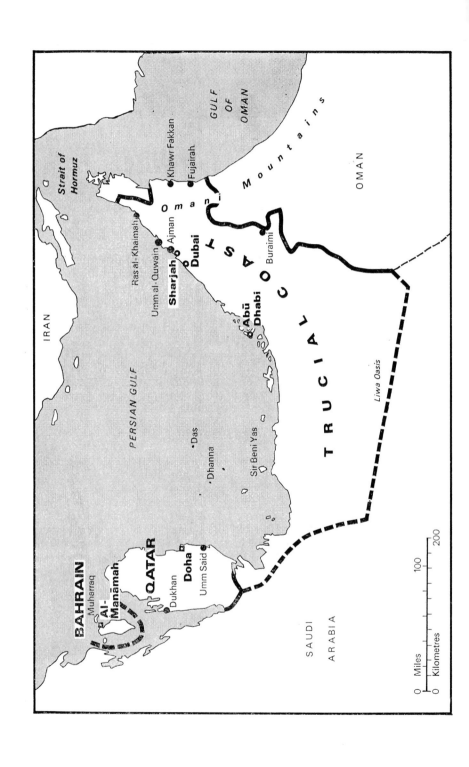

states of what is often called the 'lower Gulf', namely, the Sultanate of Oman, the seven Trucial shaikhdoms, Qatar and Bahrain.

The total population of these ten states is only about 900,000 people, of which the Sultanate of Oman alone has 6–700,000, scattered over an area about the size of Great Britain, while the islands of the Bahrain archipelago have perhaps another 200,000. The rest is divided between Qatar (about 60,000) and Abu Dhabi (about 40,000), Dubai (about 70,000) and the other Trucial shaikhdoms, some of which have as few as 5,000 inhabitants each.

Except for oil, the natural resources of these territories are insignificant. Although Bahrain's central position has enabled it to retain some commercial importance, the only territory which is able to rely today on trade rather than oil for its prosperity is the shaikhdom of Dubai. Here in the last decade or so the smuggling of gold into India has created many local fortunes.

Most of the oilfields are of recent discovery. Only Bahrain's was exploited before World War II, but its production has always been one of the smallest in the Gulf. Some of the other fields, however, are of major importance, while in some of the smaller Trucial shaikhdoms no oil has been discovered so far. There are enormous disparities in the wealth of the territories therefore, as the following table shows.

Oil

Territory	Date of first shipment	Annual output, 1969 (tons)	Approx. annual value to territory, 1969	Approx. annual value per head of population
Bahrain	1932	3·4m.	£7m.	£35
Qatar	1949	17·0m.	£40m.	£750
Abu Dhabi	1962	27·0m.	£70m.	£2,000 +
Sultanate of Oman	1967	15·0m.	£38m.	£55
Dubai	1969	5·0m.	£12m.	£170

History

At no time has a natural focus existed to draw together the disparate elements of the Gulf coasts. Unity of the region has been achieved only sporadically and through conquest: once by the Arabs after the birth of Islam, when they swept with their new religion into Persia and thus, for a time, controlled both shores; more than once by the Persians, who have from time to time occupied parts of the Arab shore; and for much of the last 150 years by Britain, through the diffuse overlordship of her Indian imperial system.

The current political situation in the Gulf, especially in the ten states with which we are concerned, is still overshadowed by the relics of that system, by which Britain made herself the traditional 'peace-keeper' among the local communities. After an association with the Sultan of Muscat (now Oman) in the Napoleonic wars with France, Britain's first political interest in the Gulf was provoked by the piracy of the tribes of the 'pirate coast' of Oman between the peninsula of Qatar and the Straits of Hormuz. A series of punitive expeditions against them resulted in 1853 in a 'perpetual maritime truce' by which the tribal rulers undertook to keep the peace at sea in return for British protection from their enemies and each other. This was the origin of the so-called 'trucial system' in the lower Gulf, from which the present Trucial states, or shaikhdoms, of Oman take their title. It was extended also to Bahrain and Qatar, while southern Persia was brought by other means within Britain's sphere of influence on the other side of the Gulf.

Kuwait was afforded formal British protection at the end of the 19th century, and with the embryonic kingdom of Saudi Arabia becoming a part of the system during World War I, and the League of Nations Mandate in Iraq being awarded to Britain at the peace settlement, British hegemony was established by 1920 throughout the Gulf.

Until then Britain's interest had been essentially maritime, but with the search for oil after World War I her concern became territorial. In the customary desert way, no land frontiers had ever been defined by the Arabs; Britain—as the protecting and peace-keeping power—was soon involved in charting and afterwards defending new lines on the map.

Gradually, as the larger states of the Gulf attained more power and self-confidence, they broke away from direct British patronage, but it was not until after World War II that the current transformation of the region began, with the coincidence of new oil discoveries and the start of Britain's general retreat from empire. Since 1961, when Kuwait became fully independent of Britain, only the ten states of the lower Gulf have continued the tradition of virtually exclusive relations with Britain. Efforts were begun there in 1968, however, to create new political structures and relationships in preparation for Britain's proposed withdrawal in 1971.

Present Political Structure

All ten states of the lower Gulf are in essence traditional Arab societies with traditional Arab political institutions. Each has an individual ruler known as the shaikh, except in the case of the Sultan of Oman, and the shaikh is generally chosen from among their number by members of the hereditary ruling family. (The rule of primogeniture does not operate in traditional Arab Society.) The rulers all hold a regular but informal public *majlis*, or council, at which tribal elders, ministers, foreign advisers, businessmen and many ordinary members of the public may discuss problems with the rulers, often of a minute and personal nature. The ruler's word is usually final. No representative political institutions in the Western sense exist; and especially in the smaller territories of the Trucial Coast no administration except that of the ruler's family has been thought necessary until lately.

The structure is therefore basically tribal, personal and patriarchal; and while it gains in intimacy from these qualities, it suffers perhaps excessively in the modern environment from administrative failures and personal jealousies. It is noteworthy that nearly all the current rulers, or their immediate predecessors, have been involved either in struggles with each other over ancient tribal disputes, or with local rivals for the succession to leadership. Tribal wars and assassinations were endemic on the Trucial Coast until 1948; and in the remoter areas of the Coast and in the interior of Oman they still occur.

The recent acquisition of oil wealth in these territories, however, has fostered the creation of rudimentary modern administrations with the aid of foreign advisers, both European and Arab. The Trucial states today, for example, contain a remarkable multi-national corps of officials and advisers including many British ex-colonial servants from the Sudan, South Arabia, India and elsewhere, Sudanese and Lebanese financial experts, Jordanian and Palestinian lawyers, and many Egyptian school-teachers of both sexes.

Much of this new administration of the Trucial Coast has been created in recent years under the aegis of the Trucial States Development Council, a co-operative body of the local rulers set up with British help and financed partly by aid from Britain and Kuwait, but increasingly since 1966 by sub-ventions from Abu Dhabi, the richest of the Trucial states themselves. Experience of this council provided the basis for the embryonic Federation of Gulf Emirates formed in 1968 at the instigation of the rulers as the first step towards replacing British security guarantees with a form of local collective security. Bahrain and Qatar joined the seven Trucial states in the Federation to provide a full federal council of nine rulers. The Sultanate of Oman, however, did not join.

In the first year of the Federation's existence agreement was reached in principle on plans of a common emblem and flag, common postal services, an official gazette and a unified defence force into which existing units of the member states would be integrated. Many formidable questions remained, however, before the Federation could be regarded as a convincing political unit; and attempts to form Arab federations elsewhere (e.g. in South Arabia, and various abortive unions between Egypt, Syria and Iraq) did not offer happy examples to the Gulf rulers. Meanwhile, the British connection remains important to all ten states. Bahrain, Qatar and the Trucial shaikhdoms rank as 'British-protected' states by virtue of the 19th century treaties. The Sultanate of Oman is legally independent of Britain, but enjoys some *de facto* British protection, partly under an exchange of letters in 1958 by which Britain undertook to train and equip the Sultan's forces in return for the use of Masirah Island as an air staging post. Internally all the states are self-governing, and although in practice British advice is often given on many matters, from finance to water supplies, it is less often taken. The chief British official is the Political Resident in Bahrain whose staff includes Political Agents in Bahrain, Qatar, Abu Dhabi and Dubai, and who also has a general oversight of British interests in Oman, where the chief British representative has the rank of Consul-General.

DEFENCE

Until 1952 the defence of all these territories depended entirely on the presence of British forces in the Gulf or their ability to get there quickly if the need arose. In that year the first modern local defence force was formed, known as the Trucial Oman Scouts. Its present strength consists of about 2,000 locally recruited Arabs, with a majority of seconded British officers and some junior Arab officers. Its duties include internal police work as well as external defence throughout the Trucial Coast. In recent years some of the responsibilities of the Scouts have overlapped with the Abu Dhabi Defence Force, recruited independently by the Ruler of Abu Dhabi. The ADDF has a mixture of Arab and British officers, and will eventually number 4,000 men. In the Sultanate of Oman little but tribal forces were available locally until 1955 when Britain agreed to assist in the reorganisation of what are now known as the Sultan of Oman's armed forces. These include a small air force and four battalions of locally recruited soldiers with a corps of seconded and retired British army officers.

Any serious threat to the frontiers of these territories, however, could be countered under existing arrangements by the direct use of British forces. Until 1952 the defence of all these territories depended entirely on the forces in Aden provided a strategic reserve for possible use in the Gulf, but since then British forces in the Gulf have been strengthened to reach a total of about 6,000 men, divided between Bahrain and Sharjah. It is these forces which are due to go in 1971, although various arrangements have been mooted for a continuing British military interest in the Gulf, from the maintenance of an emergency staff in Bahrain and Sharjah to a wider development of local forces with British training and equipment. There is also on record a pledge by the Conservative Party leadership to keep British forces east of Suez in or soon after 1971; but how and whether this will be fulfilled in practice is a matter for speculation.

INTERNAL PREOCCUPATIONS

In spite of their patriarchal structure, the life of all the Gulf states today is dominated by the importance of the oil industry, which saps and transforms the traditional institutions. In the broadest terms the changes are characteristic of the impact of money on a non-monetary society. The individualism of tribal life is undermined by the demands and opportunities of a wage economy. Technicians and civil servants are required to handle community affairs that were formerly the prerogative of traditional rulers. Frontiers have to be fixed as oil concession areas are delimited, laws have to be codified for the benefit of foreign businessmen. Schools and hospitals are built where there were none before, banks and hotels are opened, roads and water pipelines built. Inevitably, new political discontents are aroused as the traditional intimacy of ruler and ruled is broken down in this process of social change; the discontented quickly learn to look beyond their local horizons for encouragement or for the satisfaction of their demands, especially as their home territories have suddenly become so important to the rest of the world. Various forms of revolutionary 'nationalism' begin to appear, as the foundations of the old society are eroded. They tend to find fuel for agitation in the alleged monopolies of foreign oil companies, the supposed oppression of traditional rulers, and the unfashionable imperialism of British hegemony. In the recent past these discontents have been inflamed by radio propaganda and other means of subversion directed from the United Arab Republic, Syria and Iraq, whose leaders sought partly to increase their own direct influence in the Gulf and partly to embarrass the British Government in pursuit of other quarrels, such as the Suez crisis (1956), the wars in Yemen and South Arabia (1962–7) and the British Governments' alleged support of Israel (1956 and 1967). Saudi Arabia has also financed internal subversion in support of territorial claims, especially in the Buraimi oasis (1949–55) and in Oman (1954–9). After the defeat of the Arabs by Israel in 1967, however, with the consequent Egyptian withdrawal from the Yemen, most of these activities were muted, although it is possible they could again become important if circumstances seemed propitious.

Generally, the signs of political change are visible in inverse proportion to the impact of the oil industry. Nowhere in the lower Gulf have the changes been as comprehensive so far as in Kuwait, because nowhere yet has oil wealth accumulated in such massive quantities over a comparable period. But several territories are already profoundly affected.

In Bahrain, oil money has financed a modest 'welfare state' ever since the 1930s, creating a considerable white collar class whose lack of participation in the island's government has led to occasional shows of disaffection in the form of riots against the British, the local ruler, or the American-owned oil company (BAPCO-Caltex) which holds the producing concession in the islands.

In the shaikhdom of Qatar, further south, there have also been sporadic rumbles of discontent at the alleged extravagance of the ruling family and the comparative lack of advancement secured for the people by the oil money. In some of the Trucial states, the effects of the oil industry are not yet profound, but in Abu Dhabi the sheer weight of oil money has wrought startling changes since 1962. In that year, when the first oil was shipped from the off-shore field at Das Island, the shaikhdom was still to all appearances the same impoverished and traditional place that it had been for many centuries. Its ruler, Shaikh Shakhbut, was noted for his conservatism and did his utmost to stem or control the tide of change that his territory's new wealth released; yet within four years he was defeated by it. In 1966 his family sought the co-operation of the British Government to depose him in favour of his younger brother, Zaid. The operation was bloodless, and Shakhbut was exiled on a generous pension. Since then Zaid has authorised plans for modern development. These, together with the expansion of the armed forces, proved so extravagant (they included free housing for Abu Dhabi citizens, de-salination plants, water pipelines, double-lane highways across the desert, etc.) that by 1970 the country's accounts were overdrawn. Tighter financial control was introduced in that year, however, and it was expected that a favourable balance would soon be restored. Problems of investment and money distribution may cause unrest in the future, however.

Probably the most successful adaptation to wealth so far has been achieved in Dubai, where a notably shrewd ruler, Shaikh Rashid, has presided over a purely commercial triumph in which oil revenues had played no direct part up to 1968. With the discovery of a commercial field offshore, however, which went into production in 1969, Dubai was expected greatly to accelerate its accumulation of wealth.

The new riches and demands of the oil industry have also breached the protective barriers of tradition and secrecy around the Sultanate of Oman. In July 1970, the last of the traditional Sultans, Said Bin Taimur, was overthrown in a palace *coup* by his son, Qabus, because of widespread disaffection at his refusal to spend his new oil revenues (first obtained in 1967) on the country's development. One of the chief catalysts of this disaffection was the so-called Popular Front for the Liberation of the Occupied Arab Gulf (PFLOAG), a self-styled Maoist organisation, active in the southern province of Dhofar, where it received help from the Marxist Government of the neighbouring People's Republic of South Yemen (formerly South Arabia) and advice from Communist Chinese. Sultan Qabus has announced that he will introduce a constitutional form of government and proceed with economic and social development as fast as possible.

The financial developments which follow from commercial oil discoveries create new problems as well as new possibilities in the relations between the rulers of the Gulf states. Sudden acquisitions of wealth by previously poor rulers tip the scales of local power back and forth, demanding unusual forbearance from men whose suspicions of each other are already highly developed. The reconciliation of entrenched jealousies with the new realities of power is probably the most urgent internal problem that the Federation of Gulf Emirates has to face.

EXTERNAL AFFAIRS

Until 1968 the external affairs of all ten states were handled exclusively by the British Government. Since then British and local interests have coincided in encouraging the rulers to take more initiative in these affairs for themselves. Their ability to do so is limited, however, by habit, by lack of experience and resources and by the overwhelming importance of their relations with their most powerful local neighbours, Saudi Arabia and Iran.

Apart from the change in their relations with Britain, the final shape of which cannot be foreseen, the chief specific concern of the Gulf states in external affairs is with the demarcation and security of their frontiers. Many of these are still in dispute. Several Trucial states have unsettled claims against each other and Saudi Arabia and Iran have not only areas of dispute with each other but with their smaller neighbours as well. The announcement of Britain's impending withdrawal produced a flurry of disagreements over some of these claims in 1968, especially between Saudi Arabia and Iran, but a meeting between the Shah of Iran and King Faisal in Riyadh, in November of that year, produced a more amicable atmosphere and some hope of eventual agreement on all sides. Four main areas of dispute may be distinguished in the lower Gulf :

The Median Line

This is the hypothetical line in the waters of the Gulf dividing Iran's territorial waters from those of the Arab states. This line also divides the sea bed and the distribution of actual or potential oil resources therein. At issue here are two small islands near the Straits of Hormuz, Tumbs and Abu Musa, regarded by Britain and the Arab states as the possessions of Ras al-Khaimah and Sharjah respectively, but claimed by Iran. Their possession affects the course of the median line (at present to the detriment of Iran) and Iran also considers that their strategic position at the mouth of the Gulf, and within a mile or two of her coastline, makes her sovereignty there imperative to her national security.

Buraimi Oasis

This scatter of eight small oasis villages is divided between the Sultanate of Oman (two villages) and Abu Dhabi (six), but has also been claimed by Saudi Arabia since 1949. In 1952 a small Saudi force occupied part of the oasis, but it was expelled by the Trucial Oman Scouts in 1955 after international arbitration had failed to produce a solution. In 1970 the Saudi claim was advanced again at a meeting in Riyadh between Shaikh Zaid of Abu Dhabi and King Faisal and Saudi Arabia.

Sultanate of Oman

Besides the revolutionary influence of PFLOAG (see above) the Sultanate is involved in the dispute over Buraimi, and over the fate of the Kuria Muria Islands off the south coast, to which the People's Republic of South Yemen has laid claim. The relations of the Sultanate with the putative Federation of Gulf Emirates is also a matter of potential dispute as there is evidence that the Sultanate regards most of the Trucial shaikhdoms of Oman which comprise the chief membership of the Federation as traditional tributaries. There may be, therefore, an attempt to create a 'Greater Oman' under the Sultan's leadership.

The Federation of Gulf Emirates

One vexed area of dispute was solved in 1970, when Iran withdrew an old claim to sovereignty in Bahrain after a UN mission had 'ascertained' that the people of Bahrain wished to be regarded as Arabs. It was hoped this would open the way to Bahrain joining the Gulf Federation along with the Trucial States and Qatar, but this remained far from certain as the Federation continued to find difficulty in settling its internal rivalries.

GREAT POWER INTEREST

Great power interests in the lower Gulf cannot be separated from those in the Gulf area in general. The United States and the Soviet Union are both involved in parts of the Gulf already through commercial and military relationships, and with the impending withdrawal of Britain from what is left of her post-imperial position it may be expected that the super-powers will become more closely concerned in future with the political fortunes of the Gulf as a whole. The Soviet Union is the main supplier of military equipment and training to Iraq and has recently negotiated substantial military and commercial contracts with Iran. It also has opened in Kuwait the first Russian diplomatic mission on the shores of the Gulf, and in 1968 units of the Russian fleet paid their first visit to the Gulf for over half a century. These are interpreted by some observers as signs of renewed Soviet interest in an area that was traditionally coveted by the Russian Empire in the 19th century as a 'back-door' to India and influence in South Asia and which is now the world's most important source of oil.

Direct American interest is greater through the dominant position of American oil companies and the military connections of the US with Iran and Saudi Arabia. So far, however, the Americans seem anxious to avoid further physical involvement in the Gulf to replace Britain's departing forces. Instead, they are exerting their diplomacy in support of efforts to maintain stability in the area through agreements between local powers.

CONCLUSIONS

By the end of 1969 the potential for political disruption and even violence in the states of the lower Gulf still seemed considerable, but some hopeful factors had emerged. These included the creation of the Federation of Gulf Emirates, some tacit agreement between Iran and Saudi Arabia, and the possibility that Britain's physical withdrawal would at least remove one source of political discontent, especially among the more politically articulate and restive Arabs. Most of all, however, it was hoped that the importance of continuing oil revenues, at or above their current rate, would outweigh for all parties any advantage which might conceivably be gained from territorial adventures or revolutionary unrest such as could place those revenues in jeopardy. Money had become, therefore, both the major source of change and the major hope of stability in the states of the lower Gulf.

FURTHER READING

Admiralty, Naval Intelligence Division. *Iraq and the Persian Gulf*, London, 1944.
Allfree, P. S. *Warlords of Oman*, R. Hale, London, 1967.
Belgrave, Sir Charles. *The Pirate Coast*, G. Bell, London, 1966.
Busch, B. C. *Britain and the Persian Gulf 1894–1914*, Univ. of California Press, Berkeley, 1967.
Dickson, H. R. P. *Kuwait and Her Neighbours*, Allen & Unwin, London, 1956.
Holden, David. *Farewell To Arabia*, Faber & Faber, London, 1966.
Kelly, J. B. *Britain and the Persian Gulf 1795–1880*, Oxford Univ. Press, London, 1968.

Kelly, J. B. *Eastern Arabian Frontiers,* Faber & Faber, London, 1964.
Landen, R. G. *Oman Since 1856—Disruptive Modernization in a traditional Arab Society,* Princeton Univ. Press, N.J., 1967.
Marlowe, John. *The Persian Gulf in the 20th Century,* Cresset Press, London, 1962.
Monroe, Elizabeth. *Britain's Moment in the Middle East,* Chatto & Windus, London, 1963.
Phillips, Wendell. *Oman: A History,* Longmans, London, 1967.
Wilson, Sir Arnold T. *The Persian Gulf,* Allen & Unwin, London, 1954.

DAVID HOLDEN. Chief Foreign Correspondent of *The Sunday Times* since 1965. Roving correspondent of *The Times* and *The Guardian* 1960–5. Joined *The Times* 1954 and served as Middle East correspondent 1956–60. A frequent broadcaster on radio and television. Author of *Farewell to Arabia* (1966).

THE REPUBLIC OF SOUTH YEMEN

R. B. SERJEANT

EARLY HISTORY

THE South Yemen Republic is an artificial creation exemplifying the dictum that ex-colonial territories jealously preserve colonial frontiers that were dictated mainly by political expediency. Like Yemen, the country is fragmented into independent tribal units. Only the strategic and economic value of Aden port give it any significance; fisheries and a little cotton apart, it has hardly any assets.

Aden from ancient times was an entrepôt of the East-West trade; at Bir Fadl I have unearthed what looks like Syrian glass and Mesopotamian glazed pottery of about the third century AD. In the Middle Ages, Aden thrived on the India trade which was elaborately organised, with agents in every Indian Ocean port, with the international Karimi merchant group, a system of maritime customary law, and the like; but in the 16th century, through exactions of Ottoman Turkish governors, Aden lost its commerce to Mocha. The French sea captain De la Roque speaks of its ruined buildings in the early 18th century, and by 1800, Aden, subject to the Abdali sultans of Lahej, had declined through mismanagement and became no more than a little village.

The East India Company was trading in the Red Sea in the 18th and early 19th centuries and maintained a factory at Mocha to purchase coffee. New political considerations entered as Napoleon landed in Egypt in 1798 and seemed to threaten India; troops from Bombay occupied Perim, but since Perim was waterless and unsuitable for a garrison, they were moved to Aden. There they were well received by the Sultan of Lahej, and in 1802 the British sent an ambassador from Calcutta to negotiate a commercial treaty with the Sultan.

The growth of steam navigation in the 19th century rendered it imperative to find a coaling station at the south end of the Red Sea. Negotiations were in progress for purchasing Socotra when Captain Haines, who had orders to gain control of Aden against an annual payment, captured it from the Abdalis in 1839. The Sultan soon made peace and signed a treaty, being granted an annual stipend of 6,000 Maria Theresa dollars. The Abdalis thereafter made several fruitless attempts at recapturing Aden, but from 1863 relations with the British remained harmonious until Sultan Aly's defection in 1958.

At the time of Aden's capture, the Arabs formed some 44% of the popu-

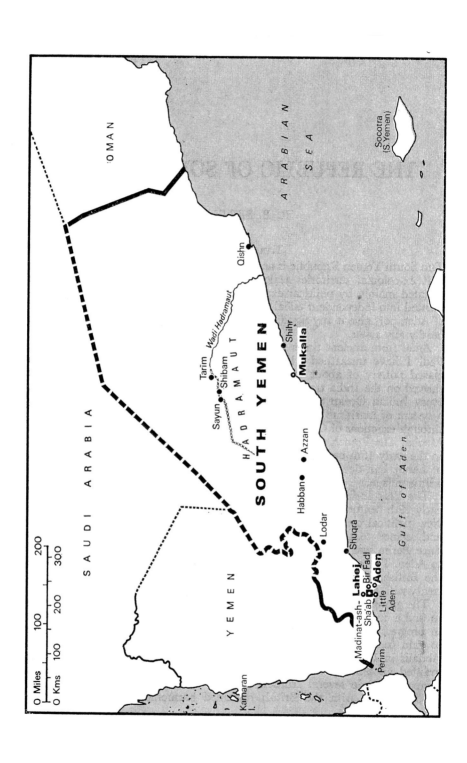

lation, outnumbering the Jewish males by under 20 men. Haines's first census in February 1839 shows the following statistics :

	Males	Females
Banians (i.e. Hindus)	35	
(Arab) servants to Banians	7	
(Jewish) servants to Banians	11	
(Somalees) servants to Banians	2	
Arabs	276	341
Jews	257	301
Somalees	26	37
Egyptians	4	
Grand total of Aden population	618	679

At the 1872 census, Arabs accounted for only 8,241 of a population of 19,289, of which Africans numbered 5,346, Indians and Jews 5,024. Aden was not, therefore, at that time a predominantly Arab city.

To secure Aden's position and keep caravan routes open for supplies, the British contracted in a series of engagements with the hinterland tribes. In the 1880s Shaikh Uthman and Khawr Maksar were purchased from the Abdali and Little Aden from the Aqrabi who had held these districts since the Middle Ages.

Egypt under the famous Pasha Muhammad Aly, in its first imperialist adventures in the Red Sea, had sent troops into Yemen, but the British dashed their hopes of winning Aden, and they had to withdraw in 1840 —like the force which President Nasser sent to occupy the Mutawakkilite Yemeni Kingdom in 1962. However the Ottoman Turks began to reappear on the scene, occupying Sanaa in 1872. Till then the British had required no frontier, though they had concluded further agreements with the Subbaihah, Fadlis, Lower Yafi'is and Hawshabis through their chiefs. Driving southwards, the Turks backed the Zaidi Imams' claims to Lahej and other districts, using disaffected tribal sections to encroach on the Abdali, Hawshabi, and Amiri confederations.

British policy aimed at creating a *cordon sanitaire* against Turkish encroachment, but the Turks themselves eventually proposed frontier demarcation, a process which went on until 1904. The British continued to extend the protected districts eastwards, concluding agreements with the Lower 'Awlaqis, Wahidis, and other tribes; at the opening of the 20th century these were extended to the Upper 'Awlaqis and to Baihan. Protectorate treaties were also arranged with the Mahri Sultan of Qishn and Socotra, and with the Sultan of Shihr and Mukalla in Hadramaut who was hereditary Jemadar of the Nizam of Hyderabad's forces. By these treaties the chiefs undertook not to alienate land to a foreign power without British permission, nor to enter into correspondence, agreement, or treaty with any foreign nation. These were voluntary undertakings, sometimes even requested by the chiefs themselves, for they wanted neither Turk nor Arab Imam. The chiefs in return received stipends, occasional presents of rifles, and entertainment when visiting Aden; but it was not intended to introduce direct British control and Aden itself was ruled from India, under a Resident, as part of the Bombay Presidency. Aden Settlement, Aden and the purchased districts occupied about 80 square miles; to it were linked Perim, and the Kuria Muria Islands, ceded to the British Crown in 1854 by the Sultan of Muscat, but inhabited by Shahra tribesmen from Oman.

The claims of the Zaidi Imams of Yemen to sovereignty over the British protected tribes were as valid as their claim to lead all Islam; that is to say, they were in practice untenable. The Zaidis occupied Fadli, Awlaqi, and even Kathiri territory in Hadramaut after the first Ottoman occupation collapsed; but their control soon vanished, or else local tribes expelled Zaidi troops. Indeed, until Mustafa Kemal abolished the Ottoman Caliphate, Hadramawt acknowledged not the Zaidi Imam, but the Turkish Caliph-Sultans' theoretical supremacy, by reciting the Friday address in mosques in his name. Yet this seemed not inconsistent with the protection treaties.

A British official publication in 1909 sums up the position at that time :

'The zone within which British influence is more immediately felt in the neighbourhood of Aden may be said to be comprised by a semi-circle having a radius of 80 miles, with the peninsula of Aden for its centre. To the eastward Britain is looked on as a kind of paramount power, which, while *recognising independence in regard to internal government*, yet is ready to prevent alienation of territory to foreign nations, or inter-tribal disputes which are carried on to the detriment of public peace or the interests of commerce.'

By competent methods a fine chain of alliances was built up, eminently satisfactory to both sides, while no British soldier or political officer was stationed outside Aden colony. This policy worked well until it was modified in the 1930s.

In July 1915 the Turks successfully invaded the Protectorate and remained in Lahej until 1919. When they left south Arabia, the Imam of the Yemen set about reconquering the country. Having never recognised the Anglo-Turkish boundary, the Imam occupied protected districts, from which he was expelled by air action in 1928 and 1934. By the treaty of Sanaa in the latter year he agreed that the frontier *status quo* should be maintained,[1] and though he never abandoned his territorial claims, this treaty provided a practical settlement until 1954.

In 1937 Aden was transferred from the Government of India to the Colonial Office. At about the same time a policy was initiated of penetration into the hinterland, the first British Resident being appointed to Hadramaut in the same year. For 30 years Hadramawt enjoyed a peace it may never have known before in history. Only after World War II did penetration, pacification and development get under way in the Eastern and Western Protectorates. With them came agricultural development, roads, education, and public health, on an ever-increasing scale. British policy aimed at creating a country which would be self-governing and more or less peaceful, even though economically it was unlikely ever to become more viable than Jordan.

NATIONALISM

In 1940 nationalist consciousness hardly existed in Aden, far less in the Protectorates. With occasional fits of violence, like the 1947 anti-Jewish riots, Aden was peaceful and contented after a century of British rule, which was admired for its justice and firmness; some people in the Protectorates would have liked to see it extended to themselves. But internal social change was taking place. The establishment of the Aden Refinery brought vastly higher standards of living and attracted tribal immigrants; the population

---

[1] By an unfortunate error in translating the English into Arabic the Imam was able to argue, though, in my opinion, without justification even in the terms of the treaty, that the *status quo* agreement applied to territory on the British side of the frontier. The treaty appears to have been drafted in English, but for some reason the Arabic text was made the authority in case of doubt as to the interpretation. The slip seems to have been as between the words *fi* and *min* which look much alike in Arabic script.

trebled in 15 years, over two-thirds being Arabs, while many were Yemeni immigrants drawn by Aden's expanding economy. In 1953, proposals to federate the sultanates of the Western Protectorate were under discussion. This alarmed Imam Ahmad of Yemen, who rightly saw that the creation of a federation would accentuate Protectorate separateness and so resorted to the tried expedient of arming Protectorate dissidents to attack peaceful districts. The 1953 proposals, he maintained, were incompatible with the Treaty of Sanaa. This in itself would have mattered little without Egyptian encouragement, but Egypt had adopted a pan-Arab attitude and its massive propaganda machine, with ever-growing intensity, spread poison everywhere through the radio, press, and education.

British policy set out to develop democratic institutions in Aden during the 1950s, to lead through the introduction of phased local representation in a legislative council (inaugurated in 1947) to ultimate self-rule—a policy which was complicated by the existence of a base at Aden of great importance. The decade also saw trade union development encouraged at first by the government. Union leaders, generally of insignificant social standing, soon saw opportunities of grasping at power that had always lain with tribal, mercantile or religious families. A group led by Abdullah al Asnag made political capital out of the fact that Yemeni immigrants had no voice in Ledgco (legislative council) elections, whereas Aden-born Indians, Jews and Somalis could vote. The true Adenese he asserted, were Yemenis (Haines's census of 1839 did not support him) and he adopted the Arab socialist line that Britain was guilty of economic oppression, following it up by attacking 'monopolistic foreign companies'. In *Yemen Workers in the Battle* he even declared : 'Any Arab region freed from colonialism and reaction must immediately join the UAR.' Mobilisation of shifting Yemeni labour against the British Government, which directly or indirectly provided its employment, brought him into headlong conflict with Britain, whose policy aimed at strengthening the Aden base for the protection of Britain's oil interests and of security in the Red Sea and Indian Ocean. The conflict was deepened by Britain's view that Soviet attempts to eliminate Western bases, and to extend Russian influence throughout the entire area, depended on Egypt's subservience to Soviet policy.

The Aden TUC, founded in 1956 through strikes and demonstrations, menaced the prosperity of the port; in 1957 a mob roused by agitators attacked the Tawahi police HQ and seven 'martyrs' (as Asnag called them) were killed. In 1960 a long-suffering government was at last forced to pass a law forbidding strikes without a declaration from an industrial court, in order to stop disruption of life in the colony for objectives unconnected with the welfare of labour. The British TUC, influenced by the Asnag group, attacked the compulsory arbitration law; the British Labour Party, ignorant of local conditions in Aden and seeing an opportunity to make political capital out of the situation, encouraged the ambitions of the Aden nationalists and initiated the policy of attacking the Federation that was to lead to ultimate disgrace and disaster.

The Federation, established in early 1959, turned out, surprisingly, a success. In 1962 it was planned that Aden should merge with it. This ought to have pleased the trade unionists, since in 1961 Asnag had attacked 'separatists' who wished to keep Aden separate from the Protectorates; but the TUC bosses, and even the Aden Association, opposed it, probably out of traditional misgivings about tribal domination. The Egyptian-engineered coup in Yemen of September 1962 found the Merger, as it was called, still undecided, but despite its unpopularity, it was forced through in a perhaps untimely way.

Aden now faced serious danger from Yemen. The danger lay, not in the Egyptian forces in Yemen, but in the persuasive power of Egyptian propaganda about the inevitability of revolution and the need for the overthrow of existing society. Besides this, the Egyptians were supplying arms to malcontents, on a scale the Imam had never been able to afford, and later set up a training centre for terrorists at Taiz and another near Baida. However, with British backing the Federation stood firm. The tribal unrest in Radfan from which the NLF (National Liberation Front) dated the 'revolution' of 14 October 1963, was crushed, and Aden remained secure enough. As late as September 1964 one could go anywhere in Aden unarmed and in safety.

British Withdrawal

There is no question that but for the election of a Labour Government in Britain, Aden could have been held, despite political mistakes and Egyptian hostility. The mere prospect of a Labour win in the 1964 election sufficed to send the nervous Fadli Sultan scurrying to Egypt. The Labour Government, after encouraging anti-Federation groups, now had to face the consequences. The Colonial Secretary, Mr Greenwood, visited Aden only to disappoint nationalists-cum-socialists without allaying Federal suspicions of Labour. Sir Kennedy Trevaskis, the architect of the Federation, was recalled and the Federation was steadily debilitated by British shilly-shallying. The nationalist leaders in Aden, Asnag and Makkawi, left to join Egyptian-sponsored organisations in Yemen. Terrorism increased but was contained, until the British decision to abandon Aden was made public in February 1966.

Instead of satisfying nationalist ambitions, Britain's abdication only complicated the struggle between rival factions. Local personalities, knowing that chaos and disaster would follow the British departure, had to consider their own political survival. They could choose to join FLOSY (Front for the Liberation of Occupied South Yemen), composed mostly of Adenese and western tribesmen, or the NLF, led by discontented teachers, a class peculiarly susceptible to propaganda on Arabism and socialism. Both organisations had been nurtured by the Egyptians in the Yemen, and liberally supplied with bazookas, mortars and grenades.

In the last months the British authorities in Aden, under orders from London to pack up and leave, chose to come to terms with the NLF rather than FLOSY, and in the bloody battle fought out between the tribal supporters of the two groups in Shaikh Uthman, the NLF emerged as victors. The British finally withdrew on 29 November 1967, and the NLF set up a government in Aden with Qahtan al-Sha'bi as its first president.

Independence

Emerging from its obscurity, the NLF was bent on socialisation and the abolition of everything 'colonialist'. Since Aden was virtually a British creation this was somewhat unrealistic. The rigid party basis of the new government was clearly manifest in such policy statements as the NLF declaration of 7 March 1968 which stated :

> 'The Revolutionary Government believes in its citizens being free to express their feelings in support of our Revolutionary Republic . . . As a safeguard for this the

South Yemen Government has now banned demonstrations, public processions, and celebrations, unless authorised by the General Command of the National Front, and unless a special permit is obtained from the Director-General of Public Security.'

In May 1968 austerity measures had to be taken to meet the economic crisis, which the NLF had maintained would not materialise, and Qahtan admitted that 'the colonialist during the last years of his presence created an artificial prosperity'. Qahtan had to discourage people from coming to seek employment in Aden as they had been doing in ever increasing numbers for so long. Missions sent to Arab and communist countries to seek aid mostly met a perfunctory response, but technical missions from communist states covered the ground already explored by British experts and raised again false hopes of mineral and oil wealth. During the year heavy increases in income tax and customs were introduced and salaries drastically cut. Popular discontent began to be openly expressed. Following the principles of its leftist *National Charter* of 1965, the NLF 'nationalised' land confiscated from Federalists by parcelling it out to its supporters. Laws were copied almost holus-bolus from Egypt, many of them not relevant at all to local conditions; a notable example was the agricultural reform law.

NLF extremists soon ran into trouble with the people and with the army, who disliked the communism of the younger men. There were insurrections in Abyan, fighting in Radfan and Baihan, and the Faridis nearly liberated the Ma'ni shaikhdom. In the Yemen, where the conservative tribal element had brought its own leftist dissidents under control, FLOSY and the Aden Federalists seemed to be making common cause, under Republican aegis, against the Aden NLF. The Yemen Republic and the NLF in South Yemen engaged in bitter radio campaigns against each other, and the prospect of unity between the two provinces became steadily more remote. In late August 1968 the first shipment of Soviet arms arrived in Aden and other Russian support followed.

Two years after achieving independence the South Yemen Republic was was in firm control only of the low country in the vicinity of Aden and towns or centres in former Federal territory. Most of the rest appeared to be reverting to anarchy in varying degrees except Hadramaut, which, with 30 years of stable British rule behind it, managed to hold together.

In international politics, South Yemen follows the line of other leftist Arab states : non-alignment, peaceful co-existence, close relations with socialist states and with Arab liberation movements. In practice this means the introduction of Russian, Yugoslav, Egyptian and North Korean 'experts'. South Yemen has shown at least sympathy with unprovoked attacks on the Oman Sultanate from its own eastern territories supported with Chinese Communist arms and Chinese trained infiltrators.

In the final resort the army is the strongest force in South Yemen but the NLF seems to have outmanœuvred and infiltrated it. I find this less surprising since my recent researches show it started as a compact, well-organised secret off-shoot of the communist-influenced PFLP of George Habash, about 1956, which nurtured it with subversive literature. More recently Maoist influence has been coming to the fore. Jobs are virtually restricted to (the very young) 'party' men, and they have fallen out with most tribes that accorded them any support, and widespread dissatisfaction is reported inside Aden and out. The stream of often ill-considered legislation from NLF headquarters in Aden is unlikely to effect much change in the society or life of the country, but the pressure, in an economy of scarcity, of the necessity to make South Yemen economically viable must affect every part of it. Unless the Suez Canal is re-opened the economic situation is likely to deteriorate rather than improve. Large-scale industrial development is hardly feasible and Aden's recovery as a highly efficient staging-post is dubious, so that tribal and local mercantile interests will have to come to an accommodation with each other to share out what limited income South Yemen can earn or attract from abroad.[2]

A factor of ever increasing economic and political importance, however, which will affect the situation in South Yemen, is the growing Russian build-up in the Indian Ocean including the former British protected island of Socotra.

FURTHER READING

Arendonk, C. Van. *Les débuts de l'Imämat Zaidite au Yemen* (trans Jacques Ryekmans), E. J. Brill, Leiden, 1960.

Cassels, Kay H. *Yemen its Early Medieval History*, Edward Arnold, London, 1892; reprint Gregg Press, Farnborough, 1969.

Hunter, F. M. *Account of the British Settlements of Aden, in Arabia*, Barnes & Noble, New York, 1968.

Ingrams, H. *Arabia and the Isles*, Murray, London, 1942; enlarged reprint, London, 1966; Praeger, New York, 3rd ed., 1966.

Ingrams, H. *The Yemen*, Murray, London, 1963; Praeger, New York, 1964.

King, G. *Imperial Outpost: Aden, Its Place in British Strategic Policy*, Oxford Univ. Press, London and New York, 1964.

Macro, E. *Yemen and the Western World*, C. Hurst & Co., London, 1968.

Naval Intelligence Division. *Western Arabia and the Red Sea*, BR 527 (Restricted), Oxford, 1946.

Paget, J. *Last Post: Aden 1964–1967*, Faber & Faber, London, 1969.

Reilly, Sir B. *Aden and the Yemen*, Colonial 343, H.M. Stationery Office, London, 1960.

Schmidt, Dana Adams. *Yemen: the Unknown War*, Holt, Rinehart & Winston, New York, 1968.

Serjeant, R. B. *The Portuguese off the South Arabian Coast*, Clarendon Press, Oxford, 1963.

Trevaskis, Sir G. K. N. *Shades of Amber*, Hutchinson, London, 1968.

Waterfield, Gordon. *Sultans of Aden*, John Murray, London, 1968.

Wenner, M. W. *Modern Yemen 1918–1960*, John Hopkins Press, Baltimore, 1967.

R. B. SERJEANT. Sir Thomas Adams' Professor of Arabic and Director of the Middle East Centre at Cambridge University. Formerly Professor of Arabic in the London School of Oriental and African Studies. Seconded as Colonial Research Fellow to Hadramawt 1947 and has since made frequent tours in South Arabia, including two in royalist Yemen and a shorter one to the Republic. Edited the BBC's *Arabic Listener* during World War II. One-time member of the Aden Protectorate Government Guards. Has written on Southern Arabia and is currently engaged on a book on the Egyptian invasion of the Yemen.

[2] The Commonwealth Development Finance Company Ltd. gave a very clear but not encouraging picture of what potentialities there were of development in a report, not for publication, made on a visit to Aden in October 1961—but even these are based on the assumption that the three main supports of the economy would continue —the presence of British forces, bunkering of ships, and entrepôt trade. Professor R. C. Tress's *Report on the Finances of Aden* of April, 1960 may be consulted.

SAUDI ARABIA

EDMOND Y. ASFOUR

HISTORICAL BACKGROUND

THE history of the Kingdom of Saudi Arabia may be traced back to the 18th century, when a religious reformer, Muhammad Ibn Abdul Wahhab (1703–91) started a religious movement known as Wahhabism in Nejd in central Arabia and was protected and sponsored by a tribal chief, Muhammad Ibn Saud who was married to his daughter. The movement preached the return of Islam to its pure form, shorn of cults and saints and aimed at the strict application of the Koran's rules in everyday life. Its puritanical spirit rebelled against adornment and demanded strict avoidance not only of alcohol and gambling but also of tobacco and any of the lighter aspects of social life. From 1740, when Abdul Wahhab and Ibn Saud joined forces, up to 1765, when Ibn Saud died, the movement spread into much of Nejd. Husain Abdul Aziz, who ruled until 1804, spread Wahhibism further, invading Iraq to the north and sacking the Shi'a centre of Kerbela (1801). The Hejaz in the west was also invaded. Taif and Mecca were captured in 1803 and Yanbo, Medina and Jeddah in the following three years.

The conquest of the Hejaz challenged the power of the waning Ottoman Empire in Arabia. The Sultan authorised Muhammad Aly of Egypt to send an expeditionary force in 1811 to subdue the Wahhabis. By 1818 the Wahhabis had been pushed back and their capital Riyadh was captured, with the Saudis accepting Ottoman suzerainty in Nejd. Ottoman and Egyptian influence remained supreme in the first half of the 19th century, and in its latter part the power of the Rashid family of Hail in north Nejd (Jabal Shammar) expanded, often with the help of the Ottomans. Taking advantage of rivalries in the house of Saud, the Rashids were able to capture Riyadh and appoint the ruler of the town. In 1891, following an unsuccessful revolt, the Wahhabi Imam Abdul Rahman Ibn Faisal al Saud had to flee Riyadh and seek refuge, first among friendly tribes and then in Kuwait, together with his son Abdul Aziz (1880–1953), who later became the first king of Saudi Arabia.

POLITICAL DEVELOPMENTS UP TO THE WAR

In 1901, Abdul Aziz, or Ibn Saud as he is generally called, supported by Mubarak of Kuwait, who was threatened by Ibn Rashid, returned to Nejd, and in January 1902, with a few hundred supporters, he captured Riyadh in a surprise night attack. His father proclaimed him ruler of Nejd and Imam of the Wahhabis. Following a decisive victory over Ibn Rashid in

271

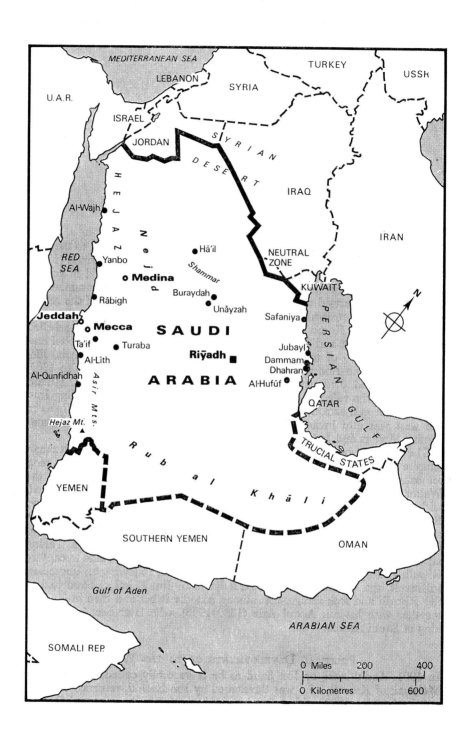

1906 all Nejd fell under his control and in 1918 he occupied the Ottoman province of Hasa on the Gulf.[1]

In World War I the British negotiated both with Ibn Saud (through Sir Percy Cox and later H. St. John Philby) and with his rival in Hijaz, the Sharif Husain (through Sir Henry McMahon and T. E. Lawrence), for their support against the Ottomans and their allies the Rashids. In return for British recognition of his independent family rule over Nejd, Hasa, Qatif and Jubail and their dependencies, territories and ports, and for protection (after consultation) against foreign aggression, Ibn Saud undertook, in the treaty of 26 December 1915,[2] not to have independent relations with foreign powers or alienate his territory, not to grant concessions without British approval, to follow British advice, to protect pilgrims and not to interfere with or attack the Gulf territories with which Britain had treaty relations; the boundaries were to be determined at a later date. During the rest of the war he fought the Rashids and the Ajmans, who were allied to the Ottomans.

The end of the war saw the disappearance of Ottoman power in the area. In a border battle at Turaba over an oasis, Ibn Saud defeated the Hejaz forces under Abdullah Ibn Husain in 1919, but was warned by Britain not to invade the Hejaz in the west. He diverted Wahhabi energies southwards and northwards, and following a brief foray in 1920 into Asir, a mountainous area lying between Hejaz and Yemen, he defeated the Rashids and occupied their capital, Hail, in the north in 1921. The northern borders with Iraq and Kuwait (including the Neutral Zone) were defined in 1922 in agreements with the two countries and with the participation of Britain. The opportunity to invade Hejaz presented itself in 1924 when British subsidies stopped and when Sharif Husain declared himself Caliph, thus incensing Wahhabi and other Moslem emotions. The Sharif's position in Hejaz had been weakened by the dispersal of part of his forces in Jordan, Syria and Iraq and by the drying-up of the British annual subsidy of £22·4 million. No international agreement or treaty afforded him protection. In August 1924 Ibn Saud attacked Taif and Mecca. Public support for Husain was weak and he declined to fight in the holy city. He abdicated in favour of his son Aly who withdrew to Jeddah. Mecca soon surrendered and after a year's siege Jeddah was also taken, along with Medina and Yanbo at the end of 1925. Aly abdicated and left for Iraq.

Ibn Saud was proclaimed King of Hejaz (in addition to his title of Sultan of Nejd and its dependencies) in January 1926 and was recognised by the Soviet Union in February. Asir in the south became a protectorate in October 1926[3] and Hejaz and Nejd were unified in January 1927, and named the

---

[1] However, in an agreement of 15 May 1914 with the Porte, said to have been found by British troops in Basra in 1914 but the existence of which was denied by the Saudis, Ibn Saud is said to have accepted the title of Wali (Governor) of Nejd for himself and his descendants, agreeing to use the Turkish flag and to allow the stationing of troops at some coastal points, and undertaking not to 'correspond about foreign affairs and international treaties or to grant concessions to foreigners' (Kelly, J. B. *Eastern Arabian Frontiers*, Faber & Faber, London, 1964, pp. 110, 149.). This agreement becomes of importance later in the dispute over Buraimi.

[2] See text in Hurewitz, ii, pp. 17–18. The treaty brought with it also a monthly payment of 5,000 British pounds which continued until 1924.

[3] Before World War I, Asir was ruled by a branch of the Moroccan Idriss family. On the death of Sayyid Muhammad Ibn Aly al Idrissi in 1923, pretenders struggled for power. Sayyid Hassan Ibn Aly, as Imam of Asir, signed a protectorate (Mecca) agreement with Abdul Aziz in October 1926 by which he placed Asir under the suzerainty of Ibn Saud in exchange for protection and life rule for himself and for 'whomsoever the House of Idrissi and the competent authorities of the Imamate may agree upon' (Hurewitz, ii, p. 148.).

Kingdom of Hejaz, Nejd and their dependencies. France recognised the new kingdom and was followed by Britain in the Treaty of Jeddah signed on 20 May 1927.[4] The feud with the Hashemites was eased with the conclusion of treaties of friendship with Iraq in 1930 and with Transjordan in 1933. The southern borders of the kingdom, named the Kingdom of Saudi Arabia in 1932, were secured in the Mecca Treaty with Yemen in 1934 following an invasion of Yemen.[5]

The five years between the treaty with Yemen and the outbreak of World War II were peaceful and a growing interest was taken in the search for oil, following its discovery in nearby Bahrain in 1932. Protracted negotiations with Britain at this time concerning the borders with Qatar and the Trucial States reached no conclusions. Of particular importance to future development was the granting in 1933 of a concession to Standard Oil of California in the eastern part of the kingdom, following the expiration of a British concession that had been granted in 1924. Exploration started in 1934 and large oil reserves were soon discovered.

INTERNAL CONSOLIDATION

Thus, before World War II started, Ibn Saud had safeguarded his kingdom through treaties with Britain and his Arab neighbours, though its southern and eastern borders were not yet fixed. Internally, he consolidated his rule after each conquest by the strict application of Wahhabi rules of conduct (with the help of the *Mutawwi'een*, patrols for the enforcement of morals), by intermarriage with daughters of tribal chieftains and by the establishment of *Ikhwan* (brethren settlements). The *Ikhwan*, a paramilitary fraternity, were established in 1912 and supported the tribal forces in Ibn Saud's wars. They shed old tribal allegiances, lived strictly according to Wahhabi rules and after the wars a large number of them settled on land supplied by Ibn Saud and with his financial help. Some hundred such settlements were established. The first and largest settlements were abandoned and the movement itself disbanded after a rebellion by two *Ikhwan* chiefs in 1927–30, which was mercilessly crushed.

The strict, sometimes harsh application of Wahhabi law and punishment resulted within two decades in the spread of internal and border security to an unprecedented degree, in a country where tribal rivalries and raids were a way of life. In 1908, for example, a rebellion instigated by Ibn Saud's cousins led not only to the defeat of the conspirators but also to the public execution of 18 out of 19 of the captured leaders. Raids across the borders of Iraq and Kuwait in 1927–8 by the Darwish, a zealous Wahhabi tribe (who disapproved of Ibn Saud's treaty with the British and of his introducing

---

[4] In the treaty Ibn Saud undertook to maintain friendly and peaceful relations with the Gulf territories who had treaty relations with Britain and to co-operate with Britain in suppressing the slave trade. The question of frontiers was referred to in the accompanying notes but remained open, Ibn Saud suspending temporarily his claim for Ma'an and Aqaba in Transjordan. The treaty, which replaced that of 1915 was valid for at least seven years and was renewed in 1936 and 1943 when it became automatically renewable for successive periods of seven years unless notice was given six months before the expiration of any period. (Hurewitz, ii, pp. 149–150.)

[5] After an unsuccessful rebellion in 1933, Hassan al Idrissi, ruler of Asir, was forced to flee to Yemen, which (together with Italy) supported him in raiding Asir. Ibn Saud invaded Yemen in 1934 and defeated Imam Yahya's forces. Italian naval forces were prevented from interfering by the British navy. In the treaty that followed, Ibn Saud, in fixing the borders, allowed the restoration of the previous borders with practically no change.

what they considered innovations) was suppressed by Ibn Saud's forces with the help of British bombers. The strict application of Koranic punishments (such as public amputation of the hand of a thief, stoning of an adultress, public decapitation of a murderer, whipping of drunkards) brought about security of person and property and banished immoral behaviour in public. Pilgrimage routes were protected and for the first time in many centuries pilgrimage ceased to be an adventure in which pilgrims risked the loss of their property if not of their lives.

THE SECOND WORLD WAR AND POST-WAR YEARS

During the war, until he declared war on Germany and Japan in March 1945, Ibn Saud maintained formal neutrality but treated with Britain and the United States. Declining revenue from pilgrimage and the virtual suspension of oil exploration and production made British and, later, US subsidies all the more welcome.[6] American influence grew fast, the way having been paved by individual missionary doctors, technical advisers (particularly K. S. Twitchell, who organised the exploitation of a gold mine at Mahd Al Dhahab), and the oil companies. In 1940 the first official American mission visited Saudi Arabia (in the company of a private agricultural mission) and in 1943 an American legation was established and two military missions arrived. In 1943 a secret agreement led to the construction early in 1946 of the Dhahran military air base. Relations were strengthened when Ibn Saud met President Roosevelt in February 1945 on board a warship in the Suez Canal. In the same year Saudi Arabia also took part in the San Francisco Conference and in the establishment of the Arab League.

The period immediately after the war was one of spectacular growth in oil production and in government revenue from oil, particularly after the precedent-setting agreement of 1950, which provided for the equal sharing of profits by the government and the oil companies, and after the nationalisation of the oil industry in Iran in 1951. (Oil revenue rose from $10 million in 1946 to $57 million in 1950 and $341 million in 1955, after which it levelled off for several years.) Despite Saudi disappointment over the US stand in the struggle for Palestine during 1948–9 these economic developments strengthened relations between the two countries. In 1951 the Dhahran air base agreement was replaced by one which extended the use of the base for five years and provided for the training of Saudi armed forces. Military aid was also granted under a mutual defence agreement of the same date. The agreement was extended and expanded in 1956 to include the establishment of a large military mission; extensive military aid was given and a military academy was established in Riyadh to train 600 officers annually. Relations with Britain were strained, however, following the dispute over the Buraimi oasis in 1949–55 (which was touched off by uncertainties about the extent of oil concession areas)[7] and, later, during the Suez war in 1956, diplomatic relations were severed.

---

[6] The British subsidy, out of a US loan to Britain, rose from £400,000 annually in 1941 to £2·5 million in 1945. Additional lend-lease was extended by the US in 1943. By comparison, oil revenue reached $3·2 million (£800,000) in 1939 and $5 million (£1·2 million) in 1945.

[7] The 1915 and 1927 treaties with Britain left undetermined the question of borders between Saudi Arabia and the adjoining territories which were in treaty relations with Britain. Extended and fruitless negotiations took place before World War II on the borders with Qatar and the Trucial States. In 1949, following disagreement

The increasing wealth of Saudi Arabia enabled it to play a growing role in the political developments in the Arab countries of the Middle East. The military effort exerted in the Palestine war of 1948 was symbolic. After that war, Ibn Saud was opposed to Abdullah's unification of a part of Palestine with Transjordan and to subsequent efforts by the Hashemites to unify Jordan, Iraq and Syria.

King Saud, who inherited the throne from his father in 1953, continued this policy of opposition to Hashemite aspirations by means of Press campaigns in the Arab countries in support of selected political personalities or parties, and by making loans to Syria to strengthen its anti-communist faction ($6 million in 1950, $10 million in 1955 and $10 million in 1956). Similarly Saudi Arabia joined Egypt and Syria in opposing the Baghdad Pact. However, in 1958 the union of Egypt and Syria and the downfall of the Hashemite monarchy in Iraq brought Jordan and Saudi Arabia (as well as Lebanon) closer to each other in opposition to the leftist régimes.

The 1960s witnessed the widening of the gulf between the two groups of Arab countries and particularly between Nasser's UAR and Saudi Arabia. The overthrow of the Imamate régime in Yemen by Abdullah al Sallal in 1962 brought immediate UAR military support to the new 'socialist' republic. A protracted war ensued between the republican-UAR forces and the royalist tribes, who were supported materially and financially by Saudi Arabia. UAR aircraft bombed border towns inside Saudi Arabia. In August 1965 Nasser visited Saudi Arabia and agreed with King Faisal (who had replaced King Saud the previous year) on the withdrawal of UAR forces from Yemen, the stoppage of Saudi aid to the royalists and the formation of a Yemeni régime acceptable to the rival factions among the Yemenis. Fighting continued, however, until a second agreement was reached in August 1967, immediately after the June war with Israel, when the withdrawal of UAR forces finally took place.

The war of June 1967, like the 1948 Palestine war, did not involve Saudi Arabia militarily. However, in accordance with the decision reached by the Arab kings and presidents in Khartoum in September 1967, Saudi Arabia undertook to contribute £50 million ($140 million) out of £135 million *p.a.* to be paid by itself, Kuwait and Libya to the UAR and Jordan until the 'effects of the aggression are removed'. It was also agreed that oil exports should continue.

Recent developments, particularly the British declaration that it will withdraw its forces from the Gulf before the end of 1971, has directed Saudi attention towards that area. Closer relations have been developed with Iran, another major power in the Gulf area; an agreement was reached in August 1968 on the median line dividing the waters of the Gulf between the two countries, and in their meetings the King and the Shah probably reached an understanding on their attitudes towards the Gulf emirates after the withdrawal of British forces. Significantly, an agreement was reached in 1967 directly with Qatar defining the long-disputed borders between the two countries.

about the extent of the ARAMCO concession discussions over the border question were restarted. The Saudi Government claimed the Buraimi Oasis, which included six small villages claimed by Abu Dhabi and two small villages claimed by Muscat. In 1952, with negotiations stalemated, a small Saudi force occupied the village of Buraimi. Arbitration during 1954–5 failed and was followed by the eviction of the Saudis by joint Abu Dhabi, Muscat and British-led Oman Levy forces. For a detailed study from the British viewpoint, see Kelly, particularly ch. 5.

CONSTITUTION AND GOVERNMENT

The form of government in the days of Ibn Saud was theocratic, the king being the Imam of the faithful as well as the absolute monarch. The law of the land is still the *Shariah* or religious Islamic law as recorded in the Koran and interpreted by the religious men. There is no written constitution besides the Koran. Tribal traditions also influenced the administration of the law; the king held his *Majlis* (council), which was open to any citizen with a complaint and gave individual judgments, and the *Ulemas* (literally savants) interpreted the law as given in the Koran and supported by the *Hadith* (sayings of the prophet). In technical matters the king had his personal advisers, including St. John Philby and several Arabs from Syria and Lebanon. The first Council of Ministers, headed by the King, was created in 1953, with the ministers largely members of the royal family and including some advisers. It had the powers to approve annual budgets, international agreements and concessions.

Under King Saud the power of the ministries grew, as well as that of Crown Prince Faisal, who was Prime Minister for long periods and exercised full power. Several factors brought about the formal transfer of power from King Saud to his half-brother Faisal in 1964. Rising consumption and development expenditures and transfer of funds abroad, when oil revenues had levelled off, particularly between 1955 and 1960, resulted in financial difficulties, large foreign debts and inflation. Prince Faisal insisted on fiscal restraint (which affected expenditure by the King and the royal family) and for monetary reform, which effectively brought back financial stability by 1962. The danger to the régime posed later by the Yemen war persuaded the majority of the royal family to confirm in March 1964 the decision of the *Ulemas* to transfer power from the king to the crown prince as regent. This was followed in November 1964 by Faisal's accession to the throne and the departure of King Saud abroad. Despite the growth of the administrative machinery since then, power of decision has remained highly centralised in the king's hands.

Administratively, the country was divided in 1963 into four provinces, Hejaz, Nejd, Asir and Eastern Province, each with an appointed governor who is charged with local administration, maintenance of order and implementation of *Shariah* judgments. A provincial council is elected to help the governor but has largely advisory functions. Municipal heads are appointed by the governor. While Riyadh is the administrative capital of the kingdom, Jeddah is the diplomatic centre and Taif is the summer residence of the king.

Justice is administered by the Chief Justice in the Department of the *Shariah*. The courts, which include courts of urgent matters, high courts and a court of appeal, are supervised by the judicial Supervisory Committee.

ECONOMIC GROWTH

Before the development of the oil industry, the bulk of the population lived at near-subsistence level. The economy was based on pastoral activities, supplemented by limited agriculture in the Asir mountains and in scattered oases, and by income from the annual pilgrimage activities in Hejaz. Fees paid by the pilgrims and a 2.5% *Zakat* tax formed a substantial part of the small government revenue. This was supplemented by subsidies from foreign governments during war periods and by small royalties from the oil concessions in the 1930s. In 1934, the year of the ARAMCO (Arabian American Oil Company) oil concession, the government budget was only 14 million riyals (about $3 million). Oil was discovered in 1937, but World War II interrupted the development of exports, which started only in 1944. However, it was not until 1950, when equal sharing of oil company profits was agreed upon, that oil revenue began to play a predominant role in the economic development of the country. Oil revenue doubled in 1950, reaching $57 million and doubled again in each of the following two years, reaching $212 million in 1952. It took ten more years and additional small revenue from Getty Oil in the Neutral Zone and Arabian Oil (Japanese) offshore[8] before revenue doubled again, reaching $410 million in 1962. In 1967, oil revenues reach $909 million and $955 million in 1968.

Gross National Product grew with the growth of oil revenue, probably at over 10% per annum, reaching about $2·2 billion in 1967, or about $500 *per capita*. About half the GNP is contributed by the oil industry. The non-oil sectors, with the exception of the government sector, have not been able to keep pace with the high rate of growth of GNP, despite intensive development in agriculture, industry, commerce and transport. The economy outside the modern oil enclave remains largely traditional, but modern establishments have grown up in and around the main cities. Similarly, the distribution of income among various localities and groups remains unequal, the disparity being widest between cities and rural areas on the one hand, and between the ruling circle and the new urban immigrants on the other. A small but growing middle class has appeared, however, in the towns and cities.

Little is known about the labour force. It is estimated that out of some 400,000 workers, one-third are employed in agriculture, one-third in government and about one-fourth in trade, finance, transport and services. Only 16,000 workers, or 4% of the total, are employed in the oil industry. A large proportion of the skilled manpower is foreign.

The oil sector accounts for practically all the exports of Saudi Arabia and almost nine-tenths of government revenue. And as has already been seen it contributes about half the total GNP. Its contribution to economic development is not limited to supplying the essential financial means but extends to training Saudis on the job and in special training programmes; it also stimulates local industry and services through local purchases and through various technical assistance services it renders. It remains, however, largely isolated from the mainstream of cultural as well as economic activity of the country.

Oil and its by-products also supply the basis for several existing or potential industries. Oil refining is largely undertaken by ARAMCO but now the government has its own refinery in Jeddah. A petrochemical complex using waste gas has been set up in Dammam and is expected to start production in 1969 at the daily rate of 1,100 tons of urea and 600 tons of fertilisers. Another refinery, a lube plant and a sulphur extraction plant are planned.

Outside oil and petrochemicals, which depend on foreign markets, the growth of industry is inhibited by the small domestic market and the scarcity

[8] In April 1965 a concession, with a participation option, was granted to the French Auxilière du Régie Autonome des Pétroles (Auxirap), and in December 1967 to the Italian AGIP, a subsidiary of ENI and also to a group of one Pakistani and two American companies.

of resources. Besides food, cement, building materials and repairs, few manufacturing industries have been able to take root. Gold mining at Mahd al Dhahab was suspended in 1954 but there are plans to exploit iron ore deposits.

Agriculture, though not highly developed, is more important than is generally thought. Animal husbandry in the age-old Bedouin tradition continues and date palms in the oases make Saudi Arabia a major producer of dates. Cereals and fruits are grown in scattered places, particularly in the south-western mountains. Both date-growing and camel-raising have suffered from a decline in the demand. The attraction of higher incomes and employment in other sectors has made it necessary for the government to support agriculture with infrastructural work, free agricultural services, free well-drilling, cheap credit and other incentives. A comprehensive survey of the water resources of the kingdom is well advanced and several small irrigation and drainage schemes have been started, notably in Al Hasa and Jizan. Shortage of water remains a principal limitation, however; hence the special interest of Saudi Arabia in water desalinisation schemes.

The scarcity of profitable investment opportunities in industry and agriculture, combined with the undeveloped infrastructure, have led to the expenditure by the government of very considerable sums in recent years on the development of the infrastructure and welfare services. The development of an extensive roads network, of ports and airports, of electricity, drinking-water systems and sewerage systems, as well as hospital, school and government buildings, has been moving apace. Services in general remain undeveloped, despite the rising demand created by pilgrims (over 300,000 per year who spend about $75 million) and by the large number of foreign teachers, government employees and technicians; the services sector (other than education and health) is normally a field for private enterprise rather than government.

Social Development

Saudi Arabia's population, numbering somewhere between four and seven million,[9] is wholly Muslim, predominantly of tribal culture, and generally follows Wahhabi rules of conduct. Variations naturally exist, as for example, between the city people of Hejaz who have had contact with the outside world through trade and pilgrims, and the more isolated, inland population of Nejd or Asir. Similarly, differences exist among townspeople (with a small but growing middle class), the settled people of agricultural areas (in the scattered oases and in the mountains of Asir) and the Bedouin who migrate with their flocks in search of grazing grounds. However, conservative and puritanical Wahhabism pervades all social life in the kingdom and has until recent years been interpreted and applied in an extremely rigid form : smoking in the street was prohibited by the *Mutawwi'een* and radio and television were not allowed. Recent years have witnessed some relaxation; shows and sports are allowed, but alcohol is still prohibited and censorship remains heavy. The growth of income and wealth in urban centres, the increased flow of Arab and foreign workers and experts, together with extensive travel by the richer class in neighbouring Arab countries and further afield, have slowly softened social rigidities, at least in private.

[9] The official figure published in the UN Yearbook is 6,990,000 in 1967, but no complete census has ever been taken. Other estimates have been of the order of 4 million.

The social system is based on the extended family or tribe, to which there are strong loyalty attachments. The position of the leading male and of other elders is very high, both in family and tribe, but women are secluded and are seen only by close family members. In the towns and villages they are heavily veiled, but among Bedouins they enjoy greater freedom and carry more responsibilities. While polygamy is allowed, it is rarely practised, particularly in cities and among the educated class. Although the slave trade was made illegal in 1936, the system of slavery survived until 1962, when all slaves (estimated at 10,000 to 15,000) were emancipated by law at a cost of £6·5 million to the government in the form of compensation.

The growth of oil revenue since 1950 has enabled Saudi Arabia to finance generous education, health and welfare programmes, bringing the benefits of modern medicine and schooling to a poor and largely illiterate population, subject to disease and suffering from malnutrition. There were virtually no hospital facilities before 1950 and only a poor health service in the cities; but by 1968 there were about 660 doctors serving in hospitals with about 6,000 beds, in addition to some 200 dispensaries for out-patients and 300 health centres in the villages, all supplying their services as well as medication free of charge. With the help of the World Health Organisation, a central laboratory, a training centre, and programmes of malaria eradication and preventive medicine were started. The development of free education was similarly extensive, particularly during the 1960s. About 400,000 children now go to school compared with one-fourth of that number a decade ago. Significantly, the first girls' school was started only in 1960 but by 1969 there were some 80,000 girls studying in 233 schools. For university education young Saudis had to go abroad until the establishment of Riyadh University in 1957. The growth of Riyadh University (which now includes eight faculties), and the establishment of the College of Petroleum and Minerals in 1963 and of Abdul Aziz University in Jeddah in 1967 have reduced greatly the dependence on foreign universities. At present about 4,300 students study in local universities and colleges, compared with about 1,500 abroad, largely in the United States. Both in education and in health the country depends to a considerable extent on foreign teachers and doctors, who come largely from other Arab countries. The supply of qualified Saudi teachers and doctors, as well as technicians and administrators in general, remains one of the serious obstacles in the way of more rapid social and economic development.

FURTHER READING

Abercrombie, T. J. 'Saudi Arabia, Beyond the Sands of Mecca', *National Geographic*, January, 1966.

Arabian American Oil Company (ARAMCO). *Yearbook*, annually.

Armstrong, H. C. *Lord of Arabia*, Barker, London, 1934; Verry, Connecticut, 1966.

Asfour, E. *Saudi Arabia: Long Term Projections*, Economic Research Institute, Beirut, 1965.

Burckhardt, J. L. *Travels in Arabia*, Colburn, London, 1829; Barnes & Noble, New York, 1968.

Lawrence, T. E. *The Seven Pillars of Wisdom*, Cape, London, 1935; Doubleday, New York, 1947.

Philby, H. St. J. B. *Diplomacy in the Near and Middle East*, 2 volumes, D. van Nostrand Co., Princeton, New Jersey, 1956.

Rihani, A. *Ibn Saud of Arabia, his People and his Land*, Constable, London, 1928.

Saudi Arabian Monetary Agency. *Annual Report*.

Sheean, V. 'King Faisal's First Year', *Foreign Affairs,* January, 1966.

Van der Meulen, D. *The Wells of Ibn Saud,* John Murray, London, 1957; Praeger, New York, 1957.

EDMOND Y. ASFOUR. Associate Professor of Economics and Director of the Economic Research Institute at the American University of Beirut 1963–7. Economist in Middle East Unit of the UN 1956–60. Author of several books and articles on the economics of Middle East countries.

SUDAN

NORMAN DANIEL

The Sudan, Kush in the Old Testament and Ethiopia to the Greeks, traces its separate history, within the overall unity of the Nile Valley, to the period of the Egyptian forts at the second cataract, roughly 2000–1700 BC. After a withdrawal associated with the Hyksos, the Egypt of the New Kingdom (1580–1100) extended its influence southward into Meroe. In the eighth century the local Meroitic dynasty conquered Egypt, ruling there as the XXVth dynasty. Two main areas of Meroitic civilisation are known, near modern Merowe and near modern Shendi, but archaeological survey is not complete. An attack on Upper Egypt by the Queen Candace, or Queen-Mother, in 23 BC, provoked Roman retaliation by the prefect Petronius. Traditionally Meroe was greatly weakened or destroyed by conquest from Axum (in modern Ethiopia) in the fourth century AD, but the sequence of events is obscure.

Converted to Christianity from the reign of Justinian, there were three Nubian successor states; the most northerly is represented in the history of art by the magnificent church frescoes from Faras; the second had its capital at Dongola, and the most southerly (Alwa) at Soba, on the east bank of the Blue Nile, south of modern Khartoum. Nubian Christianity survived in the north probably until the 15th century, but a gradual process of infiltration, intermarriage and warfare—under direct pressure from the Mameluks and also from Arab tribes themselves, under Mameluk pressure—resulted in the adoption of Islam, and of Arabic (in Dongola from the early 14th century) in the northern area and among the tribes of the eastern Sudan. The Nubian and Bija languages, however, survive and flourish to-day. In the south the kingdom of Alwa lasted longer, and fell to Arab conquest towards the end of the 15th century; the Arabs in turn were defeated, in 1504, by the Funj, an African people from further south whose origin is uncertain. The Funj Kingdom maintained its capital at Sinnar until the invasion by forces of Muhammad Aly, Viceroy of Egypt, in 1820. It was during the period of Funj rule that the conversion of the country to Islam was consolidated by a number of holy men who established teaching centres, and by the spread of the *tariqas* (religious sects or associations). It was during the later part of this period that the far west became Muslim and came under the influence of Arabic language and culture, but the sultans of Darfur had nothing to do with the Funj—war apart.

The invasion of 1820 was intended to strengthen Egyptian trade with Africa, including that in slaves, who were needed primarily as army conscripts. The early years of the *Turkiya* were unhappy; the Sudanese resented

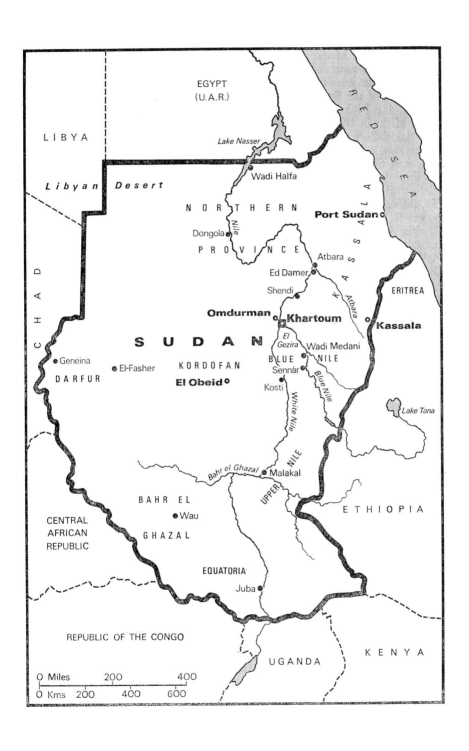

EGYPT
(U.A.R.)

LIBYA

Libyan Desert

Lake Nasser

Wadi Halfa

NORTHERN

Port Sudan

Dongola

PROVINCE

Atbara

Ed Damer

Shendi

CHAD

Omdurman

Khartoum

Kassala

ERITREA

SUDAN

El Gezira

Wadi Medani

Geneina

El-Fasher

KORDOFAN

BLUE NILE

El Obeid

Sennar

Kosti

DARFUR

Nile

Atbara

KASSALA

White Nile

Blue Nile

Lake Tana

Bahr el Ghazal

Malakal

NILE

BAHR EL

Wau

UPPER

GHAZAL

ETHIOPIA

CENTRAL
AFRICAN
REPUBLIC

EQUATORIA

Juba

REPUBLIC OF THE CONGO

UGANDA

KENYA

RED SEA

O Miles	200	400
O Kms	200	400	600

taxation, and the revolt of Nimr, *mak* of the Shendi area, who murdered the son of the Viceroy, was suppressed with severity. The capital, established initially at Wad Medani, was brought to Khartoum, at the junction of the Niles, and the machinery of modern government was introduced. In 1833 Kordofan was joined to Nubia and Sinnar, thus decisively extending the boundaries of the Sudan beyond the Nile Valley. The revolt of Muhammad Ahmad, the Mahdi, in 1881, led to the destruction of the Egyptian force under Hicks in 1883 and to the capture of Khartoum, the death of Gordon and the failure of Wolseley's relief expedition in January 1885, to the subsequent foundation of the twin city of Omdurman, across the White Nile, and finally to the death of the Mahdi from illness in the summer of the same year. The essential aim of the Mahdi was the restoration of pure Islam and the unity of Muslims, and so the supersession of existing sects. He did not consider his a nationalist movement, and he certainly did not expect it to be limited by the boundaries of the Sudan. His successor, the Khalifa Abdullāhi the T'āishi, was unable to extend the frontier beyond the point of Anglo-Egyptian resistance, and he failed to restore authority lost in the south. His rule did much to centralise government; he brought to Omdurman the western tribes on whose support he could rely, and the northern Arabs whom he could not trust. His administration was efficient, and continuous with that of the superseded régime, but the country was weakened by war and famine, and the Khalifa maintained his authority by acts of severity which alienated the most ancient areas of civilisation in the north.

The motivation of the Anglo-Egyptian reconquest under Kitchener in 1896–9 (the decisive battle of Karari, near Omdurman, took place in 1898) is disputed. It was obscured at the time by the war propaganda sincerely generated by Wingate (of Cairo Intelligence, and Kitchener's successor in the Sudan) and his assistant Slatin, and by a spirit of Christian revanchism for the death of Gordon that went against the attitudes expressed by that remarkable man in his letters and journal. We can only say that it took place in the course of the scramble for Africa, and that the Fashoda incident, immediately after the battle in 1898, released the tensions of Anglo-French rivalry for the Nile Valley. The Anglo-Egyptian condominium created in 1899 was anomalous in international law, and a source of later embarrassment to both the co-domini. Darfur was added to the Sudan in 1916, because the sultan, Aly Dinar, was supporting the Turks.

The missionary lobby had hoped for complete freedom to proselytise, but had to be content with a division of the three largely pagan southern provinces between the various mission societies, the largest of which were the CMS and the Verona Fathers. In the north, the period until the end of World War I was one of settling down to new conditions, and to government by an exiguous but highly professional service of foreign administrators. The early '20s were marked by two tendencies of great future significance. The new government had been suspicious of the Ansar (Mahdists) and had encouraged the revival of the Sufi sects, especially of the Khatmiyya, under Sayyid Aly Mirghani, with its strong Egyptian connections; but after the end of the war British hostility to the Ansar was seen to have been modified. Their Imam, Sayyid 'Abd al-Rahmān, posthumous son of the Mahdi, and himself possessed of no small charisma, now presented himself as a leader among the natural rulers of the country, claiming separate nationality for the Sudanese. This still seemed dangerous to the British, but, because they were becoming increasingly suspicious of Egyptian influence, they allowed him to build up a position of wealth and authority with its economic base in cotton estates, and boosted by government loans and contracts.

The Egyptian national movement was active and lively, and inspired a literary and political movement in the Sudan, based primarily on the graduates of Gordon College (a school chiefly for future administrators). In 1923 they joined Aly 'Abd al-Latif, a discharged junior officer who had been imprisoned the previous year for advocating 'Sudan for the Sudanese' in an unpublished article, and the White Flag League was formed. This owed something of its technique of agitation, though not its ideas, to the Communist Party. In 1924 public demonstrations coincided with the murder of Lee Stack in Egypt, and the British withdrawal of Egyptian troops from the Sudan. The Sudanese troops mutinied, but the movement was suppressed, and its final achievement was the sympathy (extending through popular songs to all social levels) with which it was remembered.

The period from 1926 to 1933 was a time of economy and of indirect rule, when Lugardism was almost an official doctrine; but the attempt to strengthen tribal leadership, to resist urban tendencies and to restrict education amounted in the long run to very little. In the southern provinces, the government, after many years of initial hesitation, accepted the missionaries' demand that the English language and the Sunday holiday should replace Arabic and Friday; and the period of indirect rule in the north was paralleled by the closure of the south to northerners, and by a policy of building up 'self-contained racial or tribal units' which in practice was largely nullified by the financial aid given to the Christian schools. No government education was undertaken there. The northern policy was reversed by Stewart Symes, who expanded educational opportunities at home and abroad, and tried to establish an alliance with the intellectual leadership. He was somewhat suspicious of the influence of Sayyid 'Abd al-Rahman. Yet by the beginning of World War II the progressives were again turning to the Egyptian movement. With the disappearance of the Italian threat from Ethiopia, the Graduates' General Congress,[1] formed in 1938, felt free in 1942 to present a memorandum which demanded, *inter alia*, self-determination after the war. The Government rejected this on the ground that the Congress did not represent the people. From this time onward the pace of political development was set by Sudanese opinion rather than by the administration, but the immediate effect was to divide the Congress. In many rural areas (especially the west) the Ansar were broadly based, and in 1945 they formed the Umma Party, which long constituted a stable political grouping. Those who opposed religious leadership were forced to look, not only to the urban bourgeoisie and proletariat, and to the northern tribes alienated by the Mahdiyya, but also, rather uneasily, for religious support to Sayyid Aly Mirghani, who maintained an ambiguous attitude to politics until his death in 1968. The *Ashigga* (full-brothers), now dominating the congress under the leadership of Ismā'īl al-Azhari, were succeeded by various groupings and alliances which can be roughly designated 'Unionists' (as favouring the union of the Nile Valley); a People's Democratic Party, specifically to represent the Khatmiyya, took final shape only just before independence.

Government did its best to keep pace. In 1946 the southern policy was reversed, and the Juba Conference of 1947 was intended to bring southern and northern development into line; but a clear understanding of the

[1] School-graduates.

dangers did not result in action adequate to avert them. In the north, the Government had established, in 1943, the Advisory Council which represented conservative Sudanese opinion, and in 1948 this was replaced by a Legislative Assembly; the Unionist groupings boycotted both, but the Umma Party provided a kind of advisory government in the Assembly, although the quality of the Assembly itself was admitted not to be high. The administration and the Umma Party shared suspicion of Egypt, and were also suspicious of each other. The Umma were pressing for self-government, and the Egyptian reaction in 1951, was to declare Farouk King of Egypt and the Sudan. The resulting international deadlock was resolved by the new Egyptian régime of 1952, and in Cairo early in the following year the Sudanese parties signed an agreement which forced the hand of the British. A general election held the same year gave the National Unionist Party a large majority.

The Government formed by Ismā'īl al-Azhari perhaps did not expect the loyalty and correctness with which the Governor-Generals now acted, and the Sudanisation programme (more radical than anything similar subsequently adopted in the Commonwealth) was completed by the summer of 1955. It was obvious that the British were indeed leaving, and that no further outside support for revolution would be needed. The Umma had meanwhile forcibly demonstrated their objection to any unity of the Nile Valley beyond the cultural unity, and so there was now unanimous support for the unilateral declaration of independence which was formalised by Parliament on 1 January 1956.

The southern politicians claimed that their consent was conditional on the subsequent creation of a federal constitution (a provisional constitution had barely been completed by 31 December). The background was as follows. As independence approached in the summer of 1955, it was seen that Sudanisation would allot few posts to southerners, and a number of conflicts with northern administrators created a crisis of confidence. In August a mutiny of the southern corps at Torit preceded a massacre, chiefly of northerners and their families. The mutineers appear to have expected British support, and when, after a fortnight of 'disturbances' across the greater part of the south, order was restored, the original mutineers had taken to the bush. They have waged guerilla war with fluctuating success ever since.

Al-Azhari was soon excluded by a coalition of the Umma and the PDP, the two sectarian parties. The results of an election held in 1958 illustrate the permanent divisions of the country. The NUP in opposition held about half as many seats as the two sectarian parties together, but the Umma had rather less than a notional combination of the NUP and PDP, the two anti-Mahdist parties. As the year wore on, there was increasing dissatisfaction with corrupt practices and political manoeuvring. Now the Umma and the NUP were negotiating a new coalition; but the Umma Prime Minister, 'Abdalla Khalīl, out of touch with Sayyid al-Siddiq (soon to succeed his father, 'Abd al-Rahmān, as Mahdist Imam), and convinced that Egypt was about to step in, preferred the seizure of power by the army on 17 November, the Commander-in-Chief, Ibrāhīm 'Abbūd, becoming President of the Supreme Council.

In general the new régime turned to orthodox economic measures to restore the finances and undertook a serious study of development projects which resulted in a ten-year plan for 1960 to 1971. The Nile Waters Agreement of 1959 with Egypt made new but expensive irrigation projects possible, but the compensation paid for the resettlement of the population of Wadi Halfa, flooded by the High Dam at Aswan, did not cover the cost. After a brief power struggle within the army there was public order for several years; there was some use of torture against communists, and most of the politicians protested and were interned in Juba for a time. On the whole, the régime was not really repressive, and it permitted a great deal of criticism. The government was in conflict with students in its last year, and tried ineffectively to extend its control over the University of Khartoum. Its most obvious failures were in its constitutional policies (a form of 'pyramidal' democracy was being introduced in its last years) and in its policies towards the south.

In the south the recommendations of an earlier international commission to readopt Arabic were put into effect from 1957 onwards, and Catholic missionaries in particular resented the absorption of church schools into a government education system. The authorities were unfamiliar with Catholic objections to undenominational education, so that mutual suspicion multiplied—suspicion on the one side of the imperialist interference of foreigners, and on the other of an Islamic persecution. Things got worse under the military régime. Senior officials were aggressive. Muslim religious schools were given the same assistance as mission schools had had under the Condominium. Restrictions on missionary activities in 1961 and the Regulating Act of 1962 gave colour to allegations of religious discrimination. The Government believed that southern politicians had allowed themselves to be manoeuvred by Catholic missionaries, and in 1964, believing that there was sufficient evidence that material help had been given to outlaws under arms, expelled all missionaries from the south (272 Catholics and 28 Protestants; the Catholics had done less to Sudanise than the Protestants). Meanwhile in 1961 a number of the mutineers arrested in 1955 were amnestied, and joined their old comrades in revolt; after a lull, the guerillas reappeared in the autumn of 1963, reorganised under the name of Anya-Nya, and early in 1964 threatened Wau, the capital of Bahr-al-Ghazal province. The régime began to pour in money and arms. Criticism of this in the north was the immediate occasion of the revolution of October 1964, when two students were killed in the course of a banned meeting.

Mounting pressure culminated in a national strike, extending to government officials, and it succeeded in expelling the military régime, because most officers were at one with their civilian relatives, and because the leading officers of the régime were unwilling to push the issue to the limit. The movement was supported by the Deputy Chief Justice, Babikr Awadalla, but its origins were spontaneous. On the 'night of the counter-revolution' the people came out into the streets in their thousands to defend the revolution, which they mistakenly believed to be threatened by an army counter-coup. A caretaker government was formed under Sirr al-Khatam al-Khalifa, a senior educationalist who believed that his function was to prepare a return to parliamentary democracy. The various party interests soon began to exploit a situation that they had not created.

Relations between northerners and southerners grew worse when a large group of southerners rioted in central Khartoum, and the same night a great number of southerners were murdered, so that all the southerners in the capital had to be brought into a football stadium for protection. Many returned to the south, where they joined the Anya-Nya or took to looting on their own account. The south had been a principal cause of the revolution, and a serious attempt to clear the ground for a settlement was made at the

Round Table Conference held in March 1965. It achieved nothing concrete, and the Anya-Nya maintained their activities throughout, so to many northerners it was disappointing; but this was largely because they had always tended to minimise the difficulties, and it was useful that the southerners said what they thought frankly, freely and publicly.

In the meantime the old political parties had edged out the progressives and revolutionaries who would have liked to see the country permanently under the guidance of the professional groups who had led the revolution. The Mahdists brought large number of Umma supporters to the capital to help force an election. An election was held and the Constituent Assembly formed, with Muhammad Ahmad Mahjūb, an experienced Umma politician of some literary distinction, as Prime Minister, and al-Azhari as Chairman of the Supreme Council. A reaction set in. Former military leaders were released from custody. Reprisals against Anya-Nya activities got out of hand, and numbers of civilians were shot in July and August at Juba and Wau. Later in 1965 the Communist Party was ineffectually banned. It was characteristic of the next few years that a committee drafted an 'Islamic constitution' which was unacceptable to southerners—and to progressives—but which all politicians supported. It was never brought to public test. There was a great deal of political manoeuvring that never reached agreement about the office of President.

Bitter rivalry developed in the Mahdi family and the Umma Party between the new Imam, al-Hādi (his brother al-Siddīq had not long survived their father) and al-Siddīq's son, al-Sādiq, to whom the family qualities of leadership had evidently descended. Mahjūb led a rump of the parliamentary party into opposition on behalf of the Imam, when, in July 1966, the coalition was reconstituted under al-Sādiq. For a brief period al-Sādiq seemed to offer the country the hope of a new approach to politics and a national leadership, but factional interests and his own dependence on sectarian support were too much for him, and after ten months he and Mahjūb again changed places. In December 1967 the PDP, which had boycotted the last election, merged with the NUP as the Democratic Unionist Party. An election was held in May 1968. The two halves of the Umma Party having run against each other (al-Sādiq's group remained the stronger, but he himself was unseated), the DUP had many more seats, although the total Umma vote was the greater. The coalition continued as before. A reconciliation of the two Umma factions came about by slow stages, and was apparently complete in April 1969; its effect on the overall political pattern was still in doubt when, on 25 May, Colonel (later Major-General) Ja'far Muhammad Nimairi announced that a new revolution under army leadership was in control.

If it is premature to evaluate the revolution of 1969, it is useful to consider it in the light of the social and political condition of the country in the later '60s. The basic economy of the Sudan has traditionally been the subsistence farming of millets, together with cattle-raising and camel-breeding in the appropriate areas. This has supported a sparse population in scattered villages, settlement modified by considerable areas of nomadism and semi-nomadism. In the west and east in particular, these conditions have favoured the sects, and people have been slow to realise the benefits they can derive from national politics. The main cash crop is cotton, grown chiefly in the Jazira, the area between the White and Blue Niles in the centre of the country, and farmed largely through a government-owned cooperative scheme. Cotton farming has produced a society comparable to that formed by industry; population is relatively dense, including urban centres of which the greatest is Wad Medani. The tenants hardly constitute a proletariat, since they employ labour; what has been created is an affluent land-using community, acutely conscious of its interests and of the advantage to be derived from political action. In this region, community development and adult education flourish, though the figures for child malnutrition, caused by unwise feeding, not by food shortage, show that learning has limits. In the regions inaccessible to irrigation, there now begins to be some awareness of the extent to which the Nile Valley—the irrigation area which is also the area of ancient civilisation—dominates the country socially and politically. In the rainwater areas the problem is conservation of water (if it did not drain away it would be more than adequate in many areas) and, though there has been a steady and increasing interest in rural water problems under successive governments, the provision of new wells has proved liable to create new areas of erosion. The local demand for regional development is likely to become stronger.

In the cities—Khartoum, with light industry and an international airport, Atbara, the railway centre, and Port Sudan, the only sea port—and even in the various administrative capitals in the provinces, there is a fairly affluent proletariat, able to take up loans on local government house building schemes, already large users of imported consumer goods, and accustomed to take political action based on class or group interests. The national medical service has on the whole been successful in providing good free medical attention (extended to the remoter areas by dispensaries), except in the south, where the fighting closed it down; nursing, unlike doctoring, hardly comes up to international standards, and there is some inevitable tension, in the Sudan as in Britain, between the public interest and the market earning capacity of private doctors. Epidemic control has been excellent, and the public health sector has been expanding. Welfare services, supplemented by private initiatives, are effective within the areas they cover, but, as elsewhere, they do not cover enough and lack co-ordination. All welfare is buttressed by the continuing strength of the extended family, which still gives shelter to the helpless, and, at the other extreme, shields the young graduate from the disadvantages of not finding suitable employment.

The political and religious divisions, of which there is so much evidence, are probably inevitable in a country of immense distances, and reflect differences of social, even more than of economic, development. The progressive trend of thought has always been much opposed to what is made to look like the last vestige of indirect rule, in the so-called 'native administration', which leaves administrative and even judicial powers in the hands of tribal leaders. The retrogressive and the divisive are seen as coinciding. One of the most consistent processes under every régime since independence has been the rapid expansion of national education. If that has meant overcrowding, sometimes gross overcrowding, it is possible to sympathise with the dilemma of a Minister of Education who can only opt for 'quality' by denying some sort of education to large numbers. There are not as many girls' schools as boys', but a comparable rate of expansion has been maintained consistently, and the number of girls at the University of Khartoum has more than trebled in a few years. It is possible to say that women have received emancipation too easily; they have the vote, and had little trouble to get it. In the larger towns at least, they have acquired freedom of movement since independence, almost without realising it. The tawb, which does not veil the face, and is as attractive as the Indian sari, though less practical, is still in use, and a guide to the degree of emancipation is whether it is drawn over the head. Overt quarrels between the Muslim Brothers and the left-wing have been concerned with women's emancipation. The Muslim Sisters, whose aim is to show that women can do everything, but in separation from men, have tried to be as active politically and socially as the Communists, to whom many women's organisations are connected—the first woman MP was a Communist. A career in public life, as a teacher—in the University of Khartoum (which is coeducational) or the school (which is not) —or as a secretary—is open to any girl; many traditional families have been slow to take advantage of some of these opportunities, but reluctance to take advantage of educational opportunity is almost unknown. Women themselves are sometimes reluctant to change the traditional pattern of ways.

The Civil Service which took over from the former administration in 1955 (and the army too) were able and highly trained. Civil servants have since been constantly recruited from the University of Khartoum, with its relatively small student intake and high standards (judged internationally or interculturally). Those who entered the service from secondary or inter-mediate school have had the chance to study at Cairo University (Khartoum branch), where evening classes for a degree in arts, economics or law have benefited many who, having had to go to work, or having failed to qualify for entrance to the University of Khartoum, still thirsted after education and the promotion to which it can lead. This is not to say that Khartoum has neglected its communal responsibilities, and its extra-mural department has expanded rapidly in recent years at all levels, offering advanced diploma work in professional subjects and, at the other extreme, the equivalent of WEA work.

How far is the structure of society in dissolution? Less so than in the West; family, local and even tribal ties remain strong, and most Sudanese, however revolutionary, want to retain the traditional humane element. Religion and sectarianism are by no means equated; there are both religious leaders and ordinary educated believers who see sectarianism as divisive and harmful. Most Sudanese respected most of the political leaders personally, but used to believe that the practice of politics, and to a lesser extent of administration, was corrupt. This may have been true in certain almost traditional matters; but corruption was most often 'altruistic', that is, on behalf of somebody else; and, though mutual back-scratching is not admir-able, it is not a rat-race. The warmth and humanity of the Sudanese has been unimpaired by modern pressures.

In the south, the Government had shown a genuine desire for reconcilia-tion, and the resettlement of refugees in 'peace villages' was successful within very strict limits. The unhappy villagers have never been allowed to be neutral; either the Anya-Nya or the army might punish them for helping the other. The Anya-Nya have always been intransigent, and seem not to want to negotiate; they have not been successful enough for long enough over a large enough area to be able to negotiate from strength; but the same can be said of the Government, which had real success in normalising large areas of the Upper Nile and Bahr al-Ghazal provinces for much of the time, but never wholly quietened Equatoria. The southern politicians in exile do not seem to command support, and the provisional government of 'the Nile' (1969) claims to be located on Sudanese soil, and has the approval of the Anya-Nya.

The revolution of May 1969 seems to fit logically into the processes of

Sudanese history. The support of members of the Communist Party caused initial alarm, but the régime seems determined to maintain its dissolution of all the old parties, without exception. It looks to renew the promise of October 1964, and its first act was to nominate civilian ministers, of whom the most senior was Babikr Awadalla. How the inevitable tensions will be solved, we do not know; but the régime has consistently adopted the 'progressive' attitude on all issues. The nationalisation of foreign firms, which had been under discussion for many years, was announced on the first anniversary of the régime in May 1970. In aligning itself with the UAR[1] (and in the posthumous military promotion of Aly 'Abd al-Latif), the régime has identified itself with the revolutionary sympathy for Egypt shown during the condominium period. It is certainly anti-Mahdist, perhaps (like the first Mahdi) anti-sectarian. Al-Sādiq al-Mahdi was early placed under arrest, and has since been exiled to Egypt. The Imam died as a result of the military attack on Aba island—where he had made himself a 'prisoner of the Vatican'—in March 1970, an attack provoked by Ansar resistance to the régime, but unexpectedly drastic; simultaneous fighting in Omdurman had a bitterness rare in the Sudan. Only time will tell whether these episodes mark the end of sectarianism.

The Anya-Nya continue on their irrepressible course, although Nimairi, who has had experience as a commander in the south, realises that they have greatly contributed to the failure of past régimes. The establishment of a Ministry for Southern Affairs, under a southern minister and staffed by southern civil servants, is important. No one politician commands the confidence of the people of the south, but the increasing extent to which southern officials and professional men in the north are gaining the respect which their predecessors failed to earn is a new factor in the long history of relations between two parts of a nation. The Minister, Joseph Garang, has said that the problem is not racial or religious, but one of equality of opportunity and of development, and this may ultimately prove to be a formula acceptable to educated opinion on both sides.

Nimairi sees himself in a line of tradition from those who fought for independence against British rule, and those who struggled against the reactionary military dictatorship and the corrupt and reactionary political parties, all now defunct, to create a new society. This is how he puts it; but it is in some such terms that his countrymen will finally evaluate his government.

FURTHER READING

Abd al-Rahim, M. *Imperialism and Nationalism in the Sudan*, Oxford Univ. Press, London, 1969.

Albino, O. *The Sudan—A Southern Viewpoint*, Oxford Univ. Press, London, 1970.

Bakheit, G. M. A. *Communist Activities in the Middle East between 1919 and 1927*, Khartoum, 1968.

Beshir, M. O. *The Southern Sudan: Background to Conflict*, C. Hurst, London, 1968; Praeger, New York, 1968.

Fadl, El S. H. *Their Finest Days*, Rex Collings, London, 1969.

Hassan, Yusuf Fadl. *The Arabs and the Sudan*, Edinburgh Univ. Press, Edinburgh, 1967.

Henderson, K. D. D. *Sudan Republic*, Ernest Benn, London, 1965; Praeger, New York, 1966.

[1] In November 1970 Sudan decided to form a federation with the UAR and Libya linking the three countries.

Hill, R. *Egypt in the Sudan, 1820–1881*, Oxford Univ. Press, London and New York, 1959.
Hill, R. *Slatin Pasha*, Oxford Univ. Press, London, 1964 and New York, 1965.
Holt, P. M. *The Mahdist State in the Sudan*, Oxford Univ. Press, London and New York, 1958.
Holt, P. M. *A Modern History of the Sudan*, Weidenfeld and Nicolson, London, 1961; Praeger, New York, 1963.

NORMAN DANIEL. On the staff of the British Council since 1947, working chiefly in the Middle East. Has spent eight years in Baghdad, fifteen months in Beirut and seven years in Khartoum. Among his publications are *Islam and the West, the Making of an Image* (1960) and *Islam, Europe and Empire* (1966). He is currently engaged on a study of cultural barriers to communications and exchange. He and his wife have always taken a special interest in the Arab World, where they have been very happy, and have one son, in an English police force.

SYRIAN ARAB REPUBLIC

ABBAS KELIDAR

EARLY HISTORY

SYRIA has always occupied a prominent place in the history of the Middle East. Its geographical and therefore strategic position has made it an attractive target as a trans-continental bridge for the movement of invading armies, as well as that of peoples from both the East and the West. Successive waves of conquest have left their cultural impressions and Syria has been able to absorb them all and in many cases to contribute to them. At one period or another, the Egyptians, Babylonians, Hittites, Greeks, Romans, Arabs and Turks have all ruled the country.

In the seventh century Damascus, the capital of Syria, fell to the invading Muslim army from Arabia. This meant the introduction of a new religion, Islam, and a new language, Arabic, constituting a new culture which has dominated the region to the present day. Within 30 years of the fall of Damascus to the Muslim Arabs the city became the capital of an empire extending from North Africa in the west to India in the east. This was the Umayyad Empire. The ease with which the Syrians accommodated themselves to the new religious and social patterns made them the masters of the Empire and their cities became great political and commercial centres. In many ways Umayyad rule emphasised Arab supremacy within Islam and therefore the Umayyad period was to have an important bearing on the movement for national revival that occurred in the 19th and 20th centuries. However, after a hundred years of supremacy Damascus was replaced by Baghdad as the centre of the Muslim Empire under the 'Abbasids.

As the 'Abbasid Empire began to disintegrate towards the end of the tenth century, Syria fell under other domination. The crusaders occupied parts of the country and established a number of kingdoms. They were driven out by the famous folk-hero of Muslim history, Salah al-Din al-Ayubi (Saladin), who united Syria with Egypt. This unity was revived by the Mamelukes of Egypt in 1260 when they incorporated Syria with their Egyptian domain. In the 16th century the Ottoman Turks occupied the country and Syria remained part of the Ottoman Empire until the end of World War I.

FOREIGN INFLUENCES

The decline of Ottoman power in the 18th and 19th centuries weakened the Turkish hold on the Arab provinces and made them the object of European

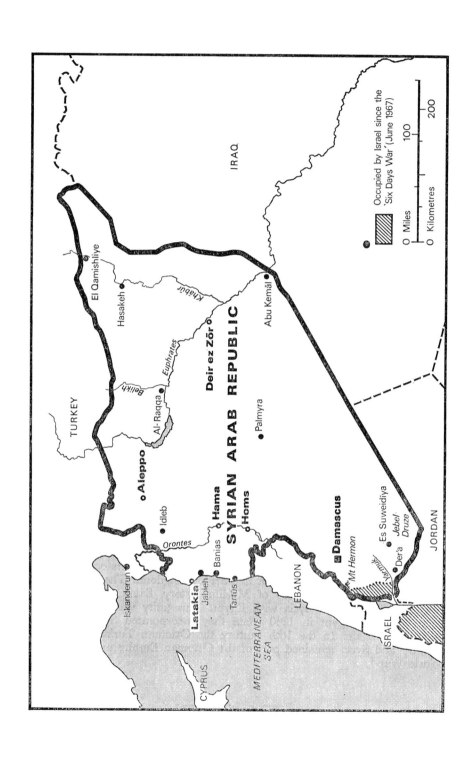

Occupied by Israel since the 'Six Days War' (June 1967)

TURKEY

IRAQ

El Qamishliye
Hasakeh
Khabur

Abu Kemāl

Deir ez Zōr

SYRIAN ARAB REPUBLIC

Euphrates
Belikh
Al-Raqqa

Aleppo
Idleb

Palmyra

Orontes

Hama
Homs

Damascus

Es Suweidiya
Jebel Druze
Der'a

JORDAN

Iskanderun
Latakia
Jableh
Banias
Tartūs

Mt Hermon

LEBANON

ISRAEL

MEDITERRANEAN SEA

CYPRUS

0 Miles   100
0 Kilometres   100   200

penetration. This took various forms, the most important of which were the extra-territorial rights secured by the Powers and known as the Capitulations. In Syria, France held a paramount position. In addition to her status as the protector of the rather large Christian Maronite community, France enjoyed considerable influence in the economic and educational spheres. But she was not alone. Russia claimed responsibility for the Christian Orthodox community while Britain did the same for the Jewish and Druze communities. Egypt continued to express an interest in Syrian affairs. In 1831 Muhammad Aly, the unchallenged ruler of Egypt, invaded Syria and appointed his son Ibrahim Pasha as governor. Ibrahim ruled the country from 1831–40, and these years were important for the Syrians. After years of Ottoman neglect, the Egyptians had some success in the introduction of stable government and economic reform. Moreover, Egyptian rule marked the first step which eventually led to the separation of the Arab countries from Turkey. Ibrahim, it seems, was encouraged by the Syrian Arabs to restore the caliphate to the Arabs, challenging the pretensions of the Turkish sultans. These ambitions were thwarted by an Anglo-Turkish agreement, whereby Ibrahim was forced to return to Egypt and Ottoman rule was restored to Syria.

The impact of the West soon made itself felt, particularly in the field of education. The missionary schools set up to teach the new learning and science of Europe attracted a number of young men, mainly Christians, whose mental and intellectual background was more receptive to the new ideas. They were to become the precursors of a new line of thought. They were assisted by the introduction of the vernacular Press and the spread of newspapers in influencing their Muslim compatriots. The rediscovery and printing of old Arabic manuscripts prompted the Muslim Arabs to examine their own condition. The cultural revival was to act as a stimulant to the religious reform movement led by Afghani and his Egyptian disciple Muhammad Abduh. A number of Syrian writers were influenced by their teaching such as Rashid Rida and Abd al-Rahman al-Kawakibi, both of whom had to leave Syria because of Turkish oppression and censorship and seek safety in British Egypt. The object of the reform movement was to strengthen the fabric of Muslim society and rejuvenate Islam so that the European onslaught on its basic tenets could be resisted.

NATIONAL STIRRINGS

It was in this field that Syria had come to occupy a leading position in the reawakening of the Arab world when the European ideas of nationalism and national self-determination began to gain a foothold in the multi-national Ottoman Empire. Although the Arab revivalist movement had some nationalist inclination it was by no means identical with the nationalist movement which dominated the politics of Central Europe at the time. However, the rise of the Young Turks in 1908 and their attempt to impose Turkish domination on the non-Turkish elements of the Empire through a policy of Turkification encouraged the Arabs, and particularly the Syrians, to express a more forthright sense of community and a corporate assertion of their national identity. Thus Syria became the centre of Arab agitation against the rule of the Young Turks and a breeding ground for political intrigue and secret societies. The aim of this kind of political activity was not so much the independence of the Arabs from the Turkish Empire as the decentralisation of authority and a share in political power.

The implications of the struggle for national liberation from the Turks were unpleasant for the Arabs since such a struggle would involve fighting against their co-religionists and would bring them into open rebellion against their caliph, the Turkish sultan, with the infidel West as their ally. It is not surprising therefore that the Arab demand for independence was muted and the Arab attitude ambivalent at the outbreak of hostilities in 1914. The nationalists wanted to neutralise the effect of the Sultan's call for a holy war (*jihad*) by associating their movement with some religious dignitaries. The Allies, especially Britain, who were concerned about the impact which such a call by the Sultan might have on the Muslims under their control, sought the same objective. None was better suited for the purpose than the guardian of the holy cities of Islam, Sharif Husain of Mecca. Thus the Sharif became Britain's choice as well as that of the leaders of the Arab independence movement. In the ensuing Husain-McMahon correspondence, the Sharif tried to extract a price for Arab co-operation against Turkey. The price was Arab independence. Though the coastal strip of Syria was excluded from the territory where the Arabs would set up their own state, Britain agreed that the Arabs would have the rest of the region as their own. Thus when the Arabs with their army entered Damascus in October 1918, they set up an Arab administration and declared Syria independent.

ANGLO-FRENCH PARTITION

Notwithstanding the terms of the controversial Husain-McMahon correspondence, the destiny of the Arab countries was in fact to be decided by the diplomatic bargaining, the conflicting promises and agreements which had been made during the war. The first and most important of these was the Sykes-Picot agreement made between Britain and France in 1916. It provided for the establishment in the Arab world of British and French zones, with an independent Arab state or federation of states divided into British and French spheres of influence. Palestine was to be an international zone. The second, which in the end was to have a greater and more dramatic effect on the destiny of the whole region, was the Balfour Declaration of 1917 promising the Jews a 'national home' in Palestine.

After the Turkish defeat Syria was in the hands of the British military, with a small French force on the coast and the army of the Sharif in the interior. The Peace Conference of 1919 decided that the Arab provinces of the defunct Ottoman Empire should be completely detached from Turkey. Instead of declaring them independent, however, the conference announced the adoption of the mandate system for some of them, a kind of trusteeship designed to lead to complete self-government and independence. Differences between Britain and France over the boundaries of the mandated territories were resolved by the agreement of San Remo in 1920, which allotted the mandate for Syria and Lebanon to France. In the meantime an Arab congress meeting in Damascus offered the crown of Syria to Amir Faisal, the second son of the Sharif, who accepted it. This action was repudiated by both Britain and France. Accordingly British troops were withdrawn and France issued an ultimatum to Faisal. A French force, after engaging Syrian troops at Maysalun, entered the capital and Faisal was forced to withdraw. A year later he became King of Iraq.

The Arabs felt that they had been betrayed by their Western allies; the charge of bad faith and betrayal was nurtured and grew, and was greatly strengthened by subsequent events in the region. The immediate reaction to the division of the Arab world into separate political entities was a cry for unity. The call for unity was expressed mainly in the Fertile Crescent, where some historical precedent for a united Arab state could be found, in Syria under the Umayyads and in Iraq under the 'Abbasids. Thus Baghdad and Damascus respectively became the advocates of Arab unity until they were overshadowed by Cairo in the 1950s. The desire for unity was strengthened by the Arab failure to resist European influence and aggravated by the loss of Palestine in 1948.

THE FRENCH MANDATE

The text of the Mandate for Syria was approved by the League of Nations in 1923, but France had started to organise the territory three years earlier. The French followed a deliberate policy of disrupting whatever national aspirations the Syrians might have entertained as a body politic. France was to accord special administrative status to the various sections of the population. The parochial feelings and the distinctive characteristics of each community were encouraged by the French authorities, and the image of France as protector and guide was fostered. Thus in 1920 an enlarged state of the Lebanon, with a majority of Christian Maronites was created, and in 1926 this became the Republic of Lebanon. The separation of Lebanon was made to safeguard the status of the Christian minority of Syria, but the population of the country was a conglomeration of minorities. There were the Druzes, the Alawites, the Kurds, the Armenians, and the Turks, in addition to the Sunni Muslim majority. Thus the territory was divided into five separate administrative units: the state of Syria incorporating Damascus and Aleppo, the state of Jabal Druze, the state of the Alawites in Latakia, a special administration for the Jazira region, and finally an autonomous government for the Sanjaq of Alexandretta. This organisation continued until 1936 when all the other regions were incorporated into Syria with the exception of Alexandretta, which was ceded by France to Turkey in 1938. In 1939, however, the original status of the various regions was restored following France's failure to ratify the Franco-Syrian Treaty of 1936. They were merged into Syria once more in 1942 following the British occupation of the country a year earlier.

The majority of Syrians made no secret of their opposition to France's policy. The Sunni Arabs, who held nationalist views, were most outspoken in their disapproval of the subdivision of their country into a number of principalities dependent on France. They campaigned for the unity of all French-mandated territory, the achievement of self-government and the unity and independence of the Arab world. They regarded all Syrians, whether they were Alawites, Christians, or Druzes, as being essentially Arab with distinctive social or religious customs due mainly to historical circumstances and geographical isolation. They resented the French measures because they were inimical to the development of an Arab Syrian nation.

While the situation in the Alawite state remained quiet, nationalist agitation in the state of Syria and French mismanagement in the Jabal Druze culminated in 1925 in a general insurrection against French rule. In the Jabal the revolt taught the French not to interfere in the social customs of the Druze community, while in Syria, where the opposition was well organised and efficiently managed by the independence movement, the National Bloc, the rebellion produced political changes. France took the first steps that were to lead in the end to self-government. The French High Commissioner ordered elections to be held and declared to the Permanent Mandate Commission that the French Government intended to negotiate a Franco-Syrian treaty similar to the Anglo-Iraqi treaty of 1922. The elections were held in July 1927 and most of the elected deputies belonged to the National Bloc. This organisation was more of a nationalist and independence movement than a political party and therefore did not possess any coherent political programme. It was an alliance of leading individuals predisposed to quarrel among themselves, not a cohesive movement. When the Assembly met, one member of the Bloc (Hashim al-Atasi) was elected Speaker and another chairman of the Constitutional Commission.

However, differences soon arose between the nationalists and the High Commissioner over the terms of the proposed constitution. The divergence of views could not be amicably resolved and the Assembly was dissolved by the French authorities. The High Commissioner issued a constitution for Syria without the offending clauses. Fresh elections were held in 1932 under the provisions of the new constitution. The majority in the new chamber were moderates, but the nationalist minority dominated the proceedings. Negotiations to conclude a treaty of alliance between the Syrian government and France started, but soon broke down over nationalist insistence that the unity of the whole of Syria should be proclaimed, France wishing to maintain the special régimes in the various regions.

In 1935 the intensification of nationalist fervour in Syria forced France to give way. A nationalist delegation arrived in Paris in 1936 to negotiate a new treaty. Under its provisions the unity of all three states, Syria, Latakia and Jabal Druze as well as the Jazira region was to be acknowledged. The treaty also provided for the transfer to the Syrian government of the rights and obligations resulting from formal agreements made by France in the name of Syria once the mandate ceased to exist and Syria was admitted to the League of Nations. Though the terms of the treaty were favourably received by the majority of Syrians and Frenchmen alike, there was some opposition to it in both countries. In Syria the extreme nationalists saw the treaty as an infringement of complete independence since it did not provide for the evacuation of French troops. In France opposition was expressed on the grounds that insufficient guarantees were given for the protection of minorities in the proposed new state. While the Syrian government succeeded in ratifying the treaty, the French found it increasingly difficult to do so. Renewed negotiations led to further concessions on the part of the Syrians but these concessions were unacceptable to the radical wing of the National Bloc, led by Shukri al-Quwatly, and caused a split in the independence movement. The French Government, faced with strong parliamentary opposition, decided to abandon the treaty. At the beginning of 1939 the French High Commissioner in Syria had to employ stringent measures to control nationalist agitation by restoring to Latakia and the Jabal their separate administration. Thus Syria had gone full circle in her search for political independence.

INDEPENDENCE ACHIEVED

The capitulation of France soon after the beginning of World War II was accompanied by the growth and spread of German influence in the area. The activities of German agents in Syria in support of the Rashid Aly régime in Iraq, contrary to the terms of the Franco-German Armistice, prompted the British military authorities in the Middle East to secure Syria against German encroachment and therefore led to the occupation of the country by a combined force of British and Free French troops. In a joint declaration the British and the Free French stated to the Syrians and Lebanese 'you will therefore be from henceforward sovereign and independent peoples and you will be able either to form yourselves into separate states or to unite into a single state'. There followed a period of negotiation between the French authorities and the government of Syria. Economic, administrative, and military measures taken during the war delayed the granting of independence and gave rise to considerable political discontent. The dissatisfaction led to the re-emergence of the National Bloc under Quwatli to resume the struggle for the liberation of Syria. In 1943 new elections were held which resulted in an overwhelming majority for the National Bloc. The victory of the Bloc was more complete in Damascus than in Aleppo where there was a split in the nationalist ranks. However in August 1943 the new Chamber met and elected Quwatli President of the Syrian Republic. The French continued to control the armed forces and tried to use this as a bargaining counter to compel the Syrian government to conclude a treaty. The Syrians however were reluctant to do so because of their earlier experience. The movement of some French troops from the Lebanese coast to Syria and the bombardment of Damascus in May 1945 led to the intervention of Britain, which issued an ultimatum to the French to cease fire. The French complied and withdrew to their barracks. This was virtually the end of French rule in Syria. In 1946, agreement was reached between Britain and France on the simultaneous withdrawal of all troops from the territory. In the same year Syria joined the United Nations and became a full member of the Arab League.

POST-INDEPENDENCE FACTIONALISM

Independent Syria has not had a very happy career. By 1946 the country had not achieved the social cohesion among its religious, tribal and ethnic groups which was essential for the formation of a modern nation. There were too many disruptive local forces hindering the integration of the minorities into a Syrian nation. The special treatment accorded by the French to the Druzes and the Alawites, and the creation of a predominantly Christian Greater Lebanon, left their mark on the country. While independence has submerged their differences to a certain extent, the ineptness of the leaders of the independence movement led to the emergence of a different kind of factionalism. This was characterised by the formation of political parties. The leaders of the nationalist movement were drawn from all parts of the country and had divergent parochial interests. They agreed to sink their differences in order to fight the French for the independence of their country. When independence was achieved, the movement lost its cohesion and the leaders were divided on personal grounds rather than over questions of policy.

The split lay in the regional rivalry between Aleppo and Damascus and took effect when the leaders of the nationalist movement from Aleppo broke away from the national leadership of President Quwatli based on the city of Damascus. The split was formalised in the election of 1947 when the Aleppo faction organised itself into the People's Party. The party represented the business interests of the merchants and bankers of Aleppo, to whom Mosul and Baghdad seemed closer and more familiar places than Damascus. This factionalism was aggravated by the interplay of Arab politics on the wider scene. In the struggle between Baghdad and Cairo for the unity and the leadership of the Arab countries the people's Party tended to support Iraq's claim, while the Quwatli faction, organised in the National Party, advocated solidarity with the Cairo-Riyadh alliance. Neither grouping had the internal political cohesion to turn it into a viable political organisation and both depended on the personal followings of their leaders. In addition to these traditional parties there were two political organisations advocating different types of nationalism. The first and less significant one was the Syrian National Social Party, commonly known as the PPS (*Partie Populaire Syrienne*), formed by Antoun Saada, a Lebanese Christian, in 1932 and operating mainly as a clandestine organisation. It was influenced by the ideas of national socialism which dominated European politics in the 1930s, and sought the unification of geographical Syria, including Iraq. The party expressed its belief in the existence of a Syrian nation, as opposed to Arab nationalism. The second was the Ba'ath Party, which came to play a prominent role not only in the politics of Syria but of the whole region. The Party was created by two Damascus secondary school teachers, Michel Aflaq and Salah al-Bitar, in 1943. In 1953 it merged with the Socialist Party of Akram al-Hawrani to constitute the Arab Ba'ath Socialist Party. The ideology of the party is derived from the mainstream of Arab nationalist thought. It seeks the unity of the Arab countries and the creation of an Arab nation. It advocates the introduction of socialism and a more equitable distribution of national wealth. Finally the party actively concerns itself with the removal of the last vestiges of Western imperialism in the Arab world, asserting positive neutralism as the basis of its foreign policy. Beside these nationalist parties there is the Syrian Communist Party, led by the most prominent Arab Communist, Khalid Bakdash.

Following the Arab-Israeli war of 1948, in which the Arabs failed to prevent the emergence of the State of Israel, and with the economic situation deteriorating amid rumours of corruption in high places, the Syrian military led by Colonel Husni al-Za'im seized power in March 1949. Under Za'im and the subsequent régimes Syria became a battleground for inter-Arab rivalry and intrigue. Za'im wavered between unity with Iraq and support for the Cairo-Riyad alliance. He chose alliance with Egypt but his break with Iraq led to another *coup* organised by the Syrian supporters of unity with Iraq in August 1949. The leader of the counter-*coup*, Sami al-Hannawi, announced the withdrawal of the army from politics and invited the veteran Hashim al-Atasi to assume the presidency. The government was dominated by the People's party, the advocates of union with Iraq. The leaders of the Ba'ath, Aflaq and Hawrani, became Ministers of Education and Agriculture respectively. However, when talks on union with Iraq were under way, the Ba'ath leaders opposed such a move on the grounds that Syrian Republican institutions should not be exchanged for Iraq's monarchy, and the status of Independent Syria should not be jeopardised by Iraq's obligation to Britain under the Anglo-Iraqi Treaty of 1930. Britain herself was not enthusiastic about the union between the two countries, which threatened her good relations with France and with Iraq's Arab rivals, Egypt and Saudi Arabia. Subjected to conflicting external and internal pressures, the government lapsed into indecision and the whole plan was shelved when the régime was overthrown by Colonel Adib Shishakli in December 1949.

SYRIA IN THE COLD WAR

Shishakli was in effective control of Syria for four years. In 1952 he abolished the Constitution of 1950 and suspended all political parties to make way for a presidential system of government, encouraging the formation of a new political organisation, the Arab Liberation Movement. His régime was marked by relative tranquillity and the completion of several economic projects in the country. Shishakli's reliance on Egypt and Saudi Arabia induced Iraq and his Syrian opponents to engineer a revolt in Jabal Druze. This culminated in an army insurrection in the Aleppo region which led to his eventual downfall in 1954.

The fall of Shishakli was followed by the restoration of republican parliamentary rule. Fresh elections were held which produced a national assembly representing the full spectrum of Syrian politics. Though the majority of deputies were Independents, the Ba'ath Party for the first time scored a remarkable popular success when about 20 of its members and sympathisers were elected. Under such circumstances the Government had to be an unstable coalition in a period when decisive action was required. In the Dulles era, cold war politics were the predominant feature of the international scene. While the West was setting up a defensive organisation to contain the march of international communism, the communist countries were bent on undermining Western influence. Arab politics were polarised between a pro-West Iraq under the monarchy and a neutralist Egypt under the leadership of Nasser's Free Officers. After a year of indecision, Syria began to drift towards Egypt under the influence of the Ba'ath leaders. Quwatli was elected to the presidency in 1955 and an economic and defence organisation was formed between Syria, Egypt, and Saudi Arabia as a counter-balance to the Baghdad Pact, which Iraq had formed with Turkey, Iran and Pakistan, backed by Britain and the United States. This marked a turning point in Syrian politics. In 1956 Syria concluded an arms deal with Czechoslovakia similar to the Egyptian-Czech deal made a year earlier which broke the Western monopoly of arms supply to the Arab states. Inside Syria the Ba'ath had been consolidating its position in the armed forces following the assassination of Adnan al-Malki, the Assistant Chief of Staff and a Ba'athist sympathiser, by a member of the PPS. The assassination made a purge of the military opponents of the Ba'ath possible. All these moves were viewed with considerable alarm in Baghdad as well as Washington. The Iraqis were concerned about the flow of their oil exports through Syria and therefore wanted to secure a friendly régime there; they also shared the American concern about communist penetration in the Arab world. They supported the organisation of a *coup* in Syria, probably to coincide with the Israeli-Anglo-French armed intervention in Egypt following the nationalisation of the Suez Canal. But the *coup* did not succeed and the ringleaders were arrested.

THE UNITED ARAB REPUBLIC

The aftermath of the armed intervention in Egypt saw the emergence of Nasser as an Arab national hero. In Syria the beginning of 1957 saw the rise of a new parliamentary group with a neutralist and radical nationalist programme emulating the policies of the Egyptian leader. Like Egypt, Syria rejected the Eisenhower Doctrine and strengthened her relations with the Soviet bloc. The Americans became so concerned about the growth of Soviet influence in Syria as to regard its development in the country as a danger to the security of Turkey and Iraq. By the end of the year Nasser had gained sufficient support in Syria to make the union of the two countries into the United Arab Republic possible.

The union was effected, at the request of the Syrians, in February 1958. Syria became the northern region of the UAR with an executive council administering the country and a joint Syrian-Egyptian cabinet under President Nasser in Cairo. The union lasted only three years. The reasons for the failure are manifold but there is little doubt that the harsh economic measures introduced into Syria to bring her economy in line with that of Egypt were chiefly to blame. Syria's interests lay in free trade and an open economy, while Egypt's lay in protection and nationalisation. Economic stringency and Egyptian mismanagement led to a *coup d'état* in Damascus and the secession of Syria from the union in September 1961.

The secessionist régime was overthrown in its turn by a military *coup* led by Ba'athist officers in March 1963, a month after Iraqi Ba'athists had ousted the Qasim régime in Baghdad. In April 1963 talks were initiated between Iraq, Syria and Egypt with a view to setting on foot a tripartite union, but the talks proved to be inconclusive. Disillusioned by the bitter experience of Syria's secession from the UAR, Nasser determined to concentrate on building up a Socialist Egypt and refused to co-operate with the Ba'athists again. The failure of the talks led to considerable recrimination between the two sides. The Syrians accused the Egyptian leader of wanting to dominate the union, while the Egyptians charged the Ba'athists with opportunism. Faced with considerable external and internal pressure the Ba'athists of both Syria and Iraq drew closer and concluded a joint defence pact in October 1963. The pact lapsed a month later when President Arif, supported by Army officers, ousted the Ba'athist régime in Baghdad.

RECENT DEVELOPMENTS

Ever since March 1963 Syria has been governed by the Ba'ath Party, but this did not interrupt the cycle of *coup* and counter-*coup* which for so long has characterised Syrian politics. Military intervention in politics breeds instability, and this in Syria has been aggravated by the vagueness of the Ba'ath ideology. The vague and often simplistic slogans of the Party have led the leaders of the Ba'ath, whether military or civilian, to interpret the policies of the party in different ways; this in turn has caused the party to degenerate into a set of rival factions, ranging from the traditional nationalist to the orthodox Marxist, which compete with each other for political power. Thus three years after the establishment of Ba'athist rule under Amin al-Hafiz and the introduction of a provisional constitution which authorised the creation of a national assembly, the radical wing of the party seized power in February 1966, causing a breach between the Syrian Regional Command of the Ba'ath and the party's Pan-Arab leadership.

Since 1966 the party has been plagued by internal discussions between the nationalists, led by Hafiz Assad, and the doctrinaires, led by Salah Jadid. And on 13 November 1970 a bloodless *coup* was staged by the military wing of the party, led by Assad.

Notwithstanding these conflicts, Ba'athist Syria has seen herself as constituting the vanguard of the Arab socialist revolution and has waged war on her opponents. These have been identified as the 'reactionaries' and include all hereditary monarchs, oligarchic political leaders, wealthy landowners and businessmen. And although Ba'athist Syria has remained the odd man out among the Arab states in their unrelenting war against Israel, she has consistently acted as the pacemaker with regard to the Palestine problem. The Syrians have opposed the summit conferences of the Arab Heads of State because they saw the futility of such gatherings, which in most cases were designed to contain the Syrians by committing them to a unified Arab policy. Ever since March 1963 when the Ba'athists came to power, Syria has been calling for the complete mobilisation of Arab resources—human and material—and advocating a policy of total confrontation with Israel. The defeat of 1967 seems to have reinforced the Syrians' belief in the soundness of their policy and thus increased their intransigence. They were the first among the Arabs to espouse the Palestinian liberation movement and therefore managed to turn the slogan of 'People's war' into something of a living reality.

Contemporary Social and Economic Structure

Syria is a country of striking contrasts. Her cities are among the oldest in the world and yet the structure of her society is still predominantly tribal and archaic. Her population of about six million is divided into many ethnic and religious groups : Arabs, Kurds and Turkomans, among whom there are Sunni Muslims, Druzes, Alawites, Ismailis, and Christians of many denominations. The great majority speak Arabic, which is the official language of the country.

For the purpose of local administration, the country is divided into nine provinces (*Muhafazat*), with a special status for the capital, Damascus. These provinces are subdivided into smaller administrative units, each responsible to the Ministry of the Interior. There are 36 districts (*qada*) and 92 sub-districts (*nahiya*).

Until recently the most powerful and coherent social groups in Syrian society have been the landowners, the tribal and feudal chiefs, and the merchant communities of Damascus and Aleppo. However, the rise, after World War II, of a new social element, namely the intelligentsia (teachers, doctors, lawyers, army officers and students), came to challenge the authority of the traditional ruling groups and supplant their political and social influence. No political group has been more active in this field than the ruling Ba'ath Party. The Ba'ath has always advocated the introduction of measures to limit the ownership of agricultural land and to nationalise industry. In many instances these measures were designed to undermine the basis of power and support of the feudal and traditional leaders of Syrian society.

These policies, coupled with the principle of 'self-management' in industry and agriculture endorsed by the sixth congress of the Ba'ath Party in 1963, constitute the basis of Syrian socialism. Thus when the Ba'ath secured power in 1963 it embarked on the implementation of its socialist programme. In May it nationalised the Arab-owned banks (foreign banks had been nationalised under the UAR) and amalgamated them in larger units under new management. Throughout 1964 a series of nationalisation decrees were announced, culminating in the takeover of about 100 industrial establishments in January 1965 which included textiles, cement, sugar, canning and food production, dyes, chemicals and soap. New boards were appointed to manage these industries, representing the employees, the Government, the Trade Unions, and the Ba'ath Party. In February the control of all imports was placed under the official Import and Export Organisation to administer Syria's internal trade, revoking the privately licensed companies.

An attempt to introduce land reform was first made in 1951 when Shishakli made the distribution of government-owned land among the peasants possible. However it was under the UAR that radical measures were taken to make the economies of the two countries, Egypt and Syria, uniform. In 1958 the law fixed the maximum limit of land ownership at 80 hectares of irrigated land and 300 hectares of unirrigated land. It was estimated at the time that the total land to be expropriated would be 275 million hectares to be distributed to about 750,000 persons or 150,000 families. The Ba'athist régime reduced the maximum limit to 15 hectares for irrigated land and 55 for non-irrigated. The limitation, however, was to be governed by such factors as the location and fertility of the land and the size of individual holdings therefore varied accordingly.

It is difficult to assess the success or the failure of these measures but there is no doubt about the antagonism they evoked among conservative and religious fundamentalist elements. The opposition acquired religious overtones since the régime derives its main support from the army, which has always been recruited from the religious and ethnic minorities; following the constant purges of its ranks, a group of Alawite officers found themselves in control of the army's higher command. The tension that had been building up ever since the Ba'athist takeover broke out first in disturbances in Homs and Banias in February 1964, spreading to Aleppo in March, and culminating in an open revolt at Hama in April which was violently suppressed. Strikes of shopkeepers and merchants followed in all the major cities, but they were broken by the threat of confiscation.

Syria is a country of considerable economic potential but political instability has not been conducive to economic development. Syria occupies an area totalling 72,000 sq. miles, a third of which consists of desert and mountains; out of an estimated area of 25,000 sq. miles regarded as cultivable, only 10,000 sq. miles are under cultivation. (The projected Euphrates dam, the first stage of which is under construction with Soviet technical and financial assistance, will lead to the irrigation of an estimated 1·5 million acres when completed.)

Syria is basically an agricultural country, where 75% of the total population (though 60% are described as urban) are still engaged in rural and agricultural activities. An extremely fertile strip extends from her borders with the Lebanon in the south into the province of Alexandretta in the north, where olives, tobacco, cotton, soft and hard fruits are grown. To the east of this strip is the mountain range of the anti-Lebanon, beyond which rainfall diminishes progressively until the desert is reached. In this region there is a wide and fertile strip of steppe-land curving northward along the Euphrates valley, where the major crops of grain and cotton are cultivated. Cotton of the medium staple variety has become of great importance to the Syrian economy. The acreage under cotton has been increasing rapidly from 195,000 in 1950 to 740,000 acres in 1966, the production of cotton rising from 35,000 tons in 1950 to 180,000 tons in 1966 (110,00 tons in 1968). Most of it is exported to Western Europe, especially Italy and France, and has assumed considerable significance in Syria's balance of payments. The grain crop too yields an exportable surplus. As with cotton, the grain crops (mainly wheat and barley) are subject to climatic conditions, especially drought, which ruined the crops of the years 1958–61. In 1967, Syria produced over a million tons of wheat and 600,000 tons of barley. Beside grain and cotton, tobacco is grown in the district of Latakia, as well as maize, rice and lentils. Livestock is in abundance. There are more than five million sheep, over half a million goats and about half a million cattle.

Syrian industry has always enjoyed the protection of the state as well as generous credit and tax facilities. Under the present régime industrialisation has become a national slogan. The main industrial centres are Damascus, Aleppo, Homs, and Latakia. The major industries are textile, which is the most important, cement, glass, chromium and asphalt. Of late, oil has become an important industry. Petroleum was first discovered in 1959, when all the concessions were granted to the General Petroleum Organisation. In 1967 the Government made an agreement with the Russians to develop the oil field at Suwaida on behalf of the Petroleum Organisation. A year later Syria started to export her oil when a 400-mile pipeline was built linking the oil field with the Mediterranean port of Tartus. The construction of an oil refinery was completed in 1959 at Homs, and a nitrogenous fertiliser plant has also been built at Homs. Futhermore Syria receives royalties from the passage of pipelines from Iraq and Saudi Arabia carrying oil to the Mediterranean terminals at Banias in Syria and Tripoli and Sidon in the Lebanon. Following protracted negotiations in 1966 the Syrian Government and the Iraq Petroleum Company signed a new agreement which gave Syria an increase of £15 million a year in annual royalties. Syrian industry, though relatively small and very new, has made a significant contribution to the national income and to a predominantly agricultural economy.

Like her cash crops of cotton and grain, Syria's foreign trade is subject to climatic conditions. Nonetheless there has been a notable though not proportional increase in both her exports and imports. While the import bill rose from £S219 million in 1951 to £S1,009 million in 1967, her exports went up from £S271 million in 1951 to £S591 million in 1966. Thus the country has been facing a chronic and increasing deficit in the balance of payments. The wide gap in the Syrian balance of trade is slightly misleading as it does not take account of oil royalties and remittances from Syrians living abroad. The barter trade agreements with the Communist countries further complicate the position. Italy is Syria's largest supplier, while the Lebanon is her most important market. The main item of her import bill is machinery for industrial and agricultural development.

Political instability has inhibited the evolution of viable political institutions in the country and therefore the system of Government is in a state of flux. The constitution of 1964 (which has been suspended since 1966) forms the official basis of the present system. The constitution guarantees basic freedoms to all Syrians but they are restricted in many cases because of the strong opposition facing the régime. The Press for instance is controlled by the Party whose newspapers al-Ba'ath and al-Thawra are the main organs; or by the professional and trade union organisations, which are in turn dominated by the Party members.

The disappearance of the traditional leadership has been accompanied by social reform. Health, education and welfare services have been provided free of charge for the poorer classes. Women have been emancipated and organised, and their gains have been consolidated since they were offered the right to vote in 1950. Workers have organised themselves in trade unions and these are now combined in a National Federation of Trade Unions.

In factories 25% of the annual profit is distributed among the workers employed.

The Syrian Government is spending large sums on economic development and on social services. The second five-year plan (1966–71) provides for the investment of £S4,997 million in agriculture and irrigation, industry and electrification, transport and communications, housing and other public utilities. In 1968 Syria added oil to her exports of agricultural produce (chiefly wheat and cotton). The Euphrates Dam, a major irrigation project which has been under discussion for many years, is now being built with Soviet aid.

In education, Syria has embarked on an ambitious programme of school building whose aim is to ensure universal literacy. There are two universities at Damascus (with 30,000 students and 650 teachers) and Aleppo (with 5,000 students and 30 teachers). In the past, Syria had a tradition of unrest among the student population, but since the assumption of power by the present Ba'athist régime the incidence of strikes and demonstrations has sharply declined.

While Syria has made substantial progress since 1945 in the fields of social and economic development, the country has been particularly subject to the political instability which has been endemic throughout the area during this period. Critical factors here are Syria's central position in the political structure of the Arab world and her deep involvement in the Palestine problem, especially since the Israelis occupied a portion of Syrian territory in 1967. It should be added that outside interference, both by other Arab countries and by the great powers, has constantly hampered the efforts of the Syrians to realise their country's full potential.

FURTHER READING

Antonius, George. *The Arab Awakening*, London, 1938.

Hitti, Philip K. *Syria: A Short History*, Collier & Macmillan, 1961.

Hourani, Albert H. *Arabic Thought in the Liberal Age 1798–1938*, Oxford Univ. Press, London, 1962.

Hourani, Albert H. *Syria and Lebanon—A Political Study*, Oxford Univ. Press, London, 1946.

Kedourie, Elie. *England and the Middle East—The Vital Years 1914–1921*, Bowes & Bowes, London, 1956.

Kerr, Malcolm. *The Arab Cold War 1958–1967*, Oxford Univ. Press, London and New York, 1965.

Longrigg, Stephen H. *Syria and Lebanon under the Mandate*. Oxford Univ. Press, London, 1958.

Seale, Patrick. *The Struggle for Syria*, Oxford Univ. Press, London and New York, 1965.

Torrey, Gordon H. *Syrian Politics and the Military 1945–1958*, Ohio State Univ. Press, 1964.

Ziadeh, Nicola A. *Syria and Lebanon*, Ernest Benn, London, 1957.

Zeine, Zeine N. *The Struggle for Arab Independence*, Khayats, Beirut, 1960.

ABBAS KELIDAR. Lecturer in Middle East Politics at the School of Oriental and African Studies, University of London since 1966. Came to England from his native Iraq in 1955. Contributes to a number of journals.

TURKEY

CLEMENT H. DODD

MODERN Turkey is the heartland of the former Ottoman Empire. One of the world's great empires, it was created by the Muslim Turks on the ruins of Byzantium, which they wore down and eventually overthrew. For many centuries the Ottoman Empire was the nearest outpost of the Islamic Middle East against the Christian West, but since the Atatürk revolution Turkey has regarded herself as essentially part of Europe, almost as an outpost now of the West. We need to look to history to understand this odd twist of fortune, to explain how Muslim Turks of Central Asian origin have come to play an almost Byzantine role.

THE OTTOMAN EMPIRE

The Turks did not suddenly burst forth on the Middle Eastern scene. They entered the Middle East as early as the ninth century, largely as mercenaries and already converted to Islam. Apart from helping to found important dynasties like that of the Seljuks, first in Baghdad and later in Konya, bands of Turks joined in the gradual war of attrition against the declining Byzantine Empire that was being waged by groups of Muslim warriors (*Ghazis*) along the frontiers. These *Ghazis* gradually extended their hold over Asia Minor. One group, led by the Osman (or Ottoman) family stood out as the most successful among them and dominated the rest. Fashioned into a state by former Seljuk and even Byzantine elements, fortified by Islam and constantly invigorated by the addition of booty-seeking Turks, the Ottoman *Ghazi* group crossed into the Balkans. There they defeated all Balkan forces sent against them, turned to consolidate their hold on Anatolia, captured Constantinople and thereby established the Ottoman Empire.

At its greatest extent in the 17th century the Empire stretched from Mecca and Medina to Budapest and included nearly all the North African littoral and large tracts of territory to the north of the Black Sea.

The end of the 17th century, however, also saw the beginning of Ottoman decline. In 1699 the Ottomans lost Hungary and a little later the province of Tabriz to Persia. By the end of the 18th century, when Russia replaced Austria as its chief enemy, the Ottoman Empire lost its lands to the north of the Black Sea. The early 19th century saw the independence of Greece and, for all practical purposes, of Egypt too. Thereafter there was a lull as the western powers struggled with Russia for influence over Europe's sick man, but between 1878 and 1914 all but the Arab provinces either fell, or were prized, away. These last were forfeited in 1918.

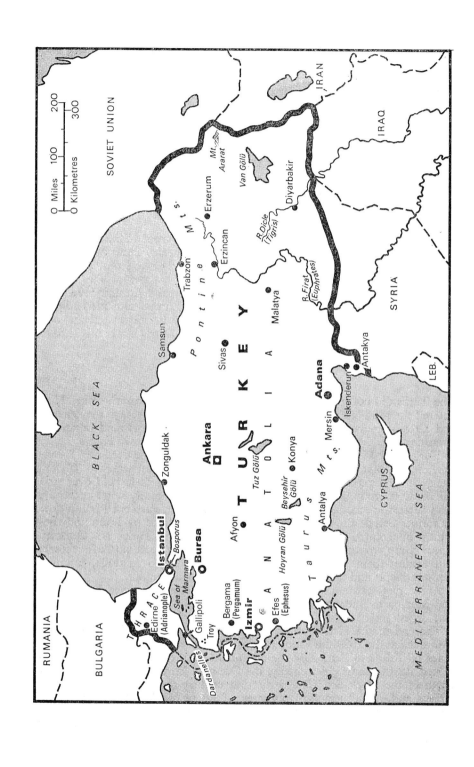

With some simplification it may be said that the Ottoman Empire declined and disintegrated for three principal reasons. Firstly, the Empire was subjected to the expansionist pressures, both territorial and economic, of the western powers and Russia, though profiting in the 19th century from European support against their great adversary. Secondly, the Empire's non-Muslim subjects, who were organised into near-autonomous nations (*millets*) under Ottoman rule, were seriously affected by the 19th century nationalist ferment; moreover nationalism also led to a desire for independence among Muslim but non-Turkish subjects of the Empire. Thirdly, the military, administrative and religious institutions of the Ottoman state entered into a steady and disastrous decline as early as the 16th century, a decline that prevented the Ottoman state from effectively facing up to and solving its external and internal problems.

After a thorough defeat on land and sea, in 1774 the Empire signed with Russia the humiliating treaty of Kutchuk Kaynarja. The Ottoman Empire now really began to reform itself. Upstart provincial landlords were brought under control and the wealth and influence of religion began to be curtailed. Led firmly from the top, modernisation began to penetrate into many fields, not least into education, now eased a little from the religious grip. A measure of equality for non-Muslims was achieved—a policy the western powers were always active in promoting. The administration began to be modernised along French lines. Young Turks started to go abroad for their education.

With increasing education, and in an age of liberalism, it was not long before a liberal critique of authoritarian reform began to appear. The Empire, it was urged, should only borrow from, not slavishly imitate, the West; it should adapt its own Islamic institutions, not abandon them.

In 1876, in response to domestic criticism and foreign pressure, the Sultan did no less than grant a constitution. By no means radical, it was nevertheless rescinded as soon as opportunity arose. This denial of freedom led in 1908 to the celebrated Young Turk revolution, which was led by the army. Freedom did not last long, but the pace of modernisation was increased during the decade the Young Turks were in power.

Republican Turkey

The allied intention after World War I was to divide up most of Turkey among the victors, but the country saved itself by waging a heroic national war of liberation under Mustafa Kemal (Atatürk). The Empire's most successful general, Kemal outmanœuvred the war-weary allies in diplomacy and outfought the occupying Greek forces in a hard-won war. It was a magnificent victory—a necessary prelude to the Atatürk revolution. Only a leader of Atatürk's stature could have forced Turkey along the road she was now to follow.

The Atatürks rejected the pre-war Young Turks, but developed their domestic policies. Equally authoritarian, they were, however, more radical. They did no less than abolish the Sultanate and Caliphate conjoined in the House of Osman. They abolished, too, the still substantial remnants of religious law. In fact, the state was ruthlessly secularised, though religious worship was not proscribed. The accent was placed on the Turkish, not the Islamic, heritage. To this end the Arabic script was discarded and the use of more truly Turkish structures and vocabulary strongly encouraged. A great merit of the language reform was that it simplified education.

To oversee these and other reforms an ostensibly democratic, but in fact authoritarian, single-party régime was established. Liberal, or religious, or separatist movements were squashed, the most dangerous being the Kurdish rebellion of 1925. People's Houses were set up as centres of education and revolutionary enlightenment, but the state was authoritarian, not totalitarian. Atatürk played a very active role as President of the Republic until his death in 1937.

After World War II, in which Turkey remained neutral until almost the end, Atatürk's lieutenant, İsmet İnönü converted the single-party régime into a multi-party system. This arose from a widespread pressure for more freedom, in part generated by the victory of the western allies, and from a general desire to align with them against the now powerful Soviet Union. In 1950, four years after the change, Atatürk's People's Party was overthrown at the polls by a new Democrat Party, which called for a less bleak attitude towards religion, more free enterprise and less repressive bureaucracy. The Democrat Party stayed in power until 1960, when they were ousted by a military coup. They too had become authoritarian in their treatment of the opposition. Moreover, they claimed an electoral legitimacy that alarmed the Atatürkist élite in the military, the bureaucracy and the universities, in whose view the electorate was being exploited.

After the trial and conviction of Democrat Party politicians (the Prime Minister and two other ministers were executed) the military, sensing their unpopularity, turned over power once more to the politicians under a new constitution. Between 1961 and 1965 coalition governments led by the People's Party under İnönü just about managed to keep the delicately poised political system in being and staved off two attempted coups in 1962 and 1963. An heir to the Democrat Party emerged in the Justice Party. When in 1965 this party came under moderate leadership, the military allowed it to assume power. Later, in the 1965 general elections, the Justice Party was returned with a substantial majority.

Turkey's foreign policy since the war has been pro-western. As a member of NATO and CENTO she has been among the strongest advocates of a firm policy towards her traditional enemy, Russia. This policy has, however, been affected by two factors. The first is Cyprus, where the United States has not taken as firm an attitude against her other ally, Greece, as Turkey would wish. The other is the resentment against American imperialism, which has developed apace among the more socialist groups, particularly the students. Both major parties are pro-Western, but they have of late tempered their attitude towards the Soviet Union.

TURKISH SOCIETY

Turkey is a country with a young and expanding population. Now some 33 million, the population has grown from under 14 million in 1927 and from nearly 28 million in 1960. The rate of growth is high at some 2·5%. Of the present population approximately 65% are under thirty-five years of age.

Turkey's population also shows a marked degree of homogeneity. There are numerous cultural and linguistic groups in Turkey, but with the exception of the Kurds in the east and the Arabs on the south-eastern border it is safe to say that they are now largely absorbed. The Kurds, however, do not amount to more than 7% of the population and the Arabs only about 1·5%. The Kurds and the Arabs have allies across Turkish frontiers but the Kurds in Persia and Iraq are minorities without political independence. The pressures on the Kurds to assimilate themselves to the general Turkish population is therefore great. Many of those who receive higher education and move into the professional classes come to regard themselves as Turks. Moreover, both Arabs and Kurds are Sunni Muslims like the Turks; although there is a sizeable group of Shi'ite Turks (*Alevis*) in Central Anatolia, theirs is no longer a disruptive influence. Nor do differences of sect as among Sunni Muslims coincide with linguistic or racial divisions.

That Turkey is still a Muslim country is a fact somewhat obscured by the strict subordination of religion to state that the Atatürk revolution brought about. Since 1950 Islam has re-emerged as a force in the country-side—as testified by the rash of mosque building that has occurred. The educated élite is mainly secular in outlook, but the newer, more technologically trained classes do not seem so positively to reject their Islamic heritage as those educated in the more classic revolutionary pattern.

Closely connected with religion is the place of women in Turkish society. Atatürk ridiculed the veil as a symbol of subjection, but dared not outlaw it; it is still to be seen, chiefly in the small towns and in the villages. What the Atatürk revolution did achieve was the introduction of a new Civil Code in 1926 which remedied women's inferior position in divorce and inheritance, limited Turks to one wife and required a civil marriage ceremony. That every so often thousands of 'illegitimate' children have to be legitimised indicates how in the countryside older traditions linger on. Turkish women have had full political rights since 1934.

The essential problem for Turkish women is not in fact a lack of legal equality, but rather a lack of education, inadequate economic opportunities to make their independence real, and the weight of custom. There are many Turkish women in the professions and in executive and clerical positions, but they occupy less than one-third of the places in middle schools and lycées and only about one-fifth of university places. Turkey still strikes the visitor as a predominantly male society.

Vital as education is for the status of women, it is also important in Turkish economic and social development generally. To take the lowest level first, statistics for 1965 show that only 48% of the Turkish population aged eleven or over is literate. The situation should slowly be remedied; it is planned that by 1971–2 all Turkish children will be receiving at least a primary education. Of the 7–18 age group 56% were attending school in 1967–8, a proportion which it is planned to increase to as much as 70% by 1972 (it was about 49% in 1961). The planners may be too sanguine, but if they are successful—and with the important proviso that the present quality is improved—then Turkey will be reaching European standards. Expansion in higher education is to be slower. The proportion of 4% in 1961 would be raised to 6·3% by 1972. In view of the expanding population, even an achievement of this size will be formidable. Literacy and schooling, it should be added, are also unevenly distributed, the less urban, and particularly the eastern, regions of the country being woefully deficient in both respects. Radio makes up for the effects of illiteracy to a certain but indeterminable extent. In 1967 there were only 85 radio sets to each thousand of population, but their use, if often for music, is widespread in coffee shops in villages and restaurants in towns.

Perhaps the most significant feature of the educational system is the present paucity of provision at secondary level. In 1964 the first stage of

311

the secondary system, the middle schools, recruited only 40% of primary school leavers. This is an important gap because of the shortage in the labour force of persons with middle school education for technical and skilled manual jobs. Once in a middle school a pupil has a very good chance of proceeding to the next secondary stage, that of the lycée, and then to institutions of higher education. Again there are plans to remedy recruitment to middle schools, but this will no doubt place great strains on the higher levels if most middle school pupils are not content to complete their education at that level.

Education is equally important in the context of Turkey's class structure. The Ottoman Empire was ruled by an educated élite, civil, military and religious. The Atatürk élite was revolutionary in its aims, but still stressed the need for an educated élite as political leaders. As government has always been highly respected in Turkey, and positions of power have always been occupied exclusively by the educated, education has always been, and still is, a prime source of social status. The traditional line of demarcation between the educated and the rest is being broken down as a variety of forms of education arise, but it has not disappeared yet.

It is not, however, the Atatürkist bureaucratic and military élite that is now accorded the highest status. Higher officials have yielded pride of place to the free professions. Doctors, engineers, lawyers and journalists are among those with the highest status. Really big businessmen (there are few), or bankers, would also qualify for the highest rank, but businessmen and industrialists in the middle reaches would generally be regarded as on a level with middle grade officials, even though they are better off financially. Teachers, particularly university teachers in the higher grades, enjoy a status like that of higher officials. Small business men and shopkeepers constitute a lower middle class; below them come the artisans and semi-skilled workers, to be followed by the mass of unskilled. Between the skilled and the unskilled there is a considerable gap.

In the towns it is probably correct to talk of a class structure—the contacts are more horizontal than vertical—but Turkey is composed mainly of villages, only 30% of the population living in towns in 1965. The differences between town and village are certainly being broken down, though when they migrate to towns many villagers often live there with other villagers and take time to integrate into urban society. If they work in towns on a seasonal basis they will often keep their families in the village, where they may well own some land. In terms of class structure it might be tentatively said that there is a correspondence between the village poor and casual manual workers in the towns, between villagers of middling wealth and town artisans or small traders, between the wealthier members of the village and, for example, merchants, contractors and hotel keepers. Very rich landowners probably rank somewhere with richer businessmen, but so much depends on their education. Many have been very influential in politics, having been courted by politicians. Incidentally, the general pattern of landholding is that of medium and small peasant proprietors, but statistics, now rather outdated, suggest that half the total cultivated area is in the hands of less than 10% of farming families.

Within the village, overall class distinctions do not really apply. There are differences in status, but not so consistently based that they lead to horizontal divisions. In ranking, the chief criterion seems to be wealth in land, but others like age, position in the family group, skills in trade and commerce, religious knowledge, and piety also count for much. Turkish rural society is

312

not egalitarian, but vertical contact perhaps makes the differences resented less than they might be.

ECONOMICS

Turkey is still a largely agricultural country, with one-third of the land under cultivation. Among a wide range of crops, wheat and then barley head the list of cereals produced. Sugar beet, cotton, tobacco, grapes, and citrus fruits are other notable and expanding products. Among livestock, sheep and goats (the latter now declining) are prominent, though not increasing very fast.

Turkey is well blessed with natural resources. There are abundant deposits of coal (nearly 7·5 million tons produced in 1966) and lignite (almost 6·5 million tons), chrome ore (689,000 tons), iron ore (1,660 million tons), copper (27,000 tons), crude petroleum (1,854,000 tons), and petroleum products (over 4·5 million tons). Production of all these minerals has increased rapidly since the end of World War II. So too has electrical power, but at 187kwh a head consumption is much below European standards. Among a variety of manufactures cement, coke, pig iron, steel ingots, sheets and pipes, woollen and cotton yarns and fabrics, sugar, superphosphate, and paper stand out. In 1966 nearly 4 million tons of cement, almost 1·5 million tons of coke, some 840,000 tons of steel ingots, and nearly three-quarters of a million tons of pig iron were produced.

When we look at the overall picture of Turkish economic development we find that the country's recent average growth has been about 6·5%. This is a little below the planned rate of 7%, but well above the normal growth rate in the 1950s of 4%–5%. With a *per caput* gross national product of only $319 ($242 in 1964) Turkey is still very poor by the European standards to which she aspires.

The main effort in Turkish economic development is in industry, which employs 1·5 million out of the total labour force of some 13·5 million. Agriculture at present contributes some 35% of the national product, but this proportion is designed to fall to 27% by the end of the present plan period, 1968–72. By then agriculture should have shown a growth rate of only 4·1%, as compared with the 12% planned for industry. The emphasis on industry has meant that the population of 10 millions mainly dependent on agriculture for its livelihood now has a *per caput* income lower in relation to incomes in other sectors than used to be the case. Increased mechanisation of agriculture has also meant that rural unemployment, or underemployment, has increased markedly, with some 200,000 people emigrating annually to the towns. For this spare manpower industrialisation is urgently needed, but despite the present emphasis on industrialisation it is estimated that two-thirds of the population will still be dependent on agriculture in 1972. In agricultural production a great deal is expected from technical improvements. One that has received much publicity is the planting of higher-yield Mexican wheat.

In order to achieve an overall annual 7% growth rate investment is called for that will absorb one-third of the GNP over the next five-year period. There is some confidence that this will be achieved. Turkey has been able to finance investment almost completely from domestic savings.

The problem Turkey has not yet been able to solve is that of foreign exchange. High rates of investment and subsequent capital goods imports have imposed an imbalance that Turkey's exports, which are largely of agricultural products, have not been able to put right. To her traditional export list of tobacco, nuts, raisins, and figs Turkey has recently added new products, like fish, citrus fruits, and cotton. There is some prospect of increasing the export of manufactured goods, but the OECD report for 1967 stresses that Turkey cannot afford to neglect her agricultural exports.

Turkey has also received considerable relief in her struggle for foreign exchange from the remittances sent home by the numerous (some 200,000) Turkish workers abroad, mainly in West Germany, but these remittances have declined of late. Another source of hard currency from which, rather surprisingly, Turkey has not as yet much profited is tourism, but greater efforts are now being made in this direction. Lovers of Turkey's lonely beauty spots and historical sites will not much relish the breaking of the tourist wave on Turkey's shores, but the ages of isolation, and relative stagnation, seem now inexorably to be drawing to a close.

POLITICS

The essential aim of the military in ushering in a new constitution in 1961 was to ensure that Turkey remained truly democratic. To this end, the new constitution included a senate and created a constitutional court. It also sought to guarantee a number of social as well as individual rights, such as the right to strike. With the military in the background this constitution has not proved to be a mere scrap of paper and there can be no doubt that it also represents the ideals of the educated élite. One new feature introduced in 1961 that has not lived up to the expectations of its sponsors has been the system of proportional representation. It has not prevented the Justice Party from obtaining a clear majority, a situation many Turks fear will lead inevitably to an abuse of power.

It is certainly true that since 1946 Turkey has enjoyed a multi-party system more in name than in actual fact. Between 1946 and 1960 the contest was essentially two-party, as it has become once more since 1965. The contest is now more real, however, than it was in the 1950s when opposition rights were seriously curtailed. Moreover, the character of the two-party struggle has changed somewhat. While the Justice Party is naturally to the right of centre, the People's Party has deliberately adopted the slogan 'left of centre' and has partly abandoned the populism that was one of its chief characteristics under Atatürk. In this rather more modern political alignment the two major parties do not have the field to themselves, however. To the far left is the still small Workers' Party, while on the right there is not only the religiously conservative Nation Party, but also a more specifically class-conscious National Action Party. Between the two centre parties there is also a recent offshoot from the People's Party, the Reliance Party, formed in 1967 from a group who did not approve the People's Party's move to the left.

In the 1969 general election the Justice Party was again returned to power, but with a reduced majority (46·5% of the poll as compared with 52·7% in 1965). The People's Party maintained its position as the chief opposition party obtaining again over a quarter of the vote, and the power of the opposition was enhanced by the success of the Reliance Party in gaining 6·6% of the poll. The Workers' Party obtained only 2·7% of the vote, a slight deterioration in its position since 1965. Many had then forecast a rapid growth for this party.

To make predictions about electoral chances is especially hazardous in the Turkish case, however, as the knowledge as yet available on the nature of political allegiance in Turkey is sketchy.

314

In the villages political allegiance seems to depend on two principal factors. It seems often to happen that groups or factions within a village will support a party because its rivals support the other. More important, perhaps, the villager is not interested in points of policy or ideology. He has definite local needs; and it seems he judges a party's fitness to govern by what it is going to provide locally, though to an extent it is true that allegiance is affected by general factors. For instance, the Justice Party obtains most support in the more developed areas of western Turkey, while the *Alevis* (Shi'ites) in Central Anatolia traditionally vote for the more secularist People's Party.

In the towns the situation must be very different from that in the villages. The evidence suggests that the lower-income groups support the Justice Party (the party is very active in practical ways of extending help to newcomers to towns) and the higher income groups the People's Party, and even the Workers' Party. Many workers have not yet broken away from the traditionalist attitudes on which the Justice Party in part relies.

Undoubtedly the most significant feature of Turkish politics is the expansion of participation since World War II. Not only is there participation through conflict between the political parties, but there is also considerable debate within political parties. In this regard, legislation inspired by the 1960 revolution and designed to make party organisation more democratic has not been without effect.

Pressure and interest groups now also participate more than formerly. Apart from the military, whose influence is ever-present, there are the 'guardians' of the Atatürk revolution, the students. They are no longer Atatürkist to a man and many interpret Atatürkism to mean socialism, whilst some, in the modern vein, reject the liberal-democratic system outright. Of late the students have become a very disruptive force, frequently going on strike, occupying university buildings and demonstrating.

The Trade Unions also speak out more and have been greatly strengthened by the right to strike. They have avoided the embraces of any one political party, preferring to bargain with the government of the day, but they are not averse to pressing the claims of candidates in elections with a working-class background.

Increased participation has also meant the involvement of new social groups. Even the political parties have been affected in this regard. Since Atatürk's times, politicians have been increasingly recruited from elements in society which were urban in origin and upbringing, less from those with an 'official' or military occupational background. The free professions, particularly the law, have steadily increased their representation in parliament. So, too, has commerce, though to a lesser degree. Higher officials are also drawn from professional families, though the extent to which they are recruited from an 'official' background is high. The personnel of politics and government is not yet widely representative of society, but has become much more so than formerly.

To sum up, it is apparent that Turkey is a purposeful state. Her rate of economic and social progress has been tolerably good and her politics stable. That she has not developed faster is usually attributed to the prevalence of traditionalist and religious attitudes and, more recently, to the bureaucratic, if dedicated, nature of the Atatürkist leadership. This is probably true, but not necessarily to be deplored. Turkey's progress has been controlled by other than materialistic concerns, a legacy perhaps of the civilisations to which she is part heir.

FURTHER READING

Coles, Paul. *The Ottoman Impact on Europe*, Thames and Hudson, London, 1968; Harcourt, Brace & World, New York, 1968.

Eren, Nuri. *Turkey Today and Tomorrow*, Praeger, New York and London, 1963.

Frey, Frederick W. *The Turkish Political Elite*, MIT Press, Cambridge, Mass., 1965.

Heyd, Uriel. *Foundations of Turkish Nationalism*, Luzac and Harvill Press, London, 1950.

Kazamias, Andreas M. *Education and the Quest for Modernity in Turkey*, Allen & Unwin, London, 1966.

Lewis, Bernard. *The Emergence of Modern Turkey*, Oxford Univ. Press, London and New York, 1961.

Mango, Andrew. *Turkey*, Thames & Hudson, London, 1968.

Robinson, R. D. *The First Turkish Republic: A Case Study in National Development*, Harvard Univ. Press, Cambridge, Mass., 1963.

Shorter, Frederic C. (ed.) *Four Studies on the Economic Development of Turkey*, Cass, London, 1967; Kelley, New York, 1968.

Szyliowicz, Joseph S. *Political Change in Rural Turkey: Erdemli*, Mouton, The Hague, 1966.

Ward, Robert E. and Rustow, Dankwart A. (eds.) *Political Modernization in Japan and Turkey*, Princeton Univ. Press, 1964.

CLEMENT H. DODD. Professor of Political Studies, University of Hull. Formerly Senior Lecturer in Government at Manchester University. A graduate in both modern history and Turkish, he has taught politics, including Middle East politics, and for three years was Visiting Professor of Government in the Middle East Technical University, Ankara. Author of *Politics and Government in Turkey* (1969), co-author of *Israel and the Arab World* (1970) and editor of *Studies in University Government and Administration* (1963).

THE UNITED ARAB REPUBLIC

TOM LITTLE

EARLIEST HISTORY

THE birth of the Pharaonic civilisation about 5,500 years ago is the historical starting point of Egypt but traces of earlier peoples provide evidence of a prehistoric period. When the ice cap withdrew northwards from Europe about 15,000 years ago it took with it the rain-bearing winds that watered the prairies of North Africa where hunting peoples lived. As the grasslands turned to desert these peoples moved away in search of rain and some found their way into the valley of the Nile where they at first continued to live as hunters. They noted in time the vegetation that grew where the annual summer flood of the Nile had watered the banks; they learned to grow edible crops and it is probable that in communal control of the Nile waters they created their first organised societies.

By 3200 BC these societies had become two 'kingdoms', one in the alluvial delta of the Nile and the other consisting of the ribbon of river bank lying to the south of it. The uniting of these two 'kingdoms' by Menes in approximately the year 3188 BC marks the beginning of Egyptian history. Within 500 years the Egyptians had acquired enough engineering skill to build the step pyramids at Saqqara, and in another 250 years the Great Pyramid at Giza, and had formed a complex government organisation covering the area from present-day Aswan to the Mediterranean Sea.

This first creative period is known as the Old Kingdom and it declined with the end of the VIth dynasty in about 2294 BC but, after about 150 years of internal troubles and disintegration, able pharaohs of the XIth and XIIth dynasties, the Middle Kingdom, reunited the country and extended their dominion to the east and south of it. So far Egypt had been protected by its deserts but in another degenerate period the Hyksos, probably a people of semitic origin, crossed the Sinai by horse and chariot and conquered the country without a battle. Thereafter Egypt was never to be free from the danger of invasion. The Amenhoteps and Thotmeses, great pharaohs of the XVIIIth dynasty, ushered in the New Kingdom in about 1570 BC by expelling the Hyksos and created an empire that reached to the Orontes, the Euphrates and the Third Cataract of the Nile, 250 miles south of the present Egyptian frontier; but in so doing they committed their country to wars against the powerful Hittites in Syria. Ramses III of the XXth dynasty was compelled to defeat a confederacy of Mediterranean peoples by land and sea in order to restore—for the last time—the Egyptian empire. By this time the Egyptians were an unwarlike people who used mercenaries and slaves to fight their wars. The empire collapsed with the death of

317

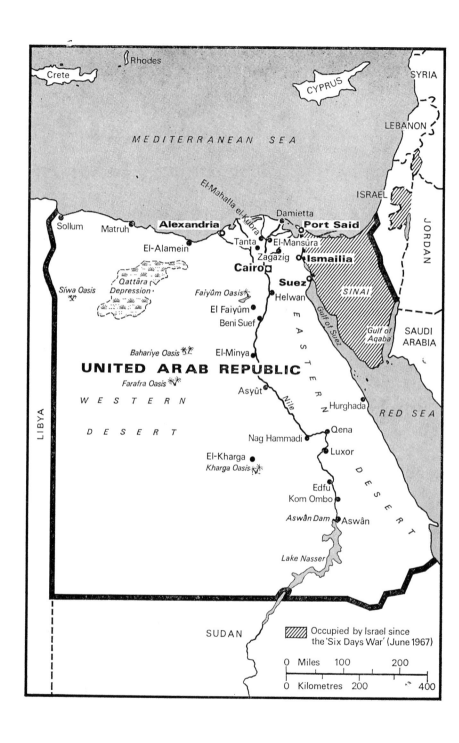

Crete

Rhodes

CYPRUS

SYRIA

LEBANON

M E D I T E R R A N E A N   S E A

ISRAEL

El-Mahalla el-Kubra

Damietta

Sollum   Matruh

Alexandria

Port Said

JORDAN

El-Alamein

Tanta

El-Mansûra

Zagazig

Ismailia

Cairo

Qattâra Depression

Faiyûm Oasis

Suez

Helwan

S I N A I

Sîwa Oasis

El Faiyûm

Beni Suef

Gulf of Suez

Gulf of Aqaba

SAUDI
ARABIA

Bahariye Oasis

El-Minya

UNITED ARAB REPUBLIC

Farafra Oasis

Asyût

E A S T E R N

W E S T E R N

LIBYA

D E S E R T

Hurghada

RED SEA

Nag Hammadi

Qena

El-Kharga

Kharga Oasis

Luxor

Nile

Edfu

Kom Ombo

D E S E R T

Aswân Dam

Aswân

Lake Nasser

SUDAN

▨ Occupied by Israel since
the 'Six Days War' (June 1967)

0   Miles   100   200

0   Kilometres   200   400

Ramses III and Egypt was in turn conquered by Libyans, Nubians, Ethiopians and Assyrians. There was a brief revival under the Saite rulers of the XXVIth dynasty between 663 and 525 BC but in that year Cambyses, the Persian Emperor, conquered and cowed the country. In 332 BC the Persians in turn yielded Egypt to Alexander the Great and after 3,000 years of existence, sometimes noble, always intelligent but often erratic, the pharaonic period ended.

In ancient Egypt Pharaoh was the peak of an administrative system which broadened downwards through the Grand Vizier and the viceroys of the provinces to the scribes and clerks. The highly developed administration was able to regulate the control of the Nile waters, organise taxation and a cattle census and provide an advanced judicial system consisting of local and high courts, with the right of appeal to the pharaoh. The ancient Egyptians' maritime skills were considerable and in course of time they built boats with timber from Lebanon using two banks of oars which carried them, it is believed, as far as the shores of India. The design of their military fortifications on the frontiers of Kush about 1500 BC was never again equalled until about AD 1300 in Europe. The solar calender of 365 days which they devised was only minutely in error and they devised what was possibly the first system of accountancy. Although medicine was in many ways primitive it was in others very advanced; there is evidence, for example, of surgery on the skull and the methods of embalming the dead showed considerable knowledge of the human body. Their pyramids were feats of architecture and engineering notable both in their mass and exactness and although they favoured the flat roof suspended on columns they knew how to use both the arch and the vault. Their artists were government servants working as a team but they often produced works of great beauty, from massive murals and sculpture to the most delicate figurines and jewellery. Their domestic buildings have entirely vanished because they were made of wood, mud and reeds, but the wall paintings reveal a remarkably sophisticated way of life in villas, set in gardens rich with flowers, which they also used to decorate the interiors. They ate meat, fish, pastries, bread and fruit and often got drunk on wine and beer. They were a gay people among whom the feminine influence was strong, possibly because inheritance was through the female side.

They spread their knowledge through their wars and to the people who conquered them; above all the Greeks benefited because in the pursuit of commerce they virtually colonised the delta area long before the pharaonic period ended. They acknowledged their debt to the Egyptians and the flowering of their art and knowledge would not have been so rapid and expansive without the Egyptian contribution.

RELIGION

The forerunners of the ancient Egyptians were pantheists and in the beginning of the pharaonic period each community in the Nile valley had its own local god in animal form to suit the hunting communities of those days. These gods merged as the communities merged, until finally Re, the god of Thebes in the Upper Kingdom, was merged with Amon to become Amon-Re, the supreme God of the known world, in the time of Thotmes III. Other gods survived beside them until finally the Isis and Osiris myth became ascendant and extended the consolations of religion to the common people. The Egyptians were deeply concerned with life after death and, as

319

their beliefs evolved, there was in all their writings from the New Kingdom onwards a growing tendency to monotheism. This was to be of supreme importance when Christianity came to the region.

GREECE AND ROME

After the brutality of Persian rule, the Egyptians considered Alexander both wise and tolerant. He remained only a year but he established a more just system of government and reaffirmed the credibility of the Egyptian religion by arranging for the oracle at Siwa to proclaim him the son of God, as the pharaohs before him had been proclaimed. The early Ptolemies, whose line inherited his conquest, did much for the country, notably in cutting two canals from the Nile to the Red Sea. The court was at Alexandria, the city which Alexander founded, and it became the most extravagant and cultured in the world. The museum was a centre of learning which attracted the great thinkers of the day, and the library, until it was destroyed by the Romans, was the finest collection of written wisdom the world had known.

Alexander and the Ptolemies nevertheless regarded Egypt as a Greek state in which all land except that belonging to the temples was the property of the ruler. He distributed it to Greeks who lived in self-governing communities and even the library and museum were denied to the Egyptians, despite their 3,000 years of civilisation. This system and quarrels within the Ptolemaic family led in time to a collapse of law and order and this was made worse by the revolts of the Egyptians. The country was run by garrison commanders and Alexandria was described by a contemporary Greek as 'exposed to the fury of the soldiery'. Weakened by disorder and popular hate the dynasty became a vassal of Rome. Cleopatra gave herself and her country to Julius Caesar and then to Augustus, but her sons did not survive to claim the inheritance. Augustus Caesar took possession of the country in 30 BC.

The Romans were absentee landlords who continued to rule through the privileged Greeks and with mercenary soldiers, all under three provincial viceroys. The Egyptians' lot improved at first under firm Roman rule, but in time the provincial administrations disintegrated in disorder, partly as a result of Egyptian resistance to the tax collectors. In the second century AD, a revolt led by native troops lasted for several years and became known to history as the Bucolic Wars. The Emperor Diocletian finally restored order, but within a few years of his abdication the provinces again collapsed in confusion. The peasants neglected the land, which was then bought by the nobles, and Egypt came to consist of vast estates ruled by private armies.

CHRISTIANITY

Christianity was now becoming an important element in the situation. Religion had remained important to the Egyptians and when St. Mark brought Christianity to Egypt, their minds, already prepared for monotheism, readily accepted it. This separated them further from the pagan Greeks and Romans, but towards the end of the second century Alexandria became a school for Hellenic Christian thinkers and within another century was second only to Rome in importance. Egyptians nevertheless provided the mass of Christians. St. Anthony is believed to have established the first monastery in the world in Egypt and early in the fourth century there were reputed to be 7,000 monks, who led resistance to paganism and therefore inspired national resistance to the pagan rulers.

Constantinople was created in AD 330 and by the time that Byzantium had inherited the power of Rome, the Church had become an instrument of state. At the Council of Chalcedon in 451 it propounded the doctrine of the dual nature of Christ, which the native Egyptian Church rejected, holding firmly to its own monophysite faith, and when the official patriarch was sent to Alexandria he was murdered. Egypt was then allowed to have two patriarchs, one the Byzantine prelate and the other the patriarch of what was now the Coptic Church of Egypt. The Byzantines persecuted the Copts and in the course of this internecine strife Alexandria decayed and the agricultural economy of the country degenerated.

ISLAM

The simplicity of the Coptic faith, together with their hatred of Byzantium, prepared the Egyptians for acceptance of the Islamic army of Amr Ibn al-As when he entered Egypt in December 639, 29 years after the Prophet Muhammad began his mission in Mecca. The Egyptians willingly yielded Alexandria to him and in 646 Egypt passed forever from the possession of Christian kings. Yet, until 1952, the Egyptians were never their own masters, being subject first to the Umayyad Caliphate of Damascus and then the 'Abbassid Caliphate of Baghdad. Even the Fatimid Caliphate, from a new line, descended from the Prophet through his daughter Fatima, which ruled the Muslim world from Egypt and founded Cairo, came from the Maghrib in North-West Africa. Its power was eroded by the Christian crusades and it was overthrown by the Kurdish forces of Salah al-Din al-Ayyoub, the Saladin of Western romance, who proclaimed himself Sultan of Egypt. He and his successor Beybars restored the dominance of Egypt but when the country was again conquered, this time by Ottoman Turks who had embraced Islam, it fell victim to the Mamelukes, descendants of the Turk, Mongol and Circassian slaves of the army of Salah al-Din. They ruled the country for 300 years.

In the pristine innocence of Islam the Copts, as people of the Book, were protected though unprivileged, but this quickly turned to oppression from which many bought their escape by turning Muslim. Their language was relegated to the sanctuaries of the Church where it remains fossilised to this day. Mameluke rule completed the country's decline despite some just and able rulers, because their communal conflicts and provincial barbarism so oppressed the long-suffering Egyptians that many of them gave up tending their land. The Black Death, which wasted Europe for two years, wasted Egypt for seven and plague returned again and again to the famine-stricken people. When Napoleon conquered Egypt at the end of the 18th century, the population was about 2·5 million whereas in pharaonic times it had been as much as 7 million.

THE NAPOLEONIC CONQUEST

Napoleon declared that he was a friend of the Sultan of Turkey, who was the Eyptians' suzerain, and had come to put an end to their sufferings at the hands of the Mamelukes; but after more than 2,000 years of subjection to foreign rulers, the Egyptians had come to the conclusion that all foreign rule was bad. To the surprise of Napoleon, they rallied to the support of the hated Mamelukes against the Christian invaders. Napoleon had to fight his way ashore at Alexandria and his forage parties were harried all the way to Cairo.

His plans to civilise the country, overcome religious prejudice, reorganise the administration and establish good government were frustrated by popular enmity. They were in any case secondary to his desire to cut British communication with India; but he failed to prevent a British landing or to defeat his prime enemies ashore. The French evacuated Egypt in 1801 and, after a short stay to restore the power of the Sultan of Turkey, the British followed them. Brief though the Napoleonic incursion was, it introduced the Egyptians to the progress of Europe, and the use of the Arabic printing press and of the printed broadsheet taught the Egyptians how to communicate more effectively. The British, by contrast, left the Mamelukes warring among themselves and with the mercenary factions of the Sultan's viceroy.

MUHAMMAD ALY THE GREAT

The Egyptians were tired of it all and in the new-found confidence born of their resistance to the French they turned in 1805 to Muhammad Aly, the leader of the Sultan's mercenary Albanians, to rid them of the whole murderous gang. This he did with deceitful ruthlessness and skill and became the Sultan's viceroy; and if he did not reward the Egyptians for their collaboration by giving them a partnership in government, he at least replaced many masters by one.

He planned to make Egypt a modern state on the European model as the foundation of his ambition and to that end he restored the power of the central government, relieving the Egyptians for the first time for centuries of provincial overlords. He restored the traditional form of government by the ruler and his *diwan*, or consultative council, and took titular possession of all lands, all taxes and all foreign trade. By this centralised control he was able to have ditches and canals cleaned and to double the number of water wheels on the Nile, so that an extra million acres of land were brought into production. He spent £12 million on starting nationalised factories and removed obstacles to trade with infidels. The people had to pay more taxes but earned more money and for many years were happy.

Muhammad Aly used French instructors to build an excellent army, with which he fought the Sultan's wars in Arabia and Greece and extended the Egyptian frontiers to Gondokoro, in the deep south of the present-day Sudan. When he quarrelled with the ungrateful Sultan, he marched his armies almost to the gates of Constantinople and the Ottoman empire might have fallen to him then if threats from Russia had not turned him back. Britain finally put an end to his ambition by imposing the Treaty of London in 1841, by which his army was restricted to 18,000 men and limits placed on his independence of the Sultan, but from it he achieved his primary aim, the hereditary right of his family to rule Egypt.

His wars had cost the country much and deprived the Egyptians of many of the benefits of his rule; but his visionary sense of the country's requirements, as symbolised in the barrage he built at the apex of the Nile delta, marks Muhammad Aly as the founder of modern Egypt. Under his rule state revenues rose from £1 million to £6 million and before his death the population was about four million.

Ibrahim, the soldier-son who had led his armies in their victorious campaigns, died in November 1848 and Muhammad Aly the following year.

His son Abbas, who succeeded him, was a reactionary of the old school who got rid of foreign advisers and traders and left the Turkish landowners to oppress their Egyptian peasants. He was murdered by his own bodyguard and his extravagant and pleasure-loving brother Said succeeded him. He brought back the foreigners in even greater numbers, incurred the first national debt (of £3,300,000 at 7%), and gave his friend Ferdinand de Lesseps the concession to build the Suez Canal on terms highly advantageous to the French, including the right to employ forced labour for four-fifths of the work.

Said died in 1863 and the unprepossessing Ismail revoked the more onerous terms of the canal concession, which had caused an international scandal over the inhuman use of forced labour; but in saving the Suez Canal Company from bankruptcy, he committed himself to an indemnity of 84 million francs for the rights he had revoked, and so found himself paying virtually the whole cost of the canal and getting next to nothing in return. Encouraged by a boom in cotton at the start of his reign, he embarked on great enterprises. He built 910 miles of railways and 500 bridges, dug 8,400 miles of canal, laid 5,000 miles of telegraph wires, built Suez village into a town, modernised Alexandria with a fine modern harbour, provided lighthouses on the Mediterranean and Red Sea coasts and built a merchant fleet of 16 ships. But these costly enterprises, combined with his personal extravagance (which earned him the soubriquet of Magnificent), brought the country to bankruptcy. Foreign powers imposed a commission of the debt and two financial controllers, one British, one French, whose combined influence brought the country largely under foreign control. When he sought to rouse the people against this system in 1879 he was deposed by the sultan at the behest of the powers.

THE BRITISH OCCUPATION

One of his extravagances was to buy from the sultan self-government in domestic affairs and the right of inheritance through the eldest sons of himself and his successors. He was succeeded therefore by his son Tewfiq, a weak man who came in foreign fetters to his throne. The national movement was by this time well-developed, both in the Turkish aristocracy which desired more power and among the Egyptians who desired more rights for themselves in their own country. A movement for the redress of the Egyptians' grievances in the army, started by an Egyptian colonel, Ahmad Bey Arabi, was used by the Turkish movement and under pressure of events turned into a full-scale army revolt, which was suppressed by British forces in 1882.

Lord Cromer, a former financial official who returned to Egypt as Consul-General, was virtually the ruler of Egypt for the next 25 years. He built an efficient administration, run by British officials, and carefully nurtured and developed the economy in order to pay the foreign debts incurred by the Khedive Ismail. The country prospered and the peasants' lot was greatly improved; but in spite of the nominal authority of the Khedive, it was essentially an alien rule, from which the Egyptian national movement was excluded. In the beginning it was closely identified with Islam by the teachings of Jamal al-Din al-Afghani, a religious teacher who came from Constantinople; but towards the end of Cromer's period in Egypt, Mustafa Kamal had given it political form with the demand for constitutional government and independence. By the time Cromer left in 1907 it had acquired a strength it was never entirely to lose.

THE SUDAN

At the time of the Khedive Ismail, the Sudan, as far as its indeterminate southern frontiers, was under the authority of Egypt and Ismail sent first Sir Samuel Baker and then General Gordon to govern it for him. In 1881 a religious teacher called Muhammad Ahmad proclaimed himself the Mahdi, the successor of the Prophet Muhammad, and raised the flag of revolt. He defeated the Egyptians everywhere and in October 1884 General Gordon, who had been sent back to the Sudan to evacuate the British and the Egyptians, was killed in Khartoum, one day before the relieving British forces arrived. It was not until 1898 that the British were able to recover the country; in January of the following year Lord Cromer raised the British and Egyptian flags over Khartoum and declared the Sudan a condominium under the Queen of England and the Khedive of Egypt. In practice it was ruled by the British until it achieved independence in 1956.

THE PROTECTORATE

Secret societies fostered by the national movement brought Egypt to a condition described by a contemporary in 1910 as 'exuberantly disorderly' and in 1913 the British sent Lord Kitchener as Consul-General to restore order. This he did by firm repressive measures; but he had begun to embark on more liberal policies to give Egyptians more part in the running of their country when he was recalled to London to command British forces in World War I. The British deposed the Khedive Abbas Hilmi and replaced him by the more co-operative Husain Kamel, who was given the title of Sultan, and Egypt was declared a Protectorate in December 1914.

This had the effect of uniting the factions of the national movement and Saad Zaghloul, a moderate who had worked with Cromer and then with Lord Kitchener, became its leader in January 1919. As a protectorate, Egypt emerged from the war in greater subjection instead of profiting from the acts of liberation which the Allies had said was the object of their war. She was not represented at the peace conference although 180,000 Egyptians had fought with the Allied armies. In 1919 the angry people revolted all over the country and many lives were lost before the revolt was suppressed by Lord Allenby, who had become High Commissioner (as the Consul-General had been called since the formation of the Protectorate).

The rebellion was nevertheless successful in forcing the British to reconsider and negotiate their position. They proposed the abandonment of the Protectorate; but Saad Zaghloul, in exile but still leader of the Wafd, as the national movement was now called, refused the attached conditions concerning the continued presence of British troops, British control over Egyptian legislation and responsibility for foreigners in the country. Lord Allenby persuaded his government to declare an end to the Protectorate unilaterally on 28 February 1922 and in April 1923 a new constitution was promulgated. Sultan Fuad who had succeeded Husain Kamel in 1917 became King Fuad with legislative powers vested in him. Saad Zaghloul returned from exile and the Wafd won 188 of the 206 parliamentary seats in the first elections in January 1924.

THE 1936 ANGLO-EGYPTIAN TREATY

The Wafd opposed the power of both King Fuad and the British. With the more recalcitrant Mustafa Nahas Pasha as its leader after Zaghloul's death, it was kept out of office by an amended and narrowed constitution until 1935, when the danger of Mussolini's imperial policy in Africa made it obvious that Egypt must unite its ranks and combine with Britain in self-defence. The Wafd won the elections under the restored constitutions and Nahas Pasha led an all-party delegation which negotiated the 1936 Anglo-Egyptian Treaty. This declared British occupation at an end but gave Britain the right to station troops in the Suez Canal Zone until both sides agreed that Egypt was ready to protect the canal herself. Britain undertook to defend Egypt against aggression.

The strong King Fuad died before the treaty was signed and was succeeded by his 17-year-old son Farouk, who soon afterwards dismissed the Wafd. This and quarrels within the Wafd Party undermined the domestic effects of the treaty. The outbreak of World War II brought 250,000 Commonwealth troops into Egypt and once again made it possible for Britain to dictate the form of government. As Farouk and his immediate advisers favoured Italy and Germany, the British imposed Nahas Pasha as Prime Minister in 1942 and this government was kept in office until 1944 when the war had passed from Egypt. This act made Farouk an implacable enemy of Britain.

The Egyptian people and all the parties demanded the total evacuation of the British but this was rejected by Britain. However, Britain did conform to the 1936 treaty by withdrawing its troops to the Canal Zone. There were sporadic disorders, which cost some lives, until in 1949 King Farouk and the Wafd decided to join forces. The king dismissed the government and in January 1950 the Wafd was re-elected, with Nahas again as Prime Minister. This combination had been made necessary by the Arab defeat by the Jews in 1948, which led to the formation of Israel; but instead of strengthening the country it combined the corruption of the palace with the corruption of the Wafd. Pandering to popular sentiment, the government declared unilaterally the unity of the Sudan and Egypt under the Egyptian crown and promoted a resistance movement against British troops in the Canal Zone. The ineffectualness of government support for this resistance was highlighted by the useless defence of the auxiliary police barracks in Ismailia on 25 January 1952, in which 47 policemen were killed. Next day the mobs took to the streets for what became known as 'the burning of Cairo' and the king again dismissed the Wafd.

THE REVOLUTION

Ever since the war powerful forces had been plotting revolution. Of these the communists were an intellectual and workers' fringe; but the Muslim Brotherhood was reputed to have about two million members, and the Free Officers movement, which included members from both of the other parties, had steadily increased its strength in the army. The Muslim Brotherhood and the Free Officers had simple (though different) concepts of socialism but were united in demanding the evacuation of the British from Egypt and the Sudan and possession of the Suez Canal. On 23 July 1952 the Free Officers overthrew the government bloodlessly and three days later sent the king into exile.

The new Government formed by the Free Officers introduced an Agrarian Reform Law which limited individual land-holding to a maximum of 200 acres. This undermined the powerful aristocracy of landowners and the junta progressively destroyed the Wafd and lesser political parties. Its refusal to submit to the dictates of the Communists and the Brotherhood brought it into conflict with both movements; it gaoled the Communists and when the Brotherhood tried to assassinate the Free Officers' leader, Colonel Gamal Abdel Nasser, on 26 October 1954, this gave Nasser the opportunity to destroy the leadership of the Brotherhood. He then moved with little impediment to the presidency of the Revolutionary Command Council, formed of the Free Officers' Executive, and finally became President of the country.

NATIONAL ASPIRATIONS ACHIEVED

Because the removal of all foreign occupation everywhere was a cardinal principal of the revolutionary officers, they sacrificed their claim to unity of Egypt and the Sudan under Egypt and signed an agreement on 12 February 1953, granting self-determination to the Sudan after a three years' transitional period. The Egyptians believed that the Sudan would choose unity; but on 1 January 1956 the Sudanese Prime Minister unilaterally declared the country to be a sovereign state independent of both Britain and Egypt. Both countries hastened to recognise the new Sudanese government.

After intermittent and sometimes stormy negotiations an Anglo-Egyptian Agreement was signed on 19 October 1954, by which Britain undertook to withdraw from the Suez Canal base by June of 1956. During the interim period there was a substantial reorientation of Egyptian policy, for several reasons. Turkey and Iraq signed a mutual defence treaty with British encouragement in January 1955 and this was bitterly opposed by President Nasser. In February 1955 Israeli forces attacked in strength and wiped out the Egyptian garrison at Gaza and in later months made several other raids. When Nasser failed to obtain the arms he required from Britain or the United States, he ordered them from Russia, with credits to be met in cotton. Russia and her allies were already purchasing by barter deals a substantial proportion of Egypt's cotton and had thus secured a firm position in Egypt. To counter this penetration, Britain, the United States and the World Bank offered, late in 1955, to provide the foreign currency requirements for the first stage of a mammoth high dam at Aswan; but when the offer was formulated in the following February, Nasser was reluctant to sign an agreement because he wanted a commitment for the entire scheme. In May 1956 Nasser recognised the People's Republic of China, which had purchased £10 million worth of cotton the previous year, thereby antagonising United States opinion, with the result that when he finally decided to accept the High Dam offer in July the United States withdrew it. Nasser retaliated by nationalising the Suez Canal Company which was an Anglo-French concern. He thus delighted the Egyptian people who saw this move as the final stage in the achievement of their national aspirations.

THE SUEZ WAR

The British and French Governments took counter-measures, ostensibly to recover international control of the canal but really designed to overthrow Nasser. They began to build up forces in Cyprus but their extreme measures received only half-hearted support from the United States; when reference to the Security Council also failed to wring concessions from Nasser, they entered into a secret agreement with Israel. Israeli forces invaded Sinai on 29 October 1956 and swept quickly towards the Suez Canal. Next day Britain and France presented an ultimatum to Israel and Egypt, instructing them to cease fire and withdraw their forces to ten miles from the canal, in default of which the two powers would intervene with sufficient strength to secure compliance. Israel naturally accepted and Egypt equally naturally refused. Britain and France vetoed a UN Security Council resolution, calling on Israel to withdraw and on all members to refrain from using force, and at the expiry of the 12-hour time-limit in the ultimatum their air forces began to bomb Egyptian airfields and other targets. The Egyptians blocked the Suez Canal by sinking ships in it and on 5 November 1956 Anglo-French forces landed in and around Port Said, killing about 650 people and wounding about 2,000. Nevertheless, Britain and France were compelled to withdraw their forces towards the end of December under pressure from the United Nations, and the Israelis withdrew behind their frontier shortly afterwards. The United Nations sent an Emergency Force (UNEF), with President Nasser's permission, to stand guard on the border. The Suez affair completed the work of the Egyptian movement begun by Muhammad Aly in 1805; as Nasser said, it 'resulted, of course, in the confirmation of our ownership of the canal, our economic independence, and the Egyptianisation of the property of the aggressor'.

The United Arab Republic

Although Suez confirmed the predominant influence of Russia in Egypt, President Nasser was worried about the way the Kremlin was using Arab communist parties to secure power in Syria and Iraq. When the powerful Ba'ath Party of Syria asked him in 1957 to unite their two countries, primarily to resist communist penetration of the army and administration, he agreed to do so, although reluctantly because he thought the move premature. The union was called the United Arab Republic and came into being in February 1958, with Nasser as President.

The union was received with unparalleled enthusiasm in Syria as else-where in the Arab world, but the problem of ruling Syria was beyond Egyptian experience. In face of growing resistance, Nasser was compelled to impose Egyptian control of the army and the intelligence services and key points in the civil administration. The ubiquitous intelligence service was particularly resented and on 28 September 1961 the Syrian Army re-volted and Nasser abandoned the experiment, although retaining for Egypt the name of United Arab Republic to symbolise Egypt's loyalty to the ideal of unity.[1]

The Yemen War

On 17 September 1962 pro-Egyptian Yemenis led by Colonel Abdullah al-Sallal overthrew the extremely reactionary régime of the Imamate in the Yemen and declared a republic. In accordance with his ideological opposition to monarchies, President Nasser sent troops to Yemen to support the new government, but the Imam Muhammad al-Badr, who had been thought dead in the ruins of his palace, arrived in Saudi Arabia with some supporters and rallied his family for a war to recover his throne. The mountainous character of the Yemen made it difficult to defeat the largely tribal forces of the royalists and Egypt was compelled to commit more and more troops

[1] In November 1970 Anwar Sadar, the UAR's new President, announced that his country had decided to form a federation linking it with Libya and Sudan. Syria has also announced her intention of joining the proposed federation.

and equipment until in 1965 there were 75,000 Egyptian soldiers in the Yemen. The failure to force a decision in the Yemen created doubts in Egypt about the wisdom of participation; the Egyptian defeat in the war with Israel in June 1967 and the withdrawal of British troops from South Arabia and Aden in November of that year settled the matter. Egyptian troops were withdrawn from the Yemen in December, with the civil war still unsettled.

THE JUNE WAR WITH ISRAEL

Relations with Israel had been greatly embittered by the Suez war of 1956 but the Egyptian frontier remained relatively undisturbed, largely because of the presence of UNEF. In 1966 and 1967 Israel made severe attacks on Jordan and Syria and President Nasser was widely blamed in the Arab world for failing to go to their assistance. An erroneous report from Russia that Israeli troops were massing near the Syrian frontier therefore led him in May 1967 to close the Strait of Tiran (giving access to the Gulf of Aqaba and the Israeli port of Eilat), to order the UN emergency force to leave the country, and to send strong reinforcements into Sinai. His belief that these actions would alert the great powers to the danger of war and lead them to restrain Israel from further action proved to be mistaken. On 5 June the Israelis destroyed the Egyptian air force on the ground and then by land and air defeated Egypt, Jordan and Syria in what became known as the Six Days War.

The destruction of the Egyptian army in Sinai made it impossible for Nasser to contemplate an early resumption of war to drive the Israelis out of his country. They were holding a line on the east bank of the Suez Canal which made it impossible to reopen the canal, which had again been blocked and had 15 foreign ships trapped in its lakes. Egypt had lost an annual income of about £80 million from the canal, as well as its oilfields in Sinai and most of its tourist trade. Nasser therefore spearheaded the campaign for a political settlement with Israel at a summit conference of Arab rulers in Khartoum in August and this became the official Arab policy. When the United Nations Security Council passed a resolution on 22 November calling for Israeli withdrawal from occupied territories, an end to the state of belligerency, and the freedom of all countries to use international waterways (i.e. giving Israel the right to use the Strait of Tiran and the Suez Canal), and appointed Mr. Gunnar Jarring as UN envoy to organise its implementation, President Nasser and King Husain of Jordan approved the resolution and supported the Jarring mission.

By the spring of 1969 the canal was still blocked and there were no signs of success for the Jarring Mission, while over many months Nasser had revealed increasing doubts about the possibility of implementing the UN resolution. He spoke with increasing frequency about the inevitability of another war with Israel, although always insisting that he would accept a political solution. Meanwhile the Russians re-equipped his army and air force and retrained them both. In July 1970 he accepted American proposals for a new approach to peace, but with manifest pessimism.

PRESIDENT NASSER

Gamal Abdel Nasser was born in Alexandria on 15 January 1918, the son of a modest post office official, but his family came from Beni Mor in the Assiut Province of Upper Egypt. He was sent to school in Cairo, where he lived with an uncle and in his boyhood took part in anti-British demonstrations. He saw in the army the instrument by which the monarchy could be overthrown and the British compelled to leave Egypt, and in 1937 he was admitted to the staff college. After his commission, he and some friends began to discuss means of liberating their country and this group became the nucleus of the Free Officers, which took organised form towards the end of World War II. It became more active after the defeat by Israel in the 1948 war and Nasser acquired pre-eminence in the executive, although officially there was no leader.

At the time of the revolution he had the rank of colonel and he took the leading role in organising the *coup d'état* of 1952. When it succeeded, the executive chose the respected General Muhammad Neguib as leader of the revolution, but he was finally ousted in 1954 and thereafter Nasser was the undoubted head of state. Differences of policy among the former executive led members one after the other to withdraw or be dismissed and in 1969 only two remained in positions of prominence in the state.

President Nasser died of a heart attack on 28 September 1970. Anwar Sadat, former vice-president, has succeeded Nasser as President.

ECONOMY

Geography
95% of Egypt is uninhabitable desert and the nation depends for its existence on the river Nile, which floods every summer with waters from the central African highlands. Its valley is a fertile strip with an average width of about six miles until it reaches Cairo and broadens into the delta; elsewhere there are a few oases, the Suez Canal Zone which is watered from the Nile, and the Mediterranean coastal strip which gets about six inches of rain a year.

The western and southern boundaries are arbitrarily drawn on 25 degrees longtitude and 27 degrees latitude and the Mediterranean and Red Sea give the country natural frontiers on the north and east, except where the Sinai desert plateau forms a land bridge between them and Asia.

Climate
In spring and summer the days are hot in the north and very hot in the tropical south but the temperature falls after sunset and gives relief. In autumn and winter in the north the days are cool and the nights often cold; even in the tropical south, where it remains pleasantly warm during late autumn and winter days, it can get cold at night. This is also true of the deserts throughout the region which cool rapidly after sunset. The country is almost rainless away from the Mediterranean coastal strip, but once every two or three years a short rainstorm will fall in the lower Nile valley.

Agriculture and Population
Egypt is an agricultural country and throughout history its primary problem has been to grow enough on its limited acreage to maintain its people. Since Muhammad Aly repaired the ravages of the economy in the early decades of the 19th century, the population has tended to grow faster than the acres which could feed it. There was an acre for every inhabitant at the end of Muhammad Aly's reign, only three-quarters when the Khedive Ismail abdicated, and in 1933, when the maximum benefits had been obtained

from the first Aswan Dam, there was only half an acre. There were 3 million inhabitants in 1805, 7 million in 1882, 13 million in 1917, 17 million in 1933, 25 million in 1952, 27 million in 1962, 30 million in 1965 and 33 million in 1970.

The Egyptians invented a simple water-lifting device called the *saqia* in pharaonic times, to raise the Nile flood to higher land which they watered by ditches. (The *saqia* can still occasionally be seen at work on the Nile banks.) This pharaonic system of using the Nile flood in 'basins' retained by low mud walls and extending the area of irrigation by simple machines remained unchanged until the British occupation, although Muhammad Aly established the principle of the next major development when he built the barrage across the Nile outside Cairo. This was intended to raise the level of the Nile by damming it and then releasing it to the delta. In 1898 the British completed the first Aswan Dam, which held the flood in the south and then controlled its release from sluices, thus providing water from the Aswan lake in winter and allowing five crops to be taken off the fertile valley in every two years. For the next few years the acreage kept up with the expansion of population but the inexorable pressure compelled more development on these lines. The Aswan dam was heightened twice, in 1912 and 1933, and by mid-century there were dams and barrages at intervals along the Nile all the way from Aswan to the delta to extend the areas of perennial (as distinct from basin) irrigation. Water storage on the Nile, however, was still limited to one year and this meant that the excess of a high flood could not be retained for use in years of low supply. Schemes to provide multi-year storage had been mooted for many years and the revolutionary government decided shortly after taking office in 1952 to authorise a scientific study by German engineers of a scheme to build a 'high dam' four miles south of the existing Aswan Dam. The foundation stone was laid by President Nasser in 1960. At the end of 1970 the dam, built with Russian aid, was completed, the huge Nasser Lake behind it providing an additional 72 million cubic yards of water for Egypt, allowing the irrigation of an extra two million acres and storage for more than one year. For the first time in many thousands of years the Nile flood, one of the most famous of natural phenomena, no longer reached lower Egypt.

Egypt grew edible crops for people and animals until Muhammad Aly introduced cotton, finding that the Nile valley was suitable for the production of the finest long and medium staple types. The British developed this cash crop until it became the mainstay of the Egyptian economy, for it paid the country to sell cotton and buy some of its food. In 1961 cotton provided 62% of Egyptian exports and cotton yarn and piece goods another 9%. Other agricultural exports are sugar, cereals, potatoes and onions.

Industry

Because of the high rate of population growth and the limitations on agricultural expansion, economic progress is now envisaged through industrial development; in the past, such development was impeded as long as industry was in private hands, because of a general lack of interest in industrial investment. Between 1930 and 1960 industrial growth continued at the average rate of about 10% a year, but was largely monopolistic in structure and until 1956 was substantially financed by foreigners, who exercised a high degree of managerial control. Sequestrations and expulsions removed almost the entire foreign element after the Suez crisis in 1956, and by 1960 Egyptian industry was almost entirely in private Egyptian hands. That year the nationalisation of industry began on a large scale and by 1969 the position was reversed : industry was almost entirely under government ownership or control.

There were good reasons for a policy of nationalisation. Before it took place there were few industries which could have survived because investment and national purchasing power were inadequate and there was a shortage of power and raw materials (except those from agriculture). Only a handful of industries have ever been competitive and even under nationalisation, with investment boosted by foreign loans and aid, industry is still not competitive. Productivity is rising rapidly but is still low by comparison with advanced countries. The justification for this apparently uneconomic policy is the country's compulsive need to break out from its constricting agricultural base.

A large part of industry derives from agriculture, notably in the production of textiles, cotton seed oil and in sugar refining; the production of fertilisers, of which Egyptian agriculture was an early and advanced user, has been greatly expanded at Aswan using power supplies from the dams. Iron and steel plants exist to utilise the ore from Aswan, and Suez was notable (until wrecked by Israeli shells after 1967) for oil refineries using crude from the fields in Sinai, the Gulf of Suez and the Red Sea coast. Since 1967 the coalfields being exploited in northern Sinai and the oilfields in southern Sinai have been in Israeli hands but new wells in the Gulf of Suez and a very promising field discovered in the western desert near Alamein have more than compensated.

The Aswan High Dam is also a major contribution to industry because the 12 mammoth turbines in the tunnels of the diversion channel can generate ten milliard kilowatts of hydro-electric power a year and this has become the motive force of the big fertiliser and other industries in Aswan and is being carried by cables right down the Nile to the delta. It has vastly expanded the hydro-electric resources on which the country more and more depends.

There has been a high rate of economic growth as a result of development planning in industry and agriculture. This was achieved by substantial national investments from the public sector which, in turn, depended greatly on foreign credits. There has been almost no private investment (the public sector provided 94% of gross investment in 1963–4) and domestic saving has, if anything, shown a slight decrease since 1956. The inadequacy of domestic saving combined with growing difficulties in obtaining foreign loans point to a probable deceleration of economic development.

The seizure of the Sinai peninsula in the June war of 1967 seriously damaged the economy, depriving the country of nearly £100 million a year. About £80 million was due to loss of revenue from the Suez Canal which was blocked (and was still closed in September 1970) and there were substantial losses from the Sinai oilfields which were in Israeli hands. The splendour of Egypt's ancient monuments gives the country a constant revenue from tourism, which the government has encouraged by building many new hotels; but the insecurity of the situation has seriously reduced this income also. A summit meeting of Arab leaders in August 1967 agreed that Saudi Arabia, Kuwait and Libya—three oil-rich countries—would together contribute £95 million a year to Egypt—and this removed the immediate pressure. Higher taxation and other austerity measures, including a cut-back on development programmes, have more than restored the pre-war economic situation.

POLITICS

Under British tutelage, Egypt acquired a system of parliamentary democracy copied from that of Britain; but it never worked properly because parliament was dominated by the powerful landowning class, the king was able to make or break governments almost at will, and the elections were seldom free. When they were free, the Wafd Party, which had overwhelming popular support from the early 1920s to the revolution of 1952, could always win. During the greater part of this period the politics of Egypt were the outcome of an uneasy balance between the king, the Wafd and the British, and the British made alliance with the party or the palace as occasion required. Other parties in the country were minority groups splintered from the Wafd or in direct alliance with the palace. When the Wafd allied itself corruptly in 1950 with King Farouk, whose degenerate conduct over a decade had brought an unpopular monarchy to its nadir, it helped to create the climate of opinion in which the army was able to seize power in 1952 without bloodshed and with popular acclaim.

The military junta which took power professed the intention of restoring the constitution, but its struggle for power against the landowners, the political parties, the communists and the Muslim Brotherhood made any form of democracy impossible. The power of the landowners was broken and the parties suppressed, but attempts were made to create an organised popular base for the revolution, first through the Liberation Rally, then the National Union and now the Arab Socialist Union, the party of the one-party state. The ASU was democratised in 1968 by elections held under universal suffrage on a pyramidal system rising from village units to the National Congress and Central Executive, the former deciding the policy of the state and the latter preparing plans for its execution. There is also a National Assembly but its role seems to be only consultative.

In 1962 President Nasser declared Egypt to be an Arab Socialist Republic in which Islam is the religion of the state. He never showed sympathy for communists, many of whom have spent years in prison; but with almost the entire economy directly or indirectly under government control, and in view of the country's substantial economic dependence on the Soviet bloc and total dependence on Russia for arms, Egypt is virtually a client-state of the USSR. This is not a position President Nasser would have chosen for himself, but it was brought about by his own 'anti-imperialist' policies and by the behaviour of the Western powers, notably towards Israel, which have created mutual antagonism.

In practice, President Nasser became the focal point of all power. For many years he completely dominated Arab public opinion far beyond the confines of his own country; he was the effective leader of the radical Arab national movement which sought to unify and socialise the Arab world and get rid of 'reactionary' Arab monarchs and rulers. The failure of the union with Syria in 1961 and his 1962-7 Yemen campaign, and finally his resounding defeat by Israel in 1967, lowered his prestige but until the time of his death he remained the most influential figure in Arab political life.

SOCIAL AFFAIRS

THE essential social fact from pharaonic times until today has been the contrast between the broad mass of poverty and the small class of rich people. 'Here a palace where reigns unbridled luxury, there a hovel swarming with people scarcely human', wrote a contemporary French observer in 1905, and if these conditions were modified over the years they were not fundamentally changed until the revolution of 1952, and they effectively controlled the social development of the country. Although more could have been done for the poor than was ever done, it remained true that the maximum sacrifices of the rich could not have met all the needs of the country in terms of health and education. Despite greater efforts to deal with these problems after 1945 there was still 75% illiteracy in 1952 and one of the highest infant mortality rates in the world.

Education

The revolutionary government has accelerated the campaign against illiteracy. Only 45% of children were receiving elementary education in 1952 but 65% were doing so in 1960 and it is expected that every child will receive some education by 1972. Even so there was still about 67% illiteracy in 1968 because of the large population of uneducated adults. From the primary schools there is a high intake into secondary schools and an unusually high admission to universities, of which there are five in Egypt. In 1966 it was realised that the industrial society being created lacked semi-skilled and skilled workers and it was decided that about 30% of primary pupils would be directed to industrial training institutes.

Health

Standards of health are still among the lowest in the world. The average life expectancy is 20 years and nearly a quarter of the children die before the age of one year in spite of determined efforts to effect improvement, and the underlying cause remains poverty. The number of doctors has been more than doubled since 1951, health centres have been established throughout the country to serve the villages, and less alarming results will be seen in mortality rates in due time. Inroads have already been made on two of the worst scourges: trachoma and bilharzia (a delibitating disease caused by a micro-organism which enters the body from stagnant Nile water). In 1967 the proportion of Egyptians suffering from bilharzia was 35% as compared with 60% in 1952 and trachoma claimed 25% as compared with 87% in 1952. Malaria is totally restricted to upper Egypt and is declining under the impact of a £23 million campaign spread over 11 years. Progress has also been made against tuberculosis although permanent results depend on a higher standard of living. The provision of clean drinking water is an important factor: in 1936 there was no potable water outside the main towns, by 1952 it had been provided for two million peasants, by 1957 for six million, and it will soon be available for the entire population.

Women

As in all Islamic countries, Egypt has seen slow but steady progress in the emancipation of women; seclusion has virtually disappeared and the veil can only be found in the most backward families. More than 60% of girls are receiving primary and preparatory education and an increasing number continue into the secondary schools and universities. The government's aim is total equality in education but its plans are still impeded by conservative families, particularly among the poor. This conservatism is seldom to be found among the new 'middle class' in the main cities, where wives more and more continue to work after marriage to maintain the family living standards. For the same reason, birth control—greatly encouraged by the government—is widely practised in this and higher strata of society. Polygamy is limited to a very small minority and with government encouragement the theologians of Islam teach that the Koran does not favour it even if it is permissible. In every respect the government seeks to encourage the equal participation of women in society. They have the vote and are encouraged to stand for parliament and the Arab Socialist Union; in 1962 there was a woman as Minister of Social Affairs. They are employed in government offices, take part with men in athletics and parade publicly with the Red Crescent and the Girl Guides.

Religion

There are just under 30 million Muslims of the Sunni (orthodox) sect of Islam and just over three million Coptic Christians. The Copts are direct descendants from the ancient Egyptians and many of the Muslims must also be because in past centuries many Copts adopted Islam for the benefits to be gained from doing so.

During most of this century Egypt has been the centre of the debate about 'modernism' or 'tradition' in Islam. This reached its peak in the 1920s and early 1930s when, on one side, an intellectual renaissance taught that the teachings of Islam left grounds for interpretation in terms of the needs of modern society, whereas traditionalists argued that the Koran and the *hadith* (the utterances of the Prophet) provided literally for the needs of all historical development. In the event Egypt became a liberal Islamic society and President Nasser himself encouraged this trend. Perhaps his most striking acts were to liberalise the role of women and to introduce secular faculties to Al-Azhar University, the stronghold of Islamic orthodoxy.

FURTHER READING

Blunt, Wilfred Scawen. *Secret History of the English Occupation of Egypt*, Martin Secker, London, 1907.

Cromer, The Earl of. *Modern Egypt*, Macmillan, London, 1908.

Fisher, W. B. *The Middle East*, Methuen, London, 1950.

Garzouzi, Eva. *Old Ills and New Remedies in Egypt*, Dar al-Maaref, Cairo, 1958.

Harris, Christina Phelps. *Nationalism and Revolution in Egypt*, Monton, The Hague, 1964.

Issawi, Charles. *Egypt in Revolution*, Oxford Univ. Press, London, 1963.

Little, Tom. *Modern Egypt*, Ernest Benn, London, 1967.

Mansfield, Peter, *Nasser's Egypt*, Penguin, London, 1969.

Nasser, Gamal Abdel. *Egypt's Liberation, The Philosophy of the Revolution*, Public Affairs Press, Washington, 1955.

O'Brien, Patrick. *The Revolution in Egypt's Economic System*, Oxford Univ. Press, London, 1966.

Rowlatt, Mary. *Founders of Modern Egypt*, Asia Publishing House, London, 1962.

Vatikiotis, P. J. *The Egyptian Army in Politics*, Indiana Univ. Press, Bloomington, 1961.

TOM LITTLE. Writer and broadcaster on Middle East affairs. Deputy correspondent of *The Times* and correspondent of *The Observer* and *The Economist* 1950–6. Starting as sub-editor, eventually became managing director of Regional News Services (Mid-East) and negotiated purchase of the rights of Reuters in the Middle East. Author of *Egypt* (1958), *High Dam At Aswan* (1965), *Modern Egypt* (1967) and *South Arabia* (1968). Has contributed the Middle East section to *The Annual Register of World Events* since 1955.

YEMEN

R. B. SERJEANT

YEMEN today means the territory in South Arabia lying north of South Yemen (Aden Federation) and south of Saudi Arabia, but in its widest sense Yemen included in the past large tracts of territory which did not belong to the state of Yemen under its recent Imams. This larger Yemen is, however, merely a geographical expression since the territory has but rarely, and only for brief periods, been united under a central government; so ambitious irredentist claims should not be treated too seriously.

Physically, Yemen consists of a strip of fairly heavily cultivated plain, the Tihamah, lying along the Red Sea, to the east of which is a tangled mass of mountain, shading off into foothills, steppe, and finally the great Arabian sand desert. On the west the rainfall is quite abundant and Yemen is the most fertile Arabian province, with about half its population consisting of farmers and settled villagers, as opposed to wandering Bedouin. Not only are the magnificent ruins of Yemen's ancient past everywhere visible, in the shape of temples and dams, with fine stone carving and inscriptions in the Himyaritic script, but its heritage of skill in architecture and masonry is still preserved in impressive buildings, great cisterns well maintained, the terraced mountain-sides and paved highways. Until the 1962 *coup* at least, a highly cultivated society ruled it, even though its culture and extensive literature were medieval in form.

Yemen has never had finite borders because it is simply a plethora of tribals units independent in themselves. The inhabitants of the Tihamah are often of African descent, not Arabs even; they have been there between two or three thousand years. The individual tribe has a loyalty within itself but not to the concept of a country or a monarch; tribes are generally hostile to their immediate neighbours. The same tribes, as early inscriptions show, have for thousands of years occupied roughly the same districts as they do today and in one way or another the tribes really control the cities, which have economic and strategic, but hardly political, importance. They dominate the other social classes, which exist as their protected subjects. As no tribal chief will tolerate the authority of his peers, the resulting impasse has been resolved by an institution with antecedents in remote antiquity: the holy family, deriving its authority from divine sources, acceptable to the haughtiest chiefs as an arbiter between them, able even to rule to a limited extent and to promulgate public morality. Power accrues to a prominent representative of such a family and if he is able, he may form a theocratic state; the example *par excellence* is the Prophet Muhammad, though certain pre-Islamic dynasties of Yemen appear also to have been theocratic rulers.

335

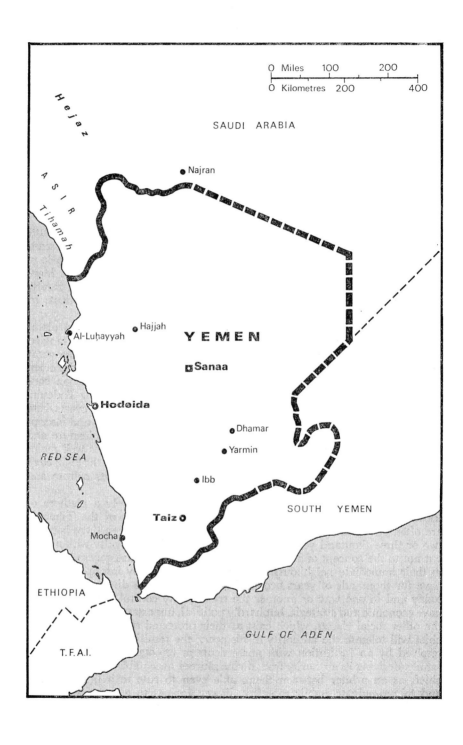

Muhammad's descendants, the Saiyids and Sharifs have maintained this role for nearly 14 centuries with varying fortunes, though the holy house has sometimes been divided within itself. The present Imam, Badr, is of Muhammad's line.

Yemen is divided between two Islamic sects, the Zaidis of the north and east, and the Shafi'is of the south and the Tihamah, reflecting a real, perhaps even a racial, division. The Zaidi warrior tribes are contrasted with the Shafi'i tribes and unwarlike peasant districts of the south. Economically the highlands and eastern steppes depend considerably on the Shafi'i districts.

Throughout Yemeni history centralised governments have also been formed in another way, when a powerful foreign invader, often with some technical superiority, has imposed his authority on the tribes; on the weakening or departure of the invader, a return to the fragmentation of tribal anarchy inevitably ensues. Just such invaders were the Aiyubids, the house of Saladin, whose successors the Rasulids, probably of Turkish descent, became identified with Yemen, giving it 200 years of security—Yemen's most brilliant age in Islamic history. In 1515 the Mameluke Sultan of Egypt despatched an expedition down the Red Sea coast to Yemen, but when the Ottoman Turks conquered the Mamelukes they annexed the province also; both boasted a military organisation vastly superior to anything in Yemen.

Modern Yemeni history really begins when the Imams, theocratic leaders of the Zaidi sect, expelled the Ottomans. Al-Qasim the Great (descended from the first Imam who arrived in Yemen in 893) started the war of independence faced by Turkish superiority in artillery, cavalry (Yemenis fight on foot), and the strong castles they held. Victorious over the Turks, their own impetus swept on the Zaidi troops to occupy the warlike 'Awlaqi and Fadli districts, Lahej, Aden, even Hadramaut, all of them Shafi'i territory— the sole occasion when the Imams achieved nominal suzerainty there. Soon the Imams found their conquests too unwieldy to control with the tribal forces at their disposal. Local chiefs reassumed power, expelling Zaidi garrisons. An Imam has no real control over the tribal contingents who respond to his call for support, and no army but a few guards, tribesmen also, so to keep tribes in order he must play one off against the other, setting (temporarily) loyal tribes against rebels. Sometimes different groups of tribes back one Imam against another.

Egypt, under its ruler Muhammad Aly in the first half of the 19th century, assumed an imperial role in the countries of the Red Sea but failed to secure Yemen and Aden. Egypt had designs on both, but the Ottoman Turks in the latter half of the century had begun to reassert themselves in Arabia. They gained control of the Hejaz, and by 1872 were strong enough to enter Sanaa, Yemen's northern capital—this marks the second Ottoman occupation of Yemen. It was constituted a province of the Ottoman empire and an administration under a Turkish governor was set up; but courageous as the Turks were, their ill-found armies suffered severely from disease and perpetual warfare with the tribes, especially the Zaidis in whose territory the traveller may still see villages destroyed by Turkish guns and never rebuilt. The Turks clashed with the Yemenis over taxation and the substitution of the Ottoman civil code for the Islamic *Shariah*. The Zaidi Imams resisted them in their mountains. In 1904 Imam Yahya, backed by Nasir Bin Ahmar, chief of the powerful Hashid confederation, succeeded his father and laid siege to Sanaa, which capitulated in 1905. Though the Turks recovered it, he besieged it again in 1911, and the Turks decided to negotiate a settlement.

The Imam's demands were in effect conceded—Yemen was divided into Zaidi and Shafiʻi districts, the Imam appointing governors in the Zaidi part while the Turkish governor appointed them in the Shafiʻi part, which the Turks seemed able to control, its inhabitants being far less difficult to handle than the Zaidis. In their southward drive, the Turks came into political conflict with Aden over tribes within the British sphere of influence; but after 30 years of border friction, the Anglo-Turkish Boundary Commission (1902–4) settled the situation, though it could not demarcate beyond Wadi Bana owing to insecurity on the northern border of the protected Yafiʻi tribe. During World War I the Turks made an incursion into the Protectorate as far as Aden, but a stalemate followed and the Turks remained there till after the Armistice.

When the Turks left after 1918, Yemen was again independent of foreign rule. Imam Yahya, as the focus of resistance and heir to a dynasty of a thousand years' duration, was the obvious successor to sovereignty. Supported by the prominent Al Wazir Saiyids and tribal chiefs, Yahya entered Sanaa and, once established, set himself to bring Yemen under his control, for it had naturally disintegrated into its component parts when the Turks left. He had first to conquer the country and this he did, sending Wazir Saiyids to take the Shafiʻi south. Hodeidah, the port of Sanaa, he took from Britain's ally the Idrisi, and not recognising the Anglo-Turkish border, invaded parts of the Aden Protectorate. These manœuvrings created friction with the British in Aden. He next dealt with the unruly Hashid confederation, his supporters and his son Ahmad (later crown-prince) and others, gaining control of eastern Yemen, including Khawlan and Maʼrib, famous for its dam. Ahmad pushed up to the north-east, overcame the Barat tribes, and in 1933 took Najran from the Makramis, an Ismaʻili group who were enemies of the Zaidis. Among the troubles and revolts of that time was the rebellion of the piratical bandit Zaraniq tribe of the south-west, which Ahmad crushed with Hashid levies. In 1934 Yahya clashed with Ibn Saud but was worsted and forced to cede territory in Asir and Najran.

Imam Yahya and his son Ahmad managed to create and maintain a state because they combined rank, personality, courage and diplomacy with an intimate knowledge of the tribes (down to the level of individuals) essential to the task. They kept an eye on their officials, especially those from Saiyid families, lest they grew too powerful, giving them spells in prison to damp any enthusiasm for revolt, but mostly freeing them later and reappointing them to office in districts where they might do least harm. The tribes, following ancient custom, gave them hostages for good behaviour. Had the Yemen remained isolated, as Imam Yahya wished, major disturbances might have been avoided. Yahya, from motives partly religious and partly political, sought to keep the Arabic Press out of Yemen, and, at first, the radio. However, he could not stop Yemenis going abroad for education and returning with the impression that Egypt and Iraq were advanced and Yemen backward, which led to the desire to 'reform' the Yemen.

Their opponents, backed by Egyptian or left-wing propaganda, accuse the Imams of all manner of evils, and especially of deliberately keeping Yemen in backwardness and economic decline, resulting in widespread misery. This reading of the situation makes no allowance for the fact that the Imams took over a state of chaos, and had to deal with a medieval polity with the means at their disposal. Acting in their own interest, they did manage to hold the balance between every other group attempting to further its own interests at the expense of others. A government's duty is to establish security;

to do this the Imams had to collect taxes and they used their northern tribes as soldiers and officials to collect from the south. In Arab countries, even the most advanced, corruption is generally widespread and accepted in public life; the very politicians who most inveigh against it are often the worst offenders once they are in power. The Imam could delegate little, in matters involving money, to the corrupt officialdom, so he was held prisoner by over-centralisation and administrative detail, unable to cope with large issues like reform. The Shafi'i districts suffered from the rapacity of officials and of the army (mainly a tax-collecting *gendarmerie*) neither of which was adequately paid through lack of sufficient financial resources. This was not the Imam's doing or wish, but he was unable to prevent it and the economy declined, while the neighbouring states, Aden Federation and Saudi Arabia, attracted thousands of Yemeni emigrants by their prosperity.

The Imams were not altogether unprogressive; they fostered education by building schools and mosques and Yemen had a surprisingly high literacy rate. They established post and telegraph offices everywhere and even set up some hospitals. It is untrue to say they built no roads, though those they did build were constructed principally for strategic reasons. They were interested in agricultural development but, for reasons beyond their control or capacity, could not arrest Yemen's economic decline.

The first stirrings against the régime in the '40s are associated with the famous Zaidi poet Zubairi, who had studied in the Azhar in Cairo, and with A. M. Nu'man, a Shafi'i of a family which had held office under the Turks. Both had been friendly with the crown prince Ahmad, but, turning against him they fled to Aden in 1944. There they founded the Yemenite Liberal Party and published a manifesto demanding reforms, essentially a moderate and reasonable document. They started a newspaper attacking Imam Yahya's government and were in touch with Saiyid Abdullah al-Wazir, who set up as Imam when Yahya was assassinated by a tribal malcontent in 1948. Ahmad, then crown-prince, escaped from Taiz to the northern citadel of Hajjah and rallied the Zaidi tribes to him; having no money to pay them he permitted them to sack Sanaa, which caused lasting grievance there. The ring-leaders were beheaded and lesser fry imprisoned, notably Nu'man, Iryani, and Ahmad al-Shami; with them was a young officer named Sallal, trained in Iraq like most officer rebels. Ahmad's punishments were drastic but just, and on the whole clement. He had the support of most public opinion in Yemen and of Aden Yemenis, as popular demonstrations against the Liberals at that time show.

Ahmad had a powerful personality. His piercing, protruberant eyes struck awe and reverence into tribesfolk, while his officials feared his wrath and swift suspicion, but he did show some ability to deal with the difficult circumstances of the time. A handicap of his latter years was an accidental addiction to morphine, but he was cured of this in 1959.

Ahmad had plenty of problems in Yemen, but he chose to add to them by provoking trouble in the Aden Protectorate. In this he was encouraged by support from the Arab League and later from Egypt, but reprisals by the 'Awdhalis and the Sharif of Baihan against his own frontiers were most effective and he had abandoned this policy by 1959. Within Yemen his more ambitious brothers intrigued against him and he nearly lost his throne to one of them in 1955. In further attempts against him, the armed forces he required to keep down recalcitrant tribes were involved; their young, semi-educated and ambitious officers were susceptible to anti-Imamic left-wing propaganda, especially from Egypt.

Ahmad was not a young man, so the question of succession was important, but Zaidis do not hold to primogeniture and Ahmad seems to have hesitated before pressing the recognition of his son Badr as heir apparent. The conservative element preferred his uncle Hasan who was therefore sent away for ten years as ambassador to Washington. The princes considered Badr incompetent to rule, but if not a personality of the calibre of his father, Badr was and is clever and open-minded. On visits abroad he saw that something must be done to modernise Yemen; looking for support elsewhere, he found it, apparently, in Egypt and Russia. Badr was responsible for introducing Egyptian instructors and Russian weapons into the schools and military establishments. He fell under the influence of the Egyptian *chargé d'affaires*, whom he consulted on all issues. His policy did not fit in with his father's aim of playing off the east against the west, obtaining thereby the reconstruction of Yemen's ports Hodeida and Mocha, and new roads. Returning from Italy in 1959, Ahmad met President Nasser at Suez, and though wisely he did not leave his ship for Egyptian soil, he is said to have told the Egyptian leader some home truths. In 1961 he boldly attacked Nasserite socialism in his famous poem, and this terminated their relationship.

Plots were now being woven around the succession; a clash between Badr, with the support of the Hashid tribes, and Hasan, backed by the Bakil, seemed likely. A conspiracy to assassinate Ahmad and Badr was thrown into confusion by Ahmad's death from natural causes, but the Egyptian *chargé d'affaires*, on instructions from Cairo, persuaded the young Egyptian-trained officers in his pay to attack Badr's house, and the *coup* of 26 September 1962 succeeded by the hair's breath. The Yemeni Liberals in Cairo had been campaigning against Imam Ahmad for some years, and a few days later Zubairi arrived in Sanaa by an Egyptian plane, along with Anwar Sadat's agent, an Egyptian of uncertain parentage called Baidani; he had served temporarily with Imam Ahmad until he dismissed him. Sallal, who preferred Russian to Egyptian aid, by a strange chance became President with the Egyptian agent Baidani as his deputy. Egyptian troops flew into Sanaa and later landed at Hodeida, bristling with Russian weapons.

Badr's uncle Hasan was the first to take up arms against the plotters, with Yemenis recruited in Saudi Arabia. Nasser for some time had run a mighty propaganda barrage against both the Imam and King Saud. So Saudi aid represented a defence measure against Egyptian aggression on the Saudis via Yemen. Badr, who had escaped from Sanaa, also took the field with Saudi support. For some months the ramshackle republic was in peril and the Egyptians badly mauled. Tribal chiefs, coming to Sanaa to receive weapons and money doled out from the Imam's magazines, would not be ruled by a clique of insignificant officers led by Sallal whom they despised; a great many of them joined the Imam, though certain prominent chiefs with a grievance became Republicans.

The Royalists found it hard to make it known, in the face of Egyptian propaganda, that they actually controlled a large part of Yemen. Although they were without tanks, planes or armour they wore the Egyptians down by sheer attrition and weakened Egypt's already shaky economy. The Egyptians could drive ill-armed tribesmen from their positions but they could never hold the country down. Neither terror, nor bribery (this was used by both sides) broke the Royalists' spirit, though allegiances fluctuated. Within the Yemen Republic itself, resistance to the Egyptian 'coloniser' grew steadily and Nasser even imprisoned prominent Republic ministers like Nu'man. Egyptian forces became so dangerously extended that Nasser resorted to the Jeddah Agreement with Faisal of Saudi Arabia and agreed to withdraw his forces—but he only used the respite to withdraw them into the defensible box formed by Hodeida, Sanaa, and Taiz. The Egyptians in 1963 had set up centres for training Aden Protectorate malcontents as terrorists, and they stepped this up when the British withdrawal was announced, hoping to have Aden fall into their hands. Except for their resounding defeat in Sinai in 1967 this might well have happened; instead they had to leave Yemen in the aftermath of the June war with Israel.

The Royalists after being within sight of capturing Sanaa from the Republicans met with severe reverses, and this for two reasons. Firstly, there was strong Russian support of the Republicans with modern arms of all descriptions including planes; secondly the Royalists fell out among themselves, Prince Muhammad Bin Husain even going so far as to depose Badr. Tiring of their squabbles, moderate Royalists led by the brilliant politician Ahmad al-Shami came to an accommodation, under Saudi aegis, with the now equally moderate, even conservative, Republican Government under President Iryani containing strong shaikhly and *qadi* elements. The Republic, after some tussles, had gained the upper hand over the extreme leftist foreign-trained group in the army and 'educated youth'. In July 1970 Britain recognised this friendly, more broadly based, Republic. There is little prospect of unity with communist-dominated South Yemen, and Yemen is preoccupied more with her economic difficulties.

FURTHER READING
(See p. 270)

THE MAGHRIB OR WESTERN ARAB WORLD

NEVILL BARBOUR

THE majority of the states of the Middle East, as we have seen, are Arabic-speaking and represent, politically and culturally, the diverse characteristics common to Arab peoples. It is therefore essential in considering the area to remember that it has a western extension in North and North-West Africa composed of five states, with a total of some 34 million inhabitants who also consider themselves part of the Arab world by language and history. This area extends westwards from the frontier of Egypt to the Atlantic and southwards across the Sahara to the negro states of Central and Western Africa. One of these states of Arabic speech, Tunisia, was formed into a unit of the Arab Caliphate from the time of the Arab conquest of Carthage in 698. The most westerly of them, known today as the Mamlakat al-Maghribiya or Moroccan Kingdom, formed a distinct political unit from about 1100; from that date its two greatest dynasties ruled over Muslim Spain and the greater part of North Africa for some 150 years. Algeria and Libya, on the other hand, date as distinct political units only from the time of the Ottoman occupation in the 16th century, while the remaining state, Mauritania, is a recent creation of French rule in Africa and was admitted as a member of the United Nations in 1961.

These five states constitute the area known to Arabs as the Maghrib. The word means 'the West', in Arabic, and is used here (as the English talk of Cornwall and Devon as the 'West Country') to denote that the area is distinguished by a certain difference of racial origin as well as by its geographical position. In spite of this the Maghrib forms a portion of the Arab world, just as Cornwall and Devon do of England. Any foreign traveller who feels at home in the Arab portions of the Middle East will feel himself equally so in the Maghrib. Though the spoken dialects of Arabic vary considerably, the language used in the press and by the government is the same as in the Middle Eastern Arab states. With regard to foreign languages, English or French are commonly understood by the educated classes in most of North Africa, together with Italian in Libya and Spanish in northern Morocco. The forms of social life and the types of architecture resemble those of the Middle Eastern Arab states; there are similar agreements and disagreements on matters of external and internal politics, and there is the same common hatred of Zionism and of the British policy which resulted in the dispossession of the greater part of the Arab population of Palestine.

The original inhabitants of the Maghrib in historical times were Berber-speaking peoples who probably came from the Nile Valley or its neighbour-hood. This population was subject to many invasions both from the Middle East and from Europe.

About 700 BC an immigrant Phoenician group founded the city of Car-thage in what is now Tunisia; as a state it came to include the present eastern Algeria, Tripolitania, the Mediterranean islands of Sicily and Malta, and in the west Cadiz in Spain and Salé in Morocco. Next came the Romans, who from 146 BC made Carthage the capital of a North African province. In AD 439 a Germanic people, the Vandals, crossed from Spain into Africa and occupied Carthage until they were displaced by the Byzantines in 535. These were followed by the Arabs who occupied and destroyed Carthage in 698 and founded a new capital at Tunis. Normans from Sicily occupied a number of Tunisian ports from 1148–60. Apart from this interruption, Arab rule continued until the 16th century; then the Spaniards, after conquering the Muslims of Granada, occupied most of the seaports from Melilla in eastern Morocco to Tripoli in Libya. After a sixty-year struggle, however, the Spaniards were displaced by Ottoman sailors and soldiers, many of European ancestry, who established three 'regencies' or military dominions : Algiers, Tunis, and Tripoli. In 1830 the French in their turn drove the Turks from Algeria. In 1882 they also took over the semi-inde-pendent Tunisia, and in 1912 Morocco, of which the northern tenth went to Spain. Morocco never came under the Turks, but many of its ports had been occupied by the Portuguese for several decades from the beginning of the 16th century. In 1911 the Italians began the invasion of Libya, which at the time was administered from Constantinople.

The Arabs had always intermarried freely with the indigenous Berber population, producing a mixed people of Arabic speech and of Muslim faith. Today it is only in the mountainous areas of Morocco, and in the Kabyle country, east of Algiers, and the Aurès, south of Biskra, that there remain considerable populations of Berber speech. There are however some Berber-speakers in southern Tunisia and in Tripolitania. Cyrenaica is entirely Arabic-speaking, though a little Berber enclave exists in the oasis of Siwa in Egypt. There is no evidence to show that the Maghrib, though part of Africa, ever had a mainly negro population, though many individuals entered the area in various capacities. Today therefore the Maghrib is over-whelmingly an Arabic-speaking area of Arab sentiment. It includes vast Saharan areas but the great majority of the population, some 34 million, increasing at the rate of two or three per cent per annum, live in a coastal strip rarely more than 100 miles wide. The principal Maghrib states today, Libya, Tunisia, Algeria, and Morocco, are all members of the Arab League, but vary considerably in national characteristics, and jealousies derived from past history give rise to some dissensions. From the Egyptian frontier to Tangier, the Maghrib has a Mediterranean frontage of some 1,500 miles, and another of some 1,200 miles on the Atlantic. Spain has for centuries possessed the ports of Ceuta and Melilla in Morocco and they are very Spanish in character. The Spanish Sahara on the Atlantic coast, 100,000 square miles, has a mere 40,000 inhabitants, akin to the Mauritanians; it contains vast potash deposits, not so far exploited.

LIBYA

Libya (810,000 square miles; population 1,650,000 in 1968) adjoins Egypt and is composed of three provinces—Cyrenaica, Tripolitania and the Fezzan, of which the latter, Saharan in character, contains a limited population of oasis dwellers. About one-third of the total population of Libya live in the most easterly province, Cyrenaica. In antiquity the Jabal al-Akhdar, the relatively well-watered plateau which contains the majority of these, was inhabited largely by Greeks, who had a prosperous agricultural and urban life. Three hundred years after the Arab conquest, however, the Fatimid ruler of Egypt, wishing to revenge himself on subjects who had rejected his rule, launched against them certain Bedouin Arab tribes, notably the Banu Sulaim. These virtually put an end to settled life in Cyrenaica, converting it into a land of nomads. In the last century it became the centre of the Sanusi movement, a Muslim religious sect based on a confraternity of which the late monarch, King Idris, was head. Only subdued by the Italians shortly before World War II, the Cyrenaicans were glad to enrol in a force organised to fight on the Allied side and in consequence received a British promise that they would not be returned to Italian rule. In the negotiations which followed the war, the Tripolitanians, who had participated less actively, found it expedient to accept Idris as King, though not themselves Sanusis, in order to share in the benefits of this promise. As ruler, Idris preferred to reside in Cyrenaica among the Sanusis, and created a new administrative capital at Beida in the Jabal al-Akhdar. The more populous and advanced province of Tripolitania lies further west, and is separated from Cyrenaica by 300 miles of desert. In the Turkish period it came to form a separate dominion with Cyrenaica under a dynasty, the Karamanlis. Limited in local resources, it lived off privateering and overland trade with West Africa, which was later killed by easier sea traffic. At the end of the Napoleonic wars Tripolitania reverted to direct rule from Istanbul until the Italian conquest of 1912.

Under King Idris the state pursued a consistently friendly policy towards Britain, though as an Arab state it refused to permit the passage of troops to share in the 1956 attack on Egypt. During the first years of independence, the state had very limited internal resources and was dependent on the leasing of bases to the USA and Great Britain and on other forms of foreign aid. With the discovery of oil in 1959 the situation was entirely changed and Libya quickly became one of the richest of all the Arab oil-bearing states. The wells are conveniently shared between the two provinces of Cyrenaica and Tripoli; and the resources thus produced made possible not only a greater independence but also the creation of a welfare state like the oil-bearing states of the Middle East. Once Libya no longer had to look to outsiders for support, the younger generation became increasingly dissatisfied with the paternalistic rule of King Idris and his deference to British views. It was always anticipated that the transition of authority to the heir, his nephew, would present difficulties. In fact his régime was overthrown by a military *coup* in 1969, when he had reached the age of 79 and was abroad undergoing treatment at a spa in Turkey. The subsequent Government, directed by young army officers, is much closer to the 'progressive' Arab states and to the communist world. It has withdrawn the military and air force facilities previously enjoyed by Great Britain and the USA. And in November 1970 it was announced that Libya intended to form a federation with Sudan and the UAR.

TUNISIA

Tunisia is the smallest in area of the Maghrib states (48,000 square miles), but with a population approaching five million is the third most populous. Situated only 50 miles from Sicily and successively the centre of Carthaginian, Roman, and then for several centuries of Arab power in North Africa, it has had a very long tradition of civilised life and its leaders today are perhaps the most modern-minded (in the West European sense) of all the Maghrib. It was from Tunis that Muslim rule was extended to Sicily from the 9th till the 11th century and it was from Tunis in the 10th century that the Fatimids, an heretical Muslim (Shi'a) dynasty achieved the conquest of Egypt and founded the city of Cairo. The later Ottoman intervention greatly diminished the relative importance of Tunisia, which from 1705 became an Ottoman dominion under the dynasty of the Husainite Beys. During the 19th century the country became virtually independent but assisted the Turkish suzerain in wartime, sending, for example, a naval detachment to the Battle of Navarino (1827) and a body of men to the Black Sea region during the Russo-Turkish war.

During this period there are many parallels, as self-governing Ottoman dominions, between the history of Tunis and that of Egypt, particularly during the reign of the Bey Ahmad (1837–1855) who introduced many reforms. As in the case of Egypt, the expensive modernising projects of the ruler led eventually to bankruptcy and so to European financial control and finally to the French occupation. As in the case of Egypt the ensuing restoration of the finances led to a national resurgence, headed from 1934 by the French-educated leader, Habib Bourguiba. By her own efforts, and taking advantage of the Moroccan and of the formidable Algerian resistance to French rule, Tunisia gained her independence in 1956 and in the following year abolished the dynasty of Ottoman origin.

Since that time Tunisia's markedly Western European outlook in many matters, notably the Congo question, Mauritania, and some aspects of the Palestine problem, has led to a number of disagreements with certain other Arab states, particularly Egypt, Algeria and Morocco. On the other hand, Tunisian support of the Algerian cause during the struggle for independence and her assertion of her own right to take over the French base at Bizerta and to buy out the French and other foreign owners of the flourishing farms mostly in the Majerda Valley, involved her in disputes with France; these resulted in her relations with the former protecting power being often surprisingly unfriendly. However, with the passage of time, these matters seem finally to be arranging themselves. On the other hand mistrust of the UAR is still a latent source of disagreement, even when on the surface relations are friendly.

Internally Tunisia is ruled by the neo-Destour Party, controlled by President Bourguiba. Apart from agriculture, Tunisia depends on its valuable phosphate mines and the production of super-phosphates, iron ore, lead and zinc. It is far from having the abundance of mineral oil which its neighbours on either side enjoy; but in the last few years supplies adequate for its own needs, leaving a surplus for export, have been found near the Algerian frontier, where they adjoin some of the Algerian fields. Tunisia has also a flourishing agriculture in the Majerda Valley and on Cape Bon, together with a valuable source of olive oil in the groves on the southern coastal area near Sfax. These however are dependent on the uncertain rainfall, so that the output varies greatly from year to year. An asset which has been enormously and very successfully developed since independence is the tourist industry; the eastern coast, previously largely deserted, now has many hotels and other facilities for tourists. Tunisia also contains many monuments of Roman antiquity such as the Colosseum at al-Djem between Sousse and

345

Sfax and the ruins of the city of Dugga between Tunis and the Algerian frontier. There is a fine Roman collection in the Bardo Museum in Tunis. From the Arab period the great Mosque of Qairawan and the reservoirs at that city are notable, while the period of the Turks and the Beys has bequeathed to the city of Tunis handsome government offices and a former Ottoman barracks which today serves as the National Library. There is also much interesting architecture, both military and domestic in Tunis and other principal towns. Other tourist attractions are the island of Jerba with its palm groves; and the oases of Gabes, Tozeur and Nefta.

ALGERIA

Algeria (*Al-Jazair*; 850,000 square miles; population, 1968, 12 million), as a distinct political unit, was brought into existence by the arrival of Turkish privateers, mostly Muslims of European origin, in the early 16th century. Soon after the capture in 1492 of Granada, the last Muslim state in Spain, the Spaniards, operating from Sicily as well as from Spain, carried the war on into Africa from Melilla eastwards, Morocco being left to Portugal. They rapidly occupied or established a protectorate over almost every port, except Tunis, as far east as Tripoli. The Hafsid Sultan of Tunis was therefore glad to accept the services of two Ottoman privateers who brought in valuable prizes of Spanish shipping, and rescued Spanish Muslims from Spain. These two men were the brothers Aruj and Kheir al-Din. They came from Mitylene and were the sons of a former Muslim soldier probably of Greek origin, married to the widow of a Greek priest. Soon, however, the Sultan began to fear that he had merely exchanged a Christian for a Muslim menace. This became clear when Aruj established himself at the hitherto insignificant port of Algiers and then died fighting the Spaniards at Tlemsen. His brother Kheir al-Din thereupon offered the territory to the Ottoman Sultan; the Sultan accepted, appointed Kheir al-Din a Sanjak Bey, and sent him 2,000 regular and 4,000 volunteer troops. This was the beginning of the three Ottoman Cjaks or military dominions in North Africa—Algiers, Tunis, and Tripoli. In the course of 15 years Kheir al-Din won such a reputation that he was named Kapudan Pasha (Lord High Admiral), with the rank of Baylerbey (Governor-General), and was given general supervision of Ottoman maritime and overseas affairs.

Formed from territory formerly more or less dependent on Tunis in the east and on Morocco or Tlemsen in the west, Algiers became the principal of the three regencies, of which Tripoli was established in 1551 and Tunis in 1574. The 60-year struggle of Spaniards and Turks for mastery in North Africa was thus ended with the establishment of Ottoman rule everywhere east of Morocco. Though the language of government now became Turkish, the ruling Ottomans never formed more than a small minority of the population. Arabs and Berbers continued to manage their own affairs, subject to the periodical payment of taxes collected by armed visitations. Algiers became a very wealthy city, mainly through the profits of privateering, and was enriched with handsome mosques and private palaces. Unlike Tunis and Tripoli it never acquired a local dynasty, though the government increasingly became of an independent nature under which the ruler or *Dey* was elected (from 1671) from the local Turks and advised by a council of ministers. Ultimately as individual privateering lost respectability in the more advanced Europe, it was confided to government management in Algiers. By the time of the French invasion of 1830 resources of this nature were virtually confined to certain sums paid by minor European powers for the safe passage of their shipping to the east.

The French invasion and régime

The French invasion was presented as an operation to end Muslim privateering and Turkish oppression of the native population of Algeria. In fact it marked the revival of French expansionism which had been interrupted by Napoleon's defeat and was an effort of the discredited government of Charles X to win the sympathy and support of the army officers. Though the destruction of Turkish power proved simple, Charles X's régime disappeared also and by degrees the expansionist tendencies of France led to the progressive occupation of the whole regency. This took a very long time. Arab resistance under Abdul Qadir was only finally defeated in 1847 and there were a number of further major risings, of which the last followed the French defeat in the Franco-Prussian War of 1870. These were succeeded by the wholesale confiscation of land and the reduction of the Algerians to a subject population, liable to restrictions of every sort.

There followed a second period from about 1880 to World War I during which old-style armed resistance ceased; a minority of well-to-do Muslim Algerians received a modern French education, while the European colonists —Spanish, Italian, and Maltese as much as French—constituted a privileged minority population. This period was marked on the part of the small group of educated Muslims by a demand for assimilation with the Europeans and equal rights for the two communities.

A third period ran from World War I till November 1954. It was marked by the refusal of the European Algerians to envisage the assimilation of the Muslim masses and by a movement for independence which originated among Algerian Muslims who had fought for France during the war or worked in French factories. This movement was promoted during World War II by the failure of the assimilationist movement and by the successes of the movements for Arab independence in the Middle East and later by the progress of similar movements in Tunisia and Morocco. Gaullist reforms and the emancipation of some thousands of Muslims proved quite insufficient. In November 1954 there began an armed resistance; this rapidly absorbed all the other elements and resulted in a struggle of more than six years. At the end of this period the Treaty of Evian formulated a settlement for an independent Algeria, by which the French Algerians would enjoy a guaranteed position. These, however, after attempting violent resistance, supported by a number of leading army officers, gave up the struggle, and 90% of them fled to Europe.

Independent Algeria

The recognition of independence was celebrated by three days of wild rejoicing and led to much paying-off of old scores. The position of the provisional Government which had been established outside Algeria was then challenged by Ahmad Ben Bella, one of the original leaders who had been imprisoned in France for nearly the whole of the rising, by Colonel Boumedienne, commander of the Algerian forces established on the Tunisian frontier outside the barrier built by the French, and by Muhammad Khider, treasurer of the funds collected for the resistance. A period of near-anarchy followed in which the provisional Government was finally displaced by the triumvirate of its three principal opponents. Ben Bella became Premier in autumn 1962 and was virtual dictator until his arbitrary methods caused him to be overthrown by Colonel Boumedienne in 1965. With the departure of the million Europeans who had controlled the economy, and because of the internal dissensions of the Algerian leaders, the country faced great difficulties. It was however aided by the revenue from oil (42,000,500 tons in 1958) and by the cessation of the need for imports hitherto demanded by the settlers. In the circumstances of the liberation it was only natural that Algeria should look for aid to the Communist countries which had helped her struggle.

Nevertheless education still depended largely on French teachers and General de Gaulle's régime went to great lengths to meet the Algerian desire to nationalise local resources and internationalise foreign aid. There were many internal troubles, but since 1960 the new Algerian state has gone a long way towards stabilisation. It strongly supports such Arab causes as Palestine and for this purpose maintains an armed force in Egypt. On the other hand it resisted the Moroccan desire to take back territory considered as an area of Moroccan influence before the French occupation. In 1970 the two countries agreed on joint exploitation of the iron ore resources, under Algerian sovereignty, in the disputed area.

Morocco

The position of Morocco (170,000 square miles; population 14 million) in the far west and its proximity to Spain caused it to be the African land most influenced by the high civilisation of al-Andalus (Muslim Spain) and also enabled it to resist the Ottoman attempt at subjugation. From about 1100 for a century-and-a-half two Moroccan dynasties ruled not only most or all of North Africa but also Muslim Spain, by which Morocco was itself very greatly influenced. This was followed by a gradual collapse and around 1500 most of the ports were occupied by Portugal, which established a virtual protectorate over the southern part of the country from Safi to Marrakesh. In the 16th century a revival occurred under the Saadian dynasty. Morocco supplied sugar to Queen Elizabeth and there was a half-hearted willingness of the protestant powers, England and the Netherlands, to utilise Moroccan aid against Spain, though without going so far as to assist a Moroccan attempt to regain Andalusia for the Muslims. The greatest Saadian Sultan, Ahmad al-Mansur (1578–1603), also established a Moroccan protectorate over the negro kingdom of Songhai on the Niger, defeating its forces by the use of Muslim refugees from Spain. There followed another period of decadence; during this Morocco retired behind the shelter of its ocean frontiers in the north and west, the mountains in the east, and the Sahara in the south. This period finally ended only in 1912 with the Franco-Spanish occupation which lasted until 1956.

During this period the possibilities of Moroccan development were fully revealed. The country's position on the Atlantic, with the High Atlas range of mountains running through it north-east from Agadir, ensures the interception of rain clouds, making it a country of substantial rivers. Those on the north run into the Atlantic after watering the coastal plain, where the greater part of the population lives; those on the south water fertile valleys and create the great palm-oasis of Tafilalet before being lost in the Sahara. the country is therefore relatively well watered. It has also one of the world's greatest reserves of mineral phosphates, besides considerable supplies of coal and iron.

Except for the brief period of the Protectorate, Morocco has been an independent country for a thousand years and its position in the far west has given it a marked individuality, though in general it shares the sentiments of the Arab world. The result of the foreign occupation was a very rapid modernisation. Beside the picturesque medieval cities there grew up modern towns such as the great port of Casablanca (al-Dar al-Baida) and the administrative capital of Rabat. The old northern capital, Fez, is one of the most interesting and picturesque of all surviving medieval cities; the old southern capital, Marrakesh, is no less interesting but far more African in character. The combination of ancient and modern civilisations, of mountain, plain and desert scenery, with a friendly population, makes the country extremely attractive.

The French protectorate, while highly efficient, ran the country by modern French-staffed departments, while the former organs of Moroccan government survived mainly as ornaments. Thus there was no local constitutional development and with the return of independence power soon reverted from the political parties to the sultan. Very soon the Istiqlal Party, which with the sultan had won back the country's independence, split into a right-wing branch, essentially Islamic and in general willing to work with the King, and a left-wing branch based on the more modern towns with the industrial workers, which desired a socialist type of government and had little love for the monarchy. In 1963 nevertheless a parliamentary system was introduced; this was however suspended by the King hardly a year later, since when the cabinets have been quite definitely selected by the monarch. Externally the chief problems have been the dispute with Algeria over territory like the Tindouf area attached to Algeria by the French, and the independence granted to Mauritania, which had formerly owed a loose allegiance to Morocco. The former problem led to frontier fighting between Morocco and Algeria in 1963, during which the Moroccans captured five Egyptian officers who were advising the Algerians. (See 'Algeria', p. 348.) In 1970 the King proposed a one-chamber constitution, which was approved by a plebiscite in spite of the opposition of the two leading parties.

MAURITANIA

Mauritania (419,000 square miles; one million inhabitants, of whom 200,000 are negroes) lies to the south of Morocco, north of the West African states. It is a mainly desert country which in the 11th century provided Morocco with one of its greatest dynasties. Later it looked to the Moroccan sultans as spiritual chiefs, and for aid against possible aggressors, though it was not administratively a portion of the kingdom. After the establishment of the Moroccan protectorate, France occupied Mauritania from 1934 and attached it to West Africa. When the French withdrew they formed the area into an independent state; in 1961 it was admitted as a member of the United Nations, in spite of Moroccan opposition which was supported by the other Arab states with the exception of Tunisia. The country contains a mountain of iron ore which is its chief natural resource and other minerals such as copper. It has a considerable tradition of Arab and Islamic learning, and shares the general Arab outlook on the Palestine problem, but the objections of Morocco have prevented its admission to the Arab League.

FURTHER READING

Barbour, Nevill. (ed.) *A Survey of North West Africa (the Maghrib)*, 2nd ed. RIIA, London, 1962.

Berque, J. *French North Africa between the World Wars*, trans. Jean Stewart, Faber & Faber, London, 1967; Praeger, New York, 1967.

Berque, J. 'Algeria', *Encyclopaedia of Islam*, vol. 1.

Bourdieu, P. *The Algerians*, Beacon Press, Boston, 1967.

Cohen, M. L. and Hahn, Lorna. *Morocco: Old Land, New Nation*, Pall Mall, London, 1966.

Gerteiny, A. G. *Mauritania*, Pall Mall Press, London, 1967; Praeger, New York, 1967.

Khadduri, Majid. *Modern Libya, a Study in Political Developments*, Johns Hopkins, Baltimore, 1963.

Moore, C. H. *Tunisia Since Independence and the Dynamics of One-Party Government*, Univ. of California Press, 1965.

NEVILL BARBOUR. Formerly Assistant Head, Eastern Services, BBC. Author of *Nisi Dominus, a Survey of the Palestine Controversy* (1946). Editor of *A Survey of North West Africa (the Maghrib)* (1959). Translator (from the Arabic) of Manfaloti's *Essays* (1931). Broadcaster on Arab affairs, and contributor to periodicals in Great Britain, USA, France, Spain, Belgium, Egypt and India.

PART THREE

POLITICAL AFFAIRS

ARAB NATIONALISM

MUNIF RAZZAZ

I

ARAB Nationalism is the driving force behind the Arabs in their struggle to create a progressive nation that can hold its own with the nations of the world.

It was born as the response to a challenge, the challenge of Western colonialism. Thus it was born with a negative character, as an attempt to struggle against alien intrusion. As it developed and approached maturity, it had first to acquire a positive character and then to become a 'liberation movement', with all the true characteristics of such movements. Irrespective of the original challenge that stimulated it, its task was to transform the backward character of its own society and to create a new and progressive Arab nation, strong, socially conscious, free and united.

II

The sense of 'belonging' to an 'Arab' entity is as old as the Arabs themselves. But this sense of 'belonging' crystallised and took form only after the advent of Islam and the Islamic conquests, when the Arabs, with a sense of a mission, confronted and defeated the Empires of the day to occupy and govern half the known world. This sense became strongest during the zenith of the Islamic Empire, and degenerated when Islamic society itself degenerated from about the tenth century onwards.

The vital energy which created the great Arab Empire and the Islamic civilisation had spent itself. The Islamic societies became stagnant, tranquil, self-satisfied societies in which every question had its answer and in which there was a complete equilibrium of political, social and cultural factors. The spirit of innovation was stifled, and any change affected only the persons of the governors and nothing else. This stagnant condition was personified by the Ottoman Empire, which included under its rule most of the Arab world.

Such a state of affairs could have lasted for ever if no new stimulus had disturbed the prevailing equilibrium. But a stimulus was provided by Western colonialism.

III

The first confrontation between the Arabs and Western colonialism occurred in the Arabian Gulf and the Indian Ocean at the beginning of the 16th century, when Albuquerque occupied the island of Hormes in the Arabian

353

Gulf in 1515. In the next four centuries the Portuguese, the Dutch, the French and the British succeeded each other in occupying the islands and the southern and eastern coasts of Arabia.

The first battles between the Arabs and the new colonialist powers were fought, not on land, but in the seas of the Indian Ocean. Before the advent of Europeans, Arabs from South Arabia had been the masters of the seaways since time immemorial. For three centuries sea battles continued between the Arabs and the new intruders, until the Arab fleet was destroyed in a decisive battle off Ras-el-Khaimah at the beginning of the 19th century. After that the whole of eastern and southern coasts of the Arabian peninsula were subjugated.

In 1797 Napoleon occupied Egypt for a short time. In 1830 the French occupied Algeria. In 1882 Tunisia and Egypt were occupied by the French and the British respectively. Later it was the turn of the Sudan, Morocco and Libya. At the end of World War I the whole Arab world was occupied, except for the interior of the Arabian peninsula itself, which was, anyhow, under British influence. The victory of colonialism was complete.

IV

The history of the Arab reaction to colonialist domination and of the development of this reaction to the present time, is the history of Arab Nationalism.

The slumbering, complacent Muslim Arab world, which had lost its driving force and was quite content with itself, and which looked at the world at large, especially the European world, as the countries of the 'Franks' and the 'infidels', was shaken by its sudden discovery of what 'Europe' and Western civilisation really meant.

The Arabs first realised the potentialities of this new civilisation from the weapons it possessed, which were quite different from anything the East had ever had.

The supremacy of the new civilisation was evident wherever the armies of the two societies faced each other. The old traditional Muslim society failed to defend itself in the face of the new danger. Its faith in its own values was shaken, and consequently its faith in the ability of the Ottoman Empire to defend the Muslim world. So the first phase of the response, that of fighting the new forces with the traditional forces, proved its failure. With the birth of the second phase there began a process of self-assessment.

V

In these circumstances it is no wonder that the first reaction to the successive defeats should be directed internally in a form of self-analysis. The supremacy of the West could not be taken at its face value. It was hard to believe that the values of the 'infidels' were better than the values of the 'faithful'. So the only acceptable explanation must be that the Muslims had for a long time distorted their own values in their own society, and that the prevailing values were really different from what Islam had taught centuries before.

This argument was strengthened by the fact that Arabs and Muslims had conquered and illuminated the world when Europe lived in the dark ages.

According to this self-criticism, what the Muslims needed was a reassessment of their own heritage, to rediscover the old values, to purify Islam from all the impurities that had been added during centuries of decay, to go back to the original sources of Arab and Muslim glory, to the pure and unadulterated teachings of Islam.

To satisfy this need, new revivalist movements were born, and were directed against the foreigners as well as against the traditional establishment and the authority of the Ottoman Empire. The Wahhabis in Arabia, the Mahdists in the Sudan and the Salafiya in North Africa were the most prominent examples of these movements in the 18th and 19th centuries. An off-shoot of this second phase of reaction was the new religious thinking in Egypt, led by Al-Afghani and Muhammad Abdu, which combined a new revived Islam with some of the values of the new European civilisation.

But this phase of the reaction, the religious revival movement, was destined to fail. It was a movement restricted by the boundaries of the traditional framework, and quite out of touch with the social changes that began to appear in society as a result of wider contacts with the West. Simple rejection of Western values proved to be useless in facing this new danger. Even half-hearted acceptance of some of these values in an attempt to modernise Islam was also bound to fail. The European avalanche could only be confronted by its own ideas and values. Once this was recognised, the third phase of the reaction was born.

VI

In the last years of the 18th century and at the beginning of the 19th, the Arab world began to have contacts with the West quite different from those it had previously had. Before, only traders in the large ports had had some contacts with foreigners, usually with the foreigners coming to the Arab ports but not the other way round.

Napoleon introduced the first Arabic Press into Egypt, along with some ideas about justice and equality, as well as new ways of life. Missionaries introduced into Lebanon and Syria, where there were large Christian minorities, foreign languages, foreign culture and opportunities for travel and study abroad.

Muhammad Aly of Egypt was the first ruler of any Arab country to realise that, in order to resist successfully the menace of the threatening Western powers, Egypt must learn a lot from them. He sent missions to Europe to study. Experts and technicians were invited to start a revolutionary reform in education, industry and the armed forces.

In Tunisia, under Khairuddin Pasha, in Lebanon with the missionary schools, in Syria, in Iraq, but also in Istanbul, the Turkish capital of the Ottoman Empire, much the same changes were taking place.

Thus a new phase was introduced into the movement of Arab awakening, characterised by the recognition that European civilisation meant, in addition to advanced arms and advancing armies, notions of freedom, justice, industry, education, modern administration and a new idea of nationalism where the bonds of common language and culture replaced the older bond of faith.

This new development was helped, first, by the recognition that traditional society in general, and the absolute authority of the Ottoman Empire in particular were responsible for the decay that had befallen the Arab world over the centuries, and for the successive defeats of Muslims in Egypt, North Africa and South Arabia. It was helped, also by the gradual changes that were taking place in the composition of society, as a result of economic

changes which brought in their wake a continuing process of modernisation.
In fact, 'modernisation', whether it applied to administration, constitutional life, civil codes, courts of justice, education or representation, was the catchword of the epoch. The movement for modernisation was strongest in Egypt, where Arabi led a revolutionary reform against the Khedive and the élite classes of Circassians, Turks and Albanians around him who held the land and controlled the government. But his revolution was smothered by the British forces which occupied Egypt in 1882.

In addition to the modernising movement there was necessarily also a search for an identity. 'Ottomanism' was no longer an appropriate description of the new national consciousness, which sprang up among the governing Turks even earlier than it did among the governed Arabs. In countries under the control of the Ottoman Empire, the search for an identity found its aim in Arab Nationalism, based on a common language, history and culture, and which rejected both the 'Ottoman' and the 'Turkish' identities. The sense of 'oneness' with the Turks was destroyed, first, naturally, among the Christian Arabs, but later among the Muslims as well.

In countries where subordination to the West came early, as in Egypt and North Africa, this need for differentiation between Arabs and Muslims did not present itself, because the main problem was the confrontation with the occupying forces. So the slogan that had to replace those of 'modernisation' and 'nationalism' was 'independence'. And this struggle for independence had to have its local character, because it was the people of a particular occupied country who were fighting against a particular occupying foreign power. And so 'Egypt for the Egyptians' was the slogan in Egypt instead of 'Arab Nationalism', and the independence of Egypt was the aim of the nationalist movement, because it was Egypt that was occupied and not the other Arab countries, and it was Britain that was the occupying power and not the Turks.

So, when World War I started, there was an Arab Nationalist movement east of Suez, directed mainly against the authority of the Ottoman Empire, and nationalist movements west of Suez directed against the Western colonialist powers. When the Ottoman Empire chose to be on the side of the Germans, the Arabs in Asia and Africa found themselves in different camps. The Asians revolted, with the help of the British, against the Turks, while the African Arabs were struggling against the Allies.

VII

The victory of the Allies, however, ended the discrepancy between the two parts of the Arab world, and unified their problems by putting them all under Western occupation. In addition, it presented them with two new problems. First, the Allies divided the whole Asian part into several small states. Second, they isolated one territory, designated for the purpose as Palestine, and promised the Jews of the world a 'national home' there.

The results of these changes were far-reaching. First, the schism in political development between the Asian and the African parts of the Arab world ended. The whole Arab world now found itself in direct confrontation with Western colonialism. The movements for independence were of necessity local and regional, and confined to the boundaries of the states concerned, but for the first time they appeared to be parts of a recognisable whole. Henceforth any national movement in any part of the Arab world found its echo in other parts. Poets in Damascus sang the praise of the Moroccan revolt of 1921–6. Others in Egypt eulogised the Syrian revolution of 1925–7. Arabs from Syria, Iraq and Jordan participated in the Palestinian revolution of 1936–8. 'Arab Nationalism' was beginning to be more than a slogan. It began to take shape in the minds and hearts of the people as a result of the unity they felt because of their common experience in the struggle against colonialism, in addition to their original unity of language, history and culture.

Secondly, Arab 'unity' was becoming a new slogan in addition to the basic slogan of 'independence'. Before the war, when all the Asian part of the Arab world was under Ottoman rule, an Arab from the Yemen could travel to Damascus—or even to Istanbul—without a passport. After the war the Fertile Crescent alone was subdivided into half a dozen separate states. And although the term 'Arab Nationalism' was first born in the Asian part, and for all practical purposes was confined, before the war to that part of the Arab world, the rationale of 'unity' which necessitated discussions about nationalism and what constituted nationalism, had to arrive at its logical conclusion, that of embracing the Arabs of Africa in the term 'Arabs'.

A third result of the new change was the transformation of the Arab Nationalist movements, whether designated as such or not, from their reformist character into armed revolutions. The frustration that befell the Arabs after the failure of the Allies to carry out their promises to the leaders of the Arab revolution of 1916 against the Turks, and the division and occupation of their lands, resulted in armed revolution everywhere. In Iraq, Syria, Jordan and Palestine, revolutions followed each other. In Morocco, Libya, Egypt and Sudan, people were struggling for independence by arms. All these revolutions were destined to fail. But they changed the character of the struggle, which had begun as reformist, concentrating on the improvement of society as a whole, politically, economically and socially, and diverted it into a new course which concentrated mainly on independence. With the beginning and the later development of this revolutionary spirit, the movement acquired its positive character and became something more than a mere reaction to a challenge.

It was against Zionism that the Arabs first took an action that involved a common responsibility. In 1932, Iraq signed a treaty with Britain by which it was regarded as independent and was admitted to the League of Nations. Egypt and Syria signed similar treaties, with Britain and France respectively, in 1936. And although this independence was incomplete, and the colonialist powers kept their armed forces in these countries and had 'rights' of interference in their foreign, financial, and economic affairs, these semi-independent states found themselves responsible not only for the development of their own countries and people, but also for helping other Arab countries in their struggle for independence. It was Palestine, where the Zionist problem with its international ramifications was the most serious of all the dangers that the Arabs faced, that most needed some kind of concerted Arab action. So it was in 1936 that the heads of the Arab states, for the first time interfered to stop the six-month-old strike and armed revolution, guaranteeing honourable negotiations with Britain. And it was in 1939 that representatives of all the Arab states, in addition to the Palestinian Arabs, participated in the round table conference in London to discuss the future of Palestine. Since then, Palestine has been the main topic around which Arab governments still gather and still feel the need for unity, in spite of all their differences.

VIII

Throughout this phase of the struggle for independence the main ideal of the various Arab national movements was borrowed from the West itself. It was, in fact, a struggle to achieve independence in order to be able to establish governments and societies on the same lines as the West. And so it was at the same time a struggle for modernisation, liberalisation, constitutional democracy, national industry, education and progress.

During this phase the search for identity was still going on. The notion of 'one Arab nation' was hardly accepted in Egypt and North Africa, although Arab responsibilities were accepted.

Social changes, except for general reform, were not in the programme of the nationalist movements. On the contrary, these movements were mainly led by wealthy landlords, successful professionals and descendants of old traditional families, who also wanted to benefit from the new financial opportunities that were opening up with the modernisation of society. So as soon as independence was achieved these leading nationalists, who became the new rulers, grabbed every available opportunity to make further gains to increase their growing wealth and their 'rights' and 'privileges'.

Until independence was achieved the national movements were devoid of any class consciousness or any overt social ends. The whole nation, except those who frankly and openly collaborated with the occupying powers, was participating in the struggle for independence.

IX

World War II was an important landmark in the development of Arab Nationalism. In fact, it was only after the war that this term could be applied in its true meaning to the Arab movements for liberation, and could be recognised as the main driving force behind the profound changes that were to overtake the Arab world.

In passing from its adolescent to its mature stage the movement underwent a revolutionary change by which it lost its simple character as a negative 'reflex action' to the colonialist challenge, and acquired the positive, spontaneous and deep-rooted character of a genuine liberation movement with a motive force of its own.

In this stage Arab Nationalism, in the narrow sense of a consciousness of belonging to one Arab nation, replaced all other narrower concepts of nationhood. Egyptianism, Algerianism, Syrianism, terms denoting previously a belief in these regional identities, have been replaced by Arabism. All regional movements, whether for independence, as in the case of Algeria, or for social revolution, as in Syria, were regarded as parts of a general Arab movement. Any progressive struggle in any Arab country had its echoes and its repercussions all over the Arab world. Israel fought with the countries of the Arab League, not with the Palestinians alone, in order to establish itself. France participated in the invasion of Egypt in 1956 in the belief that Egypt was responsible for the Algerian Revolution.

'Unity', which should have been the logical result of such a unitarian trend, was only achieved for a short period between Egypt and Syria. But 'unity in struggle' as it was called, i.e. the sense of belonging to one oppressed nation against imperialism and Zionism, was a very strong reality.

For the first time, the problem of social development was discovered and recognised, not as an aim to be attained after the success of independence movements, but as part and parcel of the movement itself. It was accepted as a problem that governed the movement's immediate rules and requirements, affected its aims and means and changed the character of the struggle itself. For the first time the importance of the class struggle within the national struggle itself was recognised.

The term 'independence' also underwent a fundamental change. Before the war it meant getting rid of the occupying power, and the national movements were content to have semi-independent states with links of tutelage to the colonial powers, and even accepted the existence of foreign armed forces and interference in the country's foreign and economic policies. After the war, the universality of colonialism, the meaning—in Leninist terms—of imperialism, the role of neo-colonialism and its ties with bourgeois capitalism, the links with other liberation movements in the third world, were all recognised and accepted. Independence became positive neutrality or non-alignment. And one of the most important aims of the Arab national movement was to struggle against foreign bases, foreign influence and interference, and against imperialism everywhere.

X

These important changes were triggered by the war and its effects on the minds of the people and on their social conditions. The war with its huge armies, its extensive front lines that cut through state boundaries and with news from all over the world reaching the peoples of the Middle East at a time when every household was trying to buy its own radio and read its own newspaper, had the effect of extending their field of vision beyond their immediate environment. The early and crushing reverses suffered by the Allies only proved to the Arabs that these strong and important world powers could also be defeated. They were not as invincible as they appeared to be.

Access to the ideas and the ideology of the Communist world introduced, for the first time in the history of the Arab world, a new element in its political education, which until then had depended mainly on Western capitalist and liberal sources. These ideas were not completely new to the Arab world. There had always been some leftists who tried to propagate these ideas, but they had failed to make any real contact with the people, because they failed to grasp the deep meaning of the changes and the contradictions that were appearing in Arab society. They were working on a dialectic that had no existence and they failed to see the real dialectical relationship between colonialism and nationalism. The class struggle was the most important thing to them at a time when the national struggle was paramount.

After the war, Arab society was ready for ideas which were socialist and Marxist in nature, especially if they were associated with ideas of nationalism.

During the war immense opportunities for employment opened up, in new industries created rapidly to supply the needs of the armed forces in the area or to make up for goods that were difficult to import, and also in services. At the same time expenditure by the armies increased. Very rapidly a new working class was created with better standards of living, better jobs and a heightened awareness and readiness to absorb and assimilate new ideas. Although higher prices swallowed up most of what was gained by the labourers, there was a definite change in the whole constitution of Arab society, with new mass immigration from the country to the cities where there were better opportunities for better paid jobs.

But side by side with this change a new, rich—very rich—middle class was also springing up, which had its connections with the ruling classes— the previous national leaders—and was trying to explore and exploit the innumerable opportunities opened up by the war and by the impending social changes and the rising standard of consumption of both public and private sectors. Corruption had never been as prevalent as it became in this period.

Popular disappointment (especially among the lower middle classes, whose salaries were more or less fixed) with the ruling and oppressing classes was immense. People were disillusioned with the new semi-independent régimes, which were led by the traditional leaders of the nationalist movement and helped by the camp followers of feudal lords, rich professionals and the social élite. These classes appeared to the people as corrupt rulers mainly interested in attending to their own vested interests and using the authority of the Government for these purposes. In fact this new ruling class was hopelessly unaware of the changes going on among the people and in the people's political consciousness during these short years during and after the war. They failed to recognise the popular yearning for better jobs, better incomes, better opportunities of education, social services, and the like.

Conflict was inevitable between régimes built on traditional and colonialist notions and designed to serve these two masters, and the new forces in a society aware for the first time of how the rest of the world lived, of the socialist struggles of the world, of the nationalist movements of Asia and Africa. This conflict could not be resolved except by a real and deep-rooted revolution, a revolution that was not only political, not only directed towards the attainment of independence or semi-independence but aiming at the complete emancipation of the masses from both external and internal bondage and the severance of any link with the old traditional and the new imperialist worlds.

The 1948 war between Israel and the Arab states, which brought the humiliating defeat of the Arabs by a handful of Jews, was the last straw that destroyed any remnants of confidence between the ruling classes on one side and the masses on the other. In addition to their other faults, these ruling classes had shown themselves incompetent as well.

Resentment against the Western powers for creating and supporting Israel, which could never be forgiven by the Arabs, was only enhanced by the defeat. The demand for an end to all Western tutelage, for the abolition of military bases and the abrogation of treaties, with a refusal to join in any military pact, became the common theme of everyday life at the popular level.

Gradually the masses began to discover the pattern in which the ruling classes, the pro-Western politicians with their vested interests in the liberal bourgeois economy, represented the agents of Western capitalism. The whole of political life began to crystallise around two centres. One was that of a ruling class at the same time reactionary, corrupt, inefficient, afraid of the emancipation of the masses, and connected directly with Western governments and capital. The other centre was that of the masses who were definitely anti-Western, anti-imperialist, anti-capitalist, anti-Zionist, and in favour of unity, freedom, socialism and neutralism. This was called, in general, 'Arab Nationalism'. The history of the Arab world during the last 20 years is the history of the conflict between these two forces.

XI

The 1948 war between Israel and the Arab states gave the Arab Nationalist movement a tremendous impetus, as did the 1967 war later on. Until then, the colonialist challenge had all the ugly characteristics of any colonialist movement; but nobody could imagine that colonialism would last for ever. Everybody knew that, sooner or later, each colony would gain its independence and would get rid of foreign forces and influence, so that the whole challenge was necessarily a temporary one.

Zionism was different. It had all the characteristics of an alien colonialist power, and, in addition, the will to stay for ever, with a racist, exclusively Jewish character, which was reluctant even to accept the presence of Arabs within its boundaries.

To the Arabs, the whole idea of Zionism was incongruous. Perhaps the fact that it seemed so inherently impracticable was one of the reasons why Arab resistance to it in its infancy was so weak and ineffectual. But with the mass immigration of the '30s, after the Nazis came to power, it was evident that the danger was real and urgent.

Since then, the struggle against Zionism has become the first concern of Arab Nationalism, replacing the struggle against the dying force of colonialism. The vicious character of Zionism came to be regarded as being far more important than any colonialism, and the struggle against it formed the practical fulcrum of the urge for Arab unity. The successive defeats of Arab régimes in their wars with Israel only succeeded in strengthening the Arabs' lack of faith in their own régimes and in augmenting their revolutionary fervour. The association of most of these rulers with the West, which created Israel and supported it through all these years, only deepened the anti-Western feeling of the masses, and increased their loss of faith in their traditional leaders.

In addition, Zionism supplied a continuous external challenge to the movement of Arab Nationalism. On the one hand this was useful in the sense that the movement was strengthened by such a challenge. On the other, it thwarted the 'positive' and 'creative' element of the movement and kept in being its 'negative' and 'reflex' character. And so, instead of a healthy growth of the Arab masses towards unity, freedom, socialism and neutralism, the whole movement was taken over and distorted by military groups which justified their existence by the imminent military menace of Zionism.

XII

These general trends of Arab Nationalism after the war were crystallised in two main streams of thought and action. One was that of the Socialist Ba'ath (Resurrection) party and the other that of Nasserism.

The Ba'ath party, through its founder Michel Aflak, built its ideological framework around three principles and three aims. The main principles were:

1. That a true nationalist movement should spring up from the masses, and should have the masses as its subject and its object, as its aim and its means. Its first revolution should be against the traditional leadership that had been based on heredity, wealth, or tribal or social connections.

By emphasising the role of the 'masses', the party avoided the term 'proletariat', because it believed that this term is an economic particularisation of a class that is specific to an industrially advanced society. In underdeveloped countries, struggling for existence and independence, masses included proletarians, but also included all the 'toiling' classes, who, by their nature, have no connections with colonial interests and indeed come into conflict with them and, because of underdevelopment, are their victims.

2. That a true nationalist movement ought not to be satisfied with 'believing in' unity, but ought to take the first step towards it by organising itself on a 'pan-Arab' nationalist basis and, by its own organisation, to refute the division of the Arab homeland.

3. That only through 'revolution' can a new progressive Arab society be built. This revolution should start within the revolutionary himself, as he rejects all that held him back in his own society, then as he reflects outward on his environment, not against colonialism alone, but against his society's backwardness as well. (This was the origin of the name 'resurrection' party.)

From these three principles developed three definite aims : unity, freedom and socialism, which became, later, the slogans of all progressive Arab movements, including Nasserism.

Nasserism was another facet of the Arab Nationalist movement. It was deeply influenced by the ideology of the Ba'ath party and it adopted its three aims as its own. In fact an alliance between the party and Nasser made unity between Egypt and Syria possible in 1958, while it was mainly the rift between them that put an end to this unity in 1961. However, Nasserism could not be the same as the Ba'ath. Starting as a military *coup d'état* and being led by as strong and pragmatic a man as Nasser, it was enslaved by its own nature. It was, in the main, a régime and not a movement. Its strength was, at the same time, its weakness. Representing the state, the strongest Arab state, with the strongest Arab leader, with its early successes against colonialism, regionalism and backwardness, it had an immense influence on the Arab masses. There was a time when the term 'Arab Nationalism' was equivalent to the term Nasserism. But Nasserism, being representative of the state and of the leader, was, by its own nature, unable to sustain itself as an organised mass movement outside the boundaries of the authority of the state, and it lacked a stable coherent ideology, as well as the spontaneity of a truly popular movement.

For some time Nasserism eclipsed the Ba'ath party and helped to create 'military factions' inside the party itself, which tried to build régimes based on military rather than on mass support.

To the Arab masses the main difference was between a party which called for revolution and social change and a régime that made the revolution and changed the society every day. To the onlookers in the Arab world it was rather a secondary question whether the revolution came from above or from below. It needed a 5 June and another defeat to show that a régime, however progressive it might be, was not a substitute for an organised mass movement.

XIII

Arab Nationalism is the driving force behind the Arabs in their struggle to create a unified progressive nation that can hold its own among the nations of the world. It was born as the response to the challenge of Western colonialism, but it has outgrown this simple reflex action and become a genuine movement on its own merits. While colonialism and its offshoots of imperialism, Zionism and apartheid continue to present the direct challenge, Arab Nationalism has appreciated the fact that the real challenge, though an indirect one, is the inner one of ensuring the development and the future of the nation.

Its main characteristics were acquired as a result of its development and its struggles. Being, mainly, a response to Western colonialism, it had to be its contradiction. And so, while it has its similarities with other anti-colonialist Asian and African liberation movements, it resembles very little other 'nationalisms' in areas that never knew direct colonial rule, such as Turkey, Afghanistan, Iran or Japan.

These characteristics have been summed up by the author as being 'free and liberal nationalism—socialistic, liberating and unifying. It has gained the deep faith of all its people and of the non-imperialist peoples the world over. It rejects aggression, imperialism, racism, exploitation, and enslavement. It adopts an independent neutral stand in international affairs and is deeply committed to international co-operation'.[1]

FURTHER READING

Abu-Lughod, I. 'The Transformation of the Egyptian Elite', *The Middle East Journal*, Summer 1967.

Antonius, George. *The Arab Awakening*, Hamish Hamilton, London, 1938; Putnam, New York, 1965.

Nusaibah, H. *The Ideas of Arab Nationalism*, New York, 1956.

Razzaz, M. *The Evolution of the Meaning of Nationalism*, Doubleday & Co., New York, 1963.

Rodinson, M. *Israel and the Arabs*, Penguin, Harmondsworth, 1968; Pantheon, New York, 1968.

Seale, P. *The Struggle for Syria*, Oxford Univ. Press, London and New York, 1965.

Zeine, Z. *Arab Turkish Relations and the Emergence of Arab Nationalism*, Beirut, 1958; Verry, Connecticut, 2nd ed., 1966.

MUNIF RAZZAZ. A member of the Ba'ath Party since 1949 and Secretary-General of the party since 1965, he resigned from his post in April 1967 after a *coup d'état* by the military faction of the party in 1966. Born in Damascus, he practised medicine in Amman, where he now lives. Co-founder of the Jordan Red Crescent Society, 1948. He is the author of several books, pamphlets and articles.

[1] Razzaz, Munif. *The Evolution of the Meaning of Nationalism*, Doubleday & Co., New York, 1963, p. 62.

POLITICAL FORCES IN THE MIDDLE EAST

FRANK STOAKES

THE POLITICS OF IDEOLOGY

IF we may distinguish crudely between the politics of material interest and the politics of ideology, it is the latter which have set the political tone of the modern Middle East.[1] For a century and more the stage has been dominated by a whole series of ideological *jihads* and crusades : the constitutional and patriotic movements in Egypt, Iran and the Ottoman Empire; the Turkish and Persian movements after World War I for national preservation, integration and development; Arab nationalism under the Ottoman Empire, continued in resistance to Western occupation, in the urge to Arab unity and in the struggle for Palestine; Arab socialist nationalism after World War II and the new Arab Left after the war of 1967; non-Arab nationalist movements in Ottoman or Arab countries, particularly now of the Kurds and Southern Sudanese; and the movements of Syrian and Lebanese nationalism. It is true that the politics of material interest have plied busily behind the scenes, sometimes independent of the politics of ideology, sometimes influencing them, sometimes part of them, and sometimes assuming them as a disguise; but the political climate has been vastly different from those countries—the Western democracies, for example—where government exists largely to reconcile and implement sectional interests.

The prominence of ideological politics is not hard to explain. When the West impinged on the area in the last century, it challenged the civilisation of the time with power and ideas alike. To meet the threat of its power, Middle Eastern reformers adopted the concept of the nation state and of constitutional or democratic rule, and they introduced a form of secular education, based on Western models, which opened the door to every other sort of modern ideology. The atmosphere of crisis, in which ideology thrives, never lifted. Foreign pressure was succeeded by foreign occupation, and occupation by concealed control; for the Arabs, the shadow of Zionism darkened and eventually took shape as Israel; internally there was misgovernment and suspected betrayal, economic stringency and a growing consciousness of social injustice. There was, in addition, widespread individual frustration and uncertainty which, we may believe, encouraged people to embrace ideology in a mood of uncompromising bitterness.

Nothing, perhaps, could have withstood this ideological flood except a sturdy system of material politics which sympathised with the aims of

[1] Israel, because of its vastly different situation, is excluded from this review.

ideology and, with reasonable success and in its own pragmatic way, tried to realise them. But political systems of this sort were lacking because the material interests of society were not strong enough to coerce or dominate the state. In the traditional Islamic system political power was autocratic and centralised; if the ruler shared it, he shared it within the ruling establishment, with the army regiments and factions which provided the physical force of government and, less frequently, with the men of religion who provided its legitimacy. Society in general—the merchants, craftsmen and villagers—had neither power nor organisation for political purposes; it was the prisoner of the state. Where exceptions existed, in the form of tribes and local warlords, these used their armed power and organisation to escape from the central political system rather than to participate in it on favourable terms. In short, society pursued its material interests in disregard of government, or by humble petition without benefit of sanctions; the realities of power were confirmed by the political culture of the time, which expected little of the ruler except order, defence and the maintenance of the prevailing ideology—Islam—and certainly favoured no public participation in government.

Social change in the modern age has had little effect on the pattern of material politics. If anything, the disparity in strength between government and society has increased. Warlords have been subdued and tribes subjugated, and those who could resist have remained, as before, outside the system. New economic and occupational groups have arisen—modern businessmen, industrial labour, clerks and administrators, the professions—but none of them, not even industrial labour, have yet developed effective sanctions against government; indeed, government has to a large extent pre-empted economic power by itself undertaking major projects of development and itself controlling the exploitation and the revenues of petroleum. Some social groups—landowners, for example—have admittedly commanded votes; but where democracy is a blueprint rather than a working mechanism, constitutions are a luxury which can be set aside at the dictate of power. Similarly it is only for short periods that social interests have been able to bribe or coopt governments to serve their will. As in the past, power is not with the public but with the army, and where there is no power material politics are an inglorious mosaic of petition and intrigue.

Ideology has been more fortunate. Its carriers have multiplied with the spread of education, whereas the proponents of material interest—tribes excepted—have been few. They have for periods achieved a certain unity and organisation, whereas material politics have divided. They have displayed a dash and daring which material politics rarely confer. And they have had power at their disposal. They have had moral power which could undermine the will of governments; the power of organised and dedicated students, which is enhanced if they are killed or mishandled by the police; the power of tribes and urban masses who could be mobilised by translating modern ideology into Islamic terms; and finally the power of the army.

The Forces of Ideological Politics

Our concern is with political forces in the sense of politically important groups. Given the ideological tone of Middle Eastern politics, we are primarily concerned with social groups in so far as they are receptive of modern ideology, as are the products of secular education; or create an ideology round themselves, like certain linguistic groups; or modify the content or spirit of an ideology because of their professional or psychological characteristics, like army officers and students; or serve as instruments of ideological politics, like labour, the urban masses, sometimes—if vicariously —the tribes and men of religion, and, again and especially, students and army officers.

Intellectuals and students

The most important political force in the modern Middle East—the force, indeed, which has moulded the Middle East in its present form—is that of the so-called intellectuals. It is they who have imported, elaborated, disseminated and tried to implement ideology, who have set themselves to modernise society and state, and who, providing Government and opposition alike, are primarily responsible for the presence or absence of national solidarity and political stability. In general terms, the 'intellectuals' are the recipients of modern, secular education at a secondary or higher level, and tend to be engaged in occupations proper to education of this type : in the professions, in state and business administration, in clerical work, in teaching, and in the commissioned ranks of the security forces; men of the highest education may also be found as merchants, industrialists, scientific farmers or simple landowners. What immediately concerns us is not the intellectuals' occupation but the education which makes them receptive of modern ideology, and in so far as their occupation blunts the edge of their ideology they are of less interest for our purpose. The educated entrepreneur, the successful doctor or the devoted scientist may well become indifferent, calculating or hostile towards the prevailing idea; businessmen who supported nationalism when it belaboured foreign monopolies sometimes lost their enthusiasm when it acquired a socialist tinge. Intellectuals with material interests tend to be suspected or rejected by the main, salaried, intellectual body, whose solidarity rests not only on education but to some extent on shared ideology and on precisely a lack of specific material interests. Its members in no way form a self-conscious economic class seeking its economic advantage. What sectional organisation they have is guild-like and divisive as between professions, and rarely operates with conspicuous vigour, except as a vehicle for the ideological politics which are common to almost all.

Students are a special section of the intellectual body, and have since the end of the 19th century played a most prominent part in ideological politics. Like the professions, but more enthusiastically, students also engage in minor political activity in pursuit of their own group interests; at a national level the main importance of this activity is the fact that organisation established for material purposes is readily turned to ideological politics and that demonstrations of protest against examination results at times end in mass riots against a régime.

The prominence of students in ideological politics needs little elucidation. Its causes include their natural energy and idealism; their proximity to the sources of political speculation; their high regard for their own capacities and for their national role in societies which are still largely illiterate; their lack of roots in the *status quo*; the permissive attitude of parents and indulgence of the general public, which stands in awe of education, together, on the other hand, with irksome social conventions; and their relative immunity from official action. Their political fervour and their great numbers, as compared with other political activists, have on occasion determined the political climate and the course of political events. Moreover schools and colleges are, as it were, the blood banks of ideology, prime nuclei of political organisation, and admirable bases of operations. In consequence, politicians have competed to enlist students in politics, as a powerful weapon against which there is no easy defence, and no other single intellectual group has been so politically versatile. So formidable are the students that revolutionary movements, eager to mobilise them when in opposition, repress them when in power or contain them in youth organisations.

Since it is the intellectuals and students who have dominated ideological politics, it may be partly to their peculiar character that ideological politics owe their tone. This has typically been one of violence, bitter zealotry and an uncompromising pursuit of the millenium, qualities common in periods of rapid change, and specifically in those groups which are spiritually, culturally, socially and economically uprooted. In these crises an ideology is seized avidly to replace the spiritual and intellectual certainty which are lost, and the organisation which embodies it offers identity and shelter and a focus for total loyalty. The targets and enemies of the new creed are pursued with a hatred which is in proportion to the anxiety of the devotee; they may deserve it or not, but the situation in any case demands a scapegoat and the creed, to serve its purpose, must provide one. In the Middle East, British and French imperialism and colonialism, American 'neo-colonialism', Zionism and the 'feudalism' of large agrarian interests have all played the part, and often in combination, as a single, diabolical conspiracy.

It is in this connection that educational and occupational distinctions among the intellectuals become directly relevant to our study. Most intellectuals are beset to some degree by these strains; but it is the less adequately educated and the less professionally secure who are the most displaced of all, and it is perhaps this intellectual proletariat whose ideology is most marked by unreasoning fantasy, a state of mind which may or may not correspond with hard political fact. Much Middle Eastern education, moreover, provides small defence against fantasy and unreason, let alone unemployment or underemployment. Learning at all levels may still, as in the past, be by rote and be quite divorced from practical life; information may be accepted or rejected according to its source rather than its plausibility or consistency; and the worker or peasant, when he is made aware of the circumstances, is often capable of shrewder political judgement. Strong conviction and weak logistic sense, reinforced perhaps by the psychological traits of a changing society, generate a perpetual opposition to government, a perpetual refusal to accept the best available and to come to terms with reality. It is on these reefs as much as anywhere that political stability has foundered.

But if the virulence of much ideological politics owes something to the nature of the participants, it is due still more to the failure of ideology to realise its ends. Modern Turkey and Iran have had long periods in which ideological aspirations were reasonably met, and the ideological tone of the time, if self-assertive, had no festering morbidity. Arab ideology, on the other hand, has an unhappier record : each victory has been overtaken by a new crisis or blighted by a new reverse. Full independence was delayed, and when achieved did not bring the expected strength and progress. Unity has proved elusive, but because the ideal exists, there can be no acceptance of smaller, viable units. The Palestine problem has brought loss and humiliation and may threaten the stability even of remote Arab states. Social reform has been blocked by social reality. The Arab intellectual is in fact the victim of recurrent political frustration and has carried his wounded ideology with dedicated obsession. From time to time some new revelation or revolution has become a source of hope; at present the new Arab Left, with its concept of the people's war, is transferring its loyalty from the leaders of Arab socialism to the Palestine guerrilla movement as the prime redemptive force in the Arab world.

Officers

The officer corps has engaged in ideological politics as enthusiastically as civilian intellectuals, and if the latter have given the Middle East its distinctive political tone, it is the officers who, by *coup d'état* or the threat of it, have given it many of its governments. With the civilian intellectuals the relationship of the officer corps is ambiguous. It shares with them that secondary level of education at which ideology is firmly implanted, and service under the Ottoman or a mandatory régime has often engendered a similar attitude of opposition towards government in general. But professional training and activity add elements which are alien to civilian thinking. These may include a belief in the armed forces as the guardian of independence, national dignity and ideological orthodoxy, in whose defence they have the right and duty to take the initiative; a regard for efficiency in government as a sacred and legitimising value, and for this and other reasons an inclination to doubt the worth of any civilian intellectual, the legitimacy of any civilian government and the intentions of any civilian politician; and an *esprit de corps*, also sacred in quality, which is sensitive to civilian control and civilian criticism. All these sentiments are apt to combine in moments of military defeat, as in the Palestine War of 1948, when the officers feel themselves martyrs to civilian inefficiency and corruption, or if governments owe their survival to armies which they curb or vilify; at times like these the army has been very prone to intervene in politics. The upper reaches of civilian intellectuals, on their side, are inclined to regard the officers as half-educated and slightly barbarous and to deny them the intellectual status to which their training, in some cases their genuine academic merit, and in others a previous professional or salaried employment should presumably entitle them. There is, in fact, a marked division between the civilian and military expression of the intellectual culture, just as the physical separation of the army in its stations makes for social division. The officers are not simply intellectuals in uniform.

Officers and civilian intellectuals are nevertheless natural if wary allies in any ideological opposition to an existing Government. For the civilian opposition, the army is the most desirable ally that exists, for it controls the most immediately effective power in society, more crushing and organised than that of tribes, more rapid in effect than that of labour or of moral pressure, more controllable than that of mob action. The only effective check to military force has been the force of a rival army faction, or that of a foreign state, as in Iraq in 1941, when a nationalist régime enjoying army support was overthrown by British invasion. For officers who regard themselves as the guardians of the state rather than its potential rulers—and the rogue individualists are if anything the exception—civilian intellectuals are necessary to conduct the government of the new era which the army inaugurates. When ideological officers and civilians have co-operated to overthrow a régime, the relative prominence of the two has varied with the situation. But even if the officers began as the tool or junior partner they have rarely remained in that position, and the relationship has usually been uneasy. At times the army has assumed power without civilian allies and has either retained it for a time or has consigned it, on probation, to a civilian government of its own choosing.

The officers differ in another respect from their civilian counterparts. Having ready power at their disposal, they can defend their own material and professional interests effectively and constitute, with the remaining tribes, the one continuously organised and forceful pressure group and the most successful exponent of material politics, as opposed to the politics of ideology. Given their exalted conception of their calling, their material politics are often interlaced with the strands of professional ideology which we have noted. Since modern armies were formed in the Middle East, there have been as many mutinies, *coups d'état* and threats of force in the cause of military honour and advantage, collective or sectional, as in the cause of political ideology. Officers have rarely, indeed, intervened in politics without the stimulus of some military grievance. Given, in whatever cause, a sense of right, and given a sense of duty to the state or nation rather than of loyalty to any government or régime, little more is needed to trigger that sort of political action which, in Britain for example, would be precluded by powerful inhibitions; and residual doubts, if they exist, are resolved when a conspiracy is threatened with discovery or a commander with transfer or retirement. In the course of time, moreover—and especially since the exploits of the Young Turk officers and of Mustafa Kemal—army intervention in politics has become almost institutionalised for both material and ideological reasons, just as in the preceding millenium it was an institutionalised means of changing government, as efficient, in its various contexts, as universal suffrage. The disposition of military groups to act in their own name or that of the whole army has at times been exploited by rogue officers, who have been as untrammelled, in an age of shifting values, by the norms of their service as their colleagues have been by norms of loyalty to a political régime. These have had their counterparts among civilian politicians, but whereas most civilians have had laboriously to forge a weapon for their purpose, the rogue officers have had one to hand.

In their material and ideological politics, officers have displayed the qualities of their profession. In conspiracy they have often been more organised, disciplined and decisive than civilians and, towards the general public, more secretive—many of the numerous military *coups* have been extraordinarily well mounted. In addition, politics between officers has sometimes been more merciful than when civilian ideology was involved. In office the army has varied in performance according to whether it displayed the temperament of soldiers or politicians. In the latter case—as with President Nasser's régime—government has differed from that of civilians mainly in so far as military organisation has stiffened administration lower down the line, not always with the expected consequences. Where, on the other hand, officers have tried to control states as they would a battalion, they have rapidly lost any prop but that of force, and even that has been whittled away by faction. But Middle Eastern armies have been prone to professional politics and ideological conspiracy, and officers who are raised to power by these means may have considerable political capacity, though this may be rather a capacity for gaining and maintaining power by division and intrigue than one (which might be supposed more typically military) for constructive programmes.

Labour and the masses

Labour has organised mainly for its sectional interests and often with severe official discouragement. Where its activities have developed ideological overtones, this has been sometimes under the far-flung influence of the state-guided Egyptian labour organisations (International Confederation of Arab Trade Unions, and Arab Federation of Petroleum Workers), sometimes under communist or similar influence as in Sudan and Iran, and sometimes under the stimulus of revolutionary governments as in Iraq and Syria. Labour has played an important political part mainly in Sudan, Aden and two of the Gulf States, Bahrain and Qatar. In the last case it paradoxically expressed the claims of a local aristocracy and not of a proletariat or an ideology.

As for the urban masses, closer examination often shows them to have more structure than might be supposed and to consist less of riff-raff than of respectable small craftsmen and traders, sometimes organised under a political boss or religious leader and sometimes stiffened by students and professional strong-arm men. The crowd, defined in this way, has played a fairly important, if sporadic part in the politics of most Middle Eastern countries. In Iraq in 1948 it caused the abrogation of a treaty with Britain and in 1952 forced a change of government. In Iran in 1953 it helped bring down the Mossadeq régime. The riots in Cairo of January 1952 marked the beginning of the end of the monarchy. The crowd, like the tribes, has sometimes been mobilised behind modern ideological causes by adapting these to traditional religious concepts.

Other divisions

Political ideology has centred mainly on established states and linguistic groups. Such, in the first case, have been Iran, and Egypt before Nasser; and, in the second, the Arabs, Turks, Persians, Kurds, Azerbaijanis and southern Sudanese. Minor foci have been the geographical region, which provided the basis of Greater Syrian nationalism, and the religious community, such as the Maronites of Lebanon, who have been the core of an ideological Lebanese patriotism. Sometimes different divisions have reinforced one another, as in Turkey, Iran, Lebanon and Southern Sudan. Religious differences, once a major source of political division, have retained prime political significance in recent times mainly when associated with political causes. Even in Lebanon, where political institutions have a formally confessional basis, sectarianism would have been of far less consequence over the last fifteen years had it not been for the rival claims of Lebanese and Arab nationalism. In Iraq the principal effect of the split between Sunni and Shi'i is now that it inhibits closer union with Sunni Arab states.

Minority nationalisms do not differ in their educational and occupational bases from those of the Arabs, Turks and Persians. Where tribes are involved, they may support the nationalist cause more from religious motives or from a distaste for all government than from the ideology which some traditional leaders come to affect. The Kurdish national movement, for example, which has recently fought such bloody battles with the forces of republican Iraq, represents a delicate alliance of intellectuals with barons, religious leaders and tribal chiefs.

Political movements and parties

There remain the specifically political groupings to consider. In general it is not organised political parties but looser political movements which have played most part in the politics of ideology. Organised mass parties have been few, and most of them have been nationalist in tone. The most important of these have been the Wafd in Egypt (1919–53); the Republican People's Party in Turkey, constituted as such in 1923–4 as the heir to a revolutionary nationalist movement, but destined to become the instrument of Atatürk's dictatorship; the Arab Socialist Renaissance ('Ba'ath') Party, initiated as a small group in 1943 to propagate an Arab nationalist socialism; the bellicose Syrian Nationalist Party, founded in 1932 to establish a Greater Syrian national state, called by a succession of names, and usually termed the 'PPS'; the *Phalanges Libanaises*, founded in 1936 to preserve Lebanon as a sovereign independent state; the Armenian 'Tashnak', founded in 1890; and the Kurdistan Democratic Party, founded in 1945. Apart from the Ba'ath Party, the most important socialist organisation has been the Tudeh Party of Iran, formally founded in 1942 and not of communist origin, though it was to be dominated by communists and to become an instrument of Soviet policy. Communist parties, competing with the more appealing ideologies of nationalism, nationalist socialism and (see below) revolutionary Islam, have had relatively little following, except for short periods. The most aggressive of them has been that of Iraq, which played an important and bloodthirsty part in the first year of the republic (1958–9) and discredited communism in the eyes of many anti-Western Arabs.

These parties account for only a minute part of the ideological activity in the area. Much of this has had no formal organisation at all, and much of it has been undertaken by small cliques of politicians (which have also constituted most of the parties of material politics) or by small study, propaganda and conspiratorial groups. One of the least institutionalised phenomena has been that of Nasserism, which swept the Arab world in the later 1950s, first as the ally and later as the enemy of the Ba'ath Party, with which it has continued to dispute leadership of Arab socialist nationalism. Although there have been minor organisations to propagate it and it has been backed by the considerable resources of the Egyptian state, Nasserism has remained essentially a climate of thought, formulated over a period in the pronouncements of the Egyptian President, realised in his policies, and representing the aspirations of most Arab Muslims and some Arab Christians of the Middle East.

One vigorous ideological movement stands apart from the main stream of political thought and is largely a reaction to it. This is political—and indeed revolutionary—Islamic fundamentalism, embodied also in Turkish and Persian political groups, but expressed most dramatically in the highly organised Muslim Brotherhood of Egypt, which was founded in 1928. The aim of the Brotherhood has been to establish a theocratic Muslim state with a socialist tinge which, it would claim, accords fully with Islamic doctrine. Its political organisation and techniques, however, owe much to European totalitarian parties, and in a number of trials it has been accused of seeking its ends by assassination and armed revolution. The Brotherhood hoped to guide and subsequently control Egyptian government after the military revolution of 1952; failing in this, it has been intermittently repressed on charges of subversion, including an attempt on the life of Nasser. It was formally suppressed in 1954, but continued to exist underground. In an admittedly religious country the Brotherhood is a reminder of the deep Muslim strains which persist beneath a modernising culture, and a warning that modern politics have failed to solve the spiritual and material problems particularly of the economic lower middle class and the lower grade of intellectuals, for whose members the Brotherhood has had a potent appeal.

EXCEPTIONS

This chapter has portrayed Middle Eastern politics as dominated, since the First World War, by an atmosphere of fervent ideology. The fervour, it has been suggested, springs partly from a failure to implement compelling political and social ideas at a time when they are mildly entertained, partly from the absence of interests more attractive than the prevailing ideologies, and from a general state of frustration, anxiety and uncertainty. Some or all of these conditions have existed in all countries under foreign rule and they have existed in many independent countries among groups which were particularly involved in social change. They have not decisively beset—or at any rate influenced—all intellectuals in these countries; there are everywhere people as balanced, pragmatic or intellectual in the ordinary sense as may be found in any area of the world, only it is not usually these who have set the political tone. Nor have these conditions been critical in countries where traditional forces have maintained a natural ascendancy, as in the Arabian states and to some degree in Sudan; or where the more vociferous ideological groups were for the moment satisfied or silenced, as in Kemalist Turkey and the Iran of Reza Shah; or where potentially ideological groups have been engaged in profitable and satisfying occupations, as to some extent in Lebanon and Kuwait; or where some more immediate preoccupation has muted the promptings of current ideology, as in Lebanon, where socialist trends have been overshadowed by confessional and regional politics.

In Turkey and Iran there have been other factors which are absent from the Arab Middle East. In both countries there has been a continued legitimacy of government, inhering in Iran in the monarchy and in Turkey in the state, and maintained through quite drastic political changes. In both countries, moreover, foreign relations and their internal implications have been significantly different from the Arab experience. Arab nationalists have assumed a single arch-fiend, vastly cunning and powerful, in the shape of Western colonialism, ex-colonialism and neo-colonialism, which, they believe, exploits Zionism and—a sure goad to emotional politics—domestic treachery to achieve its ends. The Turks have also tended in more recent times to cherish a single arch-enemy, Russia, but it could be held at bay and had no channels of domestic influence. The Persians have had two modern enemies, Russia and Britain, which commanded their indigenous tools and could not be physically withstood, but the subtlety of Persian diplomacy, which is infinite, could often frustrate them or play off one against the other: the situation was inescapable and humiliating, but not without its satisfactions. It would be nice if we could account so simply for the superior complexity and cynicism of Persian intellectual attitudes, characteristics to which the Arabs, especially of the south-east, are being increasingly exposed.

FURTHER READING

Abu Jaber, Kamel S. *The Arab Ba'ath Socialist Party*, Syracuse Univ. Press, Syracuse, 1966.

Baer, Gabriel. *Population and Society in the Arab East*, Routledge and Kegan Paul, London, 1964.

Berger, Morroe. *The Arab World Today*, Doubleday, New York, 1962.

Fisher, S. N. (ed.) *Social Forces in the Middle East*, Cornell Univ. Press, New York, 1955.

Fisher, S. N. (ed.) *The Military in the Middle East*, Ohio State Univ., Ohio, 1963.

Gibb, H. A. R. and Bowen, Harold. *Islamic Society and the West*, (2 vols), Oxford Univ. Press, London, 1950 and 1957.

Halpern, Manfred. *The Politics of Social Change in the Middle East and North Africa*, Princeton Univ. Press, Princeton, 1963.

Hourani, A. H. *Minorities in the Arab World*, Oxford Univ. Press, London, 1947.

Landau, Jacob M. *Parliaments and Parties in Egypt*, Israel Publishing House, Tel-Aviv, 1953.

Laqueur, Walter. *The Middle East in Transition*, Routledge and Kegan Paul, London, 1958.

Lerner, Daniel. *The Passing of Traditional Society: Modernizing the Middle East*, Free Press, Glencoe, 1958.

Safran, Nadar. *Egypt in Search of Political Community*, Harvard Univ. Press, Boston, Mass., 1961.

FRANK STOAKES. Lecturer in Politics at Manchester University where he is organising a programme of research into social and political change in the Middle East. One-time director of Middle Eastern Studies at St. Anthony's College, Oxford. Spent much of his life in the Middle East: in the British Embassy in Baghdad, as political officer in Iraqi Kurdistan, on attachment to the Palestine government during World War II, and in various capacities in the oil industry after the war. Co-author of *Iraq* (1958).

MARXISM AND SOCIALISM

MAXIME RODINSON

The First Appearance of Socialist Ideas

The 19th century was a decisive period for the Middle East. I have suggested that the turning point which can be detected at that time should be called 'the end of resignation'. For thousands of years, there was a high level of exploitation and oppression on the societies of the Middle East—as in all societies. There had been no lack of revolts in the past nor of plans for progress towards a more just social structure and a happier way of life. All had failed in face of the armed force at the disposition of the privileged. With the added factor of the economic stagnation which had reigned since the end of the Middle Ages, people had, by and large, become resigned.

In the 19th century, the superiority of Europe was affirmed and expressed in terms of techniques of domination. This had a double effect in the Middle East. On the one hand, a general feeling of humiliation, indignation and revolt spread to all classes. On the other hand, Europe also offered models of open and progressive societies, in which the struggle of the dissenters was intense. Those in revolt against Europe were attracted by the models Europe offered to them. By imitating the conquerors they would be able to follow their example and to throw off their yoke. They first looked for the secret of European superiority in the political field, because political liberation was the first necessity. But this implied making contact with rival political groups in Europe, of whom those most inclined to listen to the complaints of the 'under-developed' were precisely those engaged in social struggle. Thus the tide of revolt running through the Islamic world could often find an outlet in ideas of social transformation.

Islam was the dominant ideology and, in the form it took then, Islam gave little encouragement to these ideas. In the past, protest against privileges seldom included a denunciation of the privileges of wealth, which was not the principal source of power. A remedy of the evils of society was traditionally looked for in a return to the supposed purity of primitive Islam, while strict obedience to the religious law was thought to guarantee the reign of justice and social harmony.

The 1840s saw the development in Persia of a movement which challenged traditional Islam, to such an extent that certain of its members went so far as to plan the abolition of classes and of property. This was the doctrine of the Bâb, which was, possibly, not so much the first socialist movement as the last of the medieval heresies, the successor moreover of Persian movements with some socialist affinities dating from pre-Islamic days.

The beginning of socialist ideas should rather be sought in the relations

374

between the people of the Middle East and Western socialists. Just as people tried to borrow modern capitalism from the West, they also looked to the West for the secret of the struggle against capitalist privileges and, by extension, against all class privileges. Between 1833 and 1835 the Saint-Simonians sent a mission for propaganda and action to Istanbul and Egypt. In the 1840s travellers met, in Istanbul, Turks who were familiar with the trends of European socialism. In 1845 a Turk took part in the London 'Festival of Nations' organised by the European Left of socialist and communist tendencies. The great Egyptian thinker Tahtawi (1801–1873), who had lived in Paris from 1826 to 1831, gave expression to socialist ideas in an essay written in 1869.

At the same time the thrust of Middle Eastern protest was directed against European imperialist domination. Those who protested thought they would find in Islam a powerful lever with which to arouse the masses against this domination. They rejected socialist ideas as weakening national unity, as linked to irreligious ideologies and as being in any case premature. This was the attitude of the great anti-imperialist activist Jamâl ad-dîn al-Afghani in about 1870 and also that of the nationalist Egyptian with progressive ideas, Ahmad Lutfi as-Sayyid (1872–1963). Only a few intellectuals went further, following to its logical conclusion the train of scientific and positivist thought which they had borrowed from Europe : in Egypt the materialist Shibli Shmayyel, in about 1908, and the Copt Salama Musa (1887–1958), an enthusiastic disciple of the Fabian ideas of Bernard Shaw. In the cosmopolitan milieu of Salonika, the New Life (*Yeni Heyat*) group included a wing which adhered to utopian socialism.

At the beginning of the 20th century, especially among the fringe groups and the minorities, there appeared at the same time a working-class trade union movement and various social-democratic organisations in contact with the Second International. In 1886 the first Armenian social-democratic party was formed in Geneva. An embryonic proletariat, predominantly Christian and Jewish, began to organise itself in the Ottoman Empire. The same is true of Persian labourers working in the Russian Caucasus, notably at Baku. The Persian constitutional revolution, which began in 1905, allowed these socialist trade union and political organisations to develop and become firmly rooted in Persia itself. The Young Turk revolution of 1908, which had its origins in Salonika, at first allowed similar movements to develop there too, such as the Socialist Workers' Federation of Salonika, influenced by the sort of socialism of the Frenchman, Jaurès. There were a few, but only a few, Turkish Muslims in these movements. The counter-revolution in Persia and the predominance of an authoritarian Jacobinism among the Young Turks put a brutal end to all this development.

The Appeal of the Comintern

The 1914–18 War, into which the whole of the Middle East was drawn, including even theoretically neutral Persia, had considerable effects, notably by precipitating the overthrow of the Ottoman Empire, by stirring up the Arab revolt, by leading to a division of the conquered countries by the Allied conquerors and the granting of special rights to the sparse Jewish settlements in Palestine. The Russian Revolution was even more important in that it provided a model for the movement of an under-developed people against the capitalist and imperialist powers of the West and proclaimed that the end of imperialism was at hand.

Everywhere the Bolshevik movement aroused imitators. In the countries bordering on Russia, which had scarcely recovered from the revolutionary shocks of the years 1905–14 and were badly shaken by the war, armed groups arose, more or less inspired by the Russian example : in 1920 in Turkey the guerrillas of the 'Green Army' fought against the Greeks; and in Iran, with the direct help of Russian soldiers in revolt, veritable soviets even grouped together to form a republic at Ghilan and in Mazenderan.

Even without any direct connection with the Bolsheviks, there arose everywhere little groups inspired by their example and calling themselves Parties, sometimes even Communist Parties. The trade union movement took a comparatively large step forward both in Iran and in Turkey. In the Arab countries, Communism was the path chosen by small groups whose members were chiefly intellectuals and members of the minority groups. In Palestine, the Jewish community which had been reinforced since 1920, with its working-class elements of socialist tendencies who had come from Eastern Europe, provided fertile soil for the growth of socialist and trade union movements, which kept clear for the most part of communism because of the anti-Zionist attitudes of the Bolsheviks.

Soviet Russia, isolated in a hostile world, a prey to the armed intervention of the Western powers, had to find allies in the nationalist movements of the colonial world. Zinoviev, at the Congress of Eastern Peoples at Baku in 1920, called for a 'holy war' against imperialism. But this implied an alliance with movements under bourgeois or even what was called 'feudalist' direction : the rich middle class and landed proprietors of Egypt in revolt against Britain, or the Emir of Afghanistan. A direct appeal to the social struggle and to communism could only divide these movements and it seemed doubtful whether the Eastern masses could be influenced by motives that were not strictly nationalist. The theoretical discussions of the Congress of the Third International (Comintern) decided, despite the arguments of the Tartar Sultan Galiev and the Indian M. N. Roy, to treat the colonial movements simply as a contribution to the only decisive struggle, that of the proletariat of the industrial countries. In practice the communist movements were overlooked, while Soviet Russia concluded a close alliance with the Turkey of Mustafa Kemal and made a treaty with the Iran of Reza Khan, both of which had repressed communism with brutality.

The situation became stabilised along these lines. The Comintern continued to give verbal support to many small communist parties, which sometimes consisted of little more than a few émigrés settled in the USSR, and it went on spreading information about workers' movements and peasants' strikes and revolts. Emissaries brought under strict discipline all the parties which might at some stage be able to exert some influence on the internal politics of the countries concerned and which were the embryos of organisations which future events might one day allow to grow and to play an important role. These parties never enjoyed the exceptional conditions which allowed their counterparts in China and Indonesia to develop strongly. During the periods when the Comintern was recommending the tactic known as 'class against class', the local result was to advocate the internal social struggle, and thus to break up the nationalist front. In the periods when the 'united front' tactic was dominant, the alliance with the middle classes in the colonising countries meant that the national claims of the colonised countries were put into cold storage. This greatly weakened the appeal of a movement which stern measures of repression had already deprived of any means of expression, and which was torn by differences of opinion about local tactics and by the need to support one side or the other in the constant rivalry between different tendencies within Soviet communism. As some compensation the Communists were described by their very executioners as the purest representatives of an implacable social struggle against the privileges of power and wealth. Amongst the most deprived social strata, this could only encourage a certain attraction mingled with fear.

At first the movement's only hard core of militants, well-trained according to the new standards and living in the country itself, was among the Jews of Palestine. But these were especially ineffective as a result of the internal contradiction between their opposition in principle to Zionism and the fact that they belonged to a society created and maintained by Zionism. The Comintern recommended the 'arabisation' of the Party and this led to difficulties, splits, secession, indiscipline and resignations.

In 1933–4 there appeared on the scene the militants trained in the USSR along the most orthodox lines, who now replaced the former cadres, particularly in Syria and in the Lebanon under the French mandate. Arabs, and even Muslim Arabs, began to play an important part. The participation of Communists in the Popular Front Government in France in 1936 allowed the Communist Party to function legally in the Levant, to publish newspapers, to create mass organisations under communist inspiration, to develop trade unions from which the Communists derived strength. The Lebanese and Syrian Communists took over the Popular Front policy of alliance with the nationalist bourgeoisie to secure nationalist claims. This brought them some success, the more so because they constituted, especially in the Lebanon, almost the only secular and modern party rising above the conflicts between ethno-religious communities, and going beyond the restricted circle of 'notables'. Elsewhere the vigour of repression and the lack of cadres prevented developments of this type, despite the strength of social discontent expressed in strikes, peasant risings and continual troubles. The period was, above all, that of the national movement.

Between the two wars, the Communists were almost alone in standing for the social struggle. The socialism of the Second International had little appeal for the Eastern masses, except for the Jews of Palestine, and this was scarcely a recommendation for others. It provided no solution to the outstanding problem of the region, that of the struggle for national independence. In England and France, socialists took part in colonialist governments. In Iran and in Egypt, bourgeois movements claimed the title of socialists when it suited them, but had the most timid programmes of reform. Only in Iraq did intellectuals, influenced by British Fabianism, in alliance with some Communists, play a certain role after 1931. They became engaged in a military conspiracy which led to a *putsch* in 1936 and took part in the resulting government. But they were soon eliminated by their less radical allies.

FINAL FLARE-UP AND DYING DOWN OF COMMUNISM

World War II began with the two troubled years of the Soviet-German Pact, which caused considerable embarrassment inside the majority of communist parties and made their repression easier. A certain number of the old cadres were eliminated. But the German invasion of Soviet Russia in June 1941 set in motion a completely different process. The major role of the Red Army in defence and then on the offensive, with the emergence of the Soviet Union as one of the major world powers, raised the prestige of communism to the heights. Moreover even its suspicious allies, British and American, facilitated Soviet propaganda in many areas in order to win support for the Allied war effort, whilst in the Lebanon the Free French enjoyed Soviet backing against British ambitions. Soviet books and films invaded the whole of the Middle East. In addition the Soviet Union (often in common with the United States) inherited the fund of sympathy previously belonging to Germany as a great industrialised power which was not, at least to all appearances, colonialist. The alliance of the USA with England and France, and the tendency of their economies to further American political hegemony, gradually left this role to the Soviet Union alone.

Almost everywhere, the communist groups enjoyed a completely new liberty to exploit this prestige. In Turkey, leftist groups of more or less communist tendency appeared openly after 1943, and in 1946 they formed two legal parties. In Egypt, communist groups of diverse tendencies multiplied rapidly, with continual splits and partial reunifications, and played an important part in the unrest among the opposition which was arousing a large section of public opinion against the régime. They soon spread to the Sudan. In Syria and the Lebanon, where the Communist Party operated perfectly legally, publishing newspapers and inspiring trade unions and mass organisations, the Communists achieved a great success by their vigorous and decided participation in the struggle for national independence, setting aside for the time being social claims and the revolutionary vision. In Iraq, a working class leader supported by the Comintern and known under the assumed name of Fahd ('leopard') reorganised the communist movement from 1939 onwards. The movement showed itself full of vitality but ran into serious internal difficulties (rivalry between controlling factions, and the Kurdish question) at the same time as it faced a particularly severe and effective campaign of repression. In Iran especially, the protection of the Red Army (which was occupying the northern part of the country) allowed the communist Tudeh Party to develop in a spectacular way, bringing to power in Azerbaijan a democratic autonomist party led by a communist group and aiding the proclamation of the Kurdish Republic of Mahabad. Only in Palestine did world factors do little to help the task of the Communists, who were faced with the very grave problems posed by the inclination of the Jewish community in favour of the formation of a Jewish State, an idea which was condemned by the ideology of the movement. But the Arab Communists of the country freed themselves from outside influence and gained ground.

The international political policy of the USSR nipped all this growth in the bud and gave a strong reinforcement to anti-communist repression. In Turkey and in Iran, its objectives clashed with the national interest. The claims made by Stalin on Turkish territory allowed the government to forbid communist-type organisations from December 1946 onwards. In Iran, the clever Prime Minister Ghavan Saltaneh secured from Stalin the evacuation of Iranian territory in May 1946 in exchange for the promise of oil concessions. His concessions to the autonomists and the entry of three Tudeh ministers into the government were only a cover for the counter-offensive. Only a short time afterwards these ministers were dismissed and Azerbaijan and the territory of Mahabad reconquered. Turkey and Iran, thanks to the Cold War, passed under American protection. The Tudeh Party was outlawed in February 1949.

In Arab countries, the decision of the USSR in 1947 in favour of the

378

partition of Palestine, and so of the creation of a Jewish State, destroyed the standing of the communist parties, which tried to justify the Soviet attitude, albeit reluctantly. The Syrian-Lebanese Communist Party was banned and the Egyptian groups became even more divided. In Iraq, complicity with Zionism was an additional part of the indictment when the Communist leaders were arrested and brought to trial. Fahd and several others (including Jews) were hanged in 1949. The Palestinian Jews on the other hand could at last adopt an attitude more in harmony with that of their people. They showed themselves patriots and even 'hawks' in the Palestinian war of 1948. The Arab Communists of Palestine, reforming their ranks in Jordan, gained sympathy by their opposition to the annexation of the non-Israeli territory on the west bank of the Jordan by King Abdullah under the protection of Great Britain.

The Rise of New Forms of Socialism

In the Arab world, the Palestinian war finally destroyed the prestige of the ruling groups and gave a decisive reinforcement to the tendencies making for revolution.

This new revolutionary current was to be characterised by the decisive influence of Marxist ideas although the Communists, in general, played only a more or less secondary part. In the course of the preceding period, Marxist ideas had penetrated the whole range of Middle Eastern societies. Soviet prestige, the shocks suffered by the old imperialist powers, the compromises of the nationalist ruling groups on the eve or the morrow of taking over power, the increasing participation of the lower middle classes in the struggle, the recognition of problems other than that of political independence pure and simple (which by now had been achieved everywhere)—all these factors could only reinforce Marxist influence. New generations naturally looked in this direction for an ideological alternative to conservative nationalism, which was now more anxious to preserve the existing social structure than to modernise the country. The conservative elements, showing themselves indifferent to the growing misery of the masses, were ready to compromise with the former dominators who had been turned out, and they were powerless in the face of the economic system, to which was given the name of neo-colonialism, which guaranteed the subordination of these countries to the advanced capitalist nations.

Stalinism, presenting Marxist ideas in the form of an encyclopaedic and simplified dogmatic catechism, provided an attractive ideological synthesis: an up-to-date conception of the world, a universalist sociology offering the same hope to every people, an explanation of the imperialist phenomenon which was the fundamental problem for these regions, a practical method of modernisation and development, prescriptions for organisation, strategy and tactics, a theory of ethics giving moral force to secular aims to which the situation lent urgency, and even an aesthetic theory according to which the artist too had his place in the ranks of the *engagés*. To an encyclopaedic body of knowledge was added the crown of an optimistic and challenging philosophy. The younger generation of nationalists, disappointed in their elders, unsatisfied by Western ideas which offered no solution to their problems, disgusted by Western support (in practice) for the perpetuation of the old framework of society, basing their hopes on technical progress and on the kind of planned development which alone would enable modernisation to be properly oriented under the direction of national leaders, largely took over this vision of the world. Nevertheless they rejected the Stalinist ideology as leading inevitably to adherence to the communist system. For many this was unacceptable because they were still attached to old ways of thought and unwilling to make a radical overhaul of their traditional ideas, while all were afraid to tie themselves to a strategy imposed from outside. Past experience had shown the dangers of such a course. The Communists, moreover, had long since renounced all revolutionary action, often even actively opposing any pressure from the masses in that direction and asking in effect for a parliamentary régime (which would guarantee them freedom for agitation and propaganda) and for a pro-Soviet line in foreign policy. They appeared less threatening but also less original and appealing. This led to the appearance of a nationalism of Marxist tendencies which, moreover, after the end of the Zhdanov period met with more and more sympathy and understanding in the Communist world.

Socialism became so popular that even reactionary elements laid claim to its name, trying to prove that primitive Islam, in its pure form, provided a higher model of socialism. All that was needed was to return to it. The word 'socialism' became vaguely synonymous with fraternal solidarity while capitalism represented selfish cupidity or, quite simply, evil.

An example of an anti-imperialist struggle under non-communist leadership, but supported by local communists, had already been given by Mossadeq in Iran between 1951 and 1953. Its failure, which led to a firm repression of Iranian communism, showed, among other things, the necessity for a more carefully prepared organisation and ideology.

In the Arab countries, the nationalist socialist Ba'ath party became important in Syria in about 1946 and extended its branches throughout the Fertile Crescent. Allied with groups of the same tendency, in a difficult relationship with the Communists, but often supported by them in practice (at least for certain objectives), the party became an important force in the Syrian elections of 1954. In Egypt, the young soldiers who took power in 1952 at first favoured economic liberalism and the Western alliance; they were forced to adjust their ideas when they took stock of the obstacles placed by the capitalist system and Western powers in the way of their efforts to modernise their country in independence. Their leader Nasser was impelled, especially after the Suez affair in 1956, gradually to incline towards the Communist world and at the same time to try to work out an ideology under the title of 'Arab Socialism'. The nationalisation of the economy went ahead, especially after 1960. In Iraq, after the revolution of 14 July 1958, the nationalist Qasim allowed freedom of expression to socialist tendencies, at the same time preventing (with the help of the Communists) an agrarian revolution which might have led to radical socialism.

The rivalry of the three tendencies, each socialist to some extent, represented by the Ba'ath, Nasserism and Communism, unfolded amidst dramatic vicissitudes: after the Syrian-Egyptian union of 1958 to 1961, under the impulse of a temporary Nasserist-Ba'athist alliance against the Communists, came the overthrow of Qasim by a similar alliance in February 1963 with a massacre of the Communists by the Ba'ath militia. The conservatives often allied themselves with one of these movements to protect themselves against the extreme measures anticipated from the others. The Communists took on more and more the role of a supporting force, or of allies strictly confined to tasks of spreading ideological propaganda, and often found themselves brutally repressed by their erstwhile allies. As against this, the radicalisation of the other two movements and their alliance with the Communist world increased steadily, helped by the necessities of the struggle against Israel. In February 1966, the left-wing Ba'athists in Syria eliminated from power the more moderate elements of their party.

The Lebanon was prevented from following similar paths by the importance of the problem of the balance of religious communities and by the domination of an oligarchy linked to the capitalist economy. This gave rise to several interesting attempts at original socialist thought. In Jordan the conservative and pro-Western régime did not succeed in stopping the socialist forces from playing an important part in its internal politics. The Palestinians were above all preoccupied by their struggle against Israel, a struggle which became more and more exclusively their own after 1965. They were nevertheless influenced by Marxism and external factors pushed them to seek Chinese support. Some Kurd leaders of socialist outlook were impelled to seek closer relations with the Iraqi government by their own dissatisfaction with the purely nationalist and conservative positions taken up by Barzani, chief of the Kurdish movement.

The Sudan is the only Arab country where the Communist Left has been able to enjoy real working-class support. The *putsch* of 25 May 1969 has brought to power an alliance including an important group of definitely communist tendencies.

In Turkey, from about 1960 onwards, the intelligentsia of socialist tendencies formed an alliance with the bureaucracy and the army. This alliance favoured state control as against the inclination towards free enterprise of the Democratic Party, which sought support among the masses attached to religious traditionalism and challenged the moderate state socialism of Atatürk and his attempt to keep control of the national economy. The result of this was a series of military *putschs* and a political evolution which allowed the expression of socialist ideas, removing the slur previously cast on them by the link with Moscow. A Workers' Party, founded in 1961, Marxist and sympathetic to communism, was able to spread its ideas and to take a fairly independent line towards the internal discussions of the communist world.

In Israel the evolution has been quite different. A socialist party has been in power (within coalition governments) without a break since the foundation of the state. But it is a kind of socialism concerned with the defence of the interests of wage-earners within the framework of a compromise with free enterprise, and retaining a parliamentary régime as in Great Britain or Sweden. Furthermore, this defence of a social class is strictly subordinated to the national interest. The same thing applies in certain Arab countries, but the national interest impels the Arabs to resist integration with the industrial capitalist world, which threatens their freedom to take their own decisions, while Israel is looking for support precisely in this world, with which it has close ties and in which to some extent it participates. The socialists in opposition (mainly the *Mapam* Party) try to reconcile the national interest with a more vigorous drive towards a more far-reaching socialisation of the economy, and to establish links with states where this socialisation has been carried out, as well as with world revolutionary movements. They have in practice sacrificed this approach to the national interest at decisive moments, just as the majority of Jewish communists did in 1956. A tiny Jewish minority has joined the Arabs of Israel in looking for a new solution which may lead to the rejection of the Zionist principle of a State whose organic structure guarantees Jewish hegemony.

CONCLUSIONS

It can be seen that the socialist movement and the spread of Marxist ideas in the Middle East have been profoundly affected by the fundamental problems of this region, which underlie the common ambition to modernise society and to raise the standard of living in conditions of national independence. Socialism and Marxism are valued essentially as instruments for the achievement of these objectives. Their universal aspect has been placed in the background and often completely rejected in favour of a completely nationalist outlook. The model offered by the communist movement has been discredited as a result of various defects, but above all because it turned its attention to the problem of national aspirations belatedly and with too many reservations. Later on it too often subordinated these aspirations to preoccupations of world strategy, in which the security and strengthening of the Soviet Union were the prime factors. On the other hand, nationalism alone cannot satisfy societies whose struggle for independence clashes with different interests bound up with the economic and social structures of the dominant powers, and which at home have had to fight against existing privileges in the sphere of wealth and power and will have now to attack new strongholds of privilege. The Middle East will not be able to do without some socialist-type ideology, making good use of various Marxist syntheses, but also clearly incorporating among its essential values the desire for national independence.

FURTHER READING

Ahmed, Jamal Mohammed. *The Intellectual Origins of Egyptian Nationalism,* Oxford Univ. Press, London, 1960.

Berkes, Niyazi. *The Development of Secularism in Turkey,* McGill Univ. Press, Montreal, 1964.

Binder, Leonard. *The Ideological Revolution in the Middle East,* John Wiley, New York, 1964.

Haupt, Georges and Reberioux, Madeleine. (eds.) *La Deuxième Internationale et l'Orient,* Ed. Cujas, Paris, 1967.

Hourani, Albert. *Arabic Thought in the Liberal Age, 1798–1939,* Oxford Univ. Press, London, 1962.

Karpat, Kemal H. (ed.) *Political and Social Thought in the Contemporary Middle East,* Pall Mall Press, London, 1968.

Laqueur, Walter (ed.) *Communism and Nationalism in the Middle East,* 2nd ed., Routledge and Kegan Paul, London, 1958.

Laqueur, Walter. (ed.) *The Middle East in Transition,* Routledge and Kegan Paul, London, 1958.

Rodinson, Maxime. *Israel and the Arabs,* Penguin, Harmondsworth, 1968; Pantheon, New York, 1968.

Vernier, Bernard. *L'Irak d'aujourd'hui,* Armand Colin, Paris, 1963.

MAXIME RODINSON. Professor of Old Ethiopic and Old South Arabian in the Ecole Pratique des Hautes Etudes in the Sorbonne since 1955 and lecturer in Middle Eastern Anthropology. Published *Moyen-Orient,* a political monthly on the Middle East 1950–1. In charge of Oriental printed books in the Bibliothèque Nationale 1947. Spent seven years in Lebanon, first as a teacher in a Muslim High School, then as an official in the French Department of Antiquities. Member of the French Communist Party 1937–58. Has travelled widely in the Middle East. Author of *Mahomet* (1961), *Islam et capitalisme* (1966) and *Israël et le refus arabe, 75 ans d'histoire* (1968).

THE GREAT POWERS AND
THE MIDDLE EAST

IBRAHIM ABU-LUGHOD

Of all regions of the non-European world, the Middle East has had the most intimate, intense and sustained contact with Europe. And it has had continuous contact with those European countries which have for over five centuries dominated the destiny of much of the non-European world. Though the underlying motives for such contacts have varied from time to time and from country to country, it may be said that the geographic proximity of the Middle East to Europe has been a constant stimulus to interaction. As more than one observer has noted, domination of the Middle East has been the objective at one time or another of every European power or leader with any ambition to achieve world hegemony.

As a consequence of this prolonged contact an interdependent relationship has been forged between Europe and the Middle East. Although there have been mutual benefits and each has enriched the other, characteristically the relationship between the two regions has been one of hostility and antagonism; this quality has fundamentally affected the type of interdependence sought by the better elements in both societies. Historically, the initiative in establishing the contact which then gave rise to a specific type of relationship was assumed by one or another of the European powers. Only exceptionally did a Middle Eastern power take the initiative in establishing contact with Europe. When such was the case, it meant that the Middle Eastern country could determine to some extent the nature of the relationship and its outcome. Over the past millennium the Middle East twice experienced internal revolutions on a scale that enabled it to make headway. The first was when the Arab people, with the rise and subsequent spread of Islam, commanded the destiny of the Middle East and acquired power sufficient to make successful, though temporary, incursions into Europe, especially into Spain and Sicily. The second was when the Ottoman Turks assumed the leadership of the Middle East and made successful incursions into Central and Eastern Europe, although in due course Europe acquired sufficient power to regain what had been lost.

In modern times, that is from the latter part of the 18th century, the initiative has been taken entirely by Europe. The result has been the gradual loss of territory by the Middle East, the gradual loss of political and economic sovereignty by most of its countries, and the ushering in of an intellectual and ideological revolution of profound significance for the social and political system of the entire Middle East. The revolution is still going on, and the

Middle East continues to struggle to curb Europe's initiative and that of European-affiliated powers.

Three European powers have been dominant in the Middle East over the past two centuries: Great Britain, France and Russia (the Soviet Union) have consistently played critical roles in Middle Eastern affairs. Other European powers, specifically Germany and Italy, have played lesser roles, neither sufficiently sustained or significant to require much consideration in a general essay of this type. In the middle of the 20th century a European-affiliated power, namely the United States, effectively displaced Great Britain and France in playing the decisive role in shaping the outcome of the confrontation between the Middle East and the European power system.

Today the struggle for supremacy in the Middle East is triangular in nature; while the US and the Soviet Union each endeavour to assert their hegemony and thereby curb the influence of the other, the Middle East itself tries to wrest the initiative from both and to maintain its own integrity and sovereignty. In other words, in the latter part of the 20th century we observe a struggle in which the Middle Eastern states themselves, acting singly or collectively or in alliance with other competing powers, try to resist the singular control and influence of any of the great powers. Though the struggle is far from ended, the relationship between Europe and the Middle East has already undergone a transformation which is profoundly affecting the nature of the interdependence between the two regions. Though the sheer power of Europe is infinitely greater than it ever was, countervailing moral and material forces have generated a different spirit for the conduct of relations between the two. At present the Middle East experiences a higher degree of freedom of action in determining its destiny, it has greater options in its dealings with a variety of European and European-affiliated systems of thought and powers, and it has successfully established a relationship of greater equality with Europe than was possible over the past two centuries. The future promises an interaction characterised by greater mutual respect and harmony. This outcome has its roots in the evolving pattern of the interaction between the two regions in the 20th century.

GOD, GOLD AND GLORY

The involvement of the great powers in the Middle East, though effected gradually and somewhat haphazardly, was motivated by considerations of primary interests which made it imperative for those powers to seek and implement specific national policies calculated to maintain, enhance, and maximise those primary interests. These interests were differently defined at different historical periods, and no single interest could be identified as the most compelling in determining the *raison d'être* of great power involvement. The policy and style of behaviour of the great powers in the Middle East was in large measure determined at any point in time by their own definition of the cause of the involvement.

Historically speaking, the trinity of God, Gold and Glory has motivated European expansion, not only to the Middle East but to all corners of the globe. The relative importance and weight of each aspect of the trinity has differed from time to time but the three have all figured in great power involvement in the Middle East. It is not incorrect to state, even taking into account the considerable rewriting of history effected by modern historians, that the religious motive has been a constant factor in great power involvement in the Middle East. Europe's endeavour to restore the region to the realm of Christianity was epitomised by the Crusades of the Middle Ages and the confrontation with the Ottomans in the 16th and subsequent centuries. But as Europe underwent a scientific, technological and secular revolution, particularly in the wake of the French Revolution, the religious impulse was eclipsed by economic and power interests.

When Europe began to expand to other areas of the world it became important that powers with a pretension to greatness should acquire tracts of land, settle their own colonists, and directly or indirectly rule those lands. Not only was the act of possession important in terms of the prestige it conferred upon the European power, but the human and economic potential of these tracts of land added considerably to the wealth, and consequently to the power, of the colonising state. Prestige as such was joined with economic and power factors, and thus the strategic considerations of colonisation acquired considerable importance.

The adjacency of the Middle East to Europe and its critical position along the major lines of communication of the world system made the competition among the European powers for dominance in the Middle East a constant factor in Europe's changing balance-of-power system. The process of competition succeeded first in eliminating most non-European contenders and at the same time in effecting control over most countries of the region. Utilisation of the region for the advancement of the economies of the European powers followed. By the 20th century the economic motive had become primary to European involvement in the Middle East, although the other factors continued to play some role in determining the kind of involvement.

The 19th-century rivalry among the European powers accounted in part for their incursion into the Middle East, but Russia's interests and activity transcended the rivalry of other states. In addition to Russia's need for warm-water ports, it will be recalled that the Persian and Ottoman Empires extended into territories that were construed by Russia to be part of its own territorial domain. Hence Russia's attempt at dominance in the Middle East had its territorial imperative, and at that level Russia's policies and course of behaviour differed somewhat from those of Britain and France. The close relationship between church and state, which characterised the Russian political system until the October Revolution of 1917, reinforced the territorial objective of the imperialist-nationalist drive by adding a religiously conceived motive. Throughout the 19th century Russia continued to expand territorially at the expense of both Persia and Ottoman Turkey, and the tracts of land and people that came under Russia's aegis were gradually absorbed into the Russian system. The other European powers in their attempts to dominate the Middle East did not have this territorial objective, and therefore their policies once they intervened were decidedly different from those of Russia. Their attempts to control the Middle East were motivated by balance-of-power considerations and by concern for the protection or enhancement of their religious and economic interests. As the power of the Ottoman system began to decline, and as it became increasingly evident that the Ottoman system was no longer capable of resisting the encroachment of the European powers, the latter's concern was directed towards the smooth and satisfactory dismemberment of the Empire. Throughout the period of the decline, European motives and interests remained static —namely, to obtain greater economic concessions and the preservation of the Ottoman domain until its destiny could be dealt with by the ambitious European powers.

Increasingly, European involvement in the internal affairs of the Middle East took on concrete forms. The interplay of religious and power motives of the great powers resulted in the systematic application of pressure on the Ottoman Empire to grant concessions which would enable missionaries to function within the Ottoman domain, and eventually missions and missionary schools were established throughout the Middle East. Economic concessions were also obtained, and European financial houses were set up in the more important centres of trade and commerce. Land was obtained by European and European-affiliated concerns and individuals, and Europeans were invited to participate in economic development schemes deemed useful by the Ottoman government. Direct economic participation of European governments in economic activity in the Middle East also increased from the middle of the 19th century. The Middle East increasingly provided an excellent market for European exports, and thus, ironically, the efforts of the Middle East to modernise intellectually, economically and politically increased the direct involvement of the great powers.

As the Middle East countries realised that, should they fail to modernise and increase their viability they would be unable to stem the tide of European conquest, they hastened to adopt measures that would give them the strength to deal with the increasing European pressure. That these measures were reasonably successful is evident from the historical record, yet it may be stated that modernisation invited the European powers to intervene more directly and more decisively in the internal affairs of the Middle East, to forestall nascent threats to their own interests. Nowhere was this more evident than in the cases of Turkey and Egypt. As these two countries increased their programmes of modernisation, became more successful in stemming the tide of centrifugal forces, increased the effectiveness of their governing institutions, and eventually accumulated greater power, they in fact accomplished the opposite of that which they intended. Instead of warding off European pressure, they succeeded in inviting direct intervention by the European powers. By the 1880s Egypt—regardless of the diplomatic euphemisms used—was directly ruled by Great Britain, and Turkey was losing control over its own domain.

Great power control became increasingly inevitable. But one must differentiate between the types of control which the great powers exercised. Throughout the 19th century the European powers obtained favourable concessions by the indirect application of pressure. It was this indirect control that enabled the European powers to manipulate to a certain degree internal forces and governments and thereby to curb or neutralise the ambitions of rivals. Indirect control enabled missionaries and businessmen to function in a way which ultimately led to the rise of certain economic classes that owed their allegiance to Europe. An entrepreneurial class, made up predominantly of minorities and protected directly or indirectly by European powers, assumed the economic functions that were necessary for the maintenance of the European system of exploitation in the Middle East.

Yet indirect control created a degree of fission within the Middle East that eventually undermined the system. The great powers showed a greater aggressiveness towards the end of the 19th century, and the decline of Ottoman power finally rendered obsolete a system based on the subtle use of force and indirect control. It became only a question of time until the European powers would intervene more explicitly and assume direct control over the territories in question. From 1881 onward indirect control in the Middle East gave way to direct-control methods.

Several factors combined to induce the European powers to alter their method of control. In the first place, objective changes in the Middle Eastern environment not only tied the region's economic system to that of the international economy and financial system, but additionally brought in a much larger number of European personnel and 'advisers' to assist in the local modernising schemes being implemented either by national authorities or by foreign concerns. These people required additional protection, of a different type from the protection normally extended to expatriates. In the second place, the urgency of extending direct protection to European-sponsored or affiliated concerns and interests arose out of a threat that had been increasing over the years. This threat essentially came from the ranks of the nationalist reformers who succeeded in articulating a programme of social, political and economic reform that in the final analysis posed an equal challenge to the traditional governing institutions and to the European-sponsored concerns and their privileges. While most of the underpinnings of the nationalist reformers' programmes and ideology were derived from the ideology of Europe, their concrete application in the Ottoman Empire would have demanded such alterations in the system as to effect a complete break with existing traditional or European practices in the region. The nationalist reformers in part demanded a different basis for the polity; in place of the theocratic belief-system, they called for a government based on law. Instead of the authoritarian system they called for a representative government in which the duly elected representatives of the public would determine all measures of public policy. In place of citizenship by faith they called for the adoption of citizenship on the basis of the *patrie* or nation. Though such programmes had been in the making for some decades, by the latter part of the 19th century they became part of a coherent ideology for which men seeking power were willing to fight. In the process of doing so they questioned practices, in the economic and the legal realms, which enabled Europeans to make profits and to manipulate events. Additionally, they questioned the rights of European-affiliated communities to exclude the majority from the benefits that were accruing as a result of the increased economic activity in the region.

Accordingly, the young nationalist reformers posed a serious challenge to the system as it was and to those who benefited from it. In due course, as happened in Egypt by the 1870s, the partisans of reform had enough power at their disposal to topple the existing régime. It was at that point, when the traditional régime was brought to an end and thereby implicitly European interests received their first serious challenge, that a more direct alliance between the traditional classes and the Europeans was forged to combat the new forces. Then direct control as a method of protecting European and European-affiliated interest commended itself to the great powers. The full fruition of that transformation was to come about in World War I.

DIRECT EUROPEAN CONTROL

By the end of World War I direct control by Britain and France was being exercised in the Arab countries of the Middle East. Britain and the Soviet Union were exercising indirect influence in Iran. Only in Turkey (and there only against heavy odds) did Kemal Atatürk succeed in asserting real independence. While this development in the relationship between the great powers and the Middle East may have been inevitable, it is appropriate to point out that the people and the leaders of some Middle Eastern countries played significant roles in bringing about such a relationship. The nationalist movement in the Arab countries of the Middle East assumed, wrongly as it turned out, that collaboration with European powers, particularly Britain, against Ottoman power would facilitate the process of achieving independence. This assumption encouraged the Arab leadership to reach certain accords with Great Britain during World War I and made it possible for the Arabs to ally themselves with the European powers against their Ottoman sovereign. Thus the Arab revolt against the Ottoman system was launched in conjunction with the Allied effort to dismember the Ottoman Empire. That the European powers assisted materially and morally in hastening the Arab revolt is undeniable; assistance was extended on the correct assumption that the Arab revolt, regardless of its territorial, national, and ideological aspirations, would facilitate the dismemberment of the common opponent. The liaison established with the dissident Arab nationalist groups and the 'understanding' reached is commonly referred to and embodied in the Husain-McMahon agreement, which, as the Arabs understood it, committed the British Government to the cause of Arab independence after the termination of hostilities and committed the Arabs to the war on the side of the Allies.

The actual intentions of the Allies, however, were embodied in secret agreements which clearly determined the shape of the Middle East map once the war had been won. The Sykes-Picot Agreement between France and Britain (with a parallel agreement with Russia) and the 1917 Balfour Declaration not only committed these powers to the division of the Middle East among themselves, but also promised the transformation of Palestine into a Jewish national homeland. Clearly the European commitment to the Arab Revolt was tactical rather than real and was disregarded as soon as the situation permitted.

Only portions of these agreements dividing up the Middle East were implemented, however, for the postwar reality of Europe and the Middle East differed from what the three powers had anticipated. Russia's withdrawal from the war after the October Revolution removed her from the arena of competition for a number of decades, and the Soviet Union's concern with reconstruction removed it from the Middle East arena until the end of World War II. The successful resistance of the Turkish nationalists under the able leadership of Mustafa Kemal Atatürk removed Turkey proper from the domain of any ambitious European power which might entertain designs of direct control. Turkey emerged from World War I as a strong, sovereign, nationalist republic, capable of defending its national interests. From 1924 up to the present day the Turkish Republic has been successful in maintaining a relationship of equality with other powers.

Other wartime agreements had taken effect in the rest of the Middle East. The Arab countries of the Ottoman Empire were divided, although not without tension and bickering among the competing powers, essentially between Britain and France. Direct or indirect control by Britain was effected in Palestine, Transjordan, Egypt, Iraq and Iran; France retained direct control over Syria and Lebanon. Both powers rationalised their exercise of control in terms of certain international commitments. The League of Nations under the mandate system had entrusted the two powers with the task of preparing these countries for independence, except Iran, which nominally remained independent. Under the Palestine Mandate, Great Britain undertook the task of discharging the obligations embodied in the

Balfour Declaration, namely the transformation of Palestine into a Jewish national homeland.

BRITISH AND FRENCH MANDATES

In the interwar period, then, the powers shaping the destiny of the Middle East were Britain and France. Different types of control were exercised in the various countries, although in each case a special agreement was reached. French rule in Syria and Lebanon was quite direct, frequently authoritarian and on the whole regressive. This form of control was not unrelated to France's conception of its interests and role in the world. French interests in the Middle East were predominantly cultural in nature and were concerned with perpetrating France's status as an empire. In applying its control in Syria and Lebanon, France gave support to the Christian minorities of the region and fostered cultural institutions intended to serve the 'civilising mission' it conceived for itself. The French Mandate over Syria and Lebanon was a dismal failure. Economically it was harmful to the French treasury, precisely because it was imposed and maintained by force. It failed to generate the necessary economic development schemes for both countries and increased the already evident tendencies towards their further fragmentation. Finally, in Syrian eyes, it alienated part of the homeland by surrendering Alexandretta to Turkey in 1938. The French Mandate over Syria constantly faced threats of revolt, and when it was brought to an end by the combined stresses of World War II and the rising nationalist movement no one lamented its disappearance.

Britain's record is somewhat more complicated. Britain's economic interests, especially once oil became a significant factor in international production and commerce, were a determining factor in its constant attempts not only to maintain control but also to maintain a high degree of stability in the region. To accomplish this, Britain essentially followed a regional policy of maintaining an empire by treaty, which—except for Palestine—followed a single pattern. Direct control was gradually ceded to national authorities. Britain exercised her influence by enabling a client class to assume power through which Britain for all practical purposes controlled or tried to control the direction of change.

Britain's influence and control, though challenged periodically, was paramount in all Arab countries and Iran, and this supremacy was assured through temporarily acceptable treaty relations with the governing institutions of these countries until World War II.

It is perhaps arguable that Britain's role in the Middle East after World War II would have been different had it not been affected by Britain's controversial role in Palestine. It may be that the trend toward self-assertion, together with the intrusion of other powers, would of necessity have pushed Britain out, but it seems likely that Britain's responsibility in Palestine exacerbated the feeling of hostility toward a role that had never gone unchallenged. Yet the record of British accomplishment in the Middle East is not to be minimised or dismissed. It is beyond dispute that Britain rendered valuable services to the region, whether in terms of training a competent and stable cadre of civil servants and assistance in giving rise to self-governing institutions, or in terms of education and economic development schemes. That these measures were neither adequate nor satisfactory, given nationalist expectations, in no way detracts from their significance. To state and emphasise this point simply highlights a principle that is often obscured in nationalist rhetoric, namely, that an imperial power with global interests may find that its own enlightened self-interest runs parallel with the progressive development of the countries it temporarily rules. There is no question but that Britain's global and Middle East interests guided her in the implementation of policies in the region; the fact that Britain resorted to the technique of 'empire by treaty' in support of gradual change in the region confirms her estimate that ultimately British interests and their maintenance were not necessarily in conflict with the broadly conceived interests of the countries themselves.

Advent of the Super Powers

A combination of factors after World War II made fundamental changes in the nature and identity of great power involvement in the Middle East inevitable. The tremendous effect of the war itself irrevocably altered the position of the powers hitherto dominant in the Middle East. Neither France nor Britain were able to assert supremacy in the Middle East without serious challenge from competing centres of power. The emergence of the US and the Soviet Union as global super powers made the eclipse of Britain in the Middle East only a question of time, and the increased strength and viability of the nationalist drive toward radical social and economic change made a clash with what remained of Britain's power equally inevitable. The erosion of great power control and influence became part and parcel of the global struggle of the super powers for world hegemony and an objective of all nationalist movements in the region.

The nature of great power interests in the Middle East remained essentially the same, although in absolute terms they increased in value. Economically, the various development schemes launched by the national governments made it attractive for the great powers to deal on a larger scale with the Middle East countries. The increase in great power investments became quite evident as their own needs increased and as oil, the chief product of the Middle East, assumed greater importance in the world economy. Western European economies, increasingly dependent on American assistance and guidance, were planned on the basis of a continuous supply of Middle Eastern oil. Correspondingly, Soviet interests were directed toward weakening Western European economies and reducing their dependence on the United States. Thus a Soviet objective soon after the termination of World War II was not to gain possession of this vital resource but rather to deprive their opponents of it, thereby crippling them to the point where Soviet hegemony in Europe would be assured. Since the war, a constant objective of Western policies in the region has been to assure the uninterrupted flow of oil. The national governments themselves became increasingly dependent on oil revenues, although it must be added that they were not unwilling to utilise this differential dependence to exert political pressure.

No less than oil, strategy and national and global defence considerations have played a significant role in determining great power involvement and activity in the Middle East in the postwar period. The concern of the Soviet Union with pushing its frontier of security as far as possible from its own territorial domain, combined with a historic hunger for a warm-water port, made it inevitable that the Soviet Union would push for territorial concessions at the expense of some national governments in the Middle East. This motive accounts for the pressure on Iran which resulted in the establishment of the puppet state of Azerbaijan. The stationing of Soviet troops in Iran proper brought a swift response from the US and its allies. The subsequent dismantling of Azerbaijan brought to an immediate end any attempt on the part of the Soviet Union to absorb territory and thus forced it to revert to its traditional methods of disruption through the effective use of local Communist parties. The similar pressure on Turkey for the cession of part of the eastern portion of the Turkish Republic reversed a hitherto correct relationship between Turkey and the Soviet Union (it will be recalled that the Turkish nationalists had been supported by the Soviet Union, and the latter received early recognition from Turkey) which was premised on the abandonment of Czarist objectives and ambitions. Soviet pressure following World War II increased the anxieties of the Turkish Government and in the West resulted ultimately in the position stated in the Truman Doctrine, which viewed the defence of Turkey as being essential to the security of the US. Turkey was drawn into the defence networks devised by the US for European and Middle Eastern countries; and since Turkey joined NATO in 1950 its destiny has been linked with that of the US.

This external pressure on the Middle East brought about, at first with reluctance and then with eagerness, the direct involvement of the US in the Middle East. But a second and perhaps in the long run a more disruptive pressure was also brought to bear, in the form of the nationalist drive to reorganise the political and social map of the Middle East. By the 1950s nationalist movements in Iran and the Arab countries had assumed considerable force and viability. A younger generation of Arabs and Persians were clamouring for a more dignified status in the world community, greater participation in decision-making processes, and ultimately greater national integration. The nationalists had always posed a serious threat to the *status quo*, and if left alone they would have reversed the 'treaty-relations' devised to assure one or another of the great powers a preferential status in the various countries of the Middle East. While initially Great Britain would have been the first to suffer from any drastic alteration of the *status quo*, in the post-war period US interests, economic and strategic, were also threatened. The gradual weakening of Britain's global position gave the US a decisive role in the maintenance of the *status quo*. To maintain the *status quo* in the region and in an attempt to bring the region into some kind of defence network against the Soviet Union, the US over the years tried to tie up the countries with regional defence arrangements. From the stillborn Middle East Defence Pact of 1951 and the Baghdad Pact to the Eisenhower Doctrine, the countries of the Middle East figured increasingly in the calculations of the Cold War.

That the US ultimately failed to establish a defence network in the Middle East stems from a number of factors which should be mentioned. Where Soviet danger, real or imagined, was strongly felt, as it was in Turkey and Iran, policy-makers felt a certain degree of protection in allying their countries with the United States and thus were more willing to enter into treaty arrangements that would commit them to the global defence needs of the US. Where the danger was coming from sources other than the Soviet Union, the primary objective of the Middle Eastern countries was to reduce their dependence on the West. The nationalist movement in all Arab countries directed its energy to the reduction of British and American influence and intervention in the domestic affairs of the Middle Eastern states. As a result of this drive, Iraq, Egypt and Jordan, by revolutionary or evolutionary techniques, freed themselves from their subservience to Great Britain. By the end of the 1950s, with practically every country in the Middle East enjoying effective freedom in the management of its domestic and external affairs, the role of the great powers in the Middle East became primarily an aspect of the global struggle for supremacy.

EFFECTS OF NATIONALISM

In the process of achieving greater national freedom in domestic affairs, the Middle East underwent serious internal change. Where foreign concerns were not outrightly nationalised in pursuit of radical ideologies, the countries of the area nonetheless succeeded in increasing their own share in the profits of the concerns managed or owned by foreign companies. On the whole the defence concerns of the Middle Eastern countries remained in their own hands and by the late 1950s, except for Turkey and to some extent Iran, these countries were no longer formally linked to the defence needs of the great powers.

Paradoxically, as these countries attained greater freedom, the great powers reasserted themselves and their presence in a different form. Internal conflict contributed to a re-emergence of US and Soviet influence and power in the Middle East. The Arab-Israeli conflict, festering since the creation of Israel in 1948, has had a serious impact on the role which the great powers have played in the region. Internal conflict between the Arab States, resulting from the nationalist commitment to an Arab nation and to a social and political order that is decidedly modern in character, has also had an impact on the role of the great powers. By the 1960s these two critical issues accounted for the reassertion of great power involvement in the Middle East.

In part as a result of the imperative need to maintain an adequate defence against all external opponents, some Arab States initiated a policy of rapprochment with the Soviet Union. While the USSR had been consistently hostile to the nationalist movements in the region, soon after the death of Stalin it transformed its policy and began to support such nationalist movements in an attempt to undermine Western control throughout the world. Thus the interests of the nationalists and of the Soviet Union became increasingly compatible and soon resulted in agreements that appeared beneficial to both sides. Trade agreements were concluded between Egypt and the Soviet Union, and later between Syria and Iraq and the Soviet Union, and increasingly the defence needs of these countries were met by the Soviet Union. Since 1955, when the first arms agreement between the Soviet Union and Egypt was concluded, the Soviet Union has been the chief supplier of arms to what has become known as the progressive wing of the Arab world.

Correspondingly, the US either directly or indirectly became the chief supplier of arms and economic aid to the other faction of the Middle East equation. It was this kind of alignment, first brought about as a result of the desperate need for military and economic assistance without strings, that accounted in part for the embroilment of the Middle Eastern states with the global commitments of the great powers. Having once made their options clear, whether domestically (in terms of radical programmes of social and economic reconstruction) or internationally (by the adoption of a non-aligned position), it became increasingly difficult for the Middle Eastern states to stay clear of great power rivalry and intervention in the region.

In the 1960s the following picture could be drawn of the great power involvement in the Middle East. On the one hand the progressive wing in the Arab world had increasingly relied for its economic, political and military needs on the Soviet Union, and that reliance has brought about a more effective Soviet presence in the region. For the first time in modern history, the Soviet Union has become in fact a Middle Eastern power with access to facilities in the region that can be more than favourably compared to those of the other great powers. This has happened at a time when the actual influence and power of the West have been seriously weakened in the region. Paradoxically, the US, relying on its conservative backers and on Israel, is temporarily assured of being able to maintain its economic interests. But by the same token its strategic need for the Middle East has become somewhat obsolete. The overall change in the international system and the reduction of the compelling rivalry between the Soviet Union and that of the US in many ways is already having its effect on the great powers in the Middle East. The states previously committed to the defence network of the US, like Turkey and Iran, are experiencing a greater degree of freedom in dealing with the Soviet Union, whereas those that were free of any direct involvement in the defence networks of the super powers are experiencing a greater degree of difficulty in maintaining their earlier freedom of action and policy. Although all of the Middle Eastern states now enjoy relatively greater liberty to fashion their destinies than they had in the past, internal conflicts and tensions threaten to drive them in directions and to policies which might bring about more effective intervention in their affairs by the great powers.

FURTHER READING

Antonius, George. *The Arab Awakening*, Haimish Hamilton, London, 1938; Putnam, New York, 1965.

Badeau, John. *The American Approach to the Arab World*, Harper & Row, New York, 1968.

Hourani, Albert. 'The Decline of the West in the Middle East', *International Affairs*, vol. 29, nos. 1 & 2, London, 1953.

Laqueur, Walter. *The Soviet Union and the Middle East*, Praeger, New York, 1959.

Lenczowski, George. *American Interests in the Arab World*, Washington D.C., 1968.

Love, K. *Suez: The Twice Fought War*, McGraw-Hill, New York, 1969.

Monroe, Elizabeth. *Britain's Moment in the Middle East, 1914–1956*, Johns Hopkins Press, Baltimore, 1963.

Polk, William. *The United States and the Arab World*, Harvard Univ. Press, Cambridge, Mass., 1965.

Sayegh, Fayez. (ed.) *The Dynamics of Neutralism in the Arab World*, Chandler Publishers, San Francisco, 1964.

Sharabi, Hisham B. *Palestine and Israel: The Lethal Dilemma*, Van Nostrand Reinhold, New York, 1969.

Spector, Ivar. *The Soviet Union and the Muslim World, 1917–1958*, Univ. of Washington Press, Seattle, 1959.

IBRAHIM ABU-LUGHOD. Professor of Political Science and Associate Director of the programme of African Studies at Northwestern University, Evanston, Illinois. Has taught at Smith College, the University of Massachusetts and McGill University. Author of *Arab Rediscovery of Europe* (1963), co-author of *Patterns of African Development* (1967). Contributor to *The Middle East Journal, Review of Politics* and *ORBIS*. Editor of *The Arab-Israeli Confrontation: an Arab Perspective* (1970).

ZIONISM

NORMAN BENTWICH

ZIONISM is the movement of the Jewish people to return to the land of Israel —which the ancient Greeks and Romans called Palestine, after the Philistine inhabitants of the coast—to rebuild a national home there. It was a fundamental belief of the Jews, after the first Babylonian Captivity in the sixth century BC, that they would recover their homeland and rebuild the Temple in Jerusalem. The Hebrew prophets Isaiah, Jeremiah and Ezekiel strengthened that faith. Six hundred years later the Jewish people were conquered by the Romans, and the Temple of the one universal God was destroyed. They were already spread over the Middle East and other countries of the Roman Empire, and that world-wide dispersion became the permanent condition of the majority until the present day. They retained a firm faith that they would again, in the fullness of time, have a national and spiritual centre and home in the land of the Bible. A small remnant of the scattered people remained in Jerusalem throughout the ages, except for occasional expulsions. The prayers for the return were repeated thrice daily by faithful Jews, and on every occasion of joy and sorrow. Characteristic is the cry on the Passover eve, the principal family feast, 'Next Year in Jerusalem'. The long story of Jewish frustration is interspersed with the appearance of leaders claiming to be the Messiah, divinely appointed to conduct them back to the land of their ancestors.

It was not until the 19th century that an organised movement began to form agricultural 'colonies', small groups of town-dwelling Palestinians and other groups from the ghettoes of Eastern Europe. Societies were also established for this purpose in the Western countries and here they were known as Lovers (*Hovevi*) of Zion. The famous pioneer of the movement was the Anglo-Jewish philanthropist, Sir Moses Montefiore, who made seven pilgrimages from Victorian England to Palestine. He helped the Jews living in the crowded alleys of the Jewish quarter of the Old City of Jerusalem to build suburbs with gardens outside the walls, and he also acquired orange groves around Jaffa. After his death in 1884 the principal benefactor was the Frenchman, Baron Edmond de Rothschild. He came to the aid of the struggling settlers, who had for the most part no training or preparation for their new vocation; and he sent administrators and instructors to guide them. For nearly 50 years he devoted his mind and wealth to their cause. Most of the pioneers came from the Russian Empire, which contained half the Jewish people of the world and denied them civil and political rights. The first settlers were religious Jews, and the return to Palestine was associated with the fulfilment of Judaism.

Herzl and the Beginnings of Zionist Ideology

The growth of the agricultural settlement was aided by the foundation of an agricultural school near Jaffa, which was open to Arabs as well as Jews. The land was given by the Ottoman sultan, and the school was maintained by a Jewish international body, the *Alliance Israélite Universelle*. The relations of Jews and Arabs in those days were generally friendly, and Arabs were regularly employed by the Jewish farmers. A turning point in the movement of the return came, in the last decade of the 19th century, from an unexpected quarter. An Austrian Jewish publicist and playwright, Dr Theodor Herzl, was a correspondent for the Vienna daily paper, *Neue Freie Presse*, and in 1895 had reported the trial, in Paris, of the Jewish staff-officer Captain Alfred Dreyfus, who was charged—falsely, as it was proved later—with spying for the Germans. The French people reacted violently to the incident, and a virus of anti-Jewish feeling infected the country. Herzl, who hitherto had played no part in Jewish life, was overwhelmed by the outbreak in the country which Jews honoured for the French Revolution, that had accorded the rights of man to the Jews in France and in French-occupied western and southern Europe. He realised that 'emancipation'—as the idea of equal status for the Jews was called—was not a solution of the Jewish problem. The traditional hatred might break out at any time. Anti-Semitism in Western and Eastern Europe was one of the constant motives behind Zionism, and was to be terribly intensified after Hitler came to power in Germany in 1933.

Jews who wanted to preserve their religious and ethnic identity had to have their home where they would be autonomous. Herzl wrote a pamphlet, *Der Judenstaat*—the Jews' State—demanding that the Jews must procure for themselves, and occupy, an empty territory. At the time he did not know of the movement of village settlement in Palestine. His ignorance was soon remedied, and he learned quickly enough of the intense attachment of the Jewish people, particularly the oppressed masses in Eastern Europe, to Palestine. They would not accept any other land. He found that the case for a Jewish homeland in the birthplace of their religion and race had already been put eloquently by Moses Hess, a German-Jewish comrade of Karl Marx, and by the English novelist George Eliot in *Daniel Deronda*. But writing was not enough; he must summon the people to action. There must be a parliament of world Jewry which would create political and financial organs to achieve the redemption. Modern Zionism was born, and a congress was held at Basel in Switzerland in the summer of 1897. It adopted as its aim the establishment of a home in Palestine for the Jewish people, guaranteed by law. International councils were appointed and a financial instrument, the Jewish Colonial Trust, was established in England to raise the money for the granting of a charter by the Turkish Sultan confirming the right of Jews to build their home in Palestine.

A section of the Zionists had misgivings about the political and economic approach, and Herzl himself wrote that the return of the Jews to Jewishness must precede the physical return to the land. They envisaged the home in Palestine not as an autonomous sovereign state, but as a spiritual centre of the scattered people, where Jewish culture, including Judaism, would be revived. From it the creative culture would be carried to the Jewish communities of the world and would strengthen their consciousness. The philosopher of 'spiritual Zionism' was a Russian Jew, Asher Ginsberg, who wrote in Hebrew and is better known by his Hebrew pen-name Ahad Ha'am, meaning 'One of the People'. Among his disciples was Chaim Weizmann, the future President of the World Zionist Organisation and the first President of the Republic of Israel.

Herzl himself spent the last years of his life seeking the support of European potentates for the fulfilment of his vision. He asked help in turn from the Sultan of Turkey, Kaiser Wilhelm II, the Premier of the Russian Empire, the Pope, and British statesmen. He did not obtain the charter for settlement in Palestine, but he made a favourable impression on Joseph Chamberlain, then British Colonial Secretary. Chamberlain induced the government to offer to the Zionist Congress, as a land of refuge, a large territory in East Africa where Jews should have autonomy. But the Russian Jews, the largest element of the Congress, would have none of it. There should be no Zionism without Zion. Herzl died brokenhearted because of the rift. He had prophesied in 1897 that in 50 years the state would be created; he was right to the exact year.

ZIONISM UNDER THE MANDATE

The Zionist movement, not yet strong in its support from the masses except in Eastern Europe, was bitterly divided between the political followers, who wanted a charter internationally guaranteed, and those practical people who believed in steady and gradual settlement of Palestine. The annual Congress was maintained, and in 1912 Weizmann, then Reader in Chemistry at Manchester University and the leader of a cultural group of delegates, persuaded the assembly to adopt the project of a university in Palestine, which should be open to Arabs as well as Jews. It was another achievement of the cultural enthusiasts that Hebrew was adopted as the language of all primary and some secondary schools in Palestine.

With the outbreak of the war in 1914, and the Turkish alliance with Germany and Austria-Hungary, the main centre of activity of the Zionist bodies was shifted from central Europe to England. Weizmann, who moved from Manchester to London, and who made a most valuable scientific contribution to the English war effort, came to be accepted as the representative of Western Jewry to the allied powers. With his signal genius for projecting his ideas, and with the help of Herbert Samuel, who until 1917 was a member of the British cabinet, he persuaded the British Government to sponsor the claims of the Zionists for the establishment of a Jewish national home in Palestine, provided that the civil and religious rights of the other community —the Arabs—were not impaired. A declaration in that sense, which was in the form of a letter from Arthur Balfour, the foreign secretary, to Lord Rothschild, as the representative of the English Zionists, was issued in November 1917. The British Government proceeded to win the support of the Western allies, including the United States, for that policy. Zionism was then not a national movement, like that of the European peoples in the 19th century, or of the Arabs and Indians in the 20th, to get rid of a hated foreign rule. It was unique in its aim of bringing a people distributed all over the world to its historic home in the past, which was mainly occupied, though sparsely, by another branch of the Semitic race.

The first step towards implementing the Balfour Declaration was taken by the dispatch to occupied Palestine of an international commission headed by Weizmann. His meeting in 1918 with the Emir Faisal, the commander of the Arab revolt against the Turks, gave the hope—soon to be disappointed—of peaceful Jewish-Arab co-operation in the development of the Middle East.

The Zionist movement took on a fresh actuality and a fresh appeal to the Jewish people when the Mandate for the governing of Palestine was accorded to Great Britain in 1920 by the principal allied powers, and Herbert Samuel was appointed as the first High-Commissioner for the mandated territory. The appeal was naturally greatest to English-speaking Jewry, and by the terms of the Mandate the British administration recognised the Jewish Agency for Palestine, which was centred in London and presided over by Weizmann, as the body which, in co-operation with the Government, would promote and assist the establishment of the national home. In 1929 Weizmann contrived to get leading non-Zionists to participate in his agency, and so broadened its material and moral support. The Zionist Congress remained the supreme policy-making body, and its members were elected from the communities by a system of proportional representation (common in central Europe) of a number of parties : the religious *Mizrachi*, the Labour *Poalim* (workers), who were socialists, and the General Zionists, who embraced the bourgeois. Gradually, with the immigration to Palestine of manual workers, the Labour Party came to dominate the congress. The party included a religious section which combined faithful observance of the religious law with socialist doctrine. An extreme nationalist party was added : the Revisionists, who demanded that the national home should be extended to the country across the River Jordan, and who also opposed the socialist basis of democracy.

A primary Zionist purpose was to promote Jewish immigration and to organise settlement of the immigrants on the land or in industry. During the 28 years of the Mandate, the Jewish population rose tenfold from 60,000 to 650,000. The peak years were 1934 and 1935, when, under the pressure of the Hitler persecution, the number leaped to 100,000. This aroused the apprehension of the Arab population that they would then become a minority and led to the Arab revolt of 1936-9.

The Zionist bodies filled an important role in organising the immigration into Palestine and, later, Israel. Significantly the Hebrew word for immigration is *aliya*, meaning ascent, and the return to the national home has that religious and spiritual quality. The Zionist Federations, combining the different groups in each larger community, were intensely active in their country whenever a crisis arose in the relations of the Jewish Agency with the Palestine administration. Crises were frequent from 1929 until the end of the Mandate in 1948. More and more, however, the direction of policy passed from the bodies outside to the bodies in Palestine. The Executive Council of the Jewish Agency, which included representatives of the Federations, met regularly in Jerusalem after the State of Israel was declared. The Zionist Congress also held its meetings in Jerusalem. Its declining importance was marked by the decision to hold the Congress once in every four years, and more than once the interval was longer.

ZIONISM IN ISRAEL

The functions of the Zionist Organisation, once the State existed, were more controversial than they had been in the preparatory period. A bitter conflict arose between David Ben-Gurion, Prime Minister of Israel for most of the next 20 years, and the heads of the American Zionists. Ben-Gurion demanded that they should come to settle in Israel, or send members of their family to settle, now that the country was fully open and wanted settlers. Many American leaders repeated that they could not pull up their roots, but they manifested their attachment to the national home by frequent visits, investments, the support of Israel's cultural institutions, and by working for reorganisation of the Jewish system of education in America in such a way as to link it with the Israeli system. The American and English Zionists do in fact encourage Jewish youth to go to Israel, either permanently or for a year of study or work at universities or institutes of higher learning. Of those who start in this way, a growing proportion stay. The Hebrew University of Jerusalem in 1968 enrolled 1,400 students from the US and Canada, being nearly double the figure of the previous year. The heads of Diaspora Jewry retort to the Israelis, with some justice, that in the mainly secular state the knowledge of Jewish post-biblical history is weak in the young generation, and so too is the Jewishness.

The events of June 1967 undoubtedly had a twofold effect in stimulating *aliya*. On the one hand it strengthened the will for *Haluziut* (pioneering) in all Jewry; on the other hand it stimulated the religious feeling in Israeli teachers and pupils. Zionism, which was originally the expression of the national will to live, transcending the traditional 'orthodox' religion of Jewry, has now achieved its primary purpose. It has restored the historic reality of Jews as a people and a nation, and of Judaism as the religion expressing itself freely in the life of an autonomous Jewish country. If it has not yet inspired a religious revival in the Diaspora, it has fostered a heightened Jewish consciousness. The Israeli Jew nearest to prophetic stature was Martin Buber, the philosopher, who wrote in Jerusalem many books of his religious philosophy. And for him Judaism and Zionism are indissolubly linked. The Jews have the opportunity of building an ideal society as well as a national home. They have still to fulfil Herzl's behest in his book, *Alt-Neu-Land*, to conduct the administration of their homeland so that the stranger within the gates may be happy. That can be done when Israel has secured peace with the Arab peoples.

NORMAN BENTWICH, OBE, MC. Eminent barrister; Chairman, United Restitution Office since 1948. President, Jewish Historical Society 1960–2; member of Foreign Office Committee on Restitution in British Zone of Germany, 1951; Chairman, National Peace Council, 1944–6; Professor of International Relations, Jerusalem University, 1932–51; Attorney-General, Government of Palestine, 1920–31; Ministry of Justice, Cairo, 1912–15. Among his publications are *The Religious Foundations of Internationalism* (1933), *The Jews in Our Time* (1960), *Biography of Brigadier Fred Kisch* (1966).

PART FOUR

ECONOMIC AFFAIRS

NATURAL RESOURCES, ECONOMIC STRUCTURE AND GROWTH

SAMIR A. MAKDISI

The transitional phase which the Middle East, like other developing areas of the world, has entered since the end of World War II is very much in evidence in the economic field.[1] Transformation of the economic structure of the countries which this region encompasses is generally proceeding with vigour, the rate and pattern of progress varying from one country to another. While appreciable progress has been achieved by the region as a whole, the economic paths chosen by different countries have differed under the influence of economic and social considerations, and also of internal and external political developments. Regional economic co-operation has so far been very limited.

The observations which follow are intended, firstly, to convey a brief picture of the economic base upon which the growth of the countries of the region is being built and in this context their interaction with the world economy; and, secondly, to shed some light on certain aspects of the process of growth and transformation in these countries.

NATURAL RESOURCES AND ECONOMIC STRUCTURE

Looking at the region as a whole, the two prominent natural resources are agricultural land and petroleum. While other mineral deposits are available, on present evidence their regional significance as an economic resource is very limited.[2] The economic structure and growth of the region, therefore, have reflected this existing factor endowment, due allowance being made for variations in the economic characteristics of individual countries, one or two of which (as noted below) are less dependent upon agriculture and oil than upon other activities of the economy.

Agriculture accounts for a substantial portion of national income and is a major source of foreign exchange in several Middle Eastern countries; it is, furthermore, the main source of employment in most countries of the

---

[1] Any views expressed in this paper do not necessarily reflect those of the International Monetary Fund with which the author is associated.

[2] In a few countries, nevertheless, they are of significant commercial value. Turkey, for example, has exploitable quantities of iron, chrome and copper ores, coal and lignite. Jordan and the UAR exploit available phosphate deposits and the latter country also produces small quantities of chromite, iron and manganese. Iran is a minor producer of certain minerals.

region. To illustrate : excluding Lebanon and Israel as well as Kuwait and Saudi Arabia, both of which are primarily oil producing countries, the portion of domestic product originating in the agricultural sector ranged in recent years from one-fifth in Jordan and Iraq to over one-half in Sudan (see Appendix, Table 1). Available estimates for employment reveal a much larger share for agriculture in most countries of the region, reflecting the generally low productivity of agricultural labour (see Appendix, Table 2). Similarly, where oil production is not the major activity, agricultural exports are generally the principal source of export receipts.[3]

In Kuwait and Saudi Arabia (and the principalities of Bahrain, Qatar and Abu Dhabi) oil production accounts for the bulk of income as well as foreign exchange receipts; and in Iraq and Iran, where oil production is a major activity, it contributes substantially on both counts. Lebanon's economy has been greatly dependent upon foreign trade and services and the contribution of the agricultural sector to domestic production is relatively small, although as a source of employment it accounts for over one-half of the economically active population. In Israel both the trade and manufacturing sectors account for a higher portion of production than does agriculture; the percentage of the total economically active population engaged in agriculture is also relatively small. In Jordan the trade sector's contribution to domestic product has been, in recent years, of roughly the same magnitude as that of the agricultural sector. Nevertheless, the latter sector at present accounts for one-third of employment and the major portion of export receipts.

While agriculture is the mainstay of several Middle Eastern economies, the proportion of land devoted to cultivation is generally small. The ratio of arable land and land under permanent crops to total area currently amounts to about 3% in the Sudan and the UAR, 7% in Iran, 12% in Jordan, 17% to 19% in Iraq and Israel, rising to 28% in Lebanon and to about 33% in Syria and Turkey. In Kuwait and Saudi Arabia the percentage shares are negligible (see Appendix, Table 4). A major inhibiting factor to the extension of the cultivated area is the climate of the region : except on the extremities[4] the amount of rainfall is inadequate, and as is well known, the desert occupies a vast area of the Middle East. Efforts, therefore, have been made to exploit existing water resources and to expand the area under irrigation. Depending upon the availability of water and the extent to which irrigation facilities have been developed, the proportion of arable land and land under permanent crops which is currently irrigated varies widely from one Middle Eastern country to another. The UAR, on the one hand, has made extensive use of the Nile and its irrigation network is highly developed, with the result that all the cultivated area is under irrigation and crop yields are among the highest in the world. In Iran and Iraq, both of which benefit from available water resources (particularly in Iraq, where there are two major rivers, the Tigris and the Euphrates), 40% to 50% of the cultivated area is irrigated; in Israel, over one-third, in Lebanon over one-fifth and in the case of Jordan, Syria, Turkey and Sudan, the ratio varies from 5% to 11%. In Saudi Arabia the cultivated area is relatively small; the proportion which is irrigated is currently over 40%, use being made of underground water resources (see Appendix, Table 4). Nevertheless, it is apparent that with the exception of the UAR, agricultural pro-

[3] Table 3 indicates major export items of several Middle Eastern countries.
[4] Extreme north of Iran, Southern Sudan and close along the Mediterranean littoral and in Yemen.

duction is still heavily dependent upon rainfall. One consequence of this dependence is that, because of changing climatic conditions, wide variations in production may occur from one crop year to another with important repercussions on the growth of the economy.

A few countries of the region, such as Iran and Sudan, have a large agricultural potential in the extension of the rain-fed areas; for the other countries this type of expansion is much more limited. For the region as a whole, therefore, future increases in agricultural production would appear to depend more on raising the productivity of the cultivated land (generally low in comparison with more developed countries with a similar environment) than on its expansion.[5] This in turn would require heavy reliance on increasing the area under irrigation and more intensive use of irrigated land, supplemented by a more adequate exploitation of rain-fed land (e.g. more effective use of fallow,[6] improvement of crop yields), improved techniques of cultivation (proper use of fertilisers, improved seeds, control of pests and diseases), and a greater degree of agricultural mechanisation. The potential of individual countries varies. Wider possibilities for extending the irrigation network appear to exist in Iran, Iraq, Sudan and Syria than in other countries of the region, and a more intensive use of irrigated land (e.g. double cropping) seems to hold greater promise outside the UAR, in Jordan, Lebanon, Saudi Arabia, and Syria, than elsewhere.

The traditional crops of the Middle East include wheat, barley and rye mainly in the northern parts, and millet, maize and rice mainly in the southern parts. Most of them are grown for domestic consumption, but in recent years part of the production, particularly that of barley, has been diverted to export outlets.[7] A major cash crop grown in the area is cotton. It is mainly grown in the UAR, Sudan, Syria, Turkey and Iran. As a source of foreign exchange, cotton exports accounted in 1964–7 for about 32%, 48%, 47%, 24% and 25% respectively of the export proceeds (excluding oil in the case of Iran) of these countries. Another widely grown cash crop is tobacco, with Turkey accounting for the largest proportion of total production. In addition, a wide variety of fruits is grown and for some countries, such as Jordan, Lebanon and Israel, they comprise an important export item.

Petroleum resources in the Middle East currently account for one-half of proved world reserves and for about one-quarter of current world production. The largest current oil producers in the area under study are Iran, Saudi Arabia and Kuwait, followed by Iraq, the principalities of Qatar, Bahrain and Abu Dhabi combined, and the UAR. Recent discoveries in both the UAR and Syria (and especially the former country) are expected to augment their oil production substantially. The significance of petroleum to the Middle East is manifold: for those countries which are primarily oil producing, such as Kuwait, Saudi Arabia and the Arabian principalities, oil production as noted above is the principal source of income and foreign exchange; further, it is the main source of government finance and of capital formation. Iran and Iraq benefit in similar ways from oil production but, since

[5] For a very useful discussion of the problems and prospects of Middle Eastern agriculture see FAO, *Indicative World Plan for Agricultural Development, 1965–85, Near East*, vol. 1, Rome, 1966.

[6] The preceding source points out (p. 71) that in many parts of the Middle East a high proportion of the cultivated area, including irrigated lands, lies fallow during the course of the year and that effective utilisation of fallow should form one of the principal objectives in the development of rain-fed farming in the region.

[7] The UAR is a rice exporter.

their economies are more diversified, the relative contribution of oil to the economy, while substantial, is less important than in the former countries. Oil production has encouraged the establishment of petro-chemical and other industries in several of the oil producing countries which has helped to enlarge their industrial base and has contributed to expanding the pool of domestically available technical skills. Oil production has led to the establishment of oil refineries in several Middle Eastern countries, providing a local supply of fuels, and to the construction of pipelines which have brought various benefits, including the construction of refineries, to the countries through which these pipelines pass, such as Syria, Lebanon and Jordan. On a regional basis, oil production is a source of surplus capital funds from the oil-producing countries to other countries in the region, where it can be used for purposes of development. The possibilities for this type of regional co-operation are still wide, but some progress in this direction has been made, as illustrated by the activities of the Kuwait Fund for Arab Economic Development which has been contributing, albeit on a limited scale, to the investment resources of the Arab countries.

While agriculture and petroleum constitute the two basic natural resources of the Middle East,[8] and generally continue to provide the main support of its economies, the gains from the exploitation of these resources are being used to transform existing economic structures and to achieve higher levels of growth. Investments are being made in industrial and other projects, and the supply of capital goods, an essential ingredient in the process of growth, whether originating abroad or locally, is being augmented. Investments are also being made in education and the pool of domestically available skills is ever expanding. The process of growth, in other words, is changing the relative scarcity or abundance of various resources, natural, man-made, originating domestically or abroad, as well as the relative contribution of economic sectors to income and employment: Table 1 illustrates the decline in the relative contribution of agriculture to most economies of the Middle East; it is expected that as industrialisation gains further momentum, the importance of the agricultural sector will further diminish.

INTERACTION WITH THE WORLD ECONOMY

The process of growth and economic transformation in developing countries is closely linked with or dependent upon existing economic ties with the outside world, and particularly with the more advanced economies, which are the main source of needed capital goods and technical 'know-how'. Foreign trade and, more generally, international economic relations thus play a vital role in the development of less developed countries.[9] Developing countries attempt to stimulate economic growth by expanding their export sector and frequently by borrowing capital funds abroad; for some of them this dependence on world markets as outlets and as sources of supply is of the utmost importance.

The Middle East's degree of interdependence with the world economy varies from one country to another; for the region as a whole, however, several factors have tended to strengthen economic links with the outside world. Most important of these, at least in modern times, have been

---

[8] Tourism offers an important economic potential for many countries of the region on account of their geographic position and historical legacy.

[9] This is generally equally true of developed and developing countries, although the relative importance of foreign trade may vary from one country to another.

the region's natural resources. The discovery of oil, in particular, has attracted private investment on a very large scale and fostered the export markets of the oil-producing countries; the prominence of cotton in a number of Middle Eastern countries has accentuated their dependence on foreign markets, and in a few countries of the region foreign trade and services have traditionally played an important part in the economy. In addition, the geographic position of the Middle East as a link between three continents has fostered its importance in the world transport and transit system, and its historical legacy has also attracted foreign travel, which has been greatly aided by fast developments in the means of communication and transportation.

For those countries which are primarily oil-producing (Kuwait, Saudi Arabia, and the principalities of Qatar and Abu Dhabi) this dependence is of the highest order in terms of foreign markets, required capital, and the necessary technical 'know-how'. To a lesser but still substantial degree this dependence is evident in the case of countries which rely on foreign trade and services and/or the inflow of foreign capital (as Lebanon, Israel and Jordan). For countries which are dependent on cash crops (as the UAR and Syria) a change in world demand for these crops can have substantial repercussions on their economy.

A measure of the interdependence between the domestic economy and the world economy is the ratio of foreign trade to gross domestic product (GDP),[10] bearing in mind, however, that this ratio is subject to the impact of economic policy and may very well change from one period to another. Table 5 indicates the respective ratios, in recent years, of exports and imports (of goods and services) to GDP for the Middle Eastern countries. On the export side, Kuwait and Saudi Arabia have very high ratios, 65% and 70%, which reflect the dominance of oil exports in both economies.[11] They are followed by Iraq and Lebanon with export/GDP ratios of 40% and 38%, the former on account of the relative importance of oil and the latter because of substantial earnings from various services including tourism.[12] Syria, Iran, Israel and the UAR follow with ratios ranging from 19% to 26%. Despite the position of Iran as a major oil producer, the relative importance of the oil sector in the economy is not as great as in other oil-producing countries. For Jordan and Sudan, the ratios are a little lower than for the preceding group, followed by Turkey with a low ratio of about 7%.

On the import side, the highest ratio of 56% is that for Saudi Arabia, followed by Jordan, Lebanon and Israel with ratios ranging from 30% to 40%. In the case of both Israel and Jordan, whose import ratios are much higher than their export ratios, a high level of imports has been made possible by heavy reliance on foreign loans and grants. The relatively low import ratio of 23% for Kuwait is explained by its limited capacity to make use of resources made available through its export earnings. Of the remaining countries, Iran and Turkey have the lowest ratios, which are attributable

---

[10] GDP is equivalent to gross national product (GNP) less net factor income from abroad such as interest, profit and dividends. GNP is equivalent to the sum of consumption expenditures and gross domestic capital formation, private and public, and the net exports of goods and services plus the net factor income received from abroad.

[11] These ratios for both countries would have been even higher if GNP were used instead of GDP because of a substantial net outflow of factor income. For the other countries net factor income from abroad is relatively less important.

[12] Estimates of Lebanon's balance of payments for 1966 reveal that services in connection with transportation and tourism alone brought in about £L547 million compared with merchandise export of about £L584 million.

to their more diversified economies, and especially in the case of Turkey to the availability of local materials to feed its industry.

Some Aspects of Economic Growth

The real rate of growth has varied substantially from one Middle Eastern country to another; available national income estimates indicate that in the 1960s the range was from roughly 4% to 8% per annum and perhaps even higher;[13] for several countries the rate of growth has varied considerably from year to year. To a large degree this is explained by important fluctuations in agricultural production which, as noted earlier, not only accounts for a substantial portion of GDP but is still generally dependent upon rainfall. The economic growth of these countries is likely to continue to be subject in the forseeable future to important fluctuations; on the other hand, as further progress is made in extending the area under irrigation, as the economy is progressively diversified and a broader industrial base is created, their vulnerability to wide fluctuations is expected to diminish. The Middle East, moreover, is a region that has witnessed since World War II major political and social changes, which have had their impact on the rate of growth and contributed to its annual changes in individual countries. In some countries, such as Syria and the UAR, where the changes have been drastic, the structure of the economy has been profoundly influenced.[14]

Closely connected with the development of the agricultural sector has been the initiation of major land reforms in a number of Middle Eastern countries where the land tenure system had been characterised by severe inequality of land distribution, absenteeism of landlords and the poverty of farmers. These reforms took place in the UAR (1952), Syria (1958), Iraq (1958), and Iran (1960). The process of land redistribution either has already been completed or is nearing its completion; one consequence of land reform has been a reduction in the inequality of income distribution and a realignment in the class power structure of the country concerned, with important repercussions on economic policy. Land reform is one manifestation of the generally growing involvement of the government in the economic and social fields. In some countries the public sector has in fact already taken over the management of major economic enterprises, largely through acts of nationalisation (as in Syria and the UAR); since 1964 the public sector in Iraq has expanded substantially. In Turkey and Israel the public sector has been heavily involved in the management of the economy for a long time, and in other Middle Eastern countries there is abundant evidence of increased direct participation by the public sector, particularly in the field of infrastructure : creation of development agencies, banking institutions, agricultural and water schemes. In countries which are primarily oil-producing, the influence of the state is overwhelming, even if other enterprises largely belong to the private sector. In all those countries the Govern-

[13] Time series of national income estimates for most Middle Eastern countries are found in UN *Yearbook of National Accounts Statistics.*

[14] Where internal instability persisted or the private sector has feared unfavourable economic measures, capital and other resources tended to flow out. At times the region as a whole may have been affected but frequently there occurred a flow of resources from countries where political or economic instability prevailed to other countries of the region. Lebanon, for example, has been, at least until recently, a net recipient of Arab capital in search not only of investment opportunities but also of refuge from political uncertainties.

ments' economic policy, both in the development and the financial fields, has been exerting an increasing influence on the economy and its growth; in the process various instruments of economic policy have been either developed or improved upon in order to serve more adequately the economic objectives of the governments.

Most countries of the area have drawn up development plans. While some of these have been little more than a collection of projects which governments believed it desirable to implement, these plans indicate a growing consciousness on the part of governments of the need to define overall economic objectives and to influence the economic process with a view to attaining them. At the same time the private sector has played a major role in several Middle Eastern economies : in certain countries, such as Lebanon and Jordan, economic enterprises are still largely managed by this sector and until recently the private sector in other countries, such as Syria and Iraq, was mainly responsible for economic expansion. The merits of public versus private sector leadership of the economy apart, the ascendancy of the government in economic matters should, of course, be seen as part of its growing ascendancy in all aspects of a country's life. Political, social and ideological motivations have, in fact, been of paramount importance in decisions affecting the transformation of economic systems. The extent to which régimes have been ideologically motivated or the degree to which a particular ideology, in contrast to pragmatic considerations, has acted as a spark for economic and social transformation, has differed greatly from one country to another and even from one period to another in the same country.

Lastly, appreciable progress has been made in raising educational and health standards, although a number of major difficulties in this field have still to be coped with.[15] The benefits to the Middle Eastern economies of rising levels of education and health, while not directly measurable, can only be immense, particularly for those countries which initially faced very poor conditions in these fields. Table 6 illustrates some of the achievements in the field of education. For those countries which started with relatively low levels, the ratio of primary and secondary school enrolment to the corresponding population increased in the period 1950–64 from two to five times. Similarly rapid progress has been made in higher education enrolment.[16] In terms of public expenditure (and GNP) some of the Middle Eastern countries—Iraq, Syria and Turkey—have managed to increase the share of education, health and other social services, but for the region as a whole this development is not necessarily representative. One reason is that among various expenditure outlets, defence has generally been a strong competitor, not only to social services but to strictly economic projects as well.[17]

REGIONAL ECONOMIC CO-OPERATION

In practice regional economic co-operation in the Middle East has to be viewed in the context of economic relations among the Arab countries of

[15] See UN *Studies on Selected Development Problems in Various Countries of the Middle East*, New York, 1967, pp. 41–57.

[16] Taking Sudan, Syria and Turkey as examples, the number of students in higher education per 100,000 inhabitants increased from 1950 to 1965 from 4, 86, and 118 to 57, 604, and 293 respectively. (Source : UNESCO, *Statistical Yearbook, 1966*.)

[17] In recent years, according to UN data, known defence expenditures have absorbed roughly from 20% to 40% of total budgetary outlays.

the region.[18] Until recently inter-Arab economic co-operation had been very limited, despite various attempts by the Arab League in that direction. The first steps towards multilateral co-operation took place in 1953 when the Arab League drew up two economic treaties pertaining to trade (and transit) and payments among the member countries.[19] At the trade level the agreement provided essentially for the extension of preferential treatment, while transit trade among the interested parties was regulated; at the payments level, while the objective was to facilitate current and capital movement in the region, in effect they were left subject to existing regulations. Both agreements had a very limited impact and could not be considered as a serious move toward the expansion of intra-regional trade and payments.

Another step was taken in 1964 when an Arab Economic Unity Agreement (signed in 1962) was ratified by five Arab countries, establishing the Council for Arab Economic Union. The Council decided to create an 'Arab Common Market' effective from 1 January 1965, and several moves in this direction have already been taken.[20] Membership is open to all Arab states which adhered to the Agreement of 1962.

The various advantages of regional economic co-operation and ultimately integration need not be repeated here. It is enough to point, in the context of the Arab Middle East, to the wide possibilities open for a more effective utilisation of available financial resources, which would benefit individual countries as well as the region as a whole, an objective which the Kuwait Fund for Arab Economic Development has in fact been serving. On the other hand, the process of economic integration is not an easy one. Different political and economic systems prevail, and while in principle this should not prove an insurmountable obstacle, past experiences in individual countries (as well as apprehensions about the future course of events) could act as retarding factors in the endeavour to integrate economically. Nevertheless, on purely economic grounds, the region can only stand to benefit from a carefully guided process of integration.

CONCLUDING OBSERVATION

At least some of the Middle Eastern countries face at the moment (and are likely to face in the future) extremely difficult political circumstances. These political circumstances may exert an adverse influence on economic growth, by tending to diminish the share of available resources which is devoted to development projects. Of course, when the vital political interests of nations are involved, the economic problem can, understandably, assume a diminishing importance in the scale of national priorities. However,

[18] Economic relations between the Arab countries and Iran and Turkey do not benefit from any preferential treatment, while a total political and economic boycott exists between the Arab countries and Israel.

[19] 'Convention for Facilitating Trade Exchange and the Regulation of Transit Trade Between States of the Arab League' (subsequently amended several times) and 'A Convention for the Settlement of Payments of Current Transactions and the Movement of Capital Between the States of the Arab League'.

[20] Tariff reductions on intra-regional trade have been effected at a rate of 20% and 10% per annum for agricultural and manufactured commodities, respectively, and quantitative restrictions have been reduced. Further, the Agreement provides for regional co-ordination of development plans and industrial development programmes. An 'Arab Payments Union' was decided upon at the time the 'Arab Common Market' was agreed to and was planned to come into effect in 1969. The activation of an 'Arab Development Bank', which had been agreed upon by the Arab League in 1957, is also under consideration.

even if political factors are left out of account, social progress and social equality (however defined), along with economic development, are primary objectives of the countries of the region. With this spectrum of objectives, the danger of implementing a policy which may serve one objective but may conflict with the other is ever present. The care with which policies and plans need to be worked out and the economy managed cannot, therefore, be overstated, if possible conflicts between social and economic progress are to be minimised. The scope for progress is wide and would be even wider with effective and well-guided regional economic co-operation among those countries which have embarked or can embark upon such a move.

APPENDIX

TABLE 1

MIDDLE EASTERN COUNTRIES: INDUSTRIAL ORIGIN OF GROSS DOMESTIC PRODUCT AT FACTOR COST IN SELECTED YEARS (IN PERCENTAGES)

	Agriculture	Industrial Activity		Trade	Other	Total
		Total	Manufac- turing			
Iran[1]						
1960	30	28	(27)	10	32	100
1963	28	30	(30)	8	34	100
1965	28	30	(27)	8	34	100
Iraq						
1953	22	47	(8)	6	25	100
1960	17	47	(10)	6	30	100
1963	20	44	(8)	6	30	100
1965	21	45	(9)	6	28	100
Israel						
1953	12	34	(23)	—	54	100
1960	12	34	(25)	—	54	100
1963	11	36	(26)	19	34	100
1966	8	32	(24)	19	41	100
Jordan						
1959	18	7	—	22	53	100
1963	19	10	—	22	49	100
1965	23	12	—	21	44	100
1966	19	12	—	20	49	100
Lebanon						
1950	20	13	—	29	38	100
1961	18	12	—	26	44	100
1963	18	12	—	25	45	100
1966[2]	12	13	—	31	44	100
Sudan[3]						
1955	61	5	(4)	—	34	100
1960	57	5	(5)	—	38	100
1963	51	6	(5)	—	43	100
1966	54	6	(6)	—	40	100

TABLE 1—*continued*

| | Agriculture | Industrial Activity | | Trade | Other | Total |
		Total	Manufac-turing			
Syria[4]						
1953	44	12	—	14	30	100
1960	29	15	—	14	32	100
1963	36	13	—	16	35	100
1966	28	15	—	17	40	100
Turkey						
1950	49	12	(11)	—	39	100
1960	41	16	(13)	—	43	100
1963	41	16	(14)	—	43	100
1966	37	18	(16)	—	45	100
UAR						
1953	32	9	(8)	15	44	100
1958	33	19	(14)	10	38	100
1960	31	18	(14)	10	41	100
1961	25	22	(17)	10	43	100

Source: *UN Statistical Yearbook 1967*, except estimates for Jordan (1959, 1966), Lebanon (1966) and Sudan (1966) which are derived from national sources.

[1] Year beginning 21 March.
[2] Not strictly comparable with those shown for earlier years.
[3] Year beginning I July.
[4] Estimates refer to national income at 1956 prices.

TABLE 2

MIDDLE EASTERN COUNTRIES: PER CENT IN AGRICULTURE OF THE TOTAL ECONOMICALLY ACTIVE POPULATION (1965)

Country	Per cent
Iran	57
Iraq	50
Israel	12
Jordan	33
Lebanon	55
Kuwait	1
Saudi Arabia	72
Sudan	78
Syria	56
Turkey	72
UAR	55

Source: FAO, *Production Yearbook, 1967*.

TABLE 3

MIDDLE EASTERN COUNTRIES: COMPOSITION
OF COMMODITY EXPORTS (IN PERCENTAGES)

Iran[1]	*1962/3—1965/6*
Cotton, raw	25
Carpets	22
Fruits	15
Other	38
	100

Iraq[1]	*1964–6*
Dates	34
Barley	9
Raw wool	9
Cement	13
Other	35
	100

Israel	*1964–6*
Citrus fruits	16
Other agricultural exports	4
Polished diamonds	39
Other	41
	100

Jordan	*1964–7*
Fruits and vegetables	41
Phosphates	34
Other	25
	100

Lebanon	*1964–7*
Fruits and other foodstuffs	27
Textiles, textile products	9
Jewellery and precious metals	20
Other	44
	100

Syria	*1964–7*
Cotton, raw	47
Fruits and vegetables	8
Textiles	8
Barley and wheat	3
Other	34
	100

Sudan	*1964–6*
Cotton, ginned	48
Other	52
	100

TABLE 3—*continued*

Turkey	*1965–6*
Cotton	24
Fruits and nuts	21
Tobacco	21
Other	34
	——
	100

UAR	*1965/6—1966/7*
Cotton, raw	32
Cotton, yarn	8
Rice	6
Other	54
	——
	100

Source: National official publications.

[1] Excluding oil.

TABLE 4

MIDDLE EASTERN COUNTRIES: TOTAL AREA, ARABLE LAND AND LAND UNDER PERMANENT CROPS AND AREA UNDER IRRIGATION (IN 000 HECTARES)

Country	*Total Area*	*Arable land and land under permanent crops*	*Irrigated arable land and land under permanent crops*
Iran (1960)	164,800	11,593	4,651
Iraq (1964)	44,874	7,496	3,675[1]
Israel (1965)	2,070	401	152
Jordan (1965)	9,774	1,140	60
Kuwait (1966)	1,600	1	—
Lebanon (1966)	1,040	296	65
Saudi Arabia (1965)	225,330	373	162
Sudan (1954)	250,581	7,100	790[2]
Syria (1966)	18,518	6,130	508
Turkey (1966)	78,058	26,384	1,310[1]
UAR (1966)	100,000	2,780	2,780

Source: FAO, *Production Yearbook, 1967.*

[1] 1963.
[2] 1960.

TABLE 5

MIDDLE EASTERN COUNTRIES: PERCENTAGE SHARE OF
EXPORTS AND IMPORTS OF GOODS AND SERVICES IN THE
GROSS DOMESTIC PRODUCT (AVERAGE FOR 1964-6)

Country	Exports of goods and services	Imports of goods and services
Iran	21	14
Iraq[1]	40	22
Israel	20	32
Jordan	17	40
Kuwait	65	23
Lebanon[2]	38	37
Saudi Arabia[4]	70	56
Sudan	18	21
Syria[3]	26	26
Turkey	7	8
UAR[4]	19	25

Sources: Except for Lebanon, Saudi Arabia, Turkey and the UAR, *Data of UN System of National Accounts*; for Saudi Arabia and the UAR, FAO, *Indicative World Plan for Agricultural Development, 1965, Near East*, vol. II, Rome, 1966; for Lebanon and Turkey ratios are approximate, based on available national income and balance of payments estimates.

[1] Average for 1963–5.
[2] 1966 only.
[3] GNP used.
[4] Average for two years, 1962 and 1965.

TABLE 6

MIDDLE EASTERN COUNTRIES: ADJUSTED SCHOOL
ENROLMENT RATIO[1] IN SELECTED YEARS

Country	1950	1960	1964
Iran	16	30	40
Iraq	18	50	58
Israel	73	92	83
Lebanon	47[2]	66	81
Jordan	27	58	73
Kuwait	4	66	101
Sudan	5	12	16
Syria	35	45	46
Turkey	33	47	55
UAR	25	43	51

Source: UNESCO, *Statistical Yearbook, 1966*.

[1] Refers to total enrolment at the first and second levels related to the estimated population 5–19 years old.
[2] 1954.

413

FURTHER READING

Arab Development in the Emerging International Economy, papers delivered at the 56th meeting of the Princeton University Conference, 1963.

Diab, M. A. *Inter-Arab Economic Co-operation, 1951–1960*, American Univ. of Beirut, Economic Research Institute, 1963.

El-Ghonemy, M. R. (ed.) *Land Policy in the Near East*, Rome, 1967.

Issawi, Charles. 'Economic Growth in the Arab World since 1800 : Some Observations', *Middle East Economic Papers 1964*, American Univ. of Beirut, Economic Research Institute.

Kermani, T. T. *Economic Development in Action: Theories, Problems and Procedures as Applied in the Middle East*, The World Publishing Company, New York, 1967.

Polk, W. R. (ed.) *The Development Revolution, North Africa, Middle East, South Asia*, The Middle East Institute, Washington, D.C., 1963.

Society for International Development. *International Development, 1968, Accomplishments and Apprehensions*, proceedings of the Tenth Anniversary World Conference, 6–8 March, Washington D.C., 1968.

United Nations. *Studies on Selected Development Problems in Various Countries of the Middle East*, United Nations, New York, 1968, 1969 and 1970 issues.

Warriner, D. *Land Reform and Development in the Middle East—A Study of Egypt, Syria and Iraq*, 2nd end., Oxford Univ. Press, London, 1962.

SAMIR MAKDISI. A member of the staff of the International Monetary Fund since 1962. Lectured in Economics at the American University of Beirut 1959–62. Author of a number of articles, among them several examining the economies of Syria and Lebanon.

AGRICULTURE

H. BOWEN-JONES

THE diversity which is the Middle East is nowhere more apparent than in agriculture, but within the region as a whole there still exist some critical elements in the physical and social environment exerting influences which are uniform in kind if not in degree. High in this category comes the simple fact of dominant aridity, which places rain-fed agriculture and natural-grazing pastoralism at hazard and which has for millenia encouraged a turning to irrigation. Secondly, and closely associated with the fact of aridity, is the matter of ecological instability. Soil-formation is generally slow and the soils themselves tend to be deficient in important plant nutrients and vulnerable to rapid deterioration and erosion. Surface hydrology is marked by extreme fluctuation in the volume of river-flow, while groundwater is irregular in incidence and easily reduced in availability by human action. In general, cultivation and pastoralism which have been carried on extensively in the Middle East for more than five millennia have slowly but inexorably destroyed many of the capital assets of land and forests and markedly reduced the availability of water. Everywhere, save in the Nilotic tracts of Egypt, contemporary farmers now have at their disposal land which has been long over-used, even misused, in millennia during which peasant and nomad societies have struggled for survival.

The Middle East possesses some 3·5% of the world's population but its proportion of the world production of major agricultural commodities shows some significant variations. Most important perhaps is the fact that over the last 35 years the Middle East has steadily produced c.7% of the world's wheat and almost 10% of the world's barley. Of the other staple food cereals, rice and maize, the proportional contribution has remained consistently below the population ratio at 2%. Meat production has remained at between 2% and 2·5% while milk, traditionally important in a region with a strong historical element of pastoralism, has proportionately declined from c.5% of world production in the 1930s to less than half that figure in the late 1960s. With the basic foodstuffs, therefore, the Middle East as a whole shows little change in global terms and that change which has occurred has tended to show quantitative and qualitative deterioration compared with the rest of the world. Wheat and barley, usually dry-farmed and showing relatively poor returns on irrigation investment, remain the mainstay of subsistence.

A fact of equal importance is that, of the four crops to which great commercial significance has been attached by Middle Eastern states, cotton, citrus fruit, sugar and tobacco, only one, cotton, has shown a considerable increase of importance in world terms, from c.9% of world production in

415

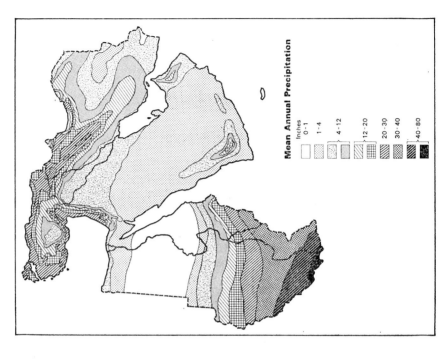

Mean Annual Precipitation

Inches
0 - 1
1 - 4
4 - 12
12 - 20
20 - 30
30 - 40
40 - 80

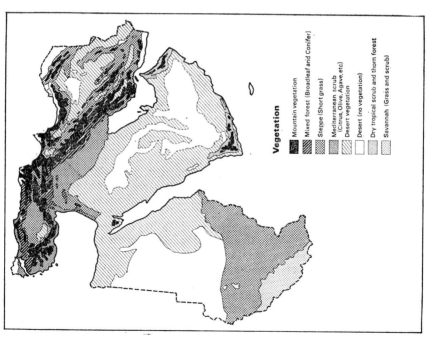

Vegetation

Mountain vegetation
Mixed forest (Broadleaf and Conifer)
Steppe (Short grass)
Mediterranean scrub (Citrus, Olive, Agave, etc)
Desert vegetation
Desert (no vegetation)
Dry tropical scrub and thorn forest
Savannah (Grass and scrub)

the 1930s to almost 14% in the late 1960s (the other main fibre, wool, has become proportionately much less important now at c.5%). Citrus fruit, the next most important cash and export crop, has increased only from c.7% to c.8% of a world production which has more than doubled in this period.

Part of the relatively disappointing lack of change in the world status of Middle Eastern agriculture results from the effect of high population growth rate in inhibiting advance from what was a low-yield base. This is reflected in the differences between the indices of total and *per caput* agricultural production (see Table 1).

TABLE 1

AGRICULTURAL PRODUCTION IN
THE NEAR EAST—VOLUMETRIC INDICES
(State of Food & Agriculture: FAO, 1968)
Average 1952–3/1956–7=100

	1952–3	*1958–9*	*1964–7*
Total Agric. Production	91	112	136
Per Caput Agric. Production	99	108	109
Total Food Production	93	118	137
Per Caput Food Production	93	107	105

Not only have the large investments in agriculture been swallowed up by the increasing population but, since much of the population increase has had to be absorbed in an already overcrowded peasant rural sector, the structural refashioning of agriculture has met many obstacles. As a result we can observe in the Middle East a complex situation containing many internal paradoxes.

First, yields are generally low for environmental and socio-technological reasons. Increased production can only be obtained in traditional terms by extending the cultivated area and expanding animal grazing grounds. This process has its limitations, as in Egypt, and is self-defeating, as in Turkey, and therefore *per caput* production stagnates or even falls. As the population increases in the countryside, holdings become smaller and emigration to the towns only partly relieves the growing pressure. The only ways out of this impasse are, first, to raise yields by the intensification of production on existing utilised land and, secondly, to increase safely the utilisable acreage. Both of these solutions require on the one hand massive capital investment in major irrigation works and on the other hand a revolution in the methods of husbandry employed by millions of peasant farmers.

Regional contrasts are of course considerable and it is to these that we must now turn. First, there is the group of essentially city-states in which agriculture has never been and is never likely to be of major economic importance. This group, including Bahrain, Kuwait, Qatar and the Trucial States, because of oil wealth now has an importance in the Arab world completely disproportionate to its population. In these relatively small territories, agricultural potential is in any case severely limited by aridity. Although the availability of capital has enabled the setting up of an extremely advanced hydroponics centre at Kuwait together with schemes for desert farming and desalination of seawater, in regional production terms agriculture may be ignored.

Secondly there is Saudi Arabia which, as is the case of Libya, has a relatively small population, an enormous oil revenue and a very large territory in which agricultural potential is severely limited. Saudi agrarian policies as in the case of Kuwait are concerned almost entirely with economic diversification, providing better living conditions in the many scattered oasis settlements of traditional farmers and pastoralists, and with deploying ample capital on resources which elsewhere would be considered sub-marginal, mainly in order to prevent the virtual depopulation of some regions. In Saudi Arabia, again as with Libya, the key lies in the exploitation of deep subterranean water.

Thirdly there is the unique case of Israel. In Israel agriculture is much more significant than the contribution to the GNP—some 7–8%—would indicate, for politico-military and for commercial reasons. Although over 82% of the Israeli population is urban dwelling, there were, in 1967, 600 Moshavim and Kibbutzim with a total population of more than 200,000, these agrarian settlements being located in strategically vulnerable as well as in potentially productive areas from the Negev to the drained lands of the former Lake Huleh. The collective Kibbutz and co-operative Moshav, together with their variants, have been established at considerable capital cost but also as a result of the pioneering zeal of the new Zionists; conventional cost-benefit analysis becomes impossible in these terms particularly since many of the skills and much of the capital have been acquired elsewhere.

Agricultural planning has therefore been based on the need for occupation of the maximum area of land and for domestic self-sufficiency for a population growing at c.3% *p.a.* In addition, the need for eliminating the annual trade deficit of almost £100 million and reducing dependence on transfer payments from abroad of c.£200 million *p.a.* has forced Israel to pay special attention to the export of agricultural commodities. As a result, exports of agricultural products total half the value of manufactured exports. The value of food and live animal exports in 1967, £54 million, was 24% of total exports, 16% being contributed by citrus alone. The index of agricultural production (c.f. Table 1) has risen from 80 in 1950 to 260 in 1968. Yields per acre are high, while production *per caput* has increased by more than 100%, the average domestic diet rating among the highest in the world. Israel serves as an example of what is technically possible under some Middle Eastern conditions but the special circumstances involved must be noted, in particular the availability of external financial income and the driving force of a siege psychology.

Iraq and the UAR may be grouped together as large territorial states, possessing great areas of riverine irrigable lands in Mesopotamia and the Nile valley and Delta, but there the resemblance ends. The UAR, agriculturally speaking, remains the gift of the Nile and, in the absence of easily exploited resources other than those of human skill and location, still derives 25% of its GDP from, and employs 60% of its labour force in, agriculture. With a total area of over one million square kilometres, almost the whole of the population of 30 million is concentrated in the 25·2 thousand square kilometres of cultivated land in the Nile Valley and Delta and the Faiyum Oasis, averaging 0·4 acres per head of population and just over two acres per agricultural worker. Outside this densely populated and intensively worked belt lies inhospitable desert which, despite a variety of technically feasible possibilities, ranging from the deliberate flooding of the Qattara depression to tapping the deep water resources lying 2,000 feet and more underground in the Nubian Sandstones, is still agriculturally useless. One of the fundamental elements in Egyptian farming is therefore the multi-cropping of the existing useable land by the development of perennial irrigation. This at present produces a cropped area (the total of land used for each crop in any one year) which is almost twice as great as the cultivated area (11 million and 6 million feddans[1] respectively). This position however has only been maintained by constructing ever more costly control works on the Nile. The High Dam at Aswan has required an investment of more than £400 million (including HEP generating costs) and will enable the conversion of 700,000 feddans from annual to perennial cultivation and the reclamation of a further one million feddans.

Together with multi-cropping have been developed all the other aspects of intensive farming, including a heavy use of fertilisers and of labour. As a result, yields per acre have reached a phenomenally high level, so high that possibilities of further increasing production in this way are virtually exhausted. The human cost of this achievement is very high—long hours of manual labour for small returns from small holdings. The land reform programme of 1952 and 1961 achieved its social objective of destroying the power of the few large landowners, but land shortage remains acute and farm holdings are still minute. It has been estimated that of the nearly five million people engaged in agriculture almost one million are redundant.

The third main characteristic of Egyptian farming is the national importance of one main cash-crop, cotton, and the prevalence of market-orientated if not fully commercial production of most other crops. Cotton, predominantly long-staple, still occupies over a quarter of the cultivated area and provides 60% of the value of Egyptian exports. Rice production, particularly important in the Delta, now provides an export surplus over and above effective domestic demand, while cane-sugar production is planned to expand shortly to the same level. Wheat and other grains are in deficit and total cereal imports are valued at c.£70 million a year. Future developments are mainly associated with export possibilities in high-income European markets for out-of-season vegetables and fruit. Agriculture in Egypt has in fact reached the ultimate point where added-value is of supreme importance, where intensity of production is associated with land shortage, extreme effort and low incomes; a point in fact where the rural population is reaching a high Malthusian level and where the national future depends entirely on a breakthrough in some other sector.

Iraq is by contrast a country of under-exploited but vast agricultural potential. With a total area of 440,000 square kilometres, of which approximately one-third can be considered cutivable, only some 23,000 square kilometres are used for agricultural purposes at any one time by the 80% of the labour force engaged in farming. The smallness of the cropped area and the low yields of most field crops largely result from the continued predominance of extensive primitive dry-farming with long fallows, this in spite of the fact that development capital is available from large oil revenues.

The reasons for this relative stagnation are complex. The new state of Iraq in 1920 had a population of some two million, concentrated around Baghdad, Basra and in the Mosul and Erbil highlands. The irrigated lands of the first two of these regions were peasant worked with primitive techniques and under chaotic tenurial arrangements. The rain-watered highlands were equally subsistence-oriented. By 1944 irrigated acreage had increased fourfold to four million acres and cash-crops such as cotton introduced. During this same period however share-tenancy of a peculiarly vicious kind became established, income from farmland was rapidly diverted into urban concerns and there was created an incentiveless class of cultivators devoid of capital, technology and opportunity.

[1] Feddan=c.1 acre.

Irrigated land potential has itself not been easy to develop. By the mid-1950s 70% of Iraq's oil revenue was already being allocated to the national development board and further major schemes for harnessing the Tigris and Euphrates are in hand, but results are slow in coming. Part of the difficulty lay and still lies with the intractability of the great rivers of Iraq and with associated hydro-ecological problems. Over the course of time these great rivers have built up their beds above the level of the surrounding plains and floods can therefore inundate thousands of square miles in a very short period. With irrigation, similarly, it is relatively easy to channel water on to lower lying land but without properly engineered drainage, mainly by pumping, irrigated land becomes waterlogged and/or affected by a build-up of soluble salts in the soil. These are the physical reasons why Iraq has been and still is a land of projects rather than agricultural performance.

In the socio-economic sector, post-1958 administrations have attempted to restore incentives and introduce improved technology through a policy of land redistribution, associated with new extension services and co-operative schemes. The ideological element in Iraqi socialism is of some importance in agricultural policy but ultimately the attitudes and values of the over one-and-a-half million cultivators (more than ten times the number employed in manufacturing) are dominant. The only important export crop is that of dates; about 60% of the crop is exported and total production makes Iraq joint world leader with the UAR in date-growing. Exports of cereals, almost entirely barley, indicate a physical surplus rather than any great commercial efficiency. Present plans for extending river control should increase the area available for perennial irrigation but a radical change in the low-level, subsistence-based structure of agriculture is necessary for any full exploitation of potential.

In Turkey and Iran, the other two non-Arab states, the physical background to agriculture is quite different. Here arid summers alternate with harsh cold winters in the central and main regions of both countries.

For environmental reasons, therefore, the great dependence on annual cereals, wheat and barley especially, is almost unavoidable and very large areas are utilisable only for unimproved rough grazing. Of the Turkish land area, about 34% is pasture land, 20% sown, 11% fallow and some 3% under fruit and vegetables; approximately 23% is under cultivation at the height of the early summer season. In Iran the proportion is much lower, only some 4% actually carrying crops with another 7% fallow and c.7% pasture and rangeland. In both countries the extensive and relatively well-watered highland ranges are rugged and even more inhospitable in winter, and the areas of relatively intensive agriculture are generally located on the peripheral lowland.

Turkey is one of the most economically diversified and advanced countries in the Middle East but agriculture still employs over half of the population and contributes c.30% of the GNP. With a population of 33 million growing at 2·5% p.a., ambitious development plans and little in the way of oil revenue, considerable attention has to be paid to the agricultural sector. Agricultural exports, raw and processed, contribute 90% of all commodity exports and production is required to continue to grow at c.4% p.a. to meet domestic requirements and to meet the large import bill resulting from heavy development investment. In Turkey, as elsewhere, this primarily means intensification and the raising of yields.

Changes in the agrarian structure are mainly dependent on the speed with which other sectors of the economy can be expanded so as to relieve a growing pressure of population in the rural areas. Food consumption *per caput*, quantitatively and qualitatively, is the second highest in the Middle East and many units of cultivation are still sufficiently large to allow for mechanisation and a reasonable rate of income and capital formation. Nevertheless, in parts of Ege, the Black Sea coast and Eastern Anatolia the position is less good; overall there is still a considerable volume of agrarian underemployment and, lastly and perhaps most important, a large proportion of land now cropped—some estimates put this as high as 50%,—should be retired from cultivation for ecological reasons. Considerable successes have been achieved with technical improvements in farming which have resulted in considerable increases in the production of cash-crops for export. In the decade 1957–67 the value of exports of cotton lint (medium staple) increased ten times, of fruit six times and of tobacco five times. The real problem areas however, Central and Eastern Anatolia, are mainly suited to land-extensive farming with low yields per acre and high yields per unit of capital and labour unit; this position can only be achieved by a reduction in the dependence on subsistence-orientated farming.

In the case of Iran, this last point is of key importance. In an even more extreme form than in Turkey, most of the cultivable area is primarily suited to capital-intensive cereal-legume production on large holdings. The regions with the greatest irrigation potential lie on the flanks of the Zagros and Elburz ranges, in the Caspian coastal lowlands, Khorasan in the north east, Khuzistan in the extreme south-west and in some of the interior basins. Irrigation has long been practised in the traditional *qanat* form, in which underground galleries tap the ground water which seeps into the many sedimentary basins from the surrounding hills and make it available for farming use. The keynote here, as also in other aspects of Iranian agriculture, is the contrast in scale, in traditional technology and landownership, between the large and the small. Individual *qanat* galleries may extend for more than 50 miles and cost £30,000–£50,000 to construct but the working unit of cultivation is predominantly very small, typically 10–12 acres in size. On these holdings, most of which are further subdivided into non-contiguous plots of half to one acre, a cereal-fallow system reduces the land actually cropped to one-third or one-half of the total holding. Most of such holdings are essentially subsistence-based, low income units supporting a technologically backward and capital-deficient peasantry.

The most significant features of the contemporary Iranian scene have been the implementation of a major land reform policy, the improvement of physical potential through large-scale irrigation schemes and an emphasis on the development of specialised commercial production. All these elements, of course, interlock with each other and with other economic sectors, and the scale and speed of development is only made possible by the size of oil revenues which now make up 50% of the State's income and are planned to supply £2,700 million to the financing of the Fourth Plan 1968–72. With a population of 28 million growing at 2·5% p.a., which needs to be supplied with foodstuffs at a level higher than at present, and with growing industrial demand for raw materials, agricultural development is expected to require c.£325 million in investment.

There have already been some successes. Cotton production has more than doubled in the last decade and is now the most important export commodity by value, excluding oil. Wheat production has become more assured as new lands are irrigated and an export surplus is now likely to become a normal feature. Sugar-beet cultivation and refining, well established in Khorasan, is now being expanded in many other regions, which, together with the cane production in the new Khuzistan development areas, makes Iran almost self-sufficient in sugar and promises a surplus for future export; in 1964 sugar was the highest value food import. Rice, tea and tobacco have also increased in production very greatly, with main centres of cultivation along the Caspian littoral. Like other sectors of the economy, agriculture is already changing radically, but whatever the availability of capital, the process of transforming the 70% of the active population engaged in agriculture is inevitably slow.

Syria, Lebanon and Jordan, traditionally regarded as parts of the Levantine sub-region of the Middle East, do in fact possess in common some of the factors which affect agricultural development. Climatically they occupy territories in the transition zone between the Mediterranean and the deserts to the south-east. Topographically, the Lebanon and anti-Lebanon mountain systems, which have high orographic precipitation, are the lands of milk and honey by contrast with the barren plains which fall away to the Euphrates and the Gulf. The differences between the agriculture of the three states are partly a matter of different balances of these two major types of terrain which lie within their borders, but to an even greater extent are a function of their individual socio-economic characteristics.

Lebanon lies wholly within the Mediterranean region; based on the relatively heavy precipitation, a varied and productive agriculture has long been established. Farming still employs c.40% of the active population but its contribution to the GNP is estimated to be 15% of the total compared with the 60% contribution made by commerce. Lebanon is *par excellence* an example of an economy dominated by the service sector which supplies some 70% of the National Income. Until recently, therefore, agriculture has developed its variety and relatively high degree of intensity and regional specialisation largely unaffected by conscious central policy-making but very much in tune with prevailing commercial attitudes.

Wheat and to a lesser extent barley are grown as staple crops in almost all regions and yields are high for the Middle East; Lebanon however remains a significant importer of cereals. Economically more significant, for domestic consumption, for supplying the 650,000 or so tourists which visit Lebanon each year, and for export, are the treecrops. The coastlands are intensively utilised for citrus fruit, tobacco, sugar cane and olives as well as for a great range of other sub-tropical fruit and vegetables. Mixed farming, including relatively high-level livestock husbandry, is predominant while most farm units are medium-sized and family-operated. In terms of production value, the citrus and apple crops represent c.60% of the total, while crude and processed products of agriculture make up c.40% of commodity exports.

As Lebanon's role as banker for the Arab oil-states has declined, more attention has had to be paid to agricultural as well as to industrial development. Under the 'Green Plan', reorganisation and reclamation are under way and the development of the Bekaa, utilising the Litani river for irrigation, is the single most important development.

The most productive agricultural region in Syria is that which is analogous to the territory of Lebanon, i.e. the provinces of Latakia, western Idleb, Hama and Homs, and the zone around Damascus and Aleppo. Away from this western area there has been until very recently little cultivation except in the highlands of northern Hasakeh and on the riverine lands along the Euphrates near Al-Rakka. Pure nomadism has declined in the semi-arid central regions, to be largely replaced by semi-sedenterisation of Bedu groups who depend on long-fallow, low-yield, subsistence cereal farming, supplemented by their low-grade livestock, chiefly sheep. The great difference in natural potential between the pluvious lands of the west and the irrigated oases on the one hand and the arid interior on the other may be illustrated thus : yields of cereals at Damascus and in Latakia and Idleb are over double those of central Aleppo, which highland Hasakeh's yields of dry-farmed legumes are three times greater.

Agriculture has long been neglected, even the rich, irrigated area of Damascus being mainly merchant-owned and share-cropper worked, with little return, investment or technological opportunity coming the way of the cultivator. Population pressure, particularly in the west, and lack of alternative opportunity have resulted in a predominance of uneconomically small working units less than five hectares in area. In the highland and pluvious zones, therefore, as in Lebanon, the pattern is generally one of diversified crops, cereals, legumes, tree- and other fruits, tobacco (especially in Latakia), together with a large range of summer vegetables, and relatively high yields per acre; however, because of pressure on land resources, *per caput* income is low. Elsewhere cultivation is extensive in type even on small to medium holdings, the crop range is small and agrarian poverty is normal. The existence of an exportable surplus of grain is more an indication of non-intensive farming and a small inelastic domestic market than of anything else. In addition to land reform legislation, two other factors have recently led to change. The first has been the encouragement given to cotton cultivation, as has happened contemporaneously in Turkey and Iran. In 1950 the area under cotton totalled some 78,000 hectares with a production of c.35,000 tons; by 1965, the highwater mark, the area had increased to 290,000 hectares and production to 290,000 tons. For the last decade cotton lint, yarn and textiles have made up c.60% of Syrian commodity exports. The second main development has been the greater attention paid to national investment in agriculture, particularly in irrigation. The current 1966–70 Five Year Plan allocates 27% of investment capital to agriculture, a total of over £93 million, of which 85% is for irrigation. With Russian assistance, the projected Euphrates dam, which will take 70% of agricultural investment capital, should provide water for c.600,000 hectares (1,500,000 acres). The total cultivated area is now c.2·8 million hectares of which c.75% are under cereals and dry-farmed legumes; the completion of the scheme in 1975 should radically alter the nature of Syrian agriculture in that the physical possibilities for intensification will be greatly expanded.

Jordanian agriculture is characterised by misfortune and distortion. The basic misfortune results from the fact that, since the creation of Israel in 1948, Jordan has possessed no part of the Palestinian coastal plain, the best favoured region in this area; in addition, since the 1967 war, she has been effectively deprived by Israeli occupation not only of the most prosperous farming land in her territory, the Judaean hills on the West Bank, but also of the use of much of the Ghor to the east of the Jordan, where considerable development investment was taking place. The distortion arises from Jordan's situation as a buffer state and a refugee zone. As a buffer State, Jordan has long received large-scale financial assistance from the West and since 1967 from Kuwait, Libya and Saudi Arabia, but much of this aid has been budgetary rather than developmental. A considerable proportion of state expenditure, derived from this external revenue, has had the effect of artificially and considerably expanding the urban market for labour and skills. Employment in agriculture has thus become secondary in importance to government employ and the alternative employment opportunities have removed much of the agrarian pressure, to the extent of producing a lower degree of intensity in farming than otherwise could have been expected. Following the June War a vast influx of refugees, who can neither be easily assimilated onto farm land nor readily absorbed in other sectors, has produced the final distortion.

The greatest potential lies in the Ghor, where until 1967 irrigation was becoming highly developed for the production of vegetables and fruit. The other main areas of intensive farming, particularly of tree crops including the olive, lay around Jerusalem, Nablus and Jericho. The impossibility of reaching international agreement concerning the use of the upper Jordan waters left the Kingdom with irrigation potential only in the Yarmuk River area and in the deep aquifers now being explored along the east and south of the Dead Sea rift.

Agriculture in non-occupied Jordan is now limited to the rain-fed areas of the highlands north-west of Amman and to the subhumid steppes which rapidly grade south and east into deserts, the traditional home of the Bedu. In the former region between 60% and 80% of the cultivated area is under wheat and barley, spring-based pseudo-oases being devoted more heavily— up to 30% in some cases—to fruit and vegetables. Holdings are predominantly small, between five and twenty acres in extent, and whether owner-occupied or share-cropped are mainly used for subsistence purposes. Jordan is now in marked deficit for all agricultural commodities. The steppe and desert areas are of little economic significance and future developments in free Jordan depend entirely on the scale on which external aid is forthcoming and on political rather than economic assessments of potential.

Equally confused is the situation at the southern extremity of the Arabian peninsula, in Yemen, South Yemen and Oman. No trustworthy statistics exist for the agricultural sector at the present day for any of these territories. In all cases farming, as distinct from nomadic pastoralism, is confined to those highland areas where orographic precipitation allows rainfed agriculture, to oasis-like valleys where surface water enables small-scale irrigation to be practised, and where, in the former Aden Protectorate, pump and flood-spate irrigation techniques were extensively developed before South Yemen became independent in 1967.

The first two types are found well developed in highland Yemen, where dry-farmed cereals including barley, millet, sorghum and oats are supplemented by tobacco and irrigated fruit crops and vegetables of considerable variety. Coffee is no longer as important as in the past and various strains of cotton are increasingly being grown. Subsistence needs dominate the whole of agriculture; prolonged recent conflicts have hindered development and politico-economic association with China has increased the obscurity which surrounds present development.

South Yemen inherited from the colonial period the busy port of Aden, whose activity depended almost wholly on sea-going trade through the Suez Canal and on commercial confidence. Since June 1967 both trade and confidence have disappeared and with them the only significant commercial market for agricultural products. In the larger ex-protectorate area, extending eastwards to Dhufar, indigenous spate-water irrigation was for long established in various parts of the Hadramaut, particularly in Lahej, and supported virtually the whole of that population not engaged in coastal commerce and fishing, i.e. c.90%. Dates, barley and sorghum remain the staple subsistence crops, together with a variety of fruit and vegetables. The bringing into production of c.50,000 acres of virgin land in the Abyan irrigation scheme area was accompanied by the development of cotton cultivation and a growing export trade. Subsequent internal conflicts, together with the decline of Aden, appear to have resulted in a considerable return to traditional crop-raising and pastoralism on a mainly subsistence basis.

The Sultanate of Oman is similarly composed of vast tracts of desert and three main zones of predominantly subsistence farming and pastoralism, the main difference lying in the availability in the Sultanate of oil-derived revenue for development purposes. In the southern province of Dhufar, the Salala embayment continues to support subsistence-based date, grain and vegetable production on a considerable scale. On the Batina coast, north of Oman, similar but smaller coastal plains maintain traditional self-sufficient farming and fishing communities. In both cases water is derived from the neighbouring hills. To the west of Oman lie the Jebel Akhdar ranges where, as in Yemen, precipitation is heavy enough to support dry-farmed barley, millets and sorghum as well as to provide seasonally adequate pasture. In the valley basins and on the lower hills, terraced and irrigated land carries treecrops and vegetables in addition. For the last decade an agricultural service has been encouraging the use of irrigation pumps and improved husbandry and crop varieties; the finances of the Sultanate now enable an acceleration of these developments, but the scale is likely to be significant only in terms of the small sedentary population.

Sudan, the last of the countries with which we are concerned, is, in complete contrast, the largest state in size of territory, the fourth largest in population and has the greatest unexploited agricultural potential. Agriculture contributes c.50% of the GNP and, including pastoralism, employs c.85% of the working population. Within this dominant sector there is however a marked contrast between commercial production, above all of cotton, and the widespread subsistence agriculture (dominant in the southern provinces) in which pastoralism plays a large part.

North of Khartoum agriculture is confined between the Nubian and Libyan deserts to a discontinuous, narrow zone along the Nile banks, a simple intensive subsistence activity. Between Khartoum and the savannah, in the intermediate zone, lies a vast tract of country in which seasonal dry-farming is possible, in which there are extensive areas of tropical clay soils and in which are available the enormous water resources of the Niles and their eastern tributaries. Here is the economic and agricultural heart of Sudan, centred in many ways on the Gezira scheme. The Gezira management board controls a total area of over 1,800,000 acres which is owned by the Government and tenant farmed; the farming and irrigation systems evolved in the Gezira have been the model for most subsequent development.

Sudan ranks sixth in the world for cotton production (mainly long-staple), and in 1968 was equal second along with Egypt for exports (over one million bales). Rotation farming, associated with cotton growing in the major schemes, has encouraged the production of durra millet, lubia beans, wheat and groundnuts. As well as meeting all domestic requirements, durra, ground-nuts and other oil seeds (in particular sesame) are now exported, these three crops providing exports to a value of between 30% and 50% of ginned cotton exports. The value of such production, together with the increasing quantity of commercially-produced dates, coffee, tobacco (the last two crops mainly in the south) and vegetables, has helped to counterbalance the drop in world cotton prices and future possibilities are enormous. The plantation-type, technologically advanced tenant-farming system seems to offer the best economic model but in the Blue Nile area many private farms, some large-scale, have also been established. In Equatoria province however this implies continued managerial domination by Muslim north-Sudanese and future developments depend entirely on the extent to which the secessionist forces in Southern Sudan exacerbate the present troubled situation.

This series of necessarily brief vignettes illustrates at least the variety of socio-economic, political and physical elements which are combined in different ways within the sub-regions of the Middle East. Overall, the most significant trends may be summarised thus. Since 1948 the Middle East has been consistently a region of food deficit and a net importer of food-stuffs, this in spite of considerable planned investment in the agricultural sector. In part this results from the rapid growth of population which, in the period 1948 to 1968, has increased by c.45 million. Part of the deficit has resulted from regionally variable increases in consumption *per caput*, a natural outcome of social welfare aspects of development plans, as in Turkey and the UAR, and of increased oil-wealth, especially in the Arab/Persian Gulf. Lastly there has been the effect of encouragement given to the production of cash-crops, industrial raw materials and exports. The highest rates of increase in production of these crops in the major agricultural countries are all far above the growth rates in the staple foodstuffs. Table 2 illustrates, albeit conservatively, part of this contrast :

TABLE 2

INCREASES IN VOLUME OF CROP PRODUCTION 1952/6–1967/8
(*in major producing areas in percentages*)

	Iraq	Iran	Syria	Sudan	Turkey	UAR
Cotton fibre	100	100	100	100	150	50
Tobacco	100	50	100	100	50	50
Tea	100	200	100	100	1,000	50
Groundnuts	100	200	100	400	1,000	100
Wheat	20	30	15	200	25	10
Barley	−10	15	40	200	10	10
Rice	40	90	−400	200	60	100

The only significant increase in foodstuffs has been in sugar, where Turkey, Iran and the UAR have considerably expanded production; this however has mainly been the result of import-substitution policies rather than the increasing of total food supplies. This is also true of much of the increase in fruit and vegetable production. Agricultural diversification is in general accompanying economic diversification but, everywhere except in Israel and the Sudan (for totally different reasons), the race between population growth and the radical modification of the surviving, dominant and traditional complex of low yield subsistence agriculture has yet to be won.

H. BOWEN-JONES, Director of the Centre for Middle Eastern and Islamic Studies, and Professor of Geography at Durham University. Carried out agricultural research in Iran, Jordan, Kuwait, Turkey and the Trucial States for, or in co-operation with, FAO and UN agencies, Ministry of Overseas Development, government agencies and British consultant firms. His publications include *Agriculture in Iran* (Volume 1, Cambridge History of Iran, 1969) and *Economic Development in the Middle East* (1969).

OIL

W. W. STEWART

THE discovery of oil in commercial quantities in the Middle East and the subsequent development of the industry to its present enormous size have taken place entirely within the present century. Today the Middle East is the greatest oil-exporting area in the world and oil is the most important economic asset of the region. Other parts of the world, notably Western Europe, Australasia, Japan and the developing countries of Southern Asia, depend upon the Middle East for the supply of the greater part of their imported requirements of oil. It was estimated in 1968 that the Middle East then held 60% of the proven reserves of oil in the world, a proportion that may well increase as further discoveries are made. In that same year the governments of the oil-exporting countries received a total sum equivalent to more than £1,400 million by way of oil revenues. These vast resources of oil have added greatly to the strategic, political and economic importance of the region.

HISTORICAL BACKGROUND AND SUMMARY OF DEVELOPMENT

For more than 5,000 years the peoples of the Middle East had been well aware of the existence of surface deposits of bitumen and of seepages of oil and gas in various parts of the region, and bitumen was used for many purposes by successive civilisations, but of the great sub-surface reservoirs of oil they naturally knew nothing at all. It was not until late in the 19th century that the demand for oil, arising from the advance of machine technology in Europe, resulted in an outside interest in the oil prospects of Iran and certain parts of the Ottoman Empire. The first important event was the result of British initiative in south-western Iran, when a large oilfield was discovered there in 1908. Smaller fields were next discovered along the Red Sea coast of Egypt, but developments in the whole region were soon interrupted by World War I. In any case, conditions then prevalent in the Ottoman Empire made any foreign commercial venture both difficult to initiate and hazardous to undertake.

The disappearance of the Ottoman Empire at the end of the war, the emergence of new countries in its place and the entry of US and French oil interests into the area all created a new situation. However, in spite of an increasing world-wide demand for oil as a source of power, development was relatively modest between the two World Wars compared with what was to happen later. In the 20 years from 1919 to 1939 the Middle East's share of total world oil production rose from about 1% to 5% only. During this

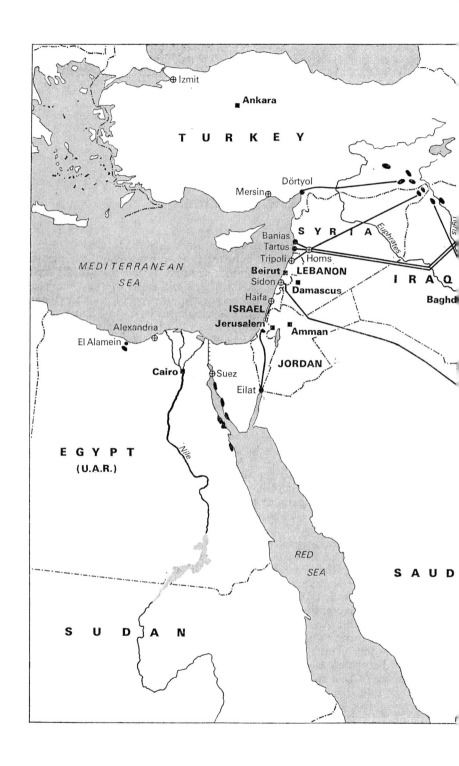

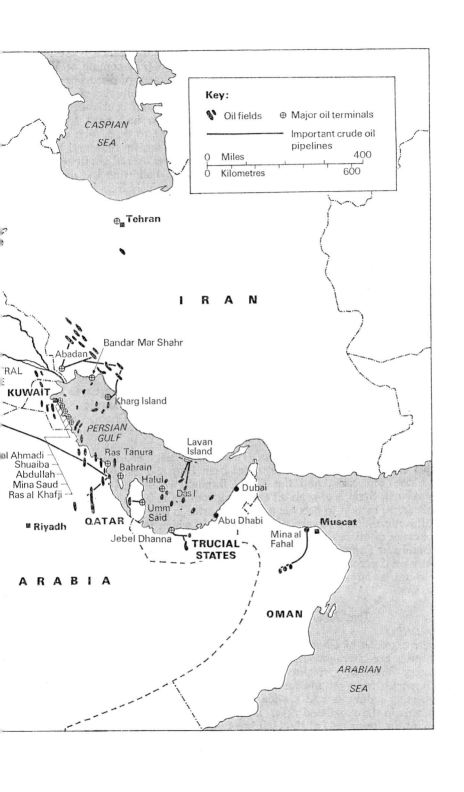

Key:

Oil fields	⊕ Major oil terminals

Important crude oil pipelines

```
0    Miles                    400
0    Kilometres               600
```

CASPIAN
SEA

Tehran

I R A N

Bandar Mar Shahr

Abadan

'RAL

KUWAIT

Kharg Island

PERSIAN
GULF

Lavan
Island

al Ahmadi
Shuaiba
Abdullah
Mina Saud
Ras al Khafji

Ras Tanura

Bahrain

Halul

Das I

Dubai

Umm
Said

Riyadh

QATAR

Abu Dhabi

Muscat

Jebel Dhanna

TRUCIAL
STATES

Mina al
Fahal

A R A B I A

OMAN

ARABIAN
SEA

time oil exports started from Iraq, Bahrain and Saudi Arabia, while there was considerable expansion of the industry in Iran. The coming of World War II in 1939 temporarily postponed the development of discoveries made in Kuwait and Qatar, but as soon as peace came again the oil industry in the whole region entered into a period of great and continuing expansion. By 1950 its share of total world production had risen to nearly 17%. Although there were local set-backs from time to time, such as those caused by the nationalisation of the industry in Iran in 1951 and by the Arab-Israeli wars of 1948, 1956, and 1967, progress overall continued in a manner which could justly be called spectacular. Following the discovery of oil in commercial quantities, exports began successively from the Kuwaiti-Saudi Neutral Zone, Abu Dhabi, Muscat and Oman (now the Sultanate of Oman), Syria and Dubai. There were also oil discoveries in the United Arab Republic (UAR), Israel and Turkey. By 1969 the Middle East's share of total world production had risen to 29%.

The Distribution of Oil Resources

The geological conditions giving rise to the accumulation of large oil deposits, a process taking many millions of years, could obviously not adapt themselves in advance to present day political frontiers. The spread of oil reserves and the benefits arising from their exploitation are necessarily uneven amongst the various countries of the region, and while the ultimate limits of oil discovery will not be reached for many years to come, these countries can conveniently be divided into three categories. Firstly, there are the oil-exporting countries whose reserves are mostly located in the vast area known geologically as the Persian Gulf geosyncline : Iran, Iraq, Kuwait, Kuwaiti-Saudi Neutral Zone, Saudi Arabia, Bahrain, Qatar, Abu Dhabi, Dubai and Oman. Secondly, there are the so-called 'transit' countries, whose geographical position places them astride the shortest route between the exporting countries and their principal markets. These are Syria, Lebanon and Jordan, which are crossed by the oil pipelines from Iraq and Saudi Arabia to the Mediterranean coast, and the UAR, through whose territory passes the Suez Canal. Syria is also an oil exporting country in her own right and the UAR seems certain to become a large exporter in due course. Finally, there are the remaining countries of the region, in which there have either been discoveries of oil in quantities as yet insufficient to satisfy internal needs, as in Israel and Turkey, or where no oil has yet been discovered.

Any brief account of oil in the Middle East must give main emphasis to the countries adjacent to the Persian Gulf, those in the first category just described.

The Persian Gulf and Adjacent Countries

The setting

Severe extremes of climate and terrain and an absence of heavy supporting industries are characteristic conditions which have to be faced by the oil industry. Vehicles, specialised equipment and supplies of all kinds need to be imported from outside for every type of oil operation. Although minor supporting industries and a wide range of services have become generally available in the populated areas, much of the exploration and development work in the lower part of the Gulf involves the maintenance of small groups and communities in remote regions almost totally devoid of local resources. The provision of management and advanced technical skills still requires the presence of foreigners, but to a greatly decreasing extent as Middle Eastern nationals gain in knowledge and experience.

Offshore drilling enterprises have to overcome formidable difficulties, both technical and logistic. These are only partly offset by the shallow depth of the waters of the Gulf, which nowhere inside the Straits of Hormuz exceeds 55 fathoms and is generally much less. However, this shallowness in turn sets further problems in the dredging of access channels and the siting of loading terminals for the huge tankers now in use.

Political problems and tensions between the various countries of the region can also affect the industry, particularly any disputes over matters of sovereignty and offshore boundaries.

The pattern of the industry and the flow of oil

The general pattern of the industry is that of production and export of crude oil on a vast scale, together with refining and export of oil products on a large but less impressive scale. Refining for local consumption is on a level sufficient to satisfy a constantly increasing demand, and there is a rapidly developing use of natural gas for internal requirements and exports as markets develop. Illustrative of this are the figures for 1969 when crude oil production amounted to 611 million tons, of which 515 million were exported as crude oil and 48 million as refined products, the balance of 48 million tons being used internally. Total refining capacity in the Gulf countries in that year amounted to just over 4% of total world capacity.

The markets for crude oil and and products are world wide. In 1969, for example, 51% of all exports went to Western Europe, 26% to Japan, 13% to Australasia, Southern Asia and elsewhere in the eastern hemisphere, 4% to the USA and the western hemisphere and 3% to Africa. Transportation of oil to eastern and southern markets is by tanker. Transportation westwards and northwards is by pipeline to the Mediterranean coast (in the case of some of the exports from Iraq and Saudi Arabia), by tanker through the Suez Canal and by tanker round the Cape of Good Hope. An interruption to the transit pipelines, such as occurred in Syria at the time of the Suez crisis in 1956 and again in 1967, is likely to cause an increase in exports by tanker from the Gulf terminals. An interruption to traffic through the Suez Canal increases the importance of the pipelines and obliges westbound tankers from the Gulf to circumnavigate the Cape. In 1967 the largest tankers which could pass through the Suez Canal fully loaded were those of about 65,000 tons deadweight, and the Canal would accept tankers in ballast of up to about 150,000 tons. By mid-1969 more than three-quarters of new tanker tonnage on order from the world's shipyards consisted of vessels exceeding 200,000 tons, and it seemed clear that the Cape route had become a permanent feature in the pattern of oil transportation from the Gulf. Experience has also shown that any interruption to the transit pipelines or the Suez Canal causes an immediate increase in imports by European consumers from alternative sources of supply, such as North Africa and Nigeria.

Governments and companies

Apart from the internal marketing of oil products, which is mostly under state control, foreign interests undertake a predominant part in the oil industry, but their status and the conditions under which they operate have been subject to continuing evolutionary change. The pioneering work of oil discovery and the subsequent development of the industry to its vast size have been almost entirely due to the efforts of the great international oil companies, representing mainly British, Dutch, US and French interests and frequently operating in partnership so as to spread the risks and heavy costs involved. Indeed, the industry could not have been started by any different means. No other agency, least of all the governments of the region, possessed the capital, technical knowledge and access to the markets of the world which were indispensable to such developments.

The early oil agreements between the governments and the companies provided for concessions over large areas for long periods. These agreements have been extensively revised in subsequent years, invariably in favour of the governments and particularly in regard to the payment provisions and the relinquishment by the companies of substantial areas over which they originally held the oil rights. The scale of payments to the host governments has moved from a simple royalty expressed in terms of gold, through a period of '50–50' division of profits, into a period where the governments' financial gain from the export of oil is significantly greater than that of the companies. The benefits brought by these companies cannot be measured only in terms of revenues paid. They have established the whole apparatus of a highly efficient industry where none existed before. As employers they have paid good wages and provided housing, industrial training, social services and welfare facilities for their workers on an impressive scale hitherto unknown in the region. They have given technical and practical help of all kinds to their host countries and have tried to integrate themselves into the national and regional life.

However, in an area of great political sensitivity and strong national consciousness the very size and importance of the concessionary companies and the enormous benefits they bring have attracted resentment and criticism. In one or two extreme cases this has led to confiscatory or restrictive action being taken against them. While the strength of feeling varies from country to country, there is a growing view in those where public opinion is articulate that foreign interests should not be allowed to predominate indefinitely in an industry which is so vital to national life. It is felt by some that the state itself should participate more actively, even in the stages of sea transportation and marketing of oil throughout the world. Against this is the realisation that the vast capital sums which would anyhow be required for entry into such 'downstream' operations are badly needed for general economic and social development at home. The foreign companies, for their part, have a natural desire to retain and expand their own business, and indeed they have built up and operate a world-wide service for the supply of oil from this area which is indispensable both to the producing and to the consuming countries.

In the meanwhile a number of state-owned oil companies have in fact been created and are in active business. Since the late 1950s other foreign companies of a wide spread of nationalities have also entered the region, having made new types of agreements by which they become partners or even contractors of the state companies, at the same time bearing the initial financial risks and being subjected to far more onerous terms than would have been contemplated a generation earlier.

Iran, Iraq, Kuwait, Saudi Arabia, Qatar and Abu Dhabi, along with Venezuela, Libya, Algeria and Indonesia, have joined the Organisation of Petroleum Exporting Countries (OPEC) which was established in 1960 for the purpose of co-ordinating and promoting the interests and aspirations of its members.

In 1968 there was also established for the same purpose the Organisation of Arab Petroleum Exporting Countries (OAPEC), membership of which was to be confined to those Arab states which derived their principal income from exports of oil. The founder members were Kuwait, Saudi Arabia and Libya.

Iran

In 1951, at a time of political turbulence in Iran, the oil industry was nationalised and the British concessionary company deprived of its rights and assets, thus bringing its operations in the country to a standstill. Iran at that time was the biggest oil producer in the region, while the Abadan refinery was the largest in the world. The National Iranian Oil Company (NIOC) was created by the Government to take over the concessionaire's properties and operate the installations, but for the next three years the industry barely functioned at all. After political changes a new Government made an agreement in 1954 with a consortium of British, Dutch, US and French oil companies, as a result of which this consortium formed two operating companies to exercise oil rights on behalf of the NIOC in a wide area in the south-west. The former British concessionaire acquired the largest single interest in the consortium and was compensated financially for its losses resulting from nationalisation.

Within a few years the consortium restored a high level of oil production and expansion has subsequently been continuous. Oil is produced from 16 or more fields, some of them of great size, in the province of Khuzistan. New discoveries have been frequent. Crude oil destined for export passes through a large pipeline system to a tanker loading terminal, perhaps the largest in the world, at Kharg Island—23 miles from the mainland. Large quantities of oil are processed by the consortium in the Abadan refinery, whence products are exported through another terminal at Bandar Mah Shahr. Abadan also provides large quantities of oil products for the local market.

Since 1957 the NIOC has entered into a number of partnerships with foreign oil companies of various nationalities including Anglo-Dutch, Italian, French, German, US and Indian (state-owned), for oil ventures in certain defined areas, mainly off-shore in the Persian Gulf. Four of the joint companies had discovered oil in commercial quantities by the end of 1969 in a total of eight new oilfields, and were exporting it from new terminals at Bandar Deylam, Kharg Island and Lavan Island. A different type of arrangement, with a French state-owned oil company acting as a contractor, had also resulted in an oil discovery.

The NIOC is concerned with numerous other oil projects. It operates refineries at Kermanshah and Tehran and a pipeline carrying oil products from Abadan to Tehran and other cities. It markets oil products internally and operates some small oil and gas fields in western and central Iran. It is a shareholder in two refineries in India and South Africa. It has made barter agreements with Eastern European countries and with Spain for the disposal of its crude oil and it owns a small fleet of tankers. It also operates medical, educational and administrative services for the oil industry generally.

As a result of an agreement between Iran and the USSR, a large pipeline was planned to be in operation by 1970 to carry natural gas from the southern oilfields to the Russian frontier, some of the gas to be used within Iran but most of it to be exported to the USSR.

Iraq

Oil is produced in Iraq by three concessionary companies which operate under common management and are owned by a group of British, Anglo-

433

Dutch, US and French oil companies, with a 5% shareholding held by the Gulbenkian interests. Major oilfields exist at Kirkuk in the north and near Basrah in the south. Oil from five northern fields is exported to tanker-loading terminals on the Mediterranean coast in Syria and Lebanon through a large pipeline system more than 550 miles in length. From the southern fields oil is loaded directly into tankers through a terminal constructed in deep water 15 miles outside the mouth of the Shatt al-Arab.

The reduction of the areas in which the concessionary companies were originally granted oil rights became, with a number of other issues, the subject of negotiation between 1958 and 1961. In the course of those negotiations the companies were prohibited from exploration work and later, when talks broke down, the government sought to settle the dispute by passing a law to deprive the companies of their rights in more than $99\frac{1}{2}\%$ of the areas, including oilfields then under development, without offering compensation. The state-owned Iraq National Oil Company (INOC) was created shortly afterwards and was later granted oil rights in the disputed areas taken from the concessionaires. In parts of these areas in the south, INOC made an agreement in 1967 for a French state-owned oil company to operate in the capacity of a general contractor. At the same time INOC made an agreement with the USSR for technical assistance, and announced that it would undertake oil production on its own account.

Refining and internal marketing of oil products are state monopolies. The principal refinery is at Daurah, near Baghdad, and there are four smaller plants in the country. Another refinery is projected for construction at Basrah.

Kuwait

The reputation of Kuwait as a country which is vastly rich in oil resources has arisen mainly from the exploitation of the prodigious oilfield of Burgan at the southern end of the country. Oil is produced from this field and from six others, both in the north and south, by a company owned in equal shares by British and US interests, whose concession originally covered the whole of Kuwait. This company has one large tanker-loading terminal on the coast at Mina al-Ahmadi, and another ten miles out at sea at which the world's largest tankers can be loaded. It also owns and operates a big refinery at Mina al-Ahmadi, from which liquefied petroleum gas as well as the normal range of oil products are exported.

The Kuwait National Petroleum Company, in which both the government and local private investors participate, was established in 1960. It has formed a partnership with Spanish interests to explore for oil in areas relinquished by the original concessionaire. It has also built a large refinery at Shu'aybah and markets oil products inside Kuwait. Another Kuwaiti company owns a small fleet of tankers.

Oil rights off-shore were granted to an Anglo-Dutch concessionaire in 1961, but exploration work was suspended in 1963 pending settlement of international boundary problems in the middle of the Gulf.

Kuwaiti-Saudi Neutral Zone

Kuwait and Saudi Arabia each possesses an undivided half interest in the Neutral Zone. Oil is produced on land from three fields by a joint organisation of two companies of US ownership, one having obtained its concessionary rights from the Government of Kuwait and the other from the Government of Saudi Arabia. One company exports its share of oil through a terminal at Mina Abdullah, located inside Kuwait itself, and the other through a terminal at Mina Saud in the Neutral Zone. Each company has built a refinery at its respective terminal, the products from which are exported.

Oil off-shore is exploited by a single Japanese concessionaire as a result of separate agreements with each of the two Governments. Each Government has a 10% shareholding in the company, which produces oil from one large field and has discovered others. The oil is loaded into tankers at sea berths and at an island platform several miles from the shore. The company has also built a refinery for export purposes at Ras al-Khafji in the Neutral Zone.

Saudi Arabia

Oil production in Saudi Arabia has so far been confined to the Eastern Province and to off-shore areas in the Persian Gulf. A concessionary company, owned by four major US oil companies, extracts oil from at least eight fields on the mainland and four under the sea-bed, some of which are of very great size and importance. Additional fields have been discovered both off-shore and on the mainland at the northern edge of the Rub'al-Khali desert. For the export of crude oil two major facilities have been constructed : a tanker-loading terminal at Ras Tanura which includes berths capable of accommodating the largest tankers afloat, and a pipeline 1,050 miles long through which the oil is pumped across Saudi Arabia, Jordan and Syria to a terminal on the Lebanese coast. Large quantities of oil are processed in a refinery at Ras Tanura, owned and operated by the same concessionary company. From here most of the resulting oil products and also liquefied petroleum gas are exported, while the rest is taken up by the local market. Further substantial tonnages of crude oil are pumped through a pipeline to the refinery at Bahrain for processing there prior to re-export.

In 1962 the Government created a state-owned General Petroleum and Minerals Organisation (Petromin), designed to participate in a wide range of oil affairs. Petromin has made agreements with French, Italian and US oil companies for exploration work in various parts of the country, including off-shore areas in the Red Sea and other territory relinquished by the original American concessionaire. In one such agreement the Government of Pakistan is also a participant. If oil is discovered in commercial quantities the company concerned is then required to enter into partnership with Petromin for its exploitation. Petromin handles all internal marketing of oil products, to which end it operates a refinery at Jeddah partly owned by private interests and intends to construct another at Riyadh. It has also formed a tanker company and other companies which undertake geophysical and drilling contracts.

Bahrain

Oil production from Bahrain is confined to a single field which is operated by a concessionaire owned by two major US oil companies. The whole of the crude oil output is normally processed in a refinery established in Bahrain under the same ownership. This refinery—one of the largest in the Middle East—receives more than three-quarters of its crude oil by pipeline from Saudi Arabia.

In 1965 another company owned by US interests began to search for oil off-shore. Bahrain shares with Saudi Arabia the oil revenues from an off-shore field operated by concessionaires in the latter country.

Qatar

Oil produced in Qatar comes from one field located on the western side of the peninsula, operated by a concessionary company owned by the same multi-national interests as those in Iraq, and from two fields off-shore to the north-east, operated by an Anglo-Dutch concessionaire. Each company has its tanker-loading terminal, one at Umm Said on the eastern coast and the other at Halul Island, 50 miles off-shore. Oil rights in both land and sea areas relinquished by the original concessionaires were awarded to another company of US ownership, which later withdrew after several years of un-successful search. Japanese interests subsequently took up part of the off-shore area.

A small topping plant at Umm Said, owned by the Government, serves the local market with oil products.

Abu Dhabi

Oil is produced in Abu Dhabi both on land and off-shore. A large field, situated in the desert about 60 miles south-west of the town of Abu Dhabi, is operated by a concessionary company which is owned by multi-national interests identical with those in Iraq and Qatar. The oil is exported through a tanker-loading terminal at Jebal Dhanna. More than 50 miles off-shore are two producing fields operated by an Anglo-French company, whose loading terminal is on Das Island.

The oil rights in areas relinquished by the above two companies have been granted to others on terms which provide for state participation if commercial oil is discovered. A partnership of US and Italian interests and also a Japanese company have been awarded areas on land, while another Japanese group is operating off-shore and struck oil in 1969.

Dubai

Exports began in 1969 from an oilfield located about 60 miles off-shore which is operated by a concessionary company owned by US, French, Spanish and German interests.

Shaikhdoms of the Trucial Coast

Included here for geographical reasons, although not yet in the same oil category as their neighbours, are the other Shaikhdoms of the Trucial Coast.

Oil concessions covering the on-shore and off-shore territories of Sharjah, Ajman, Umm al-Quwain, Ras al-Khaimah and Fujairah have been taken up from time to time by foreign companies of various nationalities, but no oil in commercial quantities has so far been discovered.

Sultanate of Oman

The existence of oil in commercial quantities in the Sultanate was confirmed in 1964. Production takes place from three fields in the interior of the country. The concessionary company, owned by Anglo-Dutch, French and the Gulbenkian interests, exports the oil through a tanker-loading terminal at Mina al-Fahal which is linked with the oilfields by a pipeline 170 miles long. Oil rights off-shore have been granted to a consortium of German and other foreign interests.

In spite of much exploration work by US companies, no commercial oil was found in the Dhofar province.

THE TRANSIT COUNTRIES

Syrian Arab Republic (Syria)

After earlier disappointments oil was discovered in 1956 in north-eastern Syria, and several other fields in the same area were located in succeeding years. The reserves are very modest in comparison with those in neighbouring

Iraq, but a pipeline has been laid 400 miles to the coast at Tartus from where exports began in 1968. The domestic oil industry in Syria was nationalised in 1965, the actual oilfields having been taken over by the Government from foreign interests several years earlier and then developed with technical assistance from the USSR. Major pipelines from Iraq and Saudi Arabia owned by the international oil companies pass through Syria, one of those from Iraq terminating at Banias where there are comprehensive storage and tanker-loading facilities. About 30 million tons of oil were loaded at Banias in 1969.

A state-owned refinery supplying products for the internal market is located at Homs, where it is well placed to draw its supplies of crude oil from one of the pipelines terminating at Banias and Tartus.

Lebanon

Both foreign and local companies have searched for oil in the Lebanon without success. The oil pipelines from Iraq and Saudi Arabia terminate respectively at Tripoli and Zahrani (near Sidon), at each of which places the oil companies have constructed extensive storage and tanker-loading facilities and a refinery. In 1969 a total of about 38 million tons of oil was loaded into tankers at the two terminals. The two refineries together supply the country's requirements of oil products.

Jordan

In spite of much exploration work by foreign oil companies, no oilfields have yet been discovered in Jordan. A refinery owned jointly by state and private interests, which meets the needs of the internal market, is located at Zerka. It is supplied with crude oil from the pipeline connecting the Saudi Arabian oilfields with the Mediterranean, which crosses Jordanian territory.

United Arab Republic (UAR)

As a result of new oil discoveries made in the 1960s the UAR is likely to become an important oil-exporting country. Exploration and production is undertaken both by the state-owned Egyptian General Petroleum Corporation (EGPC) and by foreign oil companies which enter into partnership with EGPC if they discover oil in commercial quantities. The original oilfields on the western shore of the Gulf of Suez, long since exhausted, have been replaced by others in the same area operated by EGPC. Beneath the sea-bed of the Gulf is a large field, operated by a partnership of EGPC and a US company. A string of fields along the Sinai shore of the Gulf are operated with an Italian partner; they fell under Israeli occupation after the war of June 1967. Another partnership with a US company produces oil from el-Alamein in the Western Desert, whence it is carried by pipeline to a coastal terminal near Sidi Abd al-Rahman. Natural gas has been found in commercial quantities in the Nile delta. Oil products for internal consumption are supplied by two refineries at Suez and one at Mex, near Alexandria, all owned and operated by EGPC through subsidiaries. A variety of technical assistance is provided by the USSR for the State's oil organisations.

The great significance of the Suez Canal in the transit of Middle East oil is evident from the figures for 1966. In that year tanker cargoes totalling 167 million tons passed through from south to north, of which 90% was crude oil from the Persian Gulf area destined for Europe and constituting 40% of Europe's oil imports for the year. As a result of the interruption to traffic after the war of 1967, plans were put in hand for the construction of a large transit pipeline from Suez to Alexandria.

THE OTHER COUNTRIES OF THE REGION

Turkey

The oil business in Turkey is carried on by both state-owned and private companies. Foreign companies have been permitted to participate since 1954. In spite of much exploration, production of oil is almost entirely confined to a cluster of small oilfields in the south-eastern province of Siirt. These are linked by a pipeline to Dörtyol on the Gulf of Iskanderun. By 1969 local oil production was sufficient to meet nearly 50% of the country's internal needs. However, Turkey is virtually self-sufficient in refineries, which are located at Mersin, Izmit (near Istanbul) and Batman, and another was under construction at Izmir in 1969.

Israel

Great efforts to find oil have been made in Israel by both foreign and local companies since the early 1950s, but discoveries have so far been confined to a group of small deposits in the southern coastal area, which provide declining quantities of oil never amounting to more than a very small proportion of internal requirements. Small quantities of natural gas discovered in the Negev are distributed locally for industrial use. The Government owns a large refinery at Haifa which has to rely mainly on imported crude oil delivered at Eilat in the Gulf of Aqaba and pumped to Haifa through a pipeline.

The immediate results of the Arab-Israeli war of 1967 were that Israel remained in occupation of the UAR's oilfields on the eastern side of the Gulf of Suez, and decided to construct a large transit pipeline from Eilat to Ashkelon, which would by-pass the Suez Canal.

Sudan

Some exploration for oil has taken place in the Sudan but none has been discovered. There is a refinery at Port Sudan which serves the internal market. It is owned by British and Anglo-Dutch interests and has to import its crude oil from abroad.

Yemen

Although a small amount of prospecting has been undertaken by foreign companies, mainly US and German, no oil has been found. Further efforts have been planned with Algerian co-operation.

Republic of South Yemen

Attempts made by foreign oil companies to find oil in the former Aden Protectorate were unsuccessful. Algerian assistance has since been made available. There is a large refinery at al-Bureika owned by a British company, which processes imported crude oil partly for internal consumption and bunker fuel and partly for re-export.

OIL IN THE ECONOMY OF THE MIDDLE EAST

In a region which still suffers greatly from the effect of many centuries of poverty and maladministration, the injection of the revenues arising from the exploitation of its oil resources was bound to have a dramatic if uneven impact on its social and economic life. The results really began to show themselves in the early 1950s, following the expansion of the industry after World War II and the introduction of the '50–50' profit-sharing agreements.

438

The exporting countries receive huge cash payments from the oil companies by way of royalties and taxes. These payments constitute a high proportion of the total state revenues received by the Governments from all sources. In the late 1960s this proportion was averaging as high as 50% in Iran, 58% in Iraq, 94% in Kuwait and 88% in Saudi Arabia. There is the additional benefit of large-scale local spending by the industry itself on wages, supplies, contracts and services. The oil revenues provide the governments with funds for general economic development, enabling them to create capital assets on a national scale and develop natural resources other than oil—where such exist. The money is used to finance the establishment of social services and to buttress ordinary state budgets. The oil revenues are normally received in foreign exchange, thus contributing to favourable balances of payments and the easy financing of imports. The oil-exporting countries have thus achieved international significance in trading and finance. If these revenues have also given rise to some well-publicised cases of waste and personal or national extravagance, this weakness must be put into fair perspective against the genuine achievements which are visible in all the countries where there has been time to produce results. Great and sometimes spectacular progress has been made in the fields of communications, construction of modern housing and amenities, public utilities, flood control, irrigation, light industries, and in educational and medical services. An additional but important benefit from the industry is that abundant oil is available at low cost as a source of power.

The pipeline transit countries are paid large sums by the oil companies in settlement of agreed transit dues, and also have the benefit of much local spending by the industry. These oil revenues, though important, do not have the same local economic significance as in the exporting countries. On the other hand, the Suez Canal dues received in normal times by the UAR in respect of the transit of oil tankers are of great importance to that country. The remaining countries of the region are unfortunate where oil revenues are concerned, but in those where oil has been discovered even in small quantities its value as an indigenous fuel is very great.

The uneven spread of oil resources in the region, and particularly the great wealth accruing to some of the smaller and sparsely populated Arab states in the Gulf, has inevitably caused envy in the less fortunate countries which have larger populations and an urgent need for development capital. However, the oil revenues of the exporting countries have in fact contributed greatly to a general stepping-up of economic activity throughout the Middle East, especially in the other Arab countries. It has also become the policy of some of the oil-rich states to help their less fortunate neighbours by lending money to finance particular projects and by making general financial contributions in times of special crisis.[1]

[1] See especially p. 240-1.

FUTURE PROSPECTS

During the last decade the world's consumption of oil has been increasing at an average rate of $7\frac{1}{2}\%$ annually, and this rate was generally exceeded in those areas which were the main importers of Middle East oil. Increases predicted for the succeeding decade are only a little less. The proven reserves of oil in the region are already vast, and further reserves will surely be discovered. It seems certain that there is adequate oil to supply an expanding market for a long time to come. However, the future prosperity of the oil industry in the Middle East and its ability to continue as the mainstay of the region's economy do not only require oil reserves and markets. In an area which is stricken with the Arab-Israeli dispute and subjected to many local rivalries and international pressures, the industry needs peace and reasonably stable conditions to enable it to carry on its business efficiently and to invest the huge capital sums necessary for continued expansion. There is also a need for recognition by the oil-rich governments that there is a limit to the amount of revenue which can be extracted from the industry if their oil is to remain competitive with other fuels and with oil from other producing regions. It is, however, reasonable to conclude that the degree of common interest between the oil-producing states, the oil companies and the consuming nations is so great that the long-term prospects for Middle East oil are very good indeed.

TABLE 1[2]

MIDDLE EAST OIL PRODUCTION AND REFINING CAPACITY

Year	1938	1948	1958	1968	1969	*Refining*[3] *capacity* *(million* *metric* *tons* *per* *annum)* 1969
			oil produced *(million metric tons)*			
Iran	10·4	25·3	41·0	141·5	168·1	30·0
Iraq	4·4	3·4	35·8	73·8	74·9	5·0
Kuwait	—	6·4	70·2	122·1	129·5	22·0
Kuwaiti-Saudi Neutral Zone	—	—	4·3	22·1	23·3	4·0
Saudi Arabia	0·1	19·3	50·1	141·1	148·6	19·0
Bahrain	1·1	1·5	2·0	3·8	3·8	10·0
Qatar	—	—	8·2	16·2	17·0	—
Abu Dhabi	—	—	—	24·0	28·9	—
Dubai	—	—	—	—	1·0	—
Sultanate of Oman	—	—	—	12·1	16·3	—
Turkey	—	—	0·3	3·0	3·6	7·5
Syria	—	—	—	1·0	3·0	3·0
Israel	—	—	0·1	0·1	0·1	5·5
UAR	0·2	1·9	3·2	11·3	15·0	8·5
Lebanon	—	—	—	—	—	2·5
Jordan	—	—	—	—	—	0·5
Sudan	—	—	—	—	—	1·0
Republic of S. Yemen	—	—	—	—	—	8·5
Total	16·2	57·8	215·2	572·1	633·1	127·0

[2] The figures in this table have been derived or interpreted from various monetary sources.

[3] Estimated to nearest half-million tons.

Table 2

OIL REVENUES OF MAJOR EXPORTING COUNTRIES
(in million US $)[4]

Year	1958	1968[5]
Iran	247	836
Iraq	224	476
Kuwait	425	773
Saudi Arabia	310	955
Bahrain		
Qatar	72	354
Abu Dhabi		
Sultanate of Oman	—	

Source: Petroleum Press Service.

[4] Revenue figures in this table are all shown in US dollars for the sake of uniformity.
[5] Figures given for 1968 are provisional at the time of going to press.

FURTHER READING

Hartshorn, J. E. *Oil Companies and Governments,* Faber & Faber, London, (2nd ed) 1967.

Hirst, David. *Oil and Public Opinion in the Middle East,* Faber & Faber, London, 1966; Praeger, New York, 1966.

Lenczowski, George. *Oil and State in the Middle East,* Cornell Univ. Press, New York, 1960.

Longrigg, Stephen H. *Oil in the Middle East,* Oxford Univ. Press, London and New York, (3rd ed.) 1967.

Tugendhat, Christopher. *Oil: The Biggest Business,* Eyre and Spottiswoode, London, 1968; Putnam, New York, 1968.

W. W. Stewart. Entered the oil industry in 1947. His subsequent experience included 17 years in Lebanon and Iraq, mainly in senior posts. He retired in 1968 and is now studying archaeology at the University of London.

INDUSTRIALISATION

ROBERT E. MABRO

INTRODUCTION

DEVELOPING countries lay special emphasis on industrialisation as a key factor in raising the living standards of their people and bringing about the modernisation of their economies. Discouraged by the results so far achieved, Western observers are becoming increasingly sceptical of the merits of this view. Historically, however, the relationship between industrialisation and economic development seems well-established. Whichever economic system one chooses to consider—the *laissez-faire*, capitalist régime of the 18th and 19th century in the United Kingdom, Soviet central planning, or the mixed system of Meiji Japan with its successful balance of Government intervention and free enterprise—economic progress appears to be associated with an industrial revolution. Statistical studies encompassing rich and poor countries alike point to a strong correlation between the share of industrial output in national product and *per caput* income. It is true, however, that some governments tend to identify rapid industrialisation with the concepts and symbols of national independence. They draft hasty plans and embark on ill-conceived projects, sacrificing in too many instances economic efficiency to political prestige. However numerous and disheartening, these failures should be attributed to misconceptions. They do not validate a case against the economic significance of industrialisation.

Despite great disparities in their economic background and the nature of their political régimes, most Middle Eastern countries seem to share a common belief in the virtues of modern industry, as well as current misconceptions. They are presently engaged in planning or implementing rather ambitious programmes.

HISTORICAL BACKGROUND

This interest is not new. In the late 19th century, nationalist Arab writers were advocating industrialisation as an essential means of establishing a modern, self-sufficient and independent state. At an earlier date, Egypt, with remarkable determination, and Turkey (half-heartedly perhaps) had already attempted to industrialise. The history of Muhammad Aly's ill-fated textile and military factories is well-known. Three decades later, his successor Ismail repeated the same experience with very little success. Only the sugar industry managed to survive serious obstacles and several set-backs.

These early attempts were indeed isolated ventures. The establishment of modern industry in the Middle East is a more recent phenomenon that may be back-dated to the later 1920s and 1930s—a period of timid but significant beginnings. The inter-war decades were marked by the emergence of the Misr group in Egypt, the creation of the Sümerbank and the proclamation of a Five Year Plan (1934–9) in Turkey. Small factories (textile, food, beverages) appeared for the first time in Syria and Iraq. But despite its riches and explicit concern for reforms and economic progress, Iran seems to have lagged behind during this period : in the 1930s Reza Shah launched a programme of industrial investment (sugar, textiles, cement) but his factories did not perform very well.

World War II stimulated local entrepreneurship. The Middle East was cut off from foreign sources of supplies and the local industry had to cater for the domestic market and the Allied troops. The British army helped with skills and technical expertise. The resumption of trade, after the war, enabled private investors to import machinery and equipment, and new factories were set up in Turkey, Egypt, Syria, Lebanon, Iraq and Iran. Until 1950, however, industrial expansion was proceeding at a slow pace. No country had yet embarked on large scale programmes or achieved very substantial results.

The past two decades have witnessed important changes. With the advent of revolutionary régimes (in Egypt, Iraq and Syria), the accumulation of wealth in the hands of the rulers of oil-states (Kuwait and Saudi Arabia) and an increased commitment to economic development (in all Arab countries as well as Turkey and Iran), the industrialisation drive gained momentum almost everywhere in the Middle East.

PATTERNS OF INDUSTRIALISATION

It is impossible to assess the performance of individual countries within the limits of a short essay. Middle Eastern economies are too diverse : there are considerable differences in the endowment of resources and the stage of development attained. Industry has had a relatively long history in some countries, while others have just inaugurated their first plants.

Table 1 reveals interesting differences in the structure of industrial production. The importance of metals in Turkey is worth noting (Iran has already invested in a steel plant and Iraq is planning to follow suit). Industrial output is much more diversified in Egypt, Turkey and Iran than in the rest of the area.

In the underdeveloped countries, however, industrial development tends to display some regular patterns. While some of them are ahead of others, Middle Eastern countries seem generally to follow the same path.

The first stage of industrialisation is related to *the processing of primary products for export*. In the case of agricultural commodities, only elementary operations are performed : ginning and pressing cotton (in Egypt the first gins were introduced by Muhammad Aly), grading and packaging fruits, husking rice, milling cereals, dressing skins and hides and the like. Sugar cane and tobacco may lead to more interesting ventures. Foreign demand for Turkish cigarettes once helped the establishment of a flourishing industry in Egypt and Turkey.

Oil countries may well begin with refineries and petro-chemical plants. Though most Middle Eastern countries now have their own refineries—the first was erected at Abadan as long ago as 1913—the greater part of their oil is still exported in the form of crude. The share of refined products in total output barely exceeds one-fifth. The development of a national

TABLE 1

INDUSTRIAL PRODUCTION IN SELECTED COUNTRIES OF THE MIDDLE EAST

Commodities	Units	Turkey (1967)	Egypt (1967)	Iran (1965)	Iraq (1965)	Syria (1966)	Jordan (1966)	Saudi Arabia (1966)
Iron and Steel	tons	2,400,000	330,000	—	—	—	—	—
Copper	tons	4,900	8,000	1,500	—	—	—	—
Brass products	tons	770	—	3,210	—	—	—	—
Aluminium sheets	tons	1,100	1,100	900	—	—	—	—
Cement	tons	4,250,000	2,600,000	1,400,000	1,200,000	680,000	375,000	320,000
Paper	tons	98,500	97,000	—	—	—	—	—
Tyres	pieces	1,009,000	604,000	349,000	—	—	—	—
Fertilisers	tons	327,000	1,050,000	?	—	—	?	?
Sugar	tons	672,000	363,000	360,000	46,000	91,000	—	—
Cigarettes	tons	32,275	18,000	—	—	4,000	—	—
	millions			9,670	?	?	—	—
Beer	1,000 litres	30,000	25,000	18,000	?	18,000	—	—
Cotton yarn	tons	33,000	152,000	155,000	?	36,000	—	—
Cotton fabrics	1,000 metres	172,000	104,000	423,000	50,000	—	—	—
Silk yarn	tons	—	—	—	—	6,410	?	?
Caviar	tons	—	—	3,100	290	—	—	—
Refrigerators	sets	?	25,000	38,600	—	—	—	—
TV sets	sets	?	64,000	7,400	—	—	—	—

Source: Statistical abstracts of various countries

petroleum industry is held back by a variety of constraints. The sophisticated technology and the large investments involved are often beyond domestic capabilities; foreign companies may be reluctant to co-operate since importers prefer to refine the crude in their own plants.

The next stage of industrialisation is *the transformation of raw materials into consumer goods for the local market*. The emphasis now is on import substitution : goods formerly imported from abroad are now produced at home. The range of possible industries depends on the size of the market and the availability of primary resources. In the agricultural countries of the Middle East, textiles, sugar, cigarettes, beer, tinned and processed food, leather and soft drinks were favoured by early investors and still represent an important part of industrial output today. (The desert economies of Kuwait, Saudi Arabia and Libya have less scope in these lines of production.)

The emergence of industries catering for the construction sector is characteristic of this stage. Construction opens up a number of possibilities that have been exploited almost everywhere (bricks, cement, tiles, joinery, workshops for metal and sanitary works). Small countries, like the Lebanon, have their own cement plant. The availability of raw materials, the growing importance of local markets and the high transport costs of imports favour the domestic production of these goods. Oil-producing countries should give a high priority to their construction industry : oil discoveries are always followed by a building boom. It seems strange in these circumstances that Libya has delayed so much the erection of cement factories.

These first stages of industrialisation may be characterised as the phase of free-enterprise. In most Middle Eastern countries this phase was initiated by the private sector, which succeeded in establishing a small but profitable industrial nucleus protected by natural advantages and sometimes by a tariff barrier. Interestingly enough, traditional craftsmanship played only a minor role in the development of these industries. (Local crafts did not survive Cromer's free trade policy in Egypt, and in Lebanon the once flourishing silk industry was completely destroyed by the end of World War I. In Iran, however, the carpet industry which achieved world-wide fame for the quality of its fine products, has retained its importance.) In many instances modern industry, established by technologically-minded entrepreneurs, displaced the domestic demand for handicrafts and precipitated their destruction.

Without government intervention, industrialisation generally fails to proceed beyond the first stages depicted above : the processing of primary goods for exports and of local raw materials for the domestic market. Lebanon, with its *laissez-faire* régime, is a case in point.

In the past decades, however, Middle Eastern governments assumed an increasingly important role in the management of their economies. Their involvement took a variety of forms, from nationalisation (Egypt and Syria) and comprehensive planning (Egypt) to the setting up of development boards (e.g. in Iraq), investment in state enterprises (most countries) and joint ventures with foreign companies (e.g. in Kuwait and Saudia Arabia). Besides, all governments have recourse to the classical battery of protective measures : tariffs, trade quotas and controls. Industry is exempted from taxes for periods extending over five or ten years; industrial banks are founded to provide cheap finance; imports of machinery and equipment are stimulated at subsidised prices.

Under government sponsorship, industrial development may proceed along three lines. (*a*) The traditional industries (textiles, food, cement, etc.) receive some encouragement. This is how Iraqi industrialisation, for example, got under way in the 1950s under the patronage of a development board. The first Egyptian Five Year Plan (1960–5) expanded the textile industry beyond the country's capacity. (*b*) Import substitution is taken several steps further. Semi-finished goods and manufacturers are now imported for assembly or further processing. Turkey and Egypt thus have plants for assembling cars and produce a range of consumer durables (refrigerators, gas cookers, aluminium hollow-ware, etc.) from imported raw materials and component parts. Import substitution extends to pharmaceuticals (the Egyptian pharmaceutical industry can meet 70% to 80% of the local demand), plastics, paper and some chemicals. In Iran, industrialisation has already reached this stage. With fewer resources, Iraq and Syria tend to follow the same path. (*c*) Planned economies lay special emphasis on heavy industry. Iron and steel enjoyed some priority in the early Turkish plan (1934–9) and the Egyptian Free Officers, almost from the outset, decided to build a steel mill at Helwan. (This plant was completed in the early 1960s, and with Russian help new extensions are now under way.) Heavy industry entails considerable investment in bulky and sophisticated equipment and in the complementary infrastructure : roads, harbour facilities, railway engines, pipelines, etc. The gestation period is usually long, in the sense that investors have to wait for many years before they can expect to reap financial returns. In underdeveloped countries, the private sector is generally reluctant to launch these industries and the state feels compelled to step in. It is true that, left to itself, the private sector may ignore opportunities that are beneficial to the nation as a whole because they may involve short-term pecuniary losses. Though valid in some instances, the argument should not be applied indiscriminately to justify the involvement of the state in ventures that, in the last resort, may prove wasteful both from the private and from the social point of view. In Egypt, for example, the priority given to the steel industry has been criticised, and through lack of natural advantages, the industry is likely to remain inefficient over a long period—too long perhaps for a poor country to afford. Scarce resources are diverted from more profitable uses, for instance the fertiliser industry, whose expansion—despite the presence of an excellent domestic market and good export prospects—was much delayed.

THE INDUSTRIAL STRUCTURE

Industrial development, then, is characterised by the emergence of a few large establishments owned by the state (or jointly owned with foreign participation in some oil-producing countries). The industrial sector is split between these giant firms and a large number of small, ill-equipped enterprises. Middle-sized, privately owned firms using modern technology—which played such an important role in the industrial development of the West and of Japan—have either been discouraged by nationalisation (Egypt, Iraq and Syria) or have failed to emerge in sufficient numbers (in all countries except, perhaps, Iran).

The large industrial enterprises tend to remain enclaves. They do not supply their products to other firms for further processing and they purchase very little from the small manufacturers and workshops. It is true that they absorb agricultural products and raw materials, but because they do not provide any stimulus to production in other sectors of the economy, they only succeed in displacing exports.

The middle-sized firm is more adapted to the scale of Middle Eastern markets. It is more likely to stimulate other firms by purchasing their products as inputs for its own production and by selling its own output for further processing. More efficient and thus more profitable (in relation to the capital invested), it can act as an 'engine of growth'. Private ownership is not essential for the successful performance of these firms as long as state managers are given sufficient incentives and allowed to reinvest the profits in their own enterprise.

In many Middle Eastern countries industrial development is not generated from within, but planned and stimulated from without. Scale is often confused with achievement, prestige projects with industrial power, sophisticated technology with economic efficiency. Too little attention is paid to the internal functioning of the enterprises, the inter-relationships between firms of different size and the harmonious growth of the industrial sector as an organic whole.

THE CONTRIBUTION OF INDUSTRY TO THE NATIONAL PRODUCT, EMPLOYMENT AND EXPORTS

At the present time, the contribution of industry to the gross domestic product in the Middle East ranges between 2·5% in Libya and 23% in Egypt. Table 2 provides a ranking based on available data. The figures should be interpreted carefully—they only suggest orders of magnitude—because of differences in definition and coverage of national statistics. The comparable figure for the United Kingdom is 33%.

It is clear that no Middle Eastern country has, as yet, achieved the status of an industrial economy. In the past decade, however, the manufacturing sector has been growing at a faster rate than traditional sectors—agriculture, handicrafts and the services. Egypt (to a lesser extent the same is true of Turkey and Iran) has succeeded in altering the predominantly agricultural character of its economy and it is unfortunate that further progress is being hindered by the aftermath of the June War.

TABLE 2

INDUSTRIAL PRODUCTION AS % OF GDP

Countries	Percentage
Israel	28
Egypt	23
Iran	20
Turkey	19
Syria	15
Iraq	11–12
Lebanon	12
Jordan	10
Kuwait	3–5 (estimated)
Saudi Arabia	3–5 (estimated)
Libya	2·5

Source: Statistical abstracts of individual countries

The contribution of industry to employment is small. In Egypt 11% of the labour force is currently employed in the manufacturing sector; in Libya, less than 1%. Modern plants require a comparatively small number of

447

workers to man their capital-intensive equipment. A serious problem arises in overpopulated countries suffering from a demographic explosion. Their progressive sectors—industry and oil—fail to create sufficient jobs to absorb the pool of under-employed workers and new entrants in the labour force.

The share of industrial products in total exports is also very small. Industry has not reached the stage in most Middle Eastern states where it can contribute to the balance of payment problems, a failure that may damage the development prospects of Turkey, Egypt and Syria. These countries face chronic shortages of foreign exchange. Their receipts from traditional exports are not expanding as fast as their imports, and they cannot rely on oil revenues, as can their more fortunate neighbours, to finance the growing requirements of vital foreign goods : machinery, raw materials for industry, and food.

Trade is the acid test of industrialisation. The ability to export industrial commodities may be limited by a variety of obstacles—from protection in foreign markets to the absence of proper distribution channels and a lack of initiative on the part of official trade agencies in the exporting countries. In the last resort, however, this ability depends on competitiveness. Middle Eastern industry is not efficient enough : it produces too little, at too high a price, and it cannot always compete for quality.

In the initial stages of development, poor countries must be expected to be high-cost producers. The market is small, the technology employed is not suited to their environment and skilled labour is scarce. Productivity is low, and excess capacity is the rule rather than the exception. Protection is needed; and the question is not whether, initially, a tariff barrier should be provided or not, but whether it is worth developing *certain* lines of production that may require almost indefinite protection.

CONCLUSION

In assessing the Middle Eastern performance, one should remember that industrialisation may generate long-run benefits that will outweigh short-term losses. Its utility cannot be measured in terms of private profits alone. Industry may change attitudes, create a new environment more suitable to further economic progress, and develop a wide range of skills. It may bring in capital and expertise from abroad and stimulate a number of ancillary activities : transport, internal trade, services and construction. We have already pointed out in the introduction that there is no case for an outright rejection of industrialisation as a feasible and beneficial means of economic development. But there is an urgent need for a more careful selection of projects, a rational choice of priorities and a more intelligent approach to state intervention.

Middle Eastern governments have been unable, as yet, to provide these requirements in a satisfactory manner. This is because :

(a) The selection of projects is not always wise, either because of a lack of specialist resources or because too many political considerations are allowed to interfere with the decision-making process.

(b) Industrialisation is often treated as an end in itself which must be pursued at all costs, and alternative priorities—in agriculture for example—do not receive the attention they deserve. Iraq (since 1958) is a good example of this attitude.

(c) In many cases, state intervention lacks competence and flexibility. In

Egypt, Turkey and Iraq—to name but a few countries—the successful performance of viable enterprises is hindered by an inefficient bureaucracy and by misguided policies.

It is true that mistakes and failures are difficult to avoid in the beginning. Although some Middle Eastern states—the wealthy oil producers—can afford the cost of mistakes, other countries cannot. Their people are too poor and it is the poor, in the end, who carry the burden of costly and inefficient enterprises. One can only hope that the trials and errors of first attempts will help these countries to improve the planning of their future progress.

FURTHER READING

Baldwin, George B. *Planning and Development in Iran*, Johns Hopkins, Baltimore, 1967.

Corm, Georges C. *Politique Economique et Planification au Liban 1953–63*, Beirut, 1964.

Hansen, Bent and Mazouk, Girgis. *Development and Economic Policy in the UAR (Egypt)*, North Holland Publishing Company, Amsterdam, 1965.

Mead, Donald C. *Growth and Structural Change in the Egyptian Economy*, Yale University, Illinois, 1967.

Shorter, Frederic C. and others. *Four Studies in the Economic Development of Turkey*, Cass, London, 1967.

ROBERT E. MABRO. Senior Research Officer at the Oxford University Institute of Economics and Statistics. One-time Leon Fellow of the University of London, and member of the staff of the School of Oriental and African Studies. Has lived in Egypt and France and travelled widely in the Middle East. A regular contributor to the *Journal of Development Studies, The Economic Journal* and *Projet*.

TECHNOLOGY

KEVIN G. FENELON

THOUGH the word 'technology' has now come to be associated with the most modern and sophisticated applications of scientific discovery, each age has had its own technology and in the traditional economies of the Middle East, many ingenious contrivances were devised which involved considerable technological expertise, albeit of a somewhat primitive kind. Scant attention has as yet been given to the study of the economic history of the area, but the 'industrial archaeology' of the Middle East should prove a rewarding subject for research. It is to be hoped that such studies will be undertaken before it is too late and the last vestiges of the old technology have finally disappeared.

Among these achievements of a past or passing age, perhaps the best known are the giant water-wheels of Hama in Syria, but also fascinating, though less well known, are the smaller water-wheels of the upper Euphrates in Iraq, where they are called *na'ur*. Except for the buckets made of pottery, they are entirely fabricated from wood. Specially ingenious devices are the wind-towers (*badkeer*) once numerous in Iran, Kuwait, Bahrain, Abu Dhabi and Dubai, which have openings on each side at the top to catch any breeze which may blow, whatever its direction. Connected with the rooms below, the tower creates a cooling movement of air which makes life more comfortable for the occupants. Widespread also in much the same geographical area are the underground water channels known by various names (*qanat* in Iran or *falaj* in Trucial Oman) which, after burrowing into the hills to the water sources, carry the water to farms which may be twenty or more miles distant. Both in their construction and in the choice of location of their source, considerable expertise was necessary; indeed, so sound in principle was their choice of water source that today, in places such as El Ain (Buraimi) and elsewhere in Trucial Oman, channels which had fallen into disuse and which had become choked with sand or debris are being re-opened to supply irrigation water for a reviving agriculture.

Among crafts, once flourishing and still surviving to a greater or lesser degree, there may be mentioned wooden-boat-building in the Gulf, carpet-weaving in Iran and textile manufacture in Syria and Mosul. Though the textile crafts are now practically dead, their names are still perpetuated in 'Damask' and 'Muslin', the former coming originally from Damascus and the latter from Mosul. Likewise, from Damascus came Damask steel and this city was long famed for its steel when steel-making was a small craft rather than an industry. Indeed iron and steel in the Middle East were comparatively rare materials in earlier days; as in Britain before the industrial revolution of the 18th century, only local materials would have been used to build machines or other contrivances. According to the area, the materials favoured might be wood, leather, pottery, goat skins or reeds. Irrigation devices such as the 'donkey walk' or the Euphrates water-wheels were made from wood, with buckets respectively of leather or ceramics. Perhaps the most remarkable of all adaptations of local materials are to be seen in the marshes of Iraq, where the whole economy is based on reeds : reeds provide feed for water buffaloes, reeds are used for basket-making, reeds are practically the only fuel, the houses are built of reeds and set on marshes on foundations of reeds, reeds are burned to smoke out the malaria-carrying mosquitoes. Most remarkable of all are the great cathedral-like reception houses of the shaikhs, where the only material used in their construction, apart from reeds, is a stone slab in the centre of the floor where coffee is made in enormous brass coffee pots called 'gumgum', a name onomatopoeically derived from the sound of the boiling water.

For a good many years now, however, the ancient crafts and skills have been languishing and most of them will inevitably die out before long, as the older skilled workers are not being replaced by younger men. Unfortunately the ancient skills have not been redeployed to meet the needs of the new technologies. As a result, the skilled and semi-skilled workers required in the technological industries are not locally available. These new industries are completely alien to the area and depend on foreign expertise for their operation, on foreign factories for their machinery and equipment, and on expatriates for their running and maintenance. There are, however, no insurmountable obstacles to the development of the latest, most advanced and sophisticated technologically-based enterprises, provided foreign exchange is available (as it is in the oil-rich countries) or provided that foreign capital can be persuaded to flow into the projects (as it has readily done where prospects for oil discovery appear favourable). But though a new factory, incorporating the most modern equipment, can be supplied if required as a package deal on a turn-key basis, it is far more difficult for a country to develop its own skills, supporting industries and markets within a short span of years. Tradition, inertia, and existing patterns of social organisation all militate against rapid change. It could take five years or more to train local staff to operate the factories or managers to administer them. Consider, for example, Abu Dhabi, admittedly an extreme case, which has on a *per caput* basis the highest national income in the world. In the school year, 1960–1, there were all told only 81 pupils in the schools and so, inevitably and consequently, it must take many years before the Emirate's own people are available to man the administrative, health, educational, industrial and oil sectors, even though a crash programme of adult education was introduced in 1969 and the number of school pupils soared to 5,000.

The new technologies have made their most spectacular imprint on Middle Eastern countries in oil production, oil refining, petro-chemicals and cement manufacture. All these industries require large capital investment and in respect of oil exploration and discovery, the initial costs can be high indeed. For example, it cost Petroleum Development (Oman) a sum of £60 million before the first shipment of crude oil could be made in 1967.

In this Middle Eastern development, the most rapid strides have been taken by countries bordering the Gulf, and this is not surprising, since the richest oil-fields, notably those of Iran, Saudi Arabia, Kuwait, Abu Dhabi and the Neutral Zone all border the Gulf. Further, this region has enjoyed more stable government over the past ten or fifteen years than have many of the other countries of the Middle East. Between them, they also have the largest known oil reserves in the world.

In the region, however, riches are by no means evenly spread and there are marked differences in the economic structure of the various countries. Statistics are not available for as many countries as could be wished, but the countries included in Table 1 will serve to illustrate the differences which exist among a group of countries representative of the lower Gulf. It will be observed that the percentage of persons employed in the various sectors varies greatly from country to country, indicating marked differences in industrial and economic structure.

TABLE 1

PERCENTAGE OF THE ECONOMICALLY ACTIVE POPULATION
BY ACTIVITY

Activity	Bahrain	Kuwait	Abu Dhabi	Dubai	Ras al-Khaimah
Agriculture & Fishing	8·7	1·1	7·7	6·7	50·0
Manufacture	0·8	10·0	3·0	6·4	2·0
Construction	15·6	16·1	40·1	16·8	12·4
Oil	13·0	3·9	8·3	1·7	0·5
Trade	13·9	12·9	6·1	18·5	6·2
Transport[1]	10·3	5·6	7·1	17·3	9·3
Government services	19·5	⎰ 50·4	15·5	15·2	14·6
Services	18·2	⎱	12·2	17·4	5·7

Kuwait and Abu Dhabi are rich in oil but the latter is a newcomer and hence the disproportionate number engaged in construction. Kuwait has developed its industries, many highly technological, to a greater extent than anywhere else. Bahrain is a long-established oil producer but on a relatively modest scale, and it refines all its own crude as well as a large volume of crude imported from Saudi Arabia; hence the high proportion of persons employed in the oil industry. Bahrain and Dubai—the latter now also emerging as an oil producer—are both important centres of entrepôt trade. Dubai incidentally has the distinction of being the first country in the world to develop an under-sea water-oil displacement system of oil storage.

Technological development naturally has to be attuned to the economic conditions of the country concerned. Some countries in the Middle East have enormous financial resources from the export of crude oil, as have for example Kuwait, Abu Dhabi, Iran and Saudi Arabia; but of these some, such as Kuwait and Abu Dhabi, have very small *indigenous populations*; about 250,000 in Kuwait and a mere 30,000 in Abu Dhabi. In such countries, capital-intensive industries are naturally preferred; an extreme example is the Neutral Zone shared by Kuwait and Saudi Arabia which (apart from the oil personnel) is practically unpopulated. In consequence the installations of the Arabian Oil Company there are highly automated. In Kuwait itself, there are more persons working in garages and motor repair workshops than there are in the crude oil industry of Kuwait as a whole.

In the more densely populated countries such as Egypt, Iran or Iraq, the need is for labour-intensive industries. Iran, however, has benefited from developments in nearby countries, as developments there have required

[1] Includes communications.

large numbers of unskilled labourers to undertake constructional work and other activities connected with the infra-structures. In these countries, the local populations eschew outdoor labouring and in any case they are not sufficiently numerous to meet the need, so the work is done mainly by Iranians, in much the same way as the canals and railways of England were built by Irish navvies. The Iranian labourers are migrants, coming and going as demand beckons or as the work is completed. They leave their families at home, and are content with a very modest remuneration, though this is larger than they could hope to obtain at home. As a result of the large available supply of labour in the building trades, there has been little incentive to mechanisation and there is a marked absence of even the simplest appliances such as steel scaffolding or mechanical hoists.

Technologically, the greatest asset for the development of modern industries in the Middle East lies in the enormous resources of crude oil and natural gas. The supplies available are ample for large-scale operation and the known reserves are sufficiently large to enable capital investment to be undertaken in the knowledge that the reserves will last long enough to justify the capital investment involved.

TABLE 2[2]

CRUDE OIL PRODUCTION

	1965	1966	1967	1968	1969
	Million barrels				
Iran	688	771	948	1,041	1,231
Saudi Arabia	739	873	948	1,036	1,092
Bahrain	21	23	25	28	28
Oman	—	—	21	88	120
	Million metric tons				
Iraq	64	68	60	74	74
Abu Dhabi	14	17	18	24	29
Qatar	11	14	15	16	17

Throughout the area, the oilfields have been equipped with the most efficient plant available at the time of their construction. Crude oil production involves a whole series of complex operations from scientific prospecting and drilling to transmission, including pipelines, de-gassing stations, pumping, monitoring, storage and tanker-loading.

The refineries likewise are highly complicated and the selection of their sites involves careful cost studies balancing such advantages as nearness to supply with those of nearness to markets. In refining, as in so many other large-scale enterprises, technological improvements have been rapid, and more and more elaborate or specialised equipment has had to be installed. Thus the new refinery in Kuwait's industrial area at Shuaiba, which came on-stream in November 1968, utilises a unique hydrogen process.

The most significant technological development in the Middle East during recent years has been the advance of the petro-chemical industries. Natural gas is the raw material and supplies are ample for large-scale operation.

[2] Figures are in million barrels or million metric tons according as the original data are given in volume or weight. There are approximately 7½ barrels to a metric ton but exact equivalence depends on the specific gravity of the oil.

As in practically all the technologically advanced industries there are clear economic benefits to be gained from scale, not only in capital investment costs per ton of output, but also in maintenance and other costs.

Petro-chemical plants are now operating in Iran, Kuwait, Saudi Arabia and Iraq. By mid-1972 a fifth producer is expected to come into operation when the construction of Qatar's $44 million fertiliser plant is completed. These plants consume great quantities of natural gas and whereas, only a few years ago, natural gas was a waste product to be flared away, now it is the basic material for the great industries of the Middle East.

TABLE 3

PETRO-CHEMICAL PLANTS COMPLETED OR UNDER
CONSTRUCTION, MID-1968

| Product | Productive capacity in thousand metric tons a year | | | | |
	Iran	Kuwait	Saudi Arabia	Iraq	Total
Ammonia	380	130	200	—	710
Ureas	210	180	330	—	720
Other Nitro-fertilisers	130	165	—	—	295
Sulphur	680	235	11	130	1,056
Miscellaneous	10	—	—	—	10
Total	1,410	710	541	130	2,791

Source: Baghir Mostofi, Managing Director, National Iranian Petroleum Company, in a paper read at Princeton University, October 1968.

Kuwait was the first state in the Gulf to move into the production of chemical fertilisers (previously there was only a small chemical plant at Shiraz in Iran) and it is now to be further expanded. The Kuwait Chemical Fertilizer Company's plant is located in the Shuaiba Industrial Area and is a nitrogenous fertiliser complex, utilising natural gas as its basic feedstock. Construction began in 1966 and the plant incorporated technology which at the time was among the most advanced in the world. It is concerned mainly with producing urea and ammonia sulphate for export. Two additional ammonia plants costing $60 million are now being built; one to supply ammonia for conversion into urea in Kuwait, for export; the other will be used to supply liquid ammonia for shipment to Mersin in Turkey, for further refining at a new plant constructed for 'Mediterranean Fertilizers'. Lack of trained personnel led to teething troubles when the plant went on-stream but these are now being overcome.

There appears to be no lack of the essential raw materials for the petro-chemical industry in the area and indeed so abundant is natural gas in southern Iran, that it is now being exported by pipeline to the USSR.

The most serious limitation is not lack of raw material, or difficulty in obtaining equipment from the West or from Japan, but in finding markets for the products. For their markets, the producing countries have to look eastwards where the teeming populations of Asia need fertilisers to boost their food production. Petro-chemicals are easily and cheaply transported, but a limiting factor is that of finding the necessary finance to pay for the fertilisers.

Bahrain, which has ample supplies of natural gas, has not attempted to enter the petro-chemical field but instead has made a new breakthrough with a project for large-scale aluminium smelting, a completely new industry in the Middle East. The work of constructing the smelters has now begun on behalf of a £30 million company Aluminium Bahrain (ALBA), formed for the purpose by an international consortium. A main factor in the choice of Bahrain for the project was the abundant supply of natural gas available to provide cheap fuel for the gas turbine generators. Alternative hydro-electric sites which would be conveniently situated for export are now scarce, and this has made natural gas an effective competitor with hydro-power. Other factors such as its record of political stability, its geographical situation and its traditional entrepot trading were no doubt additional factors influencing the choice of Bahrain.

In comparison with the technological advances made in the oil and chemical industries, agriculture and fisheries, the traditional mainstay of so many countries in the area, have achieved little in the way of technological advancement. Yet there are considerable possibilities for increased agricultural production in the Middle East through scientifically controlled irrigation, or overhead irrigation where applicable, or through the introduction of suitable fertilisers and insecticides, of trace elements on pastures, or of new crops and strains such as the short-stemmed varieties of wheat now being introduced elsewhere. The special problems of the arid zones, however, are being tackled in some parts of the Middle East, notably in Israel, where controlled irrigation and scientific applications of agricultural expertise are being effected. There, even sea-water is being successfully utilised for plant irrigation on open fields, though success is dependent on very carefully controlled applications quite beyond the abilities of traditional farm workers.

A recent development of considerable scientific interest is being carried out in Abu Dhabi by the University of Arizona's Environmental Research Laboratory. This is an integrated system for the production of power, water and food, designed especially for coastal desert regions. The project includes electric power generation, a de-salting plant and a controlled-environment greenhouse extending over an area of half-a-million square feet on the island of Jazirat-as-Saydiat.

Other experimental applications of new techniques are being made in scattered parts of the area, such as hydroponic cultivation in Kuwait, the harnessing of solar energy in Israel, or new methods of water distillation such as electro-dialysis. In the Gulf, the lighting authority has successfully and advantageously introduced solar batteries to light some of its buoys.

The problem of providing sufficient fresh water for domestic consumption is acute in those countries where there has been an explosive expansion in population through an influx of expatriate labour. Kuwait, which is very much in this category, has developed water distillation plants (using flash boilers which are among the largest in the world) and these distillation units are fully integrated with electricity generation and a caustic soda plant.

In the field of telecommunications, the most interesting development in the Middle East of recent date is the completion of an "Earth Station" in Bahrain which enables 24-hour contact—via communications satellites over the Indian and Pacific Oceans—to be maintained with all other earth stations in the satellite's line of sight. The Bahrain earth station is also linked with the other Gulf States by means of a tropospheric scatter system.

To sum up, it can be said that in the Middle East, the technological revolution has made rapid strides over the past ten years and indeed now some of the best equipped and most up-to-date plants in the world are to be found there. But the development is very patchy, both as regards the span of industries affected and that of the countries involved. It has been largely confined to a few industries and to a few countries. The industries are those connected with oil production and utilisation, or with transport and communications including airports, and the countries are those gifted with abundant supplies of crude oil and natural gas.

The Middle Eastern technological revolution is dependent on foreign expertise and on imported machinery and equipment. How far it can put down roots in these countries depends primarily on the rapidity with which the peoples of the countries concerned can be educated to the required standards in the new sciences and technologies, and on how far a cadre of native technicians can be built up, able and willing to become technicians and craftsmen in the oilfields, factories and other plants, working with their hands or tending the plant round-the-clock rather than confining their choice of career to office and desk jobs. No doubt in time economic forces will redress the balance when the wages of skilled or semi-skilled craftsmen rise above those for clerical and similar desk jobs, but the attainment of the required balance of occupations is a slow process. The oil companies have pioneered the way by providing technical training for skilled jobs, even sending selected craftsmen to study abroad, and a recent sign of change in attitudes has been the successful start of the Gulf Technical College in Bahrain to serve a wide region preparing students for RSA or City and Guilds examinations. General education is also of fundamental importance in a technologically-oriented society which requires a population which is both literate and numerate, but in most of the Middle Eastern countries universal education is still a goal for the future.

In one respect, however, Middle Eastern countries have an advantage over the older industrialised nations in that a late start enables them to install the most modern equipment and this puts them at an advantage *vis-a-vis* competitors in the older countries. It will be found, for example, that the soft drink factories, the breweries, cement plants, flour mills, refineries and petro-chemical plants in the Middle East are equipped with the most modern types of machinery and other plant.

In the long term, problems loom on the horizon, since oil and gas are expendable. Can they be replaced by some alternative in the area or is the Middle East to lapse back into economic stagnation and depression? These, however, are problems for the more distant future, as known reserves of crude oil and natural gas are large. Of more immediate concern is the maintenance of peace and political stability, both essential pre-requisites for any further technological developments. Granted peace and stability, there is in the meantime plenty of scope for a further rapid step forward in the technological development of new industries.

FURTHER READING

There is little literature relating to Middle East technology; useful articles occasionally appear in the following technical journals of the petroleum industry:

Petroleum Press Service, London. Monthly.
Oil and Gas Journal, Oklahoma. Weekly.
World Petroleum, New York. Monthly.
Oil and Gas International, London. Monthly.

Reference Volumes include:
Barrows, G. H. *International Petroleum Industry*, vol. 1, 'World Petroleum', New York; *International Petroleum Encyclopedia*, Petroleum Publishing Co., Oklahoma, 1970.

Kevin G. Fenelon. A Founder Fellow of the British Institute of Management, he has spent many years in the Middle East and was responsible for setting up statistical offices in Iraq, Kuwait, Bahrain and Abu Dhabi. One-time visiting Professor of Statistics and Economics at the American University of Beirut, and United Nations Expert on National Income in Jordan. Before going to the Middle East he was Assistant Secretary and Director of Statistics at the British Ministry of Food. Previously a member of the Council of the British Association for the Advancement of Science and of the Inter-Departmental Committee on Social and Economic Research. Among his many publications are *Iraq, National Income and Expenditure* (1958) and *The Trucial States. A Brief Economic Survey* (1969).

LABOUR ORGANISATION

R. L. MORRIS

INTRODUCTION

IN considering labour organisation it is convenient to extend the area covered by the Handbook to include the Arab countries of North Africa.[1] This is a vast area, for the Arab world, Turkey and Iran have a combined population of over 150 million and a space larger than China or the United States. In this area are to be found extremes of poverty and wealth, of primitive agriculture and modern industry, of tiny shaikhdoms and large nations, and a variety of social systems ranging from Marxist republicanism to traditional monarchies. One noteworthy feature is the prevalence of trade unionism, which exists everywhere except in Saudi Arabia and the Arab shaikhdoms of the southern Gulf.

Labour organisation has had a chequered history. After some false starts early in the century, it showed signs of development at the end of World War II, aided by wartime industrial expansion and by the favourable attitude of Allied occupation forces. However, in the early postwar period unions were often suppressed or controlled when Middle Eastern Governments found it necessary to move against local Communist Parties. The main expansion has taken place in the 1950s and 1960s. First, the revolutionary military régimes in Egypt, Syria and Iraq needed to mobilise popular support and established comprehensive labour movements as part of the machinery of government, although with limited success. Secondly, in the Sudan, Algeria and Aden, trade unions existing under colonial Governments were encouraged and guided by nationalist political groups seeking independence. Thirdly, even where such special factors did not apply, as in Lebanon, Kuwait and Turkey, labour has become increasingly organised in the past decade.

Although the movement has grown in size it has not been easy for unions to find an effective role in industrial relations. In the capitalist economies local employers have traditionally been hostile to any weakening of their authority while Governments have kept a close security watch to ensure that unions do not become a channel for political subversion. In socialised states the main concern has often been to ensure that the labour leadership supports the régime and to deny to political opponents the opportunity of building a power base among the workers. In such countries there may be little scope for industrial activities because labour conditions and minimum wages are

[1] The author wishes to acknowledge the help of Mr J. Skinner, British Labour Attaché at Tel Aviv, for information on Israel, and of Mr S. Cottingham, former British Labour Attaché at Teheran, for information on Turkey and Iran.

often prescribed by legislation, strike action may be forbidden, and wage levels generally may be determined by those decreed for government employment. Thus Governments of different types may tolerate, encourage or even establish a labour movement, but they all expect it to be docile. In return they accept willingly a paternalist role towards the urban worker, promulgating extensive labour legislation and setting up ministries charged with its enforcement. Furthermore, although it exists throughout the area, trade unionism affects only a small proportion of the labour force. Even if membership claims are accepted, the total can only be of the order of six million, far less than the union membership in Britain. The Middle East is still an area where economies are mainly dependent upon agriculture, where large numbers of self-employed persons are engaged in services and trade, and where family and small enterprises predominate in manufacturing.

Nevertheless, the economic importance of the sector in which labour is organised is out of all proportion to the amount of employment which it provides. In the case of the oil industry it is the main supplier of state revenue; in the case of industry, transport and commerce it is the sector of the economy which Governments are striving to expand and to modernise. Throughout this sector trade unionism is becoming accepted as essential to modern management. The lead is perhaps being taken by international oil companies disposed to follow patterns of industrial relations to which they are accustomed elsewhere in the world. But there is also a change of heart on the part of local employers who are themselves becoming more organised and more interested in the management techniques of modern industry. For their part the workers are more disposed to join unions, and to rely more on their collective bargaining strength than on the goodwill of employers and state labour legislation. The calibre of labour leadership is improving and collective contracts are more common. In the socialist states the functions of trade unions are essentially different, but there is often a need to improve the quality of management and the productivity of the worker. There is already evidence of a desire on the part of such Governments to vitalise their labour movements and to give them more real industrial responsibility.

Apart from its significance as a major factor in the efficiency of the key modern sectors of the economy, trade unionism has a role of importance to play in social development generally. There is certainly no lack of social problems in the area. In liberal states, legislative assemblies and governments are often mainly concerned with landowning, professional and merchant interests and in some cases have not shown themselves particularly responsive to workers' problems. The state may sometimes fail to implement its own labour legislation; social security may not exist or may be inadequate; public health and education services may be grossly inferior to private services; the drift from the countryside to the towns may result in bad housing conditions, extensive health problems and lack of employment opportunities. The revolutionary states have also failed to deal adequately with their social problems, despite their declared dedication to the social welfare. In fact, social problems commonly encountered in developing areas may be aggravated by the radical social policies of these states—nationalisation of industry and of commercial enterprises may result in the flight of the traditional managerial class and the entrepreneur; drastic agrarian reform may leave the rural areas without effective management and increase the drift of labour to the towns; over-expansion of traditional types of education may result in a growing pool of unemployed graduates. In the Arab world there are special social problems—economic dislocation due to the conflict with Israel; the scattering of Palestinian manpower; and the discovery of oil resources in areas far away from the main centres of population.

As they develop, trade unions may thus be expected not only to play a more effective role in industrial relations than in the past but collectively to exert a pressure in favour of social reform. In a vast area undergoing deep social transformation, with political institutions far from fully developed, with a wide variety of social systems and subject to severe internal and external pressures, it is not possible to forecast how this pressure will be exerted. Each state will adapt trade unionism and integrate it into its political structure in accordance with its own needs. What can be said is that trade unionism has grown in the Middle East and seems likely to stay and develop; that it remains a target for political groups seeking social upheaval but is increasingly dominated by moderate labour leaders seeking social reform; that governments formerly antagonistic are now encouraging its gradual development; that in many Middle Eastern areas the future trend may be away from overall state control of labour conditions, and towards better public social services and more sophisticated industrial relations; and that in some areas trade unionism may be a factor in overcoming long-standing confessional and regional divisions. Trade unionism also has a role to play internationally. In the Arab world the movement will give practical effect to the nationalist aspirations of an increasingly important sector of society and will supplement at the popular level the efforts of the Arab League to ensure co-operation between Arab States. Throughout the Middle East the organised labour movement will increasingly come into contact with the international labour field.

ARAB STATES : THE PAN-ARAB LABOUR MOVEMENT

At the centre of pan-Arab labour developments is the International Confederation of Arab Trade Unions (ICATU), formed in Damascus in 1956. It now has important labour affiliates in all Arab countries where trade unionism exists, except Libya and Tunisia, and claims a total membership of four million workers. The affiliated unions meet in congress every three years, and policy is carried out by a secretariat and by an executive council which meets as required. Additional pan-Arab labour organisations have been established for workers in the Arab oil industry, in transport and in agriculture. These are not mere industrial departments of ICATU, but independent trade union internationals, although there is naturally co-operation between them. At the professional level, there are separate pan-Arab associations for doctors, lawyers, teachers, engineers and other professional categories. All pan-Arab labour organisations are based in Cairo.

For many years the effectiveness of ICATU was impaired by political differences between Arab states, especially between Egypt and Iraq under General Qasim, and between Egypt and the Ba'athist régime in Syria. However, the war with Israel in 1967 has resulted in a reorganisation of the Confederation. Pan-Arab labour organisations have long provided technical services, including training facilities, for their affiliates and these are being strengthened. At the present juncture, however, the significance of pan-Arab labour organisations lies more in the political field than in industrial relations, for the events of 1967 have had a profound effect. The current policy of the Confederation is indeed centred on the mobilisation of Arab labour in support of the Palestinian cause. Included among its affiliates is the Palestine Workers' Federation, an organisation in exile which seeks to carry on the traditions of the Arab labour federation which existed in Palestine under the Mandate.

On the international plane the policy of the Confederation in the '50s was neutralist, in the sense that it disapproved of Arab labour links with either the West or the East. In recent years, however, its policy has changed to hostility towards the Brussels-based International Confederation of Free Trade Unions (to which many labour organisations in Western Europe are affiliated) because that body numbers amongst its affiliates the *Histadrut* of Israel. On the other hand, the Arab labour federations of Iraq and Syria are now formally affiliated to the Prague-based World Federation of Trade Unions and the present policy of ICATU is to co-operate with the World Federation on matters of common interest. In addition, since the 1967 war the national labour centres in Eastern Europe have entered into direct contact with many Arab labour organisations and are providing training facilities for Arab labour leaders.

UAR   ARAB STATES : NATIONAL LABOUR MOVEMENTS

Under the Egyptian monarchy, despite lack of official encouragement, trade unionism grew with industrialisation. In 1911 there were seven unions with 7,000 members; by 1952 there were 470 unions with 115,000 members. The pace increased after the revolution and, in 1964, 1·5 million members were reported grouped into 27 large unions. These central unions are organised on an industrial basis with area branches and numerous local committees. The central unions themselves are affiliated to a General Federation of Labour. Despite this high degree of organisation, the scope for industrial trade union action is somewhat limited because of the nationalisation of large sectors of industry and commerce. The Government itself controls conditions of work by extensive legislation and also influences the cost of living and wages through consumer subsidies, price controls, national minimum wages and wage rates in state employment. Many problems in the field of industrial relations are not yet finally solved— questions of productivity and of wage and income policy; worker participation in profits and in industrial management; the adjustment of education and training to manpower requirements; and the general role of organised labour in the civilian institutions of the socialist state.

Sudan

The Sudanese trade union movement is strong but fragmented, comprising ten federations and about 400 unions. It is virtually confined to the six northern provinces and is concentrated in the Khartoum area, although important unions exist in other key areas such as Port Sudan and Atbara. The public sector of the economy is important in Sudan and unionism is accordingly strong in government departments and public utilities. The movement has a tradition of industrial action for political purposes, dating from the days of British rule, and it was temporarily suppressed by the military régime which held power from 1958 to 1964. Communist influence was originally predominant and is still important, but many unions have links with the traditional political parties or pursue an independent line. It is not clear how their development will be affected by the change of régime in 1969.

Lebanon

The Lebanese labour movement has steadily increased in strength during the postwar period and now comprises over 100 unions with about 50,000 members. The movement is concentrated in Beirut but Tripoli and Sidon are also important centres. The strongest unions are in commerce, transport, public utilities, the oil industry, manufacturing and building. The movement has become increasingly independent of government control, but attempts to unify the movement or to reorganise it on an industrial basis have so far been unsuccessful. For its size, the movement is highly fragmented. No fewer than nine labour federations are recognised by the government as well as a confederation (which groups only four federations). This fragmentation reflects the complexity of the Lebanese social situation, with its regional and confessional differences and with competing internal and external political pressures.

Syria
The industrialisation of Syria under the French Mandate and the breaking down of traditional labour divisions based on race and religion were reflected in a growing trade union movement. In 1946 there were 50 unions with 18,000 members. In the turbulent post-independence period the unions often came into conflict with the government. From 1954 the Ba'athists controlled the movement, until 1960 when they were replaced by unionists. The movement was finally brought under Ba'athist control in 1964. Since then, the labour movement has been involved in the internal struggles between factions of the Ba'ath party, and there have been frequent changes in the leadership. The General Federation of Labour has branches in all governorates and is closely linked to the ruling party. It is formed by about 30 central (industrial) unions, with area and local committees.

Iraq
Iraqi trade unionism, which developed rapidly after the 1958 revolution, has also been a battleground for competing political groups. Initially the Communists were in control, but by 1961 they had been ousted by pro-Government leaders. These in turn were removed in early 1963 after the death of General Qasim. The Ba'athists then controlled the movement until the *coup* of November 1963 when the unions were temporarily suppressed. From 1964 to 1968 the influence of the Arab nationalist movement was strong and the leadership was sometimes in conflict with the Aref régime. With the return of the Ba'athists to power in 1968 the movement has again been reorganised.

Jordan
Refugees provided much of the labour for the industries which developed in Jordan in the '50s. Some had been trade unionists in Palestine and it was they who established the first unions. By 1957 there were 97 unions with 12,000 members. At that time the movement suffered a setback. Some of the leaders became involved in the political disturbances of that period and the unions were put under surveillance. Later the Government attitude became more relaxed and by 1967 there were 35 unions with about 16,000 members. Although concentrated in Amman, the movement spread to other towns and was developing in East Jerusalem and the West Bank area before the Israeli occupation.

Saudi Arabia
The monarchical Government of Saudi Arabia has not so far permitted trade unions, but has adopted wide-ranging paternalist labour and social policies.

Other states

In Qatar joint consultative committees exist in the oil industry. Although they have no legal basis, they are recognised by the companies and the government for purposes of industrial relations. No labour organisations exist in the Trucial States or in the Sultanate of Oman. A strong labour organisation has evolved in Kuwait, comprising workers in the oil industry and government service. At present, membership is restricted to Kuwaiti nationals.

The British colonial authorities encouraged trade unionism in Aden and a number of unions were formed. The movement later became involved in nationalist activities and was first dominated by the FLOSY group, later by the National Liberation Front. It was reorganised by the Government of South Yemen after independence. In (North) Yemen a trade union movement emerged after the establishment of the Republic. It too has become involved in the internal political struggle and has been in conflict with the republican Government.

TURKEY, IRAN AND ISRAEL

Unions appeared briefly in Turkey in 1909 and were not permitted again until 1947. Even then membership was restricted to manual workers and there were restrictions on strike action. However, a labour confederation (*Turk-Is*) was formed in 1952 and unions were allowed to federate industrially and regionally. By 1960 there were 432 unions with 283,000 members. After that date the attitude of the Government became more favourable, the 1961 Constitution and 1963 Trade Union Law providing both for freedom of association and the right to strike. By 1968 *Turk-Is* claimed a membership of 800,000.

The Turkish Government is aiming at an industrial democracy, consults *Turk-Is* on labour matters and is encouraging collective bargaining in the extensive public sector of the economy. Amongst employers the former hostility towards unionism is giving way to a more modern approach to industrial relations. Moreover, the worker is clearly looking more to the unions to protect his interests, especially in regard to job security and provision for old-age. In the political sphere, confederation policy is to avoid party affiliations, although some opposition groups seek union support.

Although the 1907 Constitution allowed freedom of association, Iran has no long tradition of trade unions for they were not permitted by Reza Shah. Some were formed under allied occupation towards the end of the war, but these were taken over by the communist Tudeh Party and suppressed in 1949. A labour law passed in 1960 provided for trade unions under certain conditions and from 1965 the Government encouraged their formation. By 1968 some 300 had been approved and registered, together with a central union. Total membership is about 100,000, and about half the workers in the oil fields are members. The Iranian Government, whilst determined to maintain its authority, wants social progress to accompany material prosperity and accepts that trade unionism is important in the context of modern industrial development. Trade unionism may, therefore, be expected to develop and to gain experience under government guidance.

Organised labour in Israel is completely dominated by the General Federation of Labour (*Histadrut*). This has 90% of the working population in membership and, since its foundation in 1920, has followed a far wider range of interests and activities than most other trade union organisations.

Despite its title, the *Histadrut* is not a federation of trade unions, for members join the central organisation directly and then an appropriate national union or collective or co-operative agricultural settlement. It is a voluntary, democratic organisation, whose elections are conducted on a basis of proportional representation, voting being for lists of candidates prepared by the various political parties. It is affiliated to the International Confederation of Free Trade Unions, takes an active interest in international labour affairs, and provides training for overseas students at its Afro-Asian Institute for Co-operation and Labour Studies in Tel Aviv.

The national activities of *Histadrut* include the administration of a workers' sick fund (which provides a comprehensive medical and hospital service for 70% of the population) and pension funds; vocational training and educational work amongst adults and young people; the management of enterprises in manufacturing industry and construction; the organisation of collective farm settlements and a network of producer, consumer and transport co-operatives; building societies; the largest insurance company in Israel and the second largest bank. Thus, apart from its trade union activities, it employs 25% of the working population, and contributes 25% to the GNP. The only other labour organisation of any significance is the National Federation of Labour sponsored by the right wing (*Herut*) party. It has about 80,000 members and runs a health insurance fund which caters for 214,000 persons.

FURTHER READING

US Department of Labour Reports on Labour Law and Practice in the Middle East, US Government Printing Office, Washington:

Labor Law & Practice in the UAR (Egypt), BLS Report No. 275, 1965.
Labor Law & Practice in Lebanon, BLS Report No. 304, 1966.
Labor Law & Practice in Saudi Arabia, BLS Report No. 269, 1964.
Labor Law & Practice in Turkey, BLS Report No. 239, 1963.
Labor Law & Practice in Iran, BLS Report No. 276, 1964.
Labor Law & Practice in Iraq, BLS Report No. 221, 1962.

Beling, W. A. *Pan-Arabism and Labor*, Harvard Univ. Press, Cambridge, Mass, 1960.
Fawzi, S. E. D. *The Labour Movement in the Sudan, 1946–1955*, Oxford Univ. Press, London, 1957.
Meynaud, J. and Salah-Bey, A. (ed.) *Trade Unionism in Africa*, Methuen, London, 1967; Barnes & Noble, New York, 1967.
Sufrin, Sidney C. *Unions in Emerging Societies, Frustration and Politics*, Syracuse Univ. Press, New York, 1964.

R. L. MORRIS. Labour Attaché based in Beirut since 1965, advises British diplomatic missions in Arab countries on social industrial and labour developments. Labour Attaché in Brazil on secondment to the Foreign Office 1958–64. Assistant Controller at the Wales Office of the Ministry of Labour 1957–8. District Officer for North and Mid-Wales 1951–7.

THE PLACE OF THE MIDDLE EAST IN WORLD TRADE

ELIZABETH COLLARD

DESPITE the political and military instability of the Middle East during the past decade, and particularly between 1964 and 1968 (the latest year for which complete trading figures are available), the astonishing feature of the place of the Middle East in the world trading pattern is its stability.

According to the International Monetary Fund, the value of world imports had reached $248,700 million in 1968 and the value of total world exports $238,000 million[1] as a result of the substantial and uninterrupted world trade expansion during the 1960s, averaging nearly 8·5% *per annum*. The trade of the Middle East countries kept up with the expansion of world trade. Imports to the Middle East as a percentage of world imports varied only very slightly during the 1964–8 period, fluctuating between 2·9% and 3·2%, while exports from the area as a percentage of world exports varied even less, fluctuating between 4·1% and 4·3% (see Tables 1 and 2).

Over a longer time span the position is much the same. Table 3 shows that exports from the area in 1938 constituted 2·7% of world trade. By 1948, however, and reflecting the growth of oil production and revenues, the Middle East's share of world exports had climbed to 3·8%. By 1955 it was 4·2% and had reached 4·3% by 1959, after which the regular pattern referred to in the previous paragraph was achieved. Table 4 shows that total imports to the Middle East, which were 3·1% of the world total in 1938, grew to 3·8% by 1948 and settled down to 3·4% by 1959, dropping slightly in later years. The primary reason for the gradual drop over the years is that there is a limit to the capacity of developing countries to absorb imports of both consumer and capital goods. The extra revenues have been invested abroad, partly in neighbouring countries.

In contrast, therefore, to the developing countries as a group, whose share in world trade has been dropping, the Middle East, itself an area composed entirely of developing countries, not only kept pace with the rest of the world in its share of overall world trade but outstripped the rest of the developing world. The share of all developing countries in world exports (excluding the communist countries) was 30% in 1948, but over the years it has declined to 27% in 1953, 22% in 1960, 21% in 1967 and 20% in 1968.

The Middle East has always been one of the most important centres of international trade, being at the cross-roads between East and West. Further-

---

[1] Import figures are higher than export figures as they include the cost of freight and insurance.

more, some of the world's most advanced trading communities have flourished in the area from time immemorial. Then came Britain's interest in an area which lay across her path to India and her eastern empire, and with the building of the Suez Canal this route became even more important, from a strategic as well as a commercial standpoint. Finally, in the 20th century, the rapid increase in oil production from the Middle East has been the underlying factor in maintaining the area's importance.

The reason for the apparently healthy trading position of the Middle East area is to be found in the extraordinary variety of countries that come under this generic title and above all in the oil wealth of a number of them. Table I shows the value of petroleum exports from these countries, which in 1968 amounted to over $6,500 million (including the Gulf States) out of total exports from the area of $9,980 million. In addition, Turkey, Israel and Jordan have all benefited from substantial amounts of foreign aid, largely for budgetary purposes, which have artificially inflated the purchasing power of these countries. Overseas credits and aid for large-scale projects such as the Aswan High Dam or the Isphahan steel mill in Iran also involve the supply of large quantities of equipment and capital goods from the West, from Japan and from Eastern Europe.

At the same time the rising standard of living, particularly in the oil-producing countries, has also led to a regularly rising demand for consumer goods, and although the rising curve is flattening out, there is no sign of the demand for consumer goods dropping. Indeed the demand is only held down by the lack of foreign exchange in some countries and by the financial stringencies caused by the June War of 1967.

The one overriding factor that links all these countries in the Middle East is that not one is master of its own destiny where world trade is concerned.

The petroleum exporting countries—Kuwait, Saudi Arabia, Iraq, Iran, Abu Dhabi, Bahrain, Qatar and now Oman and Dubai—have at present no control over the world price of crude oil or refined products and they are all engaged directly or through membership of the Organisation of Petroleum Exporting Countries (OPEC), or of the Organisation of Arab Petroleum Exporting Countries (OAPEC), in negotiating with the international oil companies for higher revenues for the oil extracted from their soil. With minor exceptions, where national oil companies are starting to market part of the oil production of the area, the oil is the property of the oil companies who market it. However, in Table 1, Total Exports of Middle East Countries, and Table 5, Middle East Imports and Exports to the Major Industrialised Countries, petroleum exports are included, as otherwise a false picture of the trading position of the countries concerned would be given. The actual *revenue* and *foreign exchange earnings* of the oil-producing countries is considerably less than the foreign exchange value of the export of crude oil from these countries, the larger part of which accrues to the oil companies. This is another reason why the value of total imports of Middle East countries is consistently less than the value of exports (see Tables 1 and 2) despite the considerable flow of aid and credits to these countries. Furthermore, Table 1 shows the complete dependence of the oil-producing countries on their oil exports. Two oil-producing countries, Iran and Iraq, are pressing ahead with industrialisation, producing mainly for their own home market at present.

The non-oil-producing countries of the area have suffered, as have all the developing countries, from the fact that the unit value of primary products

466

has risen much more slowly than the unit value of manufactured products. The World Bank estimates that the unit value (1960—100) of primary products rose to 102 in 1968, while the unit value of manufactured goods rose to 109 over the same period. The terms of trade for those Middle East countries which are dependent on one or two crops have generally been unfavourable (see Table 1) and the comparatively favourable picture for the Middle East as a whole is coloured by the rapid expansion of petroleum exports. Despite the depressed level of crude oil prices where the producing countries are concerned, the sheer volume of crude oil exports has been instrumental in keeping the proportion of Middle East trade in relation to world trade at a stable level.

Turning now to the other countries of the area, the United Arab Republic (UAR) is in fact an oil-producing country (despite the loss of the production of the Sinai oilfields which are now being exploited by Israel) but has not yet reached the stage of being a net exporter of oil. Her major exports are cotton and rice, which account for between half and two-thirds of her export earnings. Both crops are subject to blight and other pests and suffer from inadequate water supplies, but with the completion of the Aswan High Dam, the supply of water for irrigation purposes should be more reliable in the future. In spite of the 1967 War, Egypt too is pressing ahead with industrialisation and an increasing variety of goods is available for export, including textiles, cement, fruit and vegetables and also (mainly to Eastern Europe) light machinery and household goods. However, a glance at Tables 1 and 2 shows Egypt's grave trade imbalance over recent years. Egypt has received a considerable amount of aid from East and West, but not sufficient to cover the gap.

Over the years Syria has habitually imported a great deal more than she exports, although there are certain invisible items on the credit side of her balance of payments, including royalties for oil passing through pipelines over her territories. Nevertheless, Syria exports substantial quantities of agricultural products, including cotton, wool, wheat and barley and, were the years ahead to be more peaceful externally and internally, she would be capable of reducing the trade imbalance shown in the Tables.

Sudan's trade position has improved considerably over the past five years. To offset a heavy bill for imports, her main export is cotton, and cotton exports increased from a value of $92 million in 1964 to $147 million in 1968. At the same time a variety of measures has been taken to limit imports and there is now a reduced deficit and hope of a possible surplus in the current year.

The Lebanese economy is unique, and the enormous unfavourable trade balance, which has hovered around $400 million annually over the past five years, is covered by remittances from the large Lebanese communities abroad and from considerable invisible earnings from banking, insurance, tourism and other services.

The countries covered by the general heading 'Other' in Tables 1 and 2 are Yemen, Bahrain, Qatar, Oman and the Trucial States. Commercially, Abu Dhabi is the most important, with oil revenues reaching nearly £100 million in 1969. Bahrain has been exporting oil since 1934, her oil revenues gradually increasing to over £9 million annually. The regular income has been more than adequate to turn the country into a prosperous welfare state for her 200,000 inhabitants. Qatar has been exporting oil since 1949, Oman started exporting oil in 1967, and the smaller states are all hoping to become oil producers during the coming decade.

While Yemen is likely to develop into an important country in world trade in the coming years, she has not yet recovered sufficiently from the civil war to start effectively on the long overdue development of the country which will lead her to become a factor of importance in international trade. Southern Yemen is still suffering from the lop-sided nature of her economy, conditioned by her long period as Britain's main base and staging point in the Middle East from 1839–1967. While her main import is crude oil and her main export refined products, Southern Yemen remains dependent on imports for all manufactured goods and most primary products. There is some local production of cotton, vegetables and salt.

Iran stands in a category of her own. A vast country of nearly 30 million inhabitants, with a rich potential still largely unexploited, she is also one of the world's major oil-producing countries and in 1969 became the Middle East's main oil exporter, followed by Saudi Arabia and Kuwait. By contrast with these countries, however, Iran has embarked on a series of development plans and a wide variety of industries have been started. At present these industries cater largely for the expanding home market, but Iran has started to export a growing range of manufactured or made-up articles to neighbouring countries.

Three countries remain, each in a sense a 'client' state of the West—Israel, Turkey and Jordan.

Israel, with a population estimated at the beginning of 1969 to be 2·8 million (excluding the occupied Arab territories), exported goods to the value of $640 million in 1968. This total included $229 million worth of polished diamonds which had originally been imported from South Africa for polishing, so that the real figure of Israeli grown or manufactured exports is in the region of $420 million. Citrus fruit provides the other main item of Israel's exports, which include other agricultural and food products, textiles and clothing, chemicals and some industrial products. The peculiar characteristic of Israel's foreign trade is that since her creation in 1948 Israel has had a trade deficit every year, ranging between $214 and $82 *per caput*. This deficit is consistently made up by remittances from Jewish sympathisers, mainly in the United States, by German reparation payments and other grants in aid and credits, also mainly from the United States, as well as from other western countries. In 1959 the trade deficit was $251 million, in 1966 it was $354 million, in 1967 $208 million and in 1968 reached a peak of $430 million.

Jordan is a client state in another sense. After achieving political independence in 1948 she relied mainly on British subsidies for budgetary support until 1956 and the Suez crisis, after which the United States took over budgetary support, which was still running at the rate of $32 million in 1967. After the June War, when Kuwait, Saudi Arabia and Libya agreed to contribute the equivalent of £30 million annually to support Jordan until Israel evacuated her occupied territories, the United States decided to withdraw her own support of Jordan. The simple reason for the continued outside support of Jordan was that it was not possible for the country to be economically viable within the frontiers with which it found itself saddled in the aftermath of the Arab-Israeli fighting of 1948. The United Kingdom, largely responsible for this state of affairs (as a result of the Balfour Declaration and the unilateral relinquishment of the mandate in 1948), immediately undertook to provide sufficient support to ensure Jordanian independence. The main source of Jordanian income over the years, apart from overseas subsidies, has been the export of agricultural produce; this has been reduced to negligible proportions since the West Bank was occupied by Israel in 1967. The export of phosphates has been growing in recent years.

Turkey, as a member of NATO, and of the former Baghdad Pact, later transformed into CENTO, has always been supported by the West. Tables 1 and 2 show how over the years Turkey's trade deficit never fell below $100 million and in 1968 had grown to $274 million.

According to the 1969 Review of the Organisation for Economic Co-operation and Development (OECD) the flow of aid from official sources from OECD member countries, the leading industrial countries of the world, to Israel, Jordan and to Turkey was as follows:

($ million)	1965	1966	1967	1968	Average 1966–8 Official Aid Per caput $	As a % of imports
Israel	5·3	65·8	127·1	152·7	30·7	6·7
Jordan	43·3	50·6	73·1	68·9	25·9	30·8
Turkey	216·3	199·9	197·3	185·2	6·2	25·6

In addition, Israel received $277 million in 1968 from Jewish sympathisers overseas and from German reparations and receives similar amounts annually.

Other Middle East countries have received aid from OECD countries but in relation to their economies on a very much lower scale. Aid to the UAR, for example, was 5·4% of her imports between 1966–8 or at the rate of $1·4 *per caput* annually.

The major trading partners with the Middle East countries are the United Kingdom, the United States, France, West Germany, Italy, Japan and the Soviet Union. Table 5 sets out the imports and exports from the countries under discussion. The United Kingdom, Italy and Japan are the main importers, followed by France and West Germany, but the United States, while being the major exporter to the area, imports considerably less than half the value of her exports. Japan has become the major trading partner over the years, the most spectacular jump in her trade with the Middle East occurring between 1959 and 1965. The United Kingdom has substantially increased her exports to the Middle East over the past five years and despite the closure of the Suez Canal is still importing consider-able quantities of oil, more than any other Western country. Japan has, however, become the leading importer of Middle East crude.

The figures in brackets in Table 5 give the total imports and exports of the countries trading with the Middle East, and despite the volume of oil exports from the Middle East and the substantial imports of manufactured goods, the proportion of Middle East trade with her main trading partners is rather small. Again the only country with a substantial benefit to her overall balance of payments is the United States—without her Middle East trade the United States would have had an unfavourable trade balance in 1968, as she had in previous years.

Finally, it is worth noting a few special features in the overall trade picture. Israel stands completely isolated from her Arab neighbours who conduct a trade boycott against her as part of their campaign for the return of their occupied lands. Turkey really belongs to Europe as far as trade is concerned and has been accepted into 'transitional' membership with the European Economic Community (EEC), and is a member of NATO. As a member of CENTO and Regional Co-operation for Development (RCD), Turkey is linked more closely with Iran, also a member of CENTO and RCD. The Arab countries are developing their own close inter-Arab trading relation-ships through the Arab Common Market programme and a wide variety of economic arrangements through the Arab League and other inter-Arab organisations.

Thirty per cent of Israel's exports of manufactured goods go to the EEC members and a three-year trade agreement was concluded between Israel and the EEC which has been renewed as a preferential agreement, involving EEC tariff cuts of about 45%. There have been recent negotiations with the UAR and Lebanon for a preferential agreement.

It is difficult to generalise about the future prospects of the area as a whole, in view of the great variety of the countries that it embraces and of the present political uncertainties. However it seems reasonable to predict that this group of countries will be able to maintain its position in terms of world trade, and—if conditions of political stability can be restored—to make substantial headway.

TABLE 1

TOTAL EXPORTS BY MIDDLE EAST COUNTRIES 1964–8
($ millions)

($ million)	*1964*	*1965*	*1966*	*1967*	*1968*
Iran	1,254	1,303	1,309	1,930	1,879
of which:					
Petroleum	1,128	1,154	1,165	1,776	1,713
Iraq	840	882	939	828	1,043
of which:					
Petroleum	783	816	853	755	958
Israel	372	430	503	555	640
of which:					
Citrus Fruit	62	77	76	89	88·4
Diamonds	118	132	162	156	194·1
Jordan	24	28	29	32	40
of which:					
Phosphates	7	7	9	10	17
Tomatoes	3	2	5	5	6
Kuwait	1,218	1,243	1,304	1,313	1,397
of which:					
Petroleum	1,123	1,176	1,212	1,195	1,342
Lebanon	68	86	103	119	164·6
Saudi Arabia	1,180	1,400	1,650	1,786	1,945
of which:					
Petroleum	1,157	1,335	1,573	1,693	1,905
Southern Yemen	208	187	190	137	110
Sudan	197	195	203	214	232
of which:					
Cotton	92	90	100	114	147
Gum Hashab	19	21	18	24	25
Groundnuts	26	25	21	16	16

TABLE 1—*continued*

($ million)	1964	1965	1966	1967	1968
Syria	176	169	173	155	168
of which:					
Cotton	81	67	82	61	60
Wool	8	6	7	5	4
Wheat	11	2	1	—	0·2
Barley	10	12	0·9	2	49
Turkey	411	464	490	523	496
of which:					
Tobacco	90	88	107	118	93
Cotton	88	98	128	130	136
Chrome	7	8	10	7	10
Hazelnuts	50	57	53	84	76
Raisins	17	21	22	23	23
UAR	539	605	605	566	622
of which:					
Cotton	269	338	331	281	277
Rice	70	46	49	69	103
Other	670	740	880	1,000	1,230
Total Middle East	7,157	7,732	8,378	9,158	9,980
World Total	173,466	186,025	203,138	213,417	238,202
Middle East % of World	4·1	4·2	4·1	4·3	4·2

Source: International Monetary Fund

TABLE 2

TOTAL IMPORTS BY MIDDLE EAST COUNTRIES 1964-8
($ millions)

	1964	1965	1966	1967	1968
Iran	673	860	930	1,126	1,386
Iraq	413	451	493	423	404
Israel	838	832	835	769	1,081
Jordan	150	157	191	154	161
Kuwait	322	377	463	593	611
Lebanon	431	485	533	463	602
Saudi Arabia[1]	394	376	457	502	492
S. Yemen	297	301	285	200	203
Sudan	274	208	222	233	258
Syria	235	215	289	264	331
Turkey	542	577	725	691	770
UAR	934	953	916	754	700
Other	330	360	410	450	460
Total	5,833	6,152	6,749	6,603	7,396
World Total	181,735	195,708	213,928	223,832	248,737
M.E. % of World	3·2	3·1	3·2	2·9	3·0

Source: International Monetary Fund—International Financial Statistics.

[1] The figures given for 1965-8 are for the Hijri years 1964-5, 1965-6, 1966-7 and 1967-8.

471

TABLE 3

TOTAL EXPORTS FROM THE MIDDLE EAST 1938, 1948, 1955 and 1959
($ millions)

($ millions)	1938	1948	1955	1959
Iran	104·8[1]	250·9	168·8	754·5
Iraq	17·9	34·9	506·6	606·0
Israel	27·9[2]	6·2[3]	88·2	176·4
Jordan	2·8	12·4	8·0	10·0
Kuwait[4]	n.a.[8]	n.a.	n.a.	n.a.
Lebanon	—[5]	—[5]	33·3	40·0
Saudi Arabia	n.a.[6]	n.a.[6]	558·8	782·0
Southern Yemen[7]	15·7	52·3	176·5	178·0
Sudan	29·5	98·7	147·3	192·0
Syria	22·2	35·8	128·3	117·0
Turkey	115·1	196·8	313·3	355·0
UAR	147·1	591·4	397·4	461·0
Other	161·0	900·6	1,363·5	1,277·1
Total Middle East	644·0	2,180·0	3,890·0	4,949·0
Total World	23,500	57,300	93,100	115,200
Middle East % of World	2·7	3·8	4·2	4·3

[1] Nine months only
[2] This figure for Palestine
[3] Six months only
[4] Included under 'other'
[5] See Syria. Syria/Lebanon Customs Union
[6] Included under 'Other'
[7] Aden
[8] n.a. Suitable data not available

TABLE 4

TOTAL IMPORTS TO THE MIDDLE EAST 1938, 1948, 1955 and 1959
($ millions)

	1938	1948	1955	1959
Iran	69·9[1]	167·0	309·7	647·9
Iraq	45·7	183·5	272·2	326·0
Israel	55·9[2]	108·2[3]	325·6	427·0
Jordan	6·4	46·5	75·8	113·0
Kuwait[4]	n.a.	n.a.	n.a.	n.a.
Lebanon	—[5]	—[5]	217·6	255·9
Saudi Arabia	n.a.[6]	n.a.[6]	200·2	255·9
Southern Yemen[7]	29·9	110·1	207·1	205·0
Sudan	31·6	91·6	140·1	164·0
Syria	36·7	213·4	179·2	192·0
Turkey	118·8	275·0	497·6	470·0
UAR	184·0	662·5	525·2	638·2
Other	218·1	575·2	422·7	338·2
Total Middle East	797·0	2,431·0	3,373·0	4,136·0
Total World	25,400	63,400	97,900	120,700
Middle East % of World	3·1	3·8	3·4	3·4

[1] Nine months only
[2] This figure for Palestine
[3] Six months only
[4] Included under 'Other'
[5] See Syria. Syria/Lebanon Customs Union
[6] Included under 'Other'
[7] Aden

TABLE 5

MIDDLE EAST TRADE

Imports from and Exports to the Major Industrialised Countries¹
($ millions)

	1959		1965		1966		1967		1968	
	Imports	Exports	Imports	Exports	Imports	Exports	Imports	Exports	Imports	Exports
UK	554·4 (11,070)	924·6 (9,619)	727·4 (16,103)	1,196·2 (13,722)	801·9 (16,651)	975·5 (14,676)	643·4 (17,694)	941·3 (14,379)	923·0 (18,959)	1,242·2 (15,346)
USA	677·0 (14,987)	419·0 (17,383)	1,064·1 (23,186)	482·2 (27,530)	1,172·4 (27,745)	481·7 (30,430)	1,202·8 (28,745)	495·4 (31,622)	1,337·6 (35,546)	494·4 (34,660)
France	157·0 (5,081)	721·0 (5,608)	278·1 (10,343)	661·8 (10,053)	303·4 (11,843)	651·1 (10,890)	332·7 (12,381)	748·9 (11,381)	468·3 (13,939)	832·9 (12,682)
W Germany	537·9 (8,956)	513·5 (10,296)	649·2 (17,482)	673·6 (17,901)	758·3 (18,036)	707·2 (20,145)	769·9 (17,365)	808·5 (21,748)	899·4 (20,235)	926·7 (24,853)
Italy	166·5 (3,376)	472·1 (2,911)	320·9 (7,378)	890·3 (7,200)	364·8 (8,589)	957·8 (8,038)	367·9 (9,827)	1,049·3 (8,685)	435·1 (10,253)	1,034·9 (10,183)
Japan	157·5 (3,611)	378·9 (3,445)	321·9 (8,170)	1,107·9 (8,452)	389·8 (9,524)	1,249·9 (9,777)	366·2 (11,664)	1,539·5 (10,442)	496·5 (12,988)	1,827·9 (12,973)
USSR²	158·5 (5,022)	153·8 (5,387)	313·6 (7,977)	236·2 (8,093)	351·2 (7,833)	222·2 (8,753)	477·9 (8,451)	237·3 (9,552)	463·4 (9,316)	280·0 (10,528)
Netherlands	115·9 (4,144)	293·1 (3,784)	146·8 (7,460)	333·4 (6,392)	159·8 (8,016)	410·8 (6,751)	168·8 (8,336)	452·6 (7,286)	182·5 (9,291)	533·6 (8,341)
Belgium/Lux	87·7 (3,442)	167·2 (3,295)	127·5 (6,502)	244·7 (6,394)	143·1 (7,182)	254·3 (6,832)	124·2 (7,176)	160·2 (7,032)	156·9 (8,333)	375·2 (8,164)
Switzerland	66·4 (1,889)	27·4 (1,768)	121·1 (3,697)	42·4 (2,960)	138·8 (3,944)	49·0 (3,275)	143·0 (4,129)	57·7 (3,498)	163·6 (4,513)	67·2 (3,968)
Sweden	50·5 (2,418)	79·9 (2,205)	62·2 (4,377)	94·1 (3,971)	79·7 (4,582)	88·3 (4,266)	75·4 (4,701)	126·1 (4,528)	87·6 (5,182)	175·7 (4,937)
Top 7 countries total Middle East trade	2,409	3,585	3,674	5,247	4,141	5,244	4,159	5,817	5,023	6,635
Total Middle East trade			6,152	7,732	6,749	8,378	6,603	9,158	7,396	9,980
Top 7 countries % of Middle East trade	59·7%		59·7%	67·9%	61·4%	62·6%	62·9%	63·5%	67·8%	66·5%

¹ The figures in brackets are the total imports and exports of the named countries.
² The USSR figures do not include The Gulf States and Yemen.

FURTHER READING

Holden, David. *Farewell to Arabia*, Faber & Faber, London, 1966.
Musrey, Alfred G. *An Arab Common Market: a Study in Inter-Arab Trade Relations 1920–1967*, Praeger, New York, 1969.
UN Statistical Yearbook Series 1956–1968.

ELIZABETH COLLARD. Founder of Middle East Economic Digest, has also built up an economic consultancy service dealing with the Middle East. A graduate of the London School of Economics, she has travelled widely as a journalist and economist in the Middle East. Among her publications are *World Labour Comes of Age* (1946).

FOREIGN INVESTMENT AND FOREIGN AID

ROBERT E. MABRO

I

For a very long period stretching from the mid-19th century to the present time, the political and economic history of the Middle East has been intimately related to the intricate but fascinating history of foreign investment, indebtedness and aid. (To argue that foreign finance tended to play an important role does not mean that we should single out this factor as the unique or most crucial determinant of the complex of events that constitutes Middle Eastern history. Our point, precisely, is that this history is complex.) The threads are so closely interwoven that no economic study of foreign capital could avoid discussing the broader social and political issues that a long century of colonisation, struggles for independence, wars and crises inevitably does raise.

In the Middle East, foreign capital has been associated with a series of dramatic events. Let us recall the British occupation of Egypt in 1882 for which the Khedive's indebtedness offered such a convenient pretext; the nationalisation of Anglo-Iranian oil by Dr Mossadeq; the US refusal to finance the Aswan High Dam, a decision that induced a chain of reactions culminating in the Suez War of 1956. Here again, the protection of foreign investment was invoked among many other objectives to legitimise the expedition. In many instances, foreign capital was not the direct cause of political events but played a significant, albeit indirect, role as a pretext for intervention and a symbol of colonial oppression.

The history of foreign finance is one of frustration, misunderstandings and hostility. It is a history of judicial anomalies (e.g. the Capitulations), diplomatic pressures, long and protracted negotiations, one of conflicts between the powers and Middle Eastern Governments and between rival foreign interests operating in the area. The history, however, has its positive aspects too. It is illustrated by some impressive achievements : the digging and successful operation of an international waterway (Suez), the building of roads, harbours and railways in the Ottoman Empire, the discovery and production of oil. Foreign investment brought riches to desert countries (Kuwait, Saudi Arabia, other Principalities of the Gulf, Libya) and to old agricultural economies (Iraq and Iran). In the 1950s and 1960s foreign aid permitted ambitious planning in Egypt and Turkey and helped to establish Israel as a capital-intensive export-orientated economy.

To appraise the role of foreign capital in the Middle East is an extremely difficult task : we have seen that the issues raised are complex, that strong emotions have sometimes been aroused, that the achievements as well as the failures are far reaching in their consequences. But the most serious difficulty arises from the multiplicity and the sometimes conflicting nature of the criteria involved in such an appraisal. What should we value most? Economic development or political independence? Social stability or revolutionary changes? International property or a country's right to control its economic assets? Peace at any price or the struggle for some ideals or some values? Alliance with a great power or neutrality in the 'Game of Nations'? No two observers would ever agree on the weight to be given to these various objectives. The personal bias is unavoidable.

The difficulty of weighing these many criteria—one could expand the list at will—is not a purely academic problem. The ambiguity that characterises the intellectual issue has its counterpart in the ambivalence of attitudes. Most countries, whether developed or underdeveloped, have ambivalent reactions towards foreign investment—witness Servan-Schreiber and his *American Challenge*. And the same could be said about donors' attitudes in the case of foreign aid.

It is important, from the outset, to recognise that we are venturing in a field where our course may be hampered by many pitfalls. The best safeguard is to warn the reader, as we did in this introduction, of these possible dangers.

We shall concentrate on four aspects of our subject :

(1) The role played by foreign investment and indebtedness in the *past*, more precisely from 1850 to World War II, in bringing about modernisation and development in Egypt and the Ottoman Empire.
(2) The role of foreign aid, both American and Soviet, in the *present* economic development of the Middle East.
(3) The role of foreign investment (petroleum) in the oil producing states.
(4) The emergence of inter-Arab aid as a new factor and its possible role in the *future* development of the area.

II

The years 1913–14 marked the peak of an era of European financial ventures in Egypt and the Ottoman Empire. The beginnings of this era may be dated to the mid-19th century. Tables 1 and 2 disclose the amounts, the distribution and the relative size of foreign investment in the Middle East.

TABLE 1

EUROPEAN INVESTMENT IN EGYPT AND THE OTTOMAN
EMPIRE IN 1913–14 (£ millions)

| | Egypt | | Ottoman Empire | | |
	France	GB	France	GB	Germany
Public Debt	49	15	97	14·8	34·3
Private sector	81	29	35·7	9·1	21·8
	130	44	132·7	23·9	56·1

TABLE 2

INVESTMENT ABROAD FOR THE MAIN EUROPEAN
POWERS IN 1913–14

	France		Gt. Britain		Germany	
	£ million	% of total	£ million	%	£ million	%
Total amounts invested abroad	1,774	—	3,763	—	1,143	—
Investment in Egypt	130	7·3	44	6·0	—	—
Investment in Ottoman Empire	132·7	7·3	23·9	8·6	56·1	7·7

Source: Ducruet, J. *Les Capitaux Européens au Proche Orient.*

If we added, Swiss, Belgian, Dutch and Italian capital to these figures, they would probably reach the £400 million mark. The importance and the role of Europe in general—and of France in particular—as banker to the area is readily apparent.

The striking feature of this period of Middle Eastern history is that the pattern of political influence does not coincide with the pattern of investment. On the eve of World War I, France was the largest investor in both Egypt and the Ottoman Empire, but the leading political role was played by Britain in Cairo and to a lesser but still significant extent by Germany in Istanbul. The relationships between foreign capital and imperialism are not as simple as some naïve interpretations of colonial history tend to suggest. Investment was *one* element among many others in the complex struggle that determined the policies of the major powers—France, Great Britain, Germany and Russia—in the Middle East. These were rival powers. The competition involved commercial and financial interests as well as diplomatic, cultural and military ones. The influence acquired by some power in certain spheres often was the result of moves designed to counteract the role played by another State in other fields : one immediately thinks of France and Britain in Egypt. And conflicts tended to persist, especially in the financial sphere, even when general settlements were reached (e.g. the Franco–British Agreement of 1904) or when a definite pattern of political supremacy had emerged.

In Egypt and the Ottoman Empire, foreign investment took four major forms : (*a*) loans to the governments; (*b*) the Suez Canal; (*c*) railways and other means of communication; (*d*) joint-stock companies of various types.

(*a*) The Egyptian Public Debt was contracted under the Khedives Saïd and Ismaïl. Successive loans were secured on increasingly unfavourable terms. True, some of the money raised was spent on wasteful consumption. We must stress however that significant amounts were invested in agriculture and public works; these did contribute to the economic development of Egypt.

The Consolidated Debt was estimated at £91 million in 1876, the yearly interest payment at £6 million, i.e. some 60% of the government budget at that time. The Debt led to the imposition of financial control upon Egypt and, indirectly perhaps, to the loss of independence. Egypt carried for a long time the burden of her indebtedness : the financial commitments were not liquidated until 1943 ! The political consequences, some may argue, are still with us.

The Ottoman Debt, contracted under similar conditions, had a more complicated history. The foreign loans were guaranteed by the Tribute which Egypt used to pay to the Porte. As a result, a most anomalous situation arose after World War I when Egypt, an Independent State, freed from the obligation to pay a Tribute, was held responsible for the debts of the dismantled Ottoman Empire. (It is doubtful whether the Ottoman Debt contributed even in a modest way to the economic development of the Empire.)

(*b*) The history of the Suez Canal has recently deserved a thousand-page book : we cannot summarise this history in a few lines. Let us however emphasise a few points that are particularly relevant to our purpose. First, most of the foreign capital initially invested in the venture was French and, more interestingly perhaps, this capital was subscribed by a large number of very small investors. For all practical purposes, the Canal started as a joint Franco-Egyptian enterprise. Second, Egypt's loss of ownership through the sale of her shares to the British Government (1875) is not unrelated to the problem of Egypt's indebtedness which we have already discussed. Third, the Egyptian economy did not benefit very much from the Canal until its nationalisation in 1956. After this date, the Canal was important as an external source of foreign exchange but was not really integrated through productive links to the national economy. The Canal, however, enhanced Egypt's vulnerability to foreign intervention.

(*c*) Foreign investment took the form of joint ventures for the construction of railways and harbours (e.g. Beirut) in the Ottoman Empire. The most famous enterprise was the *Bagdadbahn*, in which German financial and political interests played such an important role. The *Bagdadbahn* was the object of endless rivalry and diplomatic negotiations between the European powers.

(*d*) Foreign capital was also invested in a large number of companies of various sizes and types. In 1914, some 90% of the capital invested in joint-stock companies in Egypt was owned by foreigners. (We are excluding the Suez Canal and the Egyptian branches of foreign banks. If these were included, the proportion would be much higher.) The distribution of this capital by type of activity is interesting : some 65% in financial institutions specialising in mortgage, agricultural credit, banking and insurance, 15% in commerce, 13% in real estate, 7% in transport, irrigation and manufacturing industry. In the Ottoman Empire most of the capital was invested in the railways and small but significant amounts in banks, public utilities, tobacco manufacture and mining.

The important conclusions of this analysis are : first, that foreign investment was always a *private* instrument of commerce and finance. The investors were firms or individuals motivated by profits rather than by political considerations. But the presence of foreign capital in the Middle East and its association with projects that carried political and strategic significance played an important role in the imperial policies of the powers. Second, that although the aims of foreign investors—high and secure profits—did not always coincide with the long-term interests of the host countries, there are no reasons to believe that these interests were systematically and inherently in conflict. (It is correct to assert that Egypt and the Ottoman Empire did benefit from some forms of foreign investment, but it is equally true that their economic development was hindered in many ways by the burdens of and Debt and the restrictions imposed on them by the powers.)

III

As a result of two world wars and of major transformations in both the national and the international scenes, the history of foreign capital in the Middle East has taken new turns. The main trends can be summarised as follows: after World War I, the dominance of *private* foreign investment in certain privileged fields (public utilities, financial institutions, railways, etc.), or in the form of government debt, started to decline and after World War II a new form of capital transfers known as foreign aid came into prominence. In the '30s, a field destined to acquire considerable significance was expanding as an area of investment for foreign companies: oil. In the '50s and '60s, private foreign investment in manufacturing, trade, banking and the services was severely discouraged by a wave of nationalisation in Egypt, Syria and Iraq and by the fear of political instability in other areas of the Middle East. Of course there were some exceptions. Taking an overall view, however, we can assert that two specific forms of foreign capital movements are important at present: aid and oil.

Most Middle Eastern countries—the only exceptions perhaps being two or three oil-producing States—are in need, some in urgent need, of foreign aid. In the world today, both the struggle against extreme poverty and the promotion of economic development are important objectives that no Government can afford to neglect. It is generally agreed that the transfer of resources from rich to poor countries does help in normal circumstances towards the achievement of the development goal.

During the last two decades, most Middle Eastern countries have been receiving aid in unequal and fluctuating amounts. Aid has been granted under an infinite variety of conditions and forms. The major donors and lenders are the US and the USSR, but France, Germany, the UK, Italy and some Eastern European countries can be noted among the contributors.

We cannot enter in a short essay into a full discussion of the politics and economics of aid. Rather we shall emphasise in a highly selective manner a number of points that seem important to us.

In the Middle East, as everywhere, international politics have influenced the direction and flow of aid. The most important recipients are Turkey, Egypt and Israel. Turkey has benefited from its strategic position on the south-east flank of NATO; Egypt from Nasser's political influence in the Arab world; Israel partly from its situation as a Western outpost and partly from the wide sympathies it enjoys in Europe and the US. However, even for these privileged countries the amounts received are correlated neither to the size of the population nor to the average levels of income. Egypt, the most populated and the poorest, has probably received less than Turkey and certainly far less than Israel. (Between 1949 and 1969 the long-term capital inflows into Israel must have been three or four times larger than those into Egypt. On a *per caput* basis Israel has received 30 or 40 times more foreign funds than Egypt.)

The fact that the granting of aid is often politically motivated does not necessarily affect its economic usefulness. A million pounds in the hands of the recipient are a million pounds, whatever the donor's motives. Politics become relevant to the economics of aid when it affects either the terms and conditions under which aid is granted or the regularity of the flow of funds. Uncertainty as regards the volume, timing and nature of the aid a country is hoping to receive may hinder this country's attempts to plan effectively and consistently. Some of the difficulties encountered by Egyptian and other Middle Eastern planners can be attributed to this uncertainty.

The political influence that a great power acquires in a country is not necessarily related to the volume or effectiveness of its aid programme : one can recall the relative influence of the US and the USSR in Egypt or the recent political successes of France, a small donor, in the Arab Middle East. Aid today, like private investment in the 19th century, is only *one* among many instruments in a complex game. One could argue in the light of Middle Eastern experience that the donor's threat to curtail aid as a political weapon and the recipient's threat to realign his foreign policy as a means of receiving more aid, seem to defeat, in the long-run, their stated objectives. (The US refusal to finance the Aswan High Dam drastically reduced Western influence in the area.)

The economic effects of foreign aid on Middle Eastern countries are difficult to assess. It is clear that the availability of aid has improved performance, helped the establishment of social and economic institutions, supported the efforts for raising the standard of living. There have been some spectacular achievements, such as the High Dam in Egypt, serious attempts to industrialise in Turkey, Egypt and Iran, interesting schemes of agricultural development in Syria. But it is also certain that in many cases opportunities were lost, wrong economic decisions made and funds diverted to wasteful purposes. We should recall however, that aid is a relationship involving at least two parties. (Both may share some responsibilities in the successes or deficiencies of an aid programme.) Disappointing results should not always be blamed on the recipient alone. For aid is often given in forms that suit the donors (the US give wheat because they happen to have an agricultural surplus, the USSR steel mills because these are an essential ingredient of their economic ideology) but are not always appropriate to the recipient's needs; or it is given under terms (e.g. tied aid) that may prove in the end more damaging than beneficial to the recipient's economy.

It is necessary to stress, in the face of a growing reluctance on the part of Western countries to assist developing nations, that the needs of these nations are as urgent as ever, that economic development is still an important goal and that, despite suggestions to the contrary, aid is still required. The interesting phenomenon of recent years is the emergence of the USSR as a donor not only in Egypt, Syria or Iraq, but in Turkey and Iran. It is often said that Soviet aid is not as economically interesting as the US contributions. This criticism may be true, but is certainly irrelevant when Western aid is shrinking in relative importance. Developing countries do not have many options.

IV

Foreign aid and foreign investment are the two folds of our diptych. In the Middle East today foreign private investment is overwhelmingly concentrated in one field : oil.

There is no need to elaborate on the significance of oil resources for the economies of Saudi Arabia, Kuwait, Libya, Bahrain, Qatar, Dubai, Abu Dhabi or Oman—they are a unique source of wealth; or for the economies of Iraq and Iran, where oil revenues constitute a sizeable proportion of the national income. But it is worth noting that oil does not necessarily induce economic development even when it causes considerable wealth. For development implies the transformation of a country into a modern and productive economy. But when wealth is *received* rather than *produced* the danger is that it may transform the country into a club of rentiers. If one took the long view (who knows whether oil will retain its importance in the distant future?) it would become apparent that the concern for economic development is as vital for a wealthy oil-producing country as for its less fortunate neighbours.

* * *

Any attempt to assess the significance of Middle Eastern oil for international politics should take three facts into account : that Middle Eastern oil, because of its proximity, the size of the proven reserves and the cost of exploitation, is vital to Western Europe; that few, if any, oil-producing countries could willingly afford to dispense for a long period with their oil revenues; that the relationships between the host country and foreign companies are normally dominated by this understanding of the mutual interest.

* * *

The most interesting aspect of the history of oil in the Middle East is indeed this relationship, the main features of which (and I shall draw here on the works of Professor Edith Penrose, the leading authority on this subject) I shall now discuss.

Because Governments are the sole owners of underground oil, the relationship between foreign capital and host countries is essentially a direct relationship between the companies and the State. Governments enter into agreements by which they concede the rights of exploration and production either to a single company (as in Saudi Arabia in earlier days) or to a number of competitive firms (as in Libya in more recent times). Bargaining is inherent in the relationship. After World War II, the bargaining position of governments was enhanced because many new companies were attracted to the profitable low-cost oil of the Middle East. The effects are manifold. Agreements now are more often in the form of contracts than of concessions. Governments have been able to extract a greater share in revenues (the '50-50' agreement, posted prices, etc.), to obtain the relinquishment by the companies of unexploited areas previously conceded to them, to fix targets for the level of oil production and income (Iran in 1969) and in some cases to secure equity participation in the companies (e.g. the Petromin-Auxirap partnership in Saudi Arabia). Of course, bargaining power is not absolute. Up to now, governments have failed to obtain equity participation in the major companies (ARAMCO, KOC, IPC).

The economic implication of the relationship between government and company is that all revenues from oil exports accrue directly to the State. There is no mediation through local producers as in the case of 'normal' export goods, cocoa or rubber for example. This places considerable responsibility on the governments and some, of course, are not well equipped to face it. And the absence of a significant contribution from the community to the production of its own wealth creates a situation in which incentives are weak. We suggested earlier the consequences for economic development.

The long-term problem that faces governments in their relations with companies is that of control over off-take. This is a very complex problem to which nationalisation (as Dr. Mosssadeq's attempt revealed) is no answer. Equity participation may not fulfil the hopes placed on it and the establishment of national oil companies, an interesting and promising development, is but a beginning in a very long process. Judging by the results achieved in recent years, we cannot doubt that governments will succeed in maximising the national advantage at every round of the bargaining process with the companies (without impairing the free flow of oil on which their wealth depends).

V

Oil is more than domestic wealth. It has enabled certain Middle Eastern countries to act as donors and to assist the economic development of less fortunate neighbours. In some cases, a spectacular reversal of roles has taken place over a short decade. In 1958 Libya, for example, was heavily dependent on foreign aid for the bare requirements of its economy, and Egypt ranked among the donors. In 1967 Libya became a donor country and offered to Jordan and Egypt an annual sum, larger than it had itself received from all contributors in any single year.

But the most remarkable attempt at regional economic assistance was initiated by Kuwait. The Kuwait Fund for Arab Economic Assistance was established in 1961 as an autonomous organisation. It is interesting to note that the Kuwaiti initiative took place long before the June war. It cannot be attributed to the wave of emotions that swept the Middle East in 1967. Although political motives were not altogether absent, Kuwait emphasised from the outset its serious concern for economic development. The Kuwait Fund is organised on the model of the IBRD. It follows the same practice in project appraisal, financial management, lending procedure. The organisation and policies of the Kuwait Fund have been often praised for their soundness by foreign observers. Kuwait aid is extended through other channels: the Arab African Bank, the General Authority for South Arabian and Arabian Gulf States, and through direct loans from the state. The remarkable feature of Kuwait's programme is that the sums spent have in certain years reached 8 or 9% of the country's national income.

We are happy to conclude on an optimistic note. Kuwait's experience suggests that there is within the Middle East a definite potential for self-assistance. We should add that if some countries have an abundance of capital, others (Egypt, Turkey, Lebanon) have some relative advantages in terms of the size of their market, or of their industrial experience or skill. The potential is not large enough to preclude, for the time being, the need for outside aid. But it is likely to grow. Of course many political, psychological and socio-economic factors may prevent its realisation. But it is important for all Middle Easterners to know that this potential exists. It is up to them to put it to its best advantage.

FURTHER READING

Ducruet, J. *Les Capitaux Européens au Proche Orient*, Paris, 1964.
El Mallakh, R. *Economic Development and Regional Co-operation: Kuwait*, Univ. of Chicago Press, 1968.
Hurewitz, J. C. (ed.) *Soviet-American Rivalry in the Middle East*, Praeger, New York, 1969.
Penrose, E. *The Large International Firm in Developing Countries*, M.I.T. Press, Cambridge, Mass., 1969.

PART FIVE
SOCIAL PATTERNS

TRADITIONAL ISLAMIC SOCIETY

GEOFFREY FURLONGE

I

HISTORICAL BACKGROUND

IN AD 622 the Prophet Muhammad, fleeing from mockery, abuse, and persecution in Mecca, took refuge in the North Arabian oasis of Yathrib (subsequently renamed 'Medinat an-Nabi' or City of the Prophet—'Medina' for short) and there founded a community which became a state. His intention was to create an association of men dedicated to a way of life based on the tenets of the faith which he expounded, and to the extension of its sway in the unbelieving world outside.

During the century which followed, and despite a schism which rent the community into the contending Sunni and Shi'a sects, its extent expanded spectacularly. Successive waves of its warriors, breaking forth from their desert headquarters, swept across the Middle East through Persia into Turkestan, India, and the Far East, and through North Africa and Spain into France. It is true that their repeated assaults on the Byzantine capital of Constantinople, notably those of 717 and 718, failed, and that in 732 they were checked at Poitiers by Charles Martel, with the result that they were unable to subdue any part of Eastern Europe and by the end of the 15th century had been expelled from Western Europe also. In addition the Crusader counter-assault in the 12th century established Christian control over part of the Levant. But this lasted less than a century; and in the 15th century other Muslims, the Ottoman Turks, conquered Byzantium and thus extended Islamic hegemony over an important new area. The Empire which they founded, covering the whole of the Middle East and North Africa and most of Arabia and the Balkans, gradually disintegrated during the 19th and 20th centuries until only Asia Minor was left to them; but Islam has never lost its position as the predominant religion of all these areas, except in the Balkans, Israel, and the Lebanon, and continues to command wide allegiances in central and south-east Asia, the Far East, and the continent of Africa.

ORIGINAL PRINCIPLES

The followers of Islam, as they advanced through the world, professed a faith, and were guided by principles, which had been evolved to meet the needs of an uncomplicated existence. 'Islam', which means 'resignation'—to the will of God—perfectly befitted men who lived little above the subsistence-level and whose lives were constantly endangered either by enemies or by natural circumstances such as drought, extremes of temperature, or pestilence. Its 'Five Pillars'—the essential duties incumbent upon every Muslim—

likewise responded to the mentality of a simple community. The repeated asseveration that 'God is Greatest, and Muhammad is the Prophet of God', and the five daily prayers, were clearly intended to instil into its adherents the basic tenet of the faith; the fast of Ramadan to inculcate abstinence in a race which, for all the hardness of its life, was liable to self-indulgence when given the opportunity; the almsgiving to teach mercy towards the weaker or more unfortunate, in a life which could easily breed brutality and indifference; the pilgrimage to Mecca to provide an incentive to men of narrow outlook and experience to emerge from their surroundings into an adventure which was to be planned for years ahead and looked back upon for years afterwards. To these fundamentals Muslim thinkers gradually added the elements of a moral system covering every phase of human activity, to which the believer must and did submit willingly, sure that he was thereby guaranteeing his entry into Paradise instead of his committal to everlasting hellfire.

This moral system covered not only individuals but also all aspects of human association, including that of the state. Originally Islam made no distinction between religious and temporal power. It had no priesthood to stand between the believer and Allah, who was its only head and whose Word was its only law; and its functions, forms, and constitution were to be eternal. Its *Shari'ah*, an infallible code of ethics, was intended as an instrument to reform existing society and custom, judged defective in many respects, through the enunciation of moral principles and actual legal enactments. Islam was in fact a movement of social and economic reform, backed by ethical conceptions.

In the economic field, the main principle which it laid down was that 'wealth should not be allowed to circulate only amongst the rich', from which followed a ban on all forms of usury and commercial exploitation. Its social impact was more extensive. The practice of almsgiving was insisted upon, and the *zakat* tax on grain and livestock was instituted and made obligatory in order that the poor might benefit from its proceeds. An end was made of the barbarous practice of abandoning newly-born and unwanted female children in the desert. Slavery was too deep-rooted an institution to be extirpated, but the Koran gave every encouragement to the humane treatment of slaves and to the meritorious act of freeing them, and laid down numerous rules for these purposes. Notable amongst them was the system of *mukatiba*, under which a slave working on behalf of his master might retain part of his earnings in order to amass the wherewithal to buy his freedom, and that of *tadbir*, under which a slave-owner could stipulate in his will that his slaves should be freed on his death. The use of alcohol was first restricted, then banned altogether; gambling suffered a similar fate. Elaborate rules governed the relations between the sexes : adultery by an unmarried person was punishable by a hundred lashes, by a married one by stoning to death; polygamy was restricted to four wives, and then only on condition that the husband treated them all equally; women's rights were to be 'commensurate' with men's, bearing in mind that men were the breadwinners and therefore a degree higher. Detailed rules about food included prohibitions on the consumption of corpses, blood, pork, and food offered to any God other than Allah, Jehovah, or the God of the Christians.

MODIFICATIONS

Such was the basis of Islamic society. But with the passage of time, and the widening of the Islamic community, it became modified in many important respects.

This was inevitable; for the Arabs, in whatever direction they advanced, came beyond the confines of the desert into the Sown : in the lands of the Fertile Crescent—what today are the territories of Israel, Syria and the Lebanon, and parts of Jordan; on the uplands of Kurdistan and Persia; on the plateaux and broad plains of North Africa and the Iberian Peninsula. The inhabitants of some of these areas, notably the Persians and the North African Berbers, resisted and had to be conquered; others submitted with hardly a struggle. In either event, the victors assimilated them and either did not interfere with, or in some cases adopted, their customs and habits, thus producing a variety hitherto lacking in the Islamic community.

The manner of government was particularly affected. Initially, and for the first hundred years of Islam, its realm was lightly administered by the successive caliphs, who divided it into provinces, each with a military governor and an official collector of the *zikat* tax, but left the detailed administrative organisation to the officials of the régime which Islam had replaced, provided that they were willing to conform to its basic principles. Later, however, the authority of the caliph began to be challenged by individual military governors in their provinces and was gradually whittled away until, in the middle of the 13th century, it was extinguished by the Mongol occupation of Baghdad. During the same period, the original simple form of administration developed into a bureaucracy, and the original simple way of living of the caliph tended to become progressively more luxurious. The trend was, however, abruptly reversed in the 16th century, when the Ottoman Turks occupied the Arab lands : for the Turks were dedicated to the service of Islam, and for the next 300 years their dominions were ruled more theoretically than ever before—or after.

II

THE STRUCTURE OF ISLAMIC SOCIETY

The Islamic community originally consisted of three main forms of human association : the tribe, the village, and the town or city. To examine its structure, it is necessary to consider these separately.

The Tribe

The desert way of life was inevitably conditioned by the insecurity of the nomad. Its social organisation was therefore based on the close association of individuals in the face of their common difficulties. This association was, generally speaking, on four levels : first the family, of three or more generations; then the 'lineage' or association of several families claiming a common (real or legendary) ancestor; then the sub-tribe, of two or more lineages; and finally the tribe itself.

A prominent characteristic of this organisation was egalitarianism. This derived from the precepts of the Koran, but these in turn were clearly inspired by the social conditions of the 7th century. Class distinctions existed : the camel-breeding tribes were apt to regard themselves as superior to the sheep- and goat-breeders, and in each tribe certain lineages were recognised as being of superior descent and therefore meet to provide shaikhs or leaders. But to a society whose possessions were limited by the difficulty of transporting them on migration, and where in consequence all sat on the floor together in the evenings, the Islamic conception of universal brotherhood came naturally. Shaikhs, who were chosen for merit as often as for seniority, were not rulers and usually had no right to punish; decisions affecting the

487

welfare or future of the group were normally taken by the *majlis*, a conclave of leaders, in which the Shaikh's position was that of a chairman, so that his influence was a function of his ability or personality. Visitors to the camp of King Ibn Saud in the early days of his kingdom were surprised to see lowly tribesmen approach his tent, be at once admitted, and address the great ruler as 'Abdul Aziz', without honorific.

Charity, in desert conditions, was natural and essential. Within a tribe, as Glubb Pasha has said,

> 'no human being can die of hunger or exposure. . . . No child could be unwanted and have to be cared for by a State institution. . . . Tribal solidarity will support the widow, bring up the orphan, maintain the cripple or the invalid, all in the homely environment of their native village or camp. In tribal society, old people can never complain of loneliness.'

Hospitality, on the principle of 'do as you would be done by', was equally essential and ingrained, for to refuse shelter and sustenance to one arriving from a desert journey might be equivalent to sentencing him to death. In the Arab countries, tradition, and a certain flamboyance in the Arab character, carried it well beyond the point of mere duty : to quote Glubb Pasha again,

> 'the Bedouin cannot be content to do just what is necessary. He must do ten times as much, and with a flourish and a panache as well. The guest, even if a completely unknown stranger, must be . . . entertained for three days before it is even legitimate to ask him where he came from or where he is going. Should an enemy arrive in search of him the host must, if necessary, sacrifice his life to defend his guest from injury. . . . An Arab nomad . . . will kill his last sheep to provide a banquet for a complete stranger whom he has never seen before and will never see again. . . .'

A well-known story is of the indigent Shaikh whose sole possession was a valuable stallion : when visited by two unknown people he found himself obliged to sacrifice it to provide the customary meal for them, only to find that the purpose of their visit had been to buy it for any price he cared to ask.

Individualism was another trait bred by desert conditions. From early youth boys had to learn to fend for themselves in order to survive in the wilderness, where neglect to hold on to one's camel might result in death by thirst, and a lack of watchfulness left a man prey to an enemy or a hyena. Unfortunately, with individualism also came indiscipline and combativeness : 'I against my brother; my brother and I against our cousin; our family against the world.' As a result inter-tribal feuds and raiding were, until quite recently, endemic.

This permanent condition of conflict had one curious effect : the growth of a tradition of chivalry, which taught that great deeds were more important than the winning of a battle. To overcome one's enemy after notifying him of the time and place of one's proposed attack was more meritorious than to cut him up by surprise. Champions from the two sides would engage in single combat. Young girls would be borne into battle on litters to urge on their men, but would never be harmed and, if captured, would be returned under escort. The deep Arab love for poetry often resulted in notable deeds being commemorated in verse.

The Village

Around the fringe of the desert were a series of semi-nomadic tribes, who cultivated patches of grain in the spring but became desert graziers for the rest of the year. Their organisation differed little from that of the nomads. But beyond them were the settled cultivators grouped around villages, whose social structure, though analogous to that of the tribes, differed from it in that a landowner-peasant relationship took the place of that between tribal chief and tribesman. Islamic principle ensured that there should be no class distinctions (except that landowners were on the whole regarded as superior to artisans and craftsmen), and all peasants had a common devotion to the land. This might be held communally or might belong to local or absentee landlords, whose families had either acquired it as a reward for past services, or, after the Turkish occupation, had been granted it for tax-farming purposes. The village was bound together by a network of mutual obligations, so that it could deal as a whole with the outside world. Towards the nomads, on whom the cultivators often largely depended to sell their produce but from whom they were liable to suffer depredations when the government of the day was too weak to maintain order, the village feeling was usually one of superiority not unmixed with fear. Relations with other villages, provided that they were of the same religious persuasion, were normally friendly but distant. Marriages on occasion took place between members of different villages, but were usually confined to the one. The general picture was that of a tightly-knit, inward-looking community, sometimes oppressed by landlords but self-contained and largely unaffected by the world outside.

The Towns

The majority of the towns or cities of the original Islamic Middle East— Damascus, Baghdad, Aleppo for example—were situated at the crossing of main trade-routes and served as entrepôts and markets for caravans, as well as for surrounding villagers and nomads. In addition they were the seats of the local authorities and tax-collectors; of the villages' 'absentee landlords'; of the merchants who supplied the countryside and the desert and who financed the caravans; later, of the moneylenders on whom, despite the original Islamic ban on usury, the peasant often depended. The outlook of the town-dwellers thus tended to be wider and more receptive to new ideas than that of the peasant or tribesman. In the towns, Islamic culture and the refinements of religious thought were elaborated, and political movements forged.

The urban social structure was naturally more complex than those of the desert or the villages. It was composed of a number of social strata, ranging from the civil and religious officials through the landowners to the artisans and shopkeepers. Within these classes the social organisation was based on the same principles of family and kinship as have been noted elsewhere. Indeed the larger cities were divided into quarters whose inhabitants mostly belonged to particular 'lineages' and which therefore operated rather as villages.

In these quarters, as in the villages, the interdependence of the community was manifested in almost every form of human activity. A birth would be attended not only by the midwife and the close female relatives of the prospective mother, but by as many women of the quarter as could find a pretext for being present; they would begin to assemble once the word went round that labour was beginning, and would remain in the house until it was completed, in order to congratulate the parents if the child were a boy and condole discreetly with them if it were a girl. Marriages would normally be attended by the whole population of the quarter. A death would be followed by visits to the bereaved family by every family in the quarter, men to men and women to women, the former to help with the funeral arrangements and to offer assistance if the death should have left the family in temporary straits, the women to take over the household arrangements and to help in the preparation of the funeral baked meats, in order to spare the grieving women of the family. Newcomers to the quarter would be supplied with food by the neighbours for the first week after their installation, and would then be ceremoniously called upon by every local family.

The egalitarian principle was as much observed in the towns as outside them. It was strikingly illustrated by the treatment and behaviour of the servants in some of the larger houses, who were often girls from the owners' country estates. These girls would serve guests with deference and self-effacement, but when no guests were present would sit down with the family, join in the conversation as equals, and share wholeheartedly in the life and interests of their employers, who, on their side, would feel as responsible for their welfare as for that of their own family. Another illustration of the principle was provided by the tradition in Jerusalem of Sunday picnics for the whole staffs of government offices, to be followed by round games in which all present, from the venerable head of department to the office-boy, would join.

Toleration

An Islamic principle whose operation was more evident in the towns than in the countryside or desert was that of religious and racial toleration. It had been practised since the beginnings of Islam : the original Arab armies would offer to the unbelievers whom they encountered the choice between accepting Islam, submitting and paying tribute, or fighting to the death, but would seldom attempt forcible proselytisation. Government, in the generally accepted Muslim view which long prevailed, existed only to defend cultivated lands, to maintain order, and to tax, not to coerce non-Muslims into accepting Islamic Law in matters of personal status.

This was particularly true as regards Christians and Jews. The Koran held that the followers of these two great monotheistic religions were 'People of the Book' : they believed in one God, in prophecy, and in the Day of Judgment, but had both erred, the Jews by failing to accept the revelations of both Jesus and Muhammad, the Christians by their belief that Jesus had provided the final and complete revelation and that He was God Incarnate. They were therefore to be permitted a certain status alongside the Islamic community but could not belong to it. As a result, Islamic society came to contain numerous Jewish and Christian, as well as other non-Muslim communities. Some were to be found in the countryside, notably Christians in the Lebanon, but the majority were in the towns. Particular examples were Christians in Jerusalem and Aleppo, and Jews in Baghdad. On occasion local circumstances resulted in temporary Muslim oppression of one or other of these communities, but in general they suffered little from discrimination. Jews were indeed esteemed for their special qualities, the men for their intelligence and superior education—which often included an outstanding knowledge of Arabic or Turkish—and the women for their skill in dressmaking and other feminine arts. The Christians were usually accepted on all but equal terms.

The 19th Century and After

Islamic society as described above continued without major change through the first three centuries of the Turkish overlordship of the Middle East. From the 19th century onwards, however, it suffered a process of continuous and fundamental change under the impact of new and external influences, all Western. Of these the most important can be summarised as nationalism, liberalism, and secularism.

Until the early 1830s the conception of nationalism was foreign to the Middle East, for it ran counter to the universalism of Islam. Even the word 'Turkey' was hardly used, the Ottoman Empire being described as 'The Lands of Islam' or 'The Imperial Realm'. Its Arab subjects hardly seemed conscious of being under alien domination, for they were largely left to govern themselves and felt themselves to be full members of the Islamic world to which they belonged. It was only when the Young Turks, after the 1908 Revolution, initiated a process of 'turcification' which appeared to relegate the Arabs to a second-class status that there arose a counter-movement of Arab Nationalism. This resulted, after the defeat of Turkey in 1918, in a fragmentation of the Ottoman Empire, and therefore of the Islamic world.

Liberalism, as a movement of revolt against despotism, likewise took root in Turkey in the early 19th century, but its growth was checked by Abdul Hamid's absolutism and it did not emerge until after the consolidation of the Atatürk régime between the two World Wars. In the new Arab States it proved to be a plant of uncertain growth and passed through phases of absolute and constitutional monarchy, parliamentary democracy, and military autocracy to the 'revolutionary socialism' of Egypt, Syria and Iraq in the 1950s.

Finally, Western secularism, with its rejection of theocratic control, constituted a direct challenge to the authority and influence of Islam when it began to permeate the Middle East as a concomitant of the other Western ideas. To it may be largely attributed the adoption by the Atatürk régime in Turkey of a policy which culminated, in 1928, in the excision of Islam from the Turkish Constitution and the suppression of the dervish orders; the less drastic moves made by Reza Shah in Persia against Islamic institutions there; and a progressive abandonment in the more advanced Arab countries, particularly Egypt, Syria and Iraq, of Islamic institutions which had become incompatible with modern conditions.

This trend has continued, on the whole, despite a reaction in Turkey in the 1950s which resulted in a partial restoration of Islamic authority and a similar reaction in Persia after the disappearance of Reza Shah. Throughout the Middle East Islamic tabus, notably those on usury, liquor, and gambling, have lost most of their force; comparatively few nowadays keep the fast of Ramadan or perform all their daily prayers; Koranic education no longer suffices for the needs of 20th century youth, and in almost every country of the area administration is now on a wholly secular basis.

Yet generous and thoughtful hospitality, as any visitor to the Middle East will bear witness, is still lavished on the stranger; charity towards one's neighbour was never better illustrated than by the help extended to the Arab refugees, during their mass exodus from Palestine in 1948, by Jordan families often little better off than they; perhaps best of all, free and easy intercourse between high and low, between master and servant, between ruler and subject, continues in a way which would be unthinkable in any Western society. Despite the weakening of the bonds which held together the Islamic society, its traditional qualities live on amongst its members today.

FURTHER READING

Gibb, H. A. R. *Mohammedanism*, Oxford Univ. Press, London and New York, 1953.

Hitti, Philip K. *History of the Arabs*, Macmillan, London, 1946.

Hourani, Albert, *Syria and the Lebanon*, Oxford Univ. Press, London, 1946.

Levy, Reuben. *The Social Structure of Islam*, Cambridge Univ. Press, Cambridge, 1957.

Lewis, Bernard. *The Emergence of Modern Turkey*, Oxford Univ. Press, London and New York, 1961.

FEUDALISM AND LAND REFORM

ADEL KAMAL

INTRODUCTION

IN the Middle East today 'feudalism' is generally understood to mean a land system where a small group of large, often absentee, landlords own much of the farmland while the majority of the rural population are landless and live by tenancy and hired labour on extremely unfavourable terms. Feudalism of the European type existed only at the beginning of the Ottoman Empire, in the 15th and early 16th century, and even then the feudal lords did not strictly own their fiefs—all land being the exclusive property of the State—but enjoyed the right to collect and keep the land-taxes in return for military service. This system gave way to tax-farming, which in Egypt was to last until the beginning of the 19th century and in the rest of the Middle East until the beginning of the 20th. Tax-farmers—drawn from the ranks of notables, religious dignitaries and tribal shaikhs—were given rights of tenure and the authority to collect taxes in specified districts, in return for a stipulated annual payment to the state. In the course of time tax-farmers became virtual landowners, increasingly repressive, and delivered little revenue to the treasury.

To resist European expansionism at the beginning of the 19th century more revenue was needed to modernise the army and develop the economy. Attempts were therefore made by the reforming Governments in Egypt and Turkey to replace tax-farming by direct collection but these failed everywhere in the Ottoman Empire except in Egypt.

ORIGINS OF LARGE PROPERTIES

In Egypt tax-farmers were evicted, and the land was made over to cultivators on a heritable leasehold basis. At the same time, large tracts of wasteland were transferred in full ownership to members of the ruling family and other notables for reclamation. In the early 1870s the Government began to grant ownership rights to wealthy individuals in return for several years' taxes in advance, while, on the demand side, land became an increasingly attractive asset as a result of the growing European demand for cotton. By the end of the century much of the agricultural land had passed into the hands of the rich.

Change came more slowly to the rest of the Middle East. In the second half of the 19th century, the Ottoman Governments saw the registration of State land in the names of those actually cultivating it as a way of weakening the local power of tax-farmers and of settling Bedouin tribes, especially in

Iraq and Syria. However, the reform was never fully implemented and tax-farming continued to exist until the beginning of the present century. When, from time to time, registration of titles took place, it led, paradoxically, to the creation of very large properties. The small cultivators were either intimidated into surrendering their holdings to the rich and powerful, or voluntarily had their land registered in the name of some notable, imagining the call for registration to be a preliminary to heavier taxation or conscription.

Large estates (both in Egypt and the Fertile Crescent) also arose out of grants made by the rulers to members of their families, court favourites and political supporters; others arose as a result of the seizure of peasant holdings in settlement of debts. The situation was made worse when the rich landowners gained political power : in Egypt in the 1920s, Iraq in the 1930s and Syria in the 1940s.

LAND REFORM IN EGYPT[1]

The distribution of landed property in Egypt before the overthrow of the monarchy and the introduction of land reform in September 1952 is summarised in the following table. It can be seen that $0\cdot1\%$ of the total number of landowners held nearly 20% of the country's farmland in estates of 200 feddans and over (1 feddan $= 1\cdot038$ acres) while 94% of all landowners held 35% of the area in plots of less than 5 feddans. About nine million people or 60% of the rural population did not own the land they tilled but subsisted by leasing land or working as wage labourers. Because of the high population density, competition among the peasants for the use of the land was intense and consequently rents were high and wages low.

Expropriation and redistribution

The Agrarian Reform Law directed that no one person might own more than 200 feddans, but that he could transfer a further 100 feddans to his children. The total area which became subject to requisition under this law amounted to only 434,000 feddans, barely 8% of Egypt's agricultural area. But as the revolutionary Government established its authority more firmly and gradually abandoned its conservatism for a more socialist outlook, it took over more and more land under a succession of decrees until by the mid-1960s the area liable to seizure had more than doubled, reaching 875,000 feddans or 14% of the cultivated area. The most drastic measure was taken in 1961 when the ceiling on land properties was lowered to 100 feddans per family. Landowners of expropriated land were entitled to compensation in the form of non-negotiable bonds, but in 1964 this provision was rescinded, and all existing bonds became worthless.

The expropriated land was to be distributed in holdings of two to five feddans among landless tenants, who were to pay the purchase price of the land in 30 yearly instalments plus interest, taxes and various other charges. In the course of the following decade, however, some of these charges were reduced and others abolished. By 1966, nearly 700,000 feddans or 80% of the area subject to requisition had been distributed.

Supervised co-operative societies

Expropriated land is not distributed until low-quality land, if any, has been improved and co-operative societies set up. These co-operatives, supervised

[1] This section draws heavily on Eshag, Eprime and Kamal, 'Agrarian Reform in the United Arab Republic (Egypt)', *Bulletin of the Oxford University Institute of Economics and Statistics*, May 1968.

DISTRIBUTION OF LANDOWNERSHIP IN EGYPT, 1952 and 1965

(*Owners in thousands; area in thousand feddans*)

Size-group (feddans)	Before Land Reform (1952)		Per cent of total		After Land Reform (1965)		Per cent of total	
	Owners	*Area*	*Owners*	*Area*	*Owners*	*Area*	*Owners*	*Area*
Less than 5	2,642	2,122	94·3	35·4	3,033	3,693	94·5	57·1
5 and less than 10	79	526	2·8	8·8	78	614	2·4	9·5
10 and less than 20	47	638	1·7	10·7	61	527	1·9	8·2
20 and less than 50	22	654	0·8	10·9	29	815	0·9	12·6
50 and less than 100	6	430	0·2	7·2	6	392	0·2	6·1
100 and less than 200	3	437	0·1	7·3	4	421	0·1	6·5
200 and over	2	1,177	0·1	19·7	0	0	0·0	0·0
Total	2,801	5,984	100	100	3,211	6,462	100	100

Source: UAR Central Agency for Public Mobilisation and Statistics, *Statistical Handbook, 1952–1966*, Cairo, 1967.

495

and controlled by government officials, perform the functions of the previous landowners in providing credit, in organising cultivation and in marketing. The large number of individual plots created by the division of big estates are treated as a single unit, to maintain the advantages of large-scale production.

As more experience was gained, the supervised co-operative system was extended to the entire countryside and membership was made compulsory for all farmers. The co-operatives became the sole agents for the distribution of agricultural credit and for buying and disposing of the major crops. In this way, recovery of debts was assured and poor farmers, including landless tenants, could now borrow on no other security but their crops.

The allocation of loans in cash and in kind (seeds, fertilisers, insecticides, etc.) is now governed by a quota system whereby the amount of credit that each farmer receives is determined on the basis of the size of his holding and the type of crop he plants.[2] Apart from introducing a measure of equality among farmers, the system enables the co-operatives (as the sole distributors of agricultural requisites) to implement the Government's general agricultural policy regarding the crop-rotation which it considers technically desirable.[3]

Landlord-tenant relationship

The regulation of rents represented an important aspect of the agrarian reform legislation, for it dealt with a considerable section of the rural population, numbering over four million people as against 1·5 million who had benefited from land distribution. The growing density of population had led to a rising trend in the level of rents. Another common feature of the old tenancy system had been the complete lack of security of tenure.

The reform law stipulated that cash rents should not exceed seven times the basic land-tax and that rents payable in kind should not exceed one-half of the net produce, the costs of cultivation being shared equally between landlord and tenant. In both cases, this represented an immediate reduction in rents by about one-third.

The law also provided that all leasehold contracts be concluded in writing and run for a minimum period of three years.

Effects on land productivity and incomes

There has been a steady and rapid growth in output, the average yields per acre of ten major crops rising by nearly 40% during the decade ending in 1965. In areas where there has been redistribution, the available information suggests that yields have also been rising.[4]

This was achieved by heavier use of fertilisers, by frequent spraying and by the distribution of greater quantities of selected seeds. The consolidation of fragmented holdings and the improvement of irrigation and drainage facilities were among the major reasons for the rise in productivity. Greater security of tenure may have also been a contributing factor.

The full impact of the reform was felt by only the richest and the poorest classes. A handful of rich landowners with farms of over 100 feddans lost

[2] Eshag, Eprime and Kamal, 'A Note on the Reform of the Rural Credit System in UAR (Egypt), *Bulletin of the Oxford University Institute of Economics and Statistics*, May 1967.

[3] The Government's interest in agricultural development in general is also reflected by the increasing share of investment allocated to agriculture. The proportion of total gross capital formation that was allocated to this sector rose steadily from 12% in 1952–3 to 19% in 1964–5.

[4] FAO, *World Land Reform Conference, 20 June – 2 July, 1966*, Rome, 1966.

about two-thirds of their land while a relatively small number of the land-less peasants became owners of small plots which together made up about 10% of the cultivated area in 1966. The beneficiaries enjoyed an immediate rise in their net incomes as the annual payments made to the authorities were much lower than the rents previously paid. Subsequently, their incomes increased even further, partly as a result of the reduction in their financial obligations to the authorities, but mainly as a result of a rise in gross receipts which in turn was due to a rise in both yields and prices. In 1965 their real net income was about 35% higher than it had been in 1953.

On paper, legislation for the reduction of rent meant a substantial increase in the incomes of tenant-farmers, but, owing to high population pressure, enforcement has not generally been effective. On the whole, the big land-lords who have often been denounced as 'feudalists' and 'enemies of the people' tend to observe the law to avoid getting into trouble with the Government. The small landowners, on the other hand, have no such fears and are therefore less reluctant to charge what the market can bear.

Conclusion
The Egyptian agrarian reform did not alter the distribution of landowner-ship to a very great extent (see table above), but served as a model for the con-duct of agricultural activities in general. Most of the measures adopted for the management of the distributed land—allocation of credit, marketing and technical guidance—subsequently became part of overall agricultural policy.

The success of the Egyptian reform was due to a number of factors, all stemming from the country's long experience in harnessing the waters of the Nile. Over the decades, Egypt had developed an elaborate system of irriga-tion—dams, barrages, dykes, a complex network of irrigation and drainage canals—and while doing so it had achieved high technical and administrative standards in the field of agriculture. Thus when in 1952 the agrarian reform law was enacted, there was enough expertise in the country to carry it out.

LAND REFORM IN SYRIA
The land tenure structure
Before the 1958 land reform nearly 30% of the total agricultural area con-sisted of large estates owned by only 1% of all landowners. At the other extreme, the great majority of landowners owned 15% of the area in small holdings of less than ten hectares (1 hectare=2·47 acres). About 23% of the land was owned by the state.[5] It is estimated that 70% of rural households owned no land and lived by tenancy or hired labour.

Three-quarters of the land was cultivated under various tenancy arrange-ments, and in general the higher the population density, the greater was the share of the produce taken by the landlord. In the old settled regions, where most of the peasants lived, poverty was widespread, while in the thinly populated areas more recently opened up, the position of the cultivator was very much better. Pioneering entrepreneurs of the city merchant class rented vast tracts of land from the tribal shaikhs and by investing heavily in agri-cultural machinery (tractors, irrigation pumps, etc.) converted the land from grazing to grain cultivation.[6] Because of the immobility of labour, demand for the use of the land was much less intense than in the old regions, and

[5] Zaim, Issam. 'Le Problème Agraire Syrien', *Développement et Civilisation*, Paris, 31 September 1967.
[6] Warriner, Doreen. *Land Reform and Development in the Middle East*, Oxford Univ. Press, London, 1962.

consequently the tenants' or workers' share in total production was very much higher, resulting in less extreme inequality in income distribution. It was in the old regions that land reform was a necessary condition for social change.

Land reform legislation

Syria's reform legislation was introduced following the union with Egypt in February 1958. It set a maximum limit to the ownership of land, laid down the terms of compensation and redistribution and regulated the relations between landlord and tenant. After the collapse of the union with Egypt in 1961 all land reform operations were suspended, but in 1962 the original legislation was reintroduced, with modifications largely in favour of the big landowner. In 1963 following yet another *coup d'état* the law was again changed—this time in favour of the landless cultivator.

This most recent reform law—much more drastic than its predecessors— set the maximum limit to individual ownership at between 15 and 55 hectares of irrigated land and between 80 and 200 hectares of rain-fed land.[7] Land in excess of the maximum was to be expropriated and redistributed among landless tenants in plots of up to 8 hectares of irrigated land or 30 hectares of rain-fed land.

The beneficiaries, together with other small farmers, are organised in state-supervised co-operatives which provide credit, marketing services and technical guidance. But unlike their Egyptian counterparts, they do not manage the individual holdings as one big unit with the result that there has been a transition to small-scale farming.

The reform legislation also fixed a ceiling for rents and provided security of tenure by requiring leaseholds to be drawn up in writing and to run for at least one agricultural rotation, usually three years. Eviction of tenants was made illegal except in extreme cases such as total neglect of the land.

Implementation

In 1967, 30% of the area subject to requisition had been distributed. Although in relative terms, Egypt's performance was more impressive, in absolute terms, Syria managed (with far fewer surveyors, engineers and administrators than in Egypt) to distribute 380,000 hectares or three times the area that Egypt had distributed during the first nine years of its reform. This is a commendable achievement, considering the many obstacles which Syria has to face in implementing its distribution programme. Because of regional differences in the quality of the soil and in irrigation conditions, the task of adjusting the size of holdings to the productivity of the land—to achieve a measure of equality among the beneficiaries—is more complex and therefore more time-consuming in Syria than it is in Egypt. Secondly, cultivation in Syria is on the whole much more extensive, so that heavy capital outlays are required to maintain production at the levels prevailing before the reform. Also in the newly opened-up regions population density is low, so that distribution involves large-scale investments in resettlement projects and infrastructure.[8]

Effect on Output and Incomes

The reform has so far been accompanied by an increase in total output, the

---

[1] 'Réforme Agraire, Justice Sociale, et Développement Economique en Syrie', *L'Economie et les Finances de la Syrie et des Pays Arabes*, Damascus, June 1963.

[8] Dabbagh, Salah. 'Agrarian Reform in Syria', *Middle East Economic Papers*, Beirut, 1962.

index of annual output for 1962–7 being on average 37% higher than for 1952–7. This was partly due to an increase in the area under certain crops but mainly to an improvement in land productivity. Thus the annual average yields of the three major crops, wheat, barley, and cotton, for 1962–7 were, respectively, 20%, 10% and 47% higher than for 1952–7. This sharp rise in cotton yields was due not so much to the improvement of existing soil but more to the reallocation of cotton cultivation from dry land to irrigated land.

The recipients of land have realised a substantial gain because the annual payments in respect of the purchase price of the land total only one-sixteenth of the rent previously paid to the landlords.[9] But the extent of the relative increase in their incomes varies according to the share in the produce they previously paid as tenants or share-croppers : the higher the share, the higher the percentage increase in income and vice versa. In other words, among the former tenants the poorest benefited most. Thus the impact of the reform was greatest in the old, crowded regions and lowest in the sparsely populated regions of recent settlement.

Tenants and share-croppers are in theory better off now,[10] but it is doubtful whether, in congested districts where competition for rented land is still intense, the provisions regulating conditions of tenure are observed. The solution to this problem, though extremely expensive, lies in shifting labour over to under-populated regions.

Expansion of irrigation
Until 1966 Syria's land reform had provided land for only 6% of the landless rural population, but when it is completed about 20% should have become owners. The level of output and productivity has been rising, but whether this trend will be sustained in the future is uncertain. Already there has been a steady decline in the private sector's purchases of agricultural machinery following the drastic reduction of the upper limit to landownership in 1963. Net domestic fixed capital formation in agriculture fell by 85% between 1963 and 1967. It is therefore important that the government continue the work of expansion begun by private enterprise. But the real problem in Syria is not a shortage of land but the uneven distribution of the rural population. The expansion of dry-farming under private enterprise, though important in terms of agricultural development, has done little to rectify this. The low yields and the irregularity of rainfall require that holdings be large and cultivation extensive. The expansion of irrigation, on the other hand, will permit intensive cultivation and draw more labour per land unit from areas of 'surplus'.

The Syrian Government has in fact initiated several irrigation projects, and resettlement has been under way for some time. But the most important single project is the construction of the Euphrates dam, begun in 1968. It is expected that together these projects will permit an increase of nearly one million hectares in irrigated land, raising the proportion of irrigated land

[9] The purchase price was fixed at one-quarter of the value of the land, estimated at ten times the statutory rental, payable in 40 years. If x is the rental value of the land, the annuity works out at $\dfrac{10x}{4 \times 40} = \dfrac{1}{16}x$

[10] It should be noted in this connection that, in fixing a ceiling for rents, account was taken of a host of physical conditions, such as the quality of the soil, availability of water, etc. For example, rents range from £S4 per hectare of rain-fed land in the governorate of Homs to £S103 in the irrigated parts of Latakia. See *Statistical Abstract 1967*, Syrian Arab Republic, Ministry of Planning, Damascus, 1969.

from 8% to 20% of the total cultivated area. A more balanced allocation of the peasant population will achieve what the reform cannot achieve alone.

LAND REFORM IN IRAQ

The old land tenure system

Not until the early 1930s was there a clear legal framework regulating land tenure in Iraq. In law, most of the land was the property of the state. In practice, it was held in customary tenure by tribal shaikhs and cultivated by tribesmen exercising a prescriptive right of (communal) occupation. Only a small proportion of the cultivated land was registered as permanent lease-hold, legally recognised since Ottoman times.

In an attempt to stabilise the land tenure system, successive governments in the 1930s and 1940s carried out cadastral surveys and title settlements. Titles were to be granted to those making 'productive use' of the land.[11] Strictly speaking, this should have meant the distribution of the greater part of the land amongst smaller farmers actually cultivating it. However, much of the land passed into the hands of the tribal shaikhs who had by then infiltrated parliament and gained political influence. They had also installed irrigation pumps along the river and could therefore claim to be making 'productive use' of the land. As a result, communal tenures broke up and the tribesmen's prescriptive right of occupation lapsed.

The pre-revolutionary reform

In the post-war period (1945–58) the Government launched several land-settlement schemes in an effort to tackle a variety of political and social problems arising, in part, from the extreme inequality in the distribution of land-ownership. The long-term aim of the Government was to settle all the cultivable land belonging to the state, or some 60% of Iraq's total cultivable area. In principle, this would raise peasant earnings everywhere because of the attendant decline in the man-land ratio. That seems to have been the Government's idea in attempting land reform without impinging on the existing political structure.

As it turned out, the technical and administrative complexities of the settlement programme were staggering. After 13 years of continuous effort by indigenous and foreign technicians, only a fraction of the landless labour force had been settled on an area of 1·7 million donums (1 donum = 0·618 acres).[12] Not all the new settlers were small farmers; some were retired army officers and retired civil servants. What is more significant is that half of the newly irrigated state domain was granted to influential shaikhs with a view to securing their co-operation. It looked as though effective reform could only be achieved through revolution.

Land reform legislation

In a violent coup d'état on 14 July 1958 the monarchy was overthrown and a military régime established. In September of the same year, the agrarian reform law was enacted. By then the distribution of landownership had become extremely unequal, with 2% of all proprietors holding 70% of the

[11] Hashimi, Rasool M. H. and Edwards, Alfred L. 'Land Reform in Iraq: Economic and Social Implications', Land Economics, February 1961.
[12] In the earlier stages of the programme much land went out of cultivation because of floods and soil salinisation resulting from lack of adequate dykes and drainage facilities. For a detailed account of the land settlement programme, see Adams, W. 'The Pre-Revolutionary Decade of Land Reform in Iraq', Economic Development and Cultural Change, April 1963.

land in farms of over 1,000 donums, while 70% of all proprietors owned about 3% of the land in plots of less than 30 donums. The position of share-croppers living on the vast estates—some of these ranged from 100,000 to one million donums—had deteriorated markedly.

The agrarian reform law of 1958 set the maximum size of farms at 1,000 donums for irrigated land and 2,000 donums for rain-fed land. Land above these limits was to be expropriated; after a five-year period of provisional management by the Ministry of Agrarian Reform, it was to be distributed, together with state land, among small cultivators, in holdings of between 30 and 60 donums of irrigated land and 60 to 120 donums of rain-fed land. Expropriated landowners were to be compensated, and the beneficiaries were required to pay the purchase price of their holdings in 20 annual instalments. The new owners were to join State-controlled co-operative societies which would provide agricultural inputs, farm equipment, irrigation and drainage as well as organising production and marketing. Finally, the law regulated the relationship between landlords and tenants, defining their duties and their respective shares of the produce in some detail. Eviction was prohibited.

Land reform was seen as a way of destroying the political power of the great landlords and of restoring the land to the cultivators, whose customary right of occupation had been disregarded in the 1930s and 1940s. It also seemed to promise greater productivity by providing better services through co-operation and by dividing up the enormous estates into more manageable farm units.[13]

Expropriation and distribution
In scope, the Iraqi reform was much more radical than both the Egyptian and the Syrian. Out of an area of 23·3 million donums of privately-owned land, some 7·6 million were subject to expropriation under the law. Expropriation proceeded at a rapid rate: from 1958 to 1967, over 6·8 million donums were requisitioned. In contrast, the rate of distribution was much slower: only 2·5 million donums of expropriated land and 1·3 million donums of state land had been distributed by 1967. About 6·9 million donums consisting partly of expropriated farms and partly of state domain, were managed by contract between the government and cultivators. (Most of these figures are open to question.) Thus the area brought under government control by the reform amounted to 9·7 million donums, or 40% of Iraq's farmland, the size of the entire agricultural area of Egypt. Equally impressive was the size of the rural population operating under Government control. About 54,000 families became now owners and 188,000 families became tenants of the state, together representing 30% of the total rural population in 1967.

With so much land to administer, the Iraqi civil service faced almost in-superable problems. The procedure for confiscation and distribution alone was so cumbersome—involving no less than four different departments—that it is a wonder the reform did not founder from the start. The determina-tion to forge ahead with expropriation came from the communists, who had gained control of the Ministry of Agrarian Reform. But distribution lagged seriously behind expropriation, allegedly because of the communists' opposi-tion to the formation of a *kulak* class which, once established, would resist

[13] Some of the estates were so large that the 'landowners preferred to abandon saline land and shift cultivation to new land, rather than undertake the cost of drainage'. Warriner, Doreen. *Land Reform in Principle and Practice*, Clarendon Press, Oxford, 1969.

collectivisation under state ownership. So the greater part of the expropriated land remained under the jurisdiction of the government and operated by 'temporary' tenant-farmers.

However, the stalemate continued after the communists were removed from office by the military take-over of 1963. Between 1963 and 1967 only 0·7 million donums were distributed as compared with 1·8 million donums distributed during the period of communist control. Thus the failure to distribute land more quickly cannot be attributed to communist strategy but mainly to the lack of skilled personnel. Communist policy was indeed to delay distribution, but even if it were not, distribution could not have been carried out on a wider scale. The number of trained agronomists, engineers, co-operative supervisors and accountants was far too small to provide all those entitled to land under the reform law with technical guidance, agricultural inputs, irrigation and drainage facilities and marketing services. In a harsh environment such as Iraq's, where the soil is saline and the climate dry, where the cultivator is unskilled and suspicious of the central government, especially one that is more concerned with its own survival than with carrying out reforms, the need for an adequate supply of trained technicians seems particularly urgent. The problem has been aggravated by the unsettled state of Iraqi politics. Frequent *coups d'état*, executions and sporadic violence in the streets do not provide the kind of setting in which a competent and dedicated civil service can develop.

Effects on production and incomes

Up to 1967, tenants of the state numbering 188,000 families and operating 6·9 million donums received little help from the authorities and paid little rent, if any at all. The beneficiaries numbering 54,000 families and operating 2·5 million donums were grouped into 200 co-operative societies which were ill-equipped and understaffed and could offer little beside a relatively small amount of seeds and fertilisers. Marketing services were rarely provided and rarely sought. In any case they offered no price advantage. Meanwhile, private merchants found the task of dealing with a vast number of small producers expensive and consequently paid lower prices than previously, when there were fewer producers. Irrigation pumps and drainage canals were not properly maintained, and the volume of credit remained small. In these circumstances, productivity was bound to suffer.

Of all the major crops—wheat, barley, rice and cotton—only cotton showed some improvement. The annual average of wheat yields for 1961–6 was 23% lower than the annual average for 1952–7. Production, however, was only 8% lower because of the expansion by 20% of the area sown to wheat. In the case of barley where the area remained almost unchanged, production and productivity fell by about 25%. Rice yields maintained their pre-reform level, but both area and output were 20% larger. Though cotton yields rose sharply by over 40%, output stagnated owing to the contraction in the area under cotton.

Figures for 1967 and 1968 show considerable improvement in all but the barley crop. In 1968 wheat yields recovered to the pre-reform level while production and area increased by nearly one-half. Rice yields in 1967 and 1968 surpassed by one-third the highest level ever attained before the reform. Even more dramatic was the increase in cotton yields.

Whether this is the beginning of a new trend is too early to judge. All that can be said is that since 1965, when the land reform programme was incorporated into the five-year plan, a greater effort has been made to improve farming standards. Old co-operatives have been activated and new ones established. Larger quantities of agricultural inputs have been distributed. The amount of fertilisers consumed in 1966–7 for instance was 2·5 times greater than in 1964–5.[14] Though the technical and organisational problems have not been settled by a long way—some have not even been recognised—a step forward has at last been taken toward raising agricultural productivity.

The recipients of land, whether owners or tenants of the state, gained substantially from the reform despite the fall in productivity (before 1967). The reason is simply that most of them did not pay for the land assigned to them, while the fall in productivity was not nearly big enough to cancel out the gain from the use of free land. For its part, the government lost little from the transfer of land, simply because it too did not pay much in compensation to the old landowners. In effect, the reform restored the position of the peasants, whose prescriptive right of occupation of state land had been taken away in the 1930s and 1940s.

[14] In absolute terms the amount consumed in 1966–7 was still trivial. FAO *Production Yearbook*, Rome, Vol. 21, 1967.

FURTHER READING

Baer, Gabriel. 'The Evolution of Landownership in Egypt and the Fertile Crescent', *The Economic History of the Middle East 1800–1914*, Univ. of Chicago Press, Chicago and London, 1966.

El-Akhras, Hicham. 'General Review of Syrian Agriculture in 1967', *L'Economie et les Finances des Pays Arabes*, Damascus, May 1968.

El Ghonemy, M. Riad. 'Economic and Industrial Organization of Egyptian Agriculture since 1952', *Egypt Since the Revolution*, Allen and Unwin, London, 1968.

Garzouzi, Eva. 'Land Reform in Syria', *Middle East Journal*, Washington DC, Winter–Spring 1963.

Langley, Kathleen M. 'Iraq: Some Aspects of the Economic Scene', *Middle East Journal*, Washington DC, Spring 1964.

Raphaeli, Nimrod. 'Agrarian Reform in Iraq: Some Political and Administrative Problems', *Journal of Local Administration Overseas*, April 1966.

Saab, Gabriel S. *The Egyptian Agrarian Reform 1952–1962*, Oxford Univ. Press, London and New York, 1967.

ADEL KAMAL. Research economist at the Oxford University Institute of Economics and Statistics since 1964. While in Egypt worked for the Egyptian Government as an Information Officer and contributed regularly to the English drama section of the Egyptian Broadcasting Service. Co-author of 'Rural Credit System in the UAR' and 'Agrarian Reform in the UAR' published in the *Bulletin of the Oxford University Institute of Economics and Statistics* (1967 and 1968 respectively).

EDUCATION IN THE ARAB STATES
OF THE MIDDLE EAST

ABDUL AZIZ EL-KOUSSY

INTRODUCTION

WERE it not for the fact that in the world as a whole expenditure is highest on armaments, education would certainly come first. Expenditure[1] on education is reported to be about 70%, and on health about 30%, of that on armaments. If the world has not yet come to its senses, at least it is coming to realise the importance of education and this accounts for its progress during the last 20 years. But such progress would have been much greater, and its effect on the peace and happiness of the human race would have been remarkably increased, if man were more enlightened and more rational and if he gave education top priority.

It has been observed that developments in education are almost always closely related to political developments. In this respect the Middle East presents no exception and the radical political changes that have recently taken place in the area have been accompanied by great changes in education. Most of the Arab countries have been emancipated only recently from foreign occupation. Syria and Lebanon both gained their independence in 1943 and the occupying troops were withdrawn in 1945 and 1946 respectively; the Sudan became independent in 1956; the Republic of South Yemen in 1967; Egypt acquired incomplete independence (with four reservations) in 1922, and this became complete with the withdrawal of British troops in 1954.

Long before the achievement of independence, education was being recognised in the Arab world as a potent tool for political and economic development and has since made rapid progress. The number of pupils has increased by leaps and bounds. In almost all the constitutions of all the Arab countries it has been stipulated that education is compulsory at least at the first level and it is also provided free at almost all levels in a number of countries in the region.

The eagerness of the State to spread education helped to satisfy the people's desire for it as an instrument for improving the standard of living. It was also considered essential to a liberated democratic and secure way of life. The progress of education, which was noticeable everywhere and in everyone, took place not only out of conviction but also in response to various kinds of pressure. There was the growing self-awareness, the challenge and

[1] This was quoted in the UAR daily paper *Al-Ahram*, 1968 as from a USA Official Report.

the impact of the Western rate of progress, the desire to be on a par with the rest of the world, the wide gap between political achievement and economic potential, and on top of that the population explosion. It is a familiar axiom that when progress succumbs to pressure it is likely to get out of balance. And as this happened in the Arab States it became imperative to adopt planning in the interests of a balanced development. This applied to education as well as to other areas.

It is true that some progress has been achieved; but it is also true that there is a long way yet to go and that there are various signs of imbalance. There is the disparity between quantity and quality, due to the steep rise in the number of pupils in schools, apparently accompanied by a drop in the quality. With this rapid increase in the number of pupils, the number of teachers grows at a slower rate and the number of classrooms at a slower rate still. There is also an imbalance between technical and so-called general or academic education, between what is offered by the schools and what is needed by the community and between what is needed and what is wanted. Everybody advocates, for example, the value of technical, practical and scientific education, but meanwhile academic education continues to exercise a far greater attraction. There are various other aspects of imbalance, as well as other sources of conflict. An example of the latter is the conflict that exists between conservative traditional trends and modern patterns of education; and there is also the conflict between education for independence and that for dependence.

Despite these contradictions, education has been explicitly and enthusiastically regarded in the Arab world as a powerful instrument for development, from the political, economic, cultural, social and humanitarian point of view.

General Survey[2]

Education made very little progress during the period of foreign rule. One example may be given from Egypt, where expenditure on education was only 0·8% of the total expenditure in 1882. Under public pressure this figure was increased to 4% in 40 years and it is at present more than 18%. The recent progress in terms of enrolment can also be shown in the following figures : in Syria modern primary school enrolment increased from 148,000 in 1944–5 to 647,000 in 1964–5, while in Iraq it rose from 375,000 in 1932 to 957,000 in 1964–5 and in Egypt from 380,000 in 1922 to 3·5 million in 1966–7. Enrolment in primary education in Libya was increasing at the rate of 30% annually in the late 1950s, but as school enrolment has become general the rate has gradually decreased.

Although statistically the rates of progress are very high and the total expenditure on education has enormously increased, the Arab countries in the region have not achieved what they were hoping for from education.

The total population in 1966–7 was approximately 77·6 million with a 2·6% annual rate of increase.[3] The number of children of primary school age was 12·8 million out of which 7·0 million were actually at school in 1966–7. This means that the enrolment ratio for the region is 56%, but it varies from

---

[2] All the figures are taken from official or UN reports. A few of them are estimates or calculations.
[3] The total population of the Arab world in the Middle East and the Maghrib approached 110 million in 1966–7.

90% in Lebanon to 8% in Yemen, with 71% for Iraq, 74% for Jordan and 87% for Syria.

The yearly rate of increase in primary school enrolment used to be 10% from 1950 to 1960 but it has since slowed down to 6·1%. This is still two-and-a-half times the rate of population growth, which shows that primary education is well on the way to becoming generally available, but a very great effort will be needed to achieve this within, say, 20 years.

The picture is different for secondary education, where enrolment has been increasing during the last five years at an annual rate of 17·1%, while in the previous ten years it was 13·4%. Enrolment for higher education is at present growing at a still higher rate, approximately 25% yearly. The total number of students undertaking higher education in the Arab countries of the region at present is nearly 300,000.

EDUCATION OF GIRLS

It is true that the percentage of girls attending school is not as high as the percentage of boys. In 1961 the girls in primary schools were 34·8% of the total enrolment; by 1966–7 they had become 36·1%. The difference is not as small as it may seem, since the figures given are relative and not absolute; the percentage for the absolute increase in girls' primary education is over 10%. The proportion of girls of secondary school age who actually attend secondary school ranges from 2% to 25% in the region. The percentage of girls to the total enrolment was 24·1 in 1961–2 and it reached 28·2 in 1966–7. For higher education in the UAR the girls represented 14% of the total in 1955, 17% in 1960, and 20% in 1964. In Iraq they represented 23% in 1960 and 26% in 1964.

Although these figures show a definite improvement in the educational opportunities available to girls, they also show that there still exists some resistance to the idea of women's education, especially around the age of marriage when the home becomes the main responsibility.

It is interesting at this point to mention that there is evidence that the education of women gives the society its best defence against the population explosion and this makes it a really potent weapon of social change. Recent research[4] carried out in the UAR has established the average number of living offspring, in the married lifespan of 30 years, for wives of varying degrees of education. It shows that for illiterate women the average is 8·1; for those who completed primary education, 6·9; for those who completed junior secondary, 5·9; for those who completed secondary, 5·1; and for those who passed through higher education, 3·9. Since there is, of course, no indication that fertility decreases with education, the explanation may be that when a woman is educated she likes to keep up a high standard of living which she cannot achieve unless she limits her responsibilities by controlling the size of her family. It is also obvious that the more is spent on the education of women the more is saved in the domains of health and social welfare services.

Such an argument will encourage the Arab States to make education equally available to girls and boys and to lengthen the period of compulsory education. In two countries, Jordan (1964) and Kuwait (1965), it has already been extended to cover primary and the first level of secondary school. The same trend is likely to be followed in the near future throughout the region.

[4] Shafei, A. M. N. 'The Fertility of Educated Married Women', *Journal of Educational Planning in the Arab World*, vol. VI, 1966, no. 10 (in Arabic).

PRIMARY, SECONDARY AND HIGHER EDUCATION

Another way of testing the balanced progress of education and the extent to which it realises fair opportunities among all citizens is to examine the different levels of education offered (variously referred to by educationalists as the educational 'pyramid', 'tree' or 'ladder').

The school ladder usually begins at the age of six or seven with the entrance to primary education but there are a few nurseries and kindergartens that precede this step. The number of children between the ages of three and six is estimated at 8·6 million. Of these, according to the official and UN figures, 200,000 (2·3%) have access to pre-school education, the highest percentage being in Lebanon (34·5) and in Kuwait (24·0). The Arab countries in general are gradually paying more attention to pre-school education, in order to solve the problems arising from industrialisation, urbanisation, city congestion and the flow of women to the labour market. But there are also other important factors supporting pre-primary education, such as social education and preparation for the stages to come, whether educational or otherwise.

For primary, secondary and higher education, Table 1 shows progress as well as ratios.

TABLE 1

SCHOOL ENROLMENT BY LEVEL, 1961 and 1966

Level	Enrolment 1961–2	Enrolment 1966–7
Primary	5,243,610	7,000,000
Secondary	1,120,077	2,101,400
Higher	170,000	300,000

In the Arab countries of the region in 1961, for every 100 pupils in primary schools there were 21·4 in secondary and 3·2 in higher education. The situation in 1966 was certainly very much better, since for every 100 primary school pupils there were 30·1 in secondary schools and 4·3 in higher institutes. This did not include those studying abroad in non-Arab countries. In the year 1966, for every 100 primary school pupils in France there were 74 in secondary schools; in the same year, for every 100 primary school pupils in the USA there were 61 in secondary and 19 in higher schools. Of course, in comparing the Arab countries with countries like these we must first remember that the population structure is not the same, since the proportion of young people to the total population is higher in the Arab countries than it is in any country in North America or Western Europe; but this demographic phenomenon does not account for the whole difference. It is doubtful whether all those who finish one stage of education and are capable of pursuing the stage that follows can find access to it. And if equal abilities do not somehow get equal opportunities various questions arise, related both to social justice and to waste of human resources. Looking at the above figures we can see that the Arab countries have achieved a great deal but that they still have a long way to go. They are conscious of what is needed and they are making efforts to achieve it.

Another aspect of the educational ladder is related to the number of years of schooling. The pattern of primary, junior secondary and senior secondary school years is for most Arab countries 6-3-3. But it is still 4-4-4 for Kuwait, Sudan and the Gulf region, 5-4-3 for Lebanon and 6-3-2 for Iraq. According to the Arab Cultural Agreement of 1957, the recommendations of the Arab League and a number of regional meetings, the 6-3-3 system should be the objective. The aim is also to make the corresponding parts of the ladder of equal standard, in order to facilitate as far as possible the exchange of pupils and teachers among Arab countries.

Until recently there was a great variety of primary schools which caused a lack of standardisation in instruction, and consequently a lack of real equality of opportunity. The region inherited the Koranic schools, the modern primary schools with or without foreign language instruction, and the schools, run by foreigners, with Arabic as a second language. Although such a heterogeneity was widespread in certain areas it is now disappearing. It was thus the policy of the states after independence, in order to attain unity and democracy, to aim at one primary school for all. There is of course resistance which is getting weaker in the face of the efforts of the state. Primary education is free, since it is recognised as a birthright in accordance with article 26 of the Universal Declaration of Human Rights as well as in all the constitutions of the Middle East.

The modern state primary school is co-educational, free and compulsory, and is clearly an instrument of social and political reform. The importance of primary education for the state may be seen from the fact that the expenditure on primary education as compared to total expenditure on education has shown a great increase. Egypt may be taken as an example : in 1920 the proportion was 15·4%, in 1945 it was 38·7% and in 1964–5 it reached 60%.

The curriculum for primary education still comprises separate subjects : Arabic, religion, arithmetic, science, social sciences, and practical arts and crafts. Great attention is given to foreign languages in Lebanon, to religion in Saudi Arabia and to arts and crafts in the UAR. Promotion from one class to another is effected largely through tests (with their obvious disadvantages as a means of assessment), UNRWA and UAR being exceptions. It is argued that automatic promotion makes both pupils and teachers neglect their duties. It is also argued that until we have a good system of evaluating pupils through cumulative records and have enough adjacent special schools, the system of examining, passing, failing and repeating has to be kept. Such a remedy is neither pedagogically nor economically sound.

Moving to secondary education, we find it divided into two parts, the first lasting three or four years and usually called first level general. But since it carries the pupil to further education leading to a career, this first part is intended to give the fundamental skills—linguistic, numerical, intellectual, moral, social and physical. It is also intended to bring the pupil into contact with a number of varied individual and collective practical activities through which he may discover his own abilities and tendencies and so be able to choose his future education and career.

It is on the whole agreed in the Arab countries that while primary education gives the basic skills for the all-round development of the pupil, secondary education aims at providing the country with citizens who are positive, productive and responsive to their own countries, to the sister countries in the region, and to humanity at large. Secondary education is also charged with preparing pupils for more responsibility in the economic, social and political development of the country. This first level is followed by a second level of secondary education which is usually divided into second level general and technical, the general being divided into scientific and literary, while the technical is divided into industrial, commercial, agricultural and 'feminine' (usually home economics). The Arab countries have not yet reached the most recent educational development found now in most of Europe—the unified comprehensive secondary school.

The curricula for secondary schools are formulated at ministry level by subject specialists, pedagogues and practising teachers. It was agreed at a meeting convened by the Arab League that the medium of instruction should be Arabic, that every pupil must study the history of his own country within the context of Arab history, and that he must also be given an idea of world history. Curricula are usually very carefully prepared and issued by ministerial order. There is thus uniformity for each country within a common framework for the region. The teacher is supposed to adapt his teaching to the local conditions but with standardised final examinations there is more uniformity than variation. One difficulty is that secondary general education is considered from the point of view of curriculum as a preparation for the university. This tends to make the secondary school curriculum a replica of university curricula.

With regard to the contents of the curricula, more attention is given to subjects related to natural resources, such as petrol (Saudi Arabia), cotton (Egypt), etc. The UAR is trying to make its science students more socially-minded and its humanities students more scientifically-minded. More attention is given to Arab history and Arab society. As to foreign languages, French and English are usually offered, but sometimes only one. Some subjects (science and mathematics, for example) in some countries are taught in European languages—a point of sharp disagreement, with the majority on the side of Arabic as the medium of instruction for every school subject.

Apart from UNESCO's activities in the region, the Arab League, as well as the Arab Union of Teachers' Syndicates has been holding regional meetings and conferences to discuss school curricula, textbooks, teacher preparation, and the teaching of history, geography, civics, science and mathematics. Such meetings have been effective in creating a climate where progress in education is possible.

HIGHER EDUCATION

All in all there are 26 universities in the Middle East : four in Iraq, three in Saudi Arabia, one in Jordan, five in Lebanon, three in Sudan, two in Syria, seven in Egypt and one in Kuwait. There are also more than 30 other centres for higher learning, mostly in Egypt, Lebanon, Iraq and Saudi Arabia.

Enrolment for higher education is increasing at a very high rate. The proportion of those studying humanities and arts is much higher than that of those studying sciences. Those studying humanities are in some countries more than 85% of the total enrolment, the UAR being an exception. But the proportion of Arab students specialising in humanities abroad is much smaller than that of those specialising in science, mathematics and technology.

Research has also been faring well in the Arab States. The UAR and Lebanon has each its national Centre for Scientific Research. The Cairo Centre is housing nearly 250 full-time research-workers and the Lebanese Centre is financing and co-ordinating research in various fields with 300 part-time research workers. There are also hundreds of research workers at the various universities and at a large number of highly specialised research centres. Among these are the Iraq Centre for Pedagogical and Psychological

Research, the Cairo Centre for Cancer Research, the National Centre for Criminal and Social Research, the Institutes for Petrochemical Research and many others. There is at present a ministry of scientific research in Cairo and there are ministries of higher education in Syria and Egypt, and one of their main functions is the co-ordination and orientation of research.

TECHNICAL AND SCIENTIFIC ASPECTS

It is almost unanimously agreed today that one of the important criteria for national development is the degree of interest taken in technology and science. The term 'technical education' is usually given to the industrial, the agricultural and the commercial types of schooling. There is on the whole an increase in the absolute numbers engaged in secondary technical education in some Middle Eastern countries, as can be seen in Table 2.

TABLE 2

ENROLMENT IN TECHNICAL SECONDARY SCHOOLS
IN SOME ARAB COUNTRIES

	1961–2	1966–7
Kuwait	204	1,766
Sudan	3,968	4,684
Saudi Arabia	2,644	5,274
All the Arab States in the region	146,435	168,432

This means that there is an increase in the absolute numbers, but the proportion of technical pupils to the total number at the secondary level is not showing much improvement. This may be due to two factors; first, the recent establishment of a number of universities in the region with a bias towards humanities and theoretical studies, which diverts the main stream of pupils away from technical education. Another factor is the traditional resistance which still operates against technical education. It must also be remembered that technical education is more expensive to set up than academic education.

But it is gratifying to know that in Egypt the expenditure on technical education has risen from 12% of the total expenditure on education in 1959–60 to 18·2% in 1963–4. In the Sudan, expenditure on technical education was 10·7% in 1961–2. These figures are small but it takes time to change attitudes. A study of the labour force shows that there is almost a vacuum when we come to skilled labour and middle-level manpower. There is an irresistible pressure towards university education.

It may also be mentioned that although absolute numbers for agricultural secondary education are increasing, yet for every ten pupils at the industrial schools in the region there are not more than two at the agricultural schools. This state of affairs ought to be remedied.

Now if we look into the universities we find, as has been pointed out, that the emphasis is still on arts and social sciences. They account for more than 80% of the total enrolment, the UAR being an exception, where the enrolment for these branches was 52·2% in 1966. The situation for all the Arab countries is better where students studying abroad are concerned.

Among these, arts and social sciences account for 25% of the total. This is an indication of a definite policy.

To go back to local universities, the science degrees in 1963 per 100,000 of the population were as follows :[5]

Africa	2
Europe	13
Arab States[6]	3
North America	37
Asia	2
Latin America	14

The percentage increase from 1960–4 was as follows :

Africa	25·4
Europe	47·5
Arab States	71
North America	165
Asia	17·3
Latin America	112

The percentage increase for engineering was 74·2% and it was the highest in the whole world.

To take individual countries, the increase in graduates of natural sciences from 1957 to 1963 was as follows :

UAR 207%   USA 55%   UK 66%   Philippines 164%

The percentages for engineering were as follows :

UAR 145%   USA 13%   Philippines 8%

Although the high figures mean present shortages, again they provide evidence of a definite positive interest.

There is moreover a positive movement in the direction of experimental and applied sciences, and of science as related to local resources, i.e. geology, geophysics, petroleum, chemistry, etc. There is also an attempt to reshape the content and methods of teaching mathematics, so as to benefit from the recent advances in this field.

A number of specialised research and training institutes have been established and as far as the postgraduate level is concerned the amount of research work carried out at the universities is increasing very rapidly if compared with work in the humanities.

ADULT EDUCATION AND LITERACY CAMPAIGNS

There is a general recognition of the fact that as technical standards rise, it becomes imperative for every adult working citizen to get involved in some kind of further, even life-long, education. All over the Arab countries there are such attempts in factories, government departments, syndicates, schools, universities and other institutions. For example, there are over 3,000 individuals enrolled at the American University in Cairo following some course of self-improvement. There are also training courses for health officers, for agricultural assistants, for teachers and administrators; these courses are provided by the various ministries. We have no statistics at

[5] *The UNESCO Statistical Yearbook—1965.*
[6] The Arab States mentioned here are Iraq, Jordan, Lebanon, Sudan, Syria and UAR.

present concerning such activities but it is interesting to know that training of this kind aims at improving the worker's performance, enabling him to earn a higher salary; thus it has its effect on the life of the individual, of his family and of the community. It is one effective way of democratising the nation through continuing educational opportunities.

A number of experiments are carried out at the village level by a UNESCO Regional Centre in Egypt known by the name of ASFEC.

But the most vital purpose of adult education programmes is the eradication of illiteracy. It is known that illiteracy among the population of the area ranges from 85% to 15%. It is higher among females than it is among males.

In 1961 the incidence of illiteracy in Jordan was 67·6% (among males 49·8% and among females 84·8%). In Egypt the illiteracy rate decreased from 76·2% in 1947 to 70·02% in 1960. Among males it decreased from 66·1% to 56·47% and among females from 88·2% to 83·25%.

The real danger here lies in the fact that the illiterate worker gives a poorer performance and earns much less than the literate. It has been shown in a recent study carried out in Venezuela that on average the agricultural worker who has completed primary education earns five times as much as the illiterate worker. The bearer of a secondary certificate earns 12 times as much and the bearer of a university diploma earns 30 times as much.[7]

The extent of the effort to abolish illiteracy may be seen from the fact that in the Sudan the number of adults who have learned to read and write increased from 29,365 in 1959 to 51,031 in 1963, i.e. at the yearly rate of 18·4%. The number of literacy centres increased in Kuwait from seven in 1958 to 20 in 1961, while the number of students increased from 2,429 to 6,536.

A number of experiments in what is called functional literacy have been carried out by the ASFEC Regional Centre in Egypt. The idea of functional literacy is that learning to read and write should be carried out in such a way that it fulfils a fundamentally useful purpose for the learner. The Arab countries have created a Special Fund, administered by the Arab League, for functional literacy campaigns. The Special Fund and the ASFEC Regional Centre are working closely together and great achievements are expected.

ARABISATION

One of the important aspects of education in the Arab countries is the medium of instruction. During the pre-independence period education was carried on practically everywhere in the language of the troops occupying that country. The question of arabising the medium was important both from the political and from the educational point of view. When pupils use their mother tongue for education they achieve more. They are also able to get into closer contact with their own culture and with their own problems.

The question of arabisation of education is considered in the Arab countries to comprise the following elements :

(*a*) Arabic as the medium of instruction.
(*b*) Arabic as the language of books and examinations.

---

[7] Adiseshiah, Malcolm. 'The Call of Adult Education.' A presidential address given at the Annual Conference of the Indian Adult Education Association, December 1968.

(c) The study of Arab civilisation, history, geography, civics and similar subjects, without neglecting all other studies related to other parts of the world.

(d) The teachers must be of Arab nationalities.

(e) Arab folklore, art, music and literature must also be studied.

(f) The study of the natural and human resources of the Arab world.

Besides this question of arabisation, there is also the question of Egyptianisation in Egypt, Sudanisation in the Sudan, Iraqisation in Iraq and so on. This means there is a tendency towards local emphasis within the Arab framework, all being within the world trend.

Although the general trend is towards arabisation, there are certain schools in certain countries which still continue to teach some subjects in a European language. This applies more to science, mathematics and technology in post-primary education.

PLANNING AND RESEARCH

It is of course understood that with the quantitative development of education a number of problems and imbalances occur. These can only be handled through studies, research and planning, and it is difficult in this limited space to do more than touch on these activities. But while there is an imbalance in the education of girls and boys, of adults and children, in rural and urban opportunities, in technical as opposed to academic education, in the educational output in relation to social and economic needs and the insufficiency of funds, the need for educational planning is very acute. With the help of UNESCO, a Regional Centre has been established in Beirut to carry out studies and research and conduct training for educational planning. The impact of this centre has begun to be felt in the region, with the result that ministerial units for planning have been established and in some countries the third five-year plan is now in operation.

Educational research is undertaken by bodies attached to the Ministry of Education in Syria, Jordan, Lebanon and UAR. In the UAR the unit responsible for the elaboration of the plan, the statistical unit and the documentation unit are all charged with responsibilities for carrying out research, studies and deeper analyses. There are also various institutes, with the universities and teacher-training colleges, which conduct and supervise research, most of which is for higher degrees. Mention may also be made of the recently established Psychological and Educational Research Centre in Baghdad. While the Beirut Regional Centre carries out research related to planning, the regional centre in Egypt carries out research related to literacy campaigns and community development. Naturally the research and studies carried out by the universities are different from those undertaken by the ministries.

In any case it is unanimously recognised that for the long-range improvement of education in the Arab countries, planning and research are the keynotes.

ADMINISTRATION

The Arab countries of the region have populations ranging from 32 million to a few thousand. The area of each country, the state of transport and communications and the modality of government all impose on the pattern of administration certain trends which are reflected in the administration of education. The tendency until recently was to centralise educational activities at the ministerial level and to have local administrative units for their implementation. (In two countries, Syria and Egypt, there are separate ministries of education and of higher education.) The main responsibilities of each ministry are to lay down policy; to draw up the plans, projects and programmes for the implementation of this policy; to ensure a well-balanced geographical distribution of educational services according to local needs; to estimate funds needed for executing plans and projects; to evaluate the process of education; to decide upon principles governing the role of the schools and universities in the community they serve; to draft laws, decrees and regulations; to set the required standard for the teaching staff; to decide upon suitable curricula, textbooks and educational requirements. The ministries encourage research, regulate and establish cultural relations with other countries, and co-ordinate educational activities with the activities of other ministries. The local bodies are responsible for implementing the plans. They are responsible for choosing school sites, distributing pupils and classes; applying and supervising curricula and general directives; supervising promotion examinations; providing school meals and health services. The Minister of Education is usually helped by a director general of the ministry or a small group of under-secretaries, while the Director of Education at the local level is assisted by regional controllers and district inspectors.

There are of course variations in detail, depending on the size of the country and the modality of the government. In short, the Central Ministry is responsible for the general policy and the main plan in outline, while the local authorities are responsible for implementing the plan and carrying out the directives of the Central Ministry.

It must be remembered that the majority of schools and universities in the Arab countries of the region belong to the state. Private education comprises on average about 20% of the total education system in each country; it is only in Lebanon that private institutions at all levels are in the majority.

It is the usual practice for primary education to be the total responsibility of the local authorities, except for legislation and overall planning. The appointment of teachers and headmasters and their transfer is the responsibility of the local Director of Education.

As time goes on, more responsibility is being given to the local directors, leaving the Central Ministry to handle questions of general policy, planning, research, budgeting and general directives.

AID

It is obvious that the burden of improving education and effecting substantial educational progress is a heavy one for developing countries. For this reason the Arab countries depend to a considerable extent on bilateral and international aid. Aid is mainly given for technical development and makes possible teacher-training, technical education, research, planning, innovations in education and in school buildings. In practically every Arab country there is some project for the development of one or more of these activities. Through the help of UNESCO, technical assistance, the International Development Association (IDA) and the International Bank of Reconstruction (IBRD) a great deal has already been achieved and still more is expected.

FURTHER READING

Boktor, Amin. *The Development and Expansion of Education in the UAR*, The American Univ., Cairo, 1963.
UNESCO and International Bureau of Education. *International Yearbook of Education*, IBE, Geneva, 1952–67.

ABDUL AZIZ EL-KOUSSY. Director, Regional Centre for Educational Planning and Administration in the Arab Countries. One-time Professor and Dean of the College of Education, Ein Shams University, and Technical Adviser to the Ministry of Education, Cairo. Among his many books on psychology and education are *Essentials of Psychology* (1964) and *Statistics in Psychology and Education* (1960).

WESTERNISATION IN THE ARAB WORLD

NORMAN DANIEL

THE Arab dilemma is the dilemma of any man in debt against his will; every Arab is the technological debtor of the West, and is naturally more resentful of alien intrusion just because indebted. Europeans and Arabs share a long history of reciprocal suspicion. Even today, some Europeans who live in an Arab country feel that Muslim society is alien, hostile and somehow irreconcilable; and most Arabs often have a similar feeling about the post-Christian world. The difference is that people of European stock are reassured by the thought that the technological world is their own; Arabs are correspondingly disturbed that they should not yet command it equally. They cannot feel that they enjoy even a proportionate share in the government of a world in which many groups suffer radical injustice, and not least, as they see it, their own. The old direct imperial rule has gone, and it is admitted that even indirect rule survives only in some countries. Yet somehow the mastery has remained with Europe and America. The 'developed' countries are still in power.

The inheritance is sour on both sides. Arabs today think of Christian Europe as having ceaselessly attacked them since Urban preached the First Crusade, although in fact the see-saw of mutual aggression is a good deal older and more complex than that. Europeans who dominated the world in the 19th century claimed that the technological advance which gave them the power derived from the moral superiority of the Christian religion. To the Arabs, for whom Christianity, of course, can never be better than an imperfect form of Islam, it was self-evident that a higher technology only supported the intrusion of a lower culture. The two societies are too far from each other in idiom of thought and expression to allow useful cross-fertilisation. What most appealed to the Arabs in the modern impact of Europe was the revolutionary attitude. From General Bonaparte, who had some difficulty in persuading his colleagues to manipulate Islamic sentiment, to the New Left of 1969, the revolutionary tradition has been even more contemptuous of Islam than of Christianity, but because it seems to reject the Christian past of Europe, of which, in fact, it is the product, it has made an impact upon Arab attitudes. It has seemed to offer one means of catching up with Europe. The classic statement of anti-imperialism is Hobson's, and its refinement Lenin's; and at first this seemed to offer a relatively easy solution. It was only necessary to get rid of the English or the French and all would be well. The first and simplest aim of nationalism was this, but it was not enough.

Jamal al-Din al-Afghani saw the real dilemma long ago. He said in 1882 : 'The Europeans have now put their hands on every part of the world. The

English have reached Afghanistan; the French have seized Tunisia. In reality this usurpation, aggression and conquest has not come from the French or the English. Rather it is science that everywhere manifests its greatness and power.' Unless the Arabs can make this science their own they cannot enjoy their share of power—'this true ruler, which is science, is continually changing capitals', but the capitals of science, although they have shifted from their former concentration in Western Europe to America and to Russia, have not shifted back to the Muslim world.

In the second half of the 20th century the effects of Western technological development are being felt much more widely than they were in the imperial age. This is one reason why there is more bitter resentment of Western 'imperial' influence than there was when it put the whole Arab world in shadow; resentment is learned by the young as part of their national, even of their personal, pride. Western consumer society is affecting Arab ways of living, while the Arab world has little control over the technology that shapes it. A young man growing up in the Middle East finds himself surrounded by alien artefacts: cars, buses, trams, trains, aeroplanes, tractors, even bicycles; fans, refrigerators, air-conditioners, heaters; pre-fabricated parts of buildings, cookers, sinks, plumbing materials; transistors, television sets; tinned foods, razors and razor-blades, tooth brushes, spectacles, pharmaceutical preparations; whatever is not old and traditional is foreign. Arab Governments do their best to encourage local industries to take over the manufacture of many of these things, or, if that is not possible, to assemble them or at least to package them. Sometimes the locally produced object proves inferior to the foreign import on which it is modelled, and it even happens that people will denigrate the home-made article when it is not inferior. At best it remains a copy, and cumulatively the impression is inevitably that everything modern is foreign. In fact, Western manufacturers have done more to shape daily life than a list of goods made in the West, or even modelled on the West, can measure, but, though the full extent of the technical obligation may not be realised, it is apparent to every Arab that the world into which he is born is dominated by Western technology.

Of course, the world into which every Englishman is born is dominated by the same technology, and it affects his daily life much more thoroughly; but, although its source is sometimes obviously American and it is eroding inherited ways of English life, for the most part it does not seem really foreign to him. The new world remains his own; the new facilities, the salesmanship, the mass consumption of mass products, are, or seem to be, introduced by other Englishmen; and they did indeed originate either in England, or in a society closely similar and related to English society, in America or Europe. In particular, they are welcomed by the masses for whom they are designed, and who derive the principal advantage from them.

The relation of society to consumer goods is quite different in the Middle East. The impact of a foreign technology is primarily on the urban middle class which has succeeded that tiny minority of wealthy men who were once the sole beneficiaries of material progress. It does not reach the masses, who are still too immersed in ancient ways to reap the benefit, though they envy it. The mass market has not yet been developed on the scale familiar in the West. Some of the urban proletariat and the cash-crop farmers, as consumers, are affected by the minor products of the modern world—tinned goods and razor-blades—but cannot benefit on a considerable scale, because they have little access to consumer credit. As producers they are affected, using, for example, electric pumps in irrigation, but this is no mass market.

The subsistence-farmers and the nomads would doubtless be as glad as any European to have gas cookers or refrigerators, but they could not conceive how to use them, without a revolution in their way of life. The transistor radio, which can easily be adapted to almost any form of society or way of life, has been successful wherever there is a sufficient margin of profit over subsistence. Most of the products of contemporary Western technology cannot so easily be absorbed by society as it is now constituted in the Middle East.

Although Westernisation is not just a question of the pressures of modern technology, I believe that this is the key to the problem. If there had been no technological advantage over the Arabs, they would not have been subjected to imperial aggression in the first place, or now to what is called neo-colonialism. The effect of foreign technology is international, and takes no account of Arab cultural requirements. 'The logic of the international corporation is based on the need to find large markets. . . . Once established the corporation will tend to make decisions primarily based on the economic benefit to the corporation as a whole.' This is not a Marxist speaking, but the chairman-designate of the British Institute of Management. It is the aim of every revolutionary and every nationalist Arab government to reduce imported consumer goods, for reasons of cultural as well as of economic independence.

Yet the Arabs want consumer goods, like everybody else, but they would like to make their own, and they also want heavy industry in the hope of making their own position independent. If the inevitable impression is that everything modern is foreign, the obvious inference is that the profit is foreign too. Hence the theory of neo-colonialism : the Europeans who not so long ago visibly held the jobs in government are gone, but the arrogance of commercial representatives is disliked even more, and the sight of wealth leaving the country is never palliated by the thought of benefit received from outside investment. There is particular suspicion of foreign capital beyond Arab control. This results in the demand for the nationalisation of banks and makes co-operation with the World Bank difficult. Financial orthodoxy is resented and some kind of socialist solution preferred, not because it is socialist, but because it conduces most easily to the limitation of foreign influence.

In one way this leads to a demand for more Westernisation, not less. In accordance with anti-imperialist tradition, the advice of Western experts, however sound economically, is suspect when they say that underdeveloped countries should concentrate on developing their natural agricultural resources, and leave industrial development to countries better endowed for the purpose. This is seen as a trick to rob the underdeveloped countries of the sources of power; as an example, it is said that the industrial exploitation of their oil is carried out in countries already developed, not in the countries where it is found. A highly mechanised farming may well be the best solution of many economic problems, and it may produce wealth, status and a kind of influence; but it cannot produce arms or the means of effective power. Moreover, the Hobsonian theory of the exploitation of 'colonial' markets is likely to prove true in a cultural sense at least. An agricultural country may be highly mechanised and productive, but without industry it cannot create either the machinery needed in the fields or the majority of objects in everyday use. Unless it processes its own products it will not even determine the form in which food will reach it. By exporting only raw material it must receive a cultural influence while able to impose none in

518

return. Only he to whom the technology belongs can shape the artefacts he uses.

For all these reasons the 'struggle against imperialism' and the struggle against Western influence are closely connected. The socialist states are quick to point out that this is a confirmation of Marxist theory, but, in fact, they too are seen to be 'Western'. Not only was Lenin's theory of imperialism greatly indebted to an English radical. Not only is Marxism a product of European civilisation. Not only is the USSR a rich country like other European states. Not only do Russians behave like other Europeans when they travel or live in the Arab world, keeping themselves, indeed, more strictly apart than any. The central issue from which all these points derive is that the socialist countries are as foreign and different in their ways as the non-socialist. Hence comes the demand for an 'Arab socialism' (or 'African socialism'), which can adopt anti-imperialist theory without the European forms in which it is still expressed. Hence, too, the tendency nowadays to speak of the developed North and undeveloped South, rather than of East and West.

The operation of this total foreign influence, which we may continue to call Westernisation (if only to avoid 'septentrionalisation'), is not easy to define. How far can we say that the use of European articles tends to create European behaviour? To market objects designed to satisfy needs of a different society may compel customs to conform to objects, but on the whole it seems unlikely that there would be a market at all, if the need were not naturally and spontaneously felt. Salesmanship must work on something. It is the visibly alien presence, the impression of being dependent in every detail, that is hateful, but the opposition it arouses can only be justified rationally in order to argue that local industrial production is necessary. Any industrialisation results in social change.

For example, the demands of industrial efficiency conflict with traditions of hospitality, in terms of economy, time and attitudes. Sometimes Westernisation conflicts with religion, too; for example, the requirements of industrial society conflict with the Muslim fast during the month of Ramadan. The conscientious Arab makes a point of working harder when he is fasting, partly because he is aware of outside criticism of the fast, but it is still true that overall efficiency suffers in Ramadan. Western technology tends to weaken family links, by taking up time, or by causing separations, although the links remain very strong; still, they are not as strong as they were. Younger brothers will no longer refrain from sitting down, or from smoking, in front of an elder brother, or even in front of their fathers. Such things look rather like a Western onslaught on Arab customs. They also look rather like an onslaught by the passage of time. There have been comparable changes in Europe over a few generations. Loosening of social discipline is universal. All these things would be changing and modifying anyway, as time passes and conditions change. It remains true that the old order has the additional attraction that it is an Arab order, while the new one is less obviously so.

Yet the new order might be as Arab as Western. Sometimes the Arab custom has something 'modern' to offer which an earlier phase of modernisation has destroyed in the West. For example, medical opinion is beginning to question the effect of the grim impersonal discipline and short visiting hours on the patients in our hospitals, especially in paediatrics. Arab hospitals have long been criticised because it has been impossible to discipline or even to exclude the families of patients by day or by night. Now it is beginning to look as though this offers a better basis for modernisation. It is clearly possible to mistake 'Western' for 'modern', and to lose something 'Arab' to no purpose.

Perhaps the crux is that Arabs are often accused of lacking interest in technology, and, in particular, of lacking any feeling for the maintenance of machinery. This, if true, would amount to a refusal by society to take technology seriously. Certainly the Arab world is generally less familiar from childhood upwards with mechanical activities, and so Arabs, when they undertake them, are more often at a loss than Europeans. It is true also that it is difficult in the Arab world to recruit technical students willing to 'work with their hands'. Yet these may only be world-wide troubles in an acute form. In an economy where things are made not to last, machines are nowhere receiving the loving care they need, and it does not seem impossible that the Arabs coming up may pass the Europeans going down. It is not only young Arabs who want to be engineers rather than technicians. Certainly the Arabs need to learn much about how to reward technologists, but it may be that familiarity with machines and dependence upon them will bring a natural cure for carelessness and disrespect. We have to presuppose a change to machine-mindedness, but not necessarily to being Western-minded.

For the most part, Westernisation must mean modernisation. So far as technology is concerned this is obvious enough. It is in the nature of the mass product that today's model is the economic one to sell, even in a market considered unsophisticated. So with other techniques. Every Western country seems anxious to sell its political system, which is the only system it understands; democracy, parliamentary democracy, Marxist democracy, or whatever the system may be, they have to sell abroad what they developed for the home market. The old-fashioned European 'imperialist', the Christian churches, the orthodox Communist parties and the New Left all remain convinced that their own attitudes, explanations and systems ought to be applied in all the other parts of the world. Societies can only export what they have. Neo-imperialists have less opportunity to restrict education than the old imperial powers who were notorious for this, although World Bank teams and some 'experts' have been accused of it. Patrice Lumumba University in Moscow may have started as an inferior product for people with inferior qualifications or qualities, but when the students showed themselves unwilling to accept anything less than the best, the University was quickly assimilated to normal Russian standards. Special University courses for overseas administrators in England may have been conceived in some cases as 'underdeveloped courses for underdeveloped students', but in fact they reflected existing standards, which only the new demand showed to be inadequate. So in other fields. If a revolutionary Arab Government felt that police methods adopted from, say, the English police, must be adapted to the needs of revolution, it could look for new methods and experts only to revolutionary Governments in Europe which we actively occupied by the difficulty of maintaining power, and these Governments could impart only those techniques they imposed at home. The same has applied to all the thousands of experts of all kinds provided through bilateral aid or through the agencies of the United Nations. Perhaps the experts were not always expert, but they always reflected the situation applied in the donor countries to themselves. Sometimes there has been more scope overseas to try out new techniques than at home. In Egypt, 'scientific social planning' has given sociology wider scope for experiment than it has in Europe; there has perhaps been more experimentation in the use of educational television overseas than in the countries where it began. In spite of suspicion that the West offers only an inferior article, it has in fact offered its own overspill.

To Westernise is to modernise, we need not doubt; must modernising therefore mean Westernising? The Arab world has no resources to create a wholly new technology of its own, and it would be pointless to do so even if it were possible; at most the Arabs can hope to absorb the existing Western technology and then surpass it. This is what Japan can reasonably claim to be doing, but it has done it without giving a high priority to the retention of its own characteristic culture. Yet even he who is determined to retain his own traditions at any cost may look at a car or a wireless or a refrigerator, and ask in what way this is inherently unArab or European. An Arab will point out that if geography and geology had been different, the industrial revolution might not have happened in Europe. If the Arabs had constituted the first industrial society, would their cars have been any different from the cars that in fact the West has invented—different in any essential point? Modernisation must cost the Arabs, as it has cost the West, the loss of many good things for the sake of better things, or at least for the sake of things people want more, and that more people want. If this could happen in complete isolation, the result would be the same as it is under foreign influence. If Arabs want to modernise without Westernising, they must find a kind of 'modern' which can clearly be distinguished from the overlapping 'Western'.

It is not an easy distinction to make effectively. Things and ideas that are 'culture-bound' and those that are 'culture-free' can be distinguished relatively, not absolutely. A word like 'car' has some connotation everywhere. It may not always be the same. In a very remote place it may be inseparable from the idea of a government official; but though the car is the product of a culture, it certainly also creates a culture, dictating the ways of society more and more thoroughly as more cars reach more people. In so far as it does this, it cannot be said that the car belongs in any special way to the culture from which it sprang. In so far as it is the creator of a culture, the most xenophobic member of a hostile society can only regard it as contaminated if he rejects modernisation itself. It is more likely that it is really the past, and not the present, of Western culture which he dislikes. Effectively no one objects to the inventions and manufactures; they spell safety and comfort, power and independence. Indeed, no one can stand up to their inventors without them.

A more complex case is education. The purely Koranic education of the old Islamic world was a good education from the point of view of forming the mind and training the intellect; as, too, was the classical education of Europe. The peoples of the Middle East have eagerly substituted secular education for the old scholastic kind; they thirst for it insatiably; it is the secret of secrets which, once absorbed, leads to power. Modern preoccupations have similarly forced classical education out of Europe, not because it did not train, but because it did not confer the skills that are now required, not only in medicine, and not only in biochemistry or nuclear physics or crystallography, all highly developed forms of old skills, but also in psychiatry, anthropology, sociology and linguistics, studies that are based, not on any new subject-matter, but on a new methodology. In the same category are business administration and office management, again old subjects with new methodologies, but in this case new to academic teaching. Most of these new subjects tend to be popular in the Arab world, because they are least culture-bound to the West. It may seem strange at first that this should be true of business administration, and stranger still that this should be one of the

521

subjects taught in a special faculty at el-Azhar, once and still the heart of traditional Koranic studies; but business itself is not new to the Arabs and an academic discipline based upon it is hardly newer to them than to the West. The acceptance of this sort of subject perhaps implies that it belongs to the break-up of the old order in the West, and so is less damaging to make use of in the break-up of the old Arabic culture. What we may think of as representing our current best may seem less ours, to the outside observer, than the things we are discarding; and we can even say that, from this point of view, the more modern a thing looks, the less characteristically Western it looks.

The sense of obligation an Arab student incurs towards his teacher is still strong. So far it has survived perhaps two generations—at any rate 50 years and more—of student revolt, which has a longer history in the Arab world than in the West. It would be better called student leadership of the nation. The students for the most part could count on the support of their teachers; but this is true of Western students in relation to the younger teachers, and any situation where the initiative comes from the students is destructive of one where the teacher does all the thinking. This situation is instructive, because it shows a wholly Arab development (paralleled, of course, in other areas subject to the imperialist movement of the last century) which is remarkably similar to the European and American movements, but which antedated them. Only the most extreme of the Western students can understand even the moderate among the Arabs; an average Arab student seems dangerously fanatical to a moderate British one. In spite of this, student attitudes, Arab and Western, run parallel.

Yet if the Arab tradition can naturally adopt machines, techniques (of government and revolution, of learning and teaching), and even share certain attitudes, without borrowing something specifically alien, is there really any problem at all? Can Westernisation be wholly absorbed by modernisation? That there is indeed a problem is shown by the existence of several different solutions, of which the best known and most easily defined are those of the communists and of the Muslim Brothers.

The most liberal attitude possible for a Brother to take is that 'whatever is not unIslamic is Islamic'. Whatever contradicts the Koran is obviously un-Islamic; but whereas, for example, this rules out payment of interest, the Brothers can envisage 'state capitalism', banking as a public service, loans by Agricultural Banks to farmers. They are prepared to be radical with the *sunna* and cavalier with the caliphate. When they are challenged—and by Muslims as much as by Christians—to justify the penal amputations prescribed by the Koran, they insist on those equally Koranic conditions of conviction which they are certain would normally prevent the execution of the penalty in practice, and at the same time illuminate the justice and moderation of God's word. They say that they would happily forego the traditional judicial practice of conservative society and its false interpretation of the Koranic injunctions. All this is theoretical politics; it is not practical, because, outside student and intellectual groups, the supporters of the Brothers are not radicals but conservatives. The movement is liable to violent xenophobic outbreaks, yet in theory it offers a perfectly clear solution to problems of Westernisation. It is limited by what may be argued to be the true meaning of the Koran, but it makes it possible to jettison everything in traditional Islamic culture which the Koran can be said not to require. This solution is capable of creating an entirely new society. Every imported object, and every imported idea, would be subjected to the one, simple and devastating scrutiny : if not unIslamic, i.e. not expressly forbidden by the Koran, it is acceptable. It is not likely that the experiment will ever be tried.

The communists are nationalists in the sentiments they exploit, and are not always even anti-religious. No doubt this is 'tactical', but it seems possible to detect side by side the exploitation of nationalist sentiment and a real adaptation to nationalist sentiment. The convenience of nationalism is obvious. A Western communist seems almost a contradiction in terms : an 'imperialist communist'. So far as the practical experience of Arabs goes, the working-class in Western Europe tends to be racialist. Communism can afford to confine its internationalism to the publicised official attitudes of the 'friendly countries'; to omit all analysis of capitalist society, and to allow the assumption to pass that capitalists exploit because they are imperialists, that imperialism is a natural force, like electricity, or a biological rival like viruses, needing no explanation.

Communists and nationalists often worked together in the days of revolution against imperial rule. At times they shared techniques, such as a cell organisation; and there is a very large linguistic area of shared terminology. Above all, they still share a profound and genuine suspicion of the motives of all imperialists. Communists realise that nationalism is politically and socially neutral, essentially neither a 'progressive' nor a 'reactionary' movement. Towards Muslim Brothers they are irreconcilable, because they can see the movement only as reactionary and equivalent to clericalism in Europe; but there comes a point when we can no longer be sure that the communists are not making real concessions to nationalist, and sometimes even to religious, sentiment, not so much consciously as from an unrecognised internal compulsion. It would surprise no one to find Arab communists in power deviationist or revisionist. It may well be the communists who are the Trojans and the nationalists the crew of the Horse.

Communists see no technological problem other than that which will naturally be solved when the workers control the means of production. Workers' control will imply modernisation and there will, of course, be no hesitation about adopting the necessary Western technology. In practice, the Party is preoccupied by its problems of seizing power, so often within reach, so regularly elusive; once in power, it might genuinely seek to preserve the existing working-class culture. We can too easily be tempted to ridicule this by the thought of folk-dancing displays more or less modified by Russian experts to resemble a Red Army performance. It is likely that there would be a serious and interesting attempt to retain a characteristic Arab way of living. When this has been said, it remains true that what the Communist Party really claims to offer the Arab world is an efficient revenge on the West for past humiliations, the ultimate vindication of Islamic culture, even if Islam itself should not survive.

Neither the Communist nor the Muslim Brother solution has been attempted, but there are elements of both in the thinking of different Arab governments. A stronger element than either has been the nationalist element, and nationalist solutions are the hardest to identify, because Arab nationalism is the general atmosphere of everybody's thinking, rather than a party in itself. Nationalism has a negative side; it may narrow the freedom of Arab Governments and diplomats to manoeuvre, and it often requires a doctrinal attitude apt to obscure communication with outside societies. Nationalism for the Arabs, and for other peoples living between the two tropics, is a pervasive background, like Marxism in some parts of the world and 'democracy' in others. It is so pervasive that political speeches from very different political standpoints sound alike to outside listeners. Arab nationalism is patriotism, but Arab nationalism is also xenophobia; it is a kind of jingo, but it is also the demand of dispossessed peoples for a share in the rewards of effort. It is the framework and the expression of frustration and disappointment that Arabs are unable to take an appropriate and leading part in the government of this world's affairs.

Anti-imperialism must sound anti-Western because the empires belonged to the West. The classical theory is borrowed from Hobson and Lenin, but the roots of anti-imperialism are deeper and older than either: 'The foreigners have founded neither factories nor works, for fear of suffering the fate foretold by the Arab poet, "I taught him versification but the first verse he made he made against me,"' wrote a Cairo newspaper in 1881, 'if they tell you that one is a third of two and you reply in a negative sense, they show you their cannons, and so you have to tell them they are quite right.' There has been resentment of superior force from the beginning, and a sense of being exploited; there was no need to learn these from Western analysis of imperialism. There has also always been a realisation that to modernise is a pressing necessity, and that to eject the foreigner would lose half its value if there were no social revolution; how to combine these two processes in a single effort, said Gamal Abdel Nasser shortly after coming to power, was Egypt's characteristic problem. In the last resort, the nationalist urge to vindicate the Arabs will always necessitate getting, and keeping, up to date.

The transmission of ideas from one culture to another is a complex process still not very well understood. The barriers are easier to recognise. One cultural (or national, or religious, or racial) group looks with an understanding eye upon the faults of its own members, and with a devastating criticism at the faults, often the same faults, of opposed groups. Groups are 'opposed' by no more complicated a process than existing separately, whether at a distance or side by side. Any accident may differentiate them; it need not be, though it often is, different pigmentation of the dermis, or a different language, or different customs. These things serve to mark, or are used to 'explain' the division, but the fact is that any divisive accident will do. It is this that makes the transmission of ideas very difficult. Even colleagues in one university, if there is no overwhelming majority, may be divided into mutually resentful cultural, national, racial, religious or political groupings. Groups that live side by side and serve the same purpose may still fail to communicate.

With the intransigence of nationalist sentiment and the ease with which minds can be shut to each other, how does Westernisation in fact occur? When we consider the history of the Arabs' relation with Europe, we are usually told that there is an alternation, and that as we are to them now, so they were to us in our Middle Ages. In fact it was characteristic of the Medieval Europeans to express, and presumably to feel, no obligation at all to the actual Islamic civilisation to which they owed their knowledge. In an age when the reciprocal intolerance of rival cultures was usually expressed in terms of religion, Western writers sharply distinguished Muslims from writers in Arabic, though, so far as their experience went, the two categories were effectively coterminous. To the Islamic society on their doorstep they would extend no courtesy, though Avicenna and often Averroes were given the same respect as Plato and Aristotle. These medieval writers knew exactly what they wanted, the techniques of logic, of philosophical enquiry and scholastic disputation, and the groundwork for scientific study. Once Greek and Arabic learning was in Latin, it was effectively absorbed, and isolated from cultural contamination. Is there a parallel in the Arab position to-day in face of Western achievement? Is it possible to isolate the wanted from the unwanted by translation?

Translation is precisely the key problem for the Arab universities; some teach all science subjects in Arabic, some use English or French in medicine, or in all science subjects, or a mixture of languages. Students who have to learn in a foreign language of instruction naturally tend to learn the language better than the subjects taught. It seems quite unreasonable to expect this unnatural use of a foreign language; but once we accept that the language of the university should be the language of the nation, we have quickly to insist that the Arab world cannot make do with translations only. The total body of knowledge is far too great to be translated in sufficient volume, and expands too fast for translation to keep pace.

Not that there is really any argument about this. Arabs, like the rest of us, will take all knowledge from whatever source it comes; the attitudes in which knowledge comes wrapped, they can at least try to discard. In theory, every cultural accretion can be stripped off, so that what remains can be absorbed in a form which reveals nothing of its origin. What medieval Europeans could do, Arabs can do to-day; their own past shows them as well able to borrow as other cultures are. If the Arabs cannot yet say whether 'modern' and 'Western' are synonymous, neither can anyone else. According to one theory, we are driven forward by the internal logic in events to an inevitably uniform world culture, such as the world conquerors and the ecclesiastical inquisitors failed to impose; Genghis Khan and Torquemada may prove less powerful than the salesmen of packaged goods. If this is wrong, and if in fact development in America and Western Europe, in Eastern Europe and the USSR, reveals the cultural characteristics of those areas, Arabs too can hope to modernise in a way characteristic of their own cultural history. Their profound resentment at a hundred years of political, economic and cultural interference will ensure that they will take Western technology with a minimum of Western ideas; if they must borrow much, they will borrow widely to spread the debt. They will not begin to satisfy themselves until they have reduced all borrowing to a manageable proportion, and, exploiting techniques of study shared with other cultures, can say with Abu Tammam, 'Even if our lines of descent are different, we are united in scholarship, our common father'.

FURTHER READING

Berque, J. *The Arabs, Their History and Future*, Faber & Faber, London, 1964; Praeger, New York, 1964.

Haim, S. G. *Arab Nationalism—An Anthology*, Univ. of California Press, Berkeley and Los Angeles, 1962.

Halpern, M. *The Politics of Social Change in the Middle East and North Africa*, Princeton Univ. Press, Princeton, 1963.

Hourani, A. *Arabic Thought in the Liberal Age*, Oxford Univ. Press, London, 1962.

Karpat, K. H. *Political and Social Thought in the Contemporary Middle East*, Pall Mall, Press, London, 1968.

Keddie, N. R. *An Islamic Response to Imperialism*, Univ. of California Press, Berkeley and Los Angeles, 1968.

Lewis, B. *The Middle East and the West*, Weidenfeld and Nicolson, London, 1963; Indiana Univ. Press, Indiana, 1964.

THE POSITION OF WOMEN IN MIDDLE EASTERN ARAB SOCIETY

DOREEN INGRAMS

The varying social conditions in the Arab countries of the Middle East today are strikingly reflected in the status of their women. It is possible by travelling from one country to another to observe the gradual evolution of the Arab woman from secluded dependence to complete emancipation.

The principal factor that has determined the Arab woman's place in society has been Islam, which is not only a religion but a way of life. In the Koran it is laid down that women should be modest and chaste, and should not display their charms to any men except their husbands or those within the prohibited degrees of marriage. Nothing is said about wearing a veil, nor is it ordained that women should be segregated, but purdah and the harem, customs of uncertain origin, became accepted and spread throughout the Islamic world as a means of ensuring the chastity of women. They also made women almost completely dependent on men, although under Islamic law their rights were protected in such matters as marriage, divorce and inheritance.

Marriage is a simple contract, needing only two witnesses. A man must not marry more than four wives and it is enjoined on him in the Koran that if he cannot do justice to each wife then he must take only one. A wife must be obedient to her husband, and the husband must pay the wife a dowry and provide her with suitable maintenance. There are three ways of divorcing: simple repudiation by the man, mutual consent, or a judicial dissolution which the wife can ask for on grounds such as her husband's impotence, desertion, cruelty, or failure to maintain her properly. After divorce a wife is entitled to maintenance for three months, while it is established whether she is pregnant or not, and the dowry paid by her husband belongs to her. Custody of the children is given to the mother for boys up to seven (or puberty according to some Muslim sects), and a girl to puberty (or marriage according to some sects). The father has the right of exercising supervision.

Widows and daughters must each receive a share of a man's estate, but men get double the shares of the women as it is taken for granted that men have to look after their female relatives. No one may dispose of his property by bequest beyond one-third of the estate, which ensures that neither widow nor children can be cut out of a will. Under Islamic law there is no community of property between husband and wife, and in the management and disposition of her own property a wife has complete freedom; but until a woman is educated she rarely understands financial transactions and is

526

usually dependent upon a male relative to look after her affairs. Consequently she may well be at risk in unscrupulous hands.

Many of these laws are in process of change, and polygamy is rapidly disappearing in the more progressive Arab countries. Few educated women would tolerate a second wife and although polygamy is not illegal in the Arab countries (except in Tunisia), it is more and more coming to be frowned upon and outdated. On the other hand, in the traditional countries where polygamy is still accepted it is thought reasonable for a man to marry a second wife if the first has not given him a son, and in such cases divorce is considered to be unfair to the wife as it leaves her in a much more difficult position than if she remained as one of two or more wives. Nevertheless no woman likes to share her husband; when she does so with good grace it is because she accepts the traditions of the society in which she has grown up, but polygamy is one of the first customs to be rejected by women when they become emancipated.

As in any part of the world where religious feeling is strong and deviation from religious precepts considered sinful, there are orthodox Muslims, men and women, in the Arab world who maintain a vigorous stand against attempts to modify traditional teaching, but there are also religious leaders who are prepared to reconcile religious teaching with modern trends, rather than try to curb modernity in the straightjacket of medieval Islam.

Looking at the position of women in the Arab countries as a whole, a pattern of evolution towards emancipation becomes clear, for each society has gone through, or is going through, a similar process of change. First there is the almost complete segregation of women in the harem, the acceptance of the veil, and the idea that girls must not be educated because they will then demand greater freedom, and greater freedom will lead to an amoral society. Then comes the first breach in the wall of tradition : someone quietly opens a primary school for girls, who at first will be allowed to stay at school only until they are nine or ten years old, when they have to go into purdah. The point at which secondary education for girls becomes established usually depends upon the stage that higher education has reached for boys, for when young men have been to colleges or universities they prefer to marry educated girls. Once this preference becomes fairly general, parents are willing, even anxious, to allow their daughters to stay longer at school, so as to be sure of their becoming acceptable as wives.

Having reached the stage of secondary education, it is but a short step to higher education for girls and the breach in the wall will have become wide enough for them to walk outside, however diffidently at first. This first generation of educated young women become the mothers of the next and, having led the way towards emancipation, there will be no going back for their children or grandchildren.

The Arabian peninsula, with the exception of Kuwait and to some extent of Bahrain and Aden, is the part of the Middle East that is most traditional with regard to women. This is not to say that all the women are veiled or segregated, for in many tribal societies tribeswomen are a great deal freer in these respects than women living in towns; but when the wealthiest and most important members of the society accept the veil and the harem then these are considered desirable, as they reflect the status of the head of the household. In Yemen, Southern Yemen, Oman, and most of the Gulf States, the bulk of the population is uneducated, both men and women, and until this position is radically altered there can be little change in the position of women living in those countries. Aden is an exception, for there the men have had opportunities of education for several generations, and women for two or three decades. Many Aden girls work in offices or take up professions, and in recent years the women have been active in politics and in social affairs.

Until Kuwait's immense wealth brought it suddenly and dramatically into the modern world, Bahrain was the most advanced area in the Arabian Gulf. The first primary school for girls was opened there in 1928, a secondary school in 1951 and a women's teacher-training college in 1967. Bahraini women have had the vote at 18 since 1929. As in other Arab countries, the first careers open to girls were nursing or teaching but to these broadcasting was added some years ago, and more recently girls have been working as secretaries, air hostesses, or customs inspectors.

Taking up work does not mean complete emancipation either in Bahrain, Aden, or any of the less advanced countries, for it is usual to find that a girl must go straight home after work and what she does in her leisure time will be with the consent of her parents. In such societies marriages are arranged by the parents, a traditional custom which still exists in all Arab countries among the less sophisticated families.

Although the veil is not necessarily discarded when girls go out to work, its use is becoming rarer among the younger generation. Older women who have grown up in purdah find it almost impossible to cast away the veil so that it is commonplace in Bahrain, or Aden, to see a veiled mother walking in the street with her unveiled daughter. The countries where both old and young go about unveiled are countries in which women have been emancipated for a considerable time.

Kuwait is a curiosity in the Arab world because its rapid advance from a tribal society to a modern welfare state is quite unlike anything that has happened anywhere else in the Arab Middle East, and this advance also applies to the changed status of Kuwaiti women. Only a few years ago, hardly a girl in Kuwait received education and no women went about unveiled. Today every Kuwaiti girl can go to school and continue on to university, subsequently taking up practically any work for which she is qualified. It is an astonishing jump from the veil to announcing on television in little more than ten years. Kuwaiti women are also employed in manual work and, as in the other more advanced Arab countries, the labour laws have clauses protecting their welfare. They must receive the same wage as men if they are doing the same job. They must not be employed at night, and pregnant women are entitled to thirty days leave on full pay before confinement and 40 days after it. Unlike the women in Bahrain, Kuwaiti women do not yet have the vote and women's organisations concern themselves with social and cultural activities rather than with politics.

In spite of its wealth from oil, Saudi Arabia is far more conservative than Kuwait and its women are not emancipated, probably because Saudi Arabia is the birthplace of Islam and Muslim tradition retains a firm hold in the country. Publicity about life in the Western world, with its permissive society, only reinforces the determination of most Saudi Arabians to keep girls out of mischief, married young, and fully occupied as wives and mothers. A woman inspector of schools, whose influence on female education is important, has declared that a woman's place is in the home, but that she should have sufficient education to bring up her children with a firm religious background and train them to become responsible God-fearing citizens. This attitude has official approval, for in a government publication it is said that 'As education for girls spreads, coming generations of young mothers will be in a stronger position to act as teachers to their children, by example and word, of the basic values and virtues which the community seeks to insure for itself through this tenacious adherence to Islam. And women will be in a better position to know and appreciate the rights and advantages which Muslim law, in most cases ahead of any secular law, stipulated and guaranteed for their well-being.'

The first schools for girls in Saudi Arabia were only opened about 12 years ago, but now any Saudi Arabian girl has the opportunity to go to school and, if she has the ability, to take university courses in her own home. Girls may not attend the university except for their examinations, which are held apart from the men. There are not many careers open to women except teaching, nursing, or social work. They still wear the veil and it is not easy for them to go far from home as they are not allowed to drive a car, nor to take a taxi when unaccompanied. The royal princesses play a leading part in women's social activities, the most notable of which is the Saudi Women's Renaissance Society founded in 1962 by two of King Faisal's daughters. It was established to 'raise the spiritual, intellectual, social and physical status of Saudi women . . . to organise their charitable and social activities, and prepare them to be good citizens, housewives and mothers'. It has its head-quarters in the capital, Riyadh, and among its many activities is the running of a school for blind girls, a family care service, and a women's club.

Between the largely traditional woman of the Arabian Peninsula and the modern woman of Cairo, Beirut or Baghdad, the Sudanese woman forms a bridge. Nearly half the children at school in Sudan are girls, and they are going on to the universities in increasing numbers. Opportunities are open to them in medicine, law, teaching, nursing, secretarial work, journalism, radio and television. The first woman lawyer was admitted to the Bar in 1962, and since 1964 Sudanese women have had the vote (at 18), but as yet they have little voice in public affairs, although there has been one woman elected to the National Assembly, on a university vote. There are numerous women's organisations concerned with political, social, welfare and cultural activities, including the Sudanese Women's Union which campaigns for kindergartens and adult literacy, and the National Women's Front which has a religious basis and aims at eradicating superstition and strengthening good religious practices. There is a Women's Co-operative Society which organises handicrafts in the home and their sale in government co-operative shops, a University Women's Association, and a number of benevolent and charitable organisations.

Sudanese women go out unveiled, drive cars, and lead a reasonably free life, but it is still unusual for husband and wife to go out together or for wives to be invited to official receptions with their husbands. Nor do the young girls feel any anxiety to be rid of the traditional Sudanese dress, the *taub*, a long piece of material wound round the body like a sari. University students may attend mixed classes wearing short skirts but they prefer to wear the *taub* in public as it gives them a feeling of dignity and of being respected. At the same time they campaign vigorously for equal opportunities with men, equal pay, and a greater say in public affairs.

The five remaining Arab countries of the Middle East, the United Arab Republic, Lebanon, Syria, Iraq and Jordan, have much in common as regards the position of women. In the cities and towns the veil is scarcely ever seen and many of the girls are as sophisticated as anywhere else in the world. In these countries more depends upon the attitude of individual families than upon the attitude of the state or the religious leaders as to whether a girl has complete freedom, partial freedom, or is guarded like a Victorian daughter. In Jordan, a small country where everyone knows everyone else's business, it is rather more difficult for a girl to live her own life, for instance by sharing a flat with other girls and living away from home, than it would be in Beirut or Cairo.

In all these countries, with the exception of Jordan, women have the vote at 18 or, in the case of Iraq, at 21, and in Jordan women's organisations are campaigning for votes for women. There has been a woman minister in the United Arab Republic and also one in Iraq, and at the time of writing there are eight women members of the United Arab Republic's National Assembly. Most careers are open to women, including the diplomatic service, science and engineering, and in many cases they hold senior posts without discrimination; but early marriage often cuts short promising careers, although there is a growing tendency to continue working after marriage, particularly among the highly educated women.

Women's organisations are working for changes in the laws which they consider to be unfair to them, and they have been successful in such matters as raising the age of marriage, enlarging the grounds for divorce by a wife, and altering the arrangements for the custody of children after divorce. In the United Arab Republic a woman can now divorce her husband if he takes a second wife. In Syria and Iraq marriages have to be registered, which gives parents or the bride a chance of making sure that a prospective husband is not already married.

In each of these five countries there are numerous voluntary organisations run by women dealing with social and cultural activities, such as combating illiteracy, improving the status of women in the villages, or caring for children, the handicapped, and the poor. In the United Arab Republic alone there are six thousand such organisations. Family planning clinics are spreading, particularly in the United Arab Republic, where the government has set up a Higher Family Planning Council which has the approval of the leading Muslim authority, the Rector of Al Azhar.

A look at some statistics concerned with women in the United Arab Republic shows how their position in society has altered. In 1928 there were six girls at university, in 1952 there were 6,000, and in 1961, 30,000. Women first joined the trades unions in 1928 and by 1961 there were over 500,000 women members. Women in country districts have been able to have a say in local affairs even before the townswomen, as they led a freer life; but poverty and illiteracy debarred them from taking part in national affairs until recent times, when steps have been taken through Rural Units to encourage education and other social services. But villages in Arab countries, as anywhere else, lag behind in the general advances made in the towns, and there is still a great deal to be done to improve the position of women in the villages, even in the most sophisticated countries.

The modern trend towards living in blocks of flats has changed the position of women in the Arab world by changing the whole pattern of family life, and the same problems now affect the Cairo or Beirut housewife as affect women in any modern city. She may have become more independent by living in her own home away from parents or parents-in-law, but there are no ready-to-hand baby sitters and it is no longer easy or cheap to find domestic help. Added to this the modern Arab woman faces the usual difficulties when trying to combine a job with running a home.

Questions to the problem pages of women's magazines reveal something of the society in which women live. In the Arab world they frequently show the dilemma of the girl who wants to marry someone of her own choice, or her frustration with parents who forbid her to go out alone with a young man. The answers generally, though not always, advise obedience to parents. Wives do not write about marital troubles as they are considered too private a matter to be aired publicly, nor do girls ask advice about illegitimate babies, for the permissive society is not yet as widespread, even in the most up-to-date capitals of the Arab world, as it is in the West.

It is interesting that those Arab countries which had to fight for their independence, and which led the nationalist movements of the 19th and 20th centuries, were also the countries that led the movement for the emancipation of women. It was realised that no country could take its place as an independent modern state if half of the population was out of sight and voiceless.

In much of the Arab Middle East today the women are seen and are by no means voiceless. They air their views in public, by speaking or writing; they are scientists, technicians, artists, politicians, lawyers, doctors, professors, journalists; in every field they play a part and the Arab world is the richer for their contributions.

FURTHER READING

Hodgkin, E. C. *The Arabs*, Oxford Univ. Press, London and New York, 1966.
Hoeck, Eva. *Doctor amongst the Bedouins*, Robert Hale, London, 1962.
Ingrams, Doreen. *A Time in Arabia*, John Murray, London, 1970.
Little, Tom. *Modern Egypt*, Benn, London, 1967; Praeger, New York, 1967.
Nicholson, Reynold A. *A Literary History of the Arabs*, Cambridge Univ. Press, Cambridge, 1956 and 2nd ed. New York, 1969.
Randall, Rona. *Jordan and the Holy Land*, Frederick Muller, England, 1968; International Publications Service, New York, 1968.
Sykes, John. *The Mountain Arabs*, Hutchinson, London, 1968; Chilton, New York, 1968.
Publications from Arab League Office, London. Publications from Arab Embassies, London.

DOREEN INGRAMS. Lived for many years in South Arabia (now the Republic of South Yemen). Worked in the Arabic Service of the BBC, concerned especially with the 'Woman's Programme'. Toured in many of the Arab countries making contact with women's organisations and studying the position of women in different parts of the Arab world. Author of a book examining the social, economic and political condition of South Yemen.

PART SIX

THE ARTS AND MASS MEDIA

ARABIC LITERATURE

R. B. SERJEANT

ARABIC is not merely the tongue of the Arab lands from Morocco to the Persian Gulf, but the vehicle of a literature of vast extent and great variety, imbued with its own distinctive characteristics. It has advanced even beyond the frontiers within which Arabic is written and spoken, for Arabic literature flourished in Persia, India, Malaya, Turkey, East and West Africa, and, more recently, developed schools of writings in both the Americas. Arabic has influenced the development of modern Persian, Turkish, Urdu, Malay, Swahili and Hausa, somewhat as Latin and Greek affected European languages. This literature is only possible to sketch here in briefest outline.

PRE-ISLAMIC AGE

Apart from the rock inscriptions of the Arabian peninsula, the area from which the armies of Islam came forth, the earliest form of Arabic literature known to us is the heroic poetry of the noble tribes, composed at such events as the 'Days'—the ancient battles of the Arabs, the inter-tribal clashes which are the very stuff of Arabian life. The standard Arabic verse form, the *qasidah*, was evolved in the pre-Islamic age. It consists of a variable number of *baits* (each *bait* probably originally a rhyming couplet, and independent in itself) strung together, the second hemistich of each *bait* rhyming throughout the *qasidah*. The *qasidah* opens with certain stock themes brought into a conventional sequence, as if the ancient poet was casting about as he sang among a range of thoughts before finding words for the subject, which he then declaimed.

Of prose literature virtually nothing survives, except in later tales about pre-Islamic times, and some legal documents. Some oracular utterances in rhymed prose (*saj'*) have come down from paganism, but it is not known if this *saj'* constituted a literary form. In the south-west of Arabia many thousands of inscriptions survive in languages closely akin to classical Arabic, in a script known conveniently as Himyaritic, indicating the existence of a sophisticated style of writing, but no literature remains.

DEVELOPMENT OF THE ARABIC LANGUAGE

Arabic became important because it was the language of the faith of Islam, carried by victorious Arab warriors to Spain in the west and Sind in the east, and subsequently spread, mainly by peaceful diffusion, to the other countries now Muslim in faith. The Koran consists of the inspired utterances

535

of Muhammad, founder of the Islamic faith, collected after his death from documents or individual memories. Though cast in the dialect of the holy house of Quraish, Muhammad's tribe, the Koran is considered by orthodoxy to be the word of Allah, so that a quotation from the Koran is introduced by, 'God said. . . .' In Islamic civilisation the Koran has an importance perhaps even greater than that of the Bible in Christendom, and the study of the Koran in itself gave rise to many of the earliest types of literature in Arabic.

The 114 chapters of the Koran, or parts thereof, are ascribed to Muhammad's Meccan or Medinan periods, the Meccan chapters being shorter, more declamatory, more 'prophetic' in quality than the Medinan chapters while the latter are often legalistic and revealed in some social or political context. From the outset it seems that the Koran reciters preserved in their memories the sense and application of each Koranic passage, and even the events in response to which it was revealed; as time passed and it became the book of all the Arabs and also of many non-Arabs, it grew necessary to explain words not current in ordinary speech. This led to the development of the sciences of philology and grammar, and of the correct way to intone the Koran, while explanation of its content produced vast commentaries. Though the Koran was one source of law, most Islamic law was based, theoretically, on the Prophet's customary practice or decisions in Medina. As a result there developed the tremendous literature of 'Traditions' of what Muhammad did or said. From this Tradition-collecting branched out in turn, one may say, the literature concerned with law and that section of Tradition which becomes more properly history. Law has an importance in Arabic literature and Islamic civilisation much greater than in our own; in the working out of the theoretical, practical or particular application of this law, the genius of Arabic scholars has found its highest intellectual expression. Ancillary to other fields of study, there grew up also the art of biography.

From the days of the Umayyad Caliphs at Damascus (AD 661–750) the new religion was exposed to the criticism of Christian dialectic, and had to construct a coherent system of theology to combat this; herein it was probably influenced during its first three most formative centuries by Jewish converts to Islam, and by the methods of the Jewish schools. The most formidable intellectual challenge which early Islam had to meet, however, was the force of Greek and Hellenistic thinking and science to which early Islam, no less than Christian Europe, was heir. The 'Abbasid Caliph Ma'mun (813–833) promoted the translation of Greek scientific and philosophical writings into Arabic when he set up in Baghdad the 'House of Wisdom'. At his court not only Muslim scholars were entertained but also learned Christians and Jews. Such translators as Hunain Bin Ishaq in the 9th century rendered Plato and Galen into Arabic. Some works, the original Greek of which has perished, are still extant in Arabic. Philosophical writing became a recognised scholarly activity, and mediaeval Europe knew well the names of Avicenna (Ibn Sina), Averroes (Ibn Rushd) the commentator on Aristotle, and Arabic writers on scientific subjects such as alchemy, medicine, and mathematics. The Arabic language, in order to meet the challenge of a highly cultivated and learned society, had to develop a range of technical terms and expressions unknown to the simpler Arabic of Muhammad—it was able to do this without introducing many foreign words because of the peculiar structural genius of the language.

Theological and religious literature naturally bulked large in Arabic writing, as they still do, and though they cannot be considered here, nevertheless Ghazali (d. 1111) must claim his place as a writer as well as a theologian : a professor at Baghdad who lost his faith and resigned his chair, but who, becoming a Sufi or mystic, sought to reconcile Sufism with orthodox theology in his celebrated *Revivification of the Sciences of the Faith.*

POETRY

For Arabs, poetry has an immediate and abiding appeal. Even in the Prophet's lifetime, as one can perceive in the biographies, a sort of doggerel ballad verse, probably that of the lower classes of settled folk, seems to have been current alongside the heroic tribal poetry of chivalry, of war, of love and the hunt. Poetry too was a species of propaganda, and a brilliant poem in praise of a patron of power or wealth could bring the poet a rich reward.

This was to have unfortunate consequences for Arabic poetry with its wearisome panegyrics. Tribal heroic verse hardly changed during the Umayyad period, when court life too remained very Arabian; but during the 'Abbasid period, when the capital was located in the metropolis of Baghdad and a new population of mixed antecedents, Persian, Aramean and Turkish, surrounded the court, conditions altered. 'Modern' poets of the type of the lecherous but talented Abu Nuwas mocked at the old tribal *qasidah* in smart sophisticated town verse. A little earlier, a poet of Persian descent, Bashshar Ibn Burd, is reckoned by critics the first exponent of the *badi'*, the new or invented style, which ornaments verse with metaphor and a whole range of other literary devices. Though this is restrained in Bashshar's poetry itself, it came to dominate much of Arabic verse in a fashion detrimental to the freshness and spontaneity one finds, for instance, in Abu Nuwas's winesongs.

Collections (*diwan*) of the verse of individual tribes were known even as early as the Umayyad period and 'Abbasid scholars set out to collect ancient Arabic verse with a sort of antiquarian interest. This was followed by the compilation of anthologies, of which the most notable is Abu 'l-Faraj al-Isfahani's (d. 967) 20-volume *Book of Songs*, containing ancient and modern poems, with notes on their musical setting, and a mass of biographical anecdote. Literary criticism, applied only to verse, had formulated the principle that poetry attained matchless perfection before Islam—this however was to be contradicted by Ibn Qutaibah (ninth century), the first critic to declare that verse, be it ancient or modern, should be judged by an aesthetic canon.

Two poets of the 'Abbasid era, whose lustre time has increased rather than diminished, are Mutanabbi, associated with the Hamdanid court at Aleppo, and still much read in Arab countries, though his style, the involved *badi'*, has less appeal to European taste than the boldness of thought, coupled with a somewhat destructive philosophy, of the blind Abu 'l-'Ala al-Ma'arri (hailing from a village south of Aleppo), that allows him to write, with a cynicism surprising in that age, of the three great religions of his day. His most curious writing, the *Treatise on forgiveness*, a description of a visit to Heaven and Hell to converse with the poets of olden time, has been compared with Dante's *Inferno*. The 'Abbasid period too, witnessed the spread of Sufi mystic verse, employing the metaphors of earthly passion to convey the ecstasy of divine love.

Mediaeval Spain was a major centre of Arabic and Islamic culture; through Arab Spain, often by way of Jewish intermediaries, the Greek-Arab learning of Islam reached Western Europe before Europe had direct access to Greek science and philosophy through Greek manuscripts. This is held to have had a considerable influence on mediaeval European school-men. Spanish Arabic verse has an importance and a distinctive colouring of its own, especially in the Almoravid period, when the newer forms of *muwashshahah* and *zajal*, closely associated with music and colloquial Arabic, came into general vogue. These forms originated in about the ninth century; Hispano-Arabic verse strongly affected the troubadour verse in Aquitaine and even Italian poetry. At times this Andalusian verse breaks into a curious mixture of Arabic and Romance, and it later even became a source of inspiration in its turn for Arab poets of the 20th century. Ibn Hazm (d. 1064), a talented theologian besides, is famous for a delicate work in prose and verse, the *Ring of the Dove*, a 'blend of sacred learning and pro-fane delectation', treating of the phrases, aspects and psychology of love, and even introducing the element of idealised Platonic love.

PROSE

The 'Abbasid age is rich in prose no less than verse, in secular as well as religious literature. The outstanding genius as an essayist is unquestionably al-Jahiz (d. 869), descended from the negroid clients of the Kinanah tribe. He studied the traditional Arabic 'sciences' at Basra, and became well versed in Greek philosophy and science. His large discursive *Book of Animals* is a mine of curious fact and fiction, akin in certain ways, though more scientific, to a mediaeval bestiary, and his *Book of Misers* is more revealing of Arab character and society than any other book of the time.

The essays of Jahiz are part of the large category of *adab*, polite literature or *belles-lettres*, a literature which provided the cultural pabulum for the large class of secretaries, the civil service and officials of Baghdad and other cities as well as for the educated public at large. In the latter half of the tenth century there appears with apparent suddenness a new literary genre, the *maqamah* (though it surely must have antecedents, long vanished, before it was accepted by literary circles). The hero of the *maqamah* is the learned and rascally beggar who makes his living by his wits; a sort of confidence trickster, he is always running into the narrator by whom he is exposed. The *maqamah* in rhymed prose is full of *jeux de mots* and witticisms, and its two most famous exponents are its inventor, Hamadhani, and Hariri (d. 1122) of Basra who elaborated and stereotyped it. The popularity of the *maqamah* (which is also found in mediaeval Hebrew) has only been eclipsed with the rise of modern Arabic.

History too began to form a part of *belles-lettres* towards the end of the ninth century and, whereas historians of Tabari's calibre were really collectors of Traditions, later writers begin to treat history-writing more as an organic whole. The necessity for compendia of data on the countries of the 'Abbasid empire gave an impetus towards the composition of geographies, but many strands of influence went to create this rich and interesting side of literature : Greek science, notably the works of Ptolemy, travellers' observations and tales of marvels. Idrisi, in 12th-century Sicily, was commissioned to com-pile the *Book of Roger* for the Norman King of Palermo, with accompany-ing maps, and Yaqut (d. 1229) is the author of a large geographical dic-tionary culled from many sources.

A bibliography, *The Fihrist* (988) reveals the enormous output of Arabic writing, but it is sad to observe how little of it is extant today. A tenth-century encyclopaedia, the *Treatises of the Brethren of Purity*, epitomises the thought of learned Muslim society at that time. In the tenth century also came the foundation of large libraries and of colleges of learning in capitals like Baghdad, Cairo, and Cordoba.

DECLINE OF CLASSICAL ARABIC LITERATURE

The conquest of the eastern provinces of the Caliphate by the savage and heathen Mongols, and their sacking of the capital Baghdad, struck Iraq, where Arabic literature and Islamic culture had grown and flourished so brilliantly, a blow from which it never recovered. Their murder of the 'Abbasid Caliph put an end to the Islamic theocratic state, however theoretical it was in practice during its latter phases. The centre of Islamic civilisation shifted to Egypt, while Persia (which had participated so fully in Arabic writing) turned to writing in the Persian language. There, however, as elsewhere, Arabic continued to be the language of Islamic law and theology, and Islam continued to spread far and wide into Asia and Africa.

Under the Mamelukes, a military caste of Turkish and Circassian slaves, Egypt and Syria came under a highly organised feudal military culture, sustained economically to some degree by the India trade to Europe passing through the eastern Mediterranean. As might be expected from the Mameluke régime, writing in their day includes notable works on administration, taxation, the art of war, and epistolary style. Some of the best achievement was in the field of history, in which Mameluke relations with the Venetians, Genoese and others figure in detail. The historian Maqrizi (late 14th and early 15th centuries) delved into the antiquities and topography of Egypt, and the polygraph Suyuti is credited with over 500 works, some merely short tracts. Most eminent of all is the philosopher of history and sociologist, Ibn Khaldun (d. 1406), not an Egyptian, but born in Tunis of a family of Andalusian refugees. Educated at the Qarawiyun University of Fez, an early foundation, he served with several rulers in North Africa and Spain, and for a time became chief Maliki judge in Egypt. Tamerlane, when he was besieging Damascus, invited this famous scholar to come to his camp. Ibn Khaldun's *Muqaddimah* or 'Introduction' lays down principles of historical criticism and historical theory, but he treats also of tribalism and formulates social theories based on his extensive reading and on practical political experience.

This period witnessed the rise of the great cycles of popular romances, though in origin they doubtless go back to the earliest times, as in the case of the romance of the Bedouin poet Antar. The *Sirah* of the Banu Hilal tribe is based on an historical series of migrations from Arabia to Syria and furthest North Africa; crudely printed copies may still be bought in the Arab *suqs*. In Egypt the *Thousand and One Nights* seems to have received its last accretion, the Cairene stories. It has a long and involved history, the original framework being Indian, but it is not a collection highly esteemed by Arab critics.

In Spain literature continued to flourish until, after the Reconquista, Arabic manuscripts were sought out by the conquerors and burned. What survives is of prime interest; apart from more strictly literary works, there are treatises on market law in Seville, on the mint, and the calendar of Cordova. Just over the water in Tangier the tomb of the famous globetrotter, Ibn Battutah, is still pointed out. This 14th-century geographer and scholar travelled in both eastern and western Black Africa, in Russia, India, Ceylon and China.

539

The second blow dealt to Arabic literature was the Ottoman Turkish conquest of Iraq, Syria, Egypt, western Arabia, and part of North Africa in the 16th century, which coincided, more or less, with the Portuguese diversion of much of the India trade to the Cape route and the resulting economic stress felt in countries like Egypt. Though there followed an age of stagnation, even of decline, Arabic literature still flourished in Muslim India and elsewhere—including West Africa where the full extent of its diffusion has only been realised during the last ten years. In an age of stagnation it is symptomatic that Sufi mystical literature flourished, and that as less attention was paid (possibly because of lack of patronage) to classical Arabic, colloquial Arabic came more to the fore; in this period standards of correct Arabic appear to have greatly declined.

Revival of Arabic

The brief French occupation of Egypt (1798–1801) is regarded as having given the first stimulus to the revival of Egypt and Syria. (The historian Jabarti (d. 1825), incidentally, has left us a contemporary account, through Egyptian eyes, of the French invasion.) A little later the Pasha of Egypt, Muhammad Aly (d. 1849), despatched young men of promise to train in France and Italy, including Rifa'ah al-Tahtawi, who became head of a translation bureau which turned out Arabic versions of European medical and scientific books. In 1822 a printing press was set up at Bulaq for government publications. These activities were however the precursors rather than the beginnings of the revival of Arabic as a vehicle for the transmission of vital new knowledge and ideas.

For the Arab countries as a whole the 19th century saw the impact of Western ideas and techniques and a reaction to them, but at the same time it was an age in which classical Arabic was promoted by the printing and diffusion of the major scholarly and literary writings which formed Arabic's cultural heritage.

Syria began early to come into contact with the West through missionary activities; the American Protestants opened an active mission there in 1838. Christian Arabs were able to absorb Western ideas more readily than Muslims, who started from a position of hostility to them, but though Christian missionaries made hardly any converts among the Muslim population, the attack on Islam was stimulating in that it provoked an intellectual reaction. At first the revival of Arabic was largely the work of Christian Syrians, many of whom fled to Egypt after the massacres of 1860. The 1850s and 1860s saw a rash of ephemeral journals, mainly run by Syrians. From that time the Arabic press has continuously developed and expanded, and played the principal part in firmly establishing classical or literary Arabic as the standard written language. At the same time it is in the current journals that classical Arabic has been adapted to modern use, and where experiments have been made with new literary techniques.

For the last 100 years translation and adaptation of Western literature has preoccupied even noted writers. Modern Arabic literature is so derivative, even in original work, from the literatures of Europe, French, English, and to a lesser extent Italian and Russian, that it may almost be considered as part of that literature with an Arabic colouring. Even the diction of modern Arabic prose has been affected by European idiom. If Syria, Lebanon and Egypt were the leaders of the renaissance, the smallest Arab country now has its own modern literature. The novel in a local setting has been an accepted literary genre since the first tale of contemporary Egyptian life, Husain Haikal's *Zainab*, appeared in 1914. The genre found perhaps its most original and daring author in our contemporary Nagib Mahfuz. Drama, which may be dated conveniently from the opening of the opera house in Cairo in 1869, has long been established. It still looks to Western themes, but it also draws much upon patriotic Arab traditional stories. Classical Arabic is used for heroic subjects, but colloquial Arabic is clearly essential for the sophisticated modern play.

In the 1920s and 1930s, Arabic letters were dominated by the sympathetic figure of Taha Husain, whose charming autobiography, *The Days*, may be read in English. After training in France he returned to Cairo University where he became the apostle of modernism. No doubt to shock the powerful religious conservatism of the Azhar at that time, he published in 1926 an attack on the ancient pre-Islamic poetry, suggesting that it had been forged for religious motives, which roused a storm of orthodoxy against him. His strictures on this verse are sometimes naïve and may not have much validity, but it is certainly an achievement to have combated the forces of tradition where these had stifled the critical processes of the mind.

Poetry naturally shared in the classical revival, especially in Egypt, where the most celebrated neo-classicist was Shawqi (1868–1932), the aristocratic 'prince of poets'. But, approximately contemporary with the neo-classicists, there flourished the literature of the "Emigration" in North America, using simple diction and having a strong Christian literary tradition behind it. With it is associated Gibran (1883–1932), founder of the Pen Club in 1920. It had an immense influence on the new trends in Arabic verifying when poets, dissatisfied with the *qasidah* form, traditional metres and imagery, began turning to Western literature. The Lebanese-American Amin al-Rihani experimented with 'prose verse' as early as 1905. English blank verse was copied, but a metre retained, mostly for drama. Modern poets developed post-classical verse-forms such as the Spanish *muwashshahah* and *zajal* which seem especially suitable for the theatre.

Shawqi and the neo-classicists were attacked by the younger 'Aqqad whose school enthusiastically followed English literature. They were in turn attacked by the next generation of poets. 'Aqqad opposed the short-lived but profoundly influential Apollo school founded by Abu Shadi (1892–1954). Abu Shadi was the exponent of blank verse, which is the medium employed also today by the successful playwright of Hadrami origin, 'Aly Ba Kathir.

'Free verse', over which controversy rages still, has been classified into two phases, the earlier of 1926–46, and the Iraqi school of 1947 onwards. Contemporary poets exhibit strongly the influence of Ezra Pound and T. S. Eliot. Again allusion should be made to a short-lived but important magazine, *Poetry*, founded a few years ago in Lebanon by Yusuf al-Khal. Nevertheless it should be recalled that a large section of intellectual society, though less vocal than the *avant-garde*, has no quarrel with traditional prosodic forms.

Political disaster and violent social change have profoundly stirred Arab poets; their aspirations to see the rise of a new world from the death-bed of the old are aptly represented in the popular Tammuz or Adonis theme. Some believe in political commitment (*iltizam*), usually to the political socialism of the communist poets—all too often their 'free verse' consists of tiresome slogans—nor can their rejection of the Arab cultural heritage as an irrelevance find wide acceptance.

The freedom of expression formerly enjoyed in many Arab states even under a 'feudal' régime has been arbitrarily curtailed, and increasingly writers become unable to maintain free contact with thought abroad which they once had. Lebanon is an outstanding exception in this respect, and Beirut the Middle Eastern capital in which there is today the greatest intellectual ferment.

FURTHER READING

Abdel Meguid, Abdel Aziz. *The Modern Arabic Short Story*, Cairo, 1954.

Arberry, A. J. *Moorish Poetry*, Cambridge, 1953.

Arnold, T. and Guillaume, A. *The Legacy of Islam*, Oxford Univ. Press, London and New York, 1931.

Cachia, P. *Taha Husain: His Place in the Egyptian Literary Renaissance*, London, 1956; Verry, Connecticut, 1956.

Gibb, H. A. R. *Arabic Literature*, Oxford Univ. Press, London and New York (2nd ed.), 1963.

Johnson-Davies, D. *Modern Arabic Short Stories*, Oxford Univ. Press, London and New York, 1967.

Manzalaoni, Mahmoud. *Arabic Writing Today—The Short Story*, Cairo, 1968.

Nicholson, R. A. *Literary History of the Arabs*, Cambridge Univ. Press, Cambridge and New York, 1907.

Rosenthal, F. *Ibn Khaldun, the Muqaddimah*, New York, 1958.

Schuman, L. O. *The Education of Salama Musa*, Leiden, 1961.

Serjeant, R. B. 'Arabic Poetry', *Encyclopaedia of Poetry and Poetics*, Princeton Univ. Press, Princeton, 1965.

PERSIAN LITERATURE

HUBERT DARKE

ISLAMIC Persian Literature began to flourish more than a thousand years age (ninth century AD), some 200 years after the Arab invasion of Persia. It shared in the wider Islamic heritage and the cultural background of Arabic, both of which are discussed in separate chapters of this Handbook. This very brief survey sets out to indicate the fields in which the Persian literary genius especially distinguished itself and to illustrate its nature by reference to some of the more prominent writers. Detailed reference is made only to works available in English translation.

POETRY

One of the earliest Persian poets, regarded by many present day Iranians as the greatest of all, was Firdausī (tenth century). Over a period of 25 years Firdausī composed his vast *Epic of the Kings*, which in 60,000 verses celebrates the deeds first of mythical heroes and then of historical (Sāsānian) kings and queens, from the creation of the world down to the Arab conquest in the 7th century. Comparable to the *Iliad* and the *Aeneid*, the poem breathes a spirit of patriotism, taking as its central theme the glory of Iran. One of the chief protagonists in the mythical part is Rustam, the heroic champion of the Iranians, who tragically and unknowingly kills his son, Suhrāb.

A form which almost all Persian poets have employed to some extent is the quatrain (*rubāʿī*). The most celebrated composer of *rubāʿiyāt* is the 11th century poet, ʿUmar Khayyām, who wrote no other kind of verse but these terse epigrams. (ʿUmar was not a professional poet but a professor of mathematics and astronomy.) Fitzgerald's well-known paraphrase reproduces admirably the spirit of ʿUmar's *Rubāʿiyat*, but anyone who wishes to come nearer to the letter should read the modern translation by A. J. Arberry.

To see how in the hands of a greater poet the quatrain was applied to mystical themes, one should look at those of Jalāl ad-Dīn Rūmī (13th century). Rūmī's *Masnavī* is the greatest mystical poem in Persian. Its discourse, on knowing the Divine Being and union with the Divine Beloved, is presented in a series of tales, many of them concerning legends from the Koran, traditions of the Prophet Muhammad and lives of Muslim saints. Rūmī also composed a huge corpus of shorter poems of a mystical nature. In addition there is the posthumous collection of his prose *Discourses*, which is in a sense the raw material out of which the *Masnavī* was created. An insight into the words, thoughts and deeds of Muslim mystics (Sūfīs), is provided by the *Memorial of the Saints* by ʿAttār (12th–13th century) and by Professor Arberry's general introduction to the subject.

Shīrāz, city of gardens and nightingales, produced two of Iran's best-loved poets, Sa'dī (13th century) and Hāfiz (14th century). Sa'dī composed many lyrics (*ghazals*) of high quality, but he is best known for his didactic, moralising books, the *Būstān* in verse, and the *Gulistān*, mainly in prose, but interspersed with many verses which point the moral of his anecdotes.

Sa'dī's themes are generosity, repentance, gratitude, humility, justice, love, contentment, old age. Expediency is the main lesson taught here, but a purely ethical spirit is not lacking. Sa'dī travelled much, visiting the Levant, Arabia and North Africa, and on one occasion at Jerusalem he was taken prisoner by crusaders; these experiences are reflected in his tales. He seems to have known much about the *darvīsh* (Sūfī) way of life and been in sympathy with it, but he did not attempt to expound Sūfī ideas in the way that Rūmī did.

Hāfiz is by common consent Iran's finest lyrical poet, some would say her finest poet altogether. His poems combine beauty of language, subtlety of imagery and depth of meaning to a sublime degree. Translations of 50 poems of Hāfiz have been collected in one volume, and renderings of poems by both Sa'dī and Hāfiz are included in the anthology of Persian lyrical poetry, *Immortal Rose*.

PROSE

Turning to prose works, it is especially fortunate that Juvainī's *History of the World-Conqueror* (13th century) is available in translation, as it is one of the best historical texts in Persian and among the most instructive for the general reader in that it deals with the momentous and shattering events of the Mongol invasion under Chingiz Khān and Hūlāgū Khān. Juvainī was employed as a secretary by Hūlāgū so he was an eye-witness of the events that he described; his prose style is somewhat florid but his reporting is extraordinarily vivid. These were the turbulent times in which Rūmī and Sa'dī lived, tragedies which were to be suffered all over again in the invasion of Tīmūr Lang (Tamerlane) in the 14th century.

Among the most notable works that are available in translation is the *Letter of Tansar*, a kind of political handbook in the form of advice to kings, whose origin goes back to Sāsānian (pre-Islamic) times and in the sixth century. Many Sāsānian anecdotes and sayings are quoted here and in three further books of this type which were written around the end of the 11th century. First, the *Qābūs-nāma* is one of the most delightful and amusing books in Persian. It was written by a petty prince of Tabaristān (on the southern shore of the Caspian Sea), a vassal of the Saljūqs, for the enlightenment of his son. In it he draws on the experiences of a lifetime to give paternal advice on such subjects as religion, morals, kingship, finance and marriage, always advocating expediency as the prime rule of life.

Ten years later and in very different circumstances another such book was written, this time in a more ponderous vein and on a loftier plane. This is the *Siyar al-Mulūk* of Nizām al-Mulk, written by that celebrated Prime Minister for his Saljūq (Turkish) master. His advice on matters like court ceremonial, ambassadors, spies, boon companions, arrangements for drinking parties, treatment of slaves, redress of wrongs, are often illustrated by short anecdotes. In several stories told at much greater length the writer gives free rein to his imagination and invention to create novelettes which may be counted the first prose fiction in Persian.

The third of these 'mirrors for princes' was written by the great religious thinker Ghazzālī. His *Counsel for Kings* is more academic and theoretical than the other two, which are mainly practical: its first part is a theological discourse, defining Muslim beliefs and religious principles, while the second part deals with the qualities necessary for kings, ministers and secretaries.

In a later epoch, contemporary with Rumī and Saʻdī, Nasīr ad-Dīn Tūsī (13th century) the philosopher, mathematician and astronomer, composed his *Nāsirean Ethics*, which is a highly abstract and academic ethical treatise, conceived in a profoundly philosophical and religious spirit and couched in a rather difficult and involved style. In a lighter vein, one other classical prose work of interest to the general reader is the *Marzubān-nāma* (13th century). This is a collection of animal fables, written in the ornate and affected style which the taste of the time considered appropriate for polite literature. Some of the tales may be Indian in origin, like those of the collection known as *Kalīla va Dimna*, but many have an Iranian setting, being attributed to Chosroes (*Khusrau* is a Sāsānian royal title).

THE MODERN SCENE

Literature in the Persian language has of course a continuing history up to the present day, but it is impossible in a short space to do justice to its prolific output or to consider, for instance, the Persian literature of Muslim India. Nor is the literature of the later centuries comparable in quality with writings of the recognised earlier masters.

Like all Islamic countries, Iran has been subjected to the full force of Western culture and this has profoundly influenced the development of modern Persian literature. In the present century Sadiq Hidāyat (d. 1951) stands out as Iran's greatest modern writer. The larger part of his output consists of short stories, showing the influence of Kafka and of French writers in this genre; his first work was actually written while he was studying in France. In all his work Hidāyat shows concern and compassion for the sick, the ugly, the poor, the outcast; though he was born into an aristocratic family he could write about what it feels like to be a beggar, a hunchback, a stray dog, a hungry peasant or an unattractive girl, so vividly that the reader cannot help being drawn into their sufferings. In his longer novel *The Blind Owl* he turns his attention inwards, picturing himself as a misanthropic recluse, obsessed with thoughts of death and decay, wallowing in self-pity, tortured with desires, tantalised by dreams (induced by opium), plumbing the very depths of despair. It is a repulsive but morbidly fascinating book.

FURTHER READING

Arberry, A. J. *Classical Persian Literature*, George Allen & Unwin, London, 1958.
Arberry, A. J. *Sufism: An Account of the Mystic of Islam*, George Allen & Unwin, London, 1950; Hillary House, New York, 1956.
Epic of the Kings (Shāh-nāma of Firdausī), trans. Reuben Levy, Routledge & Kegan Paul, London, 1967.
Immortal Rose (An Anthology of Persian Lyrics), trans. A. J. Arberry, Luzac, London, 1948.
Kamshad, H. *Modern Persian Prose Literature*, Cambridge Univ. Press, Cambridge, 1966.

HUBERT DARKE. Lecturer in Persian at Cambridge University. Worked for an oil company in Qatar 1954–61. Engaged in research 1950–4 and during this time travelled in India, Pakistan, Afghanistan and Iraq.

THE CULTURAL LIFE OF ISRAEL

GEOFFREY WIGODER

The Zionist movement, which evolved in the late 19th century, was composed of various strands, one of the most significant of which was known as Cultural Zionism. Crystallised by the philosopher Ahad Ha-Am (1856–1927), this maintained that Jewish cultural creativity had developed unnaturally in the Diaspora inasmuch as Jews had been living in a minority —and frequently oppressed—situation which had prevented the natural growth of a Jewish culture. This could only develop when the Jews lived in their own land, speaking their own language, and were masters of their own fate.

The external exigencies of Jewish history, together with certain aspects of internal religious and cultural development, had in fact led to the channelling of Jewish cultural and artistic potential into certain spheres. Until the advent of the period of Jewish Emancipation, when West European Jewry began to emerge from the ghettoes into which it had been confined (from the end of the 18th century), the Jewish literary genius had been primarily religio-centred (rabbinical study, religious philosophy, synagogal poetry, etc.). Artistic expression had concentrated on ritual objects and had been hampered by the tendency to invoke the second commandment's interdict on graven images. Musical talent was directed to expressions of public prayer. It was the Emancipation which released the floodgates of Jewish artistic expression and in their newfound opportunities for expression, Jews found themselves disproportionately represented in all cultural manifestations in the countries where they were living.

The return to Zion from the 1880s was accompanied by conscious efforts to harness Jewish cultural and artistic creativity to the new circumstances. One of the first struggles was for the modernisation of the Hebrew language, which for many centuries had been essentially confined to literary and liturgical expression, and its recognition as the language of the Jewish community. Simultaneously came the early gropings to find appropriate means of artistic expression for the new social and political realities. There were tensions between the newly-discovered nationalist components which led in the direction of particularism on the one hand, and on the other, the universalist pull exerted by certain aspects of Jewish tradition and also by the socialist ideology which was a powerful motivation among the first generations of Jewish settlers in the Land of Israel. The development of various trends can be discerned over the subsequent generations. The early settlers, overwhelmingly originating from an East European background, continued to reflect their area of origin. The second generation (post-World War I) began the indigenous cultural expression of the Land of Israel—

notably its pioneering aspects. The third generation, which emerged around the period of the struggle for independence (1945–9), was native-born and wholly absorbed in the emergence of the new state and a new type of Jew. The next generation has assimilated and takes for granted the discoveries of its predecessors, has abandoned their introspection and has turned to universalist movements, seeking to find its place within contemporary international artistic trends.

An added dimension has been given to this intensive activity by the varied background of the Israelis. Still basically an immigrant population, they embrace groups from countries in all parts of the world. Wherever Jews have lived throughout the centuries of their dispersion, they have been influenced by—and on occasions even imbibed deeply—their environmental culture. Each community coming to Israel has therefore brought with it traditions from its land of origin and this has contributed to the kaleidoscopic nature of the emerging expression which in certain spheres represents a meeting place, and often a synthesis, of east and west, sometimes obtained deliberately, sometimes the natural outcome of the pluralistic nature of Israeli society. One of the problems frequently discussed within Israel is that of unity versus diversity, i.e., should the integration process—including that of cultural integration—aim at producing a uniformity or is there room to preserve the individual contribution that can be made by each group by virtue of its original environmental traditions?

Less successful hitherto has been the cultural integration of the Arab elements. For one thing, the political situation has prevented an overall relationship with the culture of neighbouring countries. Inside Israel too, while there have been minor cultural developments among the Arab population, they have tended to occur with the minimum of cross-fertilisation with developments in the Jewish sector.

HEBREW LANGUAGE

At the end of the 18th century, Jewish writers in Eastern Europe began to produce modern works (novels, science textbooks) in Hebrew. The language itself was inevitably forced and artificial as a result of its long disuse. The great impetus came however from the national movement at the end of the 19th century, which ideologically allied the return to the ancestral homeland with the revival of the ancestral language as a spoken tongue. Opposition to this was encountered on various sides—the Orthodox looked on Hebrew as a holy tongue not to be defiled for secular purposes, the Yiddishists felt that Yiddish (at that time spoken by 80% of the Jewish people) should become the language of the country, while there was a cosmopolitan element which feared that the adoption of Hebrew would doom the emergent Jewish culture in the land of Israel to isolation and that the language of the country should remain within a German, French or English mainstream. The 'language war' was bitter but brief. The Hebraists, led by Eliezer Ben-Yehuda (1858–1922), the pioneer of the Hebrew language revival and compiler of its first modern dictionary, were triumphant and by the time of the British Mandate in the early 1920s Hebrew was recognised, alongside English and Arabic, as an official language of the country.

The Vaad Ha-Lashon (Language Committee), established by Ben-Yehuda, met regularly from 1904 to determine usage, pronunciation, orthography, etc. Gradually the language recovered its elasticity and was applied to all spheres of life (the Committee appointed a series of sub-committees to develop the terminology in each sphere of specialisation). Moreover the speaking of Hebrew was regarded as a national duty and at one stage a Language Protection League was established to combat the speaking of non-Hebrew tongues within a Jewish framework. Already, by the end of World War I, 40% of the Jews of the country (outside Jerusalem) were Hebrew-speaking. By 1948, 80% of the Jewish population spoke Hebrew and for over 54% it was their sole language of communication.

In 1948, Hebrew was proclaimed the language of the State of Israel. One of the early problems of the State was to teach the language to the hundreds of thousands of immigrants. Various methods were adopted—notably the *ulpan* (literally 'studio'), an intensive course lasting three to six months during which time the newcomer acquired a speaking knowledge of the language. A basic 1,000 word vocabulary was developed and served as the basis for textbooks, newspapers and special broadcasts aimed at helping the immigrant learn Hebrew. Meanwhile the Vaad Ha-Lashon received official recognition as the Hebrew Language Academy and legislation was passed in 1954 to regulate its activities and give official sanction to its decisions.

LITERATURE

Until the early part of the 20th century, little creative writing appeared in Palestine. Eastern Europe provided the focus of the Hebrew literary revival which blossomed at the end of the 19th century. Its writings soon became the modern Hebrew classics, notably the poetry of Hayyim Nahman Bialik (1873–1934) and Saul Tschernichowsky (1875–1943) and the philosophical essays of Ahad Ha-Am. Until World War I, original writing in Palestine was but a pale reflection of the great creativity in Europe. But after that war the centre of gravity rapidly shifted. For one thing, the Bolshevik Revolution heralded the closing-down of the Russian school of Hebrew writers, while the establishment of the Jewish National Home attracted to Palestine many of the intellectuals from East Europe. Bialik, Tschernichowsky and Ahad Ha-Am all spent their last years in Tel Aviv and although this was not the period of their most original work, they exerted a great influence on the development of native talent.

The first generation of writers in the country retained one foot in Eastern Europe where they had been brought up and for them the Palestinian scene was a late graft. They served as the key links between the long European experience and the new scene emerging in the Land of Israel. The outstanding names of this school are S. Y. Agnon (1888–1970), who was largely concerned with the search for faith and whose original contribution was recognised by the award of the Nobel Prize for Literature in 1966, and Hayyim Hazaz (b. 1897).

It was the next generation which based its muse primarily on the Israel experience. They too occasionally harked back to Europe but their main inspiration was drawn from the new reality—the pioneering challenge and the kibbutz experiment, the problems of settling waste lands, and the sociological and cultural aspects of the absorption of the new immigration. Outstanding here were the poets Avraham Shlonsky (b. 1900), Uri Zvi Greenberg (b. 1894) and Nathan Alterman (1910–1970), who found in the Land of Israel the answer to the rootlessness of Jewish life in the Dispersion.

It was only their successors, the generation that reached maturity around the period of Israel's War of Independence in 1948, whose experience was totally Israeli. Shocked by the fate of the Jews in Hitler's Europe and stimulated by the successful outcome of their own struggle for independence, they represented the emergent native-born (*sabra*) stereotype. Their initial self-confidence gave way after 1948 to a period of self-questioning. Once the political and military struggle had been won, there was a search for the spiritual values that would motivate the old-new state as well as answer their own individual reappraisals. They experimented in exploring Jewish history or in examining the variety of communities who had settled in Israel.

But a generation has passed since the days of the fight for the State and the latest generation is increasingly removed from the 1946–9 experience and even more from the traditional European Jewish influences. They testify to the validity of the original contention of the cultural Zionists—that the Jewish people needed their own land for cultural normalisation out of which could emerge an authentic uninhibited expression. There is an identity crisis among the new writers, whose concern is often more individual than social. Their attention is directed less towards what is particular about Israel than towards where she fits within the framework of contemporary cultural development. The traditional aspects have been assimilated and taken for granted; now the writers are exploring and imitating the currents in Western letters and becoming involved in all the current schools of literary expression. The boundaries between the European and the Israeli aspects have become blurred.

The sheer quantity of literary creativity is staggering and *per caput* book production is among the highest in the world. All literary forms are popular (the amount of verse published, for example, is surprisingly high). Most of the works appear in Hebrew but owing to the complex composition of the population, many other languages are represented. Special mention should be made of Yiddish literature. Before World War II, Yiddish literature was centred in Moscow, Warsaw and New York. The European centres were liquidated during World War II and the New York centre declined; most of the outstanding survivors have settled in Israel. Although the language itself appears doomed within a few generations, it is making its last cultural stand in Israel which is the place of publication of almost all significant new works in Yiddish as well as of its last major cultural journal.

THEATRE AND FILMS

Apart from isolated phenomena, there was no Jewish dramatic expression prior to the 19th century. When Jewish theatres began to develop in the latter part of that century, it was in Eastern Europe and the performances were in Yiddish. Theatrical performances in Palestine began at the end of the century but were still insignificant at the time of World War I.

The milestone in the establishment of Hebrew drama was the foundation of the Habimah Company in Moscow in 1917. Under the inspiration of Stanislavsky and directed by one of his associates, Vachtangov, this theatre rapidly attained an international reputation—especially for its performance of S. Anski's *The Dybbuk* (translated by Bialik from the original Yiddish). Meanwhile in Palestine a professional theatre emerged of which the first important group was the Ohel, an actors' collective emphasising the ideals of the workers' movement as well as the creation of original Hebrew drama. It began to perform in 1926, the year that Habimah left Russia as a result of an increasingly hostile attitude on the part of officialdom to the Hebrew language. Habimah toured various countries and in 1932 decided to make its permanent headquarters in Tel-Aviv with the declared objective of serving as a cultural bridge between the Jews of Palestine and Jews elsewhere.

The Habimah company dominated the Israel theatrical scene for many years but in the course of time a reaction was evoked by its stylised and dated form of acting. In 1945 a group of younger actors established a third major company, the Chamber Theatre, which was influenced by the European and American repertoires and schools of acting. They sought to introduce a contemporary international theatre and to encourage young Israeli talent in both writing and acting. The Chamber Theatre in turn influenced the other companies to adopt more realistic, flexible and popular repertoires and approaches. A further company that has made a mark in recent years is the Haifa Municipal Theatre, founded by Yoseph Millo (b. 1916) who also founded the Chamber Theatre.

Despite the great enthusiasm evinced for the theatre, especially in Tel-Aviv which is the 'arts' capital of the country, Hebrew playwriting has been disappointing. Most of the country's authors—especially the younger ones—have made at least one attempt to write a play and many of these have been incorporated into repertoires. These have generally derived from recent Israeli events or from Jewish history, but no dramatic tradition has emerged. Each new production is meticulously scrutinised by critics and public but few have come up to international standards. One frequent fault is an excess of verbiage. A few successful satires have been written by the humorist Ephraim Kishon (b. 1924) and a number of other authors have scored one-time hits but little of significance has yet appeared.

Apart from the major companies, there has been a plethora of minor and generally transient groups. Although often of short duration, these small theatres have pioneered experimental and offbeat productions. A successful trend over the past decade has been the musical. After the outstanding success of imported musicals performed in Hebrew (*My Fair Lady, Fiddler on the Roof*), a number of Israel writers and composers have turned to the medium and some of their shows have had an extended success (e.g., Yigal Mosensohn's *Casablan* and the adapation of Sami Gronemann's *King Solomon and the Cobbler*).

One particular form of theatrical entertainment has developed largely through the impetus of the army. This is provided by small troupes of actor-singer-dancers—generally between three and ten in number—who perform an informal series of songs and sketches. Initially influenced by army ensembles formed to entertain the troops, the format achieved widespread popularity. The composition of the individual groups fluctuates constantly but the performers continue to appear in varying combinations and with continuing acclaim. A number of theatrical companies appear in non-Hebrew languages. Special mention should be made of the groups appearing in Yiddish, although standards here tend to be folksy and unsophisticated.

Israel's film production was late in getting off the ground. Only a few documentaries were made in the country prior to 1948 and even after the establishment of the State, progress was slow and the films of little more than local interest. It was only in the 1960s that the industry began to come into its own. One fillip came from a number of productions made in Israel by outside companies (of which the most successful was *Exodus*). With government support, the local industry improved its facilities and a number of bright young forces emerged who began to produce films of merit. About a dozen full-length films are now produced annually, preponderantly of local interest but some of wider impact as recognised by a number of international awards.

BROADCASTING

Radio began in Palestine in 1936 when the British mandatory authorities established the Palestine Broadcasting System broadcasting in English, Arabic and Hebrew. From 1948 the Israel Broadcasting System (later the Israel Broadcasting Authority) has been responsible for the radio network which has had a considerable educational and cultural impact inside the country. Programmes were devised with the full consciousness of the educative role of the transmissions in welding together the many disparate elements in the country and giving them a common cultural experience. Primarily this impact was seen in setting standards of language (vocabulary, syntax and pronunciation) and 'radio Hebrew' has become the norm. The radio has also been utilised to promote general civics and to encourage native forms of cultural expression—by such methods as annual competitions for the best new songs, for the best new radio play, and by the popular triennial International Bible Quiz. Local musical talent has also been fostered and original works of all types commissioned.

In the early days of the State, radio programming lagged behind achievements in other spheres but rapid strides were made—partly due to the central importance of radio in the life of the country and partly because the absence of television led to a concentration and specialisation in radio when it was already being neglected in other countries. By the early 1960s Israeli radio production could be judged on international standards as was attested by awards received in international competitions.

Television has only recently reached Israel. A pilot project for schools went into operation in 1965; experimental general television started in 1968 and went into daily transmissions only late in 1969. Original production is mostly in the news and documentary spheres but Israel is only at the beginning of the road in the mastery of this medium.

MUSIC AND DRAMA

The pioneers who went to Palestine from Eastern Europe brought with them the folksongs of their countries of origin—to which they wrote Hebrew words. Up to World War I, musical activity was confined to these songs, the dancing of the *hora* (imported from Rumania) and the establishment of a couple of music schools. The 1920s saw the laying of the foundations of the country's musical life—the composer and Jewish music researcher Yoel Engel (1868–1927) arrived from Russia and pioneered music composition and music making; an opera company was founded; choirs sprang up in many parts of the country, in the villages as well as in the towns; and the first symphony orchestra came into being.

It was the large immigration from Germany in the 1930s that was largely responsible for the intensive pattern of musical appreciation which emerged in the country. The highlight was the foundation in 1936 of the Israel Philharmonic Orchestra (initially, the Palestine Symphony Orchestra) at the initiative of the violinist (Bronislaw Hubermann (1882–1947). This was at first composed entirely of refugees from Nazi Germany and its first concerts, conducted by Toscanini, became legendary. In the course of time the orchestra achieved an international reputation through its travels and recordings, while the enthusiasm it aroused necessitated the repetition of each concert in Tel Aviv up to six and eight times. Another incentive was provided by the founding of the radio orchestra in Jerusalem in 1937. In its weekly public concerts and in its other appearances and broadcasts it made especial endeavours to foster local talents. At the same time chamber music became popular and ensembles developed throughout the country—much of the talent being found on the kibbutzim. Subsequently further orchestras were founded including the Haifa Orchestra, the Army and Gadna (Army Youth) Orchestras and several chamber orchestras. Choral singing has continued to be popular and since 1952 a regular feature of musical life has been the Zimria choir festival which has brought Israeli choirs together with choirs (mainly Jewish) from overseas.

The early European nature of the folksong was tempered in the course of time by a Middle Eastern influence. Jews coming from various Arab lands, such as Yemen, brought with them a completely different tradition, essentially Arabic in form but maintaining a Jewish kernel. The two types developed side by side but also exerted a mutual influence. Other strands were provided by the Sephardi Jews who preserved traditions going back to medieval Spain and the newcomers from Western lands who introduced the chanson, jazz and, later, rock. In certain spheres religious experience penetrated the folk-music development—on the one hand, there were traditional melodies such as those developed by the *Hasidim* (the East European pietists); on the other there were compositions created for the observances developed in modern Israel, such as the agricultural festivals mentioned in the Bible and revived in the kibbutzim. No original folk-instruments have emerged but the hand-drum, recorder and accordion are in demand. The verve that characterises many of the folk-songs has led to their popularity outside Israel—primarily among Jewish communities but also often with general audiences.

Meanwhile there has been an intensive record of symphonic and chamber composition. Again the pioneers in the field came from Eastern Europe and were influenced by their early environment and Jewish musical tradition with its emphasis on minor modes. Gradually however the mood changed under the impact of the burgeoning culture in Palestine and musical life was transformed in the 1930s by the arrival of many German-Jewish composers schooled in the contemporary West European tradition with its emphasis on experiment. Here also the impact of the new environment introduced oriental elements—and in the sphere of musical composition this was not only the result of a natural, almost unconscious, absorption of such strands but a conscious effort was made by the composers of European origin to explore the oriental world of music and to wed it to western experience. They felt that here was an opportunity for original creativity by welding east and west, and they founded what they called the Mediterranean School which sought to adapt oriental styles of melody, rhythm and instrumentation to modern occidental techniques. The main composers of this school were Paul Ben-Haim (b. 1897), Oedon Partos (b. 1907), Alexander Uriah Boscovich (1908–64) and Menahem Avidom (b. 1908). The Mediterraneanists emerged in the 1940s but by the 1960s had receded or disappeared in the face of more universalistic tendencies. The younger Israeli composer tended to see himself within the mainstream of modern music. These included practitioners of the 12-tone technique (Mordecai Seter, b. 1916) and electronic music (Yosef Tal, b. 1910).

The development of folk-dancing paralleled that of folk-songs, with various groups making contributions. Apart from the *hora*, hasidic dances as well as the Arabs' *debka* became popular and were given individual interpretations. Classical ballet made little headway but modern ballet was expressed through various companies, such as the Inbal troupe of Yemenite dancers (who portrayed traditional Yemenite folklore and music through a modern interpretation) and the Bath-Sheba ballet founded by Countess Bathsheba de Rothschild.

ART

The philosopher Martin Buber, addressing the 1901 Zionist Congress, stated : 'Jewish art can come into being and flourish only together with progressive rebirth. A Jewish art can only attain perfection on Jewish soil—like Jewish culture generally.' Two years later Boris Schatz (1866–1932), who was Court Painter to the King of Bulgaria, met the Zionist leader Theodore Herzl and put forward his plan for establishing a Jewish art centre in the Land of Israel. This plan was approved by the 1905 Zionist Congress and in the following year Schatz founded the Bebalel Arts School in Jerusalem. This pioneering venture had to contend not only with the absence of encouragement on the part of the small Jewish population in Palestine but with the outright opposition of the more religious Jews. It had however the support of the Zionist movement not only for its potential aesthetic significance but because it was felt that the development of handicrafts would make an economic contribution and develop new avenues of employment.

Schatz and his early colleagues consciously endeavoured to develop a specific national style which has often been scoffed at by later and more sophisticated generations. They deliberately delved into Jewish traditions and explored the exotic aspects of the scenery and peoples of Palestine. They rejected the influences of contemporary artistic trends and emphasised the decorative rather than the pictorial. Schatz turned his attention to developing not only painting and handicrafts but also sculpture—and this was an innovation in a Jewish milieu in view of the long ban on graven images.

The turning-point came after World War I, with the immigration of a number of highly talented artists from Europe as well as the emergence of a group of younger painters, trained at Bezalel but now under the influence of the latest European schools, generally after a stay in the West—mostly in Paris. This group sought to express the reality of the Land of Israel—its light, landscape and peoples—through modern techniques, often expressionistic.

As in other cultural activities already mentioned, a further stage came with the German-Jewish immigration of the 1930s, which further internationalised the art scene. Artists among them had studied in Europe and their own involvement with the School of Paris set the keynote for the development of art inside Israel, which henceforth was involved with all the current schools, such as cubism and abstractionism. In 1941, Marcel Jancu (b. 1895), one of the founders of Dadaism, settled in the country. 1948, the year of the establishment of the State which in itself led to a greater inner security and self-confidence, saw the founding of the New Horizons group, led by Jancu and Yoseph Zaritzky (b. 1891). This proved influential in further promoting abstract art and in combating what it saw as provincialism. By the 1950s, Israeli art reflected all European styles and much of it was indistinguishable from the painting and sculpture of other countries. Artists of Middle Eastern origin as well as those on kibbutzim (where any potential artistic talent was sedulously fostered) tended to be somewhat more conservative. At this time two important artists' centres were founded—one in the picturesque ancient town of Safed, the other in Ein Hod, developed as an artists' village in the Carmel hills. One of the significant more recent developments has been in the direction of a synthesis combining both the universalistic trends predominating elsewhere in the world with some of the more particularistic attention to Jewish tradition, envisioned by the early pioneers, but now falling into an appropriate and unobtrusive perspective. Among the best-known painters of recent decades are Reuven Rubin (b. 1893) and Mordecai Ardon (b. 1896) whose works have received international recognition; Jacob Steinhardt (1887–1968), a master of the woodcut; and among the younger generation Fima (b. 1916) whose delicate abstracts were influenced by the calligraphy of his native China.

The many museums and art galleries in the country include the magnificent Israel Museum in Jerusalem (which incorporates the Bezalel art collection and a fine garden of modern sculpture as well as an archaeological wing and the Shrine of the Book, housing the Dead Sea Scrolls); the Tel-Aviv Museum (which includes a separate gallery devoted to modern art); and the Ha-Aretz Museum in Tel Aviv whose various pavilions are devoted to individual themes—e.g., glass, coins.

Sculpture progressed far more slowly than painting in view of the opposition of the religious elements in most of the big towns (Haifa was a notable exception). It flourished particularly in kibbutzim and only in the 1950s did the official ice begin to melt. Even less than in painting is there an Israeli school of sculpture but the impact of archaeological discoveries can occasionally be discerned. Abstract sculpture has come to the fore only in recent years with the French expressionists exerting a strong influence. The outstanding name of the 1930s and 1940s was Ze'ev Ben-Zvi (1904–52), and two of his pupils, Palombo (1920–66) and Itzhak Danziger (b. 1916) are the leading exponents of the succeeding generation.

From the end of the 19th century, architecture was strongly influenced by European outlooks. After World War I, a number of architects from Western Europe and Britain were active in the country; one group stressed the horizontal structure, another was influenced by expressionism, while the British school used Arab designs. The 1930s saw the arrival of the German Jewish architects, leading to a greater functionalism as well as the first modern block of flats. Town planning was often sacrificed in the early years of the State under the pressure of the mass immigration, when the urgent need was to build housing in order to get the newcomers out of tent camps and this overrode aesthetic considerations. It was only in the mid-1950s that there was a breathing-spell which enabled attention to be paid to finish externals, and landscaping. Pressure on space engendered a growing number of skyscrapers in the larger cities in the 1960s and various impressive public buildings were erected although their style reflected general western architecture rather than anything specifically Israeli.

Considerable attention has been paid to the development of home handicrafts. Many of the communities represented in the country—including the Arabs and Druzes—have individual contributions to make in this sphere and the fostering of these talents has not only proved economically desirable but has produced original work (e.g., in dress and fabric design, glass, ceramics) which in turn has made its impact on the wider artistic world.

FURTHER READING

Ariel: a quarterly review of the arts and sciences in Israel, Cultural Department of Ministry of Foreign Affairs.

Benshalom, Benzion. *Hebrew Literature between the Two World Wars*, Jewish Agency, Jerusalem, 1953.

Gradenwitz, Peter E. *Music and Musicians in Israel*, Jewish Agency, Jerusalem, 1952.

Israel Today, a series of pamphlets dealing mainly with cultural topics, Jewish Agency, Jerusalem.

Kohansky, Mendel. *The Hebrew Theatre*, Israel Univ. Press, Jerusalem, 1969.

Tammuz, B. and Wykes-Joyce, M. (eds.) *Art in Israel*, International Publications Service, 1966.

GEOFFREY WIGODER. Member of the Hebrew University's Institute of Contemporary Jewry since 1959, directs its Oral History programme and its Jewish Film Archive. Joint editor of the *Standard Jewish Encyclopaedia* and the *Encyclopaedia of the Jewish Religion*, acting editor-in-chief of the forthcoming *Encyclopaedia Judaica*. Directed Israel's overseas English broadcasts 1950–60 and external broadcasts in all languages 1960–7.

ARCHAEOLOGY

PETER J. PARR

MANY thousands of volumes have been written on the subject of Middle Eastern archaeology; what can one hope to say in the course of a few thousand words? That the subject is important is clear, and that its importance is increasing cannot be denied. The activities of professional archaeologists working in the region expand from year to year, and scarcely a season passes without a new and productive site being opened up. In the Middle Eastern capitals the national departments of antiquities grow in size and influence, while in the universities of the West the demand for instruction in Middle Eastern archaeology far exceeds the teaching resources available.

Meanwhile, the books proliferate. Such is the demand for archaeological knowledge amongst the reading public that accounts of new discoveries are by themselves unable to satisfy it, and of the dozens of new titles which regularly appear in the publishers' catalogues the greater number are concerned with the retelling of the exploits of earlier generations—the discovery of Homer's Troy or Sargon's Nimrud, the tombs of Tutankhamen and of the kings of Ur. The lives of former archaeologists have provided ready material for the biographers, and the proposal has even been made to construct a full-length film around the career of a distinguished and still-living excavator. If—as some psychologists argue—archaeology, like history, is the refuge of the misfit in society, the retreat of the escapee from the turmoil of modern life, then the plain fact is that the number of misfits and escapees is growing. Whether this is a reflection upon their own personal inadequacies or upon the deficiencies of modern society is a question which should give food for thought.

EARLY INTEREST IN ARCHAEOLOGY

An interest in the past is not, of course, a phenomenon confined to recent times, though its widespread diffusion is. It was, after all, King Ashurbanipal of Assyria who, in the seventh century BC, instructed his agents to 'hunt for the valuable tablets which are in your archives and which do not exist in Assyria and send them to me', and from this time forward the search for antiquities and for information about the past has continued. The first writers who figure in the history of this search, such as Herodotus, are, it is true, better described as anthropologists than archaeologists, though it was one of their number, Thucydides, who, in his history of the Peloponnesian War, first used purely archaeological evidence for the purposes of historical reconstruction, by postulating an Anatolian origin for the colonists of prehistoric

Delos on account of the similarity of their burial customs to those of the contemporary inhabitants of Caria on the coast of Asia Minor. Such observations and deductions are the stock-in-trade of the archaeologist today, more than two thousand years later.

But the interest of Ashurbanipal or the reasoning of Thucydides was the exception rather than the rule, and it was not until the time of the Renaissance that the real Father of Archaeology appears, in the person of Cyriac of Ancona, who in the first half of the 15th century visited Greece, Egypt and Asia Minor, copying inscriptions and making notes about the extant monuments. His enthusiasm was, naturally enough, directed mainly towards classical Greece, from where the Renaissance drew its inspiration, but it was not long before learned travellers were being attracted by more distant regions, and by the 17th century there had developed a considerable antiquarian interest in the Middle East. In the early years of that century another Italian, Pietro della Valle, journeyed across Syria and Mesopotamia, rediscovering Palmyra in the process and bringing back to Europe a collection of antiquities which aroused much comment. At the end of the same century Henry Maundrell visited Jerusalem, as had so many pilgrims before him; but the record he kept and subsequently published differed greatly from those of his predecessors in that it was activated not so much by religious sentiment as by scientific curiosity. The same scientific spirit imbued the researches of the expedition sent out to the East in 1761 by the king of Denmark to investigate, amongst other matters, archaeological remains. This project foreshadowed the more famous expedition of the 165 French scholars who, in the wake of Napoleon's army, explored the Nile valley and published, in 1809, the magnificent *Description de l'Egypte*, which set a new standard in the execution of archaeological research, and thus opened a new chapter in its history.

After this splendid achievement there was to be no looking back. The next fifty years saw a succession of explorers and learned dilettanti—many of them diplomats, like the French Consul in Mosul, Paul-Emile Botta, or the British Resident in Baghdad, Henry Rawlinson—who continued the work of compiling and collecting, though with this difference, that now a deliberate effort was made to uncover antiquities by means of excavation. By modern standards these initial attempts at archaeological digging were appallingly inadequate, though their perpetrators should not be condemned for disregarding scientific techniques which had not yet been devised. The really great achievement of this period of research lay in a different direction, namely the decipherment of the ancient languages, first the Egyptian (effectively by Champollion in 1824), then the Assyrian (by Rawlinson, Hincks and Oppert in 1857). With this new mastery over the original sources the work of interpretation moved on to a new level, at which the relics of the past could be understood, however tentatively, instead of merely contemplated.

THE BEGINNING OF PROFESSIONAL ARCHAEOLOGY

At the same time, and perhaps as a consequence of this new understanding, it may be said that the 'professionals' took over archaeological research, though it would be difficult to define exactly what is meant by that term, except that it refers to men who devoted the greater part of their active lives to a study of the past, and who became increasingly specialised in some one aspect or another of that study. Their story is too complex, and too important, to be summarised here, and it would be pointless, not to say in-

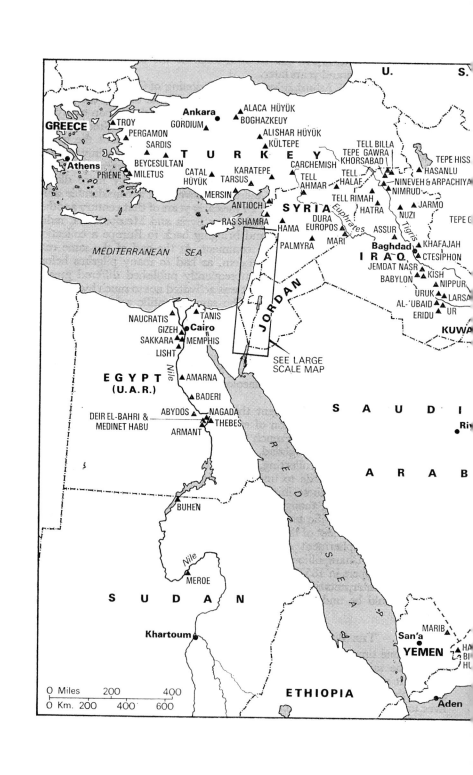

vidious, even to mention the names of some few of those scholars, when so many of them have contributed so much to our knowledge of the ancient world. Let it only be said that in the work which Schliemann began at Troy in 1870, Petrie in Egypt in 1884, and Koldewey at Babylon in 1889, there was established the framework of that discipline of archaeological fieldwork, based on close observation and meticulous recording, which is still in use today, notwithstanding the development of many new scientific techniques. It is the discipline which still guides the activities of those young men and women from our universities and museums who search out the past not only in the now well trodden valleys of the Nile, Tigris and Euphrates, but also, and increasingly, in the still little known areas of Iran, Afghanistan, and the Arabian peninsula.

The Value of Archaeology

Each of the men who, from Ashurbanipal onwards, have been diligent in a study of the relics of bygone ages will have had his own private and diverse reasons for doing so, but it is safe to say that all these reasons can be subsumed under the heading 'curiosity'. The detractors of archaeological research will add 'idle' to that heading, and make the phrase deliberately pejorative. But is an interest in the past no more than idle curiosity? To turn to the psychologists once more, many of these claim that one of the most important stabilising influences in the emotional development of the human being is a consciousness of origins and of roots, a sense of 'belonging' and of community with fellow humans. What is true for the individual is certainly true for society as a whole, and it is surely this, and not crude escapism, which explains the present widespread interest in archaeology.

As for the Middle East, there can be no doubt that it is here that the roots and origins of modern civilisation are to be found. The wheat which is now grown on the limitless prairies of North America or Australia was first cultivated in stony fields around villages on the Anatolian plateau or in the Jordan valley, some 10,000 years ago. Not long afterwards the first fortifications, temples and palaces appear, and during the course of the succeeding millennia the canons of art and architecture which are still current were first established. The alphabet which is used by the entire Western world and much of the Eastern was invented by the Canaanites in Palestine before the middle of the second millennium BC, and was propagated by Phoenicians and Greeks a thousand years later. The literature and thought of ancient Mesopotamia, Egypt, and especially of Israel has had, and continues to have, a profound influence on Western civilisation, despite the neologisms of recent years. There is no need to labour the point; the 'Cradle of Civilisation' is a description as accurate as it is hackneyed of the ancient Middle East, and the archaeologist who chooses to work in this area is obeying more faithfully than his colleagues in other fields society's demand that the roots of its being and the stages of its growth should be investigated and understood.

There is a practical side to this as well. An understanding of the past not only satisfies an emotional urge, it also helps us to understand the present. Archaeology is a form of historical research, and it is sheer nonsense to say, as some do, that history cannot, or should not, teach us anything. In his personal life man learns from his experience, and society must also learn from its collective experience, which is its history. In the process of learning a true perspective is all-important, and the great value of archaeological research is that it increases, and so improves, the historian's perspective. The progress of civilisation can be seen stretching, in the Middle East, over a period of tens of millennia, and the humility which this prospect engenders in the mind of the observer is in itself a corrective to the prevailing arrogance of modern Western man. Practical issues of present-day politics can be judged in a new light when seen against the background of this immense history; the student of the past, trained in the use of evidence and with highly developed critical faculties, can often subject current problems to a more penetrating analysis and a more judicious assessment than can his unhistorically-minded neighbour.

THE CHANGELESSNESS OF THE MIDDLE EAST

The truth of what has just been said is universal, but there is a special reason why a preoccupation with the past can help with an understanding of the present in the Middle East. In this part of the world the dichotomy of time between past and present is to a considerable extent meaningless, and one of the clearest impressions felt by the real connoisseur of the region is the degree of continuity which exists between ancient and modern. One might almost suppose that there is some sort of alchemy at work, easy to sense but hard to describe, which fuses past and present and produces a certain stability and changelessness which, however one judges it, is a powerful force to be reckoned with. The casual visitor to the area, exposed to little more than the Westernised façade of the Middle East, in the hotels and supermarkets of Cairo and Beirut, can hardly be expected to appreciate this; the idea of changelessness and stability in an area pervaded by political and social turmoil may seem wildly false. Yet it is not. A deeper acquaintance with the Middle Easterner reveals that, however appreciative he may be of the material benefits of the Western world and however skilful in adopting them, his modes of thought and his habits of behaviour remain profoundly different from those of the West.

This is something which the archaeologist, perhaps better than most, can come to understand. For the archaeologist, more than most, is in intimate contact with both the Middle Eastern past and the Middle Eastern present. His studies are directed towards the achievements—spiritual and artistic no less than technological—of the past, but his working days are spent amongst the people of the present, whose daily life he often shares and in whose ambience he often forms an important element. His explorations take him, usually on foot, over square mile after square mile of the Middle Eastern scene, looking for ancient sites but mindful of the modern farms, villages and encampments. He comes to appreciate, because he personally experiences it throughout the year, the part played by climate and natural environment in the development, past and present, of the area. When excavating he employs and trains a local labour force, learns its language and, as likely as not, finds himself involved in the personal crises—births, marriages and deaths—of his employees. Because of this, it is no accident that some of the most percipient observers of the Middle East have been archaeologists, and the name of T. E. Lawrence springs to mind only because he is the most famous. The observations which the archaeologist makes of the present are not disinterested, since from them he can learn much which helps to explain the relics of the past which are his proper concern; how an ancient building was erected or an ancient implement fashioned, and to what uses they were put, can often be inferred by reference to the buildings and implements of the neighbouring villagers. Sometimes the physical continuity between old and new is complete and utter : the village of Mishrifeh in central Syria is built on the site of ancient Qatna, and the main street of the present settlement passes through the main gate of the ancient town, still visible 3,500 years after it was built. It is when excavating in such circumstances, studying in meticulous detail and with the aid of the most advanced scientific techniques the remains of previous communities, and surrounded on all sides by the bustle and colour of the most recent, that the working of the alchemy of which we have spoken is most keenly felt, and the sense of continuity is greatest.

Such continuity, such stability, must not be confused with stagnation. The Middle East, in common with other parts of the world, has experienced its periods of stagnation, and it may be that it is only now just emerging from one of these. But the archaeologist can affirm that more often than not in ancient Mesopotamia, Egypt and the Levant continuity and innovation have gone hand in hand, and that the great innovatory movements in religious or artistic expression, in prehistoric and historic times, which have emanated in our region have been strengthened rather than hampered by the tenacious influences of the past. Whether this will be so in the future remains to be seen. The archaeologist is not a prophet and can only aspire to help in some way towards an understanding of the past, and so of the present, in this crucial part of the world. He finds it absorbing and encouraging work, since the sources at his disposal have hardly yet been touched, even after a century of activity, and there remains a multitude of sites awaiting his spade. Whatever else changes in the Middle East, of one thing we may be certain : men will still be as curious about the past as were Ashurbanipal and Cyriac of Ancona, and archaeology will prosper.

FURTHER READING

Ceram, C. W. *The World of Archaeology*, Thames and Hudson, London, 1966.
Daniel, G. *One Hundred Years of Archaeology*, Duckworth, London, 1950.
Greener, L. *The Discovery of Egypt*, Cassell, London, 1966; Viking Press, New York, 1967.
Lloyd, S. H. F. *Foundations in the Dust*, Oxford Univ. Press, London, 1947.
Parrot, A. *Discovering Buried Worlds*, S.C.M. Press, London, 1955; Dufour, Pennsylvania, 1955.
Wilkins, F. *Six Great Archaeologists*, Hamish Hamilton, London, 1961.
Woolley, Sir L. *History Unearthed*, Benn, London, 1966.

PETER J. PARR. Lecturer in Palestinian Archaeology at the London University Institute of Archaeology since 1962. Elected Fellow of the Society of Antiquaries, 1959. Directed series of excavations at the Nabataean capital of Petra in Southern Jordan from 1958–64, and is now preparing the results for publication. Senior Scholar, Secretary/Librarian and Assistant Director of the British School of Archaeology in Jerusalem, 1954–62. He is now writing a history of the Nabataeans and a general book on Petra.

ART IN THE ARAB STATES OF
THE MIDDLE EAST

NABIH KAMEL and HELEN KHAL

GENERAL BACKGROUND

THE background of contemporary art in the countries of the Middle East is in many ways similar to that of other emerging nations of the world. In the forced isolation of the age before the advent of modern communications each area of the world followed its own cultural heritage, and each knew little of what was going on elsewhere. For centuries, while Europe moved in its arts through a continuing vertical thrust of refinement that culminated in the Renaissance, lands elsewhere remained remote, their artists following paths of plastic expression significantly set apart and as ancient and unchanging as their traditions and beliefs.

It must be remembered that modern art was created in Europe, and was well into its development before its impact was felt internationally. For all other countries of the world, including the Middle East, it remains an adopted art form. This is an important factor in evaluating the tendencies of non-Western contemporary art.

Despite its comparative proximity to Europe, the Middle East remained untouched by change and foreign influence in its art forms until the early 20th century. In part, one can reasonably attribute this resistance to the fact that its artistic heritage was predominantly one of Arab origin, decisively linked with the advent of Islam in the seventh century. For too long a time this profoundly influential religion defined not only the manner of life, but also the manner of art. Although it was not always adhered to, there was established a restrictive concept that rejected any representation of the human figure. Instead, there was a concentration on the abstract and the decorative, albeit with the use of figurative animal or plant-like forms. This direction led to an abundant and highly creative architecture of mosques and palaces, and to the adornment of their interiors with the intricate geometric and Arabesque designs we still find in ample evidence today—in tiles and mosaics, in stained glass, in carpets and calligraphy.

Fifty years ago there were certainly no more than a dozen 'modern' painters and sculptors scattered throughout the entire Arab world, and the easel painting of the West was literally unknown except in the palaces of the aristocracy (mostly portraiture) or in the religious paintings imported to the scattered churches and monasteries of the area. After World War I, when the Middle East was cut up into mandates under British and French control, there was the accompanying influx of foreign educational and cultural interests. In foreign mission schools young Arab students were introduced to drawing from life and a new kind of 'picture-making' and the conversion to modern art began.

With the encouragement and assistance of a few enlightened individuals, the first selected few were sent off to Paris, Rome and London to study. Attracted initially by the Renaissance, they were in turn confronted with the revolutionary forces of impressionism, cubism and abstraction. Being young and eager, these early pioneers wasted little time with a dying classicism and moved quickly into the more lively adventure of impressionism. And they came back to their capitals—to Cairo, Beirut, Damascus, Baghdad —with minds full of new concepts, new techniques, new materials, and spirits eager for a contemporary interpretation of their own socio-cultural roots.

Today there are hundreds of artists and each country has its own art academies, its own museums, its own galleries. Though slow to awaken, government and public support is now an active presence, and modern works by local artists are increasingly found in public places, in homes, in business institutions and government buildings. Yet one can rightly say that the development of modern art in the Middle East is still passing through its adolescence; its artists have yet to reach that stage of mature inventiveness necessary to establish a valid and integrated national or area style.

Meanwhile, the creative revolt in the West persists, and having fathered an international art, now sets a pattern of 'anything goes'. This has been of little concern to Middle Eastern artists. Although they are familiar with the new inventions, with pop, op, kinetic, and the rest, although they respond to and are visually provoked by them, most are still at the stage of exploring and finding their means of self-expression through basically traditional (early modern) materials and concepts. They want to be modern, and yet they want to be themselves—and so move cautiously through their new-found creativity. Their concern becomes increasingly one of a positive identification with their own ethnic background—a concern fed to a large extent by an awakened and strong feeling of nationalism.

The impact of firmly established international styles, however, cannot be ignored for long; and to be both nationalistic and at the same time international is a challenging task. Some Middle Eastern artists begin with the international, freely adopt foreign tendencies and reject any conscious attempt at a nationalistic flavour. They want to let the cultural roots take care of themselves, believing that if the approach is sincere the roots will insist on making their presence felt. Others, however—and they are large in number—insist on a more immediate evidence of their heritage. From time to time, groups have formed in an effort to establish a consistency of form and to create a modern art that is national, but few have yet succeeded in achieving a significant influence either within their own societies or beyond their borders.

This, then, is the background that applies generally to each of the countries of the Middle East. Separately, they have their own individual development differences, their own peculiarities of form and colour expression, their own regional motivations. On the surface, differences exist, but basically the cultural area is one; closer observation reveals the underlying links of a common tradition, the background of similar social, cultural, religious and ethnic influences that provide the identifying structure of one people's art. Like a Persian carpet, the design may be an intricate composite of mosaic parts, but the whole remains intact.

EGYPT AND IRAQ

In exploring the similarities of style, it is interesting to begin on the periphery of the area. Despite the geographical distance that separates Egypt and Iraq, the art of both shows a dominating ethnic, pre-Islamic tendency. Though sometimes geometric or arabesque, the work of their artists is seldom abstract. Their main concern is with man, past and present, enduring and fatalistic. The style is largely figurative, with an imagery often borrowed from folklore and ancient mythology; or, in a more contemporary vein, from the sights and conditions of their immediate daily life. In both countries, compositional form is strongly coherent and is more one of linear definition than of a colour activity. The temperament is profoundly oriental; energy is contained and introspective, chromatic mood subdued and simple. The conception is highly regional and group-motivated, and cultural heritage is very important.

LEBANON, SYRIA AND JORDAN

When, however, we approach the central terrain that lies between the Nile and the Euphrates, certain waves of diversity begin to appear. In Lebanon, Syria and Jordan the interest in ethnic heritage diminishes; occidental tendencies are readily adopted and used with full awareness as stepping stones to a more personal expression. Although there is a conscious concern to express a common Arab identity, it is motivated more by a young, assertive pride than by any real attachment to cultural roots. The inspirational mood is rather one of a 20th century individualism unfettered by the past.

This individualism reaches its peak in Lebanon, where the intermingling of East and West, of Christian and Muslim, of old and new, has created a multi-lingual, multi-cultural, melting-pot society that is unique in the Middle East. Its artists are, equally, multi-directional and non-regional in their work, reacting with a spontaneous emotionalism to the variable elements of their immediate environment. Additionally, the dramatic visual impact of Lebanon's mountain-sea geography affords luminal and textural stimulations that lead to a preoccupation with colour. Form is of secondary interest, diverse and changing, and often without an integrated personality; it is largely open, free, colour-created, and verbose.

In sculpture, however, the link between Lebanon and the area on the periphery is close and recognisable. The three-dimensional form is decidedly eastern, closed, introspective and with an inner energy that follows a continuity of expression extending back through Islamic attitudes to the early Phœnician, Pharaonic and Mesopotamian.

The intense variety that exists in Lebanon moves in slowly diminishing waves of influence into Syria and Jordan (including Palestine). Here individualism exists, but regionalism gains importance. The artists here are as much influenced by the unchanging oriental attitudes of Iraq and Egypt as they are by Lebanon's new world diversity.

TURKEY AND IRAN

Along the northern curve of the Middle East, in Turkey and Iran, there is again a mixture of east and west. Situated on the edge of Europe and Asia, however, their art holds a much stronger occidental flavour. It is true that Islam binds them to the Middle East, but they are non-Arab in language, in race, and hence in socio-cultural attitudes. (As such, their artistic intention and identity should in fact be considered separately, rather than in relation to their adjoining Arab neighbours.) The modern art of both countries follows a complex of influences that range from a figurative romanticism to the purely non-objective, although the tendency toward abstraction plays a more prominent role. The earlier traditions of calligraphy, of miniatures and of illuminated manuscripts provide aspects of design that lend themselves favourably to a contemporary idiom, and are used as a source of inspiration today by a number of artists in both countries. Graphic line is strong and rhythmic in their hands, and they create space with an oriental, two-dimensional eye. Although interest in a nationalistic expression is occasionally voiced, few artists concern themselves seriously with it. Here the magnet of influence is Europe and the West; and many artists adopt not only a foreign art language, but take up foreign residence as well.

THE ARABIAN PENINSULA AND SUDAN

Returning to the Arab Middle East and another edge of the area, there are finally the countries of the Arabian peninsula and Sudan. Saudi Arabia, Kuwait and Yemen are still at the bare beginning of modern art, not much more than a decade old. With few exceptions, painters are still either academic, figurative or impressionistic, and their number is limited. The presence of teachers from Iraq and Egypt is beginning to leave a stylistic imprint.

The Sudan, however, is further along and rapidly developing. Although it falls within the sphere of Egyptian influence, its creative energy reveals a separate personality, a younger vigour. A stylised figuration and symbolism marks most of the painting there. But it is in the contemporary sculpture and pottery that the Sudanese artist more significantly reveals his strength of aesthetic form, at once both modern and primitive.

A FURTHER CONSIDERATION OF EGYPT, IRAQ AND LEBANON

To give a more comprehensive description of each country's progress and the characteristics of its individual artists, past and present, is beyond the scope of an article such as this. However, if only in part, it is worthwhile delving further. Therefore, without the intention of giving special interest or importance to one country over another, additional information follows on three countries: Egypt, Iraq and Lebanon, which afford a cross-section both in terms of geographic span and stylistic development.

Egypt

In University Square in Cairo stands a granite monument called 'The Awakening of Egypt'. Executed in 1920 by Mahmoud Mukhtar, it was the first modern sculpture to appear in public in Egypt, and combined in an impressive manner the static containment of the Sphinx with a new world figuration. Two years earlier, in 1918, Mahmoud Said had unveiled his first successful portrait to a group of friends; and before that in 1911, a few Egyptian painters had put together the country's first group exhibition.

These pioneer artists numbered no more than a dozen. Among them was another sculptor, Muhammad Hassan, as well as the painters, Muhammad Nagi, Yousef Kamel, Ahmad Sabry and Ragheb Ayyad. Most of them were Circassians (the Turkish minority imported to Egypt by Sultan Abdel Hamid in the mid-19th century). As such they were not, in the strict sense, Egyptian and remained largely outside the common life of the country. They studied in Europe, spent the best years of their lives there, and came back only to see Egypt through French or Italian eyes, romantically and with a foreign spirit. They achieved a high degree of accomplishment by way of impressionism and the related styles of that era, but their treatment of the subject and a borrowed chromatic scale made their work decidedly European and revealed little of the Egyptian temperament.

One exception, however, was Ragheb Ayyad. Profoundly Egyptian, he saw nothing romantic or bizarre about the people around him, and painted them in their everyday life, simply and without a western patina. He was the first to set aside impressionism and create a style at once modern and yet thoroughly Egyptian. By 1940 he had reached an admirable maturity of expression. Composition became one of graphic line, naïve and free, with contained areas of flat, subdued colour; Renaissance concepts of perspective and space were set aside, and in their place appeared an inherent sense of oriental, two-dimensional design. These elements were to have a strong influence on the works of later artists.

A second generation of artists did not begin to assert itself until almost 1950. Cut off from Europe by several years of war, creative stimulation was at a minimum, and artists worked with little inspiration beyond the still prevalent trend of a now academic impressionism. Soon after the war ended, however, the trek to Europe was resumed. There they were confronted with new art forms—social realism from Mexico, abstract expressionism from the United States, along with all the still influential innovations of the Paris school. This second generation found itself at a loss, its artistic conceptions shattered. Some of the artists were stunned and refused to believe that a new art form—alien to them—had come to stay, and they resisted change for over 15 years. Others, however, moved quickly into experimenting with the new, each artist seizing a school and unfortunately trying to make it his own. Yet a few insisted on a personal expression, and of those, the most significant was Hamed Nada.

Hamed Nada refused to join a movement. He felt, and tried to put his own vision on canvas, and succeeded admirably. His compositional balance is superb, his forms pure and innocent, his colour poetic. Working from within his own spiritual heritage, he defines his ancient land in a modern plastic idiom.

Other artists who resisted the easy path of imitation included Hamed Abdalla, Samir Refai, the late Abdel Hamid al Gazzar and Abdel Wahab Morsi. Although the technique was sometimes foreign, the flavour was certainly oriental. Also to be mentioned are the surrealists, who held their first exhibition in Egypt in 1947—notable among them are Fouad Kamel, el Telmesany and the late Ramses Younan. It is a surrealism that borders on the abstract, and contains a time-worn, past-age quality.

The dominating interest, however, remains the search for a total social expression born out of a profound involvement in the life of the land and the people. One whose work animates this social effect and has much appeal is Taheya Haleem. Her people are enduring, introspective, intensely human and at one with their environment. There is an ethereal quality about her figures; through a muted relationship of colour and form they gradually lose shape and become abstractions. This transmutation of the figurative into the abstract also occurs in Nabeeh's village scenes; his admirable use of colour tension to create depth gives a haunting mood to his work.

Other artists of interest are : Saleh Taher, whose vigorous brush handles line and colour boldly, yet sensitively; Khalil Lotfy, a metaphysical painter of luminous greys; Seif Wanly, admittedly eclectic, sees a whole new canvas in a tiny area (be it only one square inch) of someone else's work, and sets out to paint it, with accomplished technique and colour; Fouad Kamel, abandoning an earlier surrealism to become an ardent follower of American abstract expressionism, has succeeded in pushing Jackson Pollock's thoughts a little further.

Of the rising group, Omar al Nagdi, El Razzas, Hassan Soleiman, Gazbeya Serry, Zeinab Sagini, and, in graphics, Salah Reda must be mentioned. Margo Veillon and Zorian are among the leading European artists working in Egypt.

Sculpture still lags far behind painting—a curious fact when one considers Egypt's heritage of statuary. Outstanding in this field today are Samuel Henri (who now calls himself Adam), Abd al Kader Rizk (portraitist) and Gamal al Seguini. Each shows a personal sensitivity toward his material, but the trend remains totally eastern in its self-containment and inner energy.

Most exhibitions and related artistic activity are sponsored by the Egyptian Ministry of Culture; facilities for study and work are generously provided for deserving artists. Most important is the government-sponsored Alexandria Biennale, which includes works from all countries bordering the Mediterranean and is beginning to attract international attention.

Iraq

Moving across to Iraq, one finds one record of a painter in the 19th century. Abdel Kader al Rassam (the Arabic *al rassam* meaning 'one who draws or paints') was born there, began painting in Turkey, and returned to Baghdad after World War I. He died in 1952 at the age of 113 years. There were no doubt a few other lonely pioneers during al Rassam's remarkably long lifetime, but they have yet to be 'discovered'.

More definitely, the birth of modern art in Iraq occurred in the early '30s, when a few young artists set off for Europe to study. It was not until several years later, however, when they were called home by the advent of war, that their presence was actually felt in the country. Most important among them were the late Jawad Selim, both painter and sculptor, and the two painters, Faik Hassan and Hafez Droubi.

Here, too, the war years would have imposed an irritating isolation had it not been for two fortunate factors. The first, and most significant, was that during these years the artists undertook a kind of work that was to leave an indelible influence on their artistic production. Sateh al Husri, advocate, friend and patron of these artists, was then director of Iraq's archaeological museum. Wishing to give them some way of earning a living, he put them to work in his museum, restoring Iraq's antiquities and recreating authentic folkloric tableaux of costumes and customs. Through this daily intimate contact with their heritage, these artists absorbed, in a manner beyond conscious and intellectual observation, the lines, forms and colours of their past. The stimulus this provided was to leave a strong imprint on their work and on the work of their future students. The art produced in Iraq today reveals a definite style-integration that is readily recognisable—an Iraqi style—and it is no doubt the result of this museum activity.

A second influencing factor during the war years was the influx of foreign artists, refugees from Europe, mostly Polish. They brought with them new ideas, particularly about colour, and provided an additional impetus through these formative years.

In the subsequent decade, no less than three art groups were active—the 'Modern Art' group, initiated by Selim; the 'Impressionists', set up by Droubi; and the 'Vanguard', whose leader was Hassan. The energetic creativity of these three men, particularly Selim, contributed much to the dynamic and swift progression that followed; their ideas and techniques have wielded a strong influence on the plastic arts of the country for the last 20 years.

Jawad Selim's sudden death in 1961 cut short a creative power that certainly would have reached international stature had it continued. In Baghdad's Liberation Square today stands a bronze monument entitled 'Liberty'. One of Selim's last works, it is 50 metres long at the base and can be accorded the distinction of being the biggest sculptural structure to appear in Iraq in over 2,000 years. Selim had studied sculpture in England during the post-war years—the Moore, Hepworth and Armitage 'geometry of fear' years—and he was deeply inspired by the imposing drama of this new British sculpture.

As a painter, Selim's work combined a Picassoesque inventiveness of form with a Bauhaus concern for abstract colour design. Despite this geometric structure, he remained a realist, and his figures are enduringly human, warm and communicative.

Faik Hassan led his 'Vanguard' group toward a more primitive statement of colour and form. More recently, his work has taken on a semi-abstract quality, mature in technique and vibrant with a personalised colour sensitivity. He is also an excellent portraitist.

The third, Hafez Droubi, introduced into Iraqi painting a new figuration derived from cubism's segmented form, and continues to refine this approach toward an oriental interpretation.

In 1939, the Academy of Fine Arts was established in Baghdad. Today it is part of the University of Baghdad and provides an intensive programme of study in all the plastic arts, as well as music and drama. Graduates of this government school are numbered in the hundreds and include the present professionals gaining prominence in Iraq. Among them are Dhia Azzawi, who holds a degree in archaeology, borrows freely from the Iraqi past to people his 20th century compositions, and uses colour in a subdued and poetic manner with a bold sense of design. Kazem Haidar's canvases speak with a dynamic, more primary, colour contrast; his human and animal forms are large, sculpturally cut to create a stark realism. Ismail Fatah, both sculptor and painter, again bares the human form to its tragic essence. In bronze, his lonely warrior is three-dimensionally free, yet curiously caught in an inescapable isolation; the greyed and lonely whites in his canvases lock the figures with equal finality. Hashem Samarji's work is colour-motivated, textural, with an oriental symbolism. Muhammad Ghani, sculptor, works in wood, metal and stone; his forte is the female figure, the Iraqi woman, whom he portrays with a quietly rhythmic, sensual line. Others worthy of mention are Ghazi al-Saoudi, Saleh al Gumayeh and Suad Attar. Younger names attracting attention include Salem Dabaghi, Rafeh al Naseri, and Muhammad Mahredinne.

Besides painters and sculptors, Iraq is also beginning to produce some very interesting potters, again working in a style amalgamating western thought with native techniques. Notable among them is Nuha Radi, who adds jewelled ceramic colour to a provincial form turned modern.

Lebanon

In the central area of Lebanon, as mentioned earlier, diversity is the dominating characteristic of cultural life. Certain factors have determined this, most pertinent among them being that the country has for centuries been a conglomerate society of race, creed and language. More recently, during the last 50 years, the French Mandate influence left an intimate imprint on the social and cultural mores of the people, and the Christian majority acquired an orientation more western than anywhere else in the Arab world.

Public response has always been healthy in Lebanon, and an interest in art extended beyond the circles of the aristocracy. In the homes of many Lebanese today can be found portraits and landscapes executed during the early decades of this century by a handful of artists that included Saliby, Srour, Corm, the sculptor, Hoyek, and the world famous poet-painter, Khalil Gibran. Most were trained in France, and their work ranges from classicism to early impressionism, except for Gibran who studied under Rodin and followed a Blake-esque mysticism to interpret his essentially poetic vision.

In the '30s a second group began to appear—notably Caesar Jemayel, Omar Onsi, Mustafa Farouk, Saliba Doueihy and Yusuf Gsoub (sculptor). All French-trained, impressionism was an indelible influence to them (and to a later generation)—no doubt because of its emphasis on immediate colour and light response, an approach that they felt best conveyed the qualities of their landscape. A foreign artist who came to reside in Lebanon at the time must also be mentioned, particularly for his influence upon some younger painters. Georges Cyr, a Frenchman, with his expressionistic use of colour and form, did much to loosen the confining academism of an otherwise totally impressionistic tendency.

Of this group there remains today only Doueihy, who for the past 20 years has been living and working in New York. During these years he has gradually moved from impressionism to an almost abstract expressionism, and more recently to a minimal approach of flat colour and limited form statement. This last work has gained him recognition, and several US museums have acquired his paintings.

The watercolours of Onsi, who died in 1969, are perhaps the finest record of the Lebanese landscape seen through an impressionist eye. His freedom of technique and purity of colour create a fresh sparkle of sunstruck form.

Today, Lebanon's professional artists number over 100, many of them graduates of the Lebanese Academy of Fine Arts, privately established in 1939. And today these graduates are teachers to another generation in the new Institute of Fine Arts, set up by the government in 1966. A prospering economic life, a high rate of literacy, and a cosmopolitan atmosphere afford a favourable climate in Lebanon for the development of the arts. There are a number of art galleries in Beirut; exhibitions occur at a rate approaching 150 in one season, and an increasing number of artists come from neighbouring countries and from Europe to work and exhibit in Lebanon. If not in artistic production, then certainly as a show place and a market centre, Beirut has become the Paris of the Middle East.

The artistic production, however, is by no means small. Each spring the Ministry of Education sponsors a salon of painting and sculpture in which all Lebanon's artists participate. The amount of work shown is considerable, and the variety of style very wide. In speaking here about the work of individual artists, the selection will be not only on the basis of prominence, but will also point out the extent of diversity in style.

Considered by many to be the leading artist in Lebanon today is Chafic

Abboud. Although he has been living and working in Paris for the past 20 years, he has maintained a regular and close relationship with his homeland, and the quality of his painting attests to this fact. His colour is highly emotive and daring, and at the same time provokes a luminal interrelationship that is a profound expression of the Lebanese landscape. One could label Abboud as an abstract expressionist, yet his eye retains a humanism that stems from an intimate observation of the real and physical.

Among other artists who show an equal preoccupation with the emotive possibilities of colour are Amin al Bacha, who builds up his compositions in thick mosaic patches of analogous hues that combine to create an intrinsic sense of light, and Elie Kenaan, landscapist, whose rich colour and textural interest dominate the subject almost to the point of abstraction. There are also two women painters, Nadia Saikali and Yvette Ashkar, who follow a similar path of colour dynamics—Saikali moves toward a simplicity of form, yet graphic slashes of bold colour are still an important design factor; Ashkar's form is the graphic slash alone, set against, or floating in, a compatible space. (It is worth remarking here on the large number of women artists in Lebanon, almost one-quarter of the total.)

A few painters begin to search out a meaningful, oriental form and are experimenting with both linear and spatial compositions to this end. They work sometimes through Islamic concepts of design and calligraphy, intricate and abstract; sometimes figuratively through earlier Phoenician borrowings; and sometimes through the closed form tendencies that reach them from Iraq and Egypt. In this group can be found Said Akl, Wajeh Nahle, Mounir Nejm and Stelio Scamanga—the first two calligraphic, the second two most recently space-motivated toward an abstract mysticism.

Still other artists are more personal and literary. Their concern is more one of painting out a story idea, and colour and form are bent to that purpose rather than permitted their own expression. Their styles range from the primitive, to the surrealist, to the folkloric and stylised figurative. Juliana Seraphim is a surrealist, outspokenly erotic, whose ink drawings are superb in sensitivity and rhythm of line, to the point of a Gothic elegance. Khalil Zghaib, self-taught, pure primitive, has an inherent sense of design that gives his paintings of life in Lebanon a curiously living, although humourous, presence. Paul Guiragossian, who has throughout most of his career limited his subject to the human figure alone or clustered in groups of two or more, has moved from the figurative and expresses his grouped humans now with single, wide, vertical strokes of colour, still with a strong human suggestion. Farid Aouad, whose subject also is concentrated on the human, but undeniably linked with his environment, works through intimate colour and form relationships to portray his people, in cafés and on the street.

A painter-sculptor to be considered separately is Aref al Rayess. Constantly changing his style, moving from one medium to another, his is a remarkably creative energy that moves from the primitive to the pure non-objective with equal validity and power.

Sculptors in Lebanon are more numerous than in other of the area's countries. Prominent among them are the three Basbous brothers, Michel, Joseph and Alfred, who have literally turned their mountain village of Rachana into a museum of carved stone. Their styles vary from the figurative to abstractions provoked by the material itself. Two women sculptors are impressively productive. Selwa Raouda, a purely non-objective artist both in painting and sculpture, is remarkable in the sustained direction of her work. Her stone pieces are virile and mature, containing an architectonic force that is both primitive and new. Mouazzez Rawdah, who began painting ten years ago and quickly turned to sculpture, works in both stone and wood; her pieces have an imposing weight and show a high respect for the material qualities of her medium. Recently turning to metal sculpture after many years of painting is Adel Saghir—his monumental abstract pieces adorn the entrances of several of Beirut's buildings.

As mentioned earlier, there is a steady influx of foreign artists to Lebanon, and their length of residence varies from a few months to a few years. Some take up permanent residence and become an integral part of the contemporary art scene. Most important among them are John Carswell, a British sculptor, and Arthur Frick, an American painter.

HELEN KHAL. Painter and lecturer on contemporary art in the Middle East. Has taught painting at the American University of Beirut since 1961. Art critic for *The Daily Star*, Beirut 1965–8. Established the first permanent art gallery in Lebanon 1963.

NABIH KAMEL. A painter specialising in murals and portraiture; Professor of Sociology and Head of the Departments of Social Anthropology and Psychology at the Institute of Social Work, Cairo. Inspector of Education, Egyptian Education Bureau, London 1943–54.

MIDDLE EASTERN ARCHITECTURE

JOHN CARSWELL

THE Middle East has the longest tradition of architecture in the world. Some 9,000 years ago the earliest agricultural settlers built towns like ancient Jericho, with high stone walls and defensive towers, well before the invention of pottery and metal-working. The materials available were stone, mud-brick and wood, and until recently the history of architecture in the Middle East has been the record of man's ingenious attempts to exploit them.

Today, traditional methods are still used for beehive-domed houses in northern Syria, multi-storied mud-brick palaces in South Arabia, and reed huts in the marshes of southern Iraq. But like the rest of the world, the Middle East has been transformed by the use of reinforced concrete. Without it modern towns like Beirut, Ankara, Kuwait and Tehran could never have developed so swiftly; and nowadays it is hard to find a village untouched by *beton armé*.

Until this century, the Middle East had been dominated by the Ottoman Empire for more than 300 years. The great Islamic tradition of architecture lapsed, and in Turkey itself early dynamism had long since waned; the Ottomans were more interested in the maintenance of power than in building monuments. What was built was largely an echo of past grandeur, and any innovations came from the West: 18th and 19th century European architecture, even *art nouveau*, left their mark. In Iran, the spectacular building of the 17th century ended with the collapse of the Safavid dynasty, and little of consequence was subsequently erected.

The situation in those countries under Turkish rule was much the same as in Turkey itself. Random examples of derivative taste can be cited, such as the 'Azm Palace in Hama, Syria (18th century); the Turkish/Baroque restoration of the Holy Sepulchre in Jerusalem (1810); and the Opera House in Cairo (1869). After World War I, buildings in Syria and Palestine clearly show the influence of the French and British Mandates.

Architecture was not established as a separate profession in the Middle East until after the World War II. Until then engineers were generally responsible for the architectural aspect of buildings; they often acted as contractors as well.

UNITED ARAB REPUBLIC

From the time of Muhammad Aly onwards palaces, municipal buildings and private houses were built in European, often Italianate style. Mostly the work of foreigners, Egyptian architects had to be content with employment as minor government officials. The lower classes depended for building on master-masons, who frequently interpreted the Western style in their own way. The Paris Fair of 1925 had a galvanising effect on Egyptian taste; the result was an abundance of *art nouveau* iron work, ornament, and rounded balconies.

In Cairo successive town-plans appear to have cancelled each other out; Heliopolis and Garden City alone retain some semblance of order. There, and in Zamalek, private houses were built in English Tudor, French Provincial, Gothic, Far Eastern and even more bizarre styles. Some achieve real distinction, like one mid-'30s modern house on Zamalek (now the Kuwaiti Embassy). Since the Revolution, Nasser Town has been constructed, a complex of ministries and apartments with some interesting modern buildings.

Modern low-cost housing in the UAR is generally deplorable; an exception is Hassan Fathy's inspired revival of traditional mud-brick architecture for a village at Gourna, near Luxor; a similar project is underway at Kharga oasis.

In Alexandria the heavily-decorated Opera House (1921) is structurally interesting. The Cinema Royale (1939) still retains its fine period decoration, with red, black and aluminium fittings. Pastroudis cake-shop has elegant *art nouveau* details. Private houses along the coast, some very handsome, are in every style. There are few modern buildings of quality; the new Marine Terminal is ponderous to an extreme.

JORDAN

Domestic building generally consists of single-storey houses with a decent stone facing. In Amman, which has increased in size many times in the past 20 years, the new stadium, the Al Urdun Hotel, and some municipal buildings are amongst notable modern buildings; the Husain Mosque (1924) is in traditional Islamic style. On the West Bank, the Girls' Teacher Training College (UNRWA) at Ramallah is exceptionally well designed.

In Jerusalem, Government House and the Palestine Archaeological Museum (1927) are examples of Mandate architecture at its best. The museum, of intricate but practical plan, has low reliefs, and Arabic, Hebrew and English lettering carved *in situ* by Eric Gill. Most religious bodies have built relentlessly in national style, as in the French Dominican Convent of St. Etienne, and the Anglican Gothic Cathedral. In the Old City, new work has been confined largely to restoration, in particular of the Dome of the Rock, and the Holy Sepulchre.

Most municipal buildings and private houses owe much to the use of stone facing. The Intercontinental Hotel is well designed, but unfortunately sited right on the skyline of the Mount of Olives.

LEBANON

In the 19th century the typical Lebanese house was stone-built, with a pitched, tiled roof. Similar in plan to a Venetian *palazzo*, the central room on the first floor generally had a triple arched façade, with elaborate tracery. Variations of this kind of house can be seen along the whole coast of the eastern Mediterranean. Some foreign influence can be detected in the design of foreign schools and missions, such as the earlier buildings of the American

University of Beirut. In Beirut, the Saray and the arcaded street known as Ma'arad were constructed under Turkish rule in neo-oriental style.

Under the Mandate after World War I, French influence became more apparent, in schools, office buildings, domestic architecture, and even in the design of Lebanon's railway-stations. Local colour was provided by buildings like the National Museum, a monumental essay in classic Egyptian style; and a playful example in the same idiom is the Opera Cinema. The outstanding architect-engineer of the '30s was Antoine Tabet: a pupil of Auguste Perret, he was responsible for the construction of St. George's Hotel (1932), as well as the Orient Palace Hotel in Damascus. All his early buildings, including a brewery (1934) and a girls' school (1938), are simply and logically designed, and often incorporate pre-cast concrete elements.

After World War II an influx of capital from the oil states led to a building boom. Four schools of architecture were established, providing the formal training which prior to 1945 had been non-existent. A typical firm working in the early '50s was Shayer, Makdisi and Gottlieb, a combination of architect, engineer and decorator. Among the first to build in the international modern style, they were responsible for many apartment blocks, and the Alumni Club.

Innumerable buildings sprang up in the '50s, giving Beirut its unique skyline. Amongst the best are the Ghandour, Hamza, Discothèque, and Shell multi-storied apartment buildings; the Starco commercial centre; the Beirut Riyadh Bank; the American Life Insurance building; and the Artisanat handicrafts centre. The Carlton, Excelsior, Alcazar, and Byblos Hotels are well-designed (the latter with the most elegant neon Arabic sign in Beirut); less impressive is the Phoenicia, two tall blocks with pseudo-oriental balconies. The *Collège Protestante*, the School for the Blind, and individual structures in the Beirut College for Women, and the American University of Beirut merit attention. It is to be regretted that during the period of maximum expansion Beirut had no co-ordinating town plan, so that there is now a chronic lack of open space.

Outside Beirut, the new Yacht Club at Jounieh cleverly exploits a spectacular site, across the bay from the massive Casino du Liban. The Saray at Sidon uses the traditional inner courtyard plan. Amongst the best-designed private houses are those of H. Eddé, P. al Khoury, M. Philippides, and the American Ambassador, at Yarzé; M. Nakib at Hazmieh; C. Chamoun at Khaldé, and Dr. Tabbara at Rabiya. The Glidden Company on the Damascus road is a remarkable building of modest size. The Mzaar Hotel at the ski-resort of Faraya is an effective example of practical planning.

IRAQ

Turkish engineers built the Serai and army barracks in Baghdad, and a housing development at Sinak, before World War I; German engineers were responsible for the stations on the Baghdad-Istanbul railway. After the War the British built the college at Adhamiya and a cantonment in Alwiyah in colonial style. Until 20 years ago architects were either foreigners —German, Turkish, British, Syrian, even Hungarian—or Iraqis who had trained abroad, like Ahmed Mukhtar, who designed the Sporting Club at Adhamiya and a hotel in Rashid Street. Besides these, much work was simply carried out by a master-builder, or *usta mimar*, who was responsible both for the design of a building and its construction. One of these master-builders, Usta Hajji Hamoodi, is still alive.

In 1960 the School of Architecture in Baghdad opened. Iraqi architects have also studied in Europe, Britain, the United States, the USSR, and Eastern Europe. The Dean of the School of Architecture, M. S. Makiya, designed the Khulafa Mosque in Baghdad and the National Insurance Building in Kerbela; traditional patterned brickwork is cleverly used to enrich the façades. Kahtan Owni was the architect for University College, the Electricity Board administration and several interesting private houses. A. and N. Jawdat built Mansour Girls' School, and their own modern house. R. J. Chadirjee, perhaps the most talented and original architect working in the Middle East, has designed the Iraq Scientific Academy, the Veterinary College, Rafidain Bank at Sinak, the Tobacco Monopoly Administration, the 14th July and Unknown Soldier monuments, and also several striking private houses. Sensitive to traditional materials and forms, he has a very idiosyncratic style. He has also designed furniture and lighting fixtures.

SYRIA

Syria, like Lebanon, came under French influence during the Mandate. This left its trace on buildings such as the Orient Palace Hotel in Damascus (Antoine Tabet), and the National Museum. The Hotel Abu Fida in Hama is a more modest example of the same sort. The column commemorating the opening of the overland telegraph to Mecca, in Chouhada Square, Damascus, is a bizarre specimen of occidental influence. It is swathed with telegraph poles and surmounted by a scale model of the post office, all cast in bronze.

Since the war efforts have been made to rationalise the town-plans of the old sections of Damascus and Aleppo. As a result new roads have been created by demolishing old buildings; so far this has not led to any new building of particular interest. An exception is the Archaeological Museum in Aleppo.

In Damascus, the residential areas of Ain Rumaneh and Salahiyeh are well laid out with broad streets and pleasantly designed private houses with gardens. Perhaps the most imaginative architecture in Syria is to be found in pavilions for the Damascus Trade Fair, and temporary structures celebrating political events, where natural decorative talent is given full rein.

The single most impressive modern structure in Syria is the Restan Dam, on the River Orontes between Homs and Hama.

SAUDI ARABIA

Modern building in Jeddah main port and diplomatic centre, is undistinguished and limited to apartments, offices and suburban houses; traditional mud-brick houses with fretted *mashrabieh* screens are fast disappearing.

In Riyadh, the capital, many recent buildings are already uninhabitable, owing to the malfunctioning of necessary services. Poor workmanship, lack of labour and local materials, all complicate construction. The recent administration has concentrated on establishing adequate services, and architectural prospects for the future are excellent. Two good buildings are the Ministry of Petroleum, and the Government Printing Press.

Dhahran's modern airport, by Minoro Yamasaki, is outstanding in its use of Islamic motifs.

KUWAIT

Kuwait was a thriving port long before oil flowed; prosperous families dealt in pearls, and traded with India. In the walled town, carved teak doors led from the street into simple houses built round internal courtyards.

From the early '50s, a substantial amount of the oil royalties has been devoted to amenity development. First a number of schools were constructed, then municipal offices, port facilities, hospitals and private commercial buildings.

British architects predominated, designing the Power Station, the Desalination Plant, and the Sif Palace. A typical firm, Design Construction Group, successfully combines British architects with Arab engineers and contractors; they built the monumental National Bank, the Ministry of Justice and Social Affairs, and the Gulf Bank. A Lebanese group, Dar al Handasseh, built the National Petroleum Company, the Chamber of Commerce, and the Sheraton Hotel. Recently, talented young Kuwaiti architects have begun to practise.

The Town Planning authority closely controls development, and also specifies that elevations should have some sort of Islamic flavour. Private housing tends to be eclectic, incorporating every style and available finish.

PERSIAN GULF STATES

The British presence in *Bahrain* resulted in the neat development of the island, with residential suburbs under the date palms set off by magnificent gardens. The Residency, Secretariat, and Political Agent's Residence are all British-designed. Shaikh Issa Town is a praiseworthy social experiment of no great architectural interest, with the exception of two mosques.

Qatar is a more modest version of Kuwait; an interesting group of municipal buildings is offset by an enormous, badly planned hospital.

Dubai's past prosperity was based on piracy (its creek offered a hiding-place for marauders). With an anticipated oil income of $48 million, its remarkably astute ruler has decided on a vigorous policy of *laissez-faire*, making it the most sophisticated of all the Gulf towns. It has its own distinctive traditional architecture; its elegant stone and mud-brick wind towers have long been admired. The modern First National City Bank cleverly alludes to them in its façade. The ruler's palace, commercial buildings and hotels, are all in a pleasing modern style.

Until oil came to *Abu Dhabi*, there was nothing except a magnificent, rambling mud-brick fort. Now a new development houses the Petroleum Company's staff, with well-designed single storey houses and offices. There is a fine church. Several banks, all British-designed, have also been constructed.

REPUBLIC OF SOUTH YEMEN

After 1839 Aden developed as an important port and British military base. Early buildings were the Marina Hotel (*c.* 1845), two churches, barracks (1848) and the old Secretariat (1850). Arcaded verandahs with lattice screening were a characteristic feature.

Since 1950 government architects, sometimes collaborating with British firms, have built Government House, the Supreme Court, Queen Elizabeth Hospital and many schools and housing developments. The screened verandah has been frequently adapted, using modern materials but serving the same purpose of shelter from the sun without impeding cross-ventilation.

In the Governorates, such as Hadramawt, traditional architecture flourishes still. Modern hospitals have been built in Sayun, Lodar and Azzan.

ISRAEL

Zionist development began long before 1948, with 'garden cities' and settlements designed to provide a Jewish enclave in the heart of Palestine. Undoubtedly the most distinguished Jewish architect was Eric Mendelsohn; between 1934 and 1941 he built research laboratories and a machine hall at Rehovot, the Government Hospital in Haifa, the Anglo-Palestine Bank and much of Mount Scopus University in Jerusalem, as well as private houses for Weizmann, and Salman Schocken. An admirer of traditional Arab village architecture, his buildings are masterpieces of siting and suitability. In sharp contrast are the majority of domestic buildings completed since 1948, which dominate the landscape in an intrusive manner.

The practice of transforming mosques into Israeli archaeological museums, as in Beersheba, Tiberias and Jaffa, is also to be deplored.

Official buildings has been more successful. In Jerusalem the Hebrew University, National Museum, Shrine of the Book (F. Keisler) and Sculpture Garden (I. Noguchi) form a dynamic complex. In Tel Aviv the Mann Auditorium has a simple impressive façade, and the El Al building an ingenious external spiral staircase. There are many interesting scientific buildings at Rehovot. Philip Johnson designed the atomic pile at Nahal Sorek, and Oscar Niemeyer planned Haifa University.

As for the Christian minority, the new Church of the Nativity at Nazareth can be described as astonishing rather than appropriate.

IRAN

Although concrete is used increasingly, traditional brick-building techniques are still widely used throughout the country. In Isfahan, a 17th-century *khan* has been transformed into the Shah Abbas Hotel, with lavish use of traditional decoration, executed by the School of Fine Arts. Most Iranian architects train at Tehran University, or abroad in France, Italy or the United States. Houshang Seihoon, the Dean of the Architecture Faculty, has many buildings to his credit, including the striking monument to Nader Shah in Meshed.

In Tehran, 19th-century buildings such as the Golestan Palace already show Western influence. The interior of the British Residency is in unashamedly Victorian/Iranian taste. The town was replanned in the late '20s, under Reza Shah. Modern buildings of distinction include the Senate, by M. Foroughi; and the National Iranian Oil Company by A. Farmanfarmanian, who also designed the University mosque and part of the Agricultural College. There are many interesting modern houses, particularly in Chemiran.

Foreign architects have been responsible for a number of buildings. Pahlavi University in Shiraz, originally conceived by Yamasaki, was finally designed by Dana Associates. The Narmak AID Vocational Training School is a successful American-Iranian attempt at building in an indigenous style. The ingenious Iran America Society building in Tehran combines both indoor and outdoor theatres; it was designed by Brown and Daltus.

TURKEY

Since the Atatürk revolution, Turkey has attempted to express its progressive outlook through modern architecture. A pioneer was S. H. Eldem, whose work accurately reflects the dilemma most architects faced, of combining modern techniques with a respect for traditional Turkish forms. The importance of town-planning was early appreciated; whilst the results are most clearly seen in Ankara and Istanbul, almost every small town shows some sort of urban control. This usually takes the form of wide boulevards and a proliferation of public parks.

In Ankara, early examples of modern architecture are the Opera House (formerly the Exhibition Palace) and Youth Park, the University and the Railway Station. Modern Ankara's general plan was conceived by an Austrian town-planner, Jansen, after 1927. Modern apartments in the Yenisehir district are distinguished by light handling of detail and the use of colour-washed exteriors. The Atatürk memorial (1944) outside town is a solemn exercise in neo-classicism. Outstanding examples of the synthetic modern style are the Turkish History Society (1962), and the Anadolu Club.

Istanbul abounds in examples of 19th-century European taste, such as the Dolmabahçe Palace (1840); later, *art nouveau* was a popular style. The Tunel funicular railway (1873) was designed by a French engineer. In the 1950s the international modern style made its impact, particularly in the design of hotels. One of the most striking is the Hilton, designed by Skidmore, Owens and Merrill in collaboration with Eldem. Superbly landscaped, it cleverly translates traditional motifs into modern materials. Along the Bosphorus there are a number of well-designed modern houses.

In Trebizond, a new Technical University includes a school of architecture. Other notable buildings are the new museums at Karatepe, and Antalya. Both are splendidly sited.

FURTHER READING

Akcura, Tugrul. 'Turkey', *L'Architecture d'aujourdhui*, 140, Oct.–Nov., Paris, 1968.

Ashbee, C. R. 'The New Town Plan', *Jerusalem 1918–1920*, London, 1921.

Ashbee, C. R. 'An Account of the New Jewish Garden Cities . . . and the Modifications they entail in the Town Plan', *Jerusalem 1920–1922*, London, 1924.

Doe, D. B. 'The Changing Face of Aden' and 'Window and Verandah Screening in Aden', *Aden Port Trust Annual*, 47–50, 68–75.

Elhani, Aba. 'Architectural Design under Conditions of Statehood', *Ariel*, 22, Israel, 1968.

Fathy, Hassan, 'Nouveau village de Gourna', *L'Architecture d'aujourdhui*, 140, Oct.–Nov., Paris, 1968.

Fathy, Hassan, *Qurna: A Tale of Two Villages*, Ministry of Culture, Cairo.

Les Guides Bleus, *Moyen Orient*, 1956; *Egypte*, 1956; *Turquie*, 1958; Hachette, Paris.

Whittick, Arnold, *Eric Mendelsohn*, Leonard Hill, London, 1956.

JOHN CARSWELL. Has lived and worked in the Middle East since 1953, at present teaches at the American University of Beirut. Visiting Professor at St. Anthony's College, Oxford, 1958. Exhibitions of his work as an artist were held in London, 1961 and in New York, 1966. His publications include *New Julfa: The Armenian Churches and Other Buildings* (1968) and *Coptic Tattoo Designs* (1958).

ARABIC MUSIC

AFIF A. BULOS

In trying to appreciate Arabic music, it would be well in the initial stages to steer clear of almost all vocal music, so that no unnecessary barriers are created between the listener and the melody itself. He must avoid much of contemporary music, since it is largely 'phoney' Arabic music. Under the impact of Hollywood films, operatic productions and symphonic concerts in the Middle East, many so-called Arab composers consciously or unconsciously embody in their compositions extracts from European music, strung loosely together and covered with a veneer of Arabic vocal paint.

It is significant to note that while the Arabs of the seventh to the tenth centuries were too jealous of their music to allow indiscriminate borrowings from the highly developed civilisations they came in contact with, incorporating only those elements of (to them) foreign music that were akin to the nature of Arabic music, 20th century composers plunge blindly into Western music, using anything that comes within their grasp. The best way of beginning is by listening to the *qanoun*—an instrument going back to the ancient days of southern Arabia. It is trapezoid in shape, having 24 strings on which can be obtained 72 notes. The Westerner is immediately enchanted with this instrument. It has beautiful tones, similar if not superior to the harpsichord, which enable the listener to appreciate the melodic phrases with their 'unusual' rhythmic patterns and cadences. Were the Arab musician acquainted with Bach he would do justice to his music on the *qanoun*. Incidentally only a very good musician can tune this rare instrument.

Arabic music is not a collection of nomadic ditties. Such songs exist, but there is a wealth of folk song and a literature of composed music and art songs. (The *muwashshahat* of ancient Arab Spain are an example of the Arabic art song at its best. The *muwashshah* is an elegant lyric which was popular at the time, and followed a definite metrical pattern and rhyme.) But since Arabic music reached a high degree of national and artistic development before harmony and the European system of notation were evolved, it developed in a certain direction—horizontally rather than vertically as is the case with Western music. In Arabic music, there is only a melodic line played by one instrument, or by several instruments in unison, to the accompaniment of some instrument of percussion. If we compare this simple system to the enormously complex scores of European opera, where a short phrase of music will occupy a large page of lined paper and be performed by soloists, a large chorus and a symphony orchestra, we will see one of the basic differences between the two arts. In other words, harmony has made it possible in European music for the melody to be sounded by one voice or instrument, while the other parts serve to enrich it by adding harmonic depth and colour and preventing monotony. But the only harmony that exists in unadulterated Arabic music is the octave and sometimes the fourth.

Ibn Sina, the tenth century Arab theorist, defines a certain Arabic term as 'an ornament in which two consonant notes mingle in the same stroke. The noblest consonances are large intervals, and among these, the octave and the fourth are the best.' Since we may say, then, that harmony is practically absent, it takes a composer with real talent and a thorough knowledge of his medium to avoid dullness. To avoid monotony the ancient Arab composers directed their efforts towards creating new rhythmical patterns and sets of modes or scales. Manuscripts are still extant to show what songs were sung in the 'Abbasid Age and in Arab Spain but these need scholars to decipher them.

Fortunately many delightful forms such as the *doulab*—a sort of rondo— the *dawr* and *muwashshah* have been passed down to modern times by rote and have served as models for new compositions in the same form.

PRESENTATION

Before a singer begins to perform there is an instrumental prelude consisting of two parts. The first, played on either the *oud* or the *qanoun*, is exceedingly pleasant, the purpose being to establish the mood in the mind of the listener. When it finishes, a *takht* or chorus of instruments join in, in unison, and the ear that is steeped in harmonised music gets a rude shock. After that the singer improvises on the *ya leil* theme, a sort of cadenza. The only words used here are *ya leil* ('O night') and, from this invocation to darkness to come and relieve the singer from the worries of the day, the listener can judge the musical virtuosity and vocal skill of the singer. Then we come to the body of the song. This may have the form of a *muwashshah*, or a *dawr*, or a *doulab*.

The instruments included in the *takht* are the *oud*, from which the lute is copied; the *qanoun*; the *santour*, a kind of dulcimer; the *nay*, a flute played vertically, probably of Persian origin; the violin; and sometimes the flute. The instruments of percussion are the *daff* (tambourin) and the *durbakkeh*. Of late, other European instruments have been added by various arrangers.

THE QUARTER TONE

To many, Arabic music is somewhat vaguely connected with the quarter tone. Now although the smallest interval in Arabic music is the quarter tone, it does not occur in all the Arabic modes or scales, or *maqams* as they are called in Arabic, of which there are at least 14 in current use. The *Nahawand maqam* is the minor scale. The *hidjaz maqam* is obtained by lowering the second note of any minor scale half a tone and raising the fourth half a tone. The *siga maqam* and the *rast maqam* contain quarter tones. In any case in a melodic phrase the quarter tone interval seldom occurs, except as an embellishment; what we get in quarter-tone scales, however, is a three-quarter interval. Modulation between allied *maqams* may occur.

Together with this system of scales there exists also an elaborate system of rhythmical modes. In the Arabic art song the rhythmical arrangement in the first bar, or group of bars, must be exactly duplicated in all succeeding bars, or groups of bars, of the same theme.

Finally it must be noted that the foundations of European music were laid in the church, whereas Arabic music, more worldly and diverting, flourished in the houses of the wealthy and the palaces of the caliphs. And even though European music broke away from the church and grew partly under the patronage of dukes and princes, the church left a definite mark on its development. Arabic music is more sensual. Its songs are, in the main, love songs of a wistful and sensuous character and its instrumental compositions, with their strongly felt rhythms, stir the body to movement.

THEORY OF ARABIC MUSIC

According to Farmer, the Arabs possessed a theory of music long before they fell under the influence of translations from the Greek at the end of the eighth century, and the source of this theory was an older Semitic one which had influenced or formed the actual foundation of Greek theory.

The first glimpses of a definite theory of Arabic music appear in the eighth century. A certain Ibn Misjah (*fl.* 715) who had learned Persian music and had received instruction from Byzantine theorists and musicians, incorporated these borrowings into a system which came to be recognised throughout the Arabian Peninsula. Although some scholars maintain that Arabic musical theory is largely Persian, the truth is that Ibn Misjah and his successors used only those elements which could be integrated into the Arabic system.

In the middle of the ninth century, the effects of the writings of the ancient Greeks on music, which had been translated into Arabic, began to be felt. Music—*al-musiqa*—now became one of the courses studied by most learned men of this period. The theory of sound, rhythm and composition were taken up after the Greek manner. But soon Arab theorists were ahead of their Greek masters on the question of the physical bases of sound and the treatment of musical instruments.

The greatest Arab theorist was al-Farabi (897–950). Al-Farabi was not only a good mathematician and physicist but he was also a practical musician who played the *oud* and could appreciate the arts as well as the sciences. Of Turkish origin, he acquired a thorough knowledge of Greek musical theory and later studied the works of Plato and Aristotle at Baghdad. Then he moved to Aleppo, where he lived at the court of Sayfud-Dawla. Two interesting contemporaries of al-Farabi were the poet al-Mutanabbi and Abul-Faraj al-Isphahani. The latter is noted for his work : *The Great Book of Songs (Kitab al-Aghani al-Kabir)* which contains a quantity of anecdotes and biographical sketches relating to musicians, as well as an anthology of the Arabic poetry which had been set to music, down to his times. The music itself was not written down but the time signature and the fingering on the fret were given. Abul-Faraj was a descendant of the Caliphs of Baghdad and kept in touch with musicians and poets in Spain after members of his family had become rulers in Cordoba.

Other Arab theorists include Ibn Sina (Avicenna, 980–1037), who could not play on any instrument but who approached the subject from the scientific and philosophic point of view. Finally we come to Safiyud-Din Abdul-Mu'min (*fl.* 1294), a musician in the services of the last Caliph of Baghdad, who wrote two works on the theory of Arabic music, one of which (*Kitab-al-Adwar*) is in the British Museum. In his life-time, he introduced many reforms in musical theory.

Then there is al-Kindi who flourished in the ninth century, whose treatise, *Risala fi Khabar Talif al-Alhan,* is in the British Museum. In this he deals with the theory of music almost entirely as he had learned it from the Greeks. His treatise is particularly interesting in view of the definite system of phonetic notation which appears in it.

TEACHING OF ARAB MUSIC

The late King Fouad of Egypt, who was very interested in reviving and fostering Arabic art, founded a Cairo conservatory which bears his name. Here students are taught, in Arabic, the principles of harmony and the theory of both Arabic and Western music. Practical instruction in the leading instruments of the East and the West is also given. One of the rooms contains an array of various oriental instruments—mainly gifts from Egyptian and Turkish princes—as well as the quarter tone piano. The results of this admirable institution can already be felt, for it has turned out a number of intelligent young musicians who, apart from being good performers, understand the principles of their own music as well as the music of the West. When more of these young men become influential, a new day will certainly dawn for Arabic music.

In 1953 another school for the teaching of Arabic music on the same lines as the Cairo conservatory was started by the Lebanese Government in Beirut.

THE FUTURE

And what of the future? Should Arab composers blindly imitate European music and so divest Arabic music of its national character or should they dig up the musical literature of the past and reject any modifications? Will it be possible to introduce harmony, counterpoint and European forms of composition into Arabic music and yet maintain its national colour, as was the case with Russian music? There is a healthy movement in progress in Lebanon which aims at reviving old Arabic songs and presenting them with orchestral accompaniments played on an attractive mixture of Arabic and Western instruments. The parts are arranged in harmony, but the orchestration never gets too heavy for the song. This is a clear proof that through the work of experts who are steeped in both traditions it is possible to wed the best in Arabic and Western music without losing the national character of the former.

FURTHER READING

Erlanger, Baron d'. *La Musique Arabe*, Geuthner, Paris, 1930.
Farmer, H. G. *Arabian Music of the Thirteenth Century*, Verry, Connecticut, 1929.
Farmer, H. G. *Arabian Influence on Musical Theory*, Reeves, London, 1925.
Sachs, Curt. *The History of Musical Instruments*, Norton, New York, 1940.
Sachs, Curt. *Rise of Music in the Ancient World*, Norton, New York, 1943.

AFIF BULOS. Associate Professor of English at Beirut College for Women. Has lectured on Arab music in the USA, Cambridge, London, Jerusalem and Beirut. Has recorded an album of Arabic folksongs.

MASS MEDIA SYSTEMS AND
COMMUNICATION BEHAVIOUR

HAMID MOWLANA

AMONG the technological changes which have been sweeping through the Middle East in the last two decades, the development in communication has been the most fundamental and pervasive of all in its effects on the region's traditional societies. The dramatic upheavals in the economic, political and social structures of the Middle East have their origin in a radical change in the outlook of the average man on the world in which he lives. Thus, the study of the communication agencies, political behaviour, public opinion and mass media of the Middle East has rapidly accelerated in the past decade. A major factor responsible for this renewed emphasis has been the post-war interest in the developing nations with an accompanying concern for both understanding and promoting modernisation.

It is the fashion today to speak of the 'impact' of the West upon the traditional societies of the non-Western world. But the extent and depth of these societies' acceptance of the Western way of life, in all its levels, is a complex problem that cannot be measured merely by the sales figures of cars and television sets. This is not to dismiss the newly acquired habits of the peoples of the Middle East as unimportant or insignificant superficialities, but merely to point out that the theory as well as the reality of the 'impact' of the west has to be studied from the proper standpoint. Narrowing down the postulate to the central concern of this chapter, we can say the Press of the Middle East is an 'import' from the West; a product, so to speak, of the 'impact' of the West upon the Middle East.

Before the introduction of the printing press in the Middle East, communication was provided by the daily and especially the Friday meetings at the mosques, the convents of the dervishes, the coffee-houses, and the market-places. For years the spreading of news and opinion was principally the business of religious preachers in Egypt and Turkey. Especially in the fasting month of Ramadan, it was customary for theological students and many other members of the religious profession to wander from place to place preaching on current topics. In Iran, under the Safavids (1502–1736), when a more or less formalised council of ministers came into being, the *vaghaye-navis* or news-writer occupied an important place. His report in the council and the court was a major source of political intelligence. Occasionally the government news—or *akhbar* as it came to be called—was also read to the public from the stairs of mosques. The *vaghaye-navis* continued to function as a successful medium for the dissemination of news until the early 19th century.

Modern science and technology remain the most important agents of Western influence. The introduction of the printing press in the Middle East made a great change in the thinking and habits accepted for centuries by the rulers and the élite of the region. Because printing lowered the cost of education, it meant that knowledge was no longer the exclusive property of the privileged classes.

As early as the fourth decade of the 17th century the printing press had been introduced into the Middle East. For example, the first printing press in Iran was a press brought by Armenians to the city of Julfa near Isfahan. This press was found and was used by the Armenian scholar and priest, Katchadur, in 1639. The priest of the Armenian Apostolic Church prepared matrix, cast type, readied the press, paper and ink, and printed remarkably elaborate Armenian books. The movable-type printing in Julfa thus came about 190 years after printing from movable letters had first made its appearance in Germany.

In Turkey, the first printing press was established with government aid in Istanbul in 1728. However, it was to be another hundred years before newspapers were published in that country. The religious authorities opposed the introduction of the press as a European invention, but the enlightened Grand Vizir Ibrahim Pasha finally persuaded the religious authorities to give their consent to a Turkish printing press.

In Egypt, it was Napoleon who first opened that country to Western influence. In the late 18th century, he brought with him not only scientists and scholars who surveyed different aspects of Egyptian life, but also a press with Arabic and French type.

The Press and National Development

The introduction of the printing press meant that literary forms such as the newspaper could be tried out at slight financial risk. During the remaining years of the 18th century and the first half of the 19th various newspapers and periodicals were established in Egypt, Turkey, Lebanon, Iran and Syria.

In August 1798 Napoleon published the first newspaper ever to appear in Egypt, *Le Courrier d'Egypte*, which dealt mainly with political news and appeared in four pages once every four days. Two months later, in October 1798, he founded his second journal, *Le Décade Egyptien*, for scholars and administrators interested in the archaeological and literary progress of the Nile valley. Next he brought out *Al-Hawadith Al-Yawmia*, the first Arabic paper which reported daily events. Because the combined attacks by the Turks, British and native rebel forces compelled the French to evacuate the country, these publications disappeared.

Although newspapers were published by a few Frenchmen in Turkey as early as 1795 and 1826, it was not until 1831 that the first genuine Turkish newspaper, *Takvimi-Vekayieh*, a calendar of events, was established by Sultan Mahmoud II to provide closer contact with the people.

In Iran, it was Mirza Saleh Shirazi, a London-trained diplomat-scholar, who in 1837 (during the reign of Muhammad Shah, the third ruler of the Qajar Dynasty) published the first Persian newspaper. The paper, which bore the name *Akhbar*, was devoted to 'News from the East and News from the West'.

From 1858, newspapers other than official gazettes were beginning to be published in Lebanon continuously. A number of early writers and journalists who emigrated from Beirut to other Arab countries established newspapers; hence part of the reason for Lebanon's claim to be the centre of Arab journalism. The journalists emigrating from Beirut did not outnumber the indigenous founders of Arabic newspapers in Cairo, but among those who went to Egypt were a few who were conspicuously and enduringly successful and who laid the foundation of the modern Arab press for years to come.

Probably the classic example of the Lebanese influence on Egyptian journalism is *Al-Ahram*, frequently described as *The Times* of the Arab world. *Al-Ahram* was founded in Alexandria in 1876 by two Lebanese, Salim and Bishara Takla. The paper was later moved to Cairo where it has been published ever since.

Throughout the first 50 years of its existence, the press of the Middle East was restricted to official journals whose sole function was to communicate governmental announcements and proclamations and to provide certain technical knowledge for the ruling class. The press of this period lacked the diversified content associated with present-day mass media, playing little or no role in the formation of public opinion and certainly a minimal one in the dissemination of information. And since both the Arab and the non-Arab nations of the region were operating on the autocratic principle the same principle became the basis for press control.

In Iran, until the Constitutional Revolution (1905–9), the feudal and medieval system of the Qajars moulded the press into a propaganda organ. At the same time the press, despite censorship, served as a medium for the portrayal of the growing complexity of the world, as illustrated in the nature and quality of the contributed articles. The interaction between the autocratic policy of the Government in the late part of the 19th century and the inexorable social change that was taking place brought forth a hybrid Press —a weird organ of propaganda which was, at the same time, a crude kind of cinematography depicting social schism.

By the turn of the century the new tool, journalism, was in widespread social use in the Middle East. The power of the press was transferred; journalism became the weapon of men in revolution instead of men in power. This revolutionising transformation of the press in several notable cases was accomplished by political revolution. Of the three great media of propaganda in the Iranian Constitutional Revolution—the omnipresent pamphlet, the sermons of political clergy, and the newspaper press—it was the last which made the greatest gains. The press was transformed from a limited channel of communication to a genuine mass medium of enormous impact.

After the first stirrings of Egyptian and Lebanese journalism, the early years of this century saw the great struggle between nationalism and imperialism reflected almost continuously in the press. Despite the illiteracy of the mass public, the press in these countries achieved widespread circulation. In other Arab countries, the first decade of this century is pinpointed as the period when journalism began to flower in Syria, Iraq and Palestine. With the revolt of the Young Turks against the Sultan in 1908, there developed a sudden upsurge in the number of papers being published in these Arabic-speaking portions of the Turkish empire. This continued until the outbreak of World War I, when Turkey abandoned the policy of self-government for the Arabs within the Turkish empire. This nationalistic and revolutionary background to the development of the press in the Middle East— comparatively recent and unfinished as these movements were—has left a continuing impact upon the growth of mass media.

In the Middle East, the press developed in the first half of this century a new awareness of the outside world and at the same time a great degree of nationalistic self-consciousness. One finds, at the very outset of the modernisation process in the Middle East, a close connection between political and social reform and the press. It was during this period that the significance of the press both as a moulder of public opinion and as a medium of information was realised.

Throughout the turbulent history of the contemporary Middle East, the Press has found itself caught up in the turmoil of rapidly changing governments, and with the exceptions of Israel and (to a degree) Lebanon, it has had little chance for prolonged stability. In several countries, like Saudi Arabia, Syria, Jordan, Iran and Turkey, national policy has attached great importance to literacy and education—while it has paid little attention to the growth of the mass media. And because of a very low public investment, the media in the private sphere have developed more rapidly than those in the public sphere.

At the same time, in the process of political development, the institutional function of the press and the mass media has not been fully recognised in many Middle Eastern countries. Thus, the lukewarm attitude of the Government toward the mass media has been a natural concomitant of the weakness of political organisation underpinning the régime.

It seems that only Kemal Atatürk (1923–38) in Turkey, Reza Shah (1925–41) and Muhammad Mossadeq (1951–3) in Iran, and Gamal Abdel Nasser of Egypt were able to use the mass media effectively. Atatürk and Reza Shah not only developed the public concept of communication but they also used the press in its most authoritarian setting. Mossadeq's régime, based on a strong organisation of personal leadership, used the mass media with greater effectiveness as an associated instrument of action. Nasser counted heavily on the mass media revolution : 'It is true that most of our people are still illiterate. But politically that counts far less than it did 20 years ago. . . . Radio has changed everything. . . . Today people in the most remote villages hear of what is happening everywhere and form their opinion. Leaders cannot govern as they once did. We live in a new world.'[1]

The 'new world' and the change, which Nasser and other leaders spoke of, is the world reflected by the shift in modes of communicating ideas and attitudes—not the ancient media of manuscripts, dervishes and teahouses, but the mass media of picture magazines, tabloids, radio and movies are now the dominant modes.

PATTERNS OF THE MASS MEDIA SYSTEM

The press and mass media of any country contain ingredients that are endemic to their local setting, characteristics that make them special products of the social milieu from which they originate. The press and mass media in the Middle East have developed certain traits that are peculiar to the region's social and psychological framework.

The mass media systems of Lebanon and Israel are the most developed of all in the Middle East. But the area as a whole falls short of the minimum media outlets recommended by UNESCO, which include at least ten copies

[1] Nasser, Gamal Abdel. *Egypt's Liberation: The Philosophy of Revolution*, Public Affairs Press, Washington, 1955.

of daily newspapers, five radio sets, two television sets, and two cinema seats for each 100 persons. While the literacy rate has been increased during the past years, the media figures show that in a comparative study the Middle East countries have not been able to keep up their readership-audiences.

Lebanon and Israel, with their high percentage of literacy (50% and 90% respectively), have also the highest rate of media consumption, while countries like Saudi Arabia and Jordan, with their low rate of literacy (10% and 15% respectively), have the lowest number of newspaper copies and radio-TV sets in proportion to their population. Among the larger countries, only Turkey has its population fairly evenly distributed over its area. Both Iran and Egypt contain vast uninhabited deserts—but Egypt is one of the world's most densely populated countries—whereas Iran has room for growth. Thus Turkey, with its higher literacy (45%) and better distribution of its population, has better mass media than both Egypt and Iran and is only second to Lebanon and Israel.

With 46 dailies and a high readership drawn from a population of only two and a half million, the Lebanese press is the most competitive in the Middle East and is the only one in the Arab world that it still exclusively in private hands. Although a majority of newspapers and magazines continue to receive support from various political and economic groups, the press of Lebanon is relatively free from control and censorship. The government has promoted the emergence of a financially independent press and has recently proposed giving grants for the amalgamation of newspapers. The majority of newspapers are published in Arabic, but there are a number of well-edited newspapers and magazines in French, Armenian, and English. The most important and influential papers are *Al-Hayat*, *The Daily Star*, *Al-Haryda*, and *L'Orient* which are also distributed in the neighbouring countries. Lebanon, moreover, is the centre of news communication in the region. In 1969 there were more than a hundred foreign correspondents in Beirut covering an area from Tehran to Cairo.

But it is the United Arab Republic that has the most quoted and advanced newspaper press in the Arab world. The authoritative daily *Al-Ahram*, under the editorship of Muhammad Hassenein Haikal, a close friend of Nasser, has a circulation of 250,000 and is read in many Arab countries, although its distribution in Tunisia and Saudi Arabia is at present either restricted or altogether banned for political reasons. Long considered among the élite press of the world, *Al-Ahram* for years was an independent paper of high standard, with first class correspondents and writers, and ranked ahead of all competitors for reliability and responsibility. When in 1960 the press was placed by Nasser under the control of the Arab Socialist Union, journalists were required to obtain licences and publishing houses were placed under the Union's supervision. Today there are four main publishing houses, which operate as separate entities and compete with one another, but their publications and content in the area of foreign affairs reflect the views of the Government. These are Al-Ahram which publishes the daily *Al-Ahram* and a monthly economic review; Dar Al-Hilal which is concerned with magazines and publishes *Al-Mussawar*, *Hawa's* and *Al-Kawakeb*; Dar Akhbar Al-Yom which publishes the daily *Al-Akhbar* and three weeklies; and Dar Al-Gomhouriya which publishes the daily *Al-Gomhouriya*, the official organ of the Arab Socialist Union, in addition to the daily English language paper *Egyptian Gazette*, the daily French newspaper *Le Progrès Egyptien*, and the afternoon paper *Al-Missa*.

In a region of explosive politics and instability, the press of other Arab countries has developed in support of the struggle for independence and national development. Some of the Arab editors have a tradition of a relatively large degree of press freedom, in spite of oppressive censorship laws that usually go unenforced. As in most of the Middle East, the Arab Press is similar in many ways to the numerous, small, highly partisan, political party press which dominated the European and American scenes for more than half a century.

In several countries like Saudi Arabia, Kuwait, and Yemen, the mass media have had a relatively short history. In the case of Saudi Arabia, for example, because so much of the Arabian peninsula is covered by deserts, its communication system is limited to a narrow band across the centre of the country. In 1969, its six daily newspapers were published in its principal cities—Jeddah, Mecca, and Dahran. In the same year there were only eight daily newspapers in Syria, six in Kuwait, three in the Republic of South Yemen, five in Iraq, and six in Jordan. The Persian Gulf States and Yemen had no daily publications.

Apart from the wider problem of political instability, the press in these countries has had problems of its own in the areas of finance, literacy and communication. The rising cost of newsprint, for example, has affected all Arab countries. Today the price of raw newsprint in a single four page copy of a standard size Syrian newspaper represents more than 20% of the price for which the paper is sold.

In Syria, since the coming to power of the Ba'ath Arab Socialist Party, the structure of the mass media has changed and most of the country's publications are managed by political, religious or labour associations. *Al-Ba'ath* is the organ of the ruling party and its circulation of 16,000 is only second to *Al-Thawrah*, the most widely read political daily in Damascus.

In Iraq, the structure of the press was completely reorganised in 1967 by government decree; all private newspapers were closed and a total of five government-controlled papers were established. The new papers included *Al-Thawrah Al-Arabia*, the organ of the Arab Socialist Union, and *Al-Jumhuriya*, now the largest daily newspaper with a circulation of 20,000.

Similar changes were made in Jordan in 1967, when two new publishing houses were formed to publish three new daily newspapers and one weekly journal, which replaced the dozen newspapers forced to cease publication by the new press law. In each of these publishing houses the Government has a 25% holding.

The non-Arab nations of the Middle East, such as Iran and Israel, provide an excellent laboratory for the study of the intricate intermingling of the mass media and national development. In Iran, where there has always been a race between reform and revolution, the Shah has realised that a steady process of social and political reform is the only ultimate alternative to revolution. But the policy makers of the post-Mossadeq era have not used the press as a major stimulus to carry through the development plans. During this period the printed media have been ignored while the electronic media—both radio and television—have been major instruments of foreign and domestic policies.

Today two commercial and private groups—Kayhan and Ettela'at—have a virtual monopoly of the newspaper-press in Iran. With a daily circulation of 80,000 each, these two between them account for 74% of the total circulation of daily newspapers in the country. In addition to several weekly magazines for youth, children, and women, published competitively by both groups, Kayhan publishes the daily *Kayhan International* in English and

Ettela'at publishes the daily *Journal de Tehran* in French, the daily *Tehran Journal* in English, and the bi-weekly *Al-Akha* in Arabic.

Tehran dominates the press scene of Iran, as almost all daily newspapers and most of the weekly journals and magazines are published in the capital. There are a dozen general magazines of one sort or another but, ironically, the most popular and widely circulated magazine today is *Zaneh-Ruz*, a weekly magazine edited principally for women by the Kayhan group with a circulation of nearly 100,000. A unique weekly among the press of contemporary Iran is the satirical *Towfiq* (40,000) which is the paper most representative of the creative journalism of Iran during the early part of this century.

Turkey has one of the most developed press systems in the Middle East. After the revolution of 1960, the Turkish press achieved one of the longest periods of freedom in its history. But the restoration of press freedom after the revolution also created conditions favourable to the abuse of this freedom. Recognising this, the Turkish press adopted a system of self-control based on a code of ethics. A court of honour was set up to censure those violating the voluntary code of ethics.

Unlike Iran and most of the Middle East countries, Turkey has a well-distributed pattern of provincial and small-town papers. In Istanbul and Ankara, where the national papers are published, one-time family publishing houses are being turned into companies and newspaper corporations. Today the Hurriyet group, which owns the popular daily *Hürriyet* (600,000), also publishes *Yen Gazeti* and several weekly and monthly papers and has its own news agency. The Hayat group, the largest group owning periodicals, publishes the weekly illustrated magazine *Hayat* and several cinema, arts, and children's magazines. The Milliyet group publishes the influential daily *Milliyet* and several other supplements. Among the most influential and widely read publications are the daily *Cumhuriyet*, the political weekly *Akis*, and to a lesser extent *Ulus*, which supports the Republican People's Party, and *Adalet* and *Son Havadis* which give editorial support to the Justice Party.

During the past two decades of statehood, the communication system and the press of Israel have changed as rapidly as the social and demographic realities of the country itself. Having a population of only 2·7 million, Israel has 28 daily newspapers, 50 weekly publications and about 350 other periodicals appearing monthly or quarterly. With its broad range of multi-lingual news coverage, the Israeli press is one of the most vigorous systems in the Middle East. Israel has about 21 daily newspaper copies per 100 persons, double that of Lebanon, the next highest figure in the region. Besides Turkey, it is the only other country in the Middle East that produces newsprint. The high rate of literacy, an active economy, and the absence—until 1969—of television are responsible for this continued growth. Although the daily press is national in character, as are all newspapers, three are published in Tel Aviv. The three published in Jerusalem are all non-Hebrew and depend upon national circulation. Until 1968 the nearly one million Arabs living under Israeli occupation received virtually all their news from the radio. Now there are two daily newspapers in Arabic being published in Jerusalem, one by Israelis and the other by Arabs.

Party-subsidised newspapers have dominated the Israeli Press since 1948 and today only three of the regular Hebrew dailies and one-half of the foreign language dailies are independent. Reflecting the fact that a majority of Israel's population is non-native, the foreign language dailies produce about 19% of the country's total daily circulation. There are daily newspapers in Arabic, Rumanian, German, English, Hungarian, Yiddish, Polish, Bulgarian and French.

The most influential and editorially independent dailies are *Ha'aretz* and *Davar*, both published in Hebrew. These two are the most widely read of the morning papers, exceeded only by the popular afternoon newspapers, *Ma'riv* (118,000) and *Yediot Aharonot* (85,000). The leading daily newspaper in English is the *Jerusalem Post*.

The increase in literacy in the area as a whole and the relatively rapid social advances among women, matched and exceeded by advances among youth of both sexes, have given a special impetus to psychocultural transition and book reading. Thus the number of books published in several countries—among them the United Arab Republic, Iran, Syria, Turkey and Israel—has increased considerably. Paperback publications in Cairo, Tehran, Beirut and several other capital cities have added yet another dimension to the already growing mass media in the region.

The paper industry is still very small in the Middle East, and the quality of the paper is not adequate for fine editions. Imported paper is expensive, and publishers have to sacrifice details of presentation in order to keep the price of their books down. But as a whole, the prospect for printed media in a good number of the Middle East countries is not unfavourable.

THE GROWTH OF BROADCASTING AND FILMS

In most countries of the Middle East, broadcasting is a state monopoly and is financed through licence fees or government subsidies. Only Lebanon and Iran maintain private television stations supported by advertising, while radio broadcasting is exclusively government-owned and operated throughout the Middle East.

During the last decade the number of radio transmitters in the Middle East has almost doubled. However, the distribution of receivers has not progressed at the same rate. Only Iran, Lebanon, Kuwait, Syria, Egypt, Israel, and Turkey had five or more receivers per 100 persons. Most Middle Eastern broadcasting systems must serve a large population using no generally-accepted common language. Even monolingual countries like Saudi Arabia broadcast in foreign languages because their programmes are easily received in neighbouring countries. Thus many countries devote a large number of daily programmes to broadcasts directed at emigrant groups in other countries as well as to general news and background services for foreign consumption.

In some countries like Kuwait, Sudan, and Jordan, radio broadcasting has advanced more rapidly than the press and it is the primary source of news. It should be noted that the cost of radio is substantially lower than that of other media for individual governments. The development of low-cost transistors has revolutionised radio in the Middle East, and propaganda agencies —both domestic and foreign—are glad to provide audio-visual facilities for such systems. Furthermore, Governments often choose to exploit radio as a medium of national policy. Where illiteracy is so widespread, radio becomes the main means of communication. Access to a radio station is, thus, next in importance to control of the armed forces.

Being on the crossroads between Europe and Asia, the Middle East receives a significant amount of international broadcasting. Stations in Europe, India, Pakistan, Ceylon, and the Soviet Union can be clearly heard. The Voice of America has beamed daily programmes in Arabic and Persian since 1950. A survey in 1958 found a considerable knowledge of international broadcasting in Iran, indicating 'ideological sophistication—i.e., awareness of the interplay of interests and ideologies in the world arena'.[2] In the same way, such papers as the *New York Times*, *The Times* of London, and *Pravda* arrive in the major cities of the Middle East daily. On the basis of geographical factors the people of the Middle East in general are constantly exposed to international communication.

Television is establishing itself as a potent medium of information, education, and entertainment throughout the Middle East. Lebanon has the most sophisticated television system in the Middle East today and is the only country with two privately-owned national services. Next to Kuwait, Lebanon has the highest number of television receivers per 100 inhabitants. Both of the Lebanese services are largely foreign-owned. The *Compagnie Libanaise de Télévision* is owned by French interests and draws heavily on French sources, while Tele-Orient takes British and American material and has as its largest shareholder the British Thomson Organisation.

Among the growing television systems in the Middle East are those of Iran, the United Arab Republic, and Israel. In 1958, Iran had the first commercial television network in the Middle East. But in 1967, the Government decided to establish a separate national television network of its own. Today, in addition to these two networks, Iran also has a closed-circuit educational TV channel and an American armed forces TV station, both of which are in Tehran. In Israel, a state-wide television network was established in 1967 and similar projects are under way in Turkey and Jordan. And further progress in television is almost assured, especially since the medium's usefulness in education has become apparent.

The commercial television systems in Lebanon and Iran are closely patterned after European and American commercial operations. Their programmes consist largely of popular American television series dubbed in Arabic and Persian. Their locally produced programmes are also largely modelled on American quiz show and variety programmes. Cultural programmes both in radio and televison get a fair-sized audience, and the native programmes are popular. But there is a real demand for westerns, thrillers and light comedies. American, British and French-made films are continually becoming more popular. And television producers in the Middle East, as in Europe and America, are cultivating the mass audience and its tastes.

At the same time, information presented in a locally understandable form is rapidly disseminated throughout rural areas by the traditional 'grapevine'. For example, a religious leader, a school teacher, or a headman of a village, who is literate and has access to other sources such as newspapers and magazines, becomes not only the disseminator of information but also an authority who can interpret and comment on the news heard by the villagers. Thus—sometimes in conjunction—word of mouth communication and the radio continue to be the most effective means of mass dissemination in rural areas.

In recent years the leaders of the Middle East have realised the importance of audio-visual aids for both propaganda and educational purposes. In several countries, when planning television services, they have promoted film production at the same time. Although the United Arab Republic has

[2] Lerner, Daniel, *The Passing of Traditional Society: Modernizing the Middle East*, Free Press, New York, 1958, p. 382.

been the only country in the Middle East to produce feature films and motion pictures for the past two or three decades, Lebanon, Iran, and Israel have begun to make films recently. Since World War II, Turkey, Syria, Iraq, and a few other countries have been making newsreels and documentaries, but the production of both educational and cinema films has been sporadic and limited. For many years Egyptian films have been popular among the middle class and working people throughout the Middle East but the keen competition generated by French, Italian and American movies has brought this to a standstill. Thus in 1968 there were only 57 feature films produced in the Middle East, 36 of which were made in the United Arab Republic.

As might be expected, American, French, Italian, and Egyptian movies are popular among the people of the Middle East. Turkey, Iran, and Lebanon are some of the best markets for Hollywood films. But again, as is the case with newspapers and television, the cinema in the Middle East is an urban phenomenon. For example, in 1968 some 20 cinemas in Tehran provided about 75% of national seating capacity in Iran, and the pattern is similar in Beirut and Baghdad. As the consumption of film and print is concentrated in the great urban centres, many of the city workers who have neither literacy to read newspapers, nor enough cash to buy a radio, can get fairly regular access to films. But it is the farmers who are sharply cut off from the world of the cinema. Today, Israel and Lebanon have the highest rate of cinema attendance *per caput* in the Middle East.

The limitations of the cinema in the Middle East have both technical and cultural roots. In many Middle Eastern and Islamic societies, the cinema in general and foreign films in particular have been opposed by the more traditional and religious groups as corrupt and immoral. But within the past decade the barriers have been broken down to a large extent, especially in Saudi Arabia, Jordan, and the Persian Gulf States. In Iran, Syria and Turkey, film-going is now among the most popular forms of general entertainment.

CONTROL OF COMMUNICATION CHANNELS

Most of the countries in the region view the mass media as instruments of national policy, devices by which the goals of the national state or the government in power can be furthered. Such a theory of the role of the media demands control over its content. Most Middle East Governments maintain official information and news agencies which constitute in large part their communication resources on a day-by-day basis. In fact, government control of the mass media is general in the Middle East and the trend is towards more control, not less. The latest survey of press freedom around the world, conducted by the Freedom of Information Centre of the University of Missouri for the year 1966, ranked the Middle East as 'the most oppressive region of the world in regard to press freedom'.[3]

In Israel, which is a partial exception, military censorship limits freedom of expression.[4] In Lebanon, where the press enjoys a relatively high degree of freedom, the press law requires all publications to be licensed by the Ministry of the Interior. (The licence can be withdrawn if the paper tempo-

[3] Lowenstein, Ralph L., 'World Press Freedom, 1966', Freedom of Information Center Report No. 181, School of Journalism, University of Missouri, May 1967, p. 4.
[4] The *New York Times*, on February 19, 1967, reported the secret trial in Tel Aviv of two magazine editors, who were sentenced to one year in prison for publishing an article with political and security overtones. Until its disclosure by the *New York Times*, the case had not been reported in the Israeli press.

rarily suspends publication within six months of its inception.) The practice of licensing newspapers is followed in almost all Middle Eastern countries. The Turkish Press law provides penalties of up to 15 years' imprisonment for communist propaganda and among other things it penalises defamation of the president, the republic, the nation and institutions such as the army, parliament and the courts. Since the 1960 revolution, there has been an alarming number of public prosecutions of journalists. In Istanbul alone there were 152 such prosecutions in 1967, of which 33 were for obscene publications.

In many cases these controls have been justified by the governments in power on the ground that they improve the quality of journalism. Thus under the new press law, Jordanian editors are asked to satisfy certain conditions—such as to employ no less than four editors and to have a minimum amount of capital prescribed by the Government. In Iraq, management of the press is attached to the Ministry of Guidance—which allows only one independent Kurdish language paper and controls all other publications in Baghdad and elsewhere.

In Iran, with the exception of scientific, cultural and governmental publications, newspapers with a circulation of less than 3,000 and magazines with less than 5,000 are not permitted publication. According to the Reporter's Code of Journalism, the Iranian newsmen are licensed by the Ministry of Information and are not allowed to accept government employment. But these points have not been fully implemented. Criminal penalties and imprisonment are provided in the Iranian press law for publishing, among other things, anything insulting or false or libellous against the recognised religious authorities, for the offence of libel against the Shah or the Queen, for disclosing military information, and for provoking people to oppose government troops. The press law also defines the quality of education and character required in persons intending to publish newspapers or magazines. It requires, for example, that the applicant be an Iranian citizen, of at least 30 years of age, and a graduate of a college or a scholar recognised by the High Council of Education.

GENERAL CHARACTERISTICS OF THE MASS MEDIA

Throughout the turbulent history of the contemporary Middle East, the press has found itself caught up in the turmoil of rapidly changing Governments, with little hope of an enduring stability. Yet this very fact has produced a number of newspapers and periodicals of great courage and vitality, while at the same time giving rise to numerous spineless government journals and political newspapers. Although the constitutions of most countries of the Middle East have provided for freedom of the press and expression, this freedom appears to mean very little and derives what meaning it does have in each period from the philosophy of the régime currently in power.

Although the mass media have been expanding rapidly, they have not kept pace with the spread of literacy and education in the region as a whole. In particular, most rural areas of the Middle East are still badly served in the matter of communications. The mass media and literacy tend to be concentrated in the urban or more industrialised areas, leaving the countryside surrounding them untouched and unaware.

One of the most important features of the Middle Eastern audience is the significant role of word-of-mouth communication. Among the great majority person-to-person contact is still the main channel for the dissemination of information. A transistor radio, and in a few cases a television set, are the only means of modern communications in rural areas, since the majority of villagers cannot read or write.

A characteristic of the press in the Middle East is the multiplicity of newspapers in such countries as Lebanon, Iran, Turkey and Israel, which is to a large extent a reflection of the diversity of religious, political and linguistic minorities. The multilingual character of the press can be well observed by the number of publications and broadcast programmes in Armenian, French, English, as well as the local Persian, Arabic and Turkish languages.

The influence of the party press is strong throughout the area and personal journalism flourishes, providing current news with innumerable interpretations. The press of opinion has grown in strength and the informatory function of the printed media has become a secondary aim. The vast majority of newspapers are still individually owned. At the same time, this individualism has made available a variety of different journals—mostly in the non-Arab countries of the Middle East.

Among the characteristics of the mass media in the region is the high birth and mortality rate of the press. Newspapers and magazines may appear for two or three weeks, then disappear as suddenly as they had appeared. In some cases this fast sequence of birth and death has an economic reason but in many cases it is a reflection of the political and social instability of the region.

As concerns content, international and national news receive good coverage in the media but local and provincial items are poorly reported. As a whole Middle Eastern newspapers, magazines, radio-television and films are strongly influenced by their counterparts in other parts of the world. They reflect the values of the well-to-do, educated or politically powerful minority which controls the mass media. It can be said that the expectations of the people of the Middle East concerning the accuracy of their press and radio are notoriously pessimistic. Consequently the credibility of many newspapers and broadcast programmes is low.

Interestingly, the very core of the newspaper in the Middle East, usually, is in its political flavour. In the popular approach to the matter, the press is not a business but a champion permanently on guard against injustices, with a heroic destiny to fulfil. Journalists like to speak of their profession as if it were a priesthood.

A good number of journalists are also poets, novelists, or essayists. Journalism and literature are practically synonymous in most of the Middle Eastern countries, and the press is—and always has been—considered a respectable vehicle for literary productions.

And last but not least is the economic gap, which lies at the root of various attacks launched against the media as problems occur in this communication process. Because of the lack of production facilities in the region and the generally low level of the economy, the media must import much of their equipment. Since the poor network of telecommunication makes distribution both costly and haphazard, much of the news supply also comes from outside sources. Charges that the press is influenced and largely controlled by the world agencies, post-colonial ties, and governmental organisations and departments stem largely from this lack of capital within the area with which to finance indigenous news agencies and news-gathering facilities. This lack has forced the press to rely on outside sources

Increasing literacy and a growing interest in news and interpretation has

THE SIZE OF MASS COMMUNICATION SYSTEMS: DISTRIBUTION OF PRINTED MEDIA

Country	Daily newspaper number	Daily newspapers copies per 100	Total of daily, weekly and other journals	Leading newspaper with circulation	Newsprint consumption per person kg per year	News agency (date of foundation)	Books (titles published annually)
Iran	27	1·5	105	Kayhan (80,000) Eteláʻat (80,000)	0·3	Fars (1938)	985
Iraq	5	1	36	Al-Jumhuriya (20,000)	0·3	Iraqi National Agency (1959)	286
Israel	28	21	400	Haʻaretz (44,000) Maʻriv (118,000)	3·7	Israel News Agency (1923)	1,038
Jordan	2	1·8	13	Al-Destour (14,000)	0·2	—	27
Kuwait	6	0·4	25	Al-Rai Al-Amm (15,000)	—	—	113
Lebanon	46	9·7	96	Al-Hayat (25,000) L'Orient (13,500)	3·9	—	436
Persian Gulf States	—	0·4	7	Al-Jarida Al-Resmia (weekly in Bahrain)	0·3	—	—
Republic of South Yemen	3	—	12	Fataul Jazireh (10,000)	—	—	—
Saudi Arabia	6	0·4	29	Al-Bilad (15,000)	0·1	—	—
Sudan	15	0·4	—	Al-Sahafa (30,000)	0·07	—	—
Syria	8	1·9	45	Al-Thawrah (20,000) Al-Baʻath (16,000)	0·2	—	87
United Arab Republic	37	2	86	Al-Ahram (250,000)	1·3	Middle East News (1955)	3,069
Turkey	472	4·5	610	Milliyet (265,000)	0·8	Anatolia (1925)	5,442
Yemen	—	—	4	Saba (fortnightly, 10,000)	—	—	

Source: Figures have been computed from various sources (i.e., UNESCO, official government sources, and press associations) for the year 1968 unless otherwise listed.

THE SIZE OF MASS COMMUNICATION SYSTEMS: RADIO-TV, FILM AND CINEMA

Country	Radio			Television			Cinema		
	Transmitters	Receivers	Receivers per 100	Transmitters	Receivers	Receivers per 100	Number	Annual attendance per inhab.	Long film produced
Iran	22	1,700,000	7	3	150,000	0·5	238	3	—
Iraq	5	180,000	2·3	1	160,000	1·5	84	1	—
Israel	11	600,000	20	1	30,500	1·45	303	20	6
Jordan	3	64,000	3·8	—	—	—	55	3	—
Kuwait	3	350,000	157	1	75,000	34	7	—	—
Lebanon	3	451,000	27	3	170,000	10	165	14	15
Persian Gulf States	2	100,000	—	—	—	—	—	—	—
Republic of South Yemen	2	100,000	—	1	20,000	0·6	—	—	—
Saudi Arabia	4	77,000	1·3	1	35,000	0·1	—	—	—
Sudan	4	150,000	1·3	1	12,000	1·7	47	0·8	—
Syria	16	260,000	5·7	1	80,000	—	112	4	—
United Arab Republic	28	4,260,000	17	5	475,000	1·8	171	2	36
Turkey	14	2,802,721	10	1	6,000	0·01	—	—	—
Yemen	1	—	—	—	—	—	17	0·4	—

Source: Figures have been computed from various sources (i.e., UNESCO, official government sources, and press associations) for the year 1968 unless otherwise listed.

steadily widened the audience for all forms of communication. The significance and potential of the mass media in the process of social change is coming to be realised. The mass media, by focusing attention onto this change, have prompted a mood of critical self-awareness. Today as the majority of the people of the Middle East turn their eyes upon themselves, they perhaps remember that Muhammad, returning from battle, told his followers: 'You have come back from the lesser to the great struggle.' They asked, 'What is the greater struggle, O Messenger of God?' And he replied, 'The struggle within.'

FURTHER READING

Abu-Lughod, Ibrahim. 'International News in Arabic Press: A Comparative Content Analysis', *Public Opinion Quarterly*, no. 26; pp. 600–612, Winter, 1962.
Ainslie, Rosalynde. *The Press in Africa: Communications Past and Present*, Gollancz, London, 1966.
International Press Institute. *News from the Middle East*, Zurich, 1954.
Mowlana, Hamid. *International Communications: A Selected Bibliography*, Department of Communication, the American University, Washington DC, 1968.
Sommerlad, E. Lloyd. *The Press in Developing Countries*, Sydney Univ. Press, 1966.
UNESCO. *World Communication*, Paris, 1964.
UNESCO. *World Press: Newspapers and News Agencies*, Paris, 1964.
UNESCO. *World Radio and Television*, Paris, 1965.

HAMID MOWLANA. Associate Professor and Director of International Communication and Chairman of the Communication Committee at the American University in Washington, DC. Spent ten years as editor, foreign correspondent and commentator for various newspapers and television networks in the USA, Europe and the Middle East. As Editor-in-Chief of Kayhan group of Newspapers in Iran, helped to organise the Institute of Mass Communication Studies in Tehran. Author of *Journalism in Iran: A History and Interpretation* (2 vols., 1963); *International Communication: A Selected Bibliography* (1968) and *Foundations of International Communication* (1970).

INDEX

Figures in **bold type** indicate main references; those in *italics* refer to maps, statistical tables and tabulated information; the Arabic definite article (Al, El etc.) has been ignored as an element in the alphabetical arrangement of proper names, hence Al-Rashid will be found among the Rs and El-Mallakh among the Ms; the Trucial States include Abu Dhabi, Ajman, Dubai, Fujairah, Ras al-Khaimah, Sharjah and Umm al-Quwain; GDP: Gross Domestic Product; GNP: Gross National Product; ME: Middle East; UAR: United Arab Republic; UN: United Nations.